DICTIONARY OF
CONCEPTS IN LITERARY
CRITICISM
AND THEORY

DICTIONARY OF CONCEPTS IN LITERARY CRITICISM AND THEORY

Wendell V. Harris

Reference Sources for the Social Sciences and Humanities, Number 12
Raymond G. McInnis, Series Editor

Greenwood Press
New York • Westport, Connecticut • London

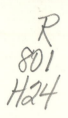

R
801
H24

Library of Congress Cataloging-in-Publication Data

Harris, Wendell V.
    Dictionary of concepts in literary criticism and theory / Wendell
V. Harris.
      p.   cm.—(Reference sources for the social sciences and
humanities, ISSN 0730–3335 ; no. 12)
    Includes index.
    ISBN 0–313–25932–1 (alk. paper)
    1. Criticism—Terminology.   2. Literature—Terminology.
3. English language—Terms and phrases. I. Title. II. Series.
PN41.H36   1992
801—dc20   91–20040

British Library Cataloguing in Publication Data is available.

Library of Congress Catalog Card Number: 91–20040
ISBN: 0–313–25932–1
ISSN: 0730–3335

First published in 1992

Greenwood Press, 88 Post Road West, Westport, CT 06881
An imprint of Greenwood Publishing Group, Inc.

Printed in the United States of America

The paper used in this book complies with the
Permanent Paper Standard issued by the National
Information Standards Organization (Z39.48–1984).

10 9 8 7 6 5 4 3 2 1

Contents

Series Foreword

In all disciplines, scholars seek to understand and explain the subject matter in their areas of specialization. The object of their activity is to produce a body of knowledge about specific fields of inquiry. As they achieve an understanding of their subject, scholars publish the results of their interpretations (that is, their research findings) in the form of explanations.

Explanation, then, can be said to organize and communicate understanding. When reduced to agreed-upon theoretical principles, the explanations that emerge from this process of organizing understanding are called concepts.

Concepts serve many functions. They help us identify topics we think about, help classify these topics into related sets, relate them to specific times and places, and provide us with definitions. Without concepts, someone has said, "man could hardly be said to think."

Like knowledge itself, the meanings of concepts are fluid. From the moment an authority introduces a concept into a discipline's vocabulary, where it is given a specific meaning, that concept has the potential to acquire a variety of meanings. As new understandings develop in the discipline, inevitably the meanings of concepts are revised.

Although this pattern in the formation of the meaning of concepts is widely recognized, few dictionaries—certainly none in a consistent manner—trace the path a concept takes as it becomes embedded in a research topic's literature.

Dictionaries in this series uniformly present brief, substantive discussions of the etymological development and contemporary use of the significant concepts in a discipline or subdiscipline. Another feature that distinguishes these dictionaries from others in the field is their emphasis upon bibliographic information.

Volumes contain about 100 entries. Consistently, entries comprise four parts. In the first part, brief statements give the current meaning of a concept. Next, discursive paragraphs trace a concept's historical origins and connotative development. In part three, sources mentioned in part two are cited, and where appropriate, additional notes briefly highlight other aspects of individual references. Finally, in part four, sources of additional information (that is, extensive reviews, encyclopedia articles, and so forth) are indicated.

Thus, with these volumes, whatever the level of their need, students can explore the range of meanings of a discipline's concepts.

For some, it is the most fundamental need. What is the current meaning of Concept X? Of Concept Y? For others with more intensive needs, entries are departure points for more detailed investigation.

These concept dictionaries, then, fill a long-standing need. They make more accessible the extensive, often scattered literature necessary to knowing a discipline. To have helped in their development and production is very rewarding.

Raymond G. McInnis

Preface

The present volume treats seventy concepts of special importance to literary theory and commentary. In determining what concepts should be included, centrality, contemporary visibility, potential for confusion between different senses of the concept, and practical bearing have been considered. By centrality is meant the importance of the concept to the understanding and definition of other concepts; by visibility, the frequency with which the concept is to be met with in contemporary criticism and theory; by potential for confusion, the likelihood that a reader familiar with only one of several partially conflicting senses would be confused by encountering a different sense; and by practical bearing, the degree to which the concept determines critical practice.

The criteria for selection listed above to some extent define what is meant by concept as opposed to term. While there is obviously no explicit boundary, rhyme royal and peripety are, rather clearly, terms; while comedy, unity, and narratology are, rather clearly, concepts. Many terms are discussed in the context of entries on concepts and are so indexed. Terms and concepts mentioned are not put in quotation marks unless there seems a possibility for confusion about whether the word itself or the term or concept to which it refers is meant; when a term is employed in a specific technical sense by a particular scholar or writer, its first appearance is italicized. Where a concept that is the subject of a separate entry is referred to in a way especially relevant to an understanding of the concept under discussion, its first mention in the entry is printed in small capital letters.

That many of the concepts treated appear to belong more to philosophy (for example, reference) or linguistics (for example, semantics) than to literary theory and commentary is the result of the degree to which approaches to literature have become interdisciplinary. I have attempted to exclude technical questions and issues not directly assimilable to literary theory or commentary; however, the line between relevance and irrelevance is always a matter of perspective.

THE INDEX

Readers are advised to consult the index before concluding that a concept or term has not been treated. Whenever two concepts seem so closely related or have been used so interchangeably that they can be more clearly and less repetitiously discussed under one entry, they have been combined under whichever seemed the most capacious or most likely to be consulted. Thus, "trope" and "figure" come together under "figure," and "semiotics" and "semiology" under "semiotics." On the other hand, where combined consideration of related concepts in the same entry has proved unduly cumbersome, each has been assigned its own entry. Thus, "reader" appears as well as "reader-response theory," and "pragmatic" as well as "pragmatism." As mentioned above, terms defined or commented on in passing also appear in the index.

QUOTATIONS

In consonance with the principle that the way something is said is part of what is said, I have included more quotations from the critical and theoretical works cited than is usual in a dictionary of this kind. Capital letters at the beginning of quoted sentences have been retained even when the quotation is incorporated into another sentence: when one goes to the source to find a passage that has been quoted, it is often of considerable help if the quotation reproduces the original form, including capital letters.

PARENTHETICAL PAGE CITATIONS

Where more than one work by an author appears in the references section of an entry, parenthetical page number citations are accompanied by a brief form of the title. In citations of Aristotle, Plato, Cicero, and Quintilian, the standard marginal numberings of their texts have been given after the volume and page of the edition cited.

OTHER GENERAL PRINCIPLES

Insofar as possible, English translations of works in other languages have been cited, and preference has been given to works available in English.

Since constant *see* references are annoying, it has seemed reasonable to allow some repetition and at times parenthetically to insert brief explanations of matters elsewhere more fully treated.

As the several senses of most of the concepts treated indicate, neutral words for use in definitions and explanations are not always available. For instance, while some senses of text are interchangeable with work, other senses mark a clear distinction. Similarly, for many purposes, though not for all, speaker, author, writer, and utterer are interchangeable; the same is true of hearer, reader, and audience, and of utterance and text. Where a particular choice among these words is not specifically required, I have used whichever seems most appropriate to the context of discussion; where necessary for clarity, I have used such expressions as hearer or reader and speaker/author. Commentary has been chosen as the comprehensive designation embracing criticism, interpretation, explication, and evaluation, as well as analyses of significance and scholarly investigations of biographical, cultural, and historical relationships.

List of Concepts

Allegory
Allusion
Author
Canon
Classic
Code
Comedy
Context
Criticism
Deconstruction
Discourse
Discourse Analysis
Epic
Evaluation
Feminist Literary Criticism
Fiction
Figure
Formalism
Genre
Genre Theory, Twentieth-Century
Hermeneutics
Historical Scholarship
Historicism
Humanism
Imagination
Intention
Interpretation
Intertextuality
Irony

Literary History
Literature
Lyric
Marxist Literary Criticism
Meaning
Metaphor
Metonymy
Mimesis
Modern
Modernism
Myth Criticism
Narrative
Narratology
New Criticism
Organic Unity
Pluralism (literary critical)
Poetics
Postmodernism
Pragmaticsm
Psychological/Psychoanalytic Criticism
Reader
Reader-Response Theory
Realism
Reference
Rhetoric
Romance
Romanticism
Structuralism
Style

THE DICTIONARY

A

___

ALLEGORY 1. To say one thing and mean another, especially where the implicit meaning is related to the explicit through parallelism or analogy. 2. As distinguished from "Romantic" symbolism defined as an insight into an intrinsic relationship between the signifier and the signified, an external comparison, often a structure of comparisons in narrative form.

There exist various definitions of allegory, but except for those that depend on the contrast between allegory and SYMBOL, *these represent not so much different senses of the term as different attempts to define what is central to the concept.*

The relationship between allegory and symbolism is complicated because, though one is often partly defined by distinguishing it from the other, both have several senses. Symbol in its largest sense evidently includes allegory; but allegory in sense 1 equally includes the concept of symbol. George Puttenham reflects the older comprehensiveness of the term allegory in The Arte of English Poesie *(1589): "The use of this figure is so large, and his virtue of so great efficacy as it is supposed no man can pleasantly utter and persuade without it. . . . Of this figure . . . we will speak first as of the chief ringleader and captain of all other figures either in Poetical or oratory science" (186).*

1. Allegory as a Greek term is generally translated as "other speaking," an essentially rhetorical designation. However, as Philip Rollinson points out, allegory came to be associated with *hyponoai*, the finding of hidden or underlying meanings. The origin of the practice of finding allegorical meanings beyond the literal meanings in Homer and in Greek myth is generally attributed to the Theagenes of the sixth century B.C. It was well established by the time of Plato, who rejected teaching children such tales as "the narrative of Hephaestus binding Here his mother, or how on another occasion Zeus sent him flying for taking her part when she was being beaten," adding, "whether they are supposed to

have an allegorical meaning or not" (2:201; 378d). The perfecting of modes of allegorizing Homer is attributed to the Stoics of the fourth and third centuries B.C. (see Pfeiffer, 10, 35, 238). The practice was then transferred to the interpretation of the Old Testament, perhaps first by Philo (first centuries B.C. and A.D.). Allegorical interpretation of the Old Testament was initiated in the New Testament itself; Christianizing allegory was applied to Greek and Roman myths throughout the medieval period. The connection between allegory, myth, and religious belief is a strong one.

The complexity of the concept of allegory can be understood only if a number of basic distinctions are kept in mind.

1a. If allegory is regarded simply as an expressive figure, the author and the interpreter who understands the allegorical meaning are participating in the same activity from different directions. The definition of Trypho (first century B.C.) is fully rhetorical: "*Allegoria* is speech which makes precisely clear some one thing but which presents the conception of another according to likeness to the greatest extent" (cited in Rollinson, 112). Longinus explicitly regards allegory as a means of pleasing and gaining attention. "*[A]llegoria* adorns speech by changing expression and signifying the same thing through a fresher expression of a different kind. For that which is commonplace, threadbare and endlessly repeated leads to satiety" (Rollinson, 111).

However, if the allegorical meaning is discovered or imposed by the interpreter, allegory becomes quite another thing, with the type depending on whether the interpreter and/or the reader of the interpreter's reading regards the allegorical meaning as discovered or imposed. The clearest example of this mode of what may be called allegorizing, as opposed to interpreting language that is presumably intended to be understood allegorically, occurs in what is known as *typological* interpretation of the Old Testament. Christian exegetes saw events of the Old Testament as types—allegorical representations—of events or teachings in the New Testament. The earliest typological allegorizations are to be found in the New Testament itself (see, for instance, Corinthians 10:1–11 and Galatians 4:22–29).

There is a complication here. The Christian writers do not appear to deny the historicity of the events recorded in the Old Testament, even though they find in them meanings of which those who actually wrote the words of the Old Testament were not aware. Nevertheless, God, who ultimately "authored" the events, is, of course, understood to have intended their meaning in intending the total history of the world. When Christians turned to the allegorizing of pagan myths, they were also finding meanings that the authors of the Greek and Latin works from which these were taken had not intended and that could not be referred to a higher power (although the formulation of these myths could be seen as distant or imperfect graspings of truths revealed only later). However, as Philip Rollinson (following James Coulter) comments, all allegorizing—that is, all discovery of allegorical meanings not recognized by the authors of the writings in which they are found—requires the imposition of the doctrines of the discoverers. Allegorizers "must first of all represent their own preconceived notions of what constitutes 'certain irrefutable truth about the nature of reality, whether physical, psychological, divine or metaphysical' " (x). Whether an interpretation is an allegorization depends on one's judgment of the intention of the author; whether a particular allegorization is judged legitimate depends on one's system of beliefs.

Two special points should be noted. First, for all the difference between the planned composition of an allegory and the allegorizing interpretation of a text that may not have been so composed, the writers of medieval and later allegory were heavily influenced by the tradition of allegorical exegesis. Second, whether practiced as creation or interpretation, allegory is a mode that can occur in a variety of genres, and not a genre in itself.

1b. A distinction made by the Venerable Bede is closely linked to that above in that it relates only to biblical interpretation. Bede differentiates verbal and factual allegory. Factual allegory, found in biblical events that, while accepted as historically true, are intended by God to be understood allegorically, is the same thing as typological interpretation. Verbal allegory in the Bible is found in the use of figures for the conveyance of divine truth—they are rhetorical figures rather than narratives of historical events, but the truth behind them is beyond doubt (the parables of Jesus are examples). Samuel Mather, whose *Figures or Types of the Old Testament* is central to American theological thought on biblical interpretation, draws the same distinction in other terms, differentiating types from allegories. "[T]here is an Historical Verity in all those typical Histories of the Old Testament. They are not bare Allegories, or parabolical Poems, such as the Song of Solomon, or Jotham's Parable . . . but they are a true Narration of Things really existent and acted in the World, and are literally and historically to be understood" (128).

1c. From the tradition of allegorical exegesis of the Bible comes the well-known differentiation of four levels: the literal; the allegorical (not to be confused with "allegorical" in the larger sense that includes this one), which illumines human life under the pattern of Christ's life; the tropological, which provides moral lessons; and the anagogical, which points toward divinely inspired truth. The fourfold categorization is attributed to John Cassian (A.D. 360–435), but is best known from Dante's letter to Can Grande. Dante writes:

> And for the better illustration of this method of exposition, we may apply it to the following verses: "When Israel went out of Egypt, the house of Jacob from a people of strange language; Judah was his sanctuary, and Israel his dominion." For if we consider the letter alone, the thing signified to us is the going out of the children of Israel from Egypt in the time of Moses; if the allegory, our redemption from Christ is signified; if the moral sense, the conversion of the soul from the sorrow and misery of sin to a state of grace is signified; if the anagogical, the passing of the sanctified soul from the bondage of the corruption of this world to the liberty of everlasting glory is signified. And although these mystical meanings are called by various names, they may one and all in a general sense be termed allegorical, inasmuch as they are different (*diversi*) from the literal or historical. (199)

1d. There is a difference between, in Rollinson's words, "allegory which has essentially two meanings, a satisfactory literal sense and some additional other meaning" and "allegory conceived as involving only one level of hidden meaning, which is to be inferred from the obscure and literally impossible text" (xx). A morally unacceptable myth, for example, is understood by an allegorical interpreter to be of the second kind.

1e. A distinction must also be drawn between figural and narrative allegory. As John MacQueen phrases it, "The myth of Orpheus is narrative allegory, but in an isolated reference, the harp of Orpheus might be used as figural allegory" (18). To take perhaps a clearer example, the personification of Time in the absence of any supporting myth or narrative is an example of figurative allegory.

1f. A threefold division that partly cuts across all the above is that between, to use James Wimsatt's terms, *topical*, *scriptural*, and *personification*. A fiction representing "the real actions of historical people" is a topical allegory. Scriptural allegories are those "written in imitation of the allegory found by medieval exegetes through the Bible" (23). Biblical parables, Kafkaesque fiction, and works like Orwell's *1984* share this classification. The last (and most common) category is comprised of allegories that simply personify abstract qualities. The first fully developed example of personification is Prudentius's *Psychomachia*.

The variety of ways of looking at allegory reflected in the above distinctions makes evident why those who set out to define allegory are so often driven back to the general form: saying one thing and meaning another. Personification is found in so many allegories that it is often taken as the defining quality. Thus Elder Olson sums up the allegorist *tout court* as "someone who uses personification and makes such abstract things as the virtues and vices into people" (593). However, while Mr. Worldly Wise is a personification, the Slough of Despond is a metaphor, and it is forcing the word to see the Absalom of Dryden's *Absalom and Achitophel* as a "personification" of the Duke of Monmouth.

Allegory is sometimes defined as an extended metaphor or a sequence of linked metaphors. For Puttenham, allegory is metaphor "extending to whole and large speeches" and thus becoming "a long and perpetual metaphor" (187). Albert Guérard defines allegory as "simile (comparison) developed into a narrative. . . . Merely a prolonged figure of speech; [it] does not imply *real* connection between the two terms of the comparison" (487). That would seem to make what has been called a figural allegory the same thing as a metaphor. However, though to describe Opportunity as a figure with a graspable forelock while bald behind seems as much metaphor as allegorical personification, to image Time as an invisible but irresistible, methodical but not wholly predictable destroyer seems more nearly an exercise in allegory. Moreover, the whole of a narrative allegory is hardly a single metaphor or even a consistently linked set of metaphors. As Jon Whitman notes, the closer the correspondences between signifier and signified, the less allegorical a narrative seems; but the more divergence, the less tenable it is (2).

2. Allegory and symbolism are used interchangeably through most of the

history of Western literature. Philip Rollinson points out that neither Philo nor
Plutarch appears to make a distinction between allegory and symbol, and writers
generally use them synonymously until the end of the eighteenth century. However, an invidious differentiation occurs when Goethe, Schlegel, and Coleridge
define allegory as mechanical and regard the resemblances on which it is based
as arbitrary rather than necessary. For instance, Coleridge writes, "by a symbol
I mean, not a metaphor or allegory or any other figure of speech or fancy, but
an actual and essential part of that, the whole which it represents" (79). (See
SYMBOL, sense 2.) C. S. Lewis accepts this distinction in *The Allegory of Love*
(1936). "The allegorist leaves the given . . . to talk of that which is confessedly
less real, which is a fiction. The symbolist leaves the given to find that which
is more real" (45). "There is nothing 'mystical' or mysterious about medieval
allegory; the poets know quite clearly what they are about and are well aware
that the figures which they present to us are fictions" (48).

There is a clear contrast between stipulative definitions of allegory as a system
of correspondences that reflects no real relationship between signified and signifer
(or between one level and another), and of the symbol as arising out of underlying
links between signifier and signified that suggest a rich variety of interrelated
meanings. However, to apply this restricted sense of allegory indiscriminately
to all those texts dating from before the end of the eighteenth century that have
been called allegorical provokes confusion. The allegorical interpretations of
pagan myth and narrative and of the Old Testament in terms of Christian religious
belief and moral doctrines evidently represent an imaginative (if frequently mis-
guided) mode of reading quite different from the translation of personifications
into the abstract concepts that an author apparently intended to represent by his
or her personifications. Moreover, at least the anagogical level of allegory can
be understood as reaching quite beyond any direct one-to-one relationship between an abstract concept and its embodiment in a more concrete literary representation.

A number of twentieth-century studies challenge the Goethe–Schlegel–Coleridge distinction. As early as 1929 Helen Dunbar's *Symbolism in Medieval
Thought* subsumes allegory and symbol under the term symbol, subdividing the
symbol into *arbitrary* or *extrinsic*, *descriptive* or *intrinsic*, and *insight* types.
The latter type is understood as "that expression of meaningful experience which
has basis in association neither extrinsic arbitrary, nor intrinsic remaining in the
realm of sense comparison, but intrinsic as expressing and reaching out toward
the supersensible" (11). "It is of the character of insight symbol to look beneath
a datum of experience to its relations in the universal pattern and in consequence
to set forth, not only the particular fact, but also that fact in its fundamental
relationships" (17). For Dunbar, Dante's allegorical levels are part of insight
symbolism. Substantial studies by Angus Fletcher (1964) and Hazard Adams
(1983) also reconflate allegory and symbolism. Robert Scholes and Robert Kellog
pursue a somewhat different approach in *The Nature of Narrative* (1966): rather
than contrasting allegory and symbol, they distinguish between "illustrative"

and "representational" narratives. *The Faerie Queene* is illustrative, while *A la recherche du temps perdu* is representative (see 107ff.).

In "The Rhetoric of Temporality" (1969), Paul de Man attempts to reverse the values generally assigned to symbol and allegory for two centuries, and argues that allegory, which always depends on and openly refers to previous uses of the signs it employs, is more truthful than the illusionary attempt of the symbol to establish unchanging identities beyond the temporal human predicament. Drawing on structuralist and deconstructionist theorizing, which shifts the focus from the question of whether the symbol can express transcendental truths or even authorial wisdom to that of whether languages can accurately express any aspect of extra-linguistic reality, de Man celebrates the honesty of allegory, in which image and substance evidently do not coincide. "Whereas the symbol postulates the possibility of identity or identification, allegory designates primarily a distance in relation to its own origin, and renouncing the nostalgia and the desire to coincide, it establishes its language from the voice of temporal difference. In so doing, it prevents the self from an illusory identification with the non-self" (191). Walter Benjamin's defense of allegory in *The Origin of German Tragic Drama* has also been influential. Benjamin refers to the Goethe-Schlegel concept of the symbol as a tyrannous usurper that "came to power in the chaos which followed in the wake of romanticism" (159). Divorcing the theological or transcendental symbol from the "plastic" symbol of literature, Benjamin opposes the momentariness of the symbol's effect to the mythical background of allegory.

References

Adams, Hazard. *Philosophy of the Literary Symbolic*. Tallahassee: Florida State University Press, 1983.

Bede. The central passage bearing on allegory from Bede's *De Schematibus et Tropis Scarae Scripturae* (early 8th century) is translated by MacQueen in his *Allegory*.

Benjamin, Walter. *The Origin of German Tragic Drama*. Trans. J. Osborne. London: NLB, 1977. Original version, 1923; German edition, 1963. "The introduction of this distorted [theological] conception of the symbol into aesthetics was a romantic and destructive extravagance which preceded the desolation of modern art criticism" (160).

Coleridge, Samuel Taylor. *The Statesman's Manual* (1816). In *Lay Sermons*. Ed. R. J. White in vol. 6 of *The Collected Works*. Ed. K. Coburn. 16 vols. London: Routledge and Kegan Paul, 1969–84.

Coulter, James. *The Literary Microcosm: Theories of Interpretation of the Later Neoplatonists*. Leiden, Netherlands: Brill, 1976. (The words quoted by Rollinson occur on p. 19.)

Dante Alighieri. *Epistle to Can Grande Della Scala* (c. 1319). In *The Letters of Dante*. Ed. and trans. Paget Toynbee. Oxford: Clarendon Press, 1920.

De Man, Paul. "The Rhetoric of Temporality." In *Interpretation, Theory and Practice*, ed. Charles Singleton. Baltimore: Johns Hopkins University Press, 1969.

Dunbar, Helen Flanders. *Symbolism in Medieval Thought and Its Consummation in the Divine Comedy*. New Haven, Conn.: Yale University Press, 1929. Offers an example of the three levels of interpretation above the literal in the Abraham and Isaac story which allegorically represents "Christ's sacrifice on Calvary," tropologically "brings to each soul knowledge of the sacrifice inevitable in the life dominated by the divine will," and anagogically "suggests the greatest height to which man can rise, the utter self-giving . . . in union with God" (20).

Fletcher, Angus. *Allegory: The Theory of a Symbolic Mode*. 1936; Ithaca, N.Y.: Cornell University Press, 1964.

Guérard, Albert L. *Preface to World Literature*. New York: Holt, 1940.

Lewis, C. S. *The Allegory of Love*. 1936; London: Methuen, 1970.

Longinus. *Art of Rhetoric*. Quoted in Appendix 2 (by Patricia Matsen) in Rollinson, *Classical Theories of Allegory and Christian Culture*.

MacQueen, John. *Allegory*. London: Methuen, 1970. Especially useful on Christian allegory.

Mather, Samuel. *The Figures or Types of the Old Testament*. 1705; New York: Johnson Reprint, 1969. A fascinating volume. "A Type is some outward and sensible thing ordained of God under the Old Testament, to represent and hold forth something of Christ in the New" (52).

Olson, Elder. "A Dialogue on Symbolism." In *Critics and Criticism: Ancient and Modern*, ed. R. S. Crane. Chicago: University of Chicago Press, 1952.

Pfeiffer, Rudolph. *History of Classical Scholarship*. Oxford: Clarendon Press, 1968.

Plato. *The Republic*. In vol. 2 of *The Dialogues*. Trans. B. Jowett. 4 vols. New York: Charles Scribner's Sons, 1907.

Puttenham, George. *The Arte of English Poesie* (1589). Ed. G. D. Willcock and A. Walker. Cambridge: Cambridge University Press, 1936. (I have regularized Puttenham's spelling.) Defines "the Courtly figure *Allegoria*" as "when we speak one thing and think another, and that our words and our meanings meet not" (186).

Rollinson, Philip. *Classical Theories of Allegory and Christian Culture*. Pittsburgh, Pa.: Duquesne University Press, 1980. An especially useful study.

Scholes, Robert, and Robert Kellog. *The Nature of Narrative*. New York: Oxford University Press, 1966.

Trypho. *On Tropes* (1st century B.C.). Quoted in Appendix 2 (by Patricia Matsen) in Rollinson, *Classical Theories of Allegory and Christian Culture*.

Whitman, Jon. *Allegory: The Dynamics of an Ancient and Medieval Technique*. Oxford: Clarendon Press, 1987. The bibliographical footnotes in the first chapter are especially valuable.

Wimsatt, James. *Allegory and Mirror*. New York: Pegasus, 1970. Good bibliographies at the end of each chapter.

Sources of Additional Information

Michael Murrin's *The Veil of Allegory* (Chicago: University of Chicago Press, 1969) contrasts the allegorical and the oratorical traditions: the orator desires to appeal to all, while the allegorist, speaking as a prophet, knows that truth cannot and perhaps should not be given to all. "The publication of *The Faerie Queene* marked a kind of apogee in the history of allegorical rhetoric, a height not reached since Dante wrote *The Divine Comedy* three hundred years earlier. It also marked the end of the allegorical tradition" (167). Murrin's *The Allegorical Epic* (Chicago: University of Chicago Press, 1980) treats Homer, Virgil, Faleria, Tasso, Spenser, and Milton. For Murrin, Virgil is the originator of the polysemous epic and Milton the last writer of true allegory. John M. Steadman's *The Lamb and the Elephant: Ideal Imitation and the Context of Renaissance Allegory* (San Marino, Calif.: Huntingdon Library, 1974) is a major treatment of allegory during the Renaissance. In contrast with Murrin, in *Dark Conceit: The Making of Allegory* (New York: Oxford University Press, 1961), Edwin Honig defines allegory very broadly, treating it as a trope, a genre, and a style. "We find the allegorical quality in a twice-told tale written in rhetorical, or figurative, language and expressing a vital belief" (12). This definition allows him to regard such writers as Hawthorne, Melville, and Kafka as allegorical.

Rosamond Tuve's *Allegorical Imagery: Some Medieval Books and Their Posterity* (Princeton, N.J.: Princeton University Press, 1966) explores the way in which specific medieval allegories were read in the sixteenth century as a means of discovering what readers of that century actually understood as allegory.

In *The Language of Allegory* (Ithaca, N.Y.: Cornell University Press, 1979), Maureen Quilligan presents an approach to allegory that is distinctive in several ways. She argues that allegory is not simply a mode that can be operative in a variety of genres but that there is a true genre of allegory; that essentially "the term 'allegory' defines a kind of language significant by virtue of its verbal ambidextrousness" (26); and that allegory ought not to be conceived in terms of levels. The third point reflects a READER-RESPONSE orientation: What has been called a higher level is "not above the literal one in a vertically organized fictional space, but is located in the self-consciousness of the reader, who gradually becomes aware, as he reads, of the way he creates the meaning of the text" (28).

ALLUSION   1. The evocation of a person, character, place, event, idea, or portion of a text through quotation (exact or approximate), implicit reference through similarity, explicit reference, or echo. Such evocation or suggestion is intended to lead the reader to bring some aspect of the referent to bear at that point of the originating text. 2. More narrowly, evocation in a specifically literary text of another such text or, by extension, of the Bible or myth.

Allusion is to be distinguished from simple imitatio, *the imitation of models of excellence advocated for instance by Roger Ascham in Book II of* The Schole-master, *though the practice of* imitatio *evidently encouraged the use of allusion.*

1. Though the term is frequently assigned stipulative definitions to fit the interests and purposes of particular discussions, in general, the term "allusion" designates the intentional but partly concealed suggestion or evocation of a prior text or of persons, places, events, objects, utterances, or texts, knowledge of which is presumed to be shared by some portion of the anticipated audience. That which is alluded to may be either topical or historical, real or fictional. The earliest use of "allusion" in this broad sense given by the *OED* is 1612, although the practice must date from the prehistory of communicative discourse.

Allusion has increasingly come to be regarded as functioning like a trope, or, in Lucy Newlyn's words, "figurative language to expand meaning through suggestion" (vii). Some allusions seem to operate as metaphors, bringing unexpected contexts or categories into association; others couple parallel situations, emotions, or attitudes, and thus more nearly resemble metonymy. A more complex consideration of metaphoric and metonymic allusion is undertaken by Ziva Ben-Porat (117–18). In either case, allusion is presumed to enrich meaning, pleasure being derived from the economy with which it does so; at times allusions may also be emulative; that is, the allusive passage may be intended to compete with that to which it alludes. Allusion so regarded can be distinguished from those cases in which the author seems not to have intended to suggest the relationship of his or her text to another whose influence is known or conjectured. This last kind of relationship—which Herman Meyer calls a *borrowing* (8), does not enrich meaning.

At the other end of a continuum is the direct reference to a text, as in "she was the stable center for all of them, a Mrs. Ramsay"; or, "he saw himself in the same position as Disraeli in 1867." The common definition of "allusion" as a tacit or covert reference would exclude such direct references, but as Carmela Perri notes in an important article ("On Alluding," 1978), such references function just as allusively as more hidden ones. Perri proceeds to argue that it is not the allusive reference (*allusion-marker* in her terms) but the referent (the *marked*) that is tacit—that is, the properties or connotations of the referent that are relevant are only tacitly specified by the context in which the alluson occurs. Thus, an allusion to Hamlet may be meant to impart (among other possibilities) melancholy, indecision, final resolution to act, or feigned madness; which of these is relevant will be implied but not overtly stated. If no connotation (only denotation) is relevant, or the relevance is stated explicitly, for Perri the case is one of simple reference, not allusion.

The broad category of allusion seems to call out for further subdivisions. Distinctions relevant to defining allusions that are more easily stated in theory than invoked in practice are those between an author's conscious recollection and unconscious incorporation of a prior text, and the related question of whether what appears to the reader to be an allusion was intended by the author to be so recognized. A third distinction—related to but different from the first two—is that between obvious or conspicuous and cryptic or hidden suggestions of other texts. Various systems of terminology have been suggested to address such distinctions, most of them drawn from the study of literary texts although applicable to discourse in general. John Hollander distinguishes between *quotation*, *allusion*, and *echo*, the last not overt and often, if not always, unconscious (64). Lucy Newlyn describes allusion as conscious and as "used by one poet to draw attention to his relationship with the other, or to make reference to a source behind his own poem which he wishes the reader to acknowledge." On the other hand, for Newlyn, an echo "is heard within the mind as distinctly recalling or reproducing an original pattern of sound, rhythm, or language" and "can either be used consciously by the poet, or be an unacknowledged presence in his writing" (viii). Though he did not explicitly give that name to what Hollander and Newman call echo, I. A. Richards used a form of the word in describing the same category in *Principles of Literary Criticism* (1925). Giving examples of two passages in Shelley that seemed to have sources in Milton, Richards described one as "echoing another poem, borrowing, as it were, Milton's voice though not his words" (216). For Michael Wheeler, allusion is the generic term for quotation and reference (3); thus, his "reference" would seem to be parallel with the "allusion" that Hollander differentiates from "quotation."

Quotations themselves can be—to use Wheeler's terms—*marked* (by quotation marks, italics, or other indications that a quotation is being made) or *unmarked*. (Wheeler's *marked* and *unmarked* are, of course, not to be confused with Perri's *marker* and *marked*.)

There is also a difference, for which there seems to be no suggested terminology, between the allusion that is a kind of bonus for the reader who recognizes it and the allusion essential to an understanding of the text (a distinction that is again reasonable in theory but that may well lead to debate in many actual cases). In the passage from *Principles of Literary Criticism* cited previously, Richards points out that (to use Newlyn's senses) the echo was not important to an understanding of Shelley's passage, while the allusion was. Again, there is evidently a difference between what seems a pattern of allusion (as explored, for example, in Wolfgang Rudat's chapters on "Allusion and Sexual Innuendo in *The Rape of the Lock*" and "The *Aeneid* in the *Knight's Tale*") and isolated allusions or echoes.

Considering the numerous distinctions of kinds and the differences in terminology outlined above, it is perhaps useful to note that allusions are most commonly regarded as consciously intended to be recognized, consciously intended to be functional, and equally allusive whether indirect (through, for example, an unmarked quotation) or direct (through, for instance, citing a text by name). They are, thus, a form of what Umberto Eco calls *overcoding* in which readers are to recognize "a surplus of content" (see 149, 269–70). Allusion so understood evidently merges at some indeterminate point into the general context that an author presumes the anticipated audience to share.

2. Most studies of allusion have been devoted more or less to allusions to literary texts that occur in texts that are themselves literary (as the phrasing in some of the quotations above suggests). Much of this attention has been given to the work of seventeenth- and especially eighteenth-century authors for whom allusion, especially allusion to Latin and Greek literature, plays a specially important role. In Reuben Brower's words, "For Dryden and for Pope allusion, especially in ironic contexts, is a resource equivalent to symbolic metaphor and elaborate imagery in other poets" (viii). As traced in detail by Harold Brooks, the way was prepared for poetry of this kind by an evolution from modernization of certain elements in Renaissance translations from Greek and Latin poetry to bolder versions by Cowley in England and imitations by Boileau in France, and then to the "imitations" of Rochester, Oldham, Swift, Pope, and Johnson, in which the skill with which the imitation finds parallels in the contemporary scene is a major source of pleasure. Constant allusion to the classics in poems not

modeled on a particular poem then occurs alongside imitations in the usual sense. Thus imitation is one boundary of allusion. That Renaissance imitation was often a means of linking present with past, of "creating ideological constructs, unblocking—within the fiction of the work—blockages in transmission" is argued by Thomas Greene in *The Light in Troy*. The richest such imitation "makes possible an emergent sense of identity, personal and cultural, by demonstrating the viability of diachronic itineraries" (19).

While Carmela Perri seems correct in arguing that the selection of possible connotations of the referent of the allusion, while tacit, is a function of the context of the allusion, how far a reader should go in pursuing the relevance of allusions to another literary work remains a question. Earl Wasserman, using as his example *The Rape of the Lock*, argues that the reader is expected to respond creatively: "the reader is not only to appreciate the poet's invention in finding appropriate allusions but is actively invited by them to exercise, within poetic reason, his own invention by contemplating the relevances of the entire allusive context and its received interpretation" (443). Wolfgang Rudat argues for even greater recognition of the "mutual commerce" between the allusion and its referent than does Wasserman. In "The Poetics of Literary Allusion," Ziva Ben-Porat develops the difference between "allusion in general" and literary allusion, suggesting that the latter includes an additional stage of actualization that seeks extensive relationships between the alluding and referenced text that are inappropriate, and indeed, often counterproductive, in ordinary allusion (111–15).

Allusion in the nineteenth and twentieth centuries has remained an important literary device in both poetry and prose, though covert references to specific passages of classical literature have become much less common and allusion in general is less frequently the major device or trope in a work.

References

Ascham, Roger. *The Scholemaster* (1570). Bk. 2, Sect. 5 ("Imitation") is reprinted in *Elizabethan Critical Essays*, ed. G. G. Smith. Oxford: Clarendon Press, 1904.

Ben-Porat, Ziva. "The Poetics of Literary Allusion." *PTL: A Journal for Descriptive Poetics and Theory of Literature* 1 (1976): 105–28. An important analysis of the difference between literary and other kinds of allusion.

Brooks, Harold F. "The 'Imitation' in English Poetry, Especially in Formal Satire, Before the Age of Pope." *Review of English Studies* 25 (April 1949): 124–40.

Brower, Reuben. *Alexander Pope: The Poetry of Allusion*. Oxford: Clarendon Press, 1959. An essential study of the importance and pervasiveness of allusion in Pope.

Eco, Umberto. *A Theory of Semiotics*. Bloomington: Indiana University Press, 1976.

Greene, Thomas M. *The Light in Troy: Imitation and Discovery in Renaissance Poetry*. New Haven, Conn.: Yale University Press, 1982.

Hollander, John. *The Figure of Echo: A Mode of Allusion in Milton and After*. Berkeley: University of California Press, 1981.

Meyer, Herman. *The Poetics of Quotation in the European Novel*. Trans. T. Ziolkowski

and Y. Ziolkowski. Princeton, N.J.: Princeton University Press, 1968. An
    important study of the function of literary allusion in the "humoristic" novel.
Newlyn, Lucy. *Coleridge, Wordsworth, and the Language of Allusion*. Oxford: Clarendon
    Press, 1986. Detailed study of the dialogue between Wordsworth and Coleridge
    which was carried on through allusion.
Perri, Carmela. "On Alluding." *Poetics* 7 (1978): 289–307. An informed, incisive,
    essential article.
Richards, I. A. *Principles of Literary Criticism*. 1925; London: Routledge and Kegan
    Paul, 1948. Pages 215–19 constitute an early twentieth-century recognition of the
    importance of allusion to meaning: "to turn the capacity for recognizing recondite
    references into a shibboleth by which culture may be estimated is a perversion to
    which scholarly persons are too much addicted" (219).
Rudat, Wolfgang E. H. *The Mutual Commerce: Masters of Classical Allusion in English
    and American Literature*. Heidelberg: C. Winter, 1985.
Wasserman, Earl. "The Limits of Allusion in *The Rape of the Lock*." *Journal of English
    and Germanic Philology* 65 (1966): 425–44.
Wheeler, Michael. *The Art of Allusion in Victorian Fiction*. London: Macmillan,
    1979.

Sources of Additional Information

For studies of allusion in individual authors, see, in addition to Newlyn and Wheeler,
Gian Biagio Conte, *The Rhetoric of Imitation, Genre, and Poetic Memory in Virgil
and Other Latin Poets*, ed. Charles Segal (Ithaca, N.Y.: Cornell University Press,
1986); U. C. Knoepflmacher, "Irony Through Scriptural Allusion: A Note on Chaucer's
Prioresse" (*Chaucer Review* 4, 1970: 180–83); Grace Landrum, "Spenser's Use of
the Bible and His Alleged Puritanism" (*PMLA* 41, 1926: 9–18); Harry Berger "The
Discarding of Malbecco: Conspicuous Allusion and Cultural Exhaustion in *The Faerie
Queene*, III, ix–x" (*Studies in Philology* 66, April 1969: 135–54); Beatrice Johnson,
"Classical Allusion in the Poetry of John Donne" (*PMLA* 43, 1928: 1098–1109);
Adelaide Tintner, *The Book World of Henry James* (Ann Arbor, Mich.: UMI Research
Press, 1987); Beverly Ann Schlack, *Continuing Presences: Virginia Woolf's Use of
Literary Allusion* (University Park: Pennsylvania State University Press, 1979); and
Intertextuality in Faulkner, ed. Michel Gresset and Noel Polk (Jackson: University
Press of Mississippi, 1985). Adelaide Tintner's *The Museum World of Henry James*
(Ann Arbor; Mich.: UMI Research Press, 1986) is an impressive study of allusions
to art in James's fiction.

Important bibliographies are Udo J. Hebel's *Intertextuality, Allusion, and Quotation:
An International Bibliography of Critical Studies* (Westport, Conn.: Greenwood Press,
1989) and "Allusion Studies: An International Annotated Bibliography, 1921–1977"
(*Style* 13, Spring 1979: 178–225), ed. Carmela Perri, et al.

While Harold Bloom's theory of influence is too eccentric to be related easily to the
broad question of allusion, his line of argument has undoubtedly made many readers
more conscious of the variety of ways in which a poet may respond to a precursor.
Perhaps the first five of the six *revisionary ratios* by which Bloom categorizes a poet's
relations to an influential precursor are most likely to manifest themselves as "echoes"
(in the sense defined previously), and the sixth, *apophrades*, as emulative allusions. See
his *Anxiety of Influence* (London: Oxford University Press, 1973) and *A Map of Misreading*
(London: Oxford University Press, 1975).

AUTHOR   The person who consciously conceives and transcribes or causes
to be transcribed the words of a TEXT.

Definition 3.a of the *OED* reads "One who sets forth written statements; the
composer or writer of a treatise or book. (Now often used to included *author-
ess*)." The opening definition is simply a restatement of the *OED* phrased in
such a way as to address quibbles over computer-generated sequences of words
and over writing to a computer disk rather than on paper. Unlike most centrally
important concepts in the field of literary study, the significant issue that the
concept of the "author" raises is not the result of competing definitions but of
the variety of explanations of the relationship between the author as the person
who holds the pen or presses keys (and eats, sleeps, loves, and pays taxes) and
the consciousness implied by the text produced.

The linking of writers' works to their biographies, in aid of either interpretation
or evaluation of the works, is obviously a long-standing practice; warnings against
it have a long tradition as well. In the *Biographia Literaria* (1817), Coleridge
adapted a letter of 1768–69 from G. E. Lessing to protest a critic's use of
biographical knowledge that is more

> than the author's publications could have told him. . . . [Such a writer] ceases to be
> a [CRITIC], and takes on him the most contemptible character to which a rational
> creature can be degraded, that of a gossip, backbiter and pasquillant . . . he steals
> the unquiet, the deforming passions of the World into the Museum; into the very
> place which, next to the chapel and oratory, should be our sanctuary, and secure
> place of refuge. (7.2:109–10)

During the debate in Oxford University over the creation of a School of English,
a frequently expressed fear was that to turn from the study of the language to
literature was to open the door to scandal and gossip. Thus Alexander Bain
wrote in 1869:

> But when a man gets into literary criticism at large, the temptation to deviate into
> matters that have no value for the predominating end of a teacher of English, is far
> beyond the lure of alcohol, tobacco, or any sensual stimulation. He runs into digres-
> sions on the life, the character, the likings and dislikings, the quarrels and friendships
> of his authors; and even gets involved in their doctrines and controversies. (213–
> 14)

Biographical background was specifically excluded by the New Critics. In their
introduction to *Understanding Poetry*, the 1938 text that spearheaded the New
Critical movement in the classroom, Cleanth Brooks and Robert Penn Warren
insist that "Emphasis should be kept on the poem as a poem" and rule out the
"study of biographical and historical materials" as a substitute for study of the
poem itself (ix, iv).

There are two major questions. The first is whether, or to what degree, the
speaker of a poem or the narrator of a novel is to be identified with the author
as person. The second question is whether, or to what degree, the attitudes and

view of life that seem to be implied by the text as a whole are to be identified with the author's.

The relation between the author and the speaker or narrator became a major issue only in this century. It has generally been resolved by distinguishing a *persona* (character, personality, or mask) assumed by the author from the author's own actions, beliefs, and habitual manner of speaking. (Donald Davie attributes the twentieth-century use of the term to Ezra Pound.) This distinction is most obvious in dramatic monologues and fiction narrated in the first person mode, least evident in LYRIC poems and novels with an external (extradiegetic) narrator. Indeed, in the lyric the question of the relation of the voice "speaking" the poem to the author tends to merge with the second question, that of the degree to which the personal attitudes toward the world implied by the text as a whole reflect the attitudes actually held by the author. T. S. Eliot's "Tradition and the Individual Talent" (1919) presents what has become the orthodox view even of the apparently personal lyric. "The progress of an artist is a continual self-sacrifice, a continual extinction of personality" (7) and "Poetry . . . is not the expression of personality, but an escape from personality " (10). That the lyric frequently presents a feeling or event as experienced by the speaker is, then, no more a guarantee that the author ever experienced the feeling or had the experience described than that the narratives of Conrad's Marlowe represent specific feelings and events experienced by Conrad. On the other hand, Donald Davie's minority position in "On Sincerity: From Wordsworth to Ginsberg" is that, despite the New Critics, much English (and American) poetry since 1780 has been "confessional" and can only be properly read as a statement of the author.

More complex is the question of the relation between the author and the opinions or worldview implied by the text as a whole. The orthodox resolution is to distinguish the author implied by the text from the author whose life had been filled, and was filled during the writing of the text, with innumerable experiences. The issue here, although related to the debate over authorial IN-TENTION, is separable from it. The question of intention asks whether the reconstruction of an author's intention from the text is possible, and if possible, privileged or even relevant. The question of authorial reflection asks whether it is possible to identify the kind of person who seems implied by the text (the reconstruction of the kind of personality and intellect that would seem most likely to lie behind the writing of the whole) with the personality of the author. The former is the question of the status of the writer's intention; the latter is the degree to which the text, including the authorial intention it may imply, represents the personality, the essential mental constitution of the author.

The debate in the mid-1920s between C. S. Lewis and E. M. W. Tillyard instructively delineates the problem that the idea of an implied author is intended to solve. Lewis wished to exclude from criticism any construction of the mind or personality of the poet. "I shall maintain that when we read poetry as poetry should be read, we have before us no representation which claims to be the poet, and frequently no representation of a *man*, a *character*, or a *personality* at all"

(4). In support of this position, Lewis argues that the poet is selecting elements of common experience (words suggesting what is "public, common, impersonal, objective") and "arranging them in a special order" (19). In his first reply, Tillyard argues for recognition of and response to the poet's personality as "some mental pattern that makes Keats Keats and not Mr. Smith or Mr. Jones. . . . And I believe we read Keats in some measure because his poetry gives a version of a remarkable personality of which another version is his life" (35). Neither Lewis nor Tillyard recognizes the possibility of an "implied author" situated between the actual poet and the order of words on the page. Again, Boris Tomashevsky writes in the essay "Thematics" (1925), "Either the tale is told objectively by the author as a simple report, without an explanation of how the events became known (the *objective* tale), or else it is told by a designated narrator who functions as a relatively specific character" (75).

Since Wayne Booth's *The Rhetoric of Fiction* (1961), it has been usual to distinguish the "implied author" from the "flesh-and-blood" author—especially, but not only, in fiction. For Booth the implied author is the author's "second self" (a term he attributes to Kathleen Tillotson). "As [the author] writes, he creates not simply an ideal, impersonal 'man in general' but an implied version of 'himself' that is different from the implied authors we meet in other men's works" (70–71). As Booth points out, "persona," "mask," and "narrator" have sometimes been employed with the general meaning he gives to "implied author," but these terms "more commonly refer to the speaker in the work who is after all only one of the elements created by the implied author and who may be separated from him by large ironies" (73). "Persona," as suggested above, most often refers to the "speaker" of a poem (Browning's Spanish monk or dying bishop) or the narrator of a story (David Copperfield, Nick Carraway). As previously noted, however, at times a poet seems to speak so completely in his or her own person, or as an external omniscient narrator seems so fused with the reader's sense of the directing intelligence behind the work, that attempting to separate the persona or narrator from the implied author is unprofitable. In principle, however, the separation remains between the implied author and the narrator, whether external (extradiegetic) or internal (intradiegetic)—between, to use perhaps less confusing terms, the implied author and what Booth calls "the teller of the tale." Something of the complexity of the composite construction that makes up the implied author had been suggested by I. A. Richards's discrimination of four kinds of meaning in *Practical Criticism* (1929). In addition to the "sense" or proposition expressed, a speaker generally has also some feelings about the proposition, an attitude toward the person or persons addressed, and an intention, "the effect he is endeavouring to promote" (181–82). The assumption that any use of language ordinarily carries all four of these "meanings" implies, of course, that they are immanent in the speaker of a poem or teller of a tale.

Without using the term implied author, in *With Respect to Readers* (1970), Walter Slatoff explores at length readers' reactions to a "presence" behind the text. Though he refers constantly to the "author's presence" or, alternatively, the "narrator's presence," Slatoff is explicit about distinguishing this presence as a psychological and logical entity from "the author considered as a biographical entity." The characteristics of the work such as "style, point of view, structure, pattern, narrative mode, and especially tone imply a controlling mind" (107). The quality of the "controlling mind" is responsible for large portions of a reader's reactions—whether positive, negative, or questioning. Slatoff gives examples of numerous differences between the "voices" that produce the authorial presence. Somewhat earlier, Reuben Brower similarly discussed the different "tones" of poems by Frost, Donne, and Hopkins in "The Speaking Voice" chapter of *The Fields of Light* (1951).

Sheldon Sacks is one of the few traditionally oriented twentieth-century critics writing after *The Rhetoric of Fiction* to have directly opposed the principle of separating the author from the personality implied by the text; in fact he insists on the importance of the reader responding to the author's beliefs and attitudes. "When we have read a good novelist's work it is as if we have had an opportunity to hear him speak to us of his beliefs and also have been able to observe for years how in fact he reacts to people we have been allowed to know performing actions whose motives have been made comprehensible to us for ends with which we sympathize or which we dislike" (271–72). The key question for Sacks is "What must this novelist have believed to have evaluated characters, acts, and thoughts in such a manner in such a work?" (68)

Current theories that seek wholly to separate text and author allow no place for an implied author. In "The Death of the Author," Roland Barthes looks to structural linguistics for the doctrine that "the whole of the enunciation is an empty process, functioning perfectly without there being any need for it to be filled with the person of the interlocutors" (145). He is indeed happy to take a further step: "Once the author is removed, the claim to decipher a text becomes quite futile. To give a text an Author is to impose a limit on that text, to furnish it with a final signified, to close the writing" (147). Michel Foucault, combining the structuralist belief that "Criticism should concern itself with the structures of a work, its architectonic forms, which are studied for their intrinsic and internal relationships" (118), with his own focus on "discursive practices" that subsume individual texts, reduces the concept of author to the "author-function." For neither Barthes nor Foucault can the personality of an author, implied or actual, be of interest. In "The Poetics and Politics of Bardicide," Richard Levin analyzes why Marxist-oriented critics are especially attracted to Barthes's proclamation of "the death of the author." That doctrine, he finds, enables Marxists "to prove . . . that the play is really saying what the critic wants it to say" without the problems of intentionalist readings (501). Further, wholly disregarding the author "enables these critics to wage—and to win—a kind of class war against the forces of evil, embodied in the text's hegemonic ideology" (502).

For theories of literature that continue to assume the necessity, or at least the value, of attributing to a consciousness the meaning derived from the structure (that is, the illocutionary force of the whole), there exists a further distinction. In the second edition of *The Rhetoric of Fiction*, Booth differentiates between the implied author of a given text and "the Career-Author," the "composite" of the implied author found in the totality of the author's works. In formulating the concept of the implied author, Booth points out that very different "second selves" are implied by Fielding's various novels (72–73), while a few pages later he speaks of the implied author of the whole of Shakespeare's plays (76). Clearly the texts of certain authors will imply much the same consciousness and attitudes, the same personality, while the implied authors found in the several texts of other writers will be much less commensurate.

References

Bain, Alexander. "On Teaching English." *Fortnightly Review* n.s. 6 (August 1869): 200–214.

Barthes, Roland. "The Death of the Author." In *Image—Music—Text*. Trans. S. Heath. New York: Hill and Wang, 1977. "We know now that a text is not a line of words releasing a single 'theological' meaning (the 'message' of the Author-God) but a multi-dimensional space in which a variety of writings, none of them original, blend and clash" (146).

Booth, Wayne. *The Rhetoric of Fiction*. 1961; 2d ed. Chicago: University of Chicago Press, 1983. Still the central document for consideration of the role of the implied reader. Excellent bibliography, brought up to 1982 in the second edition by James Phelan.

Brooks, Cleanth, and Robert Penn Warren. *Understanding Poetry*. 1938; Henry Holt, 1949.

Brower, Reuben. *The Fields of Light*. New York: Oxford University Press, 1951.

Coleridge, Samuel Taylor. *Biographia Literaria*. Ed. J. Englell and W. J. Bate. In vol. 7 of *The Collected Works of Samuel Taylor Coleridge*. Ed. K. Coburn. 16 vols. London: Routledge and Kegan Paul, 1969–84.

Davie, Donald. "On Sincerity: From Wordsworth to Ginsberg." *Encounter* 31 (October 1968): 61–66.

Eliot, T. S. "Tradition and the Individual Talent" (1919). In *Selected Essays*. New York: Harcourt, Brace and World, 1950.

Foucault, Michel. "What Is an Author?" (1969). In *Language, Counter-Memory, Practice*. Trans. D. F. Bouchard and Sherry Simon. Ithaca, N.Y.: Cornell University Press, 1977.

Levin, Richard. "The Poetics and Politics of Bardicide," *PMLA* 105 (May 1990): 491–504.

Lewis, C. S., and E. M. W. Tillyard. *The Personal Heresy: A Debate*. 1939; London: Oxford University Press, 1965. Reprinted from *Essays and Studies* 19 (1934), 20 (1935), and 21 (1936). Consists of three essays each by Lewis and Tillyard.

Richards, I. A. *Practical Criticism*. New York: Harcourt, Brace, 1929.

Sacks, Sheldon. *Fiction and the Shape of Belief: A Study of Henry Fielding*. Berkeley: University of California Press, 1964. Though Fielding is the central example, Sacks's thesis extends to the novel in general, discriminating it from the satire and the apologue.

Slatoff, Walter J. *With Respect to Readers*. Ithaca, N.Y.: Cornell University Press, 1970.
    A pioneering work on readers' responses to literary texts.
Tillyard, E. M. W. See Lewis, C. S.
Tomashevsky, Boris. "Thematics" ("Tematika," 1925). In *Russian Formalist Criticism:
    Four Essays*, ed. and trans. Lee T. Lemon and Marion J. Reis. Lincoln: University
    of Nebraska Press, 1965.

Sources of Additional Information

For a history of the word "author," and especially the relation between it and *auctores*
(authorities), see Donald E. Pease's essay on "Author" in *Critical Terms for Literary
Study*, ed. Frank Lentricchia and Thomas McLauglin (Chicago: University of Chicago
Press, 1990).

The concept of the implied author remains slippery. M. M. Bakhtin, whose writings
at times seem to divide novels between those told by a narrator-author and those told by
an internal character, specifically distinguishes between the author and any teller whatever
in a passage in "Forms of Time and Chronotope in the Novel" (in *The Dialogic Imagination,* trans. Caryl Emerson and Michael Holquist; Austin: University of Texas Press,
1981). "Even had [the author-creator] created an autobiography or a confession of the
most astonishing truthfulness, all the same he, as its creator, remains outside the world
he has represented in his work" (256). Nevertheless, the reader does respond to an
authorial level, which, in the light of the preceding quotation, is probably to be understood
as Bakhtin's equivalent of the implied author. He writes in "Discourse in the Novel"
(also included in *The Dialogic Imagination*), "Behind the narrator's story we read a
second story, the author's story; he is the one who tells us how the narrator tells his
stories, and also tells us about the narrator himself. We acutely sense two levels at each
moment in the story" (314). Wolfgang Iser's comments on the author-reader relationship
in *The Implied Reader* (1972; Baltimore: Johns Hopkins University Press, 1974) generally
identify external narrators with the author even though Iser cites Booth's distinction (see
102–3).

The idea of the implied author has been rejected by other critics. Jon-K. Adams's
Pragmatics and Fiction (Amsterdam: John Benjamins, 1985) argues that the concept of
the implied author is superfluous; the implied author cannot be part of the line of transmission from the real author to the real reader because the implied author does not speak,
and does not use language. Rather, the implied author is merely a portion of the historical
author. In *Interpretation: An Essay in the Philosophy of Literary Criticism* (Princeton,
N.J.: Princeton University Press, 1980), P. D. Juhl criticizes the concept of the implied
author (which he seems to regard as derived partially from biographical information):
"But what could be the point of giving a name ('implied author' or 'authorial personality')
to those aspects of the author which are relevant to our understanding of his work and
another (the 'real author') to those which are not and then saying that it is only the former
we are concerned with?" (191).

C

CANON 1. The five parts or activities in rhetorical composition. 2. An authoritative list of authors or works, a catalogue, intended to be complete within announced, but not necessarily evaluative, criteria. Thus a list of all an author's works constitutes the author's canon. 3. A selection of authors or works based on a norm that may be explicit or may be at least partially hidden, unconscious, or implicitly assumed. Most often, "canon" refers to those works generally assumed to be the most rewarding, to have most influenced later writers, to be part of the knowledge of the well-educated, and to be most often included in school or university curricula, thus constituting a kind of classic canon. The adjectival form, "canonical," thus designates a standard treatment of a subject, knowledge of or reference to which is expected. In recent years the assumptions behind and relationships between these criteria have been the subject of vigorous debate.

The Greek kanon *was a term applicable to standards of length and straight or upright objects and, by extension, to lists or catalogues. While "canon" seems to have carried some normative force throughout its many uses, the degree of that force varies greatly. One must keep in mind the difference between historical uses of "canon" and its present application to catalogues of texts. In both Latin and Greek, lists of texts were designated by other terms; no investigation of the concept of a canon can be restricted to the history of the use of the specific word.*

1. In its oldest application to oral or written discourse, "canon" referred to the parts of rhetorical composition regarded as essential (the five canons were invention, disposition, style, memory, and delivery).

2. The relationship of *kanon* to correctness was early implied in Christian uses of the word. "Irenaeus, in the second century, could already speak of

various familiar canons: 'the canon of truth' (in preaching), 'the canon (rule) of faith[,]' . . . and the 'ecclesiastical canon[,]' . . . expressing both true confession and correct ritual participation in the church'' (Eliade, 3:63). By the fifth century, ''canon'' was used to designate authorized lists: the accepted books of the Bible, lists of saints, and binding decisions of the Church. In such cases, the term canon meant not merely ''selected,'' however, but also ''authoritative'' (see Fowler, *Kinds of Literature*, 214). *Canon* as applied to the whole of an author's work, carries a similar, if lesser, force: a listing of an author's canon aspires to inclusiveness and authenticity (all of an author's work and only that author's work). Authority and authenticity are, of course, criteria for evaluation, but of an order different from other evaluative norms. While evaluation of style and content evidently play their part in the process of judging what is authoritative or authentic, the judgment intends to pronounce whether a given text was or was not inspired by God, or was or was not written by a particular author.

3. The first use of ''canon'' to describe a selective list of literary works appears to have been by David Ruhnken in *Historica critica oratorum Graecorum* in 1768 (Curtius, 256; Pfeiffer, 207). Where the fact of selection is explicit, as in secular uses after Ruhnken, the evaluative criteria are necessarily highlighted.

E. R. Curtius tells us that ''in Antiquity, the concept of the model author was oriented upon a grammatical criterion, the criterion of correct speech'' (250); Roger Ascham's *The Scholemaster* offers a sixteenth-century example. A passage from Bacon's *De Augmentis* (1605) lists among the purposes of criticism ''brief censure and judgment of the authors; that men may make some selection unto themselves what books to read'' and the order of studies ''that men may know in what order or pursuit to read'' (182). James (Hermes) Harris's *Philosophical Enquiry Concerning Language and Universal Grammar* (1752) includes among the tasks of criticism the search for general principles of good writing by examination of ''the most approved performances'' and the leading of readers to the finest literature: ''Indeed Critics (if I may be allowed the metaphor) are a sort of *Masters of Ceremony* in the Court of letters, thro' whose assistance we are introduced into some of the first and best company'' (*Works* 2:298). Matthew Arnold's well-known criteria for poetry include truth as well as formal excellence; the resulting ''best'' poetry ''will be found to have a power of forming, sustaining, and delighting us, as nothing else can'' (9:163). F. R. Leavis writes in the introduction to *Revaluation* (1936), ''we may say that the less important poets bear to tradition an illustrative relation, and the more important bear to it the more interesting kinds of relation: they represent significant development'' (3). The nominal criteria for selection, whether stated as grammatical correctness; stylistic felicity; the pleasurable; or the good, true, or beautiful, require agreement on the way such qualities are to be determined. Notoriously, critics have more often relied on the existence of generally shared attitudes and tastes of their time, or asserted their own personal preferences, than demonstrated and defended the privileged role of their criteria. Barbara Herrnstein Smith has argued in ''Contingencies of Value'' that the evaluative processes that produce canons ultimately respond to changing cultural functions and needs that are in constant interaction with the changing social environment.

In literature, a degree of novelty as well as conformity to tradition must always have been of importance. (In the area of religion, once the canon of sacred books is established, novelty can enter only through interpretive and critical commentary.) The opposition generated Samuel Johnson's balancing of the novel and true, Matthew Arnold's pursuit of the best that is known and thought that yet generates a current of true and fresh ideas, T. S. Eliot's concept of a tradition reordered by each work, and Harold Bloom's formulation of the struggle of creativity and individuality against belatedness.

The existence in fact of a multiplicity of canons must be acknowledged. Alastair Fowler's distinction between six different canons has quickly become almost standard. The *Official* canon "is institutionalized through education, patronage, and journalism." *Personal* canons depend on individual tastes and preferences. The *Potential* canon "in the broadest sense comprises the entire written corpus, together with all surviving oral literature"; much of it is thus not accessible in practice. The *Accessible* canon is the entire corpus to the extent one has access to it. *Selective* canons result from institutionalized reading lists and curricula. The *Critical* canon, consisting of those works and writers repeatedly discussed in books and journals is, remarks Fowler, "surprisingly narrow" ("Genre and the Literary Canon," 98–99).

As Curtius makes clear—not only in the fourteenth chapter of *European Literature and the Latin Middle Ages*, so frequently quoted on the subject of canon formation, but in the introductory chapters as well—from at least the third century when Alexandrian scholars assembled select lists of correct authors, the education one received depended on the authors included in the available curriculum. "Education becomes the medium of the literary tradition, a fact which is characteristic of Europe, but which is not necessarily so in the nature of things" (36). One sense of "classic" reduces essentially to what has been and continues to be frequently taught. Our understanding of the changes in literary values, standards of grammatical correctness, and the very meaning of the "Artes Liberales" and the vision of the world they offered is gained largely from our knowledge of curricular catalogues of accepted authors and works. For example, throughout the medieval period a pagan canon was read alongside a Christian one; to look at the apparently incongruous nature of certain of these catalogues is to recognize that what was common was a mode of reading. That is, in practice, selective canons represent the interactivity of judgments about what texts should be read and how they should be read.

Gradual recognition of the degree to which works have been selected for educational curricula on the basis of largely unexamined cultural norms or ideologies has led to the argument that the formation of the "classic," or what Fowler calls the "official," canon is a function of power: works have been evaluated in terms of their reflection of the existing power structure of society. Louis Kampf and Paul Lauter's *The Politics of Literature* (1972) is one of the earliest examples. Lauter states the point succinctly in "Race and Gender in the Shaping of the American Literary Canon": the canon "is, in short, a means by which culture validates social power" (435). Richard Ohmann's *Politics of Letters* (1987) argues that teachers of English have become servants of monopoly capitalism. The argument that the canon is a reflection of political and social power, urged initially by Marxists, has been made with considerable force by feminist critics and champions of literature written by members of minority groups. When applied to world rather than national literature, it demands attention to the literature of formerly colonized or politically marginalized cultures.

That Western literary historians, scholars, and critics—and therefore readers generally—have focused their attention on male, Caucasian writers from internationally influential countries is widely agreed. The extent to which powerful political and economic interests have encouraged this state of affairs, is, however, open to debate. It can be argued, as does G. Robert Stange in the case of Victorian poetry, that "the principal agents of canon formation are the poets themselves," reviewers, journalists, publishing houses, and the editors of anthologies (159). All these agencies may be influenced by dominant classes and ideologies, but canons do not appear to be the direct result of a single ideology or politically powerful elite directly determining evaluative judgments.

Jane Tompkins and Annette Kolodny argue for a literary history that explains why given texts do or do not have power in the world, suggesting a way to escape evaluative judgments of texts altogether—an approach formulated as long ago as 1913 by Levin L. Schucking: "what was read at a specific time in various strata and why it was read—this should be the chief question of literary history" (quoted in Holub, 50). Such an approach to the canon is implied by the "aesthetics of reception" pursued by Hans Robert Jauss, and like Schucking's, belongs to the sociology of literature.

If one accepts not only that canons are the products of evaluative choices but that all evaluations are based on the perceptions and values of a particular group, it is an easy step to the argument that all evaluative criteria are arbitrary and that no selective canon is possible that does not privilege a particular socioeconomic group. On this view, no attempt at canon building is justified. A variation on this argument is that of sophisticated contemporary theorists who point out that not only do we judge by wholly relative, often self-serving, standards, but that what we find in a work to judge depends on the critical theories we bring to it. Frank Kermode points out that the institution of criticism, especially within the academy, imposes both canonical and hermeneutic restrictions. "By the first of these expressions I mean the determination of what may or ought not to be interpreted, and by the second the decision as to whether a particular means of doing so is permissible" (74). Stanley Fish argues that "formal units are always the function of the interpretative model one brings to bear; they are not 'in' the text" (164), and thus he is "in the business of making texts and of teaching others to make them by adding to their repertory of strategies" (180). On the other hand, Howard Felperin has argued that without some agreement on a shared canon, the critical enterprise must collapse (46), and Harry Levin, who regards "our collective memory" as "our most valued patrimony," finds an agreed canon necessary to the essential "dialogue between the minds of ancestors and of contemporaries" (362).

It is perhaps the recentness of canon formation in the modern languages that makes questioning the canon seem novel. English and American literature having been generally admitted to university study only in the late nineteenth century; adjustments such as the admission of Donne to the canon of major English authors and Melville to the American seem more striking from the perspective of university departments of English than they are if considered against the long history of what the learned or educated were expected to know. From the sixth century to at least the twelfth, that a student might complete his studies without knowing Martianus Capella's *De nuptiis philologiae et mercurii* or Cassiodorus's *Institutiones* would have seemed incredible.

References

Altieri, Charles. "An Idea and Ideal of a Literary Canon." *Critical Inquiry* 10 (1983): 37–60. An able statement of a conservative position.

Arnold, Matthew. "The Study of Poetry." In vol. 9 of *The Complete Works of Matthew Arnold*. Ed. R. H. Super. 11 vols. Ann Arbor: University of Michigan Press, 1960–77.

Bacon, Francis. *The Advancement of Learning*. Ed. W. A. Wright. Oxford: Clarendon Press, 1900.

Curtius, Ernst Robert. *European Literature and the Latin Middle Ages*. Trans. W. Trask. London: Routledge and Kegan Paul, 1953. A central source.

Eliade, Mircea, ed. *The Encyclopedia of Religion*. 16 vols. New York, Macmillan 1987.

Felperin, Howard. *Beyond Deconstruction: The Uses and Abuses of Literary Theory*. Oxford: Clarendon, 1985.

Fish, Stanley. *Is There a Text in This Class?* Cambridge, Mass.: Harvard University Press, 1980.

Fowler, Alastair. "Genre and the Literary Canon." *New Literary History* 11 (1979): 97–119.

———. *Kinds of Literature*. Cambridge, Mass.: Harvard University Press, 1982.

Harris, James. *Philosophical Enquiry Concerning Language and Universal Grammar* (2 vols., 1780–81). In *The Works of James Harris, Esq*. London, F. Wingrave, 1801.

———. *Upon the Rise and Progress of Criticism* (1752). In *The Works of James Harris, Esq*. London: F. Wingrave, 1801.

Holub, Robert C. *Reception Theory: A Critical Introduction*. London: Methuen, 1984.

Jauss, Hans Robert. "Literary History as a Challenge to Literary Theory." In *Toward an Aesthetic of Reception*. Trans. T. Bahti. Minneapolis: University of Minnesota Press, 1982.

Kampf, Louis, and Paul Lauter. *The Politics of Literature*. New York: Pantheon, 1972.

Kermode, Frank. "Institutional Control of Interpretation." *Salmagundi* 43 (1979): 72–86.

Kolodny, Annette. "The Integrity of Memory: Creating a New Literary History of the

United States.'' *American Literature* 57 (1985): 291–307. An important statement of the case for rethinking the concept of the canon.

Lauter, Paul. ''Race and Gender in the Shaping of the American Literary Canon.'' *Feminist Studies* 9 (1983): 435–63.

Leavis, F. R. *Revaluation: Tradition and Development in English Poetry*. 1936; New York: Norton, 1963.

Levin, Harry. ''Core, Canon, Curriculum.'' *College English* 43 (1981): 352–62. An important statement of the function and value of conserving a traditional canon.

Ohmann, Richard. *The Politics of Letters*. Middletown, Conn.: Wesleyan University Press, 1987.

Pfeiffer, Rudolph. *History of Classical Scholarship*. Oxford: Clarendon Press, 1978.

Smith, Barbara Herrnstein. ''Contingencies of Value.'' *Critical Inquiry* 10 (1983): 1–35. An especially thoughtful discussion of the issues.

Stange, G. Robert. ''1887 and the Making of the Victorian Canon.'' *Victorian Poetry* 25 (1987): 151–68.

Tompkins, Jane. *Sensational Designs: The Cultural Work of American Fiction*. New York: Oxford University Press, 1985.

Sources of Additional Information

On the way the term came to be applied to Christian writings, see Samuel Davidson's article ''Canon'' in the *Encyclopaedia Brittanica*, 11th ed.; Rudolph Pfeiffer's *History of Classical Scholarship* (Oxford: Clarendon Press, 1968); and Bruce Kimball's *Orators and Philosophers: A History of the Idea of Liberal Education* (New York: Teachers College Press, 1986) offer valuable information on the educational canons of earlier centuries.

Efforts to include literature written by women, members of minority groups, or the politically or socially repressed are well represented by essays in *Black Studies and Literary Theory*, ed. Henry Louis Gates, Jr. (London: Methuen, 1984)—a particularly valuable collection of essays, both exploring literary theory from a black perspective and sophisticatedly analyzes texts by black authors; Dexter Fisher and Robert B. Stepto's *Afro-American Literature: The Reconstruction of Instruction* (New York: Modern Language Association of America, 1979); Marie Harris and Kathleen Aguero's *A Gift of Tongues* (Athens: University of Georgia Press, 1987); Lillian Robinson's ''Treason Our Text: Feminist Challenges to the Literary Canon'' in *The New Feminist Criticism*, ed. Elaine Showalter (New York: Pantheon 1985); Paul Lauter's *Reconstructing American Literature: Courses, Syllabi, Issues so that the work of Frederick Douglass, Mary Wilkins Freeman, Agnes Smedley, Zora Neale Hurston and Others is read with the work of Nathaniel Hawthorne, Henry James, William Faulkner, Ernest Hemingway and Others* (Old Westbury, N.Y.: Feminist Press, 1983); and David Lloyd's *Nationalism and Minor Literature* (Berkeley: University of California Press, 1987). The general political ramifications of required common texts are discussed from several points of view in Robert Scholes's ''Aiming a Canon at the Curriculum'' and the replies to that essay (*Salmagundi* 72, 1986: 101–65). A broadly conceived but uneven collection of essays on canon questions appears in *Canons*, ed. Robert von Hallberg (Chicago: University of Chicago Press, 1984). Investigations of the process of canon formation include Alan C. Golding's ''A History of American Poetry Anthologies,'' in Robert von Hallberg's *Canons* and Hugh Kenner's ''The Making of the Modernist Canon'' (*Chicago Review* 34, 1984: 49–61, and reprinted in von Hallberg's *Canons*). Christopher Clausen's ''It Is Not Elitist to

Place Major Literature at the Center of the English Curriculum'' (*Chronicle of Higher Education* 13, January 1988: A52), protests those arguments for canon revision that assume that arguments for literary merit are masked forms of validating ideological positions. Wendell Harris's "Canonicity" (*PMLA* 106, January 1991: 110–21) urges that all canons be recognized as constructions for a particular purpose.

CLASSIC   (as either adjective or substantive): 1. Of the highest class of literature; originally, highly recommended as a model. 2. A work belonging to ancient Greek or Roman literature; the most frequent form for this use is "classical." 3. A work exhibiting the characteristics generally associated with the literature of antiquity; for example, restraint, clarity, reasonableness, and stylistic decorum. Often thus opposed to "Romantic."

For brief definitions contrasting the classic and the Romantic, see the note at the end of the entry on ROMANTICISM.

1. Aulus Gellius (A.D. second century) first used the term *classicus* to distinguish the authors who may serve as models, adopting the term from *classici*, citizens of the first tax-paying class. E. R. Curtius points out that such authors were seen first as models of correct grammar and usage (249–50). This sense of the exemplariness, and hence of high quality, easily became extended to refer to works valued as wholes, not simply for their grammatical correctness. By further extension, the work that continues to be held in esteem and becomes part of what is traditionally valued, or part of a particular canon, especially a pedagogical canon, comes to be referred to as a "classic." Thus Matthew Arnold writes that "the true and right meaning of the word *classic, classical*" is that of belonging "to the class of the very best" ("Study of Poetry," 165).

What makes a work classic in this sense is evidently a matter of importance. T. S. Eliot's *What Is a Classic?* gives as criteria maturity (of the civilization, the literature, and of the author who produced the work), comprehensiveness in expressing the range of feeling of the people who speak the language, and a balance between the tradition and originality. For Eliot, Virgil is the "universal classic." In Frank Kermode's view:

> There are . . . two ways of maintaining a classic, of establishing its access to a modern mind. The first of these . . . asks what the classic *meant* to its author and his best readers, and may still mean to those who have the necessary knowledge and skill. The second is the method of accommodation, by which I mean any method by which the old document may be induced to signify what it cannot be said to have expressly stated. (40)

The true classic must be amenable to both: "It seems that on a just view of the matter the books we call classics possess intrinsic qualities that endure, but possess also an openness to accommodation which keeps them alive under endlessly varying dispositions" (44). (See also CANON.)

2. Because the models that the Renaissance delighted in discovering and imitating and that they incorporated into school curricula were those of Greek

and Roman antiquity, "classic," or more usually "classical," gradually acquired the sense of "pertaining to Greek and Roman culture." Thus Gilbert Highet's *The Classical Tradition* carries the subtitle, *Greek and Roman Influences on Western Literature*; under "classics, classical literature" in his index, one finds simply *"see* Greco-Roman literature." The noun form "classicism," which usually refers to the attempt to model writing on Greco-Roman literature, is ambiguous in connotation: whereas Sherard Vines uses the term quite honorifically in his survey *The Course of English Classicism*, Highet uses it primarily in reference to exaggerated adherence to presumed classical forms and/or rules (292).

"Classicism" as a term appears only in the nineteenth century; both "classicism" and "neo-classicism" were then employed to refer to the literature and criticism of the immediately preceding centuries (see Wellek's "Classicism in Literary History"). As understood by the neo-classicists of mid-seventeenth-century France and of eighteenth-century England and Germany, adherence to the unities, to rules about what was appropriate to a genre, and to the general or typical over the particular were essential to the kind of imitation that could give one's own work classic status. However, although Corneille, Racine, Boileau, Pope, Johnson, and Lessing are central representatives of neo-classicism, they differ from each other and from other, less influential but basically neoclassical writers. René Wellek writes that neo-classicism "attempted to discover the principles or the 'laws' or 'rules' of literature, of literary creation, of the structure of a literary work of art, and of the reader's response" (*History of Modern Criticism*, 1:12). In W. J. Bate's words, "rational determination of the absolute and ideally good in taste and morality is to be facilitated and made more authoritative by the study of the preferences and the conduct of the best in all ages, and especially classical antiquity" (24). Neo-classicism drew heavily on Aristotle and Horace, who were regarded as having reduced nature, good sense, and the resulting practice of good poets to method. In "What Is A Classic?" Charles Augustin Sainte-Beuve notes that whereas the dictionary of the Academy had in 1694 "defined a classical author merely as 'an old author strongly approved, who is an authority on the matter he treats,' " the emphasis in the 1835 edition, reflecting what by then was the conservative opposition to Romanticism, is on "strict rules" (468–69). Such rules favored didacticism, a concern for the universal and general rather than the particular, clarity of expression, decorum (as defined by the appropriate genre), and an avoidance of the enthusiastic, eccentric, and idiosyncratic.

It is nevertheless possible to stress the concern for rules too strongly in that they were simply guides toward the depiction of that which was universal and the attainment of that which was universally pleasing.

3. The Greek and Roman corpus long provided models of major genres, but in addition certain qualities of thought and style have come to be associated with it. (In discussions of neo-classicism, primary attention is most often given to the rules its spokesmen developed; in discussions of Greek and Roman literature

itself, the primary attention is most often on the qualities that seem dominant.) Matthew Arnold writes in the "Preface to the First Edition of *Poems*" that the Greeks are "the unapproached masters of the *grand style*" (5); that style he later defines in "On Translating Homer" as arising "when a noble nature, poetically gifted, treats with simplicity or with severity a serious subject" (188). Those qualities assigned to Greek literature by Arnold in the course of the 1853 and 1854 prefaces to his poems and the essay "On the Modern Element in Literature" are subordination of all parts of the work to the whole, "noble simplicity," "sanity," "adequacy" in representing the "highly developed human nature of that age," and "serenity." Other qualities commonly assigned to classic Greek and Roman literature are impersonality and clarity.

When the classical is opposed to the Romantic, the former often designates an amalgam of classical and neo-classical qualities, including especially the avoidance of enthusiasm, the pursuit of the general, restraint, impersonality, and clarity of expression. Sherard Vines formulates the difference in attitudes toward nature succinctly: "as long as man is recognized as taking nature in, rather than nature as absorbing man, the classic mode is indicated" (81). For Albert Guérard, the key words defining the classical or classicism are consistency, discipline, and restraint. The common core is *correctness*, a term perhaps best understood as appropriateness to the circumstances when applied to the exemplary works in Greek and Latin, and as following the appropriate model when applied to later, especially neo-classical, texts. Curtius defines what he calls "Standard Classicism" as "all authors and periods which write correctly, clearly, and in accordance with the rules, without representing the highest human and artistic values" (274).

The sense of classical as opposed to Romantic is not, in fact, congruent with sense 2 (pertaining to Greco-Roman literature), since, as Walter Pater pointed out, "in Greek and Roman work there are typical examples of the romantic spirit" (260). Gilbert Highet, in effect describing the contrast between Romanticism and classicism through the differences between Pindar and Horace, opposes "Inspiration and reflection; passion and planning; excitement and tranquillity; heaven-aspiring flight and a calm cruise near the ground." Nevertheless, the two very different aesthetic impulses, found in Greco-Roman poetry itself, "are not opponents, but complements and sometimes allies" (227–28). Similarly, Curtius writes, "Those who love Antiquity in all its periods and styles (a love which is certainly less common than might be supposed) are precisely those who will feel its apotheosis as the 'classical' to be empty and misleading pedantry" (250).

References

Arnold, Matthew. "Preface to the First Edition of *Poems*," "Preface to the Second Edition of *Poems*," "On Translating Homer," and "On the Modern Element in Literature." In vol. 1 of *The Complete Prose Works of Matthew Arnold*. Ed. R. H. Super. Ann Arbor: University of Michigan Press, 1960–77.

———. "The Study of Poetry." In vol. 9 of *The Complete Prose Works of Matthew Arnold*. Ed. R. H. Super. Ann Arbor: University of Michigan Press, 1960–77.

Bate, Walter Jackson. *From Classic to Romantic*. 1946; New York, Harper and Row, 1961.

Curtius, Ernst Robert. *European Literature and the Latin Middle Ages*. Trans. W. R. Trask. London: Routledge and Kegan Paul, 1953. Curtius opposes the classical not to the romantic but to the mannerist. "The mannerist wants to say things not normally but abnormally. He prefers the artificial and affected to the natural. He wants to surprise, to astonish, to dazzle" (282).

Eliot, T. S. *What Is a Classic?* London: Faber and Faber, 1945.

Guérard, Albert. Chapter 9 of *Preface to World Literature*. New York: Henry Holt, 1940.

Highet, Gilbert. *The Classical Tradition: Greek and Roman Influences on Western Literature*. 1949; New York: Galaxy, 1957.

Kermode, Frank. *The Classic: Literary Images of Permanence and Change*. New York: Viking Press, 1975.

Pater, Walter. "Postscript." In *Appreciations*. London: Macmillan, 1910.

Sainte-Beuve, Charles Augustin. "What Is a Classic?" In vol. 6 of *The Art of the Critic*, ed. Harold Bloom. New York: Chelsea House, 1988. Sainte-Beuve's own definition is a personal one: "A true classic, as I should like the term to be defined, is an author who has enriched the human mind, who has actually added to its treasures and carried it a step forward, one who has discovered some unmistakable moral truth or recaptured some eternal passion in a human heart where everything seemed known and explored" (469).

Vines, Sherard. *The Course of English Classicism*. New York: Harcourt, Brace, 1930.

Wellek, René. "Classicism in Literary History." In *Discriminations*. New Haven: Yale University Press, 1970.

———. *A History of Modern Criticism: 1750–1950*. Vol. 1. New Haven, Conn.: Yale University Press, 1955.

CODE 1. A system of rules for relating one set of phenomena to another. 2. A system of signals or signs. 3. A natural language. 4. Forms of socioeconomically determined linguistic performance. 5. A set of implicitly shared knowledge that makes it possible to understand utterances or texts. 6. A set of explicit rules for translating texts into and out of an arbitrary sign system to prevent those who do not know the rules from understanding the texts. 7. A set of values to which an individual adheres.

While "code" is at times employed to designate an element in a code, the concept of "code" in most uses is centered on the possibility of translating from one system of signification to another.

1. What Umberto Eco regards as the proper sense of "code" is derivative from the second sense given in the *OED* and dated 1809–10 from a use by Coleridge: "A system or collection of rules or regulations on any subject." As Eco points out, from the point of view of information theory, "code" can be applied to possible sets of signs or signals, possible sets of information to be conveyed by those signs or signals, and possible behavioral responses to the

signs or signals (36–37). These three systems he calls system-codes, or *s-codes*; they are to be distinguished from the code proper, which for Eco is a rule for coupling one system with another. When applied to linguistic communication, this leads to problems of semantic analysis, that is, of explaining which of the specific denotations and connotations coded in a word (sign-function) are relevant in a given use. (In simplest form, has the word "block" to do with a child's toy, an action in a football game, ropes and pulleys, a material obstruction, or the area between two sets of streets?) J. J. Katz and J. A. Fodor have answered the question through a theory of syntactic and semantic markers (see SEMANTICS) which Eco modifies: "The Revised Model aims to insert into the semantic representation all coded connotations depending on corresponding denotations as well as *contextual* and *circumstantial selections*" (105). For Eco the theory of codes excludes what is usually called the *referent* (Ogden and Richards), the *object* (C. S. Peirce), or the *bedeutung* (Frege), that is, the existing object, event, or belief to which the sign is linked, for "the codes, insofar as they are accepted by a society, set up a 'cultural' world which is neither actual nor possible in the ontological sense" (61). Thus, the rules by which code systems, including natural languages, signify are cultural constructions.

2. Regarded simply as a potential system, a "system of signals," the recognizable differentiations in a possible set of signs can be called a "code," as, more important, can those specific differentiations actually utilized by a code. Thus, the understanding of the sounds of a spoken language depends on recognizing systematic differences, such as //t// as opposed to //a//, and //ō// as opposed to //ā//. If one thinks of the senses of words as mutually limiting and defining (as are those of—to take a simplified instance—pebble, rock, and boulder both among themselves and in contrast to plants, animals, water, and so on), the total system of differences can be thought of as a code. This is, in fact, Saussure's view of language: "The linguistic fact can . . . be pictured in its totality—i.e., language—as a series of contiguous subdivisions marked off on both the indefinite plane of jumbled ideas . . . and the equally vague plane of sounds" (112).

3. The use of "code" as a synonym for a given language, including natural languages, largely derives from Roman Jakobson's celebrated essay on "Linguistics and Poetics," in which code figures as one of the "constituent factors" in any speech event (addresser, addressee, context, message, contact, or code) (353). Though Jacobson initially speaks simply of "a CODE fully, or at least partially, common to the addresser and addressee" (353), a later example cites "the lexical code of English" (356). To speak of language as a code suggests not only a one-to-one relationship like that of "tree" to "tall, woody plant," but the system by which the elements of experience are incorporated into communication and thought processes. What is coded, the distinctions between contiguous percepts made by coding, and the connotations that may become attached to elements of the code ("tall" versus "slender") all affect thought and communication.

4. The work of Basil Bernstein and his associates in England in developing

"a sociology of language" has resulted in the definition of two contrasting sets of principles that govern verbal planning and resultant language use. These Bernstein designates *elaborated* and *restricted*. "In the case of an elaborated code, the speakers will select from a relatively extensive range of alternatives and therefore the probability of predicting the pattern of organizing elements is considerably reduced. In the case of a restricted code the number of these alternatives is often severely limited and the probability of predicting the pattern is greatly increased" (1:76–77). The major significance of the difference for Bernstein is that "the lower working class, including rural groups" tends to have access only to the restricted code (1:81).

5. "Code" in the sense of a category of conventions or contexts came into use with Roland Barthes's classifications of the codes or signifying systems operating within a single text. His best-known exploration of these occurs in *S/Z* (1970), where he lists five codes: the *proairetic* (code of action), *hermeneutic* (code of puzzles), *referential* or cultural, *semic* or connotative (relying on clusters of connotations), and *symbolic* (relying on patterns, usually binary oppositions). The classification of signifying systems is, however, arbitrarily constructed: Barthes's "Structural Analysis of Narrative: Apropos of Acts 10–11" (1969) identifies twelve codes; his "Textual Analysis of a Tale by Edgar Allen Poe" (1973) omits the semic code of *S/Z* while adding the "communicative" code. According to Barthes, "The codes are simply associative fields, a supratextual organization of notations which impose a certain notion of structure"; they are "essentially cultural" ("Textual Analysis," 288). Presumably, these systems signify by calling up a reader's knowledge of external cultural attitudes and conventions of reading, or, in the largest sense, internal and external contexts. Codes can thus be thought of as describing either the kinds of knowledge the reader must, or should, bring to bear on a text, or simply the kinds of knowledge a given reader—Barthes, for instance—does bring to bear on a given text.

This usage has become loose enough to allow almost anything in a text other than a word in one of its usual denotative senses to be regarded as a code, and thus Seymour Chatman describes the personalities that readers give characters as resulting from *codes of traits* that allow the correlation of what the text tells us of them with the readers' total experience of human characters (137). Douwe Fokkema suggests a different set of five codes operating in a literary text, each code imposing its own restrictions on the author or sender (and, to the extent that they are recognized, on the reader or receiver). Fokkema's five codes are the linguistic code, which identifies the language, the literary code, which "predisposes the reader to read the text as a literary text," the generic code, the period or group code, "which directs the reader to activate his knowledge of the conventions of a period or particular semiotic community," and the idiolect of the author (8–9). When Fokkema later speaks of postmodernism as a code in itself, however, "code" here seems to be defined as the characteristics of postmodern texts, such as emphasis on the role of the reader and the rejection of any necessary relation between words and reality (38ff.).

It has become fashionable to speak of a text as "traversed by codes," an expression in which "codes" can be taken as registers, dialects, or the structure of events within the text, as well as readers' expectations based on their knowledge of genre, strategies of reading, and the culture generally.

6. The sense of "code" as a set of rules for concealing a message is not usually important for literary study except that insofar as one is concerned with the intentions of a sender (whether author or speaker), it is presumed that the sender assumes a shared set of signifying systems. The person coding a message for concealment must know that his or her receiver(s) share a (secret) set of decoding rules. Such a system is mechanical to the extent that there are rigorous rules for translation between the clear and coded text, but it is possible for the author of a literary text to plan special meanings or significances that will be available only to those who share a special knowledge or context.

All the above senses of code assume that there are systems governing the production (encoding) of texts by a writer and understanding (decoding) by a reader. (The emphasis on system is important: a dot followed by a dash is not the code for the letter "A" but rather an element of the Morse code.) The extent to which the understanding of the decoder can or should match the intention of the encoder is a matter of debate, as is the question of whether thoughts are possible prior to language. In regard to the latter, it is evident that human beings can at least use language to think about language, as happens most evidently each time a conscious choice is made between alternative modes either of expression (that is, between linguistic formulations) or of interpretation. Such considerations warn against using the term "code" carelessly and reductively. Tzvetan Todorov writes that such usage carries the risk of making us see linguistic exchange in the image of something like the work of telegraph operators: one person has a content to transmit, and encodes it with the help of a key and transmits it through the air; if contact is established, the other decodes it with the same key, thus recovering the initial content. Such an image does not correspond to discursive reality (55). A. J. Greimas and J. Courtés specifically reject the use of code in the fifth sense above: "As a borderline case, some semioticians use the term code to cover an undefined set of units which have only a slender tie with each other, based on association, with no appeal made to an underlying logico-taxonomic organization" (32).

7. H. W. Leggett's *The Idea in Fiction* (1934) makes an interesting use of the sense of "code" as applied to the beliefs and values by which an individual acts (as in "the code of a gentleman"). Leggett employs the term to designate the modes of self-definition and response that the reader comes to recognize as determining a character's actions and personality. "An individual's code embodies the standards by which he regulates his behaviour, the limitations he puts on his feelings, his beliefs, prejudices, and hopes" (71). For Leggett, the clash of codes—both between characters and within a given character—provides much of the interest of fiction. The code by which a fictional character acts may or may not be consciously recognized by that character and may or may not be

explicit in the work itself. However, a work may indeed imply the desirability of a certain code of behavior—the novels and stories of Kipling, Conrad, and Hemingway offer examples.

References

Barthes, Roland. "Structural Analysis of Narrative: Apropos of Acts 10–11" (1969) and "Textual Analysis of a Tale by Edgar Allen Poe" (1973). In *The Semiotic Challenge*. Trans. S. Heath. New York: Hill and Wang, 1988. Original French edition. 1985.

———. *S/Z*. Trans. R. Miller. New York: Hill and Wang, 1974. Original French edition, 1970.

Bernstein, Basil. *Class, Codes and Control*. 3 vols. Bernstein is the author of vol. 1 and editor of vols. 2 and 3. London: Routledge and Kegan Paul, 1971, 1973, 1975.

Chatman, Seymour. *Story and Discourse*. Ithaca; N.Y.: Cornell University Press, 1978.

Eco, Umberto. *A Theory of Semiotics*. Bloomington: Indiana University Press, 1976.

Fokkema, Douwe W. *Literary History, Modernism, and Postmodernism*. Amsterdam: John Benjamins, 1984.

Frege, Gottlob. "On Sense and Reference" (1892). In *Translations from the Philosophical Writings of Gottlob Frege*. Ed. P. Geach and M. Black. Oxford: Basil Blackwell, 1952.

Greimas, A. J., and J. Courtés. *Semiotics and Language: An Analytical Dictionary*. Trans. L. Crist, D. Patte, et al. Bloomington: Indiana University Press, 1982.

Jakobson, Roman. "Closing Statement: Linguistics and Poetics." In *Style and Language*, ed. Thomas A. Sebeok. Cambridge, Mass.: MIT Press, 1960.

Katz, Jerrold J. *Semantic Theory*. New York: Harper and Row, 1972.

Leggett, H. W. "Codes." In *The Idea in Fiction*. London: Allen and Unwin, 1934.

Ogden, C. K., and I. A. Richards. *The Meaning of Meaning*. 8th edition. New York: Harcourt, Brace, World, 1946.

Peirce, Charles Sanders. "On the Classification of Signs." In vol. 8 of *Collected Papers of Charles Sanders Peirce*. Ed. A. W. Burks. Cambridge, Mass.: Harvard University Press, 1958.

Todorov, Tzvetan. *Mikhail Bakhtin: The Dialogical Principle*. Trans. Wlad Godzich. Minneapolis: University of Minnesota Press, 1984.

Sources of Additional Information

The entry in the *Encyclopedic Dictionary of Semiotics*, ed. Thomas A. Sebeok, 3 vols. (Berlin: Mouton, 1986) is a good summary of the senses and use of "semiotics" broadly defined. Umberto Eco's chapter on "Code" in *Semiotics and the Philosophy of Language* (Bloomington: University of Indiana Press, 1986) summarizes the ways in which the meaning of the term has become "exaggeratedly generous" and develops his own more restricted meaning. Three essays in Roland Barthes's *The Semiotic Challenge*, trans. Richard Howard (1985; New York: Hill and Wang, 1988) exemplify his analyses of texts in terms of their "codes" in his sense. Robert Scholes briefly applies Barthian "codes" to Joyce's "Eveline" in *Semiotics and Interpretation* (New Haven, Conn.: Yale University Press, 1982).

COMEDY   1. That kind of drama arousing laughter and arriving at a happy ending described by Aristotle and exemplified in the extant plays of Aristophanes and Menander, and Plautus and Terence, and represented by subsequent plays that appear not too distant from the basic patterns of Greek and Roman comedy. 2. In what is largely a medieval and early Renaissance use, any work of literature that ends happily, whether or not it provokes laughter. 3. Any dramatic or narrative fiction—spoken, written, or acted—that provokes smiles or laughter.

1. That Aristotle wrote a treatise on comedy, perhaps as a second part to the existing *Poetics*, is assumed by many commentators. However, if it ever existed, the treatise is now wholly lost unless the fragment known as the *Tractatus Coislinianus* derives in part from Aristotle. Lane Cooper's *An Aristotelian Theory of Comedy* includes the *Tractatus Coislinianus* and attempts to develop a theory of comedy on Aristotelian principles; Richard Janko's translation of the *Poetics* attempts a reconstruction of the assumed second part of the *Poetics* on the basis of the *Tractatus*.

In the existing *Poetics*, Aristotle passingly describes comedy as "an imitation of men worse than the average; worse, however, not as regards any and every sort of fault, but only as regards one particular kind, the Ridiculous, which is a species of the Ugly. The Ridiculous may be defined as a mistake or deformity not productive of pain or harm to others" (15; 5:1449a). The origin of comedy was in dispute even in Aristotle's day, as was the origin of the term: Aristotle notes that the Megarians claimed that it derived from their word for village (*komē*) rather than from that for revel (*komos*). That comedy, like tragedy, developed out of performances of religious rituals is hardly in question, but the manner of development remains conjectural. Greek comedy is usually divided into Old, Middle, and New periods. The names of writers of all periods are known, together with fragments of many plays (generally preserved as quotations in other texts), but of Old Comedy only eleven plays of Aristophanes are extant, two of which ought primarily to be considered as part of Middle Comedy, of which there are no other surviving examples. The end of Old Comedy came in 404 b.c. when Athens lost its power and preeminence. Of New Comedy, the *Dyskolos* and portions of five other plays of Menander survive. Thus reconstructions of the history and characteristics of Greek comedy remain in part conjectural.

Gilbert Norwood has summarily commented:

> Comedy is that type of drama which employs action tolerably close to real life and an expression light, charming, often laughable. Allied to comedy, and often confused with it, is farce, which may be defined as exaggerated comedy: its problem is unlikely and absurd, its action ludicrous and one-sided, its manner entirely laughable. Some of the finest work included under the convenient title of "Greek comedy" should in strictness be called farce. (1)

The more riotous humor and public themes belong to Aristophanes; the more domestic, less hilarious comedy to Menander. Katherine Lever's *The Art of Greek Comedy* formulates the Aristotelian distinction in another way: "The tragic poet is concerned with the relations of human beings to those forces which lie beyond their control"; the "comic poet, on the other hand, is concerned with relations of human beings to forces or conditions which do lie within their control" (vii).

Our knowledge of Roman comedy is derived primarily from Plautus (twenty of whose plays survive) and Terence (who appears to have written only six plays, all of which survive). Since all of Terence's and the greater part of Plautus's plays were based on specific Greek originals, these Roman plays are also a prime source of our knowledge of Greek comedies. Both authors depend heavily on errors and confusions for their plots, but again the two playwrights differ, Plautus having much more liking for farce and buffoonery than Terence.

The themes and situations of Greek and Roman comedy have evidently continued on the stage not only in the Renaissance but to the present. At the same time, Aristophanes, Menander, Plautus, and Terence were sufficiently different from each other to provide a variety of models. Major conventions have constantly been altered: Roman comedy dispensed with the choruses of Greek comedy; the Renaissance moved from verse—universal in classical comedy—to prose. It is, therefore, as difficult to draw a line separating the "true" comedy from other kinds of drama as it is to reach agreement about the "true" tragedy. For instance, not all of Shakespeare's plays that are generally designated "comedies" are necessarily accepted as in fact belonging in that category. Nor is the distinction with satire at all clear-cut. Much of Aristophanes is satirical; much general as opposed to individual satire is found throughout Molière. Northrop Frye's influential analysis in *Anatomy of Criticism* ("The Mythos of Spring: Comedy") directly descends from Menander and Terence in seeing the fundamental plot of comedy as the struggle of young lovers to overcome the opposition of a parent or others whose values are astray; the lovers' eventual triumph represents the triumph of a more ideal society. He observes that both Greek and Roman comedy emphasize the importance, and not the mere convenience, of unlikely contrivances in bringing about a happy ending. "Happy endings do not impress us as true, but as desirable, and they are brought about by manipulation" (170).

The central exemplar of post-Renaissance comedy has been Molière. The most frequently cited major English playwrights for comedy are Jonson, Wycherly, Congreve, Farquhar, Goldsmith, Sheridan, Wilde, and Shaw.

2. In the Middle Ages, when stage drama as understood by the Greeks or Romans had lost its role in the culture, comedy, like tragedy, shifted its meaning. Not only was the word now applied to narratives rather than plays, but a happy ending, rather than amusement or the risible, became the primary defining characteristic. Thus could Dante call his great work *The Divine Comedy*.

3. In the first paragraph of *The Theory of Comedy*, Elder Olson writes, "I

am old-fashioned enough to mean comedy when I say comedy, and tragedy when I say tragedy: by which I mean the dramatic forms designated by such terms, and not forms which are narrative'' (3). Nevertheless, by natural extension, "comedy" has come to be applicable to all forms of literature and discourse that include a significant amount of material presumably intended to amuse and end happily. Any form of humor longer than a brief anecdote is thus likely to be called a comedy, and since the later part of the eighteenth century the novel has come to seem at least as important a vehicle for comedy as the drama. Twentieth-century studies are therefore likely to give little attention to comedy as a form, and instead try to identify the sources of laughter and/or explore the varieties within the category of the comic.

One line of explanation for laughter descends from Plato. In the *Philebus*, Socrates's analysis of the ridiculous leads Protarchus to agree with the following: "Then the argument shows that when we laugh at the folly of our friends, pleasure, in mingling with envy, mingles with pain, for envy has been acknowledged by us to be mental pain, and laughter is pleasant, and we envy and laugh at the same instant'' (3:189; 50a). The clear implication is that there is a sense of superiority, and thus malice, in laughter at ridiculous persons, whom Socrates has just defined as those who are ignorant but harmless because they lack the power to do harm (Aristotle also confines the ridiculous to those incapable of doing harm). The best-known English proponent of a similar view is Thomas Hobbes. "*Sudden Glory* is the passion which makes these *Grimaces* called LAUGHTER; and is caused either by some sudden act of their own, that pleaseth them; or by the apprehension of some deformed thing in another, by comparison whereof they suddenly applaud themselves'' (45; 1.6).

The social function of ridicule has been stressed by many, a view that brings it close to satire. Sir Philip Sidney stresses the ridiculous in persons (not, that is, in accidentals or circumstances): "Comedy is an imitation of the common errors of our life, which he representeth in the most ridiculous and scornful sort that may be; so as it is impossible that any beholder can be content to be such an one'' (41–42). Dramatists and critics of the drama have often cited the corrective function of their comedies. Thus writes John Dennis: "But can any Thing but corrupt and degenerate Nature be the proper Subject of Ridicule? And can any Thing but Ridicule be the proper Subject of Comedy?'' (2:243). A somewhat softened version is found in Henri Bergson, who notes that laughter is usually accompanied by an absence of feeling but nevertheless emphasizes the social nature of comedy: we find comedy in that which is human or that reminds us of the human, and it operates only when it can be shared. Thus, "Laughter must answer to certain requirements of life in common. It must have a *social* significance'' (65). For Bergson, laughter occurs when we perceive human inelasticity or "automatism," when characters are too rigid for the circumstances. Comedy is produced by "seeking to mould things on an idea of one's own, instead of moulding one's ideas on things" (179). Such an attitude can be described either as the result of vanity or the action of a dominant "humour," or indeed the two can be conflated. Henry Fielding announces in the preface to *Joseph Andrews* that "the only Source of the true Ridiculous (as it appears to me) is Affectation" (7); in paper number 65 of *The Covent-Garden Journal*, he associates such affectation with "throwing the Reins on the Neck of our favorite Passion, and giving it full Scope and Indulgence" (302). As Northrop Frye formulates it, the characters blocking the sought-for happy outcome of a comedy are often governed by a particular humour or otherwise obsessed. That is why comedy represents movement toward a better social state: "Illusion is whatever is fixed or definable, and reality is best understood as its negation: whatever reality is, it's not *that*" (170).

What is often regarded as the major opposing theory was stated by Kant: "Laughter is an affection arising from the sudden transformation of a strained expectation into nothing" (223). This perspective on the comedy is found in Arthur Koestler, who, after arguing that laughter is created by "the sudden clash of two swift-flowing, independent association streams" (27), continues, "Laughter is habitually called 'relieving' or 'liberating'; it is a process which discharges or 'explodes' emotional tension" (57). However, Koestler mixes in something of the Hobbesian: the "common denominator" of all forms of the jokes of which the comic consists "is usually a very faint impulse of aggression or defence manifested as malice, derision, self-assertion, or merely as an absence of sympathy with the victim of the joke" (54). Elder Olson is more specific about the form of relief involved. Comedy "removes concern" because, Olson explains in a description modeled on Aristotle's analysis of tragedy, it is "the imitation of a worthless [foolish to be concerned about] action, complete and of a certain magnitude, in language with pleasing accessories differing from part to part, enacted, not narrated, effecting a *katastasis* [relaxation] of concern through the absurd" (47). Nevertheless, it is not the thing imitated so much as the attitude taken in the imitation that produces comedy. Where tragedy "imitates an action *which it makes serious*, . . . comedy imitates an action *which it makes a matter for levity*" (36). The importance of a comic view that imposes itself on human action is frequently stated, as, for instance, by Louis Kronenberger: "Comedy is not just a happy as opposed to an unhappy ending, but a way of surveying life so that happy endings must prevail" (3).

A third approach to comedy is that of Sigmund Freud in *Wit and Its Relation to the Unconscious*, which finds the ultimate source of laughter in the energies of the unconscious. The study is primarily an analysis of brief jokes, or "wit"; Freud finds them most often in service to an inhibited craving or tendency. However, what Freud differentiates as wit, the comic, and humor, are for him all finally forms of psychic "economy," means of gratification with a minimum of personal expenditure. "All three . . . strive to bring back from the psychic activity a pleasure which has really been lost in the development of this activity. For the euphoria which we are thus striving to obtain is nothing but the state of a bygone time [childhood], in which we were wont to defray our psychic work with slight expenditure" (803).

Finally, James Feibleman's *In Praise of Comedy* (1939) constructs an interestingly broad definition of comedy as "the indirect affirmation of the ideal logical order by means of the derogation of the limited orders of actuality" (178–79). Expecting "to be tied down to actuality," when we are instead surprised by something more logical, we laugh (191). "[T]he categories of actuality are always what they have to be and seldom what they ought to be. It is the task of comedy to make this plain" (178).

While there are a range of terms that seem to mark distinctions within the overall area of the laughable—wit, humor, comedy, the comic, burlesque, farce, satire—there has hardly been unanimity in their use. Thus, on the one hand, George Meredith's well-known *Essay on Comedy and the Uses of the Comic Spirit* explicitly distinguishes comedy—the test of which is that "it shall awaken thoughtful laughter" (82)—from satire, irony, humor, and farce. For true comedy—for the sharing of the "volleys of silvery laughter" of the Comic Spirit—"A society of cultivated men and women is required, wherein ideas are current and the perceptions quick" (2). On the other hand, a writer like Morton Gurewitch makes comedy an umbrella term: "Comedy is a miscellaneous genre activated by a plurality of impulses: farce, humour, satire, and irony" (13). Nevertheless, there is a general sense of the distinctions such that "wit" occurs through clever manipulation of words and associations of thought, while "comedy" describes incongruous, ridiculous, or absurd human situations. Freud encapsulates this distinction: "Wit is made, while the comical is found" (762). "The comic" is sometimes used as an overarching term that includes the others; however, where "comedy" is employed to refer to literary texts, "the comic" can refer to analogous extraliterary sources of laughter. In comedy as a literary form, of course, the ridiculous situation is almost always blended with witty characters. "Humor," when not restricted to the "comedy of humours" in which characters are dominated by particular passions or the bents of their personalities, most frequently designates a more sympathetic or kindly laughter. "Farce" and "burlesque" are exaggerated forms of comedy, the latter most often applied when an identifiable actual person or situation is the basis. SATIRE attacks vices as opposed to follies and moves from amusing ridicule to strong contempt.

References

Aristotle. *On the Art of Poetry*. Trans. I. Bywater. Oxford: Clarendon Press, 1909.
Bergson, Henri. *Laughter in Comedy*. Ed. Wylie Sypher. Garden City, N.Y.: Doubleday Anchor, 1956. An important statement. "The comic will come into being, it appears, whenever a group of men concentrate their attention on one of their number, imposing silence on their emotions and calling into play nothing but their intelligence" (65).
Cooper, Lane. *An Aristotelian Theory of Comedy*. New York: Harcourt, Brace, 1922.
Dennis, John. "A Defense of Sir Fopling Flutter." In *The Critical Works of John Dennis*. Ed. Edward Niles Hooker. 2 vols. Baltimore: Johns Hopkins University Press, 1943.

Feibleman, James. *In Praise of Comedy: A Study in Its Theory and Practice* (1939). New
      York: Russell and Russell, 1962.
Fielding, Henry. *The Covent-Garden Journal*. Ed. B. Goldgar. Middletown, Conn.:
      Wesleyan University Press, 1988.
————. *Joseph Andrews*. Ed. Martin Battestin. Middletown, Conn.: Wesleyan University
      Press, 1967.
Freud, Sigmund. *An Essay on Wit and Its Relation to the Unconscious*. In *The Basic
      Writings of Sigmund Freud*. Ed. and trans. A. A. Brill. New York: Modern
      Library, 1938.
Frye, Northrop. ''The Mythos of Spring: Comedy.'' In *Anatomy of Criticism*. Princeton,
      N.J.: Princeton University Press, 1957. Brings together the insights of a number
      of significant earlier approaches.
Gurewitch, Morton. *Comedy: The Irrational Vision*. Ithaca, N.Y.: Cornell University
      Press, 1975.
Hobbes, Thomas. *Leviathan* (1651). Oxford: Clarendon Press, 1909.
Janko, Richard, trans. [Aristotle's] *Poetics*. Indianapolis: Hackett, 1987. Janko adds his
      reconstruction of Aristotle on comedy to his translation of the *Poetics*.
Kant, Immanuel. *Critique of Judgment*. Trans. J. H. Bernard. London: Macmillan, 1914.
Koestler, Arthur. *Insight and Outlook*. New York: Macmillan, 1949.
Kronenberger, Louis. *The Thread of Laughter: Chapters on English Stage Comedy from
      Jonson to Maugham*. New York: Alfred Knopf, 1952.
Lever, Katherine. *The Art of Greek Comedy*. London: Methuen, 1956. Begins with the
      earliest sources of comedy (600 B.C.); gives greatest attention to Aristophanes,
      but also treats Menander and the New Comedy.
Meredith, George. *An Essay on Comedy and the Uses of the Comic Spirit*. New York:
      Charles Scribner's Sons, 1897. Also included in *Comedy*, ed. Wylie Sypher.
      Garden City, N.Y.: Doubleday Anchor, 1956.
Norwood, Gilbert. *Greek Comedy*. London: Methuen, 1931. A standard survey.
Olson, Elder. *The Theory of Comedy*. Bloomington: Indiana University Press, 1968.
      Cogently presented discussion.

> Properly speaking, then, the comic includes only the ridiculous, the ludicrous, the things which
> are taken as such by analogy, the witty, and the humorous. All these, differ as they may, have
> a common characteristic: their minimization of the claim of some particular thing to be taken
> seriously, either by reducing that claim to absurdity, or by reducing it merely to the negligible
> in such a way as to produce pleasure by that very minimization. (23)

Plato, *Philebus*. In vol. 3 of *The Dialogues of Plato*. Trans. B. Jowett. 4 vols. New
      York: Charles Scribner's Sons, 1911.
Sidney, Sir Philip. *The Defence of Poesie*. Cambridge: Cambridge University Press,
      1904.

Sources of Additional Information

James E. Evans's *Comedy: An Annotated Bibliography of Theory and Criticism* (Me-
tuchen, N.J.: Scarecrow Press, 1987) lists 3,106 items, the great majority published since
1900, each of which receives a one-sentence annotation. The works included are all in
English, though the subjects treated include comedy in a number of languages.

Francis Cornford presents the theories of the development of Greek comedy that are associated with the Cambridge School of anthropology in *The Origin of Attic Comedy* (Cambridge: Cambridge University Press, 1934). The thesis is that the "canonical plot-formula [found in the plays of Aristophanes] preserves the stereotyped action of a ritual or folk drama, older than literary Comedy, of a pattern well known to us from other sources" (3). George E. Duckworth's *The Nature of Roman Comedy* (Princeton, N.J.: Princeton University Press, 1952) is a standard, very useful, source that discusses in detail the relations between Greek and Roman comedy.

A collection of comments on comedy by English writers from Ben Jonson to James Thurber is gathered in *The Idea of Comedy: Essays in Prose and Verse*, ed. W. K. Wimsatt (Englewood Cliffs, N.J.: Prentice-Hall, 1969). The introduction and conclusion by Wylie Sypher for his reprinting of the essays on comedy by Meredith and Bergson explore various modes of considering comedy (see Bergson in References above). "The ambivalence of comedy reappears in its social meanings, for comedy is both hatred and revel, rebellion and defense, attack and escape. It is revolutionary and conservative" (242).

Maurice Charney's *Comedy High and Low: An Introduction to the Experience of Comedy* (New York: Oxford University Press, 1978) is a useful survey of comedy on the stage and in the movies. Robert B. Heilman's *The Ways of the World* (Seattle: University of Washington Press, 1978), focuses on stage comedy and is largely concerned with the distinction between comedy and melodrama.

> Melodrama and comedy . . . share a large common ground: they are both ways of meeting the world—the many-sided, inconsistent, imperfect world, occasionally gratifying or fulfilling, often frustrating, and perhaps still more often seeming punishably unregenerate. Melodrama would do something about it, comedy would strive for ways of coming to terms with it. Melodrama would take arms, comedy accept. (96)

For a discussion of the theory and practice of comedy after modernism, see George McFadden's *Discovering the Comic* (Princeton, N.J.: Princeton University Press, 1982); Chapter 9 treats Barthes and Barthelme.

An interesting interpretation of comedy as an encompassing attitude toward life is that of Suzanne Langer, who contrasts comedy as the image of Fortune with tragedy as the image of Fate: "comedy is essentially contingent, episodic, and ethnic; it expresses the continuous balance of sheer vitality that belongs to society and is exemplified briefly in each individual" (*Feeling and Form*, New York: Charles Scribner's Sons, 1953, 333).

Among studies focused on laughter is J. C. Gregory's *The Nature of Laughter* (New York: Harcourt, Brace, 1924). From Gregory's "Summary and Conclusion": "The 'happy convulsion' of laughter occurs in a situation of relief" and "Laughter is a *diversion*—a pleasant expenditure upon the body of energy released from other activities" (203, 204). J. Y. T. Greig's *The Psychology of Laughter and Comedy* (London: Allen and Unwin, 1923) finds that laughter "in its beginnings at least, is somehow associated with the instinct of love" (44). Ralph Piddington's *The Psychology of Laughter* (London: Figurehead, 1933) finds laughter to be basically biologically determined, communicating "a mood in which there is no need felt for the organism to make any further adjustment to its environment beyond the one at the moment existing" (86). This reaction is then utilized as a "socially appropriate" response to situations that are mildly "subversive to the social order" (148). Both Greig's and Piddington's volumes include substantial appendices summarizing theories of laughter from Plato forward.

CONTEXT   1. Broadly, the total situation, or any aspect of the total situation (the structure of the discourse itself; the knowledge, attitudes, and beliefs the discourse evokes; or elements of the relationship between the author and audience) arguably relevant to the understanding of that which is to be interpreted (word, sentence, image, event, scene, or total discourse). 2. Everything outside the DISCOURSE itself in terms of which that discourse (in detail or as a whole) is to be understood. 3. The structure of a TEXT considered as a closed, internally interactive system. 4. In a specialized sense developed by I. A. Richards, various kinds of association that the use of a word may bring into the text. 5. For critics seeking unconscious ideological assumptions, the prevailing cultural norms of which the writer was not aware; thus for Marxist critics, the socioeconomic system on which the cultural superstructure, including literature in general, is based.

Until recently, "context" as employed in literary and rhetorical criticism was regarded as either so self-evident or, alternatively, so irrelevant, that it need not be formally defined (it is rarely found in standard dictionaries of literary terms).

1. When "the context" is said to clarify or help interpret a word or sentence, the term may simply designate anything and everything that seems relevant to deciding the sense of the word or the proposition and illocutionary force expressed by the sentence. In *The Philosophy of Rhetoric* (1936), I. A. Richards lists the usual senses of context as (a) "the words before and after a given word which determine how it is to be interpreted"; (b) "the circumstances under which anything was written or said"; (c) "the known uses of a word at the time it was written"; and (d) "anything whatever about the period, or anything else which is relevant to our interpretation of it" (32–33). All such elements in the total context of an utterance constantly function in the interpretation of whatever speech is heard or text is read, although only when interpretation is not instantaneous do we become conscious of their roles. Though words and sentences are constantly discussed in artificial isolation by logicians, grammarians, discourse analysts, and classroom teachers as examples or slices of language, the distinction between a word regarded as a lexical item or a sentence regarded as an example and working use is an essential one. The distinction between example and language-at-work has been made in various ways: for Saussure, the difference is between units of the *langue* and instances of *parole*; for some French analysts, the terms are *énoncé* and *énonciation*; Paul Ricoeur contrasts semiotics and semantics; and for H. P. Grice, the difference is between sentence meaning and utterer's meaning.

2. The major distinction between the elements constituting the total context is that between internal and external, between the structure of words making up a discourse and what Kenneth Burke has called the "extra-verbal" context in which a discourse is spoken or written (*Language*, 359). From a point of view

suggested by Saussure, the distinction can also be thought of as between relations that are *in praesentia* and those *in absentia* (123).

The *external context* is made up of background knowledge (including conventions of reading) and the immediate situation of utterance. It thus may be thought of as the historical context if "historical" is interpreted broadly enough. Curiously, the senses of context given in the *OED* do not include the external context as here defined, although that sense is partially included in the second sense listed under "contextualism": "The policy or practice, in literary criticism, of setting a poem or other work in its cultural context."

Discourse analysts have explored the forms of background knowledge rather fully. The information and attitudes that authors presumably expect of their readers is of many kinds: there is historical fact, both past and present (George Washington was the first president of the United States; the United States is bordered on the south by Mexico); brute fact (all people are mortal); institutional fact (money can be exchanged for goods); cultural beliefs and attitudes (slavery is wrong; governments should be elected); experiential knowledge (how it is to feel tired or thirsty); common skills (how to dial a telephone); knowledge of cultural issues (the question of abortion has been a major issue in the 1980s); cultural convention (one shakes hands when meeting another person; in a letter, the salutation nearly always begins "Dear _____,"), and so forth. What has come to be called "cultural literacy" consists of the informational (as opposed to experiential) elements of the total background knowledge expected of the educated adult. How much and what kind of information makes up cultural literacy is a matter of debate; clearly, what is demanded for understanding varies from text to text.

Background information is also understood to include not only isolated pieces of information but also frames, models, or schemata that allow readers to fit what they read into a framework. Readers know in a general way what it is to go to school, take a walk in the woods, or go to a restaurant; they also know the usual concomitants—desks and assignments, trees and peacefulness, or tables, waiters, and menus. Such features are assumed to be present when the associated activities are mentioned unless the reader is specifically told otherwise; they are "default" elements (see Brown and Yule, ch. 7). Similarly, certain events are assumed to cause certain effects, and certain actions to follow certain other actions. Only if the effects or subsequent actions do not follow need the reader be so informed. "Context" in the limited sense in which it is used by Ogden and Richards in *The Meaning of Meaning* is just this sense of interrelations or frames that causes a hearer or reader to assume that if *X* is mentioned, *Y* preceded or followed. In Ogden and Richards's phrasing, "A context is a set of entities (things or events) related in a certain way; these entities have each a character such that other sets of entities occur having the same characters and related by the same relation; and these occur 'nearly uniformly' " (58).

No clear line can be drawn between background information and the immediate situation, since ultimately the significance of the situation depends on background information. However, one is aware of the immediate situation (who is speaking to whom, when, where, and under what physical and cultural circumstances) in what seems to be a different way from that in which one is aware of, say, the date of the fall of Constantinople. The term "context of situation," which was apparently coined by Bronislaw Malinowski, is exemplified by his well-known example of Trobriand natives capturing fish in nets. "All the language used during such a pursuit is full of technical terms, short references to surroundings, rapid indications of change—all based on customary types of behavior, well-known to the participants from personal experience" (311). Among Kenneth Burke's five "dramatistic" terms, "scene" evidently corresponds to the immediate situation (*Grammar*, xvii).

Elements of background information have received particular attention in certain critical theories and approaches—often in terms peculiar to the approach. Thus there is a large literature about literary genres, although these are but a subclass of general discourse genres (which includes sermons, political speeches, instruction manuals); that subclass is, in turn, a subclass of cultural conventions. Charles Sanders Peirce's term for background information is "collateral observation": "by collateral observation I mean previous acquaintance with what the sign denotes. Thus if the Sign be the sentence 'Hamlet was mad,' to understand what this means one must know that men are sometimes in that strange state; one must have seen madmen or read about them; and it will be all the better if one specifically knows (and need not be driven to *presume*) what Shakespeare's notion of insanity was" (8:179).

The interpretation of tropes is generally regarded as depending on context. Wayne Booth uses the term *norms*, writing that every clue to the existence of irony "depends for its validity on norms (generally unspoken) which the reader embraces and which he infers, rightly or wrongly, that his author intends" (53). Ina Loewenberg, Ted Cohen, and John Searle are among the analysts of metaphor who have argued that the recognition and interpretation of metaphor depends on the context of the utterance. Loewenberg notes that "Any sentence can be provided contexts . . . in which it can receive either literal or metaphorical interpretations" (161).

Wolfgang Iser terms the shared conventions necessary to the speech act the *repertoire*. "The repertoire consists of all the familiar territory within the text. This may be in the form of references to earlier works, or to social and historical norms, or to the whole culture from which the text has emerged" (69). Hans Robert Jauss's concept of the "horizon of expectations," that is, the system of expectations "that arises for each work in the historical moment of its appearance, from a pre-understanding of the genre, from the form and themes of already familiar works, and from the oppositions between poetic and practical language" (22) is evidently a way of conceiving of the external context in which a given text is read in a given historical moment. One of Jauss's major theses in "Literary History as Challenge" is that "reconstruction of the horizon of expectation, in the face of which a work was created and received in the past, enables one . . . to pose questions that the text gave an answer to, and thereby to discover how the contemporary reader could have viewed and understood the work'' (28). This leads Jauss toward questions of GENRE and EVALUATION, but it also emphasizes the importance of the external contexts in determining the interest a text holds for readers in its own or later periods. Thomas Kent is similarly concerned with the relationship between context and reception. Drawing on Juri Lotman, he writes that every text has an *extra-text* ''constructed of unformulated conventions'' that ''corresponds to the elements outside of the text itself that make the text meaningful at any particular time'' (71, 70). In argumentation theory as developed by Stephen Toulmin, the concept that different fields of argument or discussion (such as physics, sports, psychology, politics, or law) define the criteria for accepting conclusions in different ways suggests that such fields function as external contexts defining meaning. Thus legal, physical, moral, and mathematical ''impossibility'' are not the same. The *heteroglossia* that Bakhtin finds in all utterances as a result of generic, professional, social, ideological, and historical differences can be regarded as reflecting the context of origination of the utterance.

When one asks what constitutes the external context of a discourse, the difficult question is how one decides what elements of that context are relevant to the interpretation of a given text. Critics following the lead of Jacques Derrida have denied the possibility of determining any limits to appropriate context—this is the major issue in the 1977 exchange between Jacques Derrida and John Searle (see DECONSTRUCTION). Jonathan Culler's formulation of the Derridean deconstructive argument is as follows:

> Context is boundless in two senses. First, any given context is open to further description. There is no limit in principle to what might be included in a given context, to what might be shown to be relevant to the performance of a particular speech act. . . . Context is also unmasterable in a second sense: any attempt to codify context can always be grafted onto the context it sought to describe, yielding a new context which escapes the previous formulation. (123–24)

This is evidently true of context understood as any information, attitude, or situation in which a reader may place a text. If context is understood not in terms of possible readers' collocations but probable authorial strategies (a distinction parallel with those between *langue* and *parole*, and between sentence meaning and utterer's meaning) an outer boundary—which is conceptually easy to understand if difficult to establish in practice—is that which the author could reasonably assume the anticipated audience to share. Thus, what rhetoricians and teachers of composition and creative writing call audience may at least as usefully be regarded as the sum of contextual elements (knowledge, attitudes, and beliefs) that the speaker or writer believes the anticipated audience or readers are likely to possess. Within this boundary the practical, if not rigorously definable, limits to relevant context result from ''the principle of local interpretation.'' As simply defined by Brown and Yule, ''This principle instructs the hearer not to construct a context any larger than he needs to arrive at an interpretation'' (59). They explicitly note that this principle ''leans heavily on the hearer's/reader's ability to utilize his knowledge of the world and his past experience of similar events in interpreting the language which he encounters" (60–61). To this must be added the assumption that authors assume this ability, knowledge, and experience in their intended readers.

3. The *internal context* is itself a structure of contexts: the syntactical position of each word; the relations between words in different sections that parallel, contrast with, or modify each other; the cumulative meaning of all the sentences to the point at which a given word or sentence occurs; and the totality of the discourse as understood after it is heard or read (that is, in the words of E. D. Hirsch, "a construed notion of the whole meaning narrow enough to determine the meaning of a part," 87). Gillian Brown and George Yule's useful alternative term for the sum of these aspects of the internal context is *co-text*.

In general, New Critical references to "context" are to the internal context; the more conservative of New Critics have striven to stay within a poetic text as totally as possible. Murray Krieger thus writes, "I find that when I am reading well the poetic context controls my experience and the meanings I see in it. To allow the poem to function referentially is to break the context. It is to allow the poem to point outside itself and thus lead me into the world of what meanings had been for me before I came to the poem" (*The New Apologists*, 20). "Contextualist" has frequently been used to describe the New Critical focus on the internal context, as, for instance by Murray Krieger in *The New Apologists for Poetry* and *The Play and Place of Criticism*, Walter Sutton in two essays in *The Journal of Aesthetics and Art Criticism* in the late 1950s, and Gerald Graff in *Poetic Statement and Critical Dogma*.

It should be recognized that most, if not all, of the elements of internal context must be understood partly in terms of elements of the external context. The description of the Court of Chancery that opens Dickens's *Bleak House* provides an essential aspect of internal context for the understanding of much that comes after it, but the scene itself is understood only in relation to a large set of attitudes and pieces of knowledge associated with words like "Lord High Chancellor," "fog," "suitors," and "November weather." Looked at another way, for the majority of critics, only those elements of the external context are relevant that are in some way invoked by the specific language of the discourse. Thus it may be argued that no purely internal context exists. Nevertheless, for certain purposes the division between internal and external contexts is useful.

4. In *The Philosophy of Rhetoric*, I. A. Richards develops another sense of context. This, which he calls *delegated efficacy*, is a kind of importation of an expanded set of relations. By associations with other words, a word is able to suggest or substitute for words not there (32). This may occur through the sharing of similar sound and similar meaning (Richards cites "flash, flare, flame, flicker, flimmer [58]") or simply the sharing of similar meanings. When one is aware of such alternative possibilities, even if not fully consciously, the alternatives are suggested along with the chosen word. "The meaning of a word on some occasions is quite as much in what it keeps out, or at a distance, as in what it

brings in'' (63). This special meaning of context parallels what Ferdinand de Saussure called *associative* relationships, that is, relationships based on either sound or meaning similarities. ''For instance, the French word *enseignement* 'teaching' will unconsciously call to mind a host of other words (*enseigner* 'teach,' *renseigner* 'acquire,' etc.; or *armement* 'armament,' *changement* 'amendment,' etc.; or *education* 'education,' *apprentissage* 'apprenticeship,' etc.)'' (123). Saussure also offers a nonlinguistic example: a Doric architectural column ''suggests a mental comparison with other (Ionic, Corinthian, etc.) although none of these elements is present in space: the relation is associative'' (124). These relationships called ''associative'' by Saussure are now generally termed ''paradigmatic.''

Richards also notes that words can import the contexts in which they most usually appear. William Empson speaks of such importations as *implications*: ''the Implication will come from an habitual context of the word (not from its inherent meaning) and will vaguely remind you of that sort of context'' (15).

5. Some theorists have applied the term *contextualist* to criticism (predominantly, but not necessarily, Marxist) that seeks precisely that which writers and audience were *not* conscious of sharing. In Howard Felperin's description of ''the most radical version of the new contextualism, . . . the 'literary' text is regarded as an indirect and elliptical expression of 'ideology,' i.e. group subjectivity or collective self-deception, and 'explained'—as distinct from 'interpreted'—by reference to a social and historical ideology about which it is silent but by which it is 'produced' '' (17).

References

Bakhtin, M. M. ''Discourse in the Novel.'' In *The Dialogic Imagination*. Austin: University of Texas Press, 1981.
Booth, Wayne. *A Rhetoric of Irony*. Chicago: University of Chicago Press, 1974.
Brown, Gillian, and George Yule. *Discourse Analysis*. Cambridge: Cambridge University Press, 1983. An excellent introduction to the aspects of discourse analysis of particular interest to students of literature.
Burke, Kenneth. *A Grammar of Motives* (1945) with *A Grammar of Rhetoric*. New York: Meridian Books, 1962.
————. *Language as Symbolic Action*. Berkeley: University of California Press, 1966.
Cohen, Ted. ''Figurative Speech and Figurative Acts.'' *The Journal of Philosophy* 71 (1975): 669–84. Reprinted in *Philosophical Perspectives on Metaphor*, ed. Mark Johnson. Minneapolis: University of Minnesota Press, 1981.
Culler, Jonathan. *On Deconstruction: Theory and Criticism after Structuralism*. Ithaca, N.Y.: Cornell University Press, 1982.
Empson, William. *The Structure of Complex Words*. New York: New Directions, n.d.
Felperin, Howard. *Beyond Deconstruction: The Uses and Abuses of Literary Theory*. Oxford: Clarendon Press, 1985.
Graff, Gerald. *Poetic Statement and Critical Dogma*. Evanston, Ill.: Northwestern University Press, 1970.
Grice, H. P. ''Utterer's Meaning, Sentence-Meaning, and Word-Meaning.'' *Foundations of Language* 4 (August 1968): 225–42. A central statement.

Hirsch, E. D., Jr. *Validity in Interpretation*. New Haven, Conn.: Yale University Press, 1967.

Iser, Wolfgang. *The Act of Reading*. Baltimore: Johns Hopkins University Press, 1978. Original German version, 1976.

Jauss, Hans Robert. "Literary History as Challenge." In *Toward an Aesthetic of Reception*. Trans. T. Bahti. Minneapolis: University of Minnesota Press, 1982.

Kent, Thomas. *Interpretation and Genre*. Lewisburg, Pa.: Bucknell University Press, 1986.

Krieger, Murray. *The New Apologists for Poetry*. Minneapolis: University of Minnesota Press, 1956. The central issues in this volume are the problems of interpreting poetry without going beyond the internal context.

———. *The Play and Place of Criticism*. Baltimore: Johns Hopkins University Press, 1967.

Loewenberg, Ina. "Identifying Metaphors." In *Perspectives on Metaphor*, ed. Mark Johnson. Minneapolis: University of Minnesota Press, 1981. Reprinted from *Foundations of Language* 12 (1975): 315–38.

Lotman, Juri. *The Structure of the Artistic Text*. Trans. R. Vroon. Ann Arbor, Michigan: Slavic Contributions, 1977.

Malinowski, Bronislaw. "The Problem of Meaning in Primitive Languages." Supplement 1 in Ogden and Richards's *The Meaning of Meaning*.

Ogden, C. K., and I. A. Richards. *The Meaning of Meaning*. 1923; New York: Harcourt, Brace and World, 1946.

Peirce, Charles Sanders. *Collected Papers*. Ed. Charles Hartshorne and Paul Weiss (vols. 1–6) and A. W. Burke (vols. 7–8). Cambridge, Mass.: Harvard University Press, 1931–35; 1958.

Richards, I. A. *The Philosophy of Rhetoric*. 1936; London: Oxford University Press, 1965.

Ricoeur, Paul. *Interpretation Theory: Discourse and the Surplus of Meaning*. Fort Worth: Texas Christian University Press, 1976. Ricoeur's emphasis is primarily on the confusions caused by the multiple senses of individual words: "it is the contextual function of discourse to screen, so to speak, the polysemy of our words and to reduce the plurality of possible interpretations, the ambiguity of discourse resulting from the unscreened polysemy of the words" (17).

Saussure, Ferdinand de. *Course in General Linguistics*. Ed. Charles Bally and Albert Sechehaye; trans. W. Baskin. New York: McGraw-Hill, 1959.

Searle, John. "Metaphor." In *Expression and Meaning*. Cambridge: Cambridge University Press, 1979.

Sutton, Walter. "The Contextualist Dilemma—or Fallacy?" *Journal of Aesthetics and Art Criticism* 17 (December 1958): 219–29.

———. "Contextualist Theory and Criticism as a Social Act." *Journal of Aesthetics and Art Criticism* 19 (Spring 1961): 317–25.

Toulmin, Stephen. *The Uses of Argument*. Cambridge: Cambridge University Press, 1958.

Sources of Additional Information

John Searle distinguishes two levels of "background" in *Intentionality* (Cambridge: Cambridge University Press, 1983). The deepest level consists of capacities, practices, or assumptions that are neither representational nor intentional in the phenomenological sense, but are rather that on which mental representation and intention depend.

> I can, for example, intend to peel an orange, but I cannot in that way intend to peel a rock or a car; and that is not because I have an unconscious belief, "you can peel an orange but you cannot peel a rock or a car" but rather because the preintentional stance I take toward oranges (how things are) allows for a completely different range of possibilities (how to do things) from that which I take toward rocks or cars. (144)

For a sociolinguistic view of background knowledge, see the chapter titled "Foundations of Knowledge in Everyday Life" in Peter L. Burger and Thomas Luckmann's *The Construction of Social Reality* (New York: Doubleday, 1966).

Roland Barthes's five codes as employed in *S/Z* (1970; trans. R. Miller; New York: Hill and Wang, 1974) can be regarded as categories of context: the code of action (*proairetic* code) consisting of the actions occurring in a narrative, the code of puzzles (*hermeneutic* code) consisting of questions raised in the course of a narrative, the cultural codes, the connotative codes (themes grouped around the character), and symbolic field (ideas). While called into existence partly by internal structure, the interpretation of each code depends finally on background information.

The term "contextualism" is employed in a somewhat unusual way by Brice Wachterhouse in the introduction to *Hermeneutics and Modern Philosophy* (Albany: State University of New York Press, 1986). Wachterhouse regards hermeneutics as "contextualist" in that a central principle of hermeneutics as he defines it is that "all understanding will necessarily be an understanding relative to the standpoint of the inquirer" (13). His antifoundationalist (relativist) emphasis falls, therefore, on neither the internal nor the external context, as discussed above, but on the context the reader chooses to regard as relevant.

CRITICISM   1. The act or process of evaluating the merit of a text. 2. The elucidation of the principles whereby evaluation should be carried out or that writers should note in order to have their work judged favorably. 3. Study of and commentary on literature generally. 4. The investigation of the origin and accuracy of texts; this nineteenth-century sense was applied primarily to the Bible. 5. In the sense employed by Matthew Arnold, the use of the best thought to be found in literary (and other) works as criteria for judgment of present questions and for freshening the mode of thought of the time. 6. The close reading, analysis, or explication of the meaning of a literary work. 7. In the sense advocated by E. D. Hirsch, all commentary on and uses of a text other than the presumptive reconstruction of the author's intended meaning.

1. and 2. In the earliest citations in the *OED* (1590, 1604), criticism carries the sense of judging and evaluating. Thus John Dennis, in the opening of *The Grounds of Criticism in Poetry* (1704): "The Design of the foresaid Treatise is, not only to retrieve so noble an Art, and to fix the Rules both of Writing and Judging, that both Reader and Writer may be at some certainty; but, to raise it to a height which it has never known before among us, and to restore it, as we find above, to all its Greatness and to all its Innocence" (unpaginated). A similar sense informs Alexander Pope's *Essay on Criticism* (1711), which is structured as a set of instructions for making proper judgments. The extension of meaning from the act of evaluation to the correct principles for evaluation can equally be found in an essay of Samuel Johnson's *Rambler* of 1751:

> It is . . . the task of criticism to establish principles; to improve opinion into knowledge; and to distinguish those means of pleasing which depend upon known causes and rational deduction, from the nameless and inexplicable elegancies which appeal wholly to the fancy, from which we feel delight, but know not how they produce it, and which may well be termed the enchantresses of the soul. (4:122)

The principles of good or pleasing writing can of course be regarded as being as valuable to the author as to the critic: certainly Pope's *Essay on Criticism* can be taken as a writer's manual. Coleridge explicitly reverses the relationship in the *Biographia Literaria*: "The ultimate end of criticism is much more to establish the principles of writing, than to furnish *rules* how to pass judgment on what has been written by others; if indeed it were possible that the two could be separated" (2:63).

This sense has never been lost, but latent in the concept of criticism as judgment is the possibility of seeking to identify the special value or pleasure of a work rather than judging the degree of value or the balance between virtues and defects. Walter Pater exemplifies this tendency, extending it, however, as in the preface to *The Renaissance*, to the pursuit of the special virtue of the individual author or artist as well as the individual work. Although George Saintsbury speaks of criticism in his *History of Criticism and Literary Taste in Europe* (1900–1904) as "that function of the judgement which busies itself with the goodness or badness, the success or ill-success, of literature from the purely literary point of view" (1:3), he continued this approach, tasting works, as has been noted, in the same way that he tasted the wines on which he was an authority. The tradition then continues in William C. Brownell (with a shift of direction): "it is the *qualities* of the writer, painter, sculptor, and not the *properties* of their productions, that are [the critic's] central concern," (17) and, later, in Helen Gardner, who writes, "The primary critical act is a judgement, the decision that a certain piece of writing has significance and value" (6), while explicitly excluding the ranking of literary works from the purposes of criticism. An intriguingly focused form of evaluative criticism is set forth in *The Rape of Cinderella* by Eugene Paul Nassar, for whom the task of evaluative criticism is to judge "to what degree the author has been successful in developing and maintaining his *tone*, that unique and complex set of attitudes he began with and builds upon" (5).

3. The tendency to use criticism as the umbrella term for all study—and thus including LITERARY HISTORY, INTERPRETATION, and HISTORICAL SCHOLARSHIP—is apparent in the five functions of the critical tradition of knowledge of Francis Bacon's *Advancement of Learning* (1605): (a) the "true correction and edition of authors"; (b) the "exposition and explication of authors"; (c) investigation of the author's times, "which in many cases give great light to true interpretations"; (d) "brief censure and judgment of the authors, that men thereby may make some election unto themselves what books to read"; and (e) the order of studies "that men may know in what order or pursuit to read" (182). In 1752

James "Hermes" Harris divided literary criticism into three species: philosophical, which seeks the general principles of good writing by examining "the most
approved performances"; historical, "through which Scholiasts, Commentators
and Explainers" make works from the past more intelligible; and corrective,
which concerns itself with restoring the accuracy of texts (2:298). A modern
instance of this usage is Northrop Frye's statement that "by criticism I mean
the whole work of scholarship and taste concerned with literature which is part
of what is variously called liberal education, culture, or the study of the humanities" (3). The concept of criticism embodied in René Wellek's *History of
Modern Criticism* is simply that "criticism is any discourse on literature" (137).

The same broad sense is routinely given retrospective application in studies
and anthologies of classical and medieval writing on literature, language, and
rhetoric, as, for example, D. A. Russell and M. Winterbottom's *Ancient Literary
Criticism*, an anthology of texts and passages from Homer and Hesiod to Menander.

4. Nineteenth-century debates over the authority of the Bible led to increasingly
sophisticated studies of composition and relationship of its books; this "textual"
or "higher" criticism to some extent reinforced the tendency to include the
reconstruction of the origin and history of a text under the term criticism.

5. Matthew Arnold's famous definition of criticism as it appears in "The
Function of Criticism at the Present Time" is "a distinterested endeavour to
learn and propagate the best that is known and thought in the world" (3:283),
where the "best that is known and thought" extends not only beyond literature
in English but, as he elucidated later in "Literature and Science," to all thought
that can be related "to our sense for conduct, to our sense for beauty" as
distinguished from scientific knowledge that does not directly so relate (10:62).
The Arnoldian sense of criticism, understood as especially embracing the criticism of literature (as, in practice, it did for Arnold), but not necessarily limited
to literature, had an enormous effect on critics of the first half of the twentieth
century, including I. A. Richards, who was concerned to differentiate the use
of language in literature from that in science; F. R. Leavis, who understood the
criticism of literature as a means of improving the culture as a whole; and the
American New Critics, who, while they saw literature as consisting of formal
structures whose value lay outside the circumstances of their composition, assumed that the study of literature had a meliorating effect on the individual and
the culture.

6. Criticism understood as an intensive analysis of a literary text regarded
ideally as a unified expression of an intellectual and emotional attitude toward
the world emerged in England and the United States in the late 1920s and 1930s.
Thus, I. A. Richards, whose *Principles of Literary Criticism* (1925) made the
communication of experiences of a harmony or balance of multiple opposed
impulses the ideal of poetry, could assume that once the experience of the poem
was properly grasped, its value was evident in the degree of equilibrium felt.
"When we have solved, completely, the communication problem, when we have

got, perfectly, the experience, *the mental condition* relevant to the poem, we have still to judge it, still to decide upon its worth. But the later question nearly always settles itself; or rather, our own inmost nature and the nature of the world in which we live decides it for us" (*Practical Criticism*, 11).

Whatever their differences, F. R. Leavis and his circle in England and the New Critics in the United States insisted on the necessity of close attention to the text while at the same time relying on an Arnoldian view of the best literature as a clarifying and purifying influence in the culture. Thus, one of the tenets of the New Critics was that only literature, through its inclusion of the human emotional response to experience, gave complete knowledge; the function of criticism, then, was to keep that knowledge before the world, and to make it available. Exemplary is Allen Tate's statement of criticism's role in "The Present Function of Criticism": "[I]n our time, as in all times, to maintain and to demonstrate the special, unique, and complete knowledge which the great forms of literature afford us" (8).

The procedure of the New Critics, then, was to approach the text as a structure of meaning complete in itself if its internal patterns were adequately attended to. As set forth in the highly influential textbook *Understanding Poetry*, by Cleanth Brooks and Robert Penn Warren, the critic should avoid all substitutes for the poem itself, "the most common ones being "Paraphrase of logical and narrative content," "Study of biographical and historical materials," and "inspirational and didactic interpretation" (iv). This stance naturally produced hostility from those for whom scholarly study of the background of a literary work or traditional literary history was the center of literary study. The New Critical position was reinforced by René Wellek and Austin Warren's widely used *Theory of Literature* (1949). Though the authors there defined literary criticism as the "study of the concrete literary works of art" (39), and thus as everything except literary history and literary theory, their distinction between *intrinsic* and *extrinsic* approaches helped to solidify a differentiation into criticism as the analysis of all the structural components of the individual work (imagery, figures, meter, style, and narrative structure), and scholarship as the investigation of the relation of literary works to biography, psychology, the history of ideas, and society. Criticism thus came to have as its central academic meaning the analysis, or explication of literary texts to elucidate meaning. Interestingly enough, however, in following the tradition of associating the center of criticism with evaluative judgment, Wellek and Warren included evaluation among the intrinsic approaches.

However, in the last twenty years, the drive to establish the fullest or most correct meaning of a text has been challenged by what Geoffrey Hartman has called the "Revisionist Reversal," which "reinvests criticism with creative potential" (8) and which, rather than "mastering" a text, reveals its indeterminacy. The "creative" emphasis recalls Oscar Wilde's "The Critic as Artist," although the style and often highly complicated modes of argument of the "revisionist" critics are much more likely to be associated with literary THEORY in one of its current senses.

7. E. D. Hirsch's 1960 *PMLA* article "Objective Interpretation" as expanded in *Validity in Interpretation* (1967) stipulatively distinguishes an author's intended *meaning* from other significances that a critic might wish to explore in the given text. In Hirsch's terminology, to attempt to understand and explain the author's meaning is to pursue *interpretation*; to pursue other questions (for example, psychological causes within and social influences on the author, applications of the text to situations not envisaged by the author, or analogies between aspects of the work and social and behavioral theories) is to pursue *criticism*. Something very much like what Hirsch calls criticism is labeled *metacriticism* by Eugene Paul Nassar (noted above as reserving "criticism" for "the evaluation of the continuity of tone"); for Nassar, metacriticism is an "assessment of the view of life of a work or its author by a critic who uses as his basis of judgment his own or other views of life" (133). Roger Fowler similarly suggests that any use of literature for "non-literary" purposes such as illustrating a social or psychological theory should be called "metacriticism" (46–47).

Note

Though "criticism" continues to have currency in senses 1, 2, 3, 6, and 7, it is notable that in the reaction against analysis of the text in isolation, the new arguments for ways of reading literature have tended to see themselves as "theory" rather than "principles of criticism"—a shift in nomenclature that points not only to the ambition of finding a ground outside literature itself but also to the desire to repudiate the conception of the relative autonomy of the text with which that term had become strongly associated. In any case, the term criticism and the attempts to articulate its subcategories remains confusing. The intrinsic/extrinsic distinction does not fully correspond to that between "meaning" and "significance," for information about the author or the historical situation in which the text appeared, including the history of ideas, may be pertinent to grasping the author's intended "meaning." "Formal" criticism (see FORMALISM), as most often understood, comes close to intrinsic criticism, but the general avoidance of specific concern with the author's intention differentiates it from Hirsch's terms understanding and interpretation.

References

Arnold, Matthew. *The Complete Prose Works of Matthew Arnold*. Ed. R. H. Super. 11 vols. Ann Arbor: University of Michigan Press, 1960–77.

Bacon, Francis. *The Advancement of Learning*. Ed. W. A. Wright. Oxford: Clarendon Press, 1900.

Brooks, Cleanth, and Robert Penn Warren. *Understanding Poetry*. New York: Henry Holt, 1938. Textbook illustrating application of New Critical approach.

Brownell, William C. *Criticism*. New York: Scribner's Sons, 1914. A small volume strongly focused on the authorial mind; the function of criticism is "to discern and characterize the abstract qualities informing the concrete expression of the artist" (16).

Coleridge, Samuel Taylor. *Biographia Literaria*. Ed. J. Shawcross. 2 vols. Oxford: Clarendon Press, 1907.

Dennis, John. *The Grounds of Criticism in Poetry* (1704). New York: Garland, 1971.

Fowler, Roger. *Modern Critical Terms*. London: Routledge and Kegan Paul, 1987.

Frye, Northrop. *Anatomy of Criticism*. 1957; Princeton, N. J.: Princeton University Press, 1971. Influential attempt to categorize the forms of which all literature partakes.

Gardner, Helen. *The Business of Criticism*. Oxford: Clarendon Press, 1959.

Harris, James. *Upon the Rise and Progress of Criticism*. Privately printed in 1752. Reprinted in *The Works of James Harris, Esq.* 2 vols. London: F. Wingrave, 1801.

Hartman, Geoffrey. *Criticism in the Wilderness*. New Haven, Conn.: Yale University Press, 1980.

Hirsch, E. D. Jr. "Objective Interpretation," *PMLA* 75 (September 1960): 463–79.

———. *Validity in Interpretation*. New Haven, Conn.: Yale University Press, 1967. Presents an argument for the possibility and importance of finding the meaning intended by the author.

Johnson, Samuel. *Yale Edition of the Works of Samuel Johnson*. Ed. W. J. Bate and A. B. Strauss. 9 vols. New Haven, Conn.: Yale University Press, 1958–71.

Nassar, Eugene Paul. *The Rape of Cinderella*. Bloomington: Indiana University Press, 1970.

Pater, Walter. *The Renaissance: Studies in Art and Poetry*. London: Macmillan, 1910.

Richards, I. A. *Practical Criticism*. New York: Harcourt, Brace, 1929.

———. *Principles of Literary Criticism*. Harcourt, Brace, 1925. The major statement differentiating literary from scientific uses of language.

Russell, D. A., and M. Winterbottom. *Ancient Literary Criticism: The Principal Texts in New Translations*. Oxford: Clarendon, 1972.

Saintsbury, George. *A History of Criticism and Literary Taste in Europe*. 3 vols. Edinburgh: Blackwood and Sons, 1900–1904. A very readable, if quite personal, survey.

Tate, Allen. "The Present Function of Criticism." In *Collected Essays*. Denver: Alan Swallow, 1959.

Wellek, René. *The Attack on Literature and Other Essays*. Chapel Hill: North Carolina University Press, 1982.

———. *A History of Modern Criticism, 1750–1950*. 6 vols. New Haven, Conn.: Yale University Press, 1955–86.

Wellek, René, and Austin Warren. *Theory of Literature*. New York: Harcourt, Brace, 1949.

Wilde, Oscar. "The Critic as Artist," In *Intentions*. London: Osgood and McIlvaine, 1891.

Sources of Additional Information

Among closely reasoned attempts to define the nature and function of literary criticism are John M. Ellis's *The Theory of Literary Criticism* (Berkeley: University of California Press, 1974) and F. E. Sparshott's *The Concept of Criticism* (Oxford: Clarendon Press, 1967). An intriguing argument against many of the usual activities of criticism is Iain McGilchrist's *Against Criticism* (London: Faber and Faber, 1982): "The core of the problem can be stated in a few words: art exists precisely to transcend those patterns of thought which criticism imposes upon it. Art exists precisely to repair the damage caused by the simplicity of analytic thought" (65).

J. E. Spingarn's "The New Criticism" in his *Creative Criticism* (New York: Henry Holt, 1917) is a historically interesting proclamation of an early twentieth-century dismissal of critical rules, genres, "all the paraphernalia of Graeco-Roman rhetoric," moral judgment, and so forth. Donald Stauffer's introductory essay in *The Intent of the Critic*, ed. Stauffer (Princeton, N. J.: Princeton University Press, 1941) usefully surveys three roles of the critic: "as an individual responding to the work of art, as interpreter to an audience, and finally as judge" (7).

A comprehensive eleven-volume anthology of criticism in the broad sense extending from Gorgias to the present is *The Art of the Critic: Literary Theory and Criticism from the Greeks to the Present*, ed. Harold Bloom (New York: Chelsea House, 1985–90). Among the commentaries on Greek and Roman criticism are G. M. A. Grube's *The Greek and Roman Critics* (London: Methuen, 1965) and Donald A. Russell's *Criticism in Antiquity* (London: Duckworth, 1981), the latter a convenient companion to D. A. Russell and M. Winterbottom's *Ancient Literary Criticism*.

D

DECONSTRUCTION A mode of reading first defined by Jacques Derrida and based on the principle that linguistic signs cannot be linked to extra-linguistic reality but are instead components of the ultimately self-contradictory structure of language. A deconstructive reading of a text is then a search for (concealed) contradictions within a text that necessarily undercut its apparent unity.

The volume of publication on Jacques Derrida and deconstruction over the last twenty years, the widely differing estimates of the value and importance of deconstruction, the tendency of disciples to repeat Derrida's key terms and techniques of writing in commentaries on Derrida and deconstruction (it has been argued that to discuss deconstruction in any other manner is to betray it), and the problems of writing about deconstruction without entering into philo-sophical questions of considerable historical and technical complexity (with particular attention to Nietzsche, Husserl, and Heidegger) make an adequate objective summary of deconstruction difficult.

Although multiple philosophical ancestors have been adduced, deconstruction as a term and a kind of writing about texts was initiated by Jacques Derrida. While his earlier writing already exhibits characteristics associated with decon-structive practices, he employs the term for apparently the first time in *Of Grammatology* (1967). Its initial appearance there is the announcement of "the destruction, not the demolition, but the de-sedimentation, the de-construction, of all the significations that have their source in that of the logos" (10). In another use relatively early in *Of Grammatology*, Derrida refers to the Platonic tradition of writing as "its dissimulation of the natural, primary, and immediate presence to the soul within the logos." The necessary form of attack on this central metaphysical tenet is, for Derrida, deconstruction. "Deconstructing this tradition will . . . not consist of reversing it, of making writing innocent. Rather of showing why the violence of writing does not *befall* an innocent language. There is an originary violence of writing because language is first, in a sense I shall gradually reveal, writing'' (37). Another somewhat explanatory use of ''deconstruction'' in Part 1 of *Of Grammatology* reads, ''To make enigmatic what one thinks one understands by the words 'proximity,' 'immediacy,' 'presence' . . . is my final intention in this book'' (70).

These several early uses of ''deconstruction'' by Derrida are here quoted because, like all his key terms, deconstruction is difficult to define. For Derrida, no language can be adequate to what it seeks to describe, and he is particularly concerned that the terms he applies to the nature of language not be understood as the names of concepts. Thus the word logos, which appears in the quotations above, is one of the many words whose Derridean definition is slippery; it roughly corresponds to an extra-linguistic guarantee of the relations between things and words, or the belief in the *presence* of extra-linguistic reality in language. It may be thought of as the assumed ground of belief that language is adequate to treat Kantian things-in-themselves; the belief itself Derrida calls *logocentrism*. The key word in the third of the above quotations, *writing*, is used in the specifically Derridean sense (sometimes called *arche-writing*) of a structure interposed between reality and the actual instance of speech or writing in the usual sense; that is, arche-writing is the system that both creates the possibility of language and excludes the possibility of its representing whatever reality may be.

The Derridean term most often invoked is the coinage *différance*, which is intended to suggest the difference between the signification of different words that constitutes their meaning, the difference between various meanings of the same word, and the infinite deferral of meaning that necessarily occurs as meaning is pursued from word to word (from difference to difference). Since the difference between two things does not in itself exist, it is, for Derrida, never present. Similarly, since that for which a sign is a sign can never be present in the sign but is the condition of the sign as sign, Derrida describes the other of the sign as the *trace*. He develops from Saussure the understanding of language as the system that makes it possible to talk about things but which, because of the arbitrary nature of the relation between a word and that to which it ''refers,'' cannot be grounded in anything besides itself. The view of the present moment as never fully present because it must contain traces of the past and future, Derrida develops from Heidegger. ''The presence-absence of the trace, which one should not even call its ambiguity but rather its play (for the word 'ambiguity' requires the logic of presence, even when it begins to disobey that logic), carries in itself the problems of the letter and the spirit, of body and soul'' (71). *Dissemination* refers to the multiple meanings to which a word is susceptible, playing on the notions of distribution and the sowing of seed, of semen. The *supplement* is in itself an example of the workings of the deconstructive thought: a supplement is added to something that is already complete, but were that something *truly* complete, it would not require a supplement. Derrida's term *parergon* works similarly—a parergon is an ornament set beside the basic work, or *ergon*; looked at against the general context as ground, it appears part of the work, but looked at with the work as ground, it appears part of the context.

The aim of the deconstructive reading, in the simplest terminology, is to reveal the *aporia*, the unresolvable contradiction necessarily produced by any use of language, and especially by undercutting central oppositions and assumed hierarchical structures. In the influential preface to her 1976 translation of Derrida's *De la Grammatologie*, Gayatri Chakravorty Spivak speaks of taking hold of any word "that seems to harbor an unresolvable contradiction" in order to "see the text coming undone as a structure of concealment, revealing its self-transgression, its undecidability" (1xxv). Texts must reveal contradictions because language can only define itself in terms of other language. E. Warwick Slinn, in one of the most clearly written explanations and defenses of Derrida, thus argues that the well-known statement in *Of Grammatology*, "There is nothing outside the text" (158), means not confinement to the particular text but rather that "there is nothing outside textuality, no referent that is not itself already part of a system of signification" (82). Within that system, deconstruction practices a double reading that sets the "conscious, voluntary, intentional relationship that the writer institutes" (*Of Grammatology*, 158) against the other senses of the words used as part of the system of language. (M. H. Abrams speaks of the first of these two readings as *construing*; the second is, of course, deconstructing.) Derrida and many of his followers insist that such double reading is not achieved by a specific method; strictly speaking, deconstruction appears as a mode of thought rather than a method or technique. However, other deconstructionist critics, especially in the United States, have produced deconstructive formulas that seem to describe a specific technique (see, for example, Jonathan Culler's summary in *On Deconstruction*, p. 150).

Since 1966, when Derrida read "Structure, Sign, and Play in the Discourse of the Human Sciences" at a Johns Hopkins University conference, his importance has steadily grown in the United States—where his influence soon became, and has remained, considerably greater than in Europe. However, the degree to which the American deconstructionists have altered the nature of the Derridean project is moot.

For a time in the early 1980s when Paul de Man, J. Hillis Miller, Harold Bloom, and Geoffrey Hartman all were members of the Yale University English department, they were regarded as the most prominent marchers under the deconstructionist banner (though Bloom and Hartman have neither claimed the name nor sought to carry out the unweaving or undoing of texts in the deconstructive manner). De Man was the earliest to enter the deconstructive camp; his essay "The Rhetoric of Blindness: Jacques Derrida's Reading of Rousseau" (included in *Blindness and Insight*, 1971) both reviews Derrida's mode of reading Rousseau and reads Derrida in a Derridean way. De Man perhaps remained closest to Derrida's manner, employing a style of much the same difficulty and taking himself with the same seriousness as does the early Derrida. However, even while pursuing deconstructive strategies in essays in *Blindness and Insight* (and especially in that essay devoted to Derrida), de Man is developing his own variation in making blindness to certain aspects of a work the necessary condition for other insights (a position not so different from the PLURALISM of the Chicago School, although based on a more subjective epistemology and stated in a more paradoxical form).

J. Hillis Miller has defined deconstruction in a way that closely echoes Spivak: "The deconstructive critic seeks to find . . . the element in the system studied which is alogical, the thread in the text in question which will unravel it all, or the loose stone which will pull down the whole building" ("Stevens' Rock," 341). However, where Derrida has tended to argue that the possibility of their opposites is implicit in the words of a text that he chooses as the point at which to begin deconstruction of that text, Miller has often imported rival senses from uses existing outside the given text. In the little example of deconstruction he contributed to the *New York Times Magazine*, he puts the sense of "undisciplined" (and implies the sense of "lewdness") alongside the sense of "luxuriousness" which most readers have found in Milton's description of Eve's "wanton ringlets"; thus she can be shown to have already fallen from the God-established order before the serpent-induced fall. In "On Edge: The Crossways of Contemporary Criticism," Miller supplements the senses of words in Wordsworth's "A Slumber Did My Spirit Seal," as Abrams points out, with senses "he has culled from diverse other texts" (Abrams, 149). In "The Critic as Host," Miller turns to etymology to deconstruct the host-parasite relation.

Among American advocates of deconstruction, two others claim particular eminence, Jonathan Culler and Barbara Johnson. Culler, who moves from a somewhat tentative endorsement in his 1979 essay on Derrida to much greater enthusiasm in his 1982 *On Deconstruction*, has given more attention to theory than to application. The two following formulations of deconstruction are typical. "Deconstruction thus undertakes a double reading, describing the ways in which lines of argument in the texts it is analysing call their premises into question, and using the system of concepts within which a text works to produce constructs, such as the *différance* and *supplement*, which challenge the consistency of that system" ("Jacques Derrida," 172).

> The effect of deconstruction is to disrupt the hierarchical relation that previously determined the concept of literature by reinscribing the distinction between literary and nonliterary works within a general literarity or textuality, and thus to encourage projects, such as the literary reading of philosophical texts and the philosophical reading of literary texts, that allow these discourses to communicate with one another. (*On Deconstruction*, 184–85)

For Barbara Johnson, "The de-construction of a text does not proceed by random doubt or arbitrary subversion, but by the careful teasing out of warring forces or signification within the text itself. If anything is destroyed in a deconstructive reading, it is not the text, but the claim to unequivocal domination of one mode of signifying over another'' (5). In her application of deconstruction in *The Critical Difference*, ''The differences *between* entities (prose and poetry, man and woman, literature and theory, guilt and innocence) are shown to be based on a repression of differences *within* entities, ways in which an entity differs from itself'' (x–xi).

The value of deconstructive double reading is one of the major points of contention among theorists. John M. Ellis argues that deconstruction achieves no intellectual progress. ''The traditional idea is questioned, subverted, and undermined—and then *retained* in order that we can focus on the act of subversion itself which, however, does not constitute a final rejection of that idea'' (262). Gregory Jay and David Miller, however, celebrate such deconstructive readings:

> What should be emphasized here is that this maneuver does not simply negate the knowledge produced by a conceptual technology any more than it tries to synthesize contradictory conclusions within some total vision. Instead, both the theoretical framework and its practical application are strategically re-marked in affiliation with unforeseen networks of metaphors, cultural attitudes, and social institutions—just as words or other symbols gain new signifying determinations from the constellation of relations that traverse them when they are placed in different texts. (7)

Another frequent objection to Derrida and deconstruction generally is that the argument equates any lack of absolute certainty with total indeterminacy. Abrams writes, ''For Derrida . . . it is a matter of all-or-nothing; there is no intermediate position on which a determinate interpretation can rest, for if no meanings are absolutely certain and stable, then all meanings are unstable and undecidable'' (136). Michael Fischer writes, ''A rigid either-or, all-or-nothing logic governs Derrida's thought: because the meaning of a text is not 'unique, univocal, rig-orously controllable, and transmittable,' it is therefore indeterminate'' (40). Robert Scholes phrases the point more broadly to take in the impurity Derrida finds in all language: ''If everything in our world is impure, insofar as we know anything about it, this means that purity is not a concept that we can use, except in a relative way: more or less pure, more or less impure. Similarly, if none of us ever experiences the pure presence of anything, then we can stop talking about pure presence as if it mattered'' (287–88). Scholes thus argues for the concept of *pragmatic presence*; we may never be wholly in the presence of each other, but the pragmatic presence that makes possible a dialogue with another person in the same room is sufficient for communication.

The same type of objection is made to Derrida's dismissal of the capacity of context to limit dissemination and thus determine meaning. Derrida has made the point a number of times. ''This is my starting point: no meaning can be determined out of context, but no context permits saturation'' (''Living On,'' 81). ''Is there a rigorous and scientific concept of *context*? . . . I shall try to demonstrate why a context is never absolutely determinable, or rather, why its determination can never be entirely certain or saturated'' (''Signature Event,'' 174). Scholes, however, charges Derrida with ignoring the grammar and syntax (part of the text's internal context), and Charles Altieri points to the way that "education in a culture" "enables us to establish criteria for appropriateness" and thus evaluate the relevance of the many aspects of any actual context (40). Derrida's concentration on the closed system of language rather than the open system of speech—as criticized, for instance, by John Boly—can be linked to the denial of the role of context, since contexts are relevant only to parole, and not to language as a system. Boly also notes that "Derrida reacts to any formal, organizing structure as if it were *ipso facto* a closed system" (154).

Deconstruction began to influence the arts, especially architecture, as early as the 1970s, and Derrida himself has touched on the relationship to the arts in his "Fifty-Two Aphorisms for a Foreward" (*Deconstruction: Omnibus Volume*, 1986) and written specifically on painting in *The Truth in Painting* (1978). To the extent that deconstruction is understood as opposing itself to MODERNISM, the architectural revolt against modernist buildings (in particular, against the "International Style" of Mies van der Rohe) easily allies itself with it. The architects Peter Eisenman, Hiromi Fujii, and Bernard Tschumi are particularly identified with deconstructive architecture. The interrelations between art, architecture, and deconstruction as a philosophical movement are interestingly explored and illustrated in the two essays by Christopher Norris and Andrew Benjamin that make up *What is Deconstruction?* and in the lavishly illustrated *Deconstruction: Omnibus Volume*. The latter includes Derrida's "Fifty-Two Aphorisms for a Foreword," an interview with Derrida, essays by deconstructive architects, and essays about deconstructive architecture.

References

Abrams, M. H. "Construing and Deconstructing." In *Romanticism and Contemporary Criticism*, ed. Morris Eaves and Michael Fischer. Ithaca; N.Y.: Cornell University Press, 1986. A reasonably objective summary of Derrida that argues against too wholehearted an adoption of deconstruction. Includes a critique of J. Hillis Miller's essay "On Edge," which is printed in the same volume together with a reply to Abrams by Miller.

Altieri, Charles. *Act and Quality*. Amherst: University of Massachusetts Press, 1981. Altieri counters deconstruction with a full-scale theory developed primarily from Wittgenstein and speech-act theory.

Boly, John. "Nihilism Aside: Derrida's Debate over Intentional Models." *Philosophy and Literature* 9 (October 1985): 152–65.

Culler, Jonathan. "Jacques Derrida." In *Structuralism and Since*, ed. John Sturrock. Oxford: Oxford University Press, 1979. A very useful introduction with brief descriptions of Derrida's major publications to 1979.

———. *On Deconstruction: Theory and Criticism after Structuralism*. Ithaca, N.Y.: Cornell University Press, 1982. The final chapter summarizes deconstructive readings of literary works by a number of critics.

Deconstruction: Omnibus Volume. Ed. Andrew Papadakis, Catherine Cooke, and Andrew Benjamin. London: Academy Editions, 1989.

De Man, Paul. *Blindness and Insight*. New York: Oxford University Press, 1971.

Derrida, Jacques. "Living On: Border Lines." Trans. J. Hulbert. In *Deconstruction and Criticism*, ed. Harold Bloom. New York: Seabury Press, 1979.

————. *Of Grammatology*. Trans. Gayatri Chakravorty Spivak. Baltimore: Johns Hopkins University Press, 1976. Originally published as *De la Grammatologie* in 1967.

————. "Signature Event Context." Trans. S. Weber and J. Mehlman. *Glyph* 1 (1977): 172–97. Originally published in Derrida's *Marges de la Philosophie*. Paris: Editions de Minuit, 1972.

————. *The Truth in Painting*. Trans. G. Bennington and I. McLeod. Chicago: University of Chicago Press, 1987. Original French edition, 1978.

Ellis, John M. "What Does Deconstruction Contribute?" *New Literary History* 19 (Winter 1988): 259–79. This essay also makes up the central portion of Chapter 3 of Ellis's *Against Deconstruction*. Princeton, N.J.: Princeton University Press, 1989.

Fischer, Michael. *Does Deconstruction Make Any Difference?* Bloomington: Indiana University Press, 1985.

> [M]y point is not simply that deconstruction is costly, but that it is unwarranted. . . . In attacking the skepticism of Derrida and others, I am, then, taking a preliminary step toward reconstituting the claim that these writers have weakened, especially Frye's claim that "the ethical purpose of a liberal education is to liberate, which can only mean to make one capable of conceiving society as free, classless, and urbane." (xiv)

Fynsk, Christopher. "The Choice of Deconstruction." In *The Textual Sublime: Deconstruction and Its Differences*. Albany: State University of New York Press, 1990.

Jay, Gregory S., and David L. Miller. "The Role of Theory in the Study of Literature?" In *After Strange Texts*, ed. Jay and Miller. University, Ala.: University of Alabama Press, 1985.

Johnson, Barbara. *The Critical Difference*. Baltimore: Johns Hopkins University Press, 1980.

Miller, J. Hillis. "The Critic as Host." *Critical Inquiry* 3 (Spring 1977): 439–47.

————. "How Deconstruction Works." *New York Times Magazine*, 9 February 1986, 25.

————. "On Edge: The Crossways of Contemporary Criticism." *Bulletin of the American Academy of Arts and Sciences* 32 (January 1979). Reprinted with a 1984 postscript in *Romanticism and Contemporary Criticism*, ed. Morris Eaves and Michael Fischer. Ithaca, N.Y.: Cornell University Press, 1986.

————. "Stevens' Rock and Criticism as Cure, II." *Georgia Review* 30 (Summer 1976): 330–48.

Scholes, Robert. "Deconstruction and Communication." *Critical Inquiry* 14 (Winter 1988): 278–95. Of Derrida's deconstruction: "the theory, insofar as it is a theory of human language, has certain serious weaknesses, and . . . there is no way to derive practical consequences from the theory, even if it were entirely convincing" (279). Scholes criticizes Derrida's identification of meaning with truth, and comments, "The powerful appeal that Derridean thought has had for American literary critics has its emotional roots in a cultural reflex of sympathy for the outlaw" (278).

Slinn, E. Warwick. "Deconstruction and Meaning: The Textuality Game." *Philosophy and Literature* 12 (April 1988): 80–87.

Spivak, Gayatri Chakravorty. "Translator's Preface" to Derrida's *Of Grammatology*. One of the most important commentaries on Derrida.

What Is Deconstruction? Ed. Christopher Morris and Andrew Benjamin, New York: St. Martin's Press, 1988.

Sources of Additional Information

The essays by Derrida that give the best introduction to his mode of thought are perhaps those gathered in *Writing and Difference*, trans. A. Bass (Chicago: University of Chicago Press, 1978, originally published 1967), especially "Structure, Sign, and Play in the Discourse of the Human Sciences" (this essay also appears in *The Languages of Criticism and the Science of Man*," ed. Richard Macksey and Eugenio Donato, Baltimore: Johns Hopkins University Press, 1970); "Signature Event Context," "Living On: Border Lines," and *Of Grammatology*, all cited in the references section; and "Différance," in *Margins of Philosophy*, trans. A. Bass (Chicago: University of Chicago Press, 1982).

An especially notorious passage at arms occurred between John Searle and Derrida in 1977. Derrida's "Signature Event Context," a deconstructive reading of J. L. Austin's *How to Do Things with Words* (*Glyph* 1, 1977, 172–97), was answered by Searle in the same number ("Reiterating the Differences," 198–208). Derrida's lengthy reply to Searle ("Limited Inc," *Glyph* 2, 162–251) is a tour de force well illustrating the resources of Derrida's rhetoric.

Richard Rorty regards philosophy not as a search for truth but rather as one part of the necessarily ever-continuing human dialogue; in "Philosophy as a Kind of Writing" (*New Literary History* 10, Autumn 1978: 141–60), Rorty's central contention is that Derrida's power comes from the realization that all philosophical writing is simply a reply to other philosophical writing. In "Deconstruction and Circumvention" (*Critical Inquiry* 14, Winter 1988: 278–95), Rorty argues against making a distinction between literature and philosophy and against regarding the task of deconstructing traditional metaphysics as particularly important. "From this point of view, there is not an urgent task called 'deconstructioning metaphysics' which needs to be performed before we can get to work on the rest of culture" (20).

Christopher Norris's devotion to explanation of and commentary on deconstruction has provided a number of helpful studies. In order of publication, these are *Deconstruction: Theory and Practice* (London: Methuen, 1982); *The Deconstructive Turn* (London: Methuen, 1983), which deals with particular issues; *Derrida* (Cambridge, Mass.: Harvard University Press, 1987); *Deconstruction and the Interests of Theory* (London: Pinter, 1988); *Paul de Man* (Cambridge, Mass.: Harvard University Press, 1988); and the essay "Deconstruction, Post-modernism and the Visual Arts" in *What Is Deconstruction?* (see References above). Although the last-named essay develops into a commentary on Derrida and the arts, it offers a very useful brief introduction to Derrida.

Joseph Riddel's "From Heidegger to Derrida to Chance: Doubling and (Poetic) Language" (*Boundary 2* 4, Winter 1976: 571–92) examines the relationships between Heidegger's hermeneutics and de Man and Derrida. Vincent Leitch's *Deconstructive Criticism* (New York: Columbia University Press, 1983) is subtitled "An Advanced Introduction"; presuming considerable acquaintance with contemporary theories, it considers Derridean deconstruction in relation to Saussure, Heidegger, Lacan, Lévi-Strauss, de Man, Miller, Hayden White, Bloom, Foucault, William Spanos, Barthes, Deleuze, Guattari, and Hartman. Stephen W. Melville's *Philosophy Beside Itself: On Deconstruction and Modernism* (Minneapolis, University of Minnesota Press, 1986) treats Derrida in relation to Hegel and then the relationship between Derrida and de Man. *Deconstruction in Context*, ed. Mark C. Taylor (Chicago: University of Chicago Press, 1986), is a collection of mostly philosophical essays with relevance to an understanding of Derrida's philosophical position.

Wallace Martin's Introduction to *The Yale Critics*, ed. Martin, Jonathan Arac, and Wlad Godzich (Minneapolis: University of Minnesota Press, 1983) provides an excellent account of the relationships of Bloom, Hartman, de Man, and Miller to deconstruction and each other. The final chapters of Art Berman's *From the New Critics to Deconstruction* (Urbana: University of Illinois Press, 1988) offer an interesting analysis of American adaptations of Derridean deconstruction. *Rhetoric and Form: Deconstruction at Yale*, ed. R. C. Davis and R. Schliefer (Norman: University of Colorado Press, 1985), includes an essay each by Miller and Hartman, and essays on Miller, Hartman, and de Man. Colin Campbell's *New York Times Magazine* essay, "The Tyranny of the Yale Critics" (9 February 1986), is a popular portrayal of the conservative reaction to deconstructive (and "revisionist") criticism. The three essays by Wayne Booth, M. H. Abrams, and J. Hillis Miller published in *Critical Inquiry* 3, 407–47, under the general title of "The Limits of Pluralism" (Spring 1977) debate the nature of deconstruction more than that of pluralism.

Michael Ryan's *Marxism and Deconstruction: A Critical Articulation* (Baltimore: Johns Hopkins University Press, 1982) seeks to delineate the relations between Derridean (as opposed to most American) deconstruction and critical (as opposed to dogmatically rigid) Marxism.

Among books and essays denying the major claims of deconstruction are Gerald Graff's "Deconstruction as Dogma" (*Georgia Review* 3, Summer: 1980: 404–21); Chapter 3 ("The Romantic Abyss") in David Novitz, ed., *Knowledge, Fiction, and Imagination* (Philadelphia: Temple University Press, 1987); Stanley Rosen's *Hermeneutics as Politics* (New York: Oxford University Press, 1987), and John M. Ellis's *Against Deconstruction* (Princeton, N.J.: University Press, 1989). Rosen's second chapter is a philosophically informed critique of Derrida's central arguments: "Underneath the Derridean playfulness . . . one finds . . . a seriousness that is in search of a doctrine, but that is not serious enough, and that therefore dissolves whatever it touches" (51). Ellis soberly assesses the arguments of both Derrida and his various expositors. Deconstruction, Ellis concludes, resists the change most needed in literary criticism, "the development of some check on and control of the indigestible, chaotic flow of critical writing through reflection on what is and what is not in principle worthwhile—that is, through genuine, rather than illusory, reflection" (159).

A reaction against de Man has resulted from the discovery of his anti-Semitic writing for pro-Nazi newspapers in the early 1940s. David Hirsch's essay, "Paul de Man and the Politics of Deconstruction" (*Sewanee Review* 96, Spring 1988, 330–38), reviews the facts and presents the case against de Man.

For an interesting statement of the possibility of something very like a deconstructive criticism published a few months before Derrida's 1966 appearance at the Johns Hopkins University conference, "The Languages of Criticism and the Science of Man," see Elder Olson's "The Dialectical Foundations of Critical Pluralism" in his *On Value Judgments in the Arts* (Chicago: University of Chicago Press, 1976), reprinted from the *Texas Quarterly* (9, Spring 1966: 202–30). In describing a philosophy employing "differential dialectics" (and the criticism that would follow from this), Olson writes:

> Let us suppose, first of all, that a philosophic system is oriented, or addressed, wholly to changing things, and employs only differential and never integrating terms. . . . This would occur if one insisted that all things are unique. . . . In the extremest view of these dialectics, the object cannot be signified, for discourse, as finite, cannot be infinitely specified; cannot be perceived, for it has changed from what we perceived even as we perceived it; cannot be

contemplated, for the same reason; and cannot be acted upon, for what we would act upon is gone before we can act. (341–42, 343)

Olson first refers to differential dialectics in "An Outline of Poetic Theory" in *Critiques and Essays in Criticism*, ed. R. W. Stallman (New York: Ronald Press, 1949).

DISCOURSE   1. Orderly, coherent thought. 2. The presentation of such thought. 3. Speech, as opposed to writing. 4. Any instance of use of language as opposed to the system of language on which use depends. 5. Spoken utterance or written texts of more than one sentence. 6. The study of effective writing. 7. In theory of narrative, the presentation or mode of telling of the story. 8. In a phrase like "discourse community," a shared set of assumptions, procedures, and specifically defined terms. 9. The interaction between language and reality that produces experience or the world-as-understood. 10. A shared understanding of a significant area of social experience within a given culture at a given time in history.

1. and 2. The general sense of "discourse" until recent years meant orderly, sequential thinking, and thus, by extension, the orderly presentation of ideas. If the Latin source, *discursum*, signified "a running to and fro," "discourse" in both French and English meant a controlled mental process, the result of which was to be an orderly, coherent, sequential setting out of ideas, as in a sermon, treatise, oration, or formal essay. Hayden White's use of the term as "that form of verbal composition" bounded by logical demonstration on one side and "pure fiction" on the other is derived from this sense (2).

3. On the other hand, discourse has frequently been employed to designate spoken as opposed to written forms of use. Thus the *OED*'s third sense: "Communication of thought by speech" and "talk, conversation."

4. A twentieth-century adaptation of "discourse" derives from its use to translate Ferdinand de Saussure's *parole*, the particular instance of language use as opposed to *langue* or the language system as a whole. "Discourse" in this sense may be applied to a single word or a single sentence as well as to the sequence of sentences to which the other uses of the word apply. Paul Ricoeur in particular contrasts discourse as an event, an act, in which linguistic choices are made, producing new combinations and initiating reference, with the system of language (*Conflict of Interpretations*, 86–87). "The system in fact does not exist. It has only virtual existence. Only the message gives actuality to language, and discourse grounds the very existence of language since only the discrete and each time unique acts of discourse actualize the code" (*Interpretation Theory*, 9). The major value of the term in this sense is its breadth: it can designate both verbal and written, literary and nonliterary uses of language. In recent years the word "text," which would seem the narrower designation, has been stretched to include any set of signs, linguistic or nonlinguistic, that one believes interpretable. In distinction, "discourse" appears limited to instances of the use of language.

5. In a similar sense, as linguists began to interest themselves in uses of

language larger than the sentence, discourse was adopted as the most appropriate word to designate any stretch of language longer than a single sentence. At the same time, since general usage until quite recently employed "utterance" primarily to refer to spoken language and "text" to written language, discourse serves as a convenient label under which to subsume both. Thus DISCOURSE ANALYSIS refers to the study of the structures of discourse in this sense.

6. In recent years there has also arisen the convention of using "discourse" to designate the object of study of the pedagogical field traditionally known as composition. For example, Timothy Crusius's *Discourse: A Critique and Synthesis of Major Theories* considers theoretical approaches to the teaching of composition, and Daniel Knapp's *Discourse: an Illustrative Reader* offers examples for use in composition courses. "Composition" having come to be identified too closely with the subject matter of high school and college courses treating the basic skills of writing, a more comprehensive word was desirable that would suggest the larger questions of theory and problems for research about how both speech and writing are constructed for specific purposes. Thus James Kinneavy wrote in 1971, "A theory of discourse will then comprise an intelligible framework of different types of discourse with a treatment of the nature of each type, the underlying logic(s), the organizational structure of this type, and the stylistic characteristics of such discourse" (4–5). Such theoretical approaches generally find it valuable to divide discourse by modes or aims: referential, persuasive, literary, and expressive (Kinneavy), or descriptive, exploratory, expository, expressive, and narrative (George Dillon).

7. In the analysis of narrative, discourse is one of the several names used to refer to the *way* in which a story is told; that is, the "how" rather than the "what." As Seymour Chatman describes the distinction, "each narrative has two parts: a story (*histoire*), the content of chain of events (actions, happenings), plus what may be called the existents (characters, items of setting); and a discourse (*discours*), that is, the expression, the means by which the content is communicated" (19). In this use, discourse is cognate with plot and *sjuzhet* as distinguished from story and fable (see NARRATOLOGY). This sense of discourse can be associated with the notion of order in sense 1 (although narrative order need be neither logically or temporally sequential) as well as the notion of actual use as opposed to the potential of a system as in senses 2 through 4.

8. As scholarly disciplines, or, more broadly, distinct modes or fields of thought or human interest, have come to be seen as defined as much by shared methodologies, criteria of validity, and terminology as by subject matter, one sense of "discourse" has become almost a synonym for the shared elements that constitute a field. Since Stephen Toulmin developed this concept of field in *The Uses of Argument* (1958) it has been pursued by argumentation theorists like Charles Willard. In this sense, the term is close to what Thomas Kuhn calls a *paradigm*.

The use of the term discourse to describe modes of thought defined by cultural assumptions has become strongly associated with the work of Michel Foucault.

In the foreward to the English translation of *The Order of Things*, Foucault writes:

> I tried to explore scientific discourse not from the point of view of the individuals who are speaking, nor from the point of view of the formal structures of what they are saying, but from the point of view of the rules that come into play in the very existence of such discourse; what conditions did Linnaeus (or Petty, or Anauld) have to fulfil, not to make his discourse coherent and true in general, but to give it, at the time when it was written and accepted, value and practical application as . . . naturalist, economic, or grammatical discourse? (xiv)

9. More broadly, philosophy and linguistics developed from the Saussurian model have argued that what we know as experience, that is, the world-as-understood (as distinguished from whatever exists prior to human sensation and cognition) results from the interaction of language and human sense reports. Thus, C. H. Knoblauch and Lil Brannon write that "Discourse enacts the world: its knowledge is not 'about' the world but is rather constitutive of the world, the substance of experience, an explanation of the self" (60).

10. If one conflates the previous two senses and thinks of a discourse community not as a particular shared set of expectations and information within a culture but as a given culture at a given time in history (for instance, Victorian England in 1860), "discourse" comprehends the shared understanding of reality in that synchronic slice of culture.

References

Chatman, Seymour. *Story and Discourse*. Ithaca, N.Y.: Cornell University Press, 1978.
Crusius, Timothy. *Discourse: A Critique and Synthesis of Major Theories*. New York: Modern Language Association of America, 1989.
Dillon, George. *Constructing Texts*. Bloomington: Indiana University Press, 1981.
Foucault, Michel. *The Order of Things*. New York: Vintage Books, 1973. Original French edition, 1966.
Kinneavy, James. *A Theory of Discourse*. 1971; New York: Norton, 1980.
Knapp, Daniel. *Discourse: An Illustrative Reader*. New York: McGraw-Hill, 1969.
Knoblauch, C. H., and Lil Brannon. Upper Montclair, N.J.: Boynton Cook, 1984.
Kuhn, Thomas. *The Structure of Scientific Revolutions*. 1962; Chicago: University of Chicago Press, 1970.
Ricoeur, Paul. *The Conflict of Interpretations*. Ed. D. Ihde. Evanston, Ill.: Northwestern University Press, 1974.
———. *Interpretation Theory: Discourse and the Surplus of Meaning*. Fort Worth: Texas Christian University Press, 1976.
Saussure, Ferdinand de. *Course in General Linguistics*. Ed. Charles Bally and Albert Sechehaye; trans. W. Baskin. 1959; New York: McGraw-Hill, 1966.
Toulmin, Stephen. *The Uses of Argument*. Cambridge: Cambridge University Press, 1958.
White, Hayden. *Tropics of Discourse: Essays in Cultural Criticism*. Baltimore: Johns Hopkins University Press, 1978.
Willard, Charles. *Argumentation and the Social Grounds of Discourse*. University: University of Alabama Press, 1983.

DISCOURSE ANALYSIS 1. Broadly, the analysis of the organizing structures of spoken or written discourse. In practice, the term is generally used
in the following more restricted senses. 2. Analysis of the ways in which
individual sentences within a discourse are related cohesively and/or coher-
ently. 3. The investigation of the way in which a hearer or reader processes—
arrives at an understanding of—a discourse, and the closely related question
of the (not wholly conscious) strategies of speakers and writers that are intended
to produce the desired understanding of their discourse. 4. The analysis of
the means by which a text as a whole produces certain effects on the reader.
5. Investigation of the effects that particular syntactic, paradigmatic, and serial
structures have on a reader by virtue of the presumably similar ways in which
discourse is processed by individuals.

*Discourse analysis has received very little attention from theorists of literature,
especially as compared with the widespread interest in the "high" or "ideological" structuralism now generally called poststructuralism. Poststructuralism
finds the individual word regarded as an element in the system of language to
be polysemous, its possible meanings self-contradictory, and its meaning a floating function of the system of language as a whole; discourse analysis, regarding
the word in the context of a particular text or utterance within a particular
situation and cultural milieu, finds determinable meaning and explicable coherence.*

*That considerable work in discourse analysis has been devoted to the exam-
ination of ordinary conversation rather than literary texts has perhaps made the
field seem irrelevant to literary critics. However, at least as much attention has
been given to texts of one sort or another as to oral speech. In effect, discourse
analysis asks a different question (or asks it of a substantially different object)
than poststructuralism, and gets a correspondingly different answer. Poststructuralism denies or brackets the processes in the minds of the individual speaker/
author and hearer/reader in the particular situation in which the text or utterance
originates, and consequently tends to dismiss questions about the determination
of intended meaning. Discourse analysis brackets everything inconsequent to
the production and reception of intended meaning in situated uses that assume
shared knowledge: all etymologies, older usages, logical entailments, and questionable hierarchies of thought of which neither producer nor interpreter is likely
to be aware. The second endeavor is at least as multidisciplinary as the first
and inspires—to judge from the amount of resulting publication—an even larger
volume of effort. The two movements seem hardly aware of each other: those
investigating text coherence rarely, if ever, cite deconstructionists; Lacanian
psychoanalytic critics rarely, if ever, cite sociolinguists.*

*The construction of grammars for describing an utterance or text is sometimes
called "text linguistics" in order to distinguish it from studies oriented toward
the relation of the text or utterance to its context, but, in general, "text linguistics" and "discourse analysis" designate the same large field of study. (See
also* TEXT.)

1. Discourse analysis, a field dating only from the 1970s, resulted from the convergence of similar interests in sociolinguistics, speech-act theory, anthropology, psychology, and ethnomethodology. Some of this work focuses on the intricate interplay of cues, rules, and shared information in ordinary conversation; some on the possibilities of constructing a "grammar" that could describe or generate properly formed texts in the way traditional grammars describe or generate properly formed sentences; and some on the role of specific elements or aspects of language (for example, markers, shifters, and registers). The range of meanings of "discourse analysis" results from the variety of fields to which investigators have primary allegiance and the variety of aspects of human communication that preoccupy them. Thus, Michael Stubbs notes that "no one is in a position to write a comprehensive account of discourse analysis. The subject is at once too vast, and too lacking in focus and consensus. . . . Anything at all that is written on discourse analysis is partial and controversial" (12).

In general, however, the varied endeavors within discourse analysis share at least one of three characteristics: (a) an interest in texts or utterances longer than the sentence; (b) a focus on how communicative activity occurs; or (c) a recognition of the essential role of context in producing meaning. In regard to (a), discourse analysts frequently note that, in Robert Longacre's words, "For too long a time, linguistics has confined itself to the study of isolated sentences, either such sentences carefully selected from a corpus or, more often than not, artfully contrived so as to betray no need for further context" (xv). Indeed, Wilbur Pickering writes, "One wonders how long a sentence grammar can continue to be theoretically defensible" (5). For Deborah Schiffrin, (b) and (c) are encompassed in the four assumptions that she takes as central to discourse analysis:

1. Language always occurs in a context.
2. Language is context sensitive.
3. Language is always communicative.
4. Language is designed for communication. (3)

In other words, discourse analysis adds a strong interest in PRAGMATICS to the syntactics and SEMANTICS of traditional linguistics.

2. A major interest has been the means of achieving cohesion, which is an intertextual matter depending on anaphoric and cataphoric (previous and subsequent) relations within a discourse, and coherence, which is primarily extratextual (dependent on knowledge external to the text) in relatively short texts. See, for instance, M. A. K. Halliday and Ruqaiya Hasan's *Cohesion in English* (1976) and Gillian Brown and George Yule's *Discourse Analysis* (1983). Cohesion alone does not produce coherence: it is easy to demonstrate that sets of sentences in which there is a clear connection from one to the next through such links as pronouns and repeated words are not necessarily coherent. The degree to which coherence is dependent on the context in which the text or utterance originates is evident once it is realized that a sequence of sentences can be

conclusively recognized as incoherent only within a context; conversely, to state the matter in another way, it is always possible, at least in theory, to imagine a context in which an apparently incoherent sequence of sentences would be coherent. As Michel Charroles phrases it:

> [G]iven a set of consecutive sentences apparently unlinked, it is always possible to construct an ad hoc situation wherein their enunciation becomes coherent—i.e., it is always possible to calculate a particular state of affairs wherein their enunciation becomes relevant (corresponds to a plausible meaning intention) because all meaning intentions are theoretically possible. (3, Charroles's italics)

("Connexity" is sometimes used as an umbrella term including both cohesion and coherence.)

3. The investigation of how the individual sentences of a discourse cumulatively link up so that coherent discourse emerges leads naturally to the processes through which the mind comes to understand the units of and the whole of a discourse. Such processing necessarily involves the constant (tentative and revisable) integration of word after word and sentence after sentence into larger structures. Thus George Dillon distinguishes three levels of reading: perception, comprehension, and interpretation (xvii–xxiii). Analysis of how coherence is pursued by the reader suggests modes of considering the strategies employed by authors. Authors' strategies, in turn, depend both on creating intertextual linkages and on assumptions about readers' extratextual knowledge. Larry Bert Jones's *Pragmatic Aspects of English Text Structure* examines the resulting authorial strategies.

> Human communication depends on assumption making. If people were not able to make assumptions regarding those to whom they speak, almost any attempt at communication would quickly break down into a shambles. Without the use of assumptions, most messages would be so laden with prefacing material, functioning to make explicit all of the cultural and experiential knowledge normally assumed in conversation, that normal communication would become impossibly cumbersome. (1–2)

Consideration of authorial assumptions leads Jones to such topics as the frames, scenes, and routines that allow a reader to fill in necessary details; the functioning of "first mentions"; and a variety of modes of authorial commentary (opinionative, explanatory, incidental, and thematic).

4. Consideration of the total structure of discourse has long been one of the purposes of literary and rhetorical commentary, but the varied assumptions and methodologies employed (Aristotelian rhetorical criticism, NEW CRITICISM, STRUCTURALISM, NARRATOLOGY) are not generally included within the term "discourse analysis." However, theories accounting for the understanding of overall structures of discourse have been built up within discourse analysis itself. An example is Teun van Dijk and Walter Kintsch's *Strategies of Discourse Comprehension* (1983): "We go from the understanding of words, to the understanding of clauses in which these words have various functions, and then to complex

sentences, sequences of sentences, and overall textual structures. But even so there is continual feedback between less complex and more complex units'' (10). Discourse analysis in this sense constantly considers not only the bidirectional relationship between parts of the discourse and the whole but sees the relationships between the discourse and the total external context.

With regard to the relation between the parts and the whole, discourse analysts have sought to find general patterns of thought and structures of expectation in discourse. (By and large, these are less rigorously determined models than those sought by early structuralism.) Robert Longacre's *Grammar of Discourse* (1983) exemplifies the subject matter of this type of discourse analysis.

> [W]e are concerned in this volume with such features as plot progression in a narrative from stage to inciting incident to further build-up to a climax of confrontation to denouement and to final resolution; with dialogue relations such as question-answer, proposal-response, remark-evaluation; with ways of combining predications according to coupling, contrast, temporal succession, temporal overlap, causation, paraphrase, and the like; and with the world of role relations such as patient, experiencer, agent, goal, and source. (xvi)

The first of the features Longacre lists, plot progression, leads, for instance, into an investigation of the ways in which peaks of interest in narrative (and, in fact, in discourse in general) are created or marked.

5. Finally, the application of what discourse analysis tells us about how discourse is understood can be applied to specific examples in order to ascertain how certain effects on readers are achieved through syntactical and larger structures. Though not drawn from discourse analysis per se, Stanley Fish's *affective stylistics* (that is, the recognition of the effects of syntactical structures that modify, surprise, or reverse readers' expectations) falls within this sense of the term. More centrally representative is George Dillon's *Language Processing and the Reading of Literature* (1978). Wolfgang Iser's studies of the way in which readers of novels fill in ''gaps'' in the text and continually develop expectations about characters and events that are either fulfilled or falsified can also usefully be regarded as a kind of macro-application of discourse analysis in this fifth sense. (See READER-RESPONSE THEORY.)

References

Brown, Gillian, and George Yule. *Discourse Analysis*. Cambridge: Cambridge University Press, 1983. A useful introduction, especially to the notions of context, information structure, cohesion, and coherence.

Charolles, Michel. ''Text Connexity, Text Coherence and Text Interpretation Processing.'' In *Text Connexity, Text Coherence: Aspects, Methods, Results*, ed. Emil Sōzer. Hamburg: Helmut Buske Verlag, 1985.

Dijk, Teun van, and Walter Kintsch. *Strategies of Discourse Comprehension*. New York: Academic Press, 1983.

Dillon, George. *Language Processing and the Reading of Literature*. Bloomington: Indiana University Press, 1978. Seeks to set forth the model of a ''generative stylistics.'' ''The way a writer chooses to frame sentences and place their elements

does affect the reader's cognitive processes in predictable ways which analysis
can explicate, but via the strategies of processing: a particular construction or
preference of a writer is important insofar as it affects processing of the text"
(xvii).

Fish, Stanley. "Literature in the Reader," *New Literary History* 2 (Autumn 1973): 123–
62. Reprinted in Fish's *Is There a Text in This Class?* Cambridge, Mass.: Harvard
University Press, 1980.

Halliday, M. A. K., and Ruqaiya Hasan. *Cohesion in English*. London: Longman, 1976.
A standard work on cohesion. Five types of "cohesion tie" are considered:
"reference, substitution, ellipsis, conjunction, and lexical cohesion."

Iser, Wolfgang. *The Act of Reading*. Johns Hopkins University Press, 1978. Original
German edition, 1976.

———. *The Implied Reader*. Baltimore: Johns Hopkins University Press, 1974. Original
German edition, 1972.

Jones, Larry Bert. *Pragmatic Aspects of English Text Structure*. Arlington, Tex.: Summer
Institute of Linguistics, 1983.

Longacre, Robert E. *The Grammar of Discourse*. New York: Plenum Press, 1983. "As
a book on discourse, this volume is dedicated to the thesis that language is language
only in context" (xv).

Pickering, Wilbur. *A Framework for Discourse Analysis*. Arlington, Tex.: Summer Institute of Linguistics, 1980.

Schiffrin, Deborah. *Discourse Markers*. Cambridge: Cambridge University Press, 1987.

Stubbs, Michael. *Discourse Analysis: The Sociolinguistic Analysis of Natural Language*.
Chicago: University of Chicago Press, 1983. A major treatment of the field which
includes discussions of several approaches to discourse analysis and the issue of
indirection (saying one thing but meaning another).

Sources of Additional Information

The four-volume *Handbook of Discourse Analysis*, ed. Teun van Dijk (London: Academic Press, 1985), provides a reasonably comprehensive view of the issues that occupy
and modes of addressing the issues that constitute discourse analysis. The opening essay
of the first volume, "Introduction: Discourse Analysis as a New Cross-Discipline," by
van Dijk, gives a useful brief history, and the second, Charles J. Fillmore's "Linguistics
as a Tool for Discourse Analysis," helpfully outlines intertextual, intratextual, and extratextual relations, defines some of the key terms, and analyzes a sample text.

Malcolm Coulthard's *An Introduction to Discourse Analysis* (London: Longmans, 1977)
is a good example of a volume focused almost wholly on oral conversation; however,
the final chapter looks briefly at the analysis of dialogue in literature.

For an example of the application of various modes of discourse analysis to a brief
text (James Thurber's "A Lover and His Lass") see *Grammars and Descriptions: Studies
in Text Theory and Text Analysis*, ed. T. van Dijk and J. Petofi (Berlin: de Gruyter,
1977). Waldemar Gutwinski's *Cohesion in Literary Texts* (The Hague: Mouton, 1976),
building on the work of Halliday and Hasan (see References above), analyzes the elements
of cohesion in excerpts from Henry James and Ernest Hemingway.

E

EPIC   1. A lengthy narrative in verse recounting heroic action; the *Iliad* and *Odyssey* of Homer and Virgil's *Aeneid* are the great classic models for the epic, while *Beowulf* and the *Nibelungenlied* are the central Teutonic examples. 2. Works having significant characteristics in common with the major exemplars of the epic. 3. Narratives of heroes in any culture or period in which the heroic code has peculiar status and in which the narratives originate in oral performance.

The following survey of three senses of epic passes over most of the vast amount of theorizing about and prescriptions for the proper structure and subject matter of epic. Voltaire's "An Essay on Epick Poetry" opens, "We have in every Art more Rules than Examples, for Men are more fond of teaching, than able to perform; so there are more Commentators than Poets" (81; 37). His comment was particularly apt for an essay on the epic. There are a number of surveys of theories of the epic; a selection of those in English will be found in "Sources of Additional Information."

1. For classical Greek culture, Homer's *Iliad* and *Odyssey* were the preeminent examples of the form of verse narrative that Aristotle understood as the epic. Aristotle offers no full description of the epic, his evident purpose in the *Poetics* being to distinguish it from TRAGEDY (4.1449b; 23.1459a–24.1460b); epic, he explains, differs in verse form (being limited to the hexameter), in length, and by virtue of its narrative, as opposed to dramatic, form. Like tragedy it should be a unified whole. The poet should remain in the background, placing the interest on the characters themselves. W. P. Ker has wryly commented that

> Aristotle wrote with very little consideration for the people who were to come after him, and gives little countenance to such theories of epic as have at various times been prevalent among the critics, in which the dignity of the subject is insisted upon.

> He does not imagine it the chief duty of an epic poet to choose a lofty argument for
> historical rhetoric. He does not say a word about the national or the ecumenical
> importance of the themes of the epic poet. His analysis of the plot of the *Odyssey*,
> but for the reference to Poseidon, might have been the description of a modern
> realistic story. (18)

Ker's irony appears to cut two ways, against those who fail to give due weight
to what Aristotle thought was or was not worth remarking in the epics of his
own culture, and against those who fail to recognize that Aristotle had in view
only the Greek epic and primarily those of Homer.

Virgil's *Aeneid*, though for the Renaissance joined with Homer in honor, is,
as gradually came to be recognized, of a distinctly different kind. Homer is
recognized as the great model of the natural, folk, or primary epic belonging to
a heroic age, and Virgil as that of the literary, artificial, or secondary epic of a
more self-conscious, civic culture. The differences have been variously formulated. The *primary* epic has been regarded as the product of a poet close to
the oral tradition and, further, close to the age and culture described, as opposed
to the poet of the *secondary* epic, who is looking back in time. The primary
epic has also been regarded as having been assembled by a poet who is able to
impose unity on a mass of existing poems and epic materials rather than by a
poet who is responsible for the whole. Scholars like C. M. Bowra and Albert
Lord locate a chief difference in the oral composition of the primary as opposed
to the composition of the secondary epics with pen and ink. The employment
of formulas that fit certain actions or events into specific metrical patterns is
evidently one of the indices of the primary epic, but Lascelles Abercrombie, W.
P. Ker, and C. M. Bowra, among others, emphasize the individualistic, fame-
seeking character of the heroes of epics of the primary group. Abercrombie
writes, "the morals of the Heroic Age are founded on individuality, and on
nothing else. In Homer, for instance, it can be seen pretty clearly that a 'good'
man is simply a man of imposing, active individuality" (12–13).

Among typical twentieth-century descriptions of the epic are the following.
John Clark (1900): "I am here giving 'epic' its most comprehensive meaning
. . . *a tale of dignity about individuals*" (1). W. Macneile Dixon (1912): "[T]he
true epic, wherever created, will be a narrative poem, organic in structure, dealing
with great action and great characters, in a style commensurate with the lordliness
of its theme, which tends to idealise these characters and actions, and to sustain
and embellish its subject by means of episode and amplification" (24). Herbert
J. Hunt (1941): "The epic poem is not easily defined. Shall we say it is that
type of poetic composition which relates the adventures of heroes who themselves, like the exploits they perform, are so magnified, so illuminated with a
significant or even supernatural glamour, as to become in some way representative of a race, a people, an age of civilization, a patriotic, religious, or moral
outlook?" (1). C. M. Bowra (1952): "An epic poem is by common consent a
narrative of some length and deals with events which have a certain grandeur

and importance and come from a life of action, especially of violent action such as war'' (*From Virgil to Milton*, 1).

Other influential descriptions are those of Georg Lukács (1920), E. M. W. Tillyard (1954), and M. M. Bakhtin (1975). In Lukács's view, the epic differs from the novel because Homer's poems (''strictly speaking his works alone are epics'') are grounded in a world that is homogeneous, rounded, and closed. ''The novel is the epic of an age in which the extensive totality of life is no longer directly given, in which the immanence of meaning in life has become a problem, yet which still thinks in terms of totality'' (30, 56). Tillyard, who seeks to define the epic by spirit rather than form, lists ''high seriousness'' of style, amplitude (which includes variety and breadth of understanding as well as length), control (producing unity), and expression of ''the feelings of a large group of people living in or near his own time'' (5–12). Bakhtin, who was, like Lukács, concerned to divide the epic from the novel, finds the epic constituted by ''a national epic past'' derived from a national tradition; that past, he argues, is separated from contemporary reality by ''absolute'' distance (13).

The canon of surviving Western texts most commonly cited as true epics has remained small, even though the writing of an epic has been an ambition of major poets through the centuries. The core of the canon of primary epics is made up of the two Homeric poems (?9th century B.C.), *Beowulf* (probably 8th century), *The Song of Roland* (?11th century), and the *Nibelungenlied* (c. 1200). The core of secondary or literary epics is represented by the *Aeneid* (19 B.C.), the *Argonautica* of Apollonius (3rd century B.C.), Lucan's *Pharsalia* (A.D. 1st century), *The Poem of the Cid* (12th century), Camões's *Lusiad* (1572), Tasso's *Jerusalem Delivered* (1575), and Milton's *Paradise Lost* (1667). (The diversity within each group represents a second set of distinctions cutting across that between primary and secondary. *Beowulf*, the *Nibelungenlied*, and *The Song of Roland* were not developed out of the Greek and Roman tradition; Camões, Tasso, and Milton are much further removed culturally from Virgil than Virgil is from Homer.) Whether *The Divine Comedy* (completed 1311?) and *The Faerie Queene* (1590/1596) are to be counted as epics has been variously argued—the first lacks the epic sort of narrative; the second is too romantic, allegorical, and episodic for acceptance by a number of scholars.

Admission to the class of epics depends—as in genre criticism generally—on the criteria emphasized. The presence of an invocation, epic similes, catalogues, and supernatural machinery have been less insisted upon in the twentieth century, but focus on the actions of a single hero, a preponderance of realism over romance (both love and magic are regarded as essentially romantic characteristics), and a nationalistic theme have all been taken as especially significant characteristics. However, each admits of exceptions or poses problems. *Paradise Lost* arguably violates all of these; the *Odyssey* and *Beowulf* are not truly nationalistic, certainly not in the sense in which the *Aeneid* and the *Lusiads* are; and the role of gods, and thus realism, in one sense varies greatly across the central epic canon.

It is further evident that the traditional high valuation of the epic has exerted its force as an element of definition: Aesthetically unsuccessful poems clearly intended to be epics are generally denied full membership in the genre. French literary history, for instance, is filled with examples. Of the many French *chansons de geste*, only *The Song of Roland* is widely given full epic status; since the Renaissance, French poets have produced scores of epics that receive the scantest of notice. Voltaire wrote in 1727, "Was I sway'd by the common Affectation of commending our native Country abroad, I would endeavour in this Place, to set off to the best Advantage, some of our *Epick* Poems; but I must frankly own, among more than fifty which I have read, there is not one tolerable" (143; 121); but Voltaire's *Henriade*, which was briefly successful, now hardly figures in histories of the genre. Herbert Hunt lists sixty French works published between 1800 and 1896 "which are really of importance or interest for the development of epic poetry as understood by nineteenth-century writers" (407). Turning to the United States, Timothy Dwight's *The Quest of Cannan* and Joel Barlow's *The Columbiad*, both recognizable as epics in terms of overall form and the second, at least, intended to provide the United States with a proper epic, figure in histories of American literature but hardly in histories of the genre.

2. *Paradise Lost* is frequently regarded as the last great or true epic, not only in English but in the Western world. On the other hand, writers have continued to produce works that they regard as epics, or as epics necessarily modified by the exigencies of their time—and critics have found it useful to apply the term to texts with certain epic-like qualities. Verse is no longer regarded as essential to the epic effect; novels of stature have especially been seen as the modern successors to the epic. Tillyard cites George Eliot's *Middlemarch* as the nineteenth-century English novel most like the epic. Joyce's *Ulysses* has, for obvious reasons, seemed to qualify as "epical" if not fully as an epic. George Steiner nominates Tolstoy: "Tolstoy asked that his works be compared to those of Homer. Far more precisely than Joyce's *Ulysses*, *War and Peace* and *Anna Karenina* embody the resurgence of the epic mode, the re-entry into literature of tonalities, narrative practices, and forms of articulation that had declined from Western poetics after the age of Milton" (9). The desire to produce or champion a great American epic has been strong. Roy Harvey Pearce gives particular attention to Whitman's "Song of Myself," Hart Crane's *The Bridge*, and William Carlos Williams's *Paterson*. Jeffrey Walker's *Bardic Ethos and the American Epic Poem* (1989) is a rhetorical analysis of Pound's *Cantos*, Crane's *The Bridge*, Williams's *Paterson*, and Olson's *Maximus Poems*; the four works are regarded as deriving from the Bardic Ethos of Whitman rather than classical models. Recently, Elaine Safer has noted the ironic use of epic devices in contemporary American novelists; she examines "the comic epics" of Barth, Pynchon, Gaddis, and Kesey.

3. As a result of twentieth-century investigations of surviving instances of the oral performance of lengthy narratives, the meaning of primary or oral epic has been extended well beyond the concepts derived so largely from Homer and

Beowulf. An important pioneer in examining the Homeric and other epics from perspectives gained from contemporary "singers" of formulaic narratives was Milman Parry, whose work with the poems of Slavic singers has been carried on by Albert B. Lord; the results appear in the latter's *Singer of Tales* (1959). Lord emphasizes that "What is important is not the oral performance but rather the composition *during* oral performance" (5).

Rather than expand the term epic, C. M. Bowra has, in effect, subsumed the primary epic under the class *heroic poetry*, which he defines in terms of a conception of the heroic centered in an individual of exceptional prowess maintaining a personal, not communal, sense of honor; and devoting himself to the pursuit of fame. "The conception of the hero and heroic prowess is widely spread, and despite its different settings and manifestations shows the same main characteristics, which agree with what the Greeks say of their heroes. An age which believes in the pursuit of honour will naturally wish to express its admiration in a poetry of action and adventure, of bold endeavour and noble examples" (2–3). Bowra's *Heroic Poetry* explores the characteristics of such poetry in something like thirty languages, and from the oldest surviving poetry to modern bards of central Europe, Asia, and the Orient.

References

Abercrombie, Lascelles. *The Epic*. London: Martin Secker, n.d. A brief but informative survey. "There is only one thing which can master the perplexed stuff of epic material into unity; and that is, an ability to see in particular human experience some significant symbolism of man's general destiny" (17).

Bakhtin, M. M. "Epic and Novel." In *The Dialogic Imagination*. Ed. Michael Holquist; trans. C. Emerson and M. Holquist. Austin: University of Texas Press, 1981.

Bowra, C. M. *From Virgil to Milton*. London: Macmillan, 1945.

———. *Heroic Poetry*. London: Macmillan, 1952.

Clark, John. *A History of Epic Poetry (Post-Virgilian)*. Edinburgh: Oliver and Boyd, 1900. A rapid survey of Later Roman, English, French, German, Italian, Spanish, and Portuguese epics.

Dixon, W. Macneile. *English Epic and Heroic Poetry*. London: J. M. Dent, 1912.

Hunt, Herbert J. *The Epic in Nineteenth-Century France*. Oxford: Basil Blackwell, 1941. "My chief aim is avowedly to sketch the history of the *humanitarian* epic in [French] Romantic poetry" (5).

Ker, W. P. *Epic and Romance: Essays on Medieval Literature*. New York: Dover, 1957. Emphasizes the difference between epic and romance. "Whatever Epic may mean, it implies some weight and solidity; Romance means nothing, if it does not convey some notion of mystery and fantasy" (4). Romance pursues wonder; the primary interest of epic is in character.

Lord, Albert B. *The Singer of Tales*. Cambridge, Mass.: Harvard University Press, 1960. "Our immediate purpose is to comprehend the manner in which [the singers] compose, learn, and transmit their epics" (vii).

Lukács, Georg. *The Theory of the Novel*. Trans. A. Rostock. Cambridge, Mass.: M.I.T. Press, 1971. Original French edition, 1920.

Pearce, Roy Harvey. "The Long View: An American Epic." In *The Continuity of American Poetry*. Princeton, N. J.: Princeton University Press, 1961.

Safer, Elaine B. *The Contemporary American Comic Epic: The Novels of Barth, Pynchon, Gaddis, and Kesey*. Detroit; Mich.: Wayne State University Press, 1988.

Steiner, George. *Tolstoy or Dostoevsky*. New York: Alfred Knopf, 1959.

Tillyard, E. M. W. *The English Epic and Its Background*. New York: Oxford University Press, 1954. Tillyard surveys classical, medieval, Renaissance, and neo-classical epical literature, both English and continental, but his primary interest is in locating those English works that exhibit the "epic spirit." The resulting list is intriguing: *Piers Plowman*, the *Faerie Queene*, *Arcadia*, *Paradise Lost*, Bunyan's *Holy War*, Pope's translation of the *Iliad*, and Gibbon's *Decline and Fall of the Roman Empire*.

Voltaire. *Essay on Epic Poetry* (1727). In *Voltaire's Essay on Epic Poetry: A Study and an Edition*, ed. and trans. Florence Donnell White. Albany, N. Y.: Brandow Printing Co., 1915. Voltaire explains the variety within the epic in a single sentence: "The best modern writers have mix'd the Taste of their Country, with that of the Ancients. Their Flowers and their Fruits, warm'd and matur'd by the same Sun, yet draw from the Soil they grow upon, their different Colours, their Flavours, and their Size" (84; 41–42). (The second page number cited here and in the text is that of the original edition.)

Walker, Jeffrey. *Bardic Ethos and the American Epic Poem*. Baton Rouge: Louisiana State University Press, 1989.

Sources of Additional Information

For a brief survey of the works widely accepted as epic together with others "having a close, sometimes direct, relation to the conventional epic," see Paul Merchant's *The Epic* (London: Methuen, 1971, vii). Merchant is particularly generous in citing modern works with one or more epical dimensions.

The work of Milman Parry on the special qualities of the oral epic, juxtaposing the performances of living "bards" or "singers" of Yugoslavia with the characteristics of Homer's epics, is described in the Introduction to *The Making of Homeric Verse: The Collected Papers of Milman Parry* (Oxford: Clarendon Press, 1971). Parry's special contribution was the demonstration of the metrical determination of the formulaic phrase to be employed: "the operative principle of Homeric style, at least in regard to the recurrent epithet, was a traditional pattern of metrical convenience rather than any sense of choosing the adjective appropriate to the immediate context" (xxvii). Essays on the oral and early written epics of fifteen different cultural traditions appear in *Heroic Epic and Saga*, ed. Felix J. Oinas (Bloomington: Indiana University Press, 1978). H. M. Chadwick's *The Heroic Age* (Cambridge: Cambridge University Press, 1912) explores both the early Teutonic and the Greek epic poems.

The existence of a poetic of epic consciously intended to avoid slavish imitation of Homer, and therefore looking to Hesiod as a second model, is argued by John Kevin Newman in *The Classical Epic Tradition* (Madison: University of Wisconsin Press, 1986). Newman finds the origin of this poetic—which was intended, among other things, to be more musical and to make the persona of the narrator more prominent—in the Alexandrian Callimachus (early third century, B.C.) and traces its influence through Apollonius of Rhodes and Virgil, and then through Dante, Chaucer, and Milton to Tolstoy, Mann, and the filmmaker Eisenstein.

William Calin's *The Epic Quest: Studies in Four Old French Chansons de Geste* (Baltimore: Johns Hopkins University Press, 1966) considers *Aymeri de Narbonne, Ami et Amile*, *Gaydon*, and *Huon de Bordeaux* as mixtures of epic and romance that achieve the sublime.

A. Bartlett Giamatti's *The Earthly Paradise and the Renaissance Epic* (Princeton, N.J.: Princeton University Press, 1966) pursues the theme of the garden paradise, finding its use becoming ambiguous in the Renaissance: "The situation reflected in earthly paradise accounts is simply another version of the human predicament of being torn between what one wants and what one can have" (85). The allegorical dimension of the epic from Virgil to Milton is treated by Michael Murrin in *The Allegorical Epic: Essays in Its Rise and Decline* (Chicago: University of Chicago Press, 1980). Andrew Fichter's *Poets Historical: Dynastic Epic in the Renaissance* (New Haven, Conn.: Yale University Press, 1982) explores "the rise of *imperium*, the noble house, race, or nation to which the poet professes allegiance" (1) in Virgil and then the Virgilian tradition as influenced by Augustine in Ariosto, Tasso, and Spenser.

A study of the ways the epic tradition bears on English Romantic Poets will be found in Brian Wilkie's *Romantic Poets and Epic Tradition* (Madison: University of Wisconsin Press, 1965); Wilkie considers Southey's *Joan of Arc*, Landor's *Gebir*, Wordsworth's *Prelude*, Shelley's *The Revolt of Islam*, Keats's *Hyperion*, and Byron's *Don Juan*.

Page Dubois's *History, Rhetorical Description and the Epic* (Cambridge: D. S. Brewer, 1982) argues "that history, man's reading of the past, is part of poetry especially in the epic, and that its use in poetry is part of the attempt to control the present and shape the future of the human community" (3).

Surveys of critical attitudes toward and pronouncements about the epic include Donald M. Foerster's *The Fortunes of Epic Poetry: A Study in English and American Criticism, 1750–1950* (Washington, D.C.: Catholic University of America Press, 1962); John P. McWilliams, Jr., *The American Epic: Transforming a Genre, 1770–1860* (Cambridge: Cambridge University Press, 1989); and H. T. Swedenberg's *The Theory of the Epic in England, 1650–1800* (Berkeley: University of California Press, 1944). The latter includes sections quoting comments by a variety of critics on major questions regarding the epic.

EVALUATION   1. Judgment of the aesthetic merit of a literary work, usually based on assumptions about the intrinsic nature of literature. 2. Judgment of the value of a literary work in terms of its fulfillment of the demands of the genre it represents. 3. Judgment of the success of a work in achieving the author's intention. 4. Judgment of the value of a literary work for the performance of a specific function.

Until well into this century, CRITICISM *was generally assumed to include, if not primarily consist of, evaluative judgments. While judgments that a work is good or bad have generally reflected evaluation understood in one of the senses distinguished above, in fact the application of any of these kinds of judgment is almost always grounded in a prior postulate about the value of literature as a whole. The value of the individual text depends, then, on the degree to which it serves the postulated value.*

1. If the literary text is regarded as an aesthetic object the contemplation of which is pleasing or produces a perception of beauty, it is but a step to the assumption that there are discoverable universal principles that produce the sense

of pleasure or beauty. Pope's *Essay on Criticism*, Ruskin's works, at least from *Modern Painters* to *The Stones of Venice*, and Arnold's various essays on poetry derive from this assumption. The philosophical treatments of aesthetic pleasure and beauty in Kant and subsequently in such writers as Schelling, Shaftesbury, Bain, and Spenser supported this assumption, although these tend to be too abstract for direct application to literature.

Early in the twentieth century, while denying a specifically aesthetic mode of response, I. A. Richards adumbrated a single principle governing the value of art, with particular attention to literature. "The most valuable states of mind . . . are those which involve the widest and most comprehensive co-ordination of activities and the least curtailment, conflict, starvation, and restriction" (59). Such states are available through art because "The artist is concerned with the record and perpetuation of the experiences which seem to him most worth having" (61). The most complete coordination of the greatest number of interests, or currents of experience, will evidently produce the finest literature.

As is well known, the New Critics looked to Richards for theoretical grounding; their favored qualities of paradox, irony, and tension are simply modes of co-ordinating complexity. René Wellek and Austin Warren's chapter on evaluation in *Theory of Literature*, a volume influential in promulgating a conception of literature that is largely New Critical, again speaks as much about the value of literature per se as about the evaluation of individual works. However, it is quite clear about the latter: "Our criterion is inclusiveness: 'imaginative integration' and 'amount (and diversity) of material integrated.' The tighter the organization of the poem, the higher its value, according to formalistic criticism" (243). This point of view is also developed in Wellek's essay "Criticism as Evaluation" in *The Attack on Literature* in which he first grounds the aesthetic experience in the recognition of "unity or organicity" and then goes on to champion "a higher organization, a tighter cohesion[,]" and greater complexity as constituting "greater artistic value." "The multiple relations we discover in a great work of art, the implications and complexities *are* a measure of value" (62). This basis for evaluation is thought of as derived from the intrinsic nature of literature; Wellek and Warren repeatedly insist that "We ought to evaluate literature in terms and degrees of its own nature" (238–39), literature being defined in reference to a single function, the production of an "aesthetic experience" that is "a form of contemplation, a loving attention to qualities and qualitative structures" (241). As Wellek writes in "Criticism as Evaluation," "the existence or rather experience of the aesthetic state seems to me undeniable. Its negation seems to me like ignoring the existence of the color red or denying that snow is white" (61).

When the Russian Formalists identified the specific literary quality as the capacity of a work to defamiliarize human experience, they were equally announcing an aesthetic principle on the basis of which literary work could be evaluated. Since defamiliarization is accomplished through novel perspectives, the creation of new devices was for them a constant literary value. Hans Robert

Jauss's view that the distance between the horizon of expectation of readers at the time of publication of a work and the structure and norms of the work itself "determines the artistic nature of the work" thus builds on the Russian Formalist position. Consequently, a text that conforms fully to the reader's expectation is " 'culinary' or light reading" (15). Much the same view is evident in Wolfgang Iser's understanding of the function of the text in guiding readers' responses toward revaluation of the customary norms of their society. In an intriguing recent book, *The Phenomenon of Literature*, Bennison Gray's evaluative standards are unequivocally stated: "There are two basic kinds of minimum standards applicable to literature: consistency of event and consistency of narration" (534). Gray applies these standards without qualification: for him, works like Fowles's *The French Lieutenant's Woman* and James's *The Turn of the Screw* are unsuccessful.

2. As Aristotle's own analysis of tragedy illustrates, rather than seeking universal principles, criticism may seek to define the peculiar excellences of individual genres and judge individual works by the degree to which they embody those excellences. Such approaches are necessarily deductive and a posteriori; that is, the principles arrived at have been deduced from extant examples of the genre that are regarded as successful. The "Chicago Critics," writing in the middle decades of this century, have argued consistently for the importance of genre in determining both interpretation and evaluation. R. S. Crane's introduction to *Critics and Criticism* explicitly sets forth their position (12–24).

3. That the proper criterion for the judgment of a work is the author's success in achieving his or her goal is a well-known assumption of Goethe and later of Croce. The same view is stated in a more technical way by Charles W. Morris in his 1939 "Esthetics and the Theory of Signs." Looking to John Dewey and George H. Mead, Morris states that "a value is a property of an object or situation relative to an interest—namely the property of satisfying or consummating an act which requires an object with such a property for its completion" (134). Therefore, "Esthetic judgment is a judgment about esthetic signs; it can be concerned in the last analysis only with the adequacy with which such a sign performs its distinctive function of presenting values through their incorporation in an appropriate sign vehicle" (149). That is, what is to be judged is the adequacy of the sign vehicle (text) to the values that the sign vehicle suggests the author intended to present. Almost always, judgment of the value of a work in terms of the author's intention is, in fact, coupled with a second judgment, implicit or explicit, about the value of the intended goal. In the words of E. D. Hirsch, "What difference does it make how well an aim is achieved if it is not a valuable aim? Not even Croce, I think, would judge a work good which perfectly achieved some perverse or idiotic aim" (118). The result is that in fact the ultimate valuation turns out to rest on the criteria appropriate to the first or fourth senses of evaluation.

The argument mounted by Wimsatt and Beardsley denying the possibility of evaluating the author's success in achieving his or her INTENTION by denying that the intention can be known has made most critics wary of trying to compare achievement and intention. However, modes of evaluation very close to this continue to be put forward. John Reichert writes in *Making Sense of Literature* (1977), "In my view . . . a full critical evaluation will consist of an analysis of the effect of the work on the reader—of precisely what sort of cognitive and emotional experience it is designed to afford—coupled, if the need arises, with justification of the value of that experience" (187–88).

4. Logical positivists have often questioned the possibility of any objective evaluation. A. J. Ayer, for example, asserts that

> such aesthetic terms as "beautiful" and "hideous" are employed, as ethical words are employed, not to make statements of fact, but simply to express certain feelings and evoke a certain response. It follows, as in ethics, that there is no sense in attributing objective validity to aesthetic judgements, and no possibility of arguing about questions of value in aesthetics, but only about questions of fact. (113)

E. E. Kellett's *The Whirligig of Taste* (1929) argues on the basis of history rather than philosophical principles that all literary judgments depend on tastes that shift in time and are peculiar to individuals.

> Thus we come back simply to this, that literary taste, like every other human faculty, is the creature of the age, circumscribed by its limitations, stirred by its passions, warped by its defects. It cannot be taken in isolation from the man as a whole. . . . Like opinion, it alters as we cross the Pyrenees, and like disease, it flourishes in one climate and decays in another. But it cannot too often be repeated that there is, in the strict sense, no spirit of the age. Each man absorbs from his environment something special to himself, and in turn gives back to it something that no other gives. (27–28)

However, the best known twentieth-century assault on the possibility of an objective evaluation of literary works is made in Northrop Frye's *Anatomy of Criticism*. For Frye, any attempt to prove one work or author better than another is "merely one more document in the history of taste" (25); he writes, "Every deliberately constructed hierarchy of values in literature known to me is based on a concealed social, moral, or intellectual analogy" (23).

One way of meeting such challenges is to declare openly that one's standard is an extrinsic one, that it is based on a social, moral, or intellectual function that literature is expected to perform. David Daiches's "The function of literature is to illuminate human experience" is a definition that serves as a norm (169). (The difference between Daiches's formulation and Richards's understanding of the power of literature to achieve harmony or Matthew Arnold's of poetry as "a criticism of life under the conditions fixed for such a criticism by the laws of poetic truth and beauty," 9:163, is a matter of degree since the nature of something largely determines its possible functions; nevertheless, there is a difference between a definition-based norm grounded in the assumed nature of a thing and one grounded in its assumed function.)

As long as the critic announces an extrinsic criterion, judgments are likely to be stated unequivocally as though made on the basis of an agreed mode of measuring aesthetic merit. Thus, F. R. Leavis can write in *The Great Tradition*:

> It is necessary to insist, then, that there are important distinctions to be made. . . . And as a recall to a due sense of differences it is well to start by distinguishing between the few really great—the major novelists who count in the same way as the major poets, in the sense that they not only change the possibilities of the art for practitioners and readers, but that they are significant in terms of the human awareness they promote; awareness of the possibilities of life. (10)

At the same time, Leavis was chary of stating his conception of the standard of judgment in any more exact terms than "awareness of the possibilities of life." "The standards of criticism are not at all of the order of the standards in the Weights and Measures Office. They are not producible, they are not precise, and they are not fixed. But if they are not effectively "there" for the critic to appeal to, the function of criticism is badly disabled" ("Standards of Criticism," 244). Much more specific has been Marxist criticism, which assumes that literature has the function of advancing the kind of society advocated by Marx and Lenin. Thus, even the Medvedev/Bakhtin volume, *The Formal Method in Literary Scholarship*, while discriminating between "ideological (extraliterary) and artistic demands and approaches," regards literary criticism as making "correct and proper social demands" on literature and the poet as having a "social assignment" (35).

However, relativism emerges once it is granted (a) that there are several possible extrinsic criteria; (b) that the judgment must take account of the response of the individual reader; or (c) that evaluative standards are shifting cultural constructs.

4a. E. D. Hirsch well represents the first type of relativism. While insisting on understanding the author's meaning as embodied in the text, Hirsch argues that the author's values need not be accepted; the bases for evaluative judgment will necessarily be extrinsic—the work may be evaluated from the point of view of political, psychological, religious, moral, or social theories, however alien these may be.

4b. The usual Anglo-American locus classicus for authorization of a personal response is the series of questions Walter Pater asks in the preface to *The Renaissance*: "What is this song or picture, this engaging personality presented in life or in a book, to *me*? What effect does it really produce on me? Does it give me pleasure? and if so, what sort or degree of pleasure?" (viii). While the thrust of the passage is toward the importance of analyzing one's own impressions of a work, the value of the work depends on the intensity and complexity of the individual's response. For Pater, the "poetic passion, the desire of beauty, the love of art for its own sake" are the greatest source of the "quickened, multiplied consciousness" he desiderates (238–39). Although this sounds like a description of an aesthetic evaluation, it essentially sets out a functional criterion.

Louise Rosenblatt, who explicitly seeks to balance Pater's emphasis on the reader's response with recognition of the control exerted by the text, nevertheless

emphasizes the importance of the reader's personal response. "In the last analysis, it is always individual readers evaluating their own personal transactions
with the text; we must recognize the uniqueness that derives from the individual's
particular selecting-out of elements from the cultural milieu, and the special
value-demands due to the unique moment in the reader's life in which the literary
transaction takes place" (153). As the previous sentence suggests, Rosenblatt
is seeking to recognize the influence of both personal experience and cultural
norms on the reader's evaluative response.

4c. Barbara Hernnstein Smith's "Contingencies of Value" strongly states the
interaction of the individual's personal "economic" system with the external
economic system of society. Evaluation, she finds, depends "on how well a
work performs desired/able functions" (26). However, what is required to perform these functions is itself largely a function of society.

> [B]y providing [the members of the community] with "necessary backgrounds,"
> teaching them "appropriate skills," "cultivating their interests," and, generally,
> "developing their tastes," the academy produces generation after generation of
> subjects for whom the objects and texts thus labeled do indeed perform the functions
> thus privileged, thereby assuring the continuity of mutually defining canonical works,
> canonical functions, and canonical audiences. (27)

That evaluative judgment can be legitimated only in terms of the specific
criteria chosen by the individual critic has become a commonplace of later
twentieth-century criticism. The principle is one stated by Coleridge in the *Biographia Literaria*: "But I should call that investigation fair and philosophical in
which the critic announces and endeavors to establish the principles, which he
holds for the foundation of poetry in general, with the specification of these in
their application to different *classes* of poetry" (2:85). One straightforward
twentieth-century formulation is Wayne Shumacher's conclusion after many
pages of discussion about the question of literary evaluation: "It may be, after
all, that the best practical course of action is to make all evaluations frankly
conditional. 'If musical sound is a quality of great poetry, then in one respect
this poem . . . ' 'If it is agreed that unity within complexity is the condition of
literary achievement . . . ' " (120).

Note

The ultimate judgment of a literary work's value has often been said to be most
authoritatively made by the winnowing of time: Valuable works are those that are regarded
as worth reading and discussing over many generations; inferior works are forgotten and
languish unread. Samuel Johnson takes this position: "The reverence due to writings that
have long subsisted arises therefore not from any credulous confidence in the superior
wisdom of past ages, or gloomy persuasion of the degeneracy of mankind, but is the
consequence of acknowledged and indubitable positions, that what has been longest known
has been most considered, and what is most considered is best understood" (60–61).
Such a view assumes universal principles of aesthetic appeal that in the long run triumph
over temporary fashions, uses, and tastes. The perspective of those who deny that there
are such principles is stated with force by E. E. Kellett: " 'Immortality,' in fact, which

writers are fond of claiming for their works, is often a matter of the merest chance, and is no more a credit to the authors than the survival of their tombstones'' (154). On the other hand, it can be argued that there is, in fact, one quality that gives continuing value to a text: sufficient richness of suggestion may allow succeeding generations to find their particular interests, demands, and criteria of value addressed. A psychologically based variation of the position that equates value with continuing interest over time is that of Norman Holland in *The Dynamics of Literary Response*. The good work, for Holland, ''embodies the fantasy with a power to disturb many readers over a long period of time and, built in, a defensive maneuver that will enable those readers to master the poem's disturbance'' (202–3).

References

Arnold, Matthew. ''The Study of Poetry.'' In vol. 9 of *The Complete Prose Works of Matthew Arnold*. Ed. R. H. Super. Ann Arbor: University of Michigan Press, 1960–77.

Ayer, A. J. *Language, Truth, and Logic*. 1936; New York: Dover, 1952.

Coleridge, Samuel Taylor. *Biographia Literaria*. Ed. J. Shawcross. 2 vols. London: Oxford University Press, 1954.

Critics and Criticism: Ancient and Modern. Ed. R. S. Crane. Chicago: University of Chicago Press, 1952.

Daiches, David. ''Literary Evaluation.'' In *Problems of Literary Evaluation*, ed. Joseph Strelka. University Park: Pennsylvania State University Press, 1969.

Frye, Northrop. *Anatomy of Criticism* (1957). Princeton, N.J.: Princeton University Press, 1971.

Gray, Bennison. *The Phenomenon of Literature*. The Hague: Mouton, 1975. Somewhat idiosyncratic but stimulating.

Hirsch, E. D., Jr. *The Aims of Interpretation*. Chicago: University of Chicago Press, 1976. The second half of this volume is focused primarily on the question of evaluation.

Holland, Norman. *The Dynamics of Literary Response*. New York: Oxford University Press, 1968.

Iser, Wolfgang. *The Implied Reader*. Baltimore: Johns Hopkins University Press, 1974. Original German edition, 1972.

Jauss, Hans Robert. ''Literary History as a Challenge to Literary Theory.'' *New Literary History* 2 (Autumn 1970): 7–37. The reception theory advocated by Jauss is interested primarily in the history of reader's responses, including evaluative responses, over time.

Johnson, Samuel. ''Preface to Shakespeare.'' In *Johnson on Shakespeare*. Vol. 7 of *The Yale Edition of the Works of Samuel Johnson*. Ed. Arthur Sherbo. New Haven: Yale University Press, 1968.

Kellett, E. E. *The Whirligig of Taste*. New York: Harcourt, Brace, 1929. An early statement of the necessary relativity of literary judgments that deserves to be better known.

Leavis, F. R. *The Great Tradition*. 1948; New York: Doubleday Anchor, 1954.

———. ''Standards of Criticism'' (1965). In *Valuation in Criticism and Other Essays*. Cambridge: Cambridge University Press, 1986.

Medvedev, P. N./M. M. Bakhtin. *The Formal Method in Literary Scholarship*. Trans. J. Wehrle. Baltimore: Johns Hopkins University Press, 1978. Originally published

under Medvedev's name, the volume has also been attributed in whole or part to
    Bakhtin.
Morris, Charles W. "Esthetics and the Theory of Signs." *The Journal of Unified Science
    (Erkenntnis)* 8 (1939–40): 131–50.
Pater, Walter. *The Renaissance*. London: Macmillan, 1910.
Reichert, John. *Making Sense of Literature*. Chicago: University of Chicago Press, 1977.
    Chapter 6 is devoted to the question of evaluation.
Richards, I. A. *Principles of Literary Criticism*. 1925; London: Routlege and Kegan
    Paul, 1948.
Rosenblatt, Louise. *The Reader, the Text, the Poem*. Carbondale: Southern Illinois Uni-
    versity Press, 1978.
Shumacher, Wayne. *Elements of Critical Theory*. Berkeley: University of California Press
    1952. The last four chapters are concerned with evaluation.
Smith, Barbara H. "Contingencies of Value." In *Canons*, ed. R. von Hallberg. Chicago:
    University of Chicago Press, 1984. Reprinted from *Critical Inquiry* 10 (1983):
    1–35.
Wellek, René. "Criticism as Evaluation" (1976). In *The Attack on Literature*. Chapel
    Hill: University of North Carolina Press, 1982.
Wellek, René, and Austin Warren. *Theory of Literature*. 1949; New York: Harcourt,
    Brace and World, 1956. Chapter 18 treats the evaluation of literature.
Winters, Yvor. *In Defense of Reason*. Denver, Colo.: Alan Swallow, 1947.

Sources of Additional Information

A wide-ranging collection of essays on the difficulties of judging the value of literary works is *Problems of Literary Evaluation*, ed. by Joseph Strelka (University Park: Pennsylvania State University Press, 1969). The section entitled "Poetics and Aesthetics" in Tzvetan Todorov's *Introduction to Poetics* (Minneapolis: University of Minnesota Press, 1981) succinctly states the argument for regarding all evaluation as the product of an interaction between the text and the individual reader. "Aesthetic judgments are propositions that strongly imply their own processes of utterance. We cannot conceive of such a judgment outside the instance of discourse in which it is made, nor in isolation from the subject articulating it" (69).

A carefully developed argument for evaluating literature in personal ethical terms (which regards form as well as subject matter and character portrayal) is made by Wayne Booth in *The Company We Keep* (Berkeley: University of California Press, 1988). Literature provides one with the means of trying out various modes of life vicariously, and can thus, Booth believes, lead the reader toward better desires.

F

FEMINIST LITERARY CRITICISM   The understanding, analysis of, and
response to literary works and/or language, and/or the institution of literary
study or literary theory from the point of view of women's experience.

*It should be noted that the term feminist criticism is routinely used to include
much more than literary criticism—frequently it signifies a critique of "patriarchal" aspects of the culture as a whole.*

*A number of broad definitions of feminist literary criticism are available from
the works of feminist critics. For Patricia Spacks it includes "any mode that
approaches a text with primary concern for the nature of female experience in
it—the fictional experience of characters, the deducible or imaginable experience
of an author, the experience implicit in language or structure" ("The Difference," 14). For Elaine Showalter, "Whether concerned with the literary representations of sexual difference, with the ways that literary genres have been
shaped by masculine or feminine values, or with the exclusion of the female
voice from the institutions of literature, criticism, and theory, feminist criticism
has established gender as a fundamental category of literary analysis" (New*
Feminist Criticism, *3). For Annette Kolodny:*

> What unites and repeatedly invigorates feminist literary criticism, then, is neither
> dogma nor method but an acute and impassioned attentiveness *to the ways in which
> primarily male structures of power are inscribed (or encoded) within our literary
> inheritance; the consequences of that encoding for women . . . and, with that, a
> shared analytic* concern *for the implications of that encoding not only for a better
> understanding of the past but also for an improved reordering of the present and
> future. ("Dancing Through," 162)*

*In Judith Fetterly's words, "To create a new understanding of our literature
is to make possible a new effect of that literature on us. And to make possible*

a new effect is in turn to provide the conditions for changing the culture that the literature reflects" (xix–xx).

Feminist criticism thus generally defined has come to include a wide variety of critical activities and theories that exist not as different senses but as possibilities, a number of which are likely to be included in any particular use of the term. There have been numerous attempts to categorize these critical approaches and theories; the resulting classifications frequently cut across one another. Discussions of feminist criticism naturally tend to shade off into the programs and issues of feminism proper, which makes coherent definition even more difficult.

Although its importance came to be fully recognized only in the 1970s, the most significant earlier twentieth-century treatment of women as writers is, by general agreement, Virginia Woolf's *A Room of One's Own* (1929). If the word "literature" is substituted for "fiction," Woolf's opening comment on her invitation to address the Cambridge women's colleges of Newnham and Girton which resulted in *A Room of One's Own* encapsulates some of the major directions in which feminist explorations of literature were to develop. "The title women and fiction might mean, and you may have meant it to mean, women and what they are like; or it might mean women and the fiction that they write; or it might mean women and the fiction that is written about them; or it might mean that somehow all three are inextricably mixed together and you want me to consider them in that light" (3–4). The book is rich in insights and quotable passages, among them Woolf's description of the probable fate to which a sister of Shakespeare with equal genius would have been driven by cultural constraints. Its major argument, however, is that the culture has rarely provided women with the essentials for successful authorship. "All I could do was to offer you an opinion upon one minor point—a woman must have money and a room of her own if she is to write fiction" (4).

A second major feminist work, Simone de Beauvoir's *The Second Sex* (1949), explores the constancy with which woman has been regarded as the Other. "She is defined and differentiated with reference to man and not he with reference to her; she is the incidental, the inessential as opposed to the essential. He is the Subject, he is the Absolute—she is the Other" (xix). Although *The Second Sex* is not primarily focused on literature, it includes the important section "The Myth of Woman in Five Authors."

Mary Ellmann's *Thinking About Women* (1968), a third influential feminist text, is a set of wry meditations on sexual stereotypes and the prevalence of what Ellmann calls "phallic criticism." Her irony is straightforward but mordant:

> Perhaps as long as sexual interest in any sense is strong, we will continue to comprehend all phenomena, however shifting, in terms of our original and simple sexual differences. . . . The persistence of the habit is even, conceivably, admirable. It might be taken as proof of the fertility of the human mind that, given so little sexual evidence, it should contrive so large a body of dependent sexual opinion. (6)

Synthesizing literary and political analysis, Kate Millett's *Sexual Politics* (1970) vigorously explores and challenges the degree to which women are dehumanized

in the works of male writers, especially Henry Miller, Norman Mailer, and
D. H. Lawrence. Carolyn Heilbrun's *Toward a Recognition of Androgyny* (1973)
uses literary examples to argue against "sexual polarization and the prison of
gender." For her, the term androgyny "defines a condition under which the
characteristics of the sexes, and the human impulses expressed by men and
women, are not rigidly defined" (ix–x). Judith Fetterly's *The Resisting Reader*
(1978) further documents the power of what Millett had called the *patriarchal
society*. Using as examples Irving's "Rip Van Winkle," Anderson's "I Want
to Know Why," Hawthorne's "The Birthmark," Faulkner's "A Rose for
Emily," Hemingway's *A Farewell to Arms*, Fitzgerald's *The Great Gatsby*,
James's *The Bostonians*, and Mailer's *The American Dream*, Fetterly charges,
"The major works of American fiction constitute a series of designs on the
female reader, all the more potent in their effect because they are 'impalpable' "
(xi). The "resistance" of the title is necessary to women because "As readers
and teachers and scholars, women are taught to think as men, to identify with
a male point of view, and to accept as normal and legitimate a male system of
values, one of whose central principles is misogyny" (xx). In their reading, as
elsewhere, women must resist "the *immasculation* of women by men" (xx). In
a uniquely different approach, Annette Kolodny's *Lay of the Land* (1985) documents the pervasiveness of the metaphor (and fantasy) of the land as woman
in American writing. "From accounts of the earliest explorers onward . . . a
uniquely American pastoral vocabulary began to show itself. . . . At its core lay
a yearning to know and to respond to the landscape as feminine" (8).

   These works of Beauvoir, Ellmann, Millett, Heilman, Kolodny, and Fetterly
belong to what Elaine Showalter calls in "Feminist Criticism in the Wilderness"
feminist reading or *feminist critique*: "it offers feminist readings of texts that
consider the images and stereotypes of women in literature, the omissions and
misconceptions about women in criticism, and woman-as-sign in semiotic systems" (182). The other type of feminist criticism Showalter here recognizes,
gynocritics, studies women as writers. This mode has early representatives in
Patricia Spacks's *The Female Imagination* (1975), Ellen Moers's *Literary Women*
(1976), Showalter's *A Literature of Their Own* (1977), Nina Baym's *Woman's
Fiction: A Guide to Novels by and about Women in America, 1820– 1870* (1978),
and Barbara Christian's *Black Women Novelists* (1980). Moers in particular
stresses that many women writers proved of greater interest once she read them
as women. Showalter's study of nineteenth- and twentieth-century British women
novelists identifies three phases in their relationship to the male tradition: the
Feminine phase of imitation of the dominant male standards (1840–1880), the
Feminist phase of protest (1880–1920), and the Female phase of self-discovery
(1920 to the present), with the latter "entering a new stage of self-awareness
about 1960" (*Literature of their Own*, 13).

   The book that did most to bring notice to Anglo-American feminist criticism
is Sandra Gilbert and Susan Gubar's *The Madwoman in the Attic: The Woman
Writer and the Nineteenth-Century Literary Imagination* (1979). Like Spacks,

Moers, and Showalter, Gilbert and Gubar examine the characteristics of women's writing. However they also draw on the Beauvoir-Millett vein of feminist criticism in stressing the evidences in Austen, Charlotte Brontë, George Eliot, Emily Dickinson, and others of the pain and effort produced by the struggle against cultural traditions that regarded women as inferior and passive and at the same time as angels, monsters, or both.

> Images of enclosure and escape, fantasies in which maddened doubles functioned as asocial surrogates for docile selves, metaphors of physical discomfort manifested in frozen landscapes and fiery interiors—such patterns recurred throughout this tradition, along with obsessive depictions of diseases like anorexia, agoraphobia, and claustrophobia. . . . We decided, therefore, that the striking coherence we noticed in literature by women could be explained by a common, female impulse to struggle free from social and literary confinement through strategic redefinitions of self, art, and society. (xi–xii)

Showalter's distinction between feminist critique and gynocritics is a useful one that corresponds fairly closely with the history of feminist criticism of the decade from the late 1960s to the late 1970s. It requires extension, however, to the earlier phase which is best represented by Beauvoir's demonstration of the male-centeredness of Western culture, and to a later phase, a rethinking of the assumptions about and theories of literature generally. Showalter explicitly added this late phase in the Introduction to *The New Feminist Criticism*: following the demonstration of the degree of misogyny in the accepted canon and "the discovery that women writers had a literature of their own," "feminist criticism demanded not just the recognition of women's writing but a radical rethinking of the conceptual grounds of literary study, a revision of the accepted theoretical assumptions about reading and writing that have been based entirely on male literary experiences" (6,8). Such rethinking would for instance include the development of the kind of aesthetic arguments Lillian Robinson calls for in *Treason Our Text* that would make it possible "to argue, in the general marketplace of literary ideas, that the novels of Henry James ought to give place—a *little* place, even—to the diaries of his sister Alice" (23).

Other classifications and oppositions within feminist criticism, however, cut across these four phases. There is, for instance, the opposition between those who envision feminist criticism as a pluralistic endeavor in which critics employ a wide range of approaches and address a variety of issues of feminist interest and those who believe that there is a central theory to which feminist critics should subscribe. Annette Kolodny's "Dancing Through the Minefield" is a central statement of the first position:

> [O]ur task is to initiate nothing less than a playful pluralism, responsive to the possibilities of multiple critical schools and methods, but captive of none. . . . Only by employing a plurality of methods will we protect ourselves from the temptation of so oversimplifying any text—and especially those offensive to us—that we render ourselves unresponsive to what Scholes has called "its various systems of meaning and their interaction." (161)

Elizabeth Meese also warns against the dangers of factions opposing each other within the total movement: "In response to the complexity resulting from multicentering moves, we need to conceive of feminist criticism, indeed as Culler suggests, all criticism, as an infinite progression that refuses to identify a center because it is always decentered, self-displacing and self-contradictory" (*Crossing*, 150). In *(Ex)Tensions* (1990) she writes:

> Perhaps most troublesome at this moment is the way in which Feminist Literary Criticism (with a proper name) seems to be staging its own internal power plays— maneuvers not unfamiliar to black, lesbian, nonacademic, and socialist feminists— as reigning Feminist scholars . . . reenact patricentric gestures of exclusion that have historically characterized "phallic" authority's production of orthodoxy or dogma. (4)

Nina Baym, who characterizes the antipluralists as "legalists" (and whose antitheoretical stance Meese rejects in the first chapter of *(Ex)Tensions*), deplores the divisions between champions of various theories to the extent that she eschews theory. "Essays in feminist journals are permeated with musts and shoulds, with homily and exhortation, and a fractiousness that at most puts 'sisterhood' under erasure and at least means that the totalizing assumptions of theory are fictions" ("Madwoman," 59). On the other hand, Cheri Register calls for a prescriptive criticism that will "set standards for what is 'good' from a feminist viewpoint," guiding both authors and critics (2). Defending Register against Elizabeth Meese, Josephine Donovan attacks "compliant 'pluralism' " for neutralizing "the radical potential of feminist criticism" (x, ix). Related to the question of pluralism is that of addressing the degree of diversity among women. The issue is mordantly phrased by Audre Lorde: "If white american [*sic*] feminist theory need not deal with the differences between us, and the resulting difference in our oppressions, then how do you deal with the fact that the women who clean your houses and tend your children while you attend conferences on feminist theory are, for the most part, poor women and women of Color?" (112). A further opposition occurs between those feminists who employ deconstruction and those who reject it (for a useful, though hardly neutral, overview of the debate, see Meese's *(Ex)Tensions*, pp. 9–28).

There is also a distinction to be made between views that seek to reduce the differences between the gender roles as much as possible and those that, while seeking to overcome male dominance, emphasize differences. For example, Simone de Beauvoir makes explicit in her introduction to *The Second Sex* that "When I use the words *woman* or *feminine* I evidently refer to no archetype, no changeless essence whatever; the reader must understand the phrase 'in the present state of education and custom' after most of my statements" (xxxv). She insists that "Woman is the victim of no mysterious fatality; the peculiarities that identify her as specifically a woman get their importance from the significance placed on them" (809). On the other hand, Patricia Spacks writes, "Changing social conditions increase or diminish the opportunities for women's action and expression, but a special female self-awareness emerges through literature in every period" (*Female Imagination*; 3). While these views are not polar (Beauvoir has in mind primarily the disabilities imposed on women by society while Spacks focuses on the positive qualities she finds in women's writing), the latter places a greater emphasis on an essential nature in women.

A parallel distinction exists between *essentialists*, who give primary emphasis to biological/psychological differences, and *nonessentialists*, who emphasize the cultural bases of woman's experience. The essentialists tend to speak of sexual differences, and the nonessentialists of gender differences. American feminist critics have most frequently had a primary concern for the total cultural situation which supports male dominance in literature as elsewhere, and which therefore is preoccupied with the history of androcentric views of women and of women's attempts to express themselves in spite of cultural pressures. A similar but more Marxist concern with cultural constraints is found among English feminists. Such focus on the ways in which culture has defined women, their reaction to such definition, and strategies for changing cultural assumptions and the associated practices is frequently referred to as *empiricist*, although clearly empirical investigations and practical protest require specific theoretical assumptions. Recent French feminism, on the other hand, has tended to focus on biological/psychological differences and to build theoretical explanatory structures.

Analysis of the language available and the customs governing discourse has been an especially fruitful form of cultural investigation. Describing the writing of the dissertation that led to her study, *Man Made Language*, Dale Spender writes, "My thesis was simple, and in my terms demonstrable. I was arguing that men controlled the language and that it worked in their favour. I could demonstrate that men had not only provided themselves with more—and more positive—words but that they ensured that they had more opportunities to use them" (x). Again, she writes, "One of the basic principles of feminism is that society has been constructed with a bias which favours males; one of the basic principles of feminists who are concerned with language is that this bias can be located in the language" (14). Her investigations led Spender "to posit the existence of a semantic rule which determines that *any* symbol which is associated with the female must assume negative (and frequently sexual—which is also significant) connotations" (19). "Gendered language" thus is language that embodies the male point of view and therefore tacitly supports male dominance. In *Feminism and Linguistic Theory*, Deborah Cameron summarizes, "The feminist view of language is reminiscent of the feminist view of sexuality: it is a powerful resource which the oppressor has appropriated, giving back only the shadow which women need to function in patriarchal society" (6).

A different mode of understanding the culturally constructed position of women arises out of Nancy Chodorow's reworking of psychoanalytical theory in such a way as to undercut its heavy dependence on biological differences. "Gender differences, and the experience of difference, like differences among women, are socially and psychologically created and situated" (4). Her position thus contrasts with those of both Sigmund Freud and Jacques Lacan. Biological, psychological, and psychoanalytical theories have received most attention in France. The attacks by Kate Millett and others on Freud (especially his emphasis on the principle of penis envy) perhaps still represent the attitude toward Freud held by most Anglo-American feminists, although Juliet Mitchell's *Psychoanalysis and Feminism* (1974) seeks to rehabilitate Freud for feminism. ''[T]he argument of this book is that a rejection of psychoanalysis and Freud's work is fatal for feminism. However it may have been used, psychoanalysis is not a recommendation *for* a patriarchal sex, but an analysis *of* one'' (xv).

The dominant French feminists tend to make use of (while partially subverting) the biological/psychoanalytical structure of Lacan, which, together with a greater interest in phenomenology and philosophy generally, has produced a much more theoretical form of feminist thought. Biological and psychoanalytical arguments are closely linked since psychoanalytical theories are heavily based on biological differences. For Lacan, who associates all language with the Symbolic Order (which he further associates with the figure of the Father), women can only express themselves through the rational, masculine language that exists and thus necessarily occupy a marginalized position. However, Hélène Cixous, Luce Irigaray, and Julia Kristeva—in different and not always compatible ways—posit and pursue a feminine form of writing (*l'écriture féminine*) that undercuts the Symbolic Order by puns, erratic punctuation, neologisms, and strategic interruptions intended to represent the pre-Oedipal Mother principle or ''thinking through the body'' as opposed to masculine intellectual discourse. This is evidently a much more radical activity than that undertaken by feminists who challenge the evidences of male dominance in particular words and syntactical structures and the assumptions about their use. (It should be noted that, at least for Cixous and Kristeva, *l'écriture féminine* is possible for both sexes, though it is most likely to be practiced by women.)

Elaine Showalter neatly sums up: ''The emphasis in each country falls somewhat differently: English feminist criticism, essentially Marxist, stresses oppression; French feminist criticism, essentially psychoanalytic, stresses repression; American feminist criticism, essentially textual, stresses expression'' (''Feminist Criticism,'' 186). Finally, feminists differ as to whether a single movement—and consequently, a single literary criticism—can embrace the interests of both heterosexual and lesbian, middle- and lower-class, white women and women of color.

References

Baym, Nina. ''The Madwoman and Her Languages: Why I Don't Do Feminist Literary Theory.'' In *Feminist Issues in Literary Scholarship*, an intriguing essay.

In other words, feminist theory addresses an audience of prestigious male academics and attempts to win its respect. It succeeds, so far as I can see, only when it ignores or dismisses the earlier paths of feminist literary study as ''naive'' and grounds its own theories in those currently in vogue with the men who make theory: deconstruction, for example, or Marxism. (45)

———. *Woman's Fiction: A Guide to Novels by and About Women in America, 1820–1870*. Ithaca, N.Y.: Cornell University Press, 1978.

Beauvoir, Simone de. *The Second Sex*. Trans. H. M. Parshley. New York: Knopf, 1953. Original French edition, 1949.

Cameron, Deborah. *Feminism and Linguistic Theory*. New York: St. Martin's Press, 1987.

Chodorow, Nancy. "Gender, Relation, and Difference in Psychoanalytical Perspective." In *The Future of Difference*, ed. H. Eisenstein and A. Jardine, Boston: G. K. Hall, 1980.

Christian, Barbara. *Black Women Novelists*. Westport, Conn.: Greenwood Press, 1980.

Cixous, Hélène, and Catherine Clement. *The Newly Born Woman*. Trans. B. Wing. Manchester: Manchester University Press, 1986.

Donovan, Josephine, ed. *Feminist Literary Criticism*. 2d ed. Lexington: Kentucky University Press, 1989. Donovan's "Afterword: Critical Revision" strongly states the political stance of feminist criticism. "The new feminist critic is not 'disinterestedly' describing cultural phenomena in the tradition of academic liberalism. She is (and knows herself to be) politically motivated by a concern to redeem women from the sloughbin of nonentity in which they have languished for centuries" (76). The volume includes "A Selected Bibliography of Feminist Literary Theory, 1975–1986" by Barbara A. White.

Ellmann, Mary. *Thinking About Women*. New York: Harcourt, Brace and World, 1968.

Feminist Issues in Literary Scholarship. Ed. Shari Benstock. Bloomington: Indiana University Press, 1987. Special issue of *The Tulsa Studies in Women's Literature* 3 (Spring/Fall 1984).

Fetterly, Judith. *The Resisting Reader: A Feminist Approach to American Fiction*. Bloomington: Indiana University Press, 1978.

The Future of Difference. Ed. Hester Eisenstein and Alice Jardine. Boston: G. K. Hall, 1980.

Gilbert, Sandra M., and Susan Gubar. *The Madwoman in the Attic: The Woman Writer and the Nineteenth-Century Literary Imagination*. New Haven, Conn.: Yale University Press, 1979.

Heilbrun, Carolyn. *Towards a Recognition of Androgyny*. New York: Knopf, 1973.

Irigaray, Luce. *Speculum of the Other Woman*. Trans. Gillian G. Gill. Ithaca, N.Y.: Cornell University Press, 1985. Original French version, 1974.

Kolodny, Annette. "Dancing Through the Minefield: Some Observations on the Theory, Practice and Politics of a Feminist Criticism." In *The New Feminist Criticism*. Reprinted from *Feminist Studies* 6 (Spring 1980): 1–25. An important and frequently attacked statement of pluralist strategy.

————. *The Lay of the Land*. Chapel Hill: University of North Carolina Press, 1985. "[A]t the deepest psychological level, the move to America was experienced as the daily reality of what has become its single dominant metaphor: regression from the cares of adult life and a return to the primal warmth of womb or breast in a feminine landscape" (6).

Kristeva, Julia. *Desire in Language: A Semiotic Approach to Literature and Art*. Trans. T. Gora, A. Jardine, and L. S. Roudiez. New York: Columbia University Press, 1980.

Lorde, Audre. *Sister Outsider*. Trumansburg, N.Y.: Crossing Press, 1984.

Meese, Elizabeth A. *Crossing the Double-Cross: The Practice of Feminist Criticism*. Chapel Hill: University of North Carolina Press, 1986.

————. *(Ex)tensions: Re-Figuring Feminist Criticism*. Urbana: University of Illinois Press, 1990.

Millet, Kate. *Sexual Politics*. Garden City, N.Y.: Doubleday, 1970.

Mitchell, Juliet. *Psychoanalysis and Feminism*. New York: Pantheon, 1974.

Moers, Ellen. *Literary Women*. Garden City, N.Y.: Doubleday, 1976. "The subject of this book is the major women writers, writers we read and shall always read whether interested or not in the fact that they happened to be women".... "Literature is the only intellectual field to which women, over a long stretch of time, have made an indispensable contribution" (xi).

The New Feminist Criticism. Ed. Elaine Showalter. New York: Pantheon, 1985.

Register, Cheri. "American Feminist Literary Criticism: A Bibliographical Introduction." In *Feminist Literary Criticism*, ed. Josephine Donovan. A useful survey of feminist criticism from a moderately militant point of view.

Robinson, Lillian. *Treason Our Text: Feminist Challenges*. Wellesley, Mass.: Working Paper No. 104, Wellesley College Center for Research on Women. 1983. A well-written statement which centers around the question, "Is the canon and hence the syllabus based on it to be regarded as the compendium of excellence or as the record of cultural history?" (13).

Showalter, Elaine. "Feminist Criticism in the Wilderness." *Critical Inquiry* 8 (1981). Reprinted in *Writing and Sexual Difference*, ed. Elizabeth Abel. Chicago: University of Chicago Press, 1982. A standard essay on feminist interests as of the early 1980s.

————. *A Literature of Their Own: British Women Novelists from Brontë to Lessing*. Princeton: Princeton University Press, 1977. "In the atlas of the English novel, women's territory is usually depicted as desert bounded by mountains on four sides: the Austen Peaks, the Brontë cliffs, the Eliot range, and the Woolf hills. This book is an attempt to fill in the terrain between these literary landmarks and to construct a more reliable map from which to explore the achievements of English women novelists" (vii).

Spacks, Patricia. "The Difference It Makes." In *A Feminist Perspective in the Academy*, ed. Elizabeth Langland and Walter Grove. Chicago: University of Chicago Press, 1981.

————. *The Female Imagination*. New York: Knopf, 1975.

Spender, Dale. *Man Made Language*. 2d ed. Winchester, Mass.: Unwin Hyman, 1985.

Woolf, Virginia. *A Room of One's Own*. New York: Harcourt, Brace, 1929.

Sources of Additional Information

Maggie Humm's *The Dictionary of Feminist Theory* (Hemel Hempstead, U.K.: Harvester Wheatsheaf, 1989) offers brief but cogent explanations of important feminist terminology and of the importance to feminists of certain persons to feminists.

For a history of the relationship of women writers to MODERNISM, see Sandra Gilbert and Susan Gubar's *No Man's Land: The Place of the Woman Writer in the Twentieth Century*, 3 vols. (New Haven, Conn.: Yale University Press, 1988-). Vol. 1, *The War of the Words*, gives "an overview of social, literary, and linguistic interactions between men and women from the middle of the nineteenth century to the present" (xii). Vol. 2, *Sexchanges*, traces "literary responses to the social and cultural metamorphoses that created the phenomenon known as modernism" (xii). Vol. 3, *Letters from the Front*, treats "the flowering of feminist modernism . . . as well as the move beyond modernism" (xii–xiii).

Histories and surveys of the feminist literary criticism almost necessarily speak from specific positions within the movement. Four rather different representatives on the genre are Cheri Register's "American Feminist Literary Criticism: A Bibliographical Introduction" (see references), Toril Moi's *Sexual/Textual Politics* (London: Routledge, 1985), Maggie Humm's *Criticism: Women as Contemporary Critics* (Brighton, U.K.: Harvester Press, 1986), and Janet Todd's *Feminist Literary History: A Defence* (Oxford: Basil Blackwell, 1988).

A significant book on women writers of the last century is Margaret Homans's *Bearing the Word: Language and Female Experience in Nineteenth Century Women's Writing* (Chicago: University of Chicago Press, 1986). "This book is about some of the particular ways in which nineteenth-century women writers wrote their relation to language by writing about the relation between women and language" (xi). "[M]y critical project in this book is to find out to what extent, and with what effects, nineteenth-century women writers of realistic novels, who wrote about women's experiences on the assumption that they could do so, also subscribed to some version of the cultural myth of women's relation to and subordination within language" (xii–xiii).

The French feminists who are generally, and largely intentionally, difficult to read (they seek a nonpatriarchal form of discourse and tend to expect considerable knowledge of Derrida and Lacan) are surveyed by several feminist writers. For various perspectives in addition to those found in the general histories of feminist literary criticism cited above, see Jane Gallop's *The Daughter's Seduction: Feminism and Psychoanalysis* (London: Macmillan, 1982); Jane Gallop and Carolyn Burke's "Psychoanalysis and Feminism in France"; Domna Stanton's "Language and Revolution: The Franco-American Dis-Connection" in *The Future of Difference* (see References above); and Pamela McCallum's "Feminist Revisions to the Literary Canon: An Overview of the Methodological Debate" in *The Effects of Feminist Approaches on Research Methodologies*, ed. Winni Tomm (Waterloo, Ont.: Wilfred Laurier University Press, 1989). Alice Jardine's *Gynesis: Configurations of Women and Modernity* (Ithaca, N.Y.: Cornell University Press, 1985) explores the relationships between French and American feminists. See also *French Feminist Thought: A Reader*, ed. by Toril Moi (Oxford: Basil Blackwell, 1988). *Writing Differences: Readings from the Seminar of Hélène Cixous*, ed. Susan Sellers (Milton Keynes: Open University Press, 1988) is a collection of essays by Cixous and members of the research seminar that exemplify Cixous's approach to literature. The essays collected in *The (M)other Tongue*, ed. S. N. Garner, C. Kahane, and M. Sprengnether, bring together feminist and psychoanalytical (both Freudian and Lacanian) approaches, emphasizing especially the preoedipal period and the figure of the Mother (Ithaca, N.Y.: Cornell University Press, 1985).

Philip M. Smith's *Language, the Sexes and Society* (Oxford: Basil Blackwell, 1985) draws on a wide variety of studies in its critique of sexist language and language-related discriminatory social structures.

A strong statement of the differences necessary to Black feminism is Barbara Omolade's "Black Women and Feminism" in *The Future of Difference* (see References above).

In conclusion, to enable black women to pursue a dialogue with white feminists, a feminist theory needs to be developed and expanded to include our priorities and experiences. We have to begin to speak of a feminism that is black in its essence and historical roots and that is not isolated from the black community. We must speak of a feminism that seeks the root cause of our oppression under capitalism and links our struggles with the liberation struggles of other peoples of color in the world. (256)

An approach that does not quite fall within any of the systems of classification or distinctions mentioned is the general focus of the essays that make up *Gender and Reading: Essays on Readers, Texts and Contexts*, ed. Elizabeth Flynn and Patrocinio Schweickart (Baltimore: Johns Hopkin University Press, 1986). Many of these adopt a reader-response approach to the differentiation of male and female reader's responses to texts. "The essays in this volume support the thesis that gender is a significant determinant of the interaction between text and reader" (xxviii). The essays by Flynn and by David Bleich, for instance, both find that male readers tend to be more detached and interact with the text less than do women.

FICTION   1. That which is feigned or invented in order to entertain and/or instruct. 2. The previous sense as restricted to prose narrative. 3. That which is feigned or pretended as an agreed practical convenience. 4. That, feigned or invented, which comes to be believed.

For definitions and terminology related to the analysis of the structure of narrative, see NARRATOLOGY. *For status of fictional objects approached through the concept of* REFERENCE, *see that entry.*

1. If both the utterer and audience or commentator (a) know that the utterance is an invention and (b) recognize that it contains propositions referring to persons, places, or things that cannot or could not have been perceived by a living person (though it will almost certainly contain propositions referring to places, persons, and/or events that can or could be so perceived), the result is what Hans Vaihinger calls an "aesthetic fiction" and Jeremy Bentham calls a fiction intended not for logic but to amuse or excite to action (18). For Bentham, such fictitious entities belong to the class of the "fabulous," that is, that of which "the same sort of picture is capable of being drawn in and preserved in the mind as of any really existing object" (xxv–xxxvi). This is the fiction generally associated with literature, whether the genre be the anecdote, invented exemplum, tale, poem, or novel. Most critical discussion has centered on narrative prose (sense 2 of the term fiction), but LYRIC as well as narrative poetry and the dramatic monologue are fictional from any point of view that does not assume the lyric is a transcript of the poet's mind at a given moment.

Explanation of the difference between texts or utterances that are fictional and those that are not proves more difficult than it seems at first, especially if a rigorous definition of fiction is attempted in such forms as "an utterance is fictional if and only if . . ." or "a statement is fictional just in case that . . ." Generally, a text is regarded as fictional if it contains any fictional statements (propositions). Most fictional texts will, of course, be made up primarily of such propositions, but as John Searle remarks, "A work of fiction need not consist entirely of, and in general will not consist entirely of, fictional discourse" (74). There is, further, a necessary distinction between what Monroe Beardsley calls "Reports" and "Reflections," the first reporting fictional events and the second commenting on them or on life generally. (Exemplary of the latter is the narrator's comment at the death of Jo in Dickens's *Bleak House*: "Dead, Right Reverends and Wrong Reverends of every order. Dead, men and women, born with heavenly compassion in your hearts. And dying thus around us every day.'')

The question of the status of fictional propositions has been approached in two major ways. The first has been the attempt to explain the status of that to which a fictional proposition has reference. Gilbert Ryle's 1933 paper on ''Imaginary Objects'' set the framework for many subsequent discussions of the essential nature of fiction (and initiates the tradition of using Mr. Pickwick as a prime exemplar of the imaginary or fictional being). For Ryle, ''Dickens' propositions are fiction just because they are not about anyone, though they pretend to be about someone'' (22). Thus, Pickwick is a *pseudo-designation* or *complex predicate* (not an object) about which there can be neither truth nor falsity. Statements about Pickwick that are external to *The Pickwick Papers* can, however, be true or false since they are propositions ''about the book or about the propositions in it'' (22). G. E. Moore, in a paper that was part of the same symposium as Ryle's, avoids the concept of the pseudo-designation, preferring to say that Pickwick is ''*the* man, having the characteristics in question, *about whom I am telling this story*.'' In contrast a historical person would appear in a text as ''*the* man, having such and such characters [*sic*], who was in such and such a place at such and such a time'' (70).

Another way of addressing the status of fictional propositions is through the distinction between *sense* and REFERENCE. In ''Sherlock Holmes smoked a pipe'' (Holmes is also a favored example of the imaginary being), ''pipe'' carries the appropriate dictionary *sense* as contextually determined without having existential *reference* to any pipe that had physical existence in any actual space at any actual time (see Harris, 100–102). To use Charles Morris's terminology, Holmes's pipe is a sign with a designatum but no denotatum, or a *type* without a *token*. Morris addresses the matter directly in ''Esthetics and the Theory of Signs'' (1939–40): ''By definition a sign must designate (''have a designatum''), but it may not actually denote anything (''may have no denotata''). . . . A designatum is thus a class of objects as determined by certain defining properties, and as a class, may be without members; the denotata are the members—if any— of the class in question'' (132–33). Monroe Beardsley similarly defines a fictional sentence as ''one that contains a proper name, or a pronoun, or a descriptive phrase . . . that does not denote anything'' (411). Barbara Herrnstein Smith, on the other hand, thinking of ''class'' in a more general way, formulates her definition of the fictional object rather differently: ''to say that an artist has represented a certain object or event is to say that he has constructed a fictive member of an identifiable class of natural ('real') objects or events'' (25).

The second major approach to explaining fictional propositions is through placing them in a different category from nonfictional uses of language, generally through regarding them as representing a special kind of SPEECH ACT. Jon-K. Adams thus argues that in fictional discourse, ''the writer attributes the words he writes to someone else. In novels this someone is usually called the narrator, and it has long been recognized that the narrator is not the writer but rather a fictional figure that performs the speech acts of the writer's text'' (12). Fiction thus does not represent a speech act in the sense of a direct interaction between the author and the reader. Gregory Currie also draws on speech-act theory, but for him fiction has the specific illocutionary force of an invitation to make-believe (as opposed to that of a request, command, or promise); propositions in fictional narrative are *fictive* illocutionary acts ("Works of Fiction," 305). "The author of fiction intends that the reader make-believe *P* where *P* is the sentence or string of sentences he utters. And he intends that the reader shall come to make-believe *P* partly as a result of his recognition that the author intends to do this" ("What Is Fiction?" 387).

For Richard Ohmann, the author of imaginative literature only pretends to report speech acts, producing what are actually quasi-speech acts since they lack the appropriateness conditions associated with true speech acts and thus lack illocutionary force. For John Searle, fiction is a "nondeceptive pseudo-performance" in which, again, while the utterance is real, the illocutionary act is pretended (65, 68). The author pretends to make an assertion that is, in fact, "nonserious" in the sense that the author is not seriously committed to it (60). Like Ryle, Searle differentiates sharply between statements about a character that occur in the narrative and those made externally: "I did not *pretend* to refer to a real Sherlock Holmes; I *really referred* to the fictional Sherlock Holmes" (72).

The discussions of fiction in terms of speech act theory noted above all focus on the author's speech act. But however the author's speech act is regarded, the narrator and characters are performing speech acts that can only be understood against the usual appropriateness conditions. Mary Louise Pratt's criticism of Ohmann's concept of quasi-speech acts can be extended to similar theories: "The real lesson speech act theory has to offer is that *literature is a context, too,* not the absence of one" (99). That is, the reader can only understand narrators' and characters' statements or speech acts by assigning them the appropriate illocutionary force within the context of the work and the culture shared by author and reader. Appropriateness conditions fully apply *within* the text.

So persistent has been the question of the truth or cognitive value of fiction that it has become integrally associated with the concept of fiction. Intentional deceit (the sense of *fiction* designating that situation in which the utterer knows the utterance to be feigned or invented but expects the hearer to believe it to be a statement about past or present reality) has rarely been of significant interest in literary commentary, but charges that fiction misleads nevertheless have a long history, beginning with Plato. Sir Philip Sidney's famous statement in *An Apology for Poetry* that since they affirm nothing, poets cannot lie, speaks to the charge of deceit but not general error in that what a reader knows to be a literary fiction may nevertheless be regarded as accurately imitating virtue or reality. That is the ground on which Plato condemned the fiction of the poets. "Then must we not infer that all poets, beginning with Homer, are only imitators; they copy images of virtue and the like, but the truth they never reach? The poet is like a painter who, as has already been observed, will make a likeness of a cobbler though he understands nothing of cobbling; and this is good enough for those who know no more than he does, and judge only by colors and figures" (2:431; 601a).

Among the more influential modern answers, that of I.A. Richards attempts to sidestep the question by assigning the pursuit of truth to the sciences. Richards, who in *Science and Poetry* (1926) quotes Thomas Love Peacock's humorous indictment of poetry as "empty aimless mockeries of intellectual exertion," is primarily concerned with the fictions of poetry rather than fiction generally, but his defense of the propositions of poetry as the emotive rather than scientific use of language (*Principles of Literary Criticism*, 267) or as *psuedo-statements* prefigures later attempts to define fiction by the logical status of its propositions and assign an extrarational value to fiction. "A pseudo-statement is a form of words which is justified entirely by its effect in releasing or organizing our impulses and attitudes" (*Science and Poetry*, 59), to which may be joined Richards's assertion that the best life for a person "will be one in which as much as possible of himself is engaged (as many of his impulses as possible). . . . And if it is asked, what does such a life feel like, how is it to live through? the answer is that it feels like and is the experience of poetry" (*Science and Poetry*, 33).

An answer that looks to rational understanding rather than emotional harmony is made by Charles Morris: "the statement that a work is 'true' might under analysis turn out to be . . . intended to affirm that the work in question actually is iconic of the value structure of a certain object or situation" (144). Other typical answers are those of Michael Scriven that fiction can be "argument by the analysis of an example" (189) and of Monroe Beardsley that "The reading of great novels shows us all sorts of motives that human beings may have, and the enormous variety of ways in which these intertwine and conflict" (430). Beardsley's general view is paralleled in David Novitz's chapter on "Fiction and the Growth of Knowledge" (in *Knowledge, Fiction, and Imagination*) which argues that fiction allows us to become aware of complexities of life and of points of view that we can try out in our own experience. It is stated in more contemporary terms by L. B. Cebak, who draws on the philosopher Hospers' distinction between propositional truth and that which is *true-to* human nature and experience (206) as well as Heidegger's concept of truth "originating" through the suggestion of a new precedent.

2. While the previous sense encompasses all forms of "literary" fiction, the brief lyric as well as the EPIC, the most common use designates fictional narrative prose—the tale, the novel, the short story. That is the relevant sense in Walter Besant's "The Art of Fiction" and Henry James's response (1884) as well as Edith Wharton's *The Writing of Fiction* (1925) and textbooks like Cleanth Brooks and Robert Penn Warren's influential *Understanding Fiction* (1943).

3. If something is known to be feigned or invented but is nevertheless believed to be a practical or convenient way of proceeding, especially in law (the legal

fiction) or science, the case is an example of what Jeremy Bentham calls a *fictional entity* (as opposed to both real entities and fabulous entities), Hans Vaihinger calls a *logical fiction*, and Frank Kermode calls a *fiction* as opposed to a *myth*. (For Kermode, fictions are both necessary and potentially dangerous: "Fictions can degenerate into myths whenever they are not consciously held to be fictive," 39.) The widely influential point of view of Thomas Kuhn's *The Structure of Scientific Revolutions* is similar to those of Bentham and Vaihinger: a scientist who believes that the paradigm he or she employs is an explanatory model that may well be replaced in the future knowingly utilizes a fiction.

Such a legal or logical fiction resembles a literary fiction in that both are intended to be understood as inventions. This parallel has been made to seem much closer by recent tendencies to emphasize the separation between language and nonlinguistic reality on the one hand and on the other to give a Kuhnian description of science as a sequence of paradigms that seek explanatory power and consistency without approaching nearer to the nature of reality. The question, then, is whether there is a difference between the fictions of literature and the fictions by which we attempt to explain reality by inserting the Kantian forms of space and time and the categories between the human understanding and the things-in-themselves. However, while a Kantian view guaranteed the construction of a common phenomenal world through denying access to things-in-themselves, a strong modern trend insists that different cultures, and to some extent different groups of individuals within each culture, build up different explanatory fictions.

4. If (a) an utterer is thought to believe an utterance, or to believe a proposition or narrative account that leads to the making of an utterance that (b) the hearer or commentator believes to be counter to fact, that which is believed by the utterer will be thought fictional in yet another sense. Examples are the individual who believes in gods or events that the hearer thinks fictional and, from the Kuhnian point of view, the scientist who believes that the current scientific paradigm (whatever it may be) represents reality. For Bentham this is another variety of the fabulous, while for Kermode it is a myth rather than a fiction.

In ideologically based criticism, this sense of the fictional may be applied to literary works in those cases in which the critic believes the author and/or intended audience hold or held a false conception of the world. Thus, a work that author and audience regard or regarded as fiction in senses 1 or 2 may also be additionally regarded from an ideological point of view as fictional in the sense of having been motivated by social, economic, or religious beliefs that ultimately reflect an omnipresent struggle for power. Whether *any* beliefs are justified is a point of ideological contention itself.

References

Adams, Jon-K. *Pragmatics and Fiction*. Amsterdam: John Benjamins, 1985.
Beardsley, Monroe C. *Aesthetics: Problems in the Philosophy of Criticism*. New York: Harcourt, Brace, 1958.

Bentham, Jeremy. Bentham's comments on fictitious entities are helpfully assembled in C. K. Ogden, *Bentham's Theory of Fictions*. 1932; Paterson, N.J.: Littlefield, Adams, 1959. The most relevant of Bentham's discussions of the fictions will be found in vol. 8 of *The Works of Jeremy Bentham*, ed. John Bowring (Edinburgh: William Tate, 1843) under the title *A Fragment on Ontology*, pp. 262–64 and 195–211.

Besant, Walter. *The Art of Fiction: A Lecture*. Boston: De Wolfe, Fiske and Co., 1884. (Published together with Henry James's essay of the same title.)

Brooks, Cleanth, and R. P. Warren. *Understanding Fiction*. New York: F. S. Crofts, 1943.

Cebak, L. B. *Fictional Narrative and Truth: An Epistemic Analysis*. Lanham, Md.: University Press of America, 1984.

Currie, Gregory. "What Is Fiction?" *Journal of Aesthetics and Art Criticism* 43 (1985): 385–92.

―――. "Works of Fiction and Illocutionary Acts." *Philosophy and Literature* 10 (1986): 304–8.

Harris, Wendell. *Interpretive Acts*. Oxford: Clarendon Press, 1988.

James, Henry. *The Art of Fiction*. Boston: De Wolfe, Fiske and Co., 1884. Published together with Walter Besant's lecture of the same title.

Kermode, Frank. *The Sense of an Ending*. Oxford: Oxford University Press, 1967. "It is not that we are connoisseurs of chaos, but that we are surrounded by it, and equipped for coexistence with it only by our fictive powers" (64).

Kuhn, Thomas. *The Structure of Scientific Revolutions*. Chicago: University of Chicago Press, 1962, 1970.

Moore, G. E. "Symposium on 'Imaginary Objects.' " *Proceedings of the Aristotelian Society*, supplementary vol. 12 (1933): 55–70.

Morris, Charles W. "Esthetics and the Theory of Signs." *The Journal of Unified Science (Erkenntnis)* 8 (1939–40): 131–50.

Novitz, David. *Knowledge, Fiction, and Imagination*. Philadelphia: Temple University Press, 1987. Novitz's "primary aim is to restore to fictional literature its former status as a functional object—allowing that a thing of beauty, bred of the imagination, may indeed instruct" (xi); the argument is made through a "romantic epistemology" (xii).

Ohmann, Richard. "Speech Acts and the Definition of Literature." *Philosophy and Rhetoric* 4 (Winter 1971): 1–19.

Plato. *The Republic*. Book 10 in vol. 2 of *The Dialogues of Plato*. Trans. B. Jowett. 4 vols. New York: Charles Scribner's Sons, 1907.

Pratt, Mary Louise. *Toward a Speech Act Theory of Literary Discourse*. Bloomington: Indiana University Press, 1977.

Richards, I. A. *Principles of Literary Criticism* (1925). London: Routledge and Kegan Paul, 1948.

―――. *Science and Poetry*. London: Kegan Paul, Trench, Trubner, 1926.

Ryle, Gilbert. "Imaginary Objects." *Proceedings of the Aristotelian Society*, supplementary vol. 12 (1933): 18–43.

Scriven, Michael. "Symposium: The Language of Fiction," *Proceedings of the Aristotelian Society*, supplementary vol. 28 (1954): 185–96.

Searle, John R. *Expression and Meaning: Studies in the Theory of Speech Acts*. Cambridge: Cambridge University Press, 1979.

FIGURE   105

Sidney, Sir Phillip. *An Apologie for Poetrie* (1595). In *Criticism: The Major Texts*, ed.
    W. J. Bate. New York: Harcourt, Brace, Jovanovich, 1970.
Smith, Barbara Herrnstein. *On the Margins of Discourse*. 1978; Chicago: University of
    Chicago Press, 1983.
Vaihinger, Hans. *The Philosophy of As If*. Trans. C. K. Ogden. 1924; London: Routledge
    and Kegan Paul, 1952.
Wharton, Edith. *The Writing of Fiction*. New York: Charles Scribner's Sons, 1925.

Sources of Additional Information

For an argument dismissing the relevance of speech-act theory to the problem of defining
the characteristics of fiction, see Kendall Walton's "Fictions, Fiction-Making, and Styles
of Fictionality" (*Philosophy and Literature* 7, Spring 1983: 78–88). Currie's "What Is
Fiction" (*Journal of Aesthetics and Art Criticism* 43; 1985: 385–92) is a reply to Walton,
while Hugh Wilder's "Intentions and the Very Idea of Fiction" (*Philosophy and Literature*
12, April 1988: 70–79) is a reply to Currie which points out the difficulties of defining
fiction in terms of the author's intentions, and finds that "Fiction is a literary tradition,
and intentions to write fiction are by-products rather than determinants of fiction" (78).
In *The Logic of Literature*, Käte Hamburger sets forth a curious but stimulating definition
of fiction that restricts it to third-person narratives (trans. M. J. Rose; Bloomington:
Indiana University Press, 1973; original German edition, 1957). For her, such fictional
narratives are distinguished from statements about reality because the narrator and that
which is narrated have only a functional, not a subject-object relation: the narrator "does
not narrate about persons and things, but he rather narrates the persons and things" (136).

For a reply to Ryle's "Imaginary Objects" (*Proceedings of the Aristotelian Society*,
supplementary vol. 12, 1933: 18–43), see Margaret Macdonald's contribution to a symposium on "The Language of Fiction" (*Proceedings of the Aristotelian Society*, supplementary vol. 28, 1954: 165–84).

The question of reference in the literary text is treated in various ways in the somewhat
miscellaneous essays collected in *On Referring in Literature*, ed. A. Whiteside and M.
Issacharoff (Bloomington: Indiana University Press, 1987).

John Wood's *The Logic of Fiction* (The Hague: Mouton, 1974) offers a highly technical
approach to the status of fiction through symbolic logic.

FIGURE   1. Any deviation from the usual form, mode of use, syntactical
placement, application, or sense of a word or of a group of words. The artistic
arrangement or employment of language. In this larger sense, "figure" includes the category of tropes. 2. In a more restricted sense, the terms figure
or scheme designate the employment of unusual or strategic arrangements of
words retaining their literal or usual meanings as opposed to the nonliteral
tropes. 3. In the tradition of biblical interpretation, the prefiguration of one
event by another; *figural* in this sense is equivalent to *typological*.

1. and 2. Although the categorization of figures—in the comprehensive
sense—into schemes and tropes, figures of speech and figures of thought, changes
in meaning and changes in form, figures of one word and figures of many, or
such divisions as "auricular," "sensable," and "sententious" has been a regular
feature at least since Cicero, there is too little correspondence between the various

categorizations to bring them into general alignment. To add to the confusion, Puttenham and others have preferred their own English terms to the classical. Thus Puttenham substitutes ''transporte'' for the Greek *metaphora* and the Latin *translatio* and prefers ''single supply'' to *zeugma*.

The general divisions, however, are between (a) schemes in which an artful arrangement of words gives force or creates pleasure in itself, (b) tropes in which changes from usual or literal meanings influence the way in which the hearer or reader thinks about the subject addressed, and (c) strategies that are neither verbal patterns nor departures from the literal. Quintilian defines a trope as ''the conversion of a word or phrase, from its proper signification to another, in order to increase its force'' (2:124; 8.6.1) or again ''an expression turned from its natural and principal signification to another, for the purpose of adorning style,'' while a figure ''is a form of speech differing from the common and ordinary mode of expression'' (2:145; 9.1.4). What Quintilian calls ''figures of thought'' in the second chapter of Book 9 are strategies like the feigning of doubt or substitution of the interrogative form for direct statement.

According to Thomas Wilson in *The Arte of Rhetorique* (1553), a trope occurs ''when the nature of wordes is chaunged from one signification to another'' and a scheme ''when they are not chaunged by nature, but only altered by speaking'' (170). Strategies like resting on a point and breaking off abruptly he calls ''colours.''

The Arte of English Poesie (1588; most often ascribed to George Puttenham) explains, ''This ornament then is of two sortes, one to satisfie and delight th'eare onely by a goodly outward shew set upon the matter with wordes, and speaches smothly and tunably running: anoather by certaine intendments or sence of such wordes & speaches inwardly working a stirre to the mynde'' (142–43; Bk. 3, Ch. 3). Puttenham further divides ''sensable'' figures into those making use of single words (e.g., ''*Metonimia* or the Misnamer,'' 180, and ''*Metalepsis* or the Farrefet,'' 183) and those ''in whole clauses or speaches'' (e.g., ''*Allegoria*, or the Figure of false semblant,'' 186, and ''*Ironia* or the Drie mock,'' 189).

Tzvetan Todorov's twentieth-century distinction between figures and tropes is the most direct: the relations of figures are *in praesentia* (visible on the page), and those of tropes *in absentia* (require mental supplementation; 21).

In addition to tropes and schemes regarded as effective when properly used, rhetoricians at times have cited specific rhetorical vices: Puttenham, for instance, lists fourteen of these, including ''*Barbarismus* or Forrein speech'' and ''*Soraismus* or the mingle mangle'' (Bk. 3, Ch. 22).

An exceptionally useful guide through the thickets of the many systems of dividing and describing figurative language is Richard Lanham's *A Handlist of Rhetorical Terms* (1968), which provides a very extensive list of terms (with their alternate names) followed by five special cross-classifications.

Most often included in listings of tropes are metaphor (including catachresis), synecdoche, metonymy, irony (or antiphrasis), hyperbole, and sometimes antonomasia and litotes. Kenneth Burke's essay ''Four Master Tropes'' has con-

FIGURE   107

tributed strongly to the contemporary emphasis on the four he finds most powerful, pervasive, and interlinked: metaphor, metonymy, synecdoche, and irony. Hayden White's Introduction to *Tropics of Discourse* argues that the steps by which the human mind comes to understand are a definite progression from metaphor to metonymy to synecdoche and then to irony, and that the modes of discourse corresponding to these represent a typology of modes of human understanding.

White is also an important representative of the many twentieth-century writers who have insisted that all uses of language are tropological inasmuch as the very objects of human discourse are constituted by tropes. A famous earlier example of this point of view is Nietzsche's statement: "What therefore is truth? A mobile army of metaphors, metonymies, anthropomorphisms, in short a sum of human relations which became poetically and rhetorically intensified" (2:180). A well-known statement by an earlier twentieth-century critic is that of I. A. Richards in *The Philosophy of Rhetoric*. "That metaphor is the omnipresent principle of language can be shown by mere observation. We cannot get through three sentences of ordinary fluid discourse without it" (92). Less well known perhaps is Jeremy Bentham's recognition of the constant figurativeness of language. Bentham observes that to say "The apple is ripe" is to say, "In this apple is the quality of ripeness," although in fact an apple is not a container and the statement is, therefore, figurative. Bentham, however, has no difficulty in distinguishing what is necessarily from what is artistically figurative.

> The discourse that, in this particular sense, is *not* figurative, is the discourse in which, for the conveyance of the immaterial part of the stock of ideas conveyed ["ripeness" is an example of immateriality], no other fictions—no other figures— are employed than what are absolutely necessary to, and which, consequently, are universally employed in, the conveyance of the import to be conveyed. When a discourse is figurative, in lieu of those, or in addition to those, other images not necessary to, and thence not universally employed in, the conveyance of the import in question, are employed. (8:331)

3. Erich Auerbach's essay "Figura" explores the use of that term as equivalent to *typus* or prefiguration in the Christian fathers from Tertullian forward.

References

Auerbach, Erich. "Figura" (1944). Trans. R. Manheim in *Scenes from the Drama of European Literature*. 1959; Minneapolis: University of Minnesota Press, 1984.
Bentham, Jeremy. *The Works of Jeremy Bentham*. Ed. John Bowring. Edinburgh: William Tait, 1843.
Burke, Kenneth. "Four Master Tropes." *Kenyon Review* 3 (Autumn 1941): 421–38.
Lanham, Richard. *A Handlist of Rhetorical Terms: A Guide for Students of English Literature*. Berkeley: University of California Press, 1968. A very valuable reference.
Nietzsche, Friedrich. "On Truth and Falsity in their Ultramoral Sense" (1873). In vol. 2 of *The Complete Works*. Trans. M. A. Mügge; ed. Oscar Levy. 1909–13; New York: Gordon Press, 1974.

Puttenham, George. *The Arte of English Poesie* (1588). Ed. G. D. Willack and A. Walker. Cambridge: Cambridge University Press, 1936. Extensive list of figures and tropes; includes as an appendix a helpful table of the figures discussed.

Quintilian. *Institutes of Oratory*. Trans. J. S. Watson. 2 vols. London: Henry G. Bohn, 1856.

Richards, I. A. *The Philosophy of Rhetoric*. 1936; London: Oxford University Press, 1981.

Todorov, Tzvetan. *Introduction to Poetics*. Trans. R. Howard. Minneapolis: University of Minnesota Press, 1981.

White, Hayden. *Tropics of Discourse*. Baltimore: Johns Hopkins University Press, 1978.

Wilson, Thomas. *The Arte of Rhetorique* (1553). Ed. G. H. Mair. Oxford: Clarendon Press, 1909.

Sources of Additional Information

Wilbur Samuel Howell's comments on the early rhetorics in England in *Logic and Rhetoric in England* (Princeton, N.J.: Princeton University Press, 1956) give useful information on the various treatments of figures and tropes therein. Arthur Quinn's *Figures of Speech: 60 Ways to Turn a Phrase* (Salt Lake City, Utah: Gibbs M. Smith, 1982) wittily explains figures of speech and provides copious examples.

FORMALISM   1. The study of literature as a field in itself, separated from questions of its relationship to historical, socioeconomic, political, and biographical backgrounds and influences; thus, major attention to the difference between literature and other uses of language and a focus on the structure of the individual work and/or the relationships between literary works. 2. As applied to the Russian Formalist group, *formalism* designates particular emphasis on defining *literariness* and the devices of literature that create interest through *defamiliarization* and in the literary devices that succeed one another as each successful mode of literary structure becomes stale. 3. As applied to the New Critics of the United States and similar critics in England and elsewhere, the term designates a particular interest in structures of imagery and symbol and the achievement of a unity or harmony in which ambiguities and tensions continue to exert their presence (see NEW CRITICISM).

1. The term formalism appears to have entered the literary vocabulary through its use as a designation for the early-twentieth-century Russian Formalists, and has been extended to include the New Critics, but the impulse toward and hostility to formalism extends further back. Matthew Arnold's concept of criticism as the propagation of the best that has been known and thought in the interest of an improved intellectual culture that would produce an improved society was clearly in opposition to what would now be called formalist principles (see "The Function of Criticism"). The struggle in the 1880s and 1890s over the introduction of a School of English Literature at the University of Oxford reveals a somewhat confused battle between the two orientations. Those who saw the study of vernacular literature as primarily of interest for the study of language and its changes (*philology* in a narrow sense) represented one kind of formalism, as did those

who warned that the formal study of English literature would lead to mere gossip about the life and times of the author. The inclusion of literature in English was achieved largely through the antiformalist Arnoldian argument for the relevance of literature as an instrument for improving society.

When used as an inclusive term for both the New Criticism and Russian Formalism, the concentration on the work in itself rather than the author's biography or the general cultural background and an understanding of the work as a unified structure are the similarities that are generally foregrounded.

2. The movement known as Russian Formalism began in 1915–16 with the founding of the Moscow Linguistic Circle and the Petersburg Society for the Study of Poetic Language (*Opojaz*), the latter giving rise to the Petrograd Institute of Art History in 1920. The most influential members of the Moscow group have proved to be Roman Jakobson and Boris Tomashevsky; the most influential of the Petersburg group, Victor Shklovsky, Boris Eichenbaum, and Yuri Tynyanov. By 1930 the pressure of Marxist orthodoxy, which insisted on viewing literature as part of the cultural superstructure reflecting the economic base, had forced the Formalists to abandon their central principles. Many of their insights, however, were transferred to the Prague Linguistic Circle, to which Roman Jakobson moved in 1920, where they reappear in somewhat modified form as part of the wider structuralist movement.

In reaction to critical commentary seeking the relationship between the literary work and the cultural context it presumably reflected, the Formalists approached literature as a separate system, looking to linguistics rather than sociology, psychology, or culture generally. From this orientation emerged certain dominant principles.

2a. Concentration on the distinguishing marks of literature. In the famous 1921 formulation of Roman Jakobson, "The object of the science of literature is not literature, but literariness—that is, that which makes a given work a work of literature" (*Noveyshaya russkaya poeziya*, 11).

2b. Justification of literature as a means of *defamiliarizing* what has become so routinely a part of life that it is no longer really seen. A well-known statement of 1917 in Shklovsky's "Art as Technique" states: "The technique of art is to make objects 'unfamiliar,' to make forms difficult, to increase the difficulty of and length of perception because the process of perception is an aesthetic end in itself and must be prolonged" (12). Whether the primary purpose of defamiliarization (*ostranenie*) was simply the creation of an aesthetic effect or had the larger purpose of giving fresh perceptions of ordinary experience is a a matter of debate. René Wellek writes: "[T]he formalists do not deny art its great social function; they rather broaden and redefine it. Over and over again they assert that 'the purpose of art is to make us see things, not to know them. Art is there to awaken us from our usual torpor' " (129). On the other hand, for Fredric Jameson, *ostranenie* is a "purely formal concept" meant to identify literariness (52).

2c. Preoccupation with the technical *devices* of literature (such as form of narration, plot structuring, treatment of time, and creation of sound patterns). This led to a concept of the work as a unified structure, which led further to the concept that each work is unified around a dominant device or group of elements. In other terminology, the *dominant* is that which is *foregrounded*.

2d. The conception of literature as an autonomous system, which leads to an emphasis on the conventions of literature. "I write," said Shklovsky in 1923, "about the conventions of art" (quoted in Erlich, 163).

2e. Primary focus on the sound rather than the thought in poetry. Metaphors are seen primarily as parts of patterns, not modes of thought. Krystyna Pomorska insists: "The works of the Opojaz scholars eloquently show that their interest was focused strictly upon the nature of sound and sound patterns in literature" (27). She quotes from Shklovsky: "In the enjoyment of the meaningless 'transrational word' the articulatory side, a sui generis *dancing of the speech organs* causes most of the enjoyment which poetry brings" (30). Eichenbaum believes that even in a prose narrative like Gogol's "The Overcoat," the sound is more important than any content (see Pomorska, 33).

2f. "Motivation" of the principal structural devices is by aesthetic rather than realistic or intellectual purposes: the aim of the device is simply to create the work, not to express a thought. According to Shklovsky, "The story is, in fact, only material for plot formulation. The plot of *Eugene Onegin* is, therefore, not the romance of the hero with Tatyana, but the fashioning of the subject of this story as produced by the introduction of interrupting digressions" ("Sterne's *Tristram Shandy*," 57). Jameson puts the issue concisely: "For the Formalists everything in the work exists in order to permit the work to come into being in the first place" (82).

2g. Such emphasis on the importance of structural devices undercuts the importance of characterization, the characters themselves being simply devices.

2h. An interest in the way in which conventions arise, become normative, and then fade as they become stale, reaction against the (currently) normative in literature being essential to the continuing power of literature to sharpen perception. Literary history thus becomes a record of the creation of novelty through a process internal to literature. A famous summation of this view of literary history is Shklovsky's principle of "the canonization of the junior branch." "When the 'canonized' art forms reach an impasse, the way is paved for the infiltration of the elements of non-canonized art, which by this time have managed to evolve new artistic devices" (quoted in Erlich, 227). Ann Jefferson sums this up, "[N]ew Works have to revive the perceptibility of literature either by defamiliarizing over-familiar techniques . . . or else by foregrounding a previously non-functional device. In other words, changes in literature depend not on the personal circumstances or the psychological make-up of an author, but on the pre-existing forms of literature" (32). In reviewing the development of the Formalists, Eichenbaum writes (1926):

> Given our understanding of literary evolution as the dialectical change of forms, we
> did not go back to the study of those materials which had held the central position

in the old-fashioned historical-literary work. We studied literary evolution insofar
as it bore a distinctive character and only to the extent that it stood alone, quite
independent of other aspects of culture. ("Theory," 136)

Judgments of a specific work are to be made on the basis of its position in the
history of literature since the "literariness" of a text is a function of the freshness
of its devices (again the specific orientation of the Formalists is highlighted by
comparison with Matthew Arnold's warning in "The Study of Poetry" against
the "historic estimate").

2i. Viewing literary history as a succession of devices led to the demotion of
the role of the author. Thus, Shklovsky: "Art is not created by the individual
will, by the genius. The creator is simply the geometrical point of intersection
of forces operative outside him" (quoted in Erlich, 221).

Their concern for the ways in which literary language deviates from the norms
of practical usage led the Russian Formalists to close analyses of poetic structure,
especially of sound. According to Erlich, "The domain in which the Formalist
concepts were used to greatest advantage was undoubtedly the theory of versification" (182). However, the major influence of the Formalists outside Russia
has been on the theory of narrative fiction. Thus, Vladimir Propp's *Morphology
of the Folktale* (1928), which is formalist in its concentration on the structural
components of the folktale, initiated a new direction in the study of narrative
that was absorbed by STRUCTURALISM and became one of the foundations of
NARRATOLOGY. Exemplary also is the work of Boris Tomashevsky, as in his
essay "Thematics," which outlines analytical concepts not yet fully integrated
into the narratology of Genette and Barthes since they concern content as well
as structure. In addition to distinguishing story and plot (*fabula* and *sjuzhet*,
story material and its structuring in the actual narrative), Tomashevsky examines
the nature of narrative *motifs*, that is, the irreducible parts of a work, distinguishing those that are essential to the story (*bound* motifs) from those that are
not essential but that are likely to reflect contemporary literary conventions (*free*
motifs), and those that change situations (*dynamic* motifs) from those that do
not (*static* motifs). Motifs cannot simply be dropped into a work; they require
motivation, which is defined as "the network of devices justifying the introduction of individual motifs or groups of motifs" (78). Motivations may be
either *compositional*, that is, related to the conduct of the plot, or *realistic*, that
is, provided to give the illusion of reality.

Russian Formalism is frequently discussed primarily for its role in helping
prepare the way for structuralism through its rejection of the relevance of an
author's biography and elevation of formal structuring over thought content, but
the two modes of analysis should not be confused. The structures of interest to
the Russian Formalists were those of individual works, not of larger patterns
reflecting in the work. René Wellek comments, "The Russian concept of form
or structure is always confined to a work of art or to groups of works of art and
is not, as in Lévi-Strauss or Lucien Goldmann, an analogous large-scale social
structure" (133). "Formalist" was not the adjective that the group chose for

themselves; it should, in any case, be understood as referring to pursuit of the specific form of the individual work, not universal structures. Eichenbaum wrote in 1924, "We are not 'Formalists' but, if you will, specifiers" (quoted in Steiner, 17). Russian Formalism can be seen, then, as not only one ground of structuralism but as influencing the rather different direction taken by Mikhail Bakhtin, who followed the Formalists in avoiding the early Marxist reduction of literature to the reflection of the social superstructure and exploring the way narrative expresses divergent social voices rather than simply the view of the author.

References

Arnold, Matthew. "The Function of Criticism at the Present Time" (1864). In vol. 3 of *The Complete Prose Works of Matthew Arnold*. Ed. R. H. Super. Ann Arbor: University of Michigan Press, 1962–77.
————. "The Study of Poetry" (1880). In vol. 9 of *The Complete Prose Works*.
Bakhtin, Mikhail. See *Problems of Dostoevsky's Poetics*, ed. and trans. Caryl Emerson (Minneapolis: University of Minnesota Press, 1984. Also see *The Dialogic Imagination*, ed. Michael Holquist, and trans. C. Emerson and M. Holquist. Austin: University of Texas Press, 1981.
Eichenbaum, Boris. "The Theory of the Formal Method" (1926). In *Russian Formalist Criticism: Four Essays*.
Erlich, Victor. *Russian Formalism: History—Doctrine*. The Hague: Mouton, 1955. The first comprehensive book on Russian Formalism in English. Essential.
Jakobson, Roman. *Noveyshaya russkaya poeziya* (Newest Russian Poetry). Prague: 1921. The constantly quoted comment on literariness appears, for instance, in Eichenbaum's essay in "The Theory of the Formal Method," p. 107.
Jameson, Fredric. *The Prison-House of Language: A Critical Account of Structuralism and Russian Formalism*. Princeton, N.J.: Princeton University Press, 1972. The section entitled "The Formalist Projection" is an insightful critique from a Marxist point of view. Jameson is particularly critical of the Formalists' emphasis on synchronic structure at the expense of diachronic process.
Jefferson, Ann. "Russian Formalism." In *Modern Literary Theory*, ed. Ann Jefferson and David Robey. London: B. T. Batsford, 1986. Provides a good summary.
Pomorska, Krystyna. *Russian Formalist Theory and Its Poetic Ambience*. The Hague: Mouton, 1968. The first chapter is specifically on Russian Formalism; especially useful in its discussion of the Formalist treatment of poetry.
Propp, Vladimir. *Morphology of the Folktale* (1928). Trans. Laurence Scott. 1958; Austin: University of Texas Press, 1968.
Russian Formalist Criticism: Four Essays. Ed. and trans. L. T. Lemon and M. J. Reis. Lincoln: University of Nebraska Press, 1965. Includes four very important Formalist texts: Victor Shklovsky's "Art as Technique" (1917) and "Sterne's *Tristram Shandy*: Stylistic Commentary" (1921), Boris Tomashevsky's "Thematics" (1925), and Boris Eichenbaum's "The Theory of the 'Formal Method' " (1927). Useful introduction comparing the New Critics and the Russian Formalists.
Shklovsky, Victor. "Art as Technique" and "Sterne's *Tristram Shandy*: Stylistic Commentary" in *Russian Formalist Criticism: Four Essays*.
Steiner, Peter. *Russian Formalism: A Metapoetics*. Ithaca, N.Y.: Cornell University Press, 1984. Steiner surveys the different principles held by various Formalists and views

the development of Formalism in terms of three metaphors: the machine, the organism, and the system.

Tomashevsky, Boris. "Thematics" in *Russian Formalist Criticism: Four Essays*.

Wellek, René. "Russian Formalism" (1971). In *The Attack on Literature and Other Essays*. Chapel Hill: University of North Carolina Press, 1982. Originally appeared in *Arcadia* 6 (1971): 175–86. A bit dated, but a good survey of the relations of Formalism to other literary movements in Russia and elsewhere, with a summary list of major interests and publications.

Sources of Additional Information

In addition to Wellek and Jefferson (see References above), good general surveys of the theory of narrative are to be found in Robert Scholes's *Structuralism: An Introduction* (New Haven, Conn.: Yale University Press, 1974, pp. 74–91) and the first chapter of Jurij Striedter's *Literary Structure, Evolution, and Value: Russian Formalism and Czech Structuralism Reconsidered* (Cambridge, Mass.: Harvard University Press, 1989). Striedter also develops the differences between Formalism and structuralism. Also see Chapters 2 and 3 of Tony Bennett's *Formalism and Marxism* (London: Methuen, 1979). Bennett argues that "the Formalists should be viewed more seriously and sympathetically by Marxist critics than has hitherto been the case" and that "many of the difficulties in which Marxist criticism currently finds itself can be traced to the fact that it has never clearly disentangled its concerns from those of traditional aesthetics" (3).

Only a small part of Russian Formalist criticism has been translated into English; because of the difficulty of finding such translations, I have listed the Formalist essays in the collections cited. *Russian Formalism: A Collection of Articles and Texts in Translation*, ed. J. E. Bowlt and Stephen Bann (Brighton, U.K.: Dolphin Press, 1973) includes Shklovsky's "The Resurrection of the Word" (1914), "On the Connection Between Devices of *Syuzhet* Construction and General Stylistic Devices" (1919), and "Poetry and Prose in Cinematography (1927); A. A. Reformatsky's "An Essay on the Analysis of the Composition of the Novella" (1922); and Boris Eichenbaum's "Literature and Cinema" (1926). *Twentieth-Century Russian Literary Criticism*, ed. Victor Erlich (New Haven, Conn.: Yale University Press, 1975) includes Shklovsky's "Pushkin and Sterne: *Eugene Onegin*" (1923) and "Parallels in Tolstoy" (1923); Eichenbaum's "Pushkin's Path to Prose" (1924) and "On Tolstoy's Crises" (1924); Tynyanov's "Dostoevsky and Gogol" (1929); Zhirmunsky's "The Passion of Aleksandr Blok" (1921); and Jakobson's "On a Generation that Squandered Its Poets."

Readings in Russian Poetics, ed. by L. Matejka and K. Pomorska (Cambridge, Mass.: MIT Press, 1971) is a rich collection containing Eichenbaum's "The Theory of the Formal Method" (1927), "Literary Environment" (1929), and "O. Henry and the Theory of the Short Story" (1927); Tomashevsky's "Literature and Biography" (1923); Tynyanov's "On Literary Evolution" (1927), "Rhythm as the Constructive Factor of Verse" (1924), and "The Meaning of the Word in Verse" (1924); Tynyanov and Jakobson's "Problems in the Study of Literature and Language" (1928); Jakobson's "The Dominant" (1935); Jakobson and Petr Bogatyrev's "On the Boundary between Studies of Folklore and Literature" (1913); Propp's "Fairy Tale Transformation" (1928); Brik's "Contributions to the Study of Verse Language" (1927); Voloshinov's "Reported Speech" (1930); Bakhtin's "Discourse Typology in Prose" (1929); Trubeckoy's "Afanasij Nikitin's *Journey Beyond the Three Seas*" (1926); and Shklovsky's "The Mystery Novel: Dickens's *Little Dorrit*" (1925). German translations from the Formalists appear in *Texte der*

Russischen Formalisten, 2 vols, ed. W. Kosny (Munich: Wilhelm Fink, 1969); French translations of fourteen selections have been published as *Théorie de la littérature*, ed. T. Todorov (Paris: Seuil, 1965).

The Formal Method in Literary Scholarship, written by P. N. Mevedev, Mikhail Bakhtin, or both (trans. A. J. Wehrle; Baltimore: Johns Hopkins University Press, 1978), is a Marxist criticism of Formalism that nevertheless contrives to incorporate some of the strengths of Formalism in the Marxist theory it presents. "The literary structure, like every ideological structure, refracts the generating socioeconomic reality, and does so in its own way. But, at the same time, in its 'content,' literature reflects and refracts the reflections and refractions of other ideological spheres (ethics, epistemology, political doctrines, religion, etc.)" (16–17). "The work cannot be understood outside the unity of literature. But this whole unity and the individual works which are its elements cannot be understood outside the unity of ideological life" (27).

Robert L. Belknap's "Plotlets and Schemes" in *Russian Formalism: A Retrospective Glance*, ed. R. L. Jackson and S. Rudy (New Haven, Conn.: Yale Center for International and Area Studies, 1985) points out the diversity of definitions of *sjuzhet, fabula,* and *tema*, all of which can be translated as "plot." On this matter, see also Tzvetan Todorov's "Some Approaches to Russian Formalism" in *Russian Formalism*, ed. by Bann and Bowlt (see References above).

Ewa M. Thompson's *Russian Formalism and Anglo-American New Criticism* explores the differences between the two movements (The Hague: Mouton, 1971).

G

GENRE   1. A class, kind, genus, or species of literature. 2. One of the three prime, natural, or universal genres: EPIC, dramatic, and LYRIC.

One of the problems in considering the meaning, history, or theory of genre is the variety of terminological distinctions. Aristotle's eidos *is translated both as "species" and as "kind." The term genre, brought into English to avoid the vagueness and extra-literary resonances of words like kind, class, and type, is hardly a definitive term in French, where it has a variety of meanings. Some commentators restrict "genre" to a few broad forms and others use it to refer to an intermediate level, while still others use it to refer to categorizations at any level. The uses of "mode" are yet more various.*

So many are the systems by which varieties of literature have been grouped and so inconsistent are the resulting lists that a brief summary of historical attitudes toward genre seems more useful than the detailing of categorization after categorization. For twentieth-century theories of genre, see the entry below.

1. Explicit categorization of literary kinds is found at least as early as Plato. In *The Republic*, Plato's categorization of all poetry as "simple narration, or imitation, or a union of the two" in *The Republic* (215; 392d)—one of the earliest examples of the classification of literature—is intended to bring all three together as forms of imitation. (An alternative phrasing of Plato's distinction is "authorial, figural, and mixed.") In the opening sentence of the *Poetics*, Aristotle's statement, "Our subject being Poetry, I propose to speak not only of the art in general but also of its species and their respective capacities" suggests that it is understood that poetry is made up of kinds (all of which, Aristotle immediately reminds the reader, are modes of imitation). Aristotle's criteria for distinguishing between the kinds are three: differences in means (verse or prose, with or without musical accompaniment), objects (representation of persons better than, worse than, or

on a level with ordinary humanity), and manner of imitation (alternation of narrative and dialogue, pure narrative, or dramatic presentation). In the classical Greek period, literature was almost synonymous with poetry. Within poetry, tragic and comic dramas, epics, and satyr plays were the basic categories. In the more diffuse area of what was most frequently called *melic* poetry (all that was not epic or dramatic), more distinct kinds—distinguished by meter as well as subject and/or purpose—were needed: lyric, elegiac, dithyrambic, satiric, and so forth. Such distinctions were also made by the Romans. Cicero is content to divide poetry into tragic, comic, epic, melic, and dithyrambic; Horace names epic, elegiac, iambic, lyric, comic, tragic, and satiric; Quintilian treats epic, pastoral, elegiac, satiric, iambic, lyric, comic, and tragic. Rosalie Colie comments on what is known of the cataloguing of the great library at Alexandria (founded 310 B.C.): "literary works were organized by groups, sometimes thematic[,] . . . sometimes metrical, sometimes topical; within a given group, works were organized by author when known, then generically" (11). By the time of the destruction of that library in A.D. 642, a considerable array of generic names was available.

The medieval period was much less interested in the niceties of genre distinction; the terms were retained, but their listing by various medieval commentators suggests little interest in more than names for discriminating subjects. John of Garland writes: "[O]ne kind of historical narrative is an Epithalamium, which is a wedding poem. Another is an Epicedium, which is a plain song apart from a burial. . . . Another is an Apotheosis, which is a poem that celebrates deification or the coming of a soul to glory. Another is a Bucolic, which is about cowherding. Another is a Georgic, which is about agriculture" (101–3).

Renaissance enthusiasm for classical literature extended to an enthusiastic retrieval and imitation of classical genres. J. C. Scaliger's careful discrimination of better than a hundred genres is the greatest monument to the significance of genre in the fifteenth and sixteenth centuries. Colie's *The Resources of Kind* explores in detail the delight in distinguishing genres according to classical models, the repeated warnings against the mixing of genres, and the paradoxical nonchalance with which the classical genres were, in fact, mixed. Of particular interest in the seventeenth century is Thomas Hobbes's division of poetry into the three genres that he associates with the court, the city, and the country: heroic, scommatic, and pastoral. His subdivision of each of these into narrative and dramatic yields epic and tragedy, satire and comedy, and pastoral and pastoral comedy.

The neo-classical period is generally understood to have been more cautious about the mixing of genres and at the same time interested in a lesser number of kinds of poetry. However, Ralph Cohen argues, in "On the Interrelation of Eighteenth-Century Literary Forms," that the neo-classical forms or kinds were understood to modify each other and produce new forms. The nineteenth century's interest in genre is characterized by greater emphasis on poetry that is neither dramatic nor narrative—that is, the lyric in the broad sense—by greater recognition of historical changes in the genres and large-scale systems of thought linking the three "universal" genres to psychological, philosophical, or evolutionary principles (see sense 2). Reaction against such ambitious speculations resulted in a general disinclination to give serious consideration to genre in the early twentieth century, a tendency reinforced by the rise of New Criticism, in which the emphasis on the autonomous internal structure of a text discouraged the exploration of the relations between individual text and genre. The counterreaction begins about mid-century in the midst of the insistence on the importance of generic distinctions by the Chicago Neo-Aristotelian School, and was signalized in Germany by Emil Staiger's *Grundbegriffe des Poetik* (1946), as in the United States, Canada, and England by Northrop Frye's *Anatomy of Criticism* (1957).

2. Well before the nineteenth century, the division of all types of literature into the three universal or prime kinds—epic, dramatic, and lyric—which is suggested by the opening of Aristotle's *Poetics* but not made doctrine there (Aristotle almost totally ignores what would have been called melic, now lyric, poetry) was beginning to take place. Irene Behrens's *Die Lehre von der Einteilung der Dichtkunst* (1940) makes Charles Batteaux's volume of 1746 the major impetus; René Wellek, citing Behrens approvingly, goes on to point to the German post-Kantian speculation in Schiller and the Schlegels; Paul Hernadi, also citing Behrens, writes that "Around 1800, the Schlegel brothers, Schelling, Goethe, Jean Paul Richter, Hegel, and other German writers and philosophers finally established something like a doctrine of holy trinity in modern genre criticism" (193). However, Alastair Fowler puts the origin in Francisco Casales at the beginning of the seventeenth century, or even Minturno in the middle of the sixteenth. In any case, this positing of epic, dramatic, and lyric as the overarching genres required the extension of the meaning of lyric and the elevation of its status into something like equality with the other two. A famous statement is that of Goethe: "There are only three genuine natural forms of literature: the straightforward narrative, the enthusiastically excited, and that expressed through dramatic characters: epic, lyric, and drama" (5:223). Much of the examination of and commentary on the three forms during the nineteenth century related them to larger philosophical structures. For instance, Hegel's logical system (in which thesis and antithesis yield a synthesis) incorporated the three genres by making drama the synthesis of epic objectivity and lyric inwardness. This "third and last mode of presentation conjoins the two previous ones into a new whole in which we see in front of us both an objective development and also its origin in the hearts of individuals" (2:1038). The most common correlation is with the three great divisions of time: the epic looks to the past, the lyric belongs to the present, and the drama focuses attention on the future as scene leads on to scene. The multiple correlations made by Eneas Sweetland Dallas exemplify the potential of such analogues. For Dallas the dramatic represents the modern Western period, the epic the antique Greek, and the lyric the primitive Eastern. Moreover, among other triadic correlations, the

dramatic is linked to the present, plurality, and the Beautiful; the epic with the past, totality, and the True; and the lyric with the future, unity, and the Good. The tradition continues in Emil Staiger's *Grundbegriffe der Poetik* (1946), where the three genres are associated with the divisions of time, the essential human faculties, and the process of human development. The lyric relates to the past, childhood, and the emotional; the epic to the present, youth, and the represent-ative; and the dramatic to the future, maturity, and the logical. Staiger further suggests that the lyric is to be correlated with the syllable, the epic with the word, and the dramatic with the sentence, the argument for which is summarized by Heather Dubrow: "Like a syllable, the lyric is an expressive form that carries no meaning and fulfills no purpose; like a word, the epical defines an object; like a sentence, the dramatic is concerned with the relationship between subject and verb, or actor and action" (104).

The general association of the three universal genres with past, present, and future found in nineteenth-century German idealists and their heirs seems as much analogical as historical. A more truly evolutionary perspective was adopted by writers at the end of the century under the influence of theories of biological evolution. Two of the best known are those of J. A. Symonds and Ferdinand Brunetière. Symonds's "On the Application of Evolutionary Principles to Art and Literature" (1888) had already been given exemplification in his *Shakspere's Predecessors in the English Drama* (1884). The theory, which blends the Dar-winian idea of the evolution of species with the childhood, maturity, and death of the individual, assumes that each nation and each genre goes from birth to a point of fullest development and then declines. "[E]ach particular polity, each specific form of art, has, like a plant or animal, its destined evolution from a germ, its given stock of energy, its limited supply of vital force. . . . Granted favouring circumstances and no thwarting influence, it will pass through the phases of adolescence, maturity, and old age. But it cannot alter its type" ("Application," 10). Therefore, "Criticism seeks the individuality imprisoned in the germ, exhibited in the growth, exhausted in the season of decline" (11). After the undoubted culminative achievement of Shakespeare, decline is irre-versible. "We . . . who regard the evolution of the Drama from the vantage-ground of time, see that in Shakspere the art of sixteenth-century England was completed and accomplished" (*Shakspere's Predecessors*, 5). Symonds is often spoken of as though he insisted on applying his three-phase model in all cir-cumstances. However, he notes in *Shakspere's Predecessors*, "The succession in time of the stages I have tried to indicate must not be insisted on too harshly"; and in the later essay ("On the Application"); he finds that by his own time the arts of Europe have become hybrids between nations, with the result that "Per-sonal capacity, the liberty of individual genius, the caprice of coteries, assert themselves with more apparent freedom in these circumstances. The type does not expire, because the type has become capable of infinite modification" (55). At about the same time in France, Ferdinand Brunetière was similarly treating genres as biological species that differentiate themselves as do natural species;

they move from the simple to the complex, develop to mature perfection, and then decline.

That the three universals represent basic modes of literary response but are not to be confused with true genres, that is, artistic patterns or models, as argued by Karl Viëtor in 1931, is restated and urged by Claudio Guillén in *Literature as System* (121–22).

References

Aristotle. *Poetics*. Trans. I. Bywater. Oxford: Clarendon Press, 1909.

Behrens, Irene. *Die Lehre von der Einteilung der Dichtkunst*. Halle, E. Germany: Niemeyer, 1940.

Brunetière, Ferdinand. *L'Evolution des genres dans l'histoire de la littérature*. Paris: Hachete, 1890.

Cohen, Ralph. "On the Interrelation of Eighteenth-Century Literary Forms." In *New Approaches to Eighteenth-Century Literature*, ed. Phillip Harth. English Institute Essays. New York: Columbia University Press, 1974.

Colie, Rosalie L. *The Resources of Kind: Generic Theory in the Renaissance*. Ed. B. K. Lewalski. Berkeley: University of California Press, 1973. An exceptionally rich little volume.

Dallas, Eneas Sweetland. *Poetics*. London: Smith, Elder, 1852.

Dubrow, Heather. *Genre*. London: Methuen, 1982. Considers both the functions of genre and the history of genre theory. Useful bibliography.

Fowler, Alastair. *Kinds of Literature: An Introduction to the Theory of Genres and Modes*. Cambridge, Mass.: Harvard University Press, 1982. Essential.

Frye, Northrop. *Anatomy of Criticism*. Princeton, N.J.: Princeton University Press, 1957.

Goethe, Johann Wolfgang. *West-Ostlicher Divan*. In *Sämtliche Werke*, vol. 5. Ed. Konrad Burdach. Stuttgart and Berlin: J. G. Cotta, 1902–7.

Guillén, Claudio. *Literature as System*. Princeton, N.J.: Princeton University Press, 1971. The essay "On the Uses of Literary Genre" is an especially salient analysis.

Hegel, Georg Wilhelm Friedrich. *Aesthetics: Lectures on Fine Art*. Trans. T. M. Knox. 2 vols. Oxford: Clarendon Press, 1975. (The lectures were given in 1823, 1826, and 1828–29.) The brief citations generally given to Hegel's commentary on the different genres of poetry do not at all adequately represent the insights and stimulating suggestions in these pages.

Hernadi, Paul. "Order Without Borders: Recent Genre Theory in the English-Speaking Countries." In *Theories of Literary Genre*, ed. Joseph Strelka. University Park: Pennsylvania State University Press, 1978.

Hobbes, Thomas. Letter to Davenant of January 10, 1650 (cited as "The Answer to the Preface to Gondibert"). In vol. 6 of *The English Works of Thomas Hobbes*. Ed. W. Molesworth. 11 vols. London: John Bohn, 1840.

John of Garland. *The 'Parisiana Poetria' of John of Garland*. Ed. and trans. T. Lawler. Yale Studies in English no. 182. New Haven, Conn.: Yale University Press, 1974.

Plato. *The Republic*. In vol. 2 of *The Dialogues of Plato*. Trans. B. Jowett. New York: Charles Scribner's Sons, 1911.

Scaliger, J. C. *Poetices Libra Septem*. Lyons, 1561.

Staiger, Emil. *Grundbegriffe der Poetik*. Zurich: Atlantis Verlag, 1946.

Symonds, John Addington. "On the Application of Evolutionary Principles to Art and

Literature" (1888). In *Essays Speculative and Suggestive*. London: Chapman and Hall, 1893.

———. *Shakspere's Predecessors in the English Drama*. London: Smith, Elder, 1884.

Wellek, René. "Genre Theory, the Lyric, and *Erlebnis*." In *Discriminations*. New Haven, Conn.: Yale University Press, 1970. A substantial essay.

Sources of Additional Information

The three volumes of *The Growth of Literature* by H. Munro Chadwick and N. Kershaw Chadwick (Cambridge: Cambridge University Press, 1932) survey the oral literature of a variety of cultures. The whole of this literature is divided into five major types (corresponding to genres). The first three are "Type A: Narrative Poems"; "Type B: Poems dealing with situation or emotion, and consisting wholly or mainly of speeches"; and "Type C: Poems of didactic interest" (p. 28). The others are Type D, celebration poetry; and Type E, "personal" poetry or "poetry relating to the poet's own feelings or experiences, or to persons in immediate relationship with him, or to things which have come under his observation but which are not of general significance" (42).

For exemplification and discussion of variations on the genres (or subgenres) of classical poetry, see Francis Cairns's *Generic Composition in Greek and Roman Poetry* (Edinburgh: Edinburgh University Press, 1972). Examples include: *anathematikon* (dedication), *genethliakon* (birthday poem), *flagitatio* (demand for return of one's property), and *soteria* (rejoicing for escape from danger or illness).

Hans Robert Jauss's "Theory of Genres and Medieval Literature" in his *Toward an Aesthetic of Reception*, trans. T. Bahti (Minneapolis: University of Minnesota Press, 1982) develops an original taxonomy of medieval literature and argues that "No perceptible historical continuity exists between the forms and genres of the Middle Ages and the literature of our present" (108).

Irvin Ehrenpreis's *The Types Approach to Literature* (New York: King's Crown Press, 1945) reviews twenty-six different divisions of genre, sketches the approach to genre implicit or explicit in certain important American scholars, gives considerable space to evolutionary concepts of genre, and reports on genre-organized college and high school courses of the time. Ehrenpreis makes the interesting point that the convenience of generic distinctions in school curricula has given genre part of its prominence. For a more recent survey of sixty theories of genre grouped under four classes (expressive, pragmatic, structural, and mimetic), see Paul Hernadi's *Beyond Genre: New Directions in Literary Classification* (Ithaca, N.Y.: Cornell University Press, 1972).

The chapter "Literary Genres" in René Wellek and Austin Warren's *Theory of Literature* (New York: Harcourt Brace, 1949) offers a general overview of the kinds of problems that have been raised by theories of genre.

GENRE THEORY, TWENTIETH-CENTURY   1. A philosophically or historically derived classification of literary works. 2. An argument for or demonstrations of the importance of generic categories. 3. An elucidation of a limited number of literary kinds or genres as the basis for differentiating the genre of literature from among the set of genres making up human discourse.

See also GENRE. *Genre theories are often divided into two groups: the philosophical or deductive and the historical or inductive. The first categorizes genres of literature in terms of logically derived possibilities, often based on principles*

drawn from psychological or philosophical theories; the second categorizes them
on the basis of historically existing kinds. Genre theories may also be grouped
according to the sorts of taxonomic criteria invoked or by the degree to which
they recognize historical changes in genres. The grouping here adopted as most
useful is by primary purpose, the three purposes being equivalent to three dif-
ferent senses in which the term genre theory is used.

Attempts both to improve the ways in which genres are categorized and to
defend the importance of generic categories have been motivated first by evident
inconsistencies in the historical designations of genres and by the outright re-
jection of the notion of genre that is at least partly the result of these deficiencies.
Albert Guérard succinctly sums up the historical situation: "Blind chance, the
prestige of a few masters, the dogmatism of a few pedants, have combined to
give us a nomenclature remarkably incomplete as well as perverse" (225). The
best-known denial of the principle of genre is that of Benedetto Croce: "From
the theory of artistic and literary kinds derive those erroneous modes of judgment
and of criticism, thanks to which, instead of asking before a work of art if it be
expressive and what it expresses[,] . . . they ask if it obey the laws of epic or of
tragedy, of historical painting or of landscape" (36–37). While Croce's 1909
attack is directed against the use of generic definitions as rules, Joel Spingarn
in 1911 announces the total denial of the principle of generic categorization:
"Poets do not really write epics, pastorals, lyrics[,] . . . they express themselves,
and this expression is their only form" (23). For Maurice Blanchot in 1959,
"A book no longer belongs to a genre; every book arises from literature alone"
(293).

1. There have been any number of approaches to the revision of the generic
map, most of them replete with criticism of the inadequacy of other attempts.
An interesting approach taken in the first half of the twentieth century by Albert
Guérard insists that each prime genre is characterized by its own spirit as well
as form while recognizing that a work may incorporate the spirit of one genre
in the form of another. Guérard therefore adapts an approach that he credits to
Eduard von Hartmann, and arrives at nine genres: the lyrical lyric, the epic lyric,
the dramatic lyric, the lyrical epic, and so forth. (René Wellek and Austin
Warren's recommendation that genres be defined by both inner and outer form
is an alternate way of phrasing Guérard's concern for both form and spirit;
Heather Dubrow's conception of host genres reflects another way of viewing the
incorporation of elements of one genre in the form of another.) The Chicago or
Neo-Aristotelian critics who flourished in the 1940s and 1950s, and especially
R. S. Crane and Elder Olson, untiringly insist on the importance of correctly
identifying the genre to which a work belongs. Crane and Olson insist on drawing
a radical distinction between mimetic and didactic poetry. The first gives pleasure
through imitation; the second, while employing many of the devices of mimetic
poetry, seeks to inculcate a thesis. Mimetic poetry "does not engage our interest
and emotions in particulars of the action in order to instruct us generally," writes
Olson; "on the contrary it instructs us about particulars of the characters and

actions in the poem in order to engage our emotions and interest us in behalf of these very characters and actions'' (''William Empson,'' 67. See also pp. 588–94 of Olson's ''A Dialogue on Symbolism'' and pp. 156–60 in Crane's *The Languages of Criticism and the Structure of Poetry*). This dichotomy between the mimetic and didactic has been so much discussed that it is sometimes forgotten that the Chicago critics relied on a variety of generic distinctions, such as Olson's four kinds of action (''Outline,'' 560). Crane argues against the rigid application of genres; genres or forms are simply aids to understanding. Using Gray's *Elegy* as an example, Crane says of the sort of critic he favors: ''He would have no favorite hypothesis of structure as such, but would know merely that among short poems which, like the *Elegy*, evoke in us serious emotions, the shaping principle may be of several essentially distinct types, each of them generating distinct artistic problems for the poet'' (175). The critic is then to use ''his theory of possible principles of structure in short poems simply to furnish him with the distinctions he needs if he is not to substitute a structure of his own for the structure Gray achieved'' (176).

Among Anglo-American theories of genre, that of Northrop Frye is best known. Frye's *Anatomy of Criticism* (1957) reaches well beyond theories of genre as these have generally been understood to categorize the kinds of literature from four major intersecting perspectives. Frye's modes categorize five degrees of the hero's power of action; his mythoi align the four seasons and correspond to the comic, romantic, tragic, and satiric. The forms Frye actually labels genres are distinguished by their essential form of presentation (acted, recited, spoken as if in soliloquy, or presented on the printed page—the last is prose fiction, added by Frye to the traditional prime kinds, drama, epic, and lyric, respectively). The fourth taxonomy discriminates four types of symbolism. Frye's recognition of subcategories within many of his types further refines, and complicates, his total system. The result is a set of cross-cutting categories intended to describe the full range of literary possibilities, on the one hand, and allow a very specific description of individual texts, on the other. Robert Scholes has modified elements of Frye's system as applied to prose fiction, and derived seven *modes* (117–38). These reflect ''the quality of the fictional world'': satire, picaresque, comedy, history, sentiment, tragedy, and romance, which he arranges into a unique *V*-shaped diagram (Scholes reserves *genre* for what are often called *subgenres*). On the other hand, while recognizing the value of regarding genres as tending toward a system in which they are mutually defined, Claudio Guillén finds no fundamental or necessary system but rather any number of systems dependent on the time and culture.

> I will suggest that the history of literature . . . is characterized not so much by the operation of full systems as by a tendency toward system or structuration. Thus it appears that the historian is led to evaluate, for every century or phase in the history of his subject, the precise scope of a limited, persistent, profound ''will to order'' in the slowly but constantly changing domain of literature as a whole. (376)

In further contrast to Frye and Scholes, who attempt to delineate specific sets of classificatory terminology, in *Kinds of Literature* (1982), Alastair Fowler is like Guérard in proposing a set of categorizations that recognize that genres are characterized dually (for Fowler, the duality is of "form and substance"); unlike Guérard, he does not attempt to set out the appropriate number of categories in each set. Using genre as a synonym for characterizing category generally, Fowler calls historical genres *kinds*; kinds modified by "additional specification of content" are *sub-genres*. A *mode* is a "selection or abstraction from a kind" (roughly, a mode seems to be a modification of a kind by the specification of certain characteristics, not wholly unlike Guérard's adjectival *spirits*, modifying nominal forms as in "dramatic lyric"); *constructional types* are formal characteristics that may appear in a variety of kinds such as catalogues or linked sequences.

Fowler is particularly concerned to remind his readers that genres carrying the same name in different historical periods may be very different and proposes that kinds should perhaps be used in association with a date (for example, 1600 comedy as opposed to 1700 comedy). The radical changes in what may seem to be the same genre is a point made by Coleridge in his early nineteenth-century lectures on Shakespeare. "If the tragedies of Sophocles are in the strict sense of the word tragedies, and the comedies of Aristophanes comedies, we must emancipate ourselves of a false association from misapplied names, and find a new word for the plays of Shakespeare" (1:197). Such recognition of changes within genres, which a system like Frye's largely negates, is equally insisted on by Rosalie Colie.

2. Major commentaries on generic theory may focus wholly or primarily on the functions of genres, and thus, on the value of recognizing them. The first chapter ("Literary Genres") of Tzvetan Todorov's *The Fantastic* argues the necessity of generic understanding in that "Any description of a text . . . is a description of genre" (7). Like almost all twentieth-century genre theorists, Todorov emphasizes the necessity of flexibility in the application of generic description: "*every* work modifies the sum of possibilities, each new example alters the species" (6). He suggests that any structure of genres must be based on three aspects: the verbal (including the speaker and persons spoken to), the syntactic (the "logical, temporal, and spatial" relations within the text), and the semantic (the themes); he does not, however, go on to develop such a generic scheme.

Perhaps the most absolute argument for the recognition of the genre of a given text is that of E. D. Hirsch, who makes all understanding of meaning (by which Hirsch means the author's intended meaning) contingent on correctly identifying the genre of the text. In Hirsch's use of the term, the *intrinsic genre* of a text is finally a genre really applicable to that text alone. The intrinsic genre "is that sense of the whole by means of which an interpreter can correctly understand any part in its determinacy" (86). This does not quite mean that any change in a text would alter its genre, although Hirsch's intrinsic genres are very narrow indeed. However, the reader begins the process of determining the intrinsic genre by establishing the larger kinds of genres to which the work may belong and then progressively narrowing the field.

The function of genre theory as one of, if not the, major means of grasping the whole in terms of which the parts of the literary texts are to be understood is generally accepted. Alastair Fowler, whose *Kinds of Literature* falls into this second sense or kind of genre theory as much as into the first, says succinctly, "We identify the genre to interpret the exemplar" (38). Heather Dubrow expands the point: "genre, as many students of the subject have observed, functions much like a code of behavior established between the author and his reader" (2) and is analogous to an invitation letting an invited guest know whether to expect a formal dinner party, a convention banquet, or a picnic.

David H. Richter's "Pandora's Box Revisited" and John Reichert's "More than Kin and Less than Kind" represent in brief the increasingly common position that the purpose of genres is not to define (much less to provide rules), but to suggest perspectives. Richter proposes that "we might employ one set of generic distinctions to help us answer one sort of question, another set to answer a wholly different question" (477). For Reichert, once it is recognized that genres are not mutually exclusive classes but rather generally understood categories that interact and overlap—"it is misleading to speak at all of *the* genre to which a work belongs" (65)—the application of genres simply provides a guide to intelligent reading and discussion of literary works. "These observations suggest that the value of genre theorizing is chiefly preparatory, heuristic, pedagogical" (76). Adena Rosmarin has carefully articulated a similar understanding of genre, which she then applies to the dramatic monologue in *The Power of Genre* (1985). Her position is that "once genre is defined as pragmatic rather than natural, as defined rather than found, and as used rather than described, then there are precisely as many genres as we need, genres whose conceptual shape is precisely determined by that need" (25). Texts are to be read *as if* they belonged to particular usefully chosen genres. "The primary act of the generic critic is suppositional and metaphoric: let us explain this literary text by reading it in terms of that genre" (40). (It should be noted that Rosmarin uses "deductive" to mean the movement from the chosen genre to the work—"asserting particular instances of the traits stated or implied by the posited genre," 41; and not, as the word deductive usually means in the context of genre theory, the derivation of a set of genres from a theoretical principle.) Drawing on the work of E. H. Gombrich, Rosmarin argues that the schemas ("genres," as she uses the term) are necessary to the author as well as serving as pragmatic aids to the reader; that is, they enable the author to get started. This again is a common theme in contemporary genre theory. Scholes writes, "The writing process is generic in this sense: every writer conceives of his task in terms of writing he knows" (130). Claudio Guillén emphasizes the creative rather than merely imitative value of genres for the writer when he observes that "a preexistent form can never be simply 'taken over' by the writer or transferred to a new work. The task of form-making must be undertaken anew all over again" (111).

Fowler sums up, "If genre is of little value in classification, what then is it good for? This book has set out the idea that it is a communication system, for the use of writers in writing, and readers and critics in reading and interpreting" (256).

Together with Fowler's book, Rosalie Colie's *The Resources of Kind* and Heather Dubrow's *Genre* offer the widest-ranging commentaries on the value of the audience's expectations about genre for the author. Focused on the English Renaissance, Colie's book explores the large degree to which Renaissance authors were conscious of generic distinctions while nonchalantly departing from these. After exemplifying both tendencies, she examines "what the *literary* gain may be, both in having genres and in refusing to allow generic categories to dictate or predestine the size, scope, content, and manner in any particular literary work" (103). It is obvious that departures from generic conventions are only recognizable, and thus effective as strategies, if the generic conventions are known, but Colie demonstrates in great detail the ways in which Renaissance authors played on their readers' generic expectations. Dubrow, who helpfully surveys the functions of genre and the history of generic theory, concludes by suggesting the value not only of more attention to the functioning of readers' generic expectations but of the generic approach to understanding the changes in individual authors' uses of genre over their careers, the relations of fashions in genre to social and political movements and large-scale modes of thought in particular historical periods, and in organizing literary history.

Fowler's, Dubrow's, Guillén's, and Colie's studies argue in different ways the point made by Colie's final sentence: "Significant pieces of literature are worth much more than their kind, but they are what they are in part by their inevitable kind-ness" (128).

3. Rather than either developing a taxonomy of genres or investigating the functions of generic distinctions, some critics have directed their efforts in such a way that, while dividing literature into major kinds (usually two), they define literature itself. In a sense, such efforts are radical questionings of Aristotle's subsumption of all art under the principle of imitation. Käte Hamburger thus finds that there are two genres, the fictional or mimetic and the lyric. The feature they share is that neither makes statements about reality (neither is directed toward the "object-pole"), though they avoid such statement in different ways. Henri Bonnet similarly finds only two fundamental genres, fiction and poetry. While poetry expresses the inner self, "the novelist gets away from the self, in order to reach the individual *in the others*" (8). The two forms correspond to the "dual aspect" of the human individual: "corporeal and spiritual" (12). (As in many generic systems, the most common meanings of terms are here modified; what Bonnet calls fiction may be written in verse, just as what he calls poetry may be written in prose.) Bennison Gray, after developing his definition of a work of literature as "the unverifiable moment-by-moment statement of an event," dismisses the traditional names of genres in favor of five species that fit tidily under that definition: unmediated monologue and dialogue, and unmediated script, story, and serial (215).

References

Blanchot, Maurice. *Le livre à venir*. Paris: Gallimard, 1959. The translation of the passage quoted is from Tzvetan Todorov's "The Origin of Genres," *New Literary History* 8 (Autumn 1976): 159.

Bonnet, Henri. "Dichotomy of Artistic Genres." Trans. A. Grava. In *Theories of Literary Genre*, ed. Joseph Strelka. University Park: Pennsylvania State University Press, 1978.

Coleridge, Samuel Taylor. *Coleridge's Shakespearean Criticism*. Ed. Thomas M. Raysor. 2 vols. London: Constable, 1930.

Colie, Rosalie L. *The Resources of Kind: Generic Theory in the Renaissance*. Ed. Barbara K. Lewalski. Berkeley: University of California Press, 1973. A standard reference.

Croce, Benedetto. *Aesthetics*. Trans. D. Ainslie (1909). New York: Noonday Press, 1964.

Crane, R. S. *The Languages of Criticism and the Structure of Poetry*. Toronto: University of Toronto Press, 1953.

Dubrow, Heather. *Genre*. London: Methuen, 1982.

Fowler, Alastair. *Kinds of Literature: An Introduction to the Theory of Genres and Modes*. Cambridge, Mass.: Harvard University Press, 1982. An important book.

Frye, Northrop. *Anatomy of Criticism*. Princeton, N.J.: Princeton University Press, 1957.

Gray, Bennison. *The Phenomenon of Literature*. The Hague: Mouton, 1975.

Guillén, Claudio. *Literature as System*. Princeton, N.J.: Princeton University Press, 1971.

Guérard, Albert. *Preface to World Literature*. New York: Henry Holt, 1940.

Hamburger, Käte. *The Logic of Literature*. Trans. M. J. Rose. Bloomington: Indiana University Press, 1973.

Hirsch, E. D., Jr. *Validity in Interpretation*. New Haven: Yale University Press, 1967.

Olson, Elder. "A Dialogue on Symbolism." "An Outline of Poetic Theory," and "William Empson, Contemporary Criticism, and Poetic Diction." In *Critics and Criticism*, ed. R. S. Crane. Chicago: University of Chicago Press, 1952.

Reichert, John. "More than Kin and Less than Kind: The Limits of Genre Theory." In *Theories of Literary Genre*, ed. Joseph Strelka. University Park: Pennsylvania University Press, 1978.

Richter, David H. "Pandora'a Box Revisited: A Review Article." *Critical Inquiry* 1 (December 1974): 453–78.

Rosmarin, Adena. *The Power of Genre*. Minneapolis: University of Minnesota Press, 1985.

Scholes, Robert. *Structuralism in Literature*. New Haven, Conn.: Yale University Press, 1974.

Spingarn, J. E. "The New Criticism" (1911). In *Creative Criticism*. New York: Harcourt, Brace, 1931.

Todorov, Tzvetan. *The Fantastic: A Structural Approach to a Literary Genre*. Trans. R. Howard. Cleveland; Ohio: Press of Case Western Reserve University, 1973.

Wellek, René, and Austin Warren. *Theory of Literature*. 3d ed. New York: Harcourt, Brace, and World, 1956.

Sources of Additional Information

For a helpful guide to the organization and thought of Northrop Frye's *Anatomy of Criticism* (see References above), see Robert D. Denham's *Northrop Frye and Critical*

Method (University Park: Pennsylvania State University Press, 1978). In *Beyond Genre: New Directions in Literary Classification* (Ithaca, N.Y.: Cornell University Press, 1972), Paul Hernadi develops a set of sixteen "modes of poetic discourse" that are intended to improve on Frye while retaining the principle of intersecting classifications (four major modes, four perspectives, three types of scope, and three moods).

Jonathan Culler's *Structuralist Poetics* (Ithaca, N.Y.: Cornell University Press, 1975) is an interpretation of structuralism that emphasizes the conventions that readers bring to literature and treats genre as such a convention. "If a theory of genres is to be more than a taxonomy it must attempt to explain what features are constitutive of functional categories which have governed the reading and writing of literature" (137).

Thomas Kent's *Interpretation and Genre* (Lewisburg, Pa.: Bucknell University Press, 1986) interestingly contrasts synchronic and diachronic dimensions of genre.

> On the formal or synchronic level, formulated conventions establish specific, formal standards against which any particular text may be compared. On the cultural or diachronic level, unformulated conventions reflect the assumptions and values of a specific audience or reader, and they help establish the meaning and significance given to a text by a specific audience of reader at a particular moment in history. (39)

Herman P. Saloman's "Observations on the Definition, Evolution, and Separation of Genres in the Study of French Literature" and Klauss Weissenberger's "Morphological Genre Theory: An Answer to Pluralism of Forms" discuss twentieth-century French and German genre theory respectively; both are included in *Theories of Literary Genre*, ed. by Joseph Strelka (University Park: Pennsylvania State University Press, 1978).

H

HERMENEUTICS 1. The translation of something not understood into an understandable form, that is, a form which is assimilable to the cognitive interrelation of language, conventions, and practices already achieved; interpretation. 2. The interpretation of Biblical texts. 3. The interpretation of any text. 4. The human interpretation of anything whatever, from sense impressions to cultural structures, together with the investigation of the assumptions, practices, and limits of various hermeneutic methods and theories. 5. The exploration of the assumptions and implications of cultural structures and practices, especially of the ideologies embodied. (See also INTERPRETATION.)

1. The broad meaning of hermeneutics has been available from early Greek and is often conjecturally assumed to be related to the role of Hermes in translating the messages of the gods into human language. It could thus be applied to interpretation or clarification in any domain—as by Aristotle in *Peri Hermenais*, which treats the grammatical structure of statements as logical subject and predicate.

2. The earliest sustained applications of interpretive principles to texts were in Biblical exegesis; accordingly, "hermeneutics" has long been associated with Biblical commentary. Gerald Bruns's "The Problem of Figuration in Antiquity" is a useful account of hermeneutical principles developed by Philo, Origen, and Augustine, and especially their willing acceptance of allegorical interpretations. Thus, Philo: "We must make up our minds that [everything] is figurative and involves deeper meanings" (2:313 [Sect. 167]). Bruns paraphrases a central principle of Origen's as follows: "When you know that something is wrong with what you are reading—that is, when you discover that what is written is garbled, contradictory, unbelievable, or even when it contains an obvious scribal error—*then* you know that it is trying to speak to you, or (more accurately) that it is trying to draw you into its secrets" (153). Central to Augustine is the principle

"that whatever appears in the divine Word that does not literally pertain to virtuous behavior or to the truth of faith you must take to be figurative" (87–88 [Bk. 3, Sect. 10]). The principle of Matthias Flacius Illyricus in *Clavis Scripturae Sacrae* (1567) that each passage in the Scriptures should be understood in such a way as to reflect the internal coherence of the whole of the Scriptures belongs to the same hermeneutical tradition (quoted in Mueller-Vollmer, 2). Such principles necessarily produce an allegorical form of hermeneutics that assumes hidden meanings and readily constructs figurative meanings to address difficult or apparently scandalous passages in such a way as to produce consistency.

3. It is generally agreed that in the Renaissance the newly intense study of Greek and Latin texts, the Protestant need for Biblical interpretation not dependent on ecclesiastical authority, and revived interest in philosophical questions led to more conscious concern with hermeneutical methods. By the eighteenth century these methods were being codified by J. M. Chladenius in *Introduction to the Correct Interpretation of Reasonable Discourses and Books* (1742). By general consent, however, Friedrich Schleiermacher's lectures on hermeneutics, begun in 1819, laid the foundation for the general field of hermeneutics as since understood, giving impetus toward the creation of a method that would be applicable to all texts. Schleiermacher's division of the process of understanding into the grammatical (in relation to language) and technical (in relation of the author's individuality) or, in later terminology, linguistic and psychological, marks two major currents in the development of hermeneutics. "[E]ach person represents one locus where a given language takes shape in a particular way, and his speech can be understood only in the context of the totality of the language. But then too he is a person who is a constantly developing spirit, and his speaking can be understood as only one moment in this development in relation to all others" (98). Schleiermacher's two canons of grammatical interpretation are that "[a] more precise determination of any point in a given text must be decided on the basis of the use of language common to the author and his original public" (117) and "[t]he meaning of each word of a passage must be determined by the context in which it occurs" (127). His statement of the goal of technical interpretation is "nothing other than a development of the beginning, that is, to consider the whole of the author's work in terms of its parts and in every part to consider the content as what moved the author and the form as his nature moved by that content" (148). Schleiermacher is also responsible for the formulation of what has come to be known as the "hermeneutic circle": "Complete knowledge always involves an apparent circle, that each part can be understood only out of the whole to which it belongs, and vice versa" (113). The whole direction of Schleiermacher's hermeneutics then is toward the reconstruction of the meaning the author must have intended to be literally understood (that is, without any assumption of esoteric meanings).

The adaptations and modifications of the Schleiermacherian tradition effected by Johann Droysen, Philip August Boeckh, Wilhelm Dilthey, and other theorists of philological hermeneutics cannot here be pursued in any detail. Boeckh is responsible for the distinction between the task of hermeneutics as the understanding of the subject in itself and that of criticism as "not to understand a subject in itself but to discover the relations between several subjects" (45–46). Dilthey explicitly formulated the concept of the hermeneutic circle in which the fact that the part is understood only in relation to the whole and the whole only in relation to the parts that make it up leads to a constant alternation between focus on an aspect of a text and focus on an interpretive hypothesis embracing the whole of the text. Dilthey's concept of hermeneutics also moved the goal toward the recreation of *lived experience* (*Erlebnis*) and *life-expression* (*Lebensäusserung*) and away from an understanding of the specific grammatical (linguistic) formulation. The Introductions to Kurt Mueller-Vollmer's *The Hermeneutic Reader* and Richard Palmer's "Allegorical, Philological, and Philosophical Hermeneutics" offer valuable summaries of hermeneutic systems from Schleiermacher to Gadamer. Specific, still-debated issues that have arisen within the tradition of philological hermeneutics are set out in the latter part of the discussion of sense 4.

One of the most influential contemporary statements of hermeneutics in the tradition descending from Schleiermacher has been E. D. Hirsch's argument for the possibility and importance of determining the intention of the author. Though it is impossible to be certain in the case of any specific text that one is correctly interpreting the author's intended meaning, argues Hirsch, in principle it is always possible to do so through appropriate attention to the text, the genre, and the original context. The choice between different possible interpretations is to be made through a "logic of validation" that seeks to narrow the class to which the text belongs, and thus narrow the interpretive possibilities as far as possible. That much of what interests a reader may result from perspectives on the text that have nothing to do with the author's intention is recognized by Hirsch; these interests are not however part of the *meaning* but rather constitute a portion of the text's possible *significances*.

Richard Palmer names the whole tradition stemming from Schleiermacher through Dilthey *philological* as opposed to the *allegorical hermeneutics* that dominated the earlier and the *philosophical hermeneutics* that has come to dominate in the second half of this century. Philological hermeneutics emphasizes "grammar, history, genre, and the psychology of the author" (24). Such philological interpretation does not seek "to unlock a secret meaning hidden (often purposely) from the multitude" but seeks rather "what must have been the originally intended meaning in the original context of its utterance" (26–27). The emphasis on the problem of interpreting texts whose origins are distant or culturally alien has been central to hermeneutics from the beginning. Interestingly, the basic level of interpretive processing through which words are understood as combining to make up propositions and propositions are understood in relation to the larger sections of the text is now generally regarded as the object of DISCOURSE ANALYSIS, not hermeneutics.

4. The fourth sense in which hermeneutics has come to be used is both more comprehensive and more specifically oriented toward philosophical issues than sense 1. Contemporary hermeneutical thought, or philosophical hermeneutics, is the result of the convergence of several forces or conditions. The first is a tendency to push the concept well beyond the interpretation of language. The process by which the mind judges or interprets bare sense impressions (*percepts* in Peircean terminology) so that they become nameable or classifiable perceptions (of a tree, or music, or the smell of wood smoke) can be regarded as part of the subject of hermeneutics. Moreover, something like Friedrich Nietzsche's view has come to prevail: "I am convinced of the phenomenalism of the *inner* world also: everything that reaches our consciousness is utterly and completely adjusted, simplified, schematised, interpreted" and " 'Inner experience' only enters consciousness when it has found a language which the individual can *understand*— that is to say, a translation of a certain condition into conditions with which he is *familiar*"; thus "facts are precisely what is lacking, all that exists consists of *interpretations*" (15:7, 11, 12). Similarly, as Kenneth Burke points out as early as *Counter-Statement* (1931) and develops more fully in *The Philosophy of Literary Form* (1941), each individual interprets each experiential situation strategically, that is, in terms of his/her own values and goals. More philosophically stated, Edmund Husserl's phenomenological analysis regards all objects as constituted by human intentionality. (In Husserlian phenomenology, all conscious thought and desire must be understood as having, or *intending*, an object; such objects may or may not have actual existence.) All such explanations of the way raw sense impressions or, more complexly, physical, social, and cultural situations are given meaning by the individual can be argued to be at least partly parallel to the interpretation of texts.

The second impetus toward the rapprochement of hermeneutics and speculative philosophy is the number of moot issues in hermeneutical literature, issues that have both been cast in the form of direct oppositions and argued to be in complementary or dialectical relationships. One issue, made clearly visible in Schleiermacher's distinction between grammatical and technical (author-oriented) hermeneutics, is the importance or even validity of considering the individuality of the author. By defining hermeneutics as the understanding of the text, not the presentation or explanation of that understanding to others, Schleiermacher raises the question of the relation between the two activities. Is one's understanding of a text one thing and the exegetical process of explaining or explicating it another, a process that necessarily imports anachronistic interests? Further, his very quest for a general hermeneutics opened the still-argued question of its possibility, of whether in fact each field must have its own hermeneutic principles.

By framing his hermeneutics around the difference between "explanation" (*erklären*) as the goal of the physical sciences and "understanding" (*verstehen*) as the goal of the human sciences, Dilthey gives prominence to the question of the degree of difference between the two. Dilthey's emphasis on the psychological aspect of interpretation sharpens the grammatical/technical difference in a way that emphasizes the much-to-be-debated question of the importance or validity of considering the author's individuality, beliefs, and intentions. Dilthey moves toward the psychological pole so that, as Paul Ricoeur has put it, the question becomes "not *what* a text says, but *who* says it" (*Hermeneutics and the Human Sciences*, 52). All these questions seem to demand a larger framework for their resolution than can be provided by hermeneutics regarded as a system of principles for understanding texts.

The third current driving changes in the conception of hermeneutics has been Martin Heidegger's adoption of the word to describe his quest for *Dasein* (Being-in-the-world) in *Being and Time* (1927). The Husserlian phenomenology that Heidegger builds upon but seeks to transcend thus becomes linked to hermeneutics to such an extent that philosophical hermeneutics is sometimes called "phenomenological" hermeneutics. Heidegger's own frequently quoted statement in the introduction to *Being and Time* is the following: "The phenomenology of Dasein is *hermeneutic* in the primordial signification of the world, where it designates this business of interpreting" (62). Hubert Dreyfus has summed up the final result of Heidegger's hermeneutic quest as follows: "By a double use of the hermeneutic circle, hermeneutic phenomenology strips away our disguises and makes manifest the preontological understanding of being as *unheimlich* which is hidden in each person's awareness and in our public practices, thus revealing the deep truth of our condition" (73). While Heidegger's philosophical hermeneutics discovers a rootlessness lying deep in the human mind, his emphasis on the historicity of all understanding of the existential world denies the possibility of discovering the intended meaning of texts of earlier periods.

Hans-Georg Gadamer's development of hermeneutics in *Truth and Method* (1960) is also phenomenological, but rather than searching for "Being," he pursues the relation of the total historical context to the construction of meaning. Accepting Heidegger's belief in the impossibility of understanding earlier historical contexts, Gadamer argues: "the reconstruction of the original circumstances, like all restoration, is a pointless undertaking in view of the historicity of our being" (149). The understanding of an earlier text consists then in a fusion of the original historical "horizon" with the present one (*Horizontverschmelzung*). Gadamer thus raises from another direction one of the problems of historicism: the degree to which earlier periods (and other cultures) can be known and the degree to which the fusion of horizons privileges present beliefs and attitudes. The fact of this fusion is, for Gadamer, the source of the interest of a later period in a text. Since such interests dependent on later historical situations are the source of "significance" for Hirsch, Hirsch's argument for the determinacy of intended meaning and Gadamer's for the historical relativity of meaning represent two major contemporary hermeneutical directions. Gadamer's identification of understanding as the fusion of original with present meanings also undercuts much of the traditional difference between understanding and explication. Thus Gadamer writes that German romanticism "has taught us that understanding and interpretation are ultimately the same thing" (350).

Paul Ricoeur's hermeneutics is grounded more in allegorical than philosophical hermeneutics. Thus, "[i]nterpretation . . . is the work of thought which consists in deciphering the hidden levels of meaning in the apparent meaning, in unfolding the levels of meaning implied in the literal meaning" (*Conflict of Interpretations*, 13). However, like other philosophical hermeneuts, Ricoeur pursues interpretation well beyond the text, into the unconscious with Freud and into cultural structures with Nietzsche and Marx. These three for Ricoeur were masters of the "suspicious" hermeneutics that looks always for meanings hidden beneath the surface. Moreover, where the Schleiermachian tradition sought to recover the consciously intended meaning of texts, Ricoeur recognizes unconscious meanings across human experience.

A personal definition of hermeneutics that wholly undercuts the sense of understanding as finding the meaning of texts or discourses is that of Richard Rorty as set forth in *Philosophy and the Mirror of Nature*. For Rorty, "[t]he dominating notion of epistemology is that to be rational, to be fully human, to do what we ought, we need to be able to find agreement with other human beings" (316), or again, "[h]ermeneutics is not 'another way of knowing'— 'understanding' as opposed to (predictive) 'explanation' " (356). . . . Rather it is a form of edification through which we find "new, better, more interesting, more fruitful ways of speaking" (360). Rorty's use of "hermeneutics" is strongly questioned by Rüdiger Bubner in "Hermeneutics: Understanding or Edification?" "Edifying philosophy forgets the task of clarifying the concrete issues that are crucial to everyone's understanding and left unilluminated by those who mix philosophy with empty rhetoric or the vagueness of quasipoetical language" (38). In any case, Rorty, like at least the early Heidegger, cancels the possibility of a metaphysics while celebrating hermeneutics, or, from the point of view of hostile critics, puts hermeneutics in the place of metaphysics.

5. The opposition between the methods and goals of the physical sciences and those of the human sciences, between explanation of physical laws and the understanding of human experience as formulated by Dilthey, has produced a continuing debate between those with the programmatic goal of one unified science and those who, like Gadamer, insist on separation. This debate has largely taken the form of argument about the relation between the social/behavioral and the physical sciences and thus does not substantively address the interpretation of literary texts. However, the latter twentieth-century movement to redefine the humanities and the social sciences under the rubric "human sciences" has necessarily implied a relevance for literary study.

Gadamer's belief that both the traditions of the past and the "prejudices" of the moment to which they have led profitably interact to produce understanding has led to another confrontation. Jürgen Habermas, speaking from a position founded in the Neo-Marxian Frankfurt School, has challenged Gadamer for being satisfied with understanding rather than proceeding to a critique of the ideologies revealed. (See CRITICISM.) Moreover the product of hermeneutical inquiry is necessarily biased. "Hermeneutical understanding cannot enter into a question without prejudice; on the contrary it is unavoidably biased by the context in which the understanding subject has first acquired his schemata of interpretation" (quoted in Mueller-Vollmer, *The Hermeneutics Reader*, 295–96). The belief that hermeneutics should go beyond interpretation to the practical activity of restructuring society, found not only in Habermas but in writers representing various forms of Marxism, can be distinguished as a "cultural" hermeneutics. It can also be regarded as the addition of "application" to the pair "understanding" and "explication."

Karl-Otto Apel and Paul Ricoeur both attempt to resolve the apparent opposition between understanding and explanation as well as that between Gadamerian hermeneutics and the call for criticism in the Frankfurt School sense by making the apparently conflicting positions complementary. The main thrust of Apel's argument is against the "scientistic" belief that the methods and basic assumptions of science are not subjective; Ricoeur focuses on "the matter of the text" as belonging to neither author nor reader and on the productive "tension between proximity and distance" (*Hermeneutics and the Human Sciences*, 61–62).

It is perhaps worth noting that, as Apel implies, such a role for hermeneutics returns in its own way to what Schleiermacher originally meant by saying that the task of hermeneutics is "[t]o understand the text at first as well as and then even better than its author" (112), that is, "to consider the content as what moved the author and the form as his nature moved by that content" (148) or, in other words, as the effect of the total historical context on the author as well as his individual treatment of the elements of that context to which he/she responded. Apel's words are, "all understanding, to the extent that it does succeed, has to understand an author better than he understands himself, in that it reflectively surpasses the author in his world- and self-understanding (in Hegel's sense) and does not merely reconstruct his spiritual experiences by reexperiencing them in his imagination" ("Scientistics," 338). To understand the text as well as the author would seem to mean to understand *what* the text was intended to say; to understand it better than the author would seem to be to understand *why* those intentions developed and *how* they reflect the historical situation as understood from a present perspective. The "how" and "why" now appear to be the major preoccupation of what is usually thought of as hermeneutical theory, though certain theorists like Kurt Mueller-Vollmer are calling for a return to hermeneutics as a method of interpreting texts, rather than a philosophical or socially programmatic endeavor (see Mueller-Vollmer's "Understanding and Interpretation: Toward a Definition of Literary Hermeneutics").

In *Hermeneutics as Politics* Stanley Rosen argues that the whole direction pursued by philosophical hermeneutics is political in nature and that thinkers like Apel cannot avoid the political consequences of the reduction of all theory to interpretation. Rorty's vision of the clarifying power of edifying dialogue in place of battles over objective truth offers no comfort to Rosen. "Edifying hermeneutics is the exoteric doctrine of the will to power, an instrument of the cunning of reason, a stage in the dialectical self-destruction of bourgeois civilization'' (193).

References

Apel, Karl-Otto. "Scientistics, Hermeneutics, Critique of Ideology: An Outline of a Theory of Science from an Epistemological-Anthropological Point of View." Trans. L. G. DeMichiel. In *The Hermeneutics Reader*.
———. *Understanding and Explanation: A Transcendental-Pragmatic Perspective*. Trans. G. Warnke. Cambridge, Mass.: MIT Press, 1984.
Augustine. *On Christian Doctrine*. Trans. D. W. Robertson, Jr. Indianapolis: Bobbs-Merrill, Library of the Liberal Arts, 1958.
Boeckh, August. *On Interpretation and Criticism*. Trans. J. P. Pritchard. Norman: University of Oklahoma Press, 1968. Portions are reprinted in *The Hermeneutics Reader*.
Bruns, Gerald. "The Problem of Figuration in Antiquity." In *Hermeneutics: Questions and Prospects*, ed. Gary Shapiro and Alan Sica. Amherst: University of Massachusetts Press, 1984. A lucid account.
Bubner, Rüdiger. "Hermeneutics: Understanding or Edification?" In *Phenomenology and the Social Sciences*, ed. H. N. Mohanty. Supplement to *Philosophical Topics* 12 (1981).
Burke, Kenneth. *Counter-Statement* (1931). Chicago: University of Chicago Press, 1957.
———. *The Philosophy of Literary Form*. Baton Rouge: Louisiana State University Press, 1941.
Chladenius, Johann Martin. *Einleitung zur richtigen Auslegung vernünftiger Reden und Schriften*. Leipzig, 1742. A translation of a portion of Chladenius by Carrie Asman-Schneider appears in *The Hermeneutics Reader*.
Dreyfus, Hubert. "Beyond Hermeneutics: Interpretation in Late Heidegger and Recent Foucault." In *Hermeneutics: Questions and Prospects*, ed. Gary Shapiro and Alan Sica. Amherst: University of Massachusetts Press, 1984. A helpful discussion of Heidegger for the uninitiated. Dreyfus's essay should, however, be considered together with Richard E. Palmer's comments on it in the same volume ("On the Transcendability of Hermeneutics").
Gadamer, Hans-Georg. *Truth and Method* (1960). Trans. and ed. G. Barden and J. Cumming. New York: Seabury Press, 1975.
Habermas, Jürgen. "On Hermeneutics' Claim to Universality." Trans. Jerry Dibble. In *The Hermeneutics Reader*. English translation of the essay in *Hermeneutik und Ideologiekritik: Theorie-Diskussion*. Frankfurt: Suhrkamp Verlag, 1971.
Heidegger, Martin. *Being and Time*. Trans. J. Macquarrie and E. Robinson. New York: Harper and Row, 1962. Helpfully indicates the pagination of the later German editions.
The Hermeneutics Reader: Texts of the German Tradition from the Enlightenment to the Present. Ed. Kurt Mueller-Vollmer. New York: Continuum, 1985. The introduction is a useful summary of the German hermeneutic tradition; most of the selections are central to an understanding of this tradition. Includes informative headnotes and bibliography.
Hirsch, E. D. *Validity in Interpretation*. New Haven, Conn.: Yale University Press, 1967.

Includes Hirsch's original 1960 formulation of his position and an appendix on his differences with Gadamer.

Kresic, Stephanus. *Contemporary Literary Hermeneutics and Interpretation of Classical Texts*. Ottawa: Ottawa University Press, 1981.

Mueller-Vollmer, Kurt. "Understanding and Interpretation: Toward a Definition of Literary Hermeneutics." In *Literary Criticism and Philosophy*, ed. Joseph Strelka. University Park: Pennsylvania State University Press, 1983.

Nietzsche, Friedrich. *The Will to Power*. Vols. 14 and 15 of *The Complete Works of Friedrich Nietzsche*. Edited by O. Levy. 18 vols. 1909–11; New York: Russell and Russell, 1964.

Palmer, Richard. "Allegorical, Philological, and Philosophical Hermeneutics: Three Modes in a Complex Heritage." In *Contemporary Literary Hermeneutics and Interpretation of Classical Texts*, ed. S. Kresic. An incisive survey.

Philo Judaeus. *That the Worse Is Wont to Attack the Better*. In vol. 2 of *Philo*. Trans. F. H. Colson and G. H. Whitaker. Loeb Classical Library. London: Heinemann, 1929.

Ricoeur, Paul. *The Conflict of Interpretations: Essays in Hermeneutics*. Ed. Don Ihde. Evanston, Ill.: Northwestern University Press, 1974.

————. *Hermeneutics and the Human Sciences*. Ed. and trans. J. B. Thompson. Cambridge: Cambridge University Press, 1981.

Rorty, Richard. *Philosophy and the Mirror of Nature*. Princeton, N.J.: Princeton University Press, 1979.

Rosen, Stanley. *Hermeneutics as Politics*. New York: Oxford University Press, 1987.

Schleiermacher, Friedrich. *Hermeneutics: The Handwritten Manuscripts by F. D. Schleiermacher*. Ed. Heinz Kimmerle, trans. J. Duke and J. Forstman. Missoula, Mont.: Scholars Press, 1977. A portion of these notes for Schleiermacher's lectures has been reprinted in *The Hermeneutics Reader*. Another translation from Kimmerle's German transcription by Jan Wojcik and Roland Haas appeared in *New Literary History* 10 (1978): 1–15.

Sources of Additional Information

Richard Palmer's *Hermeneutics: Interpretation Theory in Schleiermacher, Dilthey, Heidegger, and Gadamer* (Evanston, Ill.: Northwestern University Press, 1969) presents major philosophical issues that have arisen in the major line of hermeneutic theorists from a Gadamerian point of view.

Wilhelm Dilthey's "The Rise of Hermeneutics," trans. Frederic Jameson (*New Literary History* 3, 1972: 229–44) offers the history of hermeneutics to his own time from Dilthey's point of view. *Wilhelm Dilthey: Selected Writings*, ed. H. P. Rickman (Cambridge: Cambridge University Press, 1976) is an especially useful collection since passages of relevance to hermeneutic issues are scattered through many of the eighteen volumes of Dilthey's *Gesammelte Schriften* (Göttingen-Stuttgart: Vanderhoeck and Ruprecht, 1914–17).

Both Peter Szondi's essays on hermenutics in *On Textual Understanding*, trans. H. Mendelsohn (Manchester: Manchester University Press, 1986) and Kurt Mueller-Vollmer's "Understanding and Interpretation: Toward a Definition of Literary Hermeneutics" in *Literary Criticism and Philosophy* (see References above) argue against the overly psychological approach of Dilthey, and the latter critiques the conflation of understanding and explanation (or explication) in Gadamer as well. Both, in effect, return to Schleiermacher as the proper foundation for a hermeneutics focused on textual understanding rather than larger philosophical issues.

David Linge's introduction to his translation of Gadamer's *Philosophical Hermeneutics* (Berkeley: University of California Press, 1976) gives a useful overview of Gadamer's mode of thought in which hermeneutical understanding is mediation, not reconstruction. Georgia Warnke's *Gadamer: Hermeneutics, Tradition and Reason* sympathetically presents Gadamer's thought in relation to that of other hermeneutical writers, especially Hirsch and Rorty.

The question of the relationship between explanation in the physical sciences and understanding in the human sciences is explored in Joseph Bleicher's *Contemporary Hermeneutics: Hermeneutics as Method, Philosophy, and Critique* (London: Routledge and Kegan Paul, 1980) and Stephan Strasser's *Understanding and Explanation* (Pittsburgh, Pa.: Duquesne University Press, 1985). The debate between Gadamer and Habermas is analyzed by Rüdiger Bubner in "Theory and Practice in the Light of the Hermeneutic-Criticism Controversy" (*Cultural Criticism* 2, 1974: 337–52). Roy J. Howard's *The Three Faces of Hermeneutics* (Berkeley: University of California Press, 1982) is an incisive survey of three "avenues" of hermeneutic thought as presented primarily through the works of Wittgenstein, Habermas, and Gadamer.

A very clear, and strongly supportive, outline of the philosophic hermeneutics of Heidegger, Gadamer, and Rorty is to be found in Brice Wachterhauser's introductory essay in *Hermeneutics and Modern Philosophy*, ed. Brice Wachterhauser (Albany: State University of New York Press, 1986). He especially emphasizes the importance of historicity and linguisticality. Historicity involves the claim "that the very meaning and validity of any knowledge-claim is inextricably intertwined with the historical situation of both its formulators and evaluators" (7); and "in transcending the limitations of any one mode of speaking and seeing, we never transcend the fundamental linguisticality (*Sprachlichkeit*) of our understanding" (10). An approach that tries to go beyond both Heidegger and Derrida, making the understanding of the world more difficult than either, is found in John Caputo's *Radical Hermeneutics* (Bloomington: Indiana University Press, 1987). "Radical hermeneutics situates itself in the space which is opened up by the exchange between Heidegger and Derrida, an exchange which generates another and more radical reading of Heidegger and another, more hermeneutic reading of Derrida" (5).

Hans Robert Jauss suggests an interesting reversal of the philological tendency to approach a text first from its historical context; for Jauss, the historically reconstructive reading becomes the third step, necessarily preceded by an aesthetic response generated in the process of reading and a retrospective exegesis of the whole ("Literature and Hermeneutics," *What Is Criticism?* ed. Paul Hernadi, Bloomington: Indiana University Press, 1981).

HISTORICAL SCHOLARSHIP   In the broad field of literary studies, the pursuit and knowledge of the linguistic, historical, and biographical information necessary for the interpretation of a text as it is likely to have been understood in its own time.

Historical scholarship is not a term likely to receive definition in a dictionary of literary terms, but it covers a wide range of scholarly activities that have historically been the center of literary studies. The phrase became common in the years during which the American New Critics and certain English congeners were seeking to make a clear distinction between CRITICISM as the analysis (and sometimes evaluation) of the individual text and studies of the historical context in which a work was produced and/or the biography of the AUTHOR who produced it. The need for such a term and its scope becomes clearer when viewed against the changing uses of the sometimes competing terms LITERARY HISTORY, HISTORICISM, and philology.

"Literary history," which is an ambiguous term in several ways, suggests, and is used to designate, studies of changes in literature over time more often than the investigation of the individual historical contexts of a text or group of texts. Philology, an older, broad sense of which corresponds with historical scholarship as defined above, developed a narrow meaning in the nineteenth century, when it came to be identified, particularly in England, with the study of language per se, either the history of the development of one or more languages or, as comparative philology, the study of the relations between languages and the development of distinct languages from a common root language. The *locus classicus* for the most extended sense in which philology is identified with all seven of the liberal arts is Martianus Capella's *De nuptiis Philologiae et Mercurii* (On the Marriage of Philology and Mercury), written in the fifth century A.D. Examples in the *OED* adequately document the continued use of philology with this large scope. Cited from Thomas Fuller's *Worthies of England* (1662) is, "Philology properly is terse and polite learning, *melior literatura. . . .* But we take it in the larger notion, as inclusive of all human liberal studies." The 1776 citation from George Campbell's *Philosophy of Rhetoric* reads: "All the branches of philology, such as history, civil, ecclesiastic, and literary: grammar, languages, jurisprudence, and criticism." Campbell's use is especially interesting since it is evidently derived from Francis Bacon's treatment of "literary history," which corresponds to "the general state of learning" (6:183). James Harris's *Philological Inquiries in Three Parts* states in the beginning, "Philology should hence appear to be of a most *comprehensive* character, and to include not only all Accounts of *Criticism* and *Critics*, but of everything connected with *Letters*, be it *Speculative* or *Historical*" (3). However, by the time of Johnson's *Dictionary* (1755), the meaning is already beginning to contract. Under "Philological" one finds a quotation from Watts: "Studies, called *philological*, are history, language, grammar, rhetoric, poetry, and criticism," but "Philology" yields simply "Criticism; grammatical learning."

As a result of the growth of an intense interest in the origin and development of language during the nineteenth century, which received its major impetus from Herder's *On the Origin of Language* (1772), philology became more and more identified with the technical study of language, that is, what is now most commonly referred to as linguistics. It is especially significant that the Dewey Decimal System of library classification, first published in 1876, totally separated philology, the subdivisions of which (in the 400 range) are all linguistic, from literature (which was assigned the 800s). In 1879 John Peile defined philology in his "primer" to the subject as "the science which teaches us what language is. The philologist deals with the words which make up a language, not merely to learn their meaning, but to find their history.'' The real subject of philological study, said Peile, is the ''unceasing change and development of language'' (5).

That philology, which had been especially closely identified with knowledge of the culture and literature of Greece and Rome as well as Greek and Latin, was regarded by the 1880s as comprising no more than the study of language is evidenced by the fact that those who sought to add the formal study of literature in modern languages (including, of course, English) at Oxford saw themselves as fighting against not only the classicists but the philologists. On the one hand, Henry Nettleship urged ''that philology is a necessary adjunct to the academical study of literature, that the academical study of literature, without philology, is a phantom which will vanish at the dawn of day'' (15). On the other hand, Thomas Case, the Wayneflete Professor of Moral Philosophy, feared the new interest in the ancestors of modern English: ''An English School will grow up, nourishing our language not from the humanity of the Greeks and Romans, but from the savagery of the Goths and Anglo-Saxons. We are about to reverse the Renaissance'' (101).

However, the broader sense of philology has never been wholly lost, and as *OED* citations again testify, protests against the narrower sense have been continual. The eleventh edition of the *Encyclopaedia Britannica* (1910) distinguishes between a literary and a linguistic philology, though the great preponderance of the articles addresses the latter. Norman Foerster's ''The Study of Letters'' (1941) refers to a linguistic and a literary philology, placing them both under the rubric of ''literary scholarship.'' As a more recent example, Tzvetan Todorov, after identifying philology with *literary exegesis*, divides the latter into ''two wings, the one linguistic and the other historical.'' In regard to the historical branch, he continues, ''a discourse acquires its meaning only within a particular context, and it is incontestable that a better knowledge of this context is pertinent to the comprehension of the discourse'' (xxix–xxx). Foerster's literary philology and Todorov's historical exegesis are pretty much what R. S. Crane defined as the role of the philologist in ''Principles of Literary History,'' written in 1950 and published in 1967. The ''way of the philologist,'' writes Crane, ''consists in the literal exegesis and comparison of texts in terms of the material traits of their content and form in a context of the circumstances of their composition; its essential instruments are textual and historical criticism, grammar (including prosody), the grammatical parts of logic, and bibliography in the traditional sense'' (''Principles,'' 2:47). Whether termed ''literary philology'' or ''historical scholarship,'' the purpose of the endeavor is to establish the CONTEXT in which texts were written as a means of determining as fully as possible their meaning at the time (meaning is here used in the Hirschean sense of ''the author's intended verbal meaning''; for further discussion of this point, see MEANING).

The importance of the original context was the central issue in the debates over the relative values of criticism (understood as analysis of the meaning conveyed by the structure of the text in itself) and historical scholarship (or "literary history" used in this sense) in the 1930s and 1940s. The best-known and most influential statement of the new emphasis on criticism is R. S. Crane's "History versus Criticism in the Study of Literature": "However vigorously on occasion we may have professed our allegiance to criticism, it has not been criticism but history to which we have devoted our really serious energy and thought" (2:20). Thus, "it is our fault that of the seniors who have had the advantage of majoring in our departments . . . [a majority] show themselves, when put to the test . . . incapable of intelligently discussing an imaginative work in terms appropriate to its nature" (2:21). The remedy Crane proposes is systematic work in the theory of the arts and especially literature and "exercises in the reading and literary *explication* of literary texts" (2:22, 23).

Crane's position was echoed in particular by members of the New Critical movement. Crane's argument, as paraphrased by John Crowe Ransom, is "that historical scholarship has been overplayed heavily in English studies, in disregard of the law of diminishing returns, and that the emphasis must now be shifted to the critical." For Ransom this means that "the students of the future must be permitted to study literature, now merely about literature" (330). One more example may be taken from Cleanth Brooks's "Literary History vs. Criticism" of 1940:

> The average English professor . . . has been trained (if he comes from one of our better universities) in linguistics and the history of literature. He possesses a great deal of information, valuable and interesting in its own right, and of incalculable value for the critic. But he himself is not that critic. He has little or no knowledge of the inner structure of a poem or drama (this is not to say that he does not know the past critical generalizations on it!); he is ignorant of its architecture; in short, he often does not know how to *read*. (405)

On the other hand, none of the replies to the call for more criticism as opposed to historical scholarship was more resounding than Crane's own partial palinode of 1957, "Criticism as Inquiry; or, The Perils of the 'High Priori Road.' " "I was one of those who, in the middle thirties, were urging strongly that criticism be given a better show in our university departments of literature. Since then, observing the course which the dominant academic criticism has taken, I have been tempted very often to think that, if this is what criticism has to be, we might be better off with less of it" (2:44). The fault, writes Crane, is in the "dialectical fallacy," "the tacit assumption that what is true in your theory as a dialectical consequence must also be, or tend to be, true in actuality" (2:40).

In England, the most illuminating controversy over what is essentially the same issue occurred when F. W. Bateson's article on the importance of the "literary context" roused F. R. Leavis to reply. "The discipline of contextual reading, as defined and illustrated in the preceding paragraphs," wrote Bateson, "should result in the reconstruction of a human situation that is demonstrably implicit in the particular work under discussion" (19). Leavis replied, "I do indeed . . . think that the study of literature should be associated with extra-literary studies. But to make literary criticism *dependent* on the extra-literary studies . . .

in the way Mr. Bateson proposes is to stultify the former and deprive the latter of the special profit they might have for the literary student'' (174). (For further consideration of the issue, see CONTEXT.)

Essentially the same issue still exercises scholars, critics, and theorists, though it is formulated somewhat differently. Rather than whether or to what degree the reconstruction of historical context is useful or necessary to the interpretation and/or evaluation of a literary work, the question has shifted to the relative importance of the meaning of a text at the time of its writing and its meaning to later generations of readers. Those who reject the possibility of any determinate meaning question the possibility of reconstructing an intended meaning. E. D. Hirsch argues against confusing the interpretation of intended meaning with the assignment of significances of interest to the critic. It should be noted that one can assign to a text a significance other than its meaning (in the senses Hirsch gives to these terms) within its own historical context as well as in the present context. Hans Robert Jauss argues for the validity of the meanings of a text both in its original context and through the history of its reception to the present, to include the meanings generated by that history itself. Robert Weimann, employing a different terminology, is concerned with the dialectic between past significance and present meaning.

Each of these positions has further ramifications; some of these are discussed under MEANING, HISTORICISM, and DECONSTRUCTION.

References

Bacon, Francis. *Advancement of Learning* (1605). Vol. 6 of *The Works of Francis Bacon*. Ed. J. Spedding, R. L. Ellis, and D. D. Heath. Boston: Taggard and Thompson, 1863.

Bateson, F. W. ''The Function of Criticism at the Present Time.'' *Essays in Criticism* 3 (January 1953): 1–27.

Brooks, Cleanth. ''Literary History vs. Criticism.'' *Kenyon Review* 2 (Fall 1940): 403–12.

Case, Thomas. *An Appeal to the University of Oxford Against the Proposed School of Modern Languages*. Cited in David J. Palmer, *The Rise of English Studies*. London: Oxford University Press, 1965, 101.

Crane, R. S. ''Criticism as Inquiry; or, The Perils of the 'High Priori Road.' '' In *The Idea of the Humanities*, vol. 2. Chicago: University of Chicago Press, 1967.

———. ''History versus Criticism in the Study of Literature.'' In vol. 2 of *The Idea of the Humanities*. Reprinted from *English Journal* (College Edition) 24 (1935).

———. ''Principles of Literary History.'' In vol. 2 of *The Idea of the Humanities*.

Foerster, Norman. ''The Study of Letters.'' In *Literary Scholarship: Its Aims and Methods*. Chapel Hill: University of North Carolina Press, 1941.

Harris, James. *Philological Inquiries in Three Parts*. London: C. Nourse, 1781.

Hirsch, E. D., Jr. *Validity in Interpretation*. New Haven, Conn.: Yale University Press, 1967.

Jauss, Hans Robert. ''Literary History as a Challenge to Literary Theory.'' *New Literary History* 2 (Autumn 1970): 7–37.

Leavis, F. R. "The Responsible Critic; Or, The Function of Criticism at Any Time."
    Scrutiny 19 (Spring 1953): 162–83.
Nettleship, Henry. *The Study of Modern European Languages and Literature.* Oxford:
    Parker, 1887.
Peile, John. *Philology.* New York: Appleton, 1879.
Ransom, John Crowe. "Criticism, Inc." In *The World's Body* (1938). Port Washington,
    N. Y.: Kennikat Press, 1964.
Todorov, Tzvetan. *Introduction to Poetics.* Trans. R. Howard. Minneapolis: University
    of Minnesota Press, 1981.
Weimann, Robert. *Structure and Society in Literary History.* Charlottesville: University
    Press of Virginia, 1976.

Sources of Additional Information

In his *Encyclopaedie und Methodologie der philologischen Wissenschaften* (Berlin,
1877), August Boeckh argues against the separation of philology and history. "Repeated
examination of the true nature of philological activity, with all arbitrary and empirical
barriers removed and viewed in its highest universality, makes clear that philology (or
what is the same thing, history) is *the knowledge of what is known*" (see the translation
of the first section of the *Encyclopaedia* [from the 1886 edition] by J. P. Pritchard entitled
On Interpretation and Criticism, Norman: University of Oklahoma Press, 1968, p. 8).

For the story of the struggle to establish literature in the vernacular as a "School" at
Oxford and "Tripos" at Cambridge, see Stephen Potter's *The Muse in Chains* (London:
J. Cape, 1937) and David Palmer's *The Rise of English Studies* (London: Oxford Uni-
versity Press, 1965). For the long struggle between historical scholarship, philology in
the narrow sense, and criticism in the United States, see the first twelve chapters of
Gerald Graff's *Professing Literature: An Institutional History* (Chicago: University of
Chicago Press, 1987).

Sidney Lee's 1913 "The Place of English Literature in the Modern University," in
Elizabethan and Other Essays, ed. F. S. Boas (Oxford: Clarendon Press, 1929), interestingly documents the common view of the divisions of the study of English literature
early in the century: criticism, history, philology, and "composition or practical experiment in the art of expression on the part of the student" (5). Of the contemporary
understanding of philology: "The main theme of English study is English literature. . . .
Literature is the mistress of the household, language the chief handmaiden. . . . Verbal
structure is secondary to mental substance" (3).

For the influence of Romantic Philology in England, see Linda Dowling's *Language
and Decadence in the Victorian Fin de Siècle* (Princeton, N.J.: Princeton University
Press, 1986).

HISTORICISM   1. The belief that the meaning and value of anything resides
in its history and that the history can be reconstructed. 2. The belief that all
human formulations of truth or value, and all human institutions, are to be
understood relative to their historical context; this belief and attempts to apply
it are often called German Historicism (in this sense sometimes called *historism*). 3. Emphasis on the constant alterations in beliefs, attitudes, and
institutions through recorded history and the resulting relativism of all judgments. 4. The belief that the study of history will reveal laws or cycles that

explain the course of human or social development and make it possible to predict the direction of future development. 5. As New Historicism, an emphasis on (a) the diversity of social currents in any given period, (b) the inescapable coloring of any understanding of the past by the modes of thought of the present in which the historian is operating (as in sense 3), and (c) the understanding of society as essentially political, that is, as a structure of power seeking to contain challenges to power.

1. The term historicism has been employed with various, sometimes opposed, senses in history, philosophy, theology, economics, and literature. Several uses not relevant to literature have been omitted here (succinct summaries of the manifold definitions that have been assigned will be found in Harry Ritter's *Dictionary of Concepts in History*, the essay ''The Meaning of Historicism'' by Dwight Lee and Robert Beck, and *The Encyclopedia of Philosophy*). The last work sums up what has been proposed as the general meaning, subsuming most of the senses in which the term has been employed, as ''the belief that an adequate understanding of the nature of anything and an adequate understanding of its value are to be gained by considering it in terms of the place it occupied and the role it played within a process of development'' (4:24). It should, nevertheless, be borne in mind that the degree to which a text must be understood in terms of the original historical milieu and the degree to which it should be evaluated in terms of that context are separable questions.

Most applications to phenomena in the field of literature, however, have carried one of the more specific senses that follow.

2. *Historismus*, sometimes translated as ''historism,'' but most often as ''historicism,'' is the name retrospectively given by the twentieth-century historian Friedrich Meinecke to a doctrine of individuality associated with Goethe, Herder, Schleiermacher, and the historian Leopold von Ranke that denied the possibility of universal laws to history. As developed in the twentieth century, this historicism accepts from Vico the general concept of distinct ages—necessary for historical periodization—together with the sense that a pattern underlies the major currents of thought in each age. Erich Auerbach, who spoke for the main current of historicism between the two world wars, wrote, ''If we assume with Vico that every age has its characteristic unity, every text must provide a partial view on the basis of which a synthesis is possible'' (*Literary Language*, 19). Further:

> For [Vico] the world of the nations . . . embraces not only political history but also the history of thought, of expression (language, literature, the fine arts), religion, law, and economics. Because all these follow from the cultural state of human society in a given period and consequently must be understood in relation to one another or cannot be understood at all, an insight into one of these facets of human creativity at a given stage of development must provide a key to all the others at the same stage. (*Literary Language*, 8)

The original thrust of historicism in this sense was as much against the imposition of any uniform aesthetic as an assertion of the possibility of understanding the uniqueness of each period. Thus Auerbach, like Herder, saw historicism as "the conviction that every civilization and every period has its own possibilities of aesthetic perfection; that the works of art of the different peoples and periods, as well as their general forms of life, must be understood as products of variable individual conditions, and have to be judged each by its own development, not by absolute rules of beauty and ugliness" ("Vico," 184).

The endeavor of literary scholars to understand the beliefs and attitudes and reconstruct the general frame of reference of authors and readers of an earlier period and different nationality, language, or cultural history has frequently been called "historicist" in a looser sense. Thus W. K. Wimsatt, speaking for the New Criticism of the middle decades of this century, refers to previous Anglo-American criticism as "historicist" ("Battering," 186).

3. Emphasis on the uniqueness of each historical period may lead not to the formulation of methods of recovering an earlier mode of thought but rather to questioning the very possibility of doing so and thus to various degrees of relativism. In E. D. Hirsch's words, "The earlier emphasis on individuality which had given significance to the study of other cultures in their own right became, by one or two turns of the Hegelian gyre, an emphasis on the impossibility of studying other cultures in their own right" (41). Strongly skeptical relativism is sometimes distinguished as radical historicism. Three issues emerge in the debate between historicism in sense 2 and radical historicism. The first is the degree to which there is a human mental constitution sufficiently common through the centuries to allow the reconstruction of the thought and attitudes, or worldviews, of other times and cultures. The belief that there is such a common mental structure is sometimes seen as a defining characteristic of a HUMANISM, which is especially associated with historicism; this is frequently now called *essentialism*. An especially straightforward statement of essentialism is to be found in George Saintsbury's reply to objections to "judging ancient literature from modern points of view." The true critic, for Saintsbury, "endeavours—a hard and ambitious task!—to extract from *all* literature, ancient, medieval, and modern, lessons of its universal qualities, which may enable him to see each period *sub specie aeternitatis*" (1:8).

The second issue is the related question whether or in what degree it is possible to overcome the historical position of the later interpreter, scholar, or reader. To the degree that this is not possible, reconstructions of the thought of an earlier period will be different in every successive period. Relativism can be more optimistic: Erich Auerbach wrote, "For historical relativism is relative in two respects: of the material and of those who are striving to understand it. It is a radical relativism, but that is no reason to fear it. The area in which we move in this effort at understanding is the world of men, to which we ourselves belong" (*Literary Language*, 12). Or again, R. G. Collingwood:

> [I]n history, as in all serious matters, no final achievement is possible. [Nevertheless,] [t]his is not an argument for historical skepticism. It is only the discovery of a second dimension of historical thought, the history of history: the discovery that the historian

himself, together with the here-and-now which forms the total body of evidence available to him, is a part of the process he is studying, has his own place in that process, and can see it only from the point of view which at this present moment he occupies within it. (248)

René Wellek and Austin Warren's *Theory of Literature* (1942) similarly argues for a ground between "false relativism and false absolutism," which they term "perspectivism" (43).

Finally, there is contention over the importance of understanding events and productions of the earlier period as those would have been understood at the time (assuming that such understanding is to some extent possible). The attempt to understand the past in its own terms is sometimes pejoratively referred to as antiquarianism.

The principles involved in debates over the degree to which historicism as a program proves impossible because its assumptions necessarily imply a historical relativism or is irrelevant to humanity's real interests evidently extend far beyond the field of literature. However, the issues have been, and continue to be, central to literary theory. Some degree of HISTORICAL SCHOLARSHIP (or philology in its broadest sense) has always been assumed to be requisite for literary understanding. Even the insistence of the Anglo-American New Critics that the proper object of literary study is the literary work itself assumed a knowledge of the meaning of words as used at the time of writing. At the same time, even for those who are most confident of the possibility of an adequate reconstruction of historical context, this effort has almost always been regarded as propaedeutic to an aesthetic appreciation. In the words of George Edward Woodberry in 1913, "The end given being to realize the state of a man at a past moment—it may be in China or Peru—the office of historical criticism seems an indispensable preliminary" and "I am not disposed to relinquish historical criticism; nay, rather I must cling to it as my only hope of qualifying myself to undertake that purely aesthetic criticism by which I may at last become one with the soul of the artist and see his vision with the meaning and atmosphere it had to himself" (53, 55). Northrop Frye answers the question in a substantially similar manner: texts, like other cultural artifacts, are to be read in two ways: "From a purely historical point of view . . . cultural phenomena are to be read in their own context without contemporary application. We study them as we do the stars." However, for Frye, such study should be counterbalanced by "ethical criticism," which "deals with art as a communication from the past to the present" (24). These two activities again partly parallel E. D. Hirsch's distinction between *meaning* and *significance* (see MEANING). The debate in the field of literature has, in fact, largely been over the kinds and amount of historical scholarship necessary to understand a text.

The relevance of past literature to the present raises another kind of question. If a literary work is only to be understood in its own historical period, and if the mentalities of periods differ substantially, can the work be relevant if read in a way not originally intended, and should it be so read? Again, even early-twentieth-century critics with strong historical leanings like George Woodberry have recognized that readers' responses will necessarily be governed in part by their own historical situation and, indeed, will be partly personal. New Critics like W. K. Wimsatt also recognize the confluence of the past, the present, and the personal in understanding literature. "To understand the heroism of Henry or the irony of Pope and Dryden we have to draw upon historical information and linguistic glosses. But we have to draw equally upon the modern world and our own experience. We find the meaning of heroism and of irony ultimately in the objects of our own experience and in our own minds" ("History," 255).

4. Karl Popper gave the name historicism to the belief that there is a knowable human destiny and that the future development of society can be predicted. "I mean by 'historicism' an approach to the social sciences which assumes that *historical prediction* is their principal aim, and which assumes that this aim is attainable, by discovering the 'rhythms' or the 'patterns,' the 'laws' or the 'trends' that underlie the evolution of history" (3). Popper's immediate targets were fascism and Marxism, but his analysis of historicism as he defined it was directed against all attempts to impose massive changes on a society by means of any large-scale social theory. Historicism in Popper's sense is rarely found in theories of literature per se; that is, predictions about the way the literary forms or subject matter must develop in the future have generally been, at the most, short-range extrapolations from contemporary trends. However, certain varieties of MARXIST LITERARY CRITICISM predict the general direction literary creation or *production* must follow as it reflects the economic and political changes they anticipate.

5. The term New Historicism has been taken from its use by Stephen Greenblatt in the 1982 introduction to a collection of essays, *The Power of Forms in the English Renaissance*. "[M]any of the present essays give voice, I think, to what we may call the new historicism, set apart from both the dominant historical scholarship of the past and the formalist criticism that partially displaced this scholarship in the decades after World War Two" (5). Greenblatt points to three differences between the "old" historicists and the "New Historicism." First, the older historicists attempted to sum up the whole of an age as a unified set of beliefs and attitudes, while the New Historicists emphasize the tensions, and more specifically, the struggles for power within a culture at any period (E. M. W. Tillyard's *The Elizabethan World Picture* has become their standard example of the older historicism).

The second difference is the New Historicists' insistence that interpretation of the past is a function of the historical situation of the interpreter. Thus:

> The earlier historicism tends to be monological; that is, it is concerned with discovering a single political vision, usually identical to that said to be held by the entire literate class or indeed the entire population. . . . This vision, most often presumed to be internally coherent and consistent, though occasionally analyzed as the fusion of two or more elements, has the status of an historical fact. It is not thought to be the product of the historian's interpretation, nor even of the interests of a particular social group in conflict with other groups. (5)

The general perspective thus summarized depends substantially on the work of Michel Foucault. However, Greenblatt's phrase "political vision" and the reference to "interests of a given social group" point to a third characteristic, the interpretation of all tensions, all disagreements, and ultimately all action as evidence of struggles for political power. Here the influence of Foucault's understanding of history as the product of the struggle for power and the Marxist interpretation of history as class struggle join with the concern for the interpreter's frame of reference that goes back at least to Wilhelm Dilthey and to the problem of the unity of the historical period (already called into question by the history of ideas as understood by A. O. Lovejoy).

Characteristics other than those originally cited by Greenblatt have come to be associated with the New Historicism. One is the denial of *essentialism*; human culture is seen as the product of socioeconomic structures and therefore of power relationships. Thus, Jonathan Dollimore's *Radical Tragedy* challenges "the idea that 'man' possesses some given, unalterable essence which is what makes 'him' human, which is the source and *essential* determinant of 'his' culture and its priority over conditions of existence" (250). Second, since culture is a construct, literature is regarded not simply as a reflection of the culture but as an agent in bringing about changes. Third, the older historicist's view that the texts and events of a period cast light on other texts and events because of the unity of a cultural moment is shifted frequently into arguments for the parallelism between one text or event and a text or incident that seems wholly foreign but helps illustrate the power relations of the time. Focus on an event or nonliterary text is regarded by most New Historicists as an application of what the anthropologist Clifford Geertz has called "thick description." Frequently, New Historicist criticism is overtly political in its judgment and its explicit aim of bringing about social change. Thus, Walter Cohen's "Political Criticism of Shakespeare" opens with a wholly political evaluation of New Criticism: "The dominance of New Criticism depended in part on the pervasive upper class anti-communist offensive often localized as McCarthyism"; it closes with the statement, "A politically serious criticism has no option but to connect concern with the job with ongoing, larger movements for social change" (19, 39). Perhaps the most comprehensive criticism to date of the New Historical assumptions and arguments is offered by Edward Pechter in "The New Historicism and Its Discontents: Politicizing Renaissance Drama" (1987).

Considerable discussion has occurred over the degree of newness in New Historicism, of which Brook Thomas's "The New Historicism and other Old-Fashioned Topics" serves as a good example. One may, indeed, return to René Wellek's 1949 "Literary History" for the view that "Literature is not simply determined by social evolution; it is itself a center of forces, and influences the trends of society" (111) and its suggestion that scholars "look for the essence of a work of art in a system of signs and implicit norms existing as social facts in a collective ideology just as, for instance, the system of language exists" (117).

New Historicism arose in the field of Renaissance studies, but very quickly also began to be visible in the work in other literary periods. In part its appeal seems to have come from the perception among many critics and scholars that not only STRUCTURALISM but DECONSTRUCTION and the entire set of critical strategies associated with poststructuralism were just as formalist and as separated from ordinary human interests and experience as the Russian Formalist and New Critical approaches to literature. One result of the rapid growth of interest in New Historicism has been an equally rapid broadening of the meaning of the designation, followed by attempts to develop distinctions between different goals lumped under the same term. Increasingly, practitioners who have been regarded under the umbrella of New Historicism are divided into a (largely English) group called *cultural materialists* who operate under a strong Marxist imperative and a (largely American) group whose analysis of power relations is less manifestly Marxist. Stephen Greenblatt, who calls his own approach *cultural poetics* in the 1980 *Renaissance Self-Fashioning* (1980), continues to prefer that label in his 1988 *Shakespearean Negotiations*. "Cultural poetics" is there defined as "study of the collective making of distinct social practices and inquiry into the relations among the practices" (5). The New Historicist movement shows every sign of continuing to develop in divergent directions. As Hayden White has written of the New Historicists, "What they have specifically discovered . . . is that there is no such thing as a specifically historical approach to the study of history, but a variety of such approaches, at least as many as there are positions on the ideological spectrum" ("New Historicism," 302).

References

Auerbach, Erich. *Literary Language and Its Public in Late Latin Antiquity and in the Middle Ages*. New York: Pantheon, 1965. Original German edition, 1958. The introduction is especially valuable as a statement of earlier-twentieth-century historicism.
————. "Vico and Aesthetic Historicism." In *Scenes from the Drama of European Literature* (1959). Minneapolis: University of Minnesota Press, 1984. Reprinted from *Journal of Aesthetics and Art Criticism* 8 (December 1949): 110–11. Sympathetic presentation of Vico's belief that "we are capable of re-evoking human history from the depth of our own consciousness" (190).
Cohen, Walter. "Political Criticism of Shakespeare." In *Shakespeare Reproduced*, ed. J. Howard and M. O'Connor. London: Methuen, 1987. Strongly political. Includes a bibliography of political studies of Shakespeare in the 1980s.
Collingwood, R. G. *The Idea of History*. Oxford: Clarendon Press, 1946. An important statement of the relativity of historical interpretation which nevertheless does not deny historical knowledge and of the mind's capacity to reflect on its own operation. "The philosophizing mind never simply thinks about an object, it always, while thinking about any object, thinks also about its own thought about that object" (1).
Dollimore, Jonathan. *Radical Tragedy*. Brighton, U.K.: Harvester Press, 1984.
Encyclopedia of Philosophy. Ed. Paul Edwards. 8 vols. New York: Macmillan, 1967.

Foucault, Michel. *The Archaeology of Knowledge*. Trans. A. M. S. Smith. London: Tavistock, 1970.

———. *The Order of Things: An Archaeology of the Human Sciences*. London: Tavistock, 1970.

Frye, Northrop. *Anatomy of Criticism*. Princeton, N.J.: Princeton University Press, 1957.

Geertz, Clifford. *The Interpretation of Cultures*. New York: Basic Books, 1973.

Greenblatt, Stephen. *Renaissance Self-Fashioning*. Chicago: University of Chicago Press, 1980. The brief introduction is generally taken as the first promulgation of the intent of New Historicism.

———. *Shakespearean Negotiations*. Berkeley: University of California Press, 1988.

———. "Towards a Poetics of Culture." In *The New Historicism*, ed. Harold Veeser. London: Routledge, 1989.

Hirsch, E. D. *Validity in Interpretation*. New Haven, Conn.: Yale University Press, 1967. Argues a position basic to historicism in its most common, nonpejorative meaning. "It is one thing to say blankly that we can never 'truly' understand the texts of a past age; it is quite another thing to venture the less absolute and no doubt true conception that we sometimes cannot possibly acquire all the cultural givens necessary for understanding an old text" (40).

Lee, Dwight, and Robert Beck. "The Meaning of 'Historicism.' " *American Historical Review* 59 (1954): 568–77.

Meineke, Friedrich. *Historism: The Rise of a Classic Outlook* (1936). Trans. J. E. Anderson. New York: Herder and Herder, 1972.

Pechter, Edward. "The New Historicism and Its Discontents: Politicizing Renaissance Drama." *PMLA* 102 (May 1987): 292–302. After a critical evaluation of various aspects of New Historicism, Pechter concludes, "Anyone who, like me, is reluctant to accept the will to power as the defining human essence will probably have trouble with the critical procedures of the new historicists and with their interpretive conclusions" (301).

Popper, Karl. *The Poverty of Historicism*. Boston: Beacon Press, 1957. Historicism as Popper defines it always desires a vast ("holistic") transformation of society; against this "Utopian" project which, he believes, must always end in repression, Popper proposes "piecemeal social engineering" (64).

The Power of Forms in the English Renaissance. Ed. S. Greenblatt. Norman, Okla.: Pilgrim Books, 1982.

Ritter, Harry. *Dictionary of Concepts in History*. New York: Greenwood Press, 1986.

Saintsbury, George. *A History of Criticism and Literary Taste in Europe*. 3 vols. Edinburgh: William Blackwood and Sons, 1900–1904.

Thomas, Brook. "The New Historicism and Other Old-Fashioned Topics." In *The New Historicism*, ed. Harold Veeser. London: Routledge, 1989.

Wellek, René. "Literary History." In *Literary Scholarship*, ed. N. Foerster. Chapel Hill: University of North Carolina Press, 1949.

Wellek, René and Austin Warren. *Theory of Literature*. 1942; New York: Harcourt, Brace and World, 1956.

White, Hayden. "New Historicism: A Comment." In *The New Historicism*, ed. Harold Veeser. London: Routledge, 1989.

———. *Tropics of Discourse: Essays in Cultural Criticism*. Baltimore: Johns Hopkins University Press, 1978. Sees all representations of history as relative but does not find this necessarily vitiating. "The historian *shapes* his materials, if not in accordance with what Popper calls (and criticizes as) a 'framework of preconceived ideas,' then in response to the imperatives of narrative discourse in general'' (102).

Wimsatt, W. K. "Battering the Object." In *Day of the Leopards*. New Haven, Conn.: Yale University Press, 1976. Reprinted from *Contemporary Criticism*, ed. M. Bradbury and D. Palmer. London: Edward Arnold, 1970.

———. "History and Criticism." In *The Verbal Icon*. Lexington: University Press of Kentucky, 1954. Originally appeared in *PMLA* 66 (February 1951): 21–31.

Woodberry, George Edward. "Two Phases of Criticism: Historical and Esthetic." In *Criticism in America*. New York: Harcourt, Brace, 1924.

Sources of Additional Information

Georg G. Iggers's *The German Conception of History: The National Tradition of Historical Thought from Herder to the Present* (1968; Middletown, Conn.: Wesleyan University Press, 1983) is an excellent scholarly survey of the origins and vicissitudes of German Historicism with an important bibliography. One of Iggers's concerns is the degree to which historicists prepared the way for German fascism.

For a clear reflection of what is now called an essentialist view of humanity, see Norman Foerster's "Literary Scholarship and Criticism" (*English Journal*, College Edition, 25, 1936: 224–32). The critical study of literature seeks "the understanding of those timeless elements in literary art which transcend historical phenomena and which correspond to whatever is enduring in human nature" (224). The problems of dividing history into periods or blocks are examined by Claudio Guillén in "Second Thoughts on Currents and Periods" in *The Disciplines of Criticism*, ed. P. Demetz, T. Greene, and L. Nelson (New Haven, Conn.: Yale University Press, 1968).

Geoffrey Green's *Literary Criticism and the Structures of History: Erich Auerbach and Leo Spitzer* (Lincoln: University of Nebraska Press, 1982) is a useful discussion of the influence of historicism on these two figures.

For a comparison of the kind of historicism represented by Ranke and Auerbach with the principles of the history of ideas, see the first chapter of Arthur O. Lovejoy's *The Great Chain of Being* (1936; Cambridge, Mass.: Harvard University Press, 1964). Essentially, the history of ideas is interested primarily in philosophical ideas, not the systems in which these are combined in specific periods.

René Wellek and Austin Warren, in *Theory of Literature* (1949; New York: Harcourt, Brace, 1956) suggest "perspectivism" as an alternative to absolute relativism or absolute historicism in sense 2. "In practice, such clear-cut choices between the historical and the present-day point of view are scarcely feasible. . . . We must be able to refer a work of art to the values of its own time and of all the periods subsequent to its own" (43). Hans Robert Jauss's "Literary History as a Challenge to Literary Theory" (*New Literary History* 2, Autumn 1970: 7–37; reprinted as the first chapter in *Toward an Aesthetic of Reception*, trans. T. Bahti, Sussex, U.K.: Harvester, 1982) similarly attempts to mediate between a historicism that seeks to understand a work wholly in its original context and the criticism of the work in terms of its present significance—the history of a work's reception is a history of the responses elicited by each of the "horizons of expectation" that it enters.

Fredric Jameson's attack on the historicism represented by Herder, Ranke, Auerbach, and others ("Marxism and Historicism," *New Literary History* 11, Autumn 1979: 41–72) slightly antedates general awareness of the New Historicist's opposition to that earlier historicism. Jameson offers an interesting categorization of five kinds of historicism: *genetic*, *teleological*, *existential* (that described under the second definition above, as derived from Herder and Ranke), *schizophrenic* (Nietzschean denials of the possibility of understanding history), and *Marxist*.

Helpful summary essays on the New Historicism are Louis Montrose's "Renaissance Literary Studies and the Subject of History" and Jean E. Howard's "The New Historicism in Renaissance Studies," both in *English Literary Renaissance* 16 (Winter 1986: 5–12 and 13–43, respectively). The essentially political variety of New Historicism, frequently distinguished as *cultural materialism*, is presented from various points of view in *Political Shakespeare: New Essays in Cultural Materialism*, ed. Jonathan Dollimore and Alan Sinfield (Manchester, U.K.: Manchester University Press, 1985). From the Foreword: " 'Materialism' is opposed to 'idealism': it insists that culture does not (cannot) transcend the material forces and relations of production"; further, cultural materialism "registers its commitment to the transformation of a social order which exploits people on grounds of race, gender, and class" (viii).

For additional criticism of New Historicism from different points of view, see Howard Felperin's "Making it 'Neo': The New Historicism and Renaissance Literature" (*Textual Practice* 1, Winter 1987: 262–76) and Frank Lentricchia's "Foucault's Legacy–A New Historicism?" in Harold Veeser, ed., *The New Historicism* (London: Routledge, 1989).

Judith Newton's "History as Usual? Feminism and the 'New Historicism' " (*Cultural Critique* 9, Spring 1989: 87–121) argues that "feminists contributed in a crucial way to perspectives which have been largely appropriated and popularized by men" (97).

HUMANISM 1. The rediscovery and pursuit of classical learning in the Renaissance. 2. The Renaissance emphasis on human experience rather than on divine order, and on philosophical, scientific, and aesthetic rather than theological interpretations and evaluations of human experience. 3. Devotion to the study of Greek and Roman literature and philosophy and, by extension, later arts and letters. 4. The argument that truth is relative to human experience as developed by a specific philosophy of PRAGMATISM. 5. As what came to be known as the New Humanism, a moral philosophy founded on the difference between the human and the natural, especially animal, world, and emphasizing the ability of human beings to control their responses to experience. 6. Opposition to the cold reason of science with an insistence on the intuitive, emotional, and/or imaginative, especially as fostered by literary study. 7. The rejection of religious beliefs in favor of the critical exercise of human reason (secular humanism). 8. In recent decades, the name for any of several beliefs or attitudes opposed by advocates of political and social change, especially by those accepting Marxist principles (see MARXIST LITERARY CRITICISM).

Various sets of interrelations between these senses are evident. 1 and 2 look to different though related characteristics of the Renaissance period, foreshadowing a continuing difference between senses of the word relating it primarily to the study and knowledge of certain subjects (the humanities) and those relating it primarily to an attitude toward specific principles by which to interpret the world. Senses 3 and 7 are extrapolations from senses 1 and 2.

The passage most frequently cited in connection with definitions of humanism is from the second-century Latin writer Aulus Gellius; it is perhaps best to give it here, since, under diverging interpretive emphases, it is claimed as the authority for most of the senses listed.

> Those who have spoken Latin and have used the language correctly do not give to the word humanitas *the meaning which it is commonly thought to have, namely, what the Greeks call* [philanthropia], *signifying a kind of friendly spirit and good-feeling towards all men without distinction; but they gave to* humanitas *about the force of the Greek* [paideia]; *that is, what we call* eruditionem institutionemque in bonas artes, *or "education and training in the liberal arts." Those who earnestly desire and seek after these are most highly humanized. For the pursuit of that kind of knowledge, and the training given by it, have been granted to man alone of all the animals, and for that reason it is termed* humanitas, *or "humanity." (13:17)*

1. That a major part of the rebirth later named the Renaissance was knowledge of and devotion to Greek and Roman learning is a commonplace; what continues to be debated are the relative strengths of various attitudes toward life that accompanied this. Whatever is regarded as the dominant characteristic of the Renaissance is likely to be called humanism. A scholar like Oscar Kristeller places the emphasis on the pursuit of a liberal education. He writes, "I have been unable to discover in the humanist literature any common philosophical doctrine, except a belief in the value of man and the humanities and in the revival of ancient learning" (22). Kristeller points to the sense of the term *Humanismus* as "a program and ideal of classical education" and to *Humanista* as designating "the professor or teacher or student of the humanities" (9). This sense of humanism gives preponderance to the study of what Gellius calls the *bonas artes*, which essentially include the broad base of knowledge expected of the good orator. Bruce Kimball writes:

> [W]hat united the Renaissance humanists was primarily their common commitment to an educational ideal based on the classical literature of antiquity, especially the writings of Cicero and Quintilian.... [Further,] [f]or their program of education, the Renaissance humanists took the name *studia humanitatis* or *studia humaniora*, terms that Cicero and Gellius had coined and equated with *artes liberales* and that, by the fifteenth century, had come to mean the disciplines of grammar, rhetoric, poetry, and history, often combined with moral philosophy. (77–78)

2. As a corollary to the influence of Greek and Roman philosophy and literature, the intellectual leaders of the Renaissance have traditionally been seen as progressively more interested in things secular than sacred. W. J. Bouwsma sums up the Renaissance attitude as understood from the later nineteenth century until somewhere in the middle of the twentieth: "It was individualistic, anti-scholastic, and anti-Christian" with a "shift of attention from heaven to earth." However, as Bouwsma goes on to say, more recent scholarship has found greater continuity between the Renaissance and medieval periods. Douglas Bush argues as early as 1939 that the "classical humanism of the Renaissance was fundamentally medieval and fundamentally Christian" (68). Rather than stressing anti-

Christian elements, the authors of *The Emergence of Liberal Humanism* (W. H. Coates et al.) speak of opposition to a "theocentric civilization" and "the sensed conviction that religion did not provide the sole solution to the problem of organizing human life" (4). In any case, the term humanism has seemed a natural one to express the shift of intellectual focus in the Renaissance toward the human and away from the divine.

3. As a result of the importance given to the literature of Greece and Rome by the Renaissance, humanism came to have the continuing sense of devotion to classical learning, to the achievements of civilization, and eventually to literature in the vernacular as well. Humanism and the love and study of the humanities (regarded as those subjects neither scientific nor directly utilitarian) are often regarded as synonymous. E. K. Rand uses the word in this sense: "A humanist is one who has a love of things human, one whose regard is centered on the world about him and the best that man has done; one who cares more for art and letters, particularly the art and letters of Greece and Rome, than for the dry light of reason or the mystic's flight into the unknown" (102).

4. In the first decades of this century F. C. S. Schiller and William James engaged in a sustained effort to identify their particular form of PRAGMATISM with humanism. For both, pragmatism recognized that the human knowledge of reality must always be contingent and relative. There is a reality that is what it is, but human knowledge of it always depends on our human concerns, and is always incomplete. One of James's summations of pragmatism reads, "A new opinion counts as 'true' just in proportion as it gratifies the individual's desire to assimilate the novel in his experience to his beliefs in stock" (36). Of his own similar formulation of pragmatism, Schiller comments, "The method we have observed; it is empirical, teleological, and concrete. Its spirit is a bigger thing, which may fitly be denominated Humanism. . . . Humanism is really in itself the simplest of philosophic standpoints; it is merely the perception that the philosophic problem concerns human beings striving to comprehend a world of human experience by the resources of human minds" (12). Or in James's words, "Mr. Schiller . . . proposes the name of 'Humanism' for the doctrine that to an unascertainable extent our truths are man-made products" (116–17).

5. The New Humanism associated with Paul Elmer More and Irving Babbitt looks back to ethical standards formulated in antiquity, but its specific doctrines are phrased in new terms. Both insist on the development of disciplined responses to experience. In "What Is Humanism?" (1907), Babbitt refers to Gellius's comments on *humanitas* to discriminate humanism from humanitarianism, the second lacking the discipline and selectivity of the first. "[T]the word really implies doctrine and discipline, and is applicable not to men in general but only to a select few" (4). In an essay of 1913, More insisted that a duality of the human consciousness makes possible the control of impulses and responses that distinguish humans from animals. "Beside the flux of life there is also that within man which displays itself intermittently as an inhibition upon this or that impulse, preventing its prolongation in activity, and making a pause or eddy, so to speak,

in the stream. This negation of the flux we call the inner check . . . a restraint upon the flux exercised by a force contrary to it'' (247–48). The strong moral bent of the New Humanism is apparent in More's assertion that "Happiness is the feeling that accompanies the governing of our impulses by the inner check. Repentance and remorse are the feelings that accompany insufficient exercise of the inner check'' (252). More and Babbitt both believed that personal control was forwarded by the study of literature, especially classical literature, and Norman Foerster carries the identification with the study of literature and criticism in the Arnoldian sense even further. Citing Matthew Arnold's distinction between the personal, historical, and real estimates of a literary work, Foerster continues, "The real estimate is that of . . . the humanists, who seek to transcend not only the personal but also the historical estimate and to attain a judgment in terms of permanently human values'' (xii).

6. The New Humanist insistence on the radical distinction between humanity and not only the other animals but the rest of the natural world led to a heightened opposition between them and "naturism,'' as stated, for example, by Norman Foerster. "Nature, apparently blind and pitiless, indifferent to all that we value most, affords no light in our search for a *modus vivendi* in a state of society'' (160). Regarding science as the study of the natural world, Foerster and others warned against the mere weighing and measuring of science. Humanism here, then, is defined as opposition to the natural world and the science that devotes itself to its exploration.

7. By extension from sense 2, humanism has been employed in the twentieth century to designate the rejection of any theistic belief, together with a concomitant commitment to the resources of human reason. The New Humanists are among those for whom humanism includes the rejection of religious belief; this was the source of the strong opposition from T. E. Hulme and, in a milder way, from T. S. Eliot. Hulme's "Humanism and the Religious Attitude'' (1924) argued that humanism is totally inadequate because it does not recognize original sin and assumes the possibility of progress toward perfectibility. The humanist refuses "to believe any longer in the radical imperfection of either Man or Nature. This develops logically into the belief that life is the source and measure of all values, and that man is fundamentally good'' (47). Eliot objected, "In the actual Humanist position there is, as I have tried to show, on the one hand an admission that in the past Humanism has been allied with religion, and on the other hand a faith that it can in the future afford to ignore positive religion'' (430). In the concluding essay in *The Humanist Alternative* (1973), Paul Kurtz sums up humanism: "if it is anything, [it] is committed to a method of free inquiry and to the use of critical intelligence'' (182). For Kurtz this entails that "Humanism cannot in any fair sense of the word apply to one who still believes in God as the source and creator of the universe'' (177). Similarly, H. J. Blackham's *Humanism* (1976) opens, "Twenty years ago 'humanist' was not generally applied to people who held the kind of views described in this book. Now it is the commonest term used in reference to those who do not profess recognized

religious belief.'' (2) Jean-Paul Sartre found congruence between his *existential atheism* and humanism in the denial by both that either nature or God defines the human essence. ''There is no other universe except the human universe, the universe of human subjectivity. This relation of transcendence as constitutive of man (not in the sense that God is transcendent, but in the sense of self-surpassing) with subjectivity (in such a sense that man is not shut up in himself but forever present in a human universe)—it is this that we call existential humanism'' (55).

On the other hand, the same kind of alliance between humanism (as a concern for the proper evaluation of secular interests) and religious belief that Douglas Bush found in the Renaissance is claimed by twentieth-century believers like Jacques Maritain.

8. Humanism has long been an honorific term—it has been claimed by religion, atheism, existentialism, and pragmatism. However, the values associated with humanism (in one or another of its senses) have come under increasing attack in the second half of this century. Perhaps the most influential questioning originated in Martin Heidegger's ''Letter on Positivism'' (1947). Where William James valued pragmatism and humanism for dispensing with metaphysics, Heidegger, who sought to undermine the entire ground of traditional metaphysics, found what he defines as humanism still dependent on metaphysics. ''Every determination of the essence of man that already presupposes the interpretation of being without asking about the truth of Being, whether knowingly or not, is metaphysical. The result is that what is peculiar to all metaphysics, specifically with respect to the way the essence of man is determined, is that it is ''humanistic.'' Accordingly, every humanism remains metaphysical'' (202). Heidegger, however, saw humanism not as an evil or destructive force but simply as inadequate. He writes, ''the thinking in *Being and Time* is against humanism. But this opposition does not mean that such thinking aligns itself against the humane and deprecates the dignity of man. Humanism is opposed because it does not set the *humanitas* of man high enough'' (210).

''Humanism'' has since acquired strongly pejorative senses for certain political, philosophical and literary-critical schools; various senses of humanism are disvalued by various writers. Michel Foucault's ''Revolutionary Action: 'Until Now' '' (1977) identifies humanism with political oppression: ''In short, humanism is everything in Western civilization that restricts *the desire for power:* it prohibits the desire for power and excludes the possibility of power being seized'' (221–22). Regarding the twentieth-century cultural situation in general, Elizabeth Bruss commented in 1982: ''The long romance with humanism, the delight in the masterful imposition of human form on the chaos of nature, had turned sour'' (17). With Heidegger somewhere in the background, Jonathan Dollimore condemns ''essentialist humanism'' for failure to accept difference and change. ''Anti-humanism and its declared objective—the decentering of man—is probably the most controversial aspect of Marxist, structuralist and post-structuralist theory'' (249). John Fekete sees ''bourgeois humanism'' as exerting ''a profoundly repressive ideological influence,'' as supporting a cultural status quo.

In our time, when the existing social forms stand between the possibility of realizing the dreams of humanity (the hopes of the past) and the actuality of the nightmare evolving daily within those forms (the shapes of the past): the fetish of achieved form bears an affirmative relation to the ideology of perpetual domination, and it must accept responsibility in the reproduction of a counter-revolutionary society. (xxii)

References

Babbitt, Irving. "What Is Humanism?" In *Literature and the American College* (1907). Chicago: Gateway Editions, 1956. An important statement of New Humanist principles.

Blackham, Harold John. *Humanism*. 2d. rev. ed. New York: International Publications Service, 1976. An argument for basing an ethical worldview on a nontheistic humanism.

Bouwsma, William James. *The Culture of Renaissance Humanism*. Washington, D.C.: American Historical Association, 1973. A useful summation of shifts in the understanding of the Renaissance.

Bruss, Elizabeth. *Beautiful Theories*. Baltimore: Johns Hopkins University Press, 1982.

Bush, Douglas. *The Renaissance and English Humanism*. Toronto: University of Toronto Press, 1939. Insists on the continuing importance of religious belief in Renaissance humanism.

Coates, Willson Havelock, Hayden V. White, and J. Salwyn Schapiro. *The Emergence of Liberal Humanism: An Intellectual History of Western Europe*. New York: McGraw-Hill, 1966.

Dollimore, Jonathan. "Beyond Essentialist Humanism." in *Radical Tragedy*, ed. J. Dollimore, Brighton, U.K.: Harvester Press, 1984.

Eliot, T. S. "Second Thoughts About Humanism" (1932). In *Selected Essays*. New York: Harcourt, Brace, 1950. See also "The Humanism of Irving Babbitt" (1927) in this volume.

Fekete, John. *The Critical Twilight*. London: Routledge and Kegan Paul, 1977.

Foerster, Norman. *Toward Standards: A Study of the Present Critical Movement in American Letters*. New York: Farrar and Rinehart, c. 1930. A forceful presentation of New Humanist judgments.

Foucault, Michel. "Revolutionary Action: 'Until Now.' " In *Language, Counter-Memory, Practice*. Trans. D. Bouchard and S. Simon. Ithaca, N.Y.: Cornell University Press, 1977.

Gellius, Aulus. *The Attic Nights* (c. A.D. 145). Trans. J. C. Rolfe. Loeb Classical Library. London: Heinemann, 1927.

Heidegger, Martin. "Letter on Humanism" (1947). Trans. F. A. Capuzzi and J. G. Gray. In *Martin Heidegger: Basic Writings*. Ed. David Krell. New York: Harper and Row, 1977.

Hulme, T. E. "Humanism and the Religious Attitude." In *Speculations*. New York: Harcourt, Brace, 1924.

The Humanist Alternative: Some Definitions of Humanism. Ed. P. W. Kurtz. London: Pemberton Books, 1973.

James, William. "Pragmatism and Humanism." In *Pragmatism* (1907). Cambridge, Mass.: Harvard University Press, 1975.

Kimball, Bruce. *Orators and Philosophers*. New York: Teachers College Press, 1986.

A useful survey of the "Idea of a Liberal Education" from the fifth century B.C. to the present.

Kristeller, Paul Oscar. *Renaissance Thought: The Classic, Scholastic, and Humanist Strains*. New York: Harper and Row, Harper Torchbook, 1961. A standard source.

Maritain, Jacques. *Integral Humanism* (1936). Trans. J. W. Evans. Notre Dame: University of Notre Dame, 1973.

More, Paul Elmer. "Definitions of Dualism." In *The Drift of Romanticism*. Shelburne Essays, 8th Series. Boston: Houghton Mifflin, 1913.

Rand, E. K. *Founders of the Middle Ages* (1928). Cambridge, Mass.: Harvard University Press, 1929.

Sartre, Jean-Paul. *Existentialism and Humanism* (1946). Trans. P. Mairet. London: Methuen, 1948.

Schiller, F. C. S. *Studies in Humanism*. London: Macmillan, 1919. An important supplement to William James's better-known essays on pragmatism and humanism.

Sources of Additional Information

For an interpretation that strongly emphasizes the religious aspects of the Renaissance and views humanism proper as ending with the Renaissance, see Giuseppe Toffanin's *History of Humanism* (New York: Las Americas, 1954).

R. S. Crane's "The Idea of the Humanities," in vol. 1 of *The Idea of the Humanities* (2 vols.; Chicago: University of Chicago Press, 1967) is a major statement on the conception of the humanities as the arts "which deal with those aspects of human experience that differentiate man most completely from the animals, to the end that individual men may actualize as fully as possible their potentialities as men" (7–8).

William James's essays "Humanism and Truth" and "The Essence of Humanism" in *The Meaning of Truth* (1909; Cambridge, Mass.: Harvard University Press, 1975) supplement his treatment of humanism and pragmatism in the volume *Pragmatism* (1907; Cambridge, Mass.: Harvard University Press, 1975).

The state of the debate between the New Humanists and their opponents in 1930 is represented by two collections of essays. The essays *Humanism and America*, ed. Norman Foerster (New York: Farrar and Rinehart, 1930) argue the case for the New Humanism; *The Critique of Humanism*, ed. C. Hartley Grattan (New York: Brewster and Warren, 1930) attacks it from various directions. The list of contributors to the Grattan volume includes Edmund Wilson, Malcolm Lowry, Kenneth Burke, R. P. Blackmur, Yvor Winters, and Lewis Mumford. Walter Sutton's "The New Humanism" in *Modern American Criticism* (Englewood Cliffs, N.J.: Prentice-Hall, 1963) is a helpful, though largely hostile, summary of the New Humanism.

For a full-scale argument for humanity's ability to solve its own problems through a form of humanism, see Corliss Lamont's *Humanism as a Philosophy* (New York: Philosophical Library, 1949).

I
_____

IMAGINATION   1. In Plato's *Republic*, by implication no more than the capacity to copy or imitate that which is presented by the senses. 2. In Plato's *Phaedrus*, the operation of divine inspiration in the poet or rhapsode. 3. The capacity to recall images that have been presented by the senses. 4. The capacity to create symbols representing truths unavailable to the senses. 5. The faculty or activity of creating fictions. 6. That which mediates between the raw stimulus of the senses and the understanding to produce perceptions. 7. That which links associations into a train. 8. The activity of the mind that unifies, blends, and produces symbols for which no concept is finally adequate. 9. The activity of the unconscious mind.

In literary study, especially in the twentieth century, the term imagination is most often linked in some way to Coleridge's definition, which distinguishes it from fancy *(roughly definition 6 above). However, imagination and the Greek and Latin terms generally so translated* (phantasia, eikasia, *and* imaginatio) *have a long history prior to Coleridge, and imagination has been used in a considerable variety of ways since, most of which are tangentially, if not directly, related to the literary or aesthetic use. The meaning and ramifications of the concepts of the imagination held by Plato, Aristotle, Dante, Kant, and Coleridge (and even Hobbes and Locke) are the subject of continuing debate, and the complexities are such that any brief summary of their positions is a kind of travesty.*

1. Plato's concept of poets and artists as imitators, expressed through Socrates in Book 10 of *The Republic*, essentially denies them such creative power as the imagination in its usual senses implies. The poet's imitation, or *eikasia*, is just the copying of that which is presented to the senses, which in turn is only an imperfect copy of the ideal. Thus Socrates expects and receives assent to his

question, "Imitation is only a kind of play or sport, and the tragic and epic poets are imitators in the highest degree?" (2:433; 602b). "The imitative art is an inferior who marries an inferior, and has inferior offspring" (2:439; 603b).

2. However, the divine phantasy granted to the poet or rhapsode in the *Phaedrus* presumably goes beyond any such imitation, and is thus an anticipation of the notion of the imagination as transcending the ordinary activities of the mind: "There is also a third kind of madness, which is a possession of the Muses; this enters into a delicate and virgin soul, and there inspiring frenzy, awakens lyric and all other numbers." However, for Plato this is not actually a power of the mind but a power that descends from outside: "he who, not being inspired and having no touch of madness in his soul, comes to the door and thinks he will get into the temple by the help of art—he, I say, and his poetry are not admitted" (1:550; 45a). Plato's view of the imagination is complicated; it alters over time, or at least between different dialogues, according to his purpose. Murray Wright Bundy, who attempts a chronological tracing of Plato's treatment of the imagination, concludes: "Here was a theory of subjective art as the work of phantasy; of realistic art as a kind of imagination; of symbolic art as the result of a higher activity of the imagination; and finally of inspired poetry and prophecy as the product of the perfect union of divine and human phantasy" (58).

3. For Aristotle, *phantasy* named the activity of recalling stored images that had been present to the senses: "imagination is the faculty in virtue of which we say that an image presents itself to us" (125; 428a). Quintilian represents this view when describing the ability to call up especially vivid images: "What the Greeks call *phantasiai* we call *vision*; images by which representations of absent objects are so distinctly represented to the mind, that we seem to see them with our eyes, and to have them before us" (1:247; Bk. 6, Ch. 2, Sect. 29). This remained a central sense in which the terms fancy or imagination were employed until close to the end of the eighteenth century. In the first of his *Spectator* essays on the imagination (No. 411, June 21, 1812), Joseph Addison writes:

> [B]y the Pleasures of the Imagination, I mean only such Pleasures as arise originally from Sight, and . . . I divide these Pleasures into two kinds: My Design being first of all to Discourse of those Primary Pleasures of the Imagination, which entirely proceed from such Objects as are before our Eyes; and in the next place to speak of those Secondary Pleasures of the Imagination which flow from the Ideas of visible Objects, when the Objects are not actually before the Eye, but are called up into our Memories, or form'd into agreeable Visions of Things that are either Absent or Fictitious. (3:537)

As Donald Bond points out, it was the limitation of the imagination to a mechanical function that seemed to require that such ideas as justice and God be innate (5:254–55).

4. For Neoplatonism and for Dante (at least in the view of Bundy), the imagination was understood as the source of symbols that transcended the ordinary processes of the mind. Bundy argues that Dante makes the imagination

responsible for insights that go beyond the world of sense in the *Inferno* and *Purgatorio*, to be replaced by faith in the *Paradiso*, where no human faculties are equal to communicating the final vision. Blake's view of the imagination is much the same as that of Neoplatonism: "This World of Imagination is Infinite & Eternal, whereas the world of Generation, or Vegetation, is Finite and Temporal. There Exist in that Eternal World the Permanent Realities of Every Thing we see reflected in this Vegetable Glass of Nature" (830).

5. However, writers such as Bacon saw imagination simply as the source of fictions. In *The Advancement of Learning*, Bacon writes that "Poesy . . . doth truly refer to the Imagination; which, being not tied to the laws of matter, may at pleasure join that which nature hath severed, and sever that which nature hath joined, and so make unlawful matches and divorces of things." The result is "Feigned History," the use of which "hath been to give some shadow of satisfaction to the mind of man in those points wherein the nature of things doth deny it" (6:202–3).

6. As R. L. Brett points out, the imagination was also thought of as the means by which the mind processed sensations into concepts (43–44). Immanuel Kant's positing of three kinds of imagination disentangled certain confusions while complicating the concept. For Kant, the reproductive imagination recalled and copied, while the productive imagination mediated between sense reports and the concepts of the understanding. The aesthetic imagination, on the other hand, mediated between the ideas of the Reason (which are not linked to the phenomenal world) and the concepts of the Understanding (which are so linked).

7. For James Mill and others holding an associationist view of the mind, the imagination was simply the linking of ideas. "Imagination is not a name of any one idea. I am not said to imagine, unless I combine ideas successively in a less or greater number. An imagination, therefore, is the name of a *train*. I am said to have an imagination when I have a train of ideas" (239).

8. Coleridge's famous distinction between the fancy (which is pretty much Kant's reproductive imagination), the primary imagination (more or less Kant's productive imagination), and the secondary imagination (something like Kant's aesthetic imagination) described the three faculties or activities as follows. Fancy is "no other than a mode of Memory emancipated from the order of time and space. . . . [E]qually with the ordinary memory the Fancy must receive all its materials ready made from the law of association." The primary imagination is "the living Power and prime Agent of all human perception"—that is, it links the bare sense report to a concept: a portion of what is stimulating the eye becomes a dog, or a tree, or a waterfall. The secondary imagination "dissolves, diffuses, dissipates, in order to recreate; or where this process is rendered impossible, yet still at all events it struggles to idealize and unify" (2:202).

That Coleridge's distinction was not dependent wholly on Kant or the subsequent German idealists is shown by Walter Jackson Bate and J. M. Bullitt, who find earlier examples in William Duff, James Beattie, Dugald Stewart, Mrs. Piozzi, and the Edgeworths.

The contrast between fancy and imagination has been closely explored and vigorously championed in the twentieth century by I. A. Richards (see especially *Coleridge on the Imagination*) and others. On the other hand, the grounds of the distinction have been questioned by critics like Barbara Hardy, who asks of its actual application, "Will we not find ourselves, nine times out of ten, in a critical limbo where there is only the evidence of an enormous versatile creative power which refuses to stand still long enough for us to fix either label?" (344).

9. In a lively survey of theories over the centuries, E. S. Dallas points out the vagueness with which the concept of the imagination has been treated. "Whereas in common parlance and in popular opinion imagination is always referred to as a great power, the authorities in philosophy resolve it away. It is some other faculty, or a compound of faculties. It is reason out for a holiday; it is perception in a hurry; it is memory gone wild; it is the dalliance of desire; it is any or all of these together" (181–82). Accordingly, Dallas proposes that "the imagination or fantasy is not a special faculty but that it is a special function," that is, what Dallas calls the "Hidden Soul," the unconscious play of the mind.

References

Addison, Joseph. *Spectator*. Paper no. 411 for 21 June 1712. In vol. 5 of *The Spectator*, Ed. Donald F. Bond. 5 vols. Oxford: Clarendon Press, 1965. *Spectator* papers numbers 411 through 421 constitute a comprehensive discussion of the imagination by Addison.

Aristotle. *De Anima*. Trans. R. D. Hicks. London: Cambridge University Press, 1907. The page number of the quotation in this edition is followed by the standard marginal citation.

Bacon, Francis. *Of the Advancement of Learning: The Works of Francis Bacon*. Ed. J. Spedding, R. L. Ellis, and D. D. Heath. 15 vols. Boston: Taggard and Thompson, 1853.

Bate, Walter Jackson, and J. M. Bullitt. "Distinctions Between Fancy and Imagination in Eighteenth-Century English Criticism." *Modern Language Notes* 60 (January 1945): 8–15.

Blake, William. *Poetry and Prose of William Blake*. Ed. Geoffrey Keynes. London: Nonesuch Press, 1927.

Bond, Donald F. "The Neo-Classical Psychology of the Imagination." *ELH* 4 (December 1937): 245–64.

Brett, R. L. *Fancy and Imagination*. London: Methuen, 1969.

Bundy, Murray Wright. *The Theory of Imagination in Classical and Medieval Thought*. University of Illinois Studies in Language and Literature, vol. 12, nos. 2–3. Urbana: University of Illinois, 1927. A major survey.

Coleridge, Samuel Taylor. *Biographia Literaria*. Ed. J. Shawcross. 2 vols. Oxford: Clarendon, 1907.

Dallas, E. S. *The Gay Science*. 2 vols. London: Chapman and Hall, 1866.

Hardy, Barbara. "Distinction Without Difference: Coleridge's Fancy and Imagination." *Essays in Criticism* 1 (October 1951): 336–44.

Mill, James. *Analysis of the Phenomena of the Human Mind*. Vol. 1. Ed. J. S. Mill. 2 vols. London: Longmans, Green, Reader and Dyer, 1869.

Plato. *The Dialogues of Plato*. Trans. B. Jowett. 4 vols. New York: Charles Scribner's
    Sons, 1911. Citations to Plato include first the volume and page number in this
    edition and then the standard (Stephanus) marginal numbering of Plato's text.
Richards, I. A. *Coleridge on Imagination*. London: Kegan Paul, Trench, Trubner, 1934.

Sources of Additional Information

A. S. P. Woodhouse's "Romanticism and the History of Ideas" (in *English Studies
Today*, ed. C. L. Wrenn and G. Bullough, London: Oxford University Press, 1951)
focuses on the conception of the imagination in England during four periods as represented
by Bacon, Hobbes, Addison, and the Romantics.

Both the senses in which imagination is employed and the functions of imagination
have been categorized by important thinkers in ways that do not readily fit with the major
senses outlined above. Thus, John Ruskin begins his three chapters on the imagination
in the second volume of *Modern Painters* (in *The Works of John Ruskin*, vol. 4, ed. E.
T. Cook and A. Wedderburn, 39 vols., London: George Allen, 1903) with a loose
definition: "Briefly, the power of the human mind to invent circumstances, forms, or
scenes, at its pleasure, may be generally called 'imagination' " (4:220). However, he
then defines the imagination in terms of the modification of the objects of external creation
by the mind of the artist before declaring that "the essence of the Imaginative faculty is
utterly mysterious and inexplicable" (4:224) and then outlining three functions of the
imagination that eventually are summed up as "Associative of Truth, Penetrative of
Truth, and Contemplative of Truth" (4:313).

In *Interpretations of Poetry and Religion* (1900; New York: Scribner's, 1927), George
Santayana employs the term in what is best understood as an attentuated form of sense
4. "The imagination . . . must furnish to religion and to metaphysics those large ideas
tinctured with passion, those supersensible forms shrouded in awe, in which alone a mind
of great sweep and vitality can find its congenial objects" (6). Wallace Stevens's *The
Necessary Angel* (New York: Vintage, 1951) insists on the interrelation of imagination
and reality: the imagination is part of the reality we experience; the reality we experience
is partly shaped by the imagination. In *Principles of Literary Criticism* (London: Kegan
Paul, Trench, Trubner, 1925) I. A. Richards gives six meanings of imagination including
"the use of figurative language," "inventiveness," and "sympathetic reproducing of
other people's states of mind" (251).

INTENTION   1. Plan, design; the hoped for, aimed at, purposefully pursued
    result of a text. 2. The meaning of a text as embodied in the work itself. 3.
    From the point of view of the editing of texts, what the author intended as
    the text. 4. As a term in phenomenology, the act of directing consciousness
    toward an object, either existing or imaginary.

1. The frequent assumption that the success of a literary work should be judged
by the author's success in accomplishing his or her purpose is generally understood to imply (though it need not) that the intent or purpose can be known from
evidence at least partly external to the work. A standard example is Pope's "In
every work regard the writer's end, / Since none can compass more than they
intend" (11:255–56). In Norman Foerster's words (1941): "From *some* point
of view [the scholar] must learn to deal with the three questions framed by Goethe.

'What did the author propose to himself? Is what he proposes reasonable and sensible? And how far has he succeeded in carrying it out?' '' (25). Ananda K. Coomaraswamy's statement of this form of intentionalism (well-known because it is a reply to the best-known denial of the relevance of external evidence) is, "The only possible literary criticism of an already existing and extant work is one in terms of the ratio of intention to result" (48). Coomaraswamy believes an author's statement of intention is valid for this purpose. It will be noted that Goethe's questions as endorsed by Foerster and Coomaraswamy's formulation address evaluation rather than interpretation. Erich Auerbach has summed up the concomitant belief in the interpretive efficacy of biographical information. "The simple fact that a man's work stems from his existence and that consequently everything we can find out about his life serves to interpret the work loses none of its relevance because inexperienced scholars have drawn ridiculous inferences from it" (12). The assumption that knowledge of an author's life is, in one degree or another, important for the interpretation of the author's works has a long history, providing much of the motivation for biographies of authors from the Classical period to the present. Coomaraswamy quotes Plato (*Laws* 668c) as the first source: "If we are to be connoisseurs of poems we must know in each case in what respect they do not miss their mark. For if one does not know the essence of the work, what it intends, and of what it is an image, he will hardly be able to decide whether its intention (*boulesis*) has or has not found the mark" (42).

2. The best-known statement that evidence external to the literary work is not determinative of the author's intention is the 1945 essay "The Intentional Fallacy" by W. K. Wimsatt and Monroe Beardsley. This essay was, in fact, developed from their entry on "Intention" in Joseph Shipley's *Dictionary of World Literature* (1943), which states their basic position: "the meaning of a work resides within the work; no judgment of intention has relevancy unless corroborated by the work itself, in which case it is supererogatory" (329). The key statement of "The Intentional Fallacy," "that the design or intention of the author is neither available nor desirable as a standard for judging the success of a work of literary art," was directed, as Wimsatt and Beardsley specifically say, at the view that "In order to judge the poet's performance, we must know *what he intended*" (3–4). The essay was widely taken to mean (a) that the original "design or intention of the author" is not the appropriate standard either for judging merit or determining meaning (a position the authors explicitly later endorsed), and (b) that it was impossible to discuss authorial intention (which they later explicitly denied). Wimsatt wrote in 1968 that "[w]hat we meant in 1945, and what in effect I think we managed to say, was that the closest one could ever get to the artist's intending or meaning mind, outside his work, would still be short of his *effective* intention or *operative* mind as it appears in the work itself and can be read from the work" ("Genesis," 36). The construction of the "effective intention" or verifiable intent in the mind of the authors themselves was the goal of the interpreter, not the reconstruction of what had been in the

mind of the author at the time of composition. In a succinct formulation from Wimsatt's "History and Criticism" (1951), "The poet himself is taken as artist, not as intender, but as accomplisher" (*Verbal Icon*, 263). In discussing intention in his *Aesthetics* (1958), Beardsley later restated the position in terms of the illegitimacy of confusing internal and external evidence of authorial intention. Despite these clarifications, however, until recently the enormously influential "The Intentional Fallacy" has been seen as exiling from respectable literary commentary all reference to an author's intention. The exclusion of authorial intention has been frequently understood as an article of New Critical belief (see NEW CRITICISM), even though the New Critics frequently referred to authorial (that is, effective, active, or accomplished) intention.

If intention is understood as the effective or achieved intention represented in the work itself, Wimsatt and Beardsley's position is not strongly opposed to that of E. D. Hirsch, for whom the verbal meaning that is the object of interpretation is "whatever someone has willed to convey by a particular sequence of linguistic signs and which can be conveyed (shared) by means of those linguistic signs" (31). The primary difference is that Hirsch is much more specific about what kinds of external evidence are useful in seeking the author's intended meaning. P. D. Juhl, who goes further than Hirsch in insisting that all interpretation logically implies authorial meaning, defines such intention in a way close to that of the authors of "The Intentional Fallacy."

> In speaking of what an author intended to convey by his work, I do not mean what he *planned* to write or convey. Nor am I using the term "intention" in the broader sense of "motive" in which it may include, for example, his desire to achieve fame or other causal factors. . . . Rather I am using the term in the sense of an author's intention in writing a certain sequence of words—in the sense, that is, of what he meant by the words he used. (14)

Hirsch and Juhl are both speaking of what Michael Hancher calls *active intention*. Hancher's 1972 essay, "Three Kinds of Intention," suggests the term *programmatic intention* for "the author's intention to make something or other," and *active intention* as the "intention that the *thing* one has made *mean* (and be taken to mean) something or other" (829, 831).

Four questions necessarily remain even if it is agreed that the author's accomplished intention, or an intention that can reasonably be attributed to the structure of propositions that make up the text, is to be equated with the text's MEANING. (a) Are the two formulations of intention just given, both of which seem implied by the whole of Wimsatt's and Beardsley's discussion of the topic, equivalent? (b) What is the source of the difference between the intended and realized intentions? (c) Can a text actually be interpreted wholly internally—that is, with no reference to context beyond the text? And if some context is necessary to interpretation, where does the line between internal and external evidence fall? (d) If our understanding of what a text conveys or means is understood as an "intent" in any sense, that is, if the understanding of a text is the construction of an author's intent as realized in the text, are there not different kinds of intent to be considered?

2a. To answer ''yes'' to the first question and identify the author's realized or accomplished intention with the meaning discoverable in the text assumes that language use is accepted as having the goal of communicating, either directly or by implication, a proposition or series of propositions, and assumes moreover that this intention is largely recoverable. The first assumption has been challenged—in its application to literature—by Northrop Frye. ''[A] poet's intention is centripetally directed. It is directed towards putting words together, not toward aligning words with meanings'' (86). The assumption is also denied by structuralists and deconstructionists. An example of the structuralist challenge is the argument of Roland Barthes in ''The Death of the Author.'' ''[W]riting is the destruction of every voice, of every point of origin. Writing is that neutral, composite, oblique space where our subject slips away, the negative where all identity is lost'' (142), for ''Linguistically, the author is never more than the instance writing, just as I is nothing more than the instance saying I: language knows a 'subject,' not a person'' (145). Jacques Derrida, the founder of deconstructive modes of thought (see DECONSTRUCTION), seeks to sever the text from the author, reader, and any specific context. ''To be what it is, all writing must, therefore, be capable of functioning in the radical absence of every empirically determined receiver in general'' (180). ''For a writing to be a writing it must continue to 'act' and to be readable even when what is called the author of the writing no longer answers for what he has written'' (181). ''Every sign . . . can be *cited*, put between quotation marks; in doing so it can break with every given context, engendering an infinity of new contexts in a manner which is absolutely illimitable'' (185). While structuralist and deconstructionist positions deny the possibility of determinate communication partly by denying either the relevance of context or its recovery, the antihistorical position, which has a long history, asserts not the impossibility of determinate communication, but both the essentiality of context for interpretation and the impossibility of adequately recovering the original context of the construction of a text (see HISTORICISM).

Nevertheless, many critics, ignoring such arguments, have continued to assume that an author necessarily writes with a purpose or intention and that whatever other meanings or significances a reader finds, an author intends a text to convey a meaning which is, in principle, recoverable. Support for this position may be drawn from the field of the philosophy of language, especially the work of H. P. Grice, whose analysis of meaning is grounded in the distinction between *natural* meaning, in which meaning refers to a symptom or effect of a cause (smoke means fire, high interest rates mean scarce money), and *non-natural* meaning (meaning$_{nn}$), which refers to a human agent's intent to communicate. That is, '' 'A meant$_{nn}$ something by x' is (roughly) equivalent to 'A intended the utterance of x to produce some effect in an audience by means of the recognition of his intention,' '' where *utterance* refers to any use of signs (385). Walter Davis makes ''the simple observation that when an artist composes he does so with a general purpose or end in view. If he didn't, there is no way he could get started'' (5). An essay of 1982 by Steven Knapp and Walter B. Michaels entitled ''Against Theory'' drew considerable comment by jumping over or leaving aside the entire debate over the ambiguities of the word intention, the assumptions of historicism, and the indeterminacy of meaning on either structuralist or deconstructionist grounds to announce flatly that ''the meaning of a text is simply identical to the author's intended meaning'' (724).

2b. Differences between an author's prospective intention and the realized intention may evidently be due to a failure of craftsmanship—authors may not be able to convey what they hope to convey or believe they have conveyed. Only a little less obvious is the difficulty of speaking of an author's plan or design; Joel Spingarn's observation that ''the poet's aim must be judged at the moment of the creative act, that is to say, by the art of the poem itself, and not by vague ambitions which he imagines to be his real intentions before or after the creative work is achieved'' (25) sounds much like the position of Wimsatt and Beardsley, but what is ''the moment of the creative act''? Is it the moment the author decides to write a given work, the moment the first words are written, some point in the actual writing, or the moment the last words are written?

Part of the New Critics' distrust of external evidence such as a writer's prospective or even retrospective, statement of intention is based in a particular concept of the creative process. For instance, critics like John Crowe Ransom and Murray Krieger define the concept of creation as, in Krieger's words, a ''creative power which achieves its ends by working in a resistant medium.'' (93). The resistance of the language itself and of the internal context the author is bringing into existence necessarily contribute to the shape of what is created. ''[T]his give-and-take struggle must be seen to be involved throughout the entire composition of the poem, from the first line to the last of the first draft to the last. As the struggle develops, the initial rough idea grows in precision and depth'' (73). Ransom's concept of the poem as having logical content surrounded by irrelevant texture had earlier produced a similar formulation. ''Total intention is the total meaning of the finished poem, which differs from the original logical content by having acquired a detail which is immaterial to this content, being everywhere specific, or local, or particular, and at any rate unpredictable'' (224).

2c. The question of whether in fact it is possible to interpret a text in itself—on the basis of internal evidence only—was acknowledged from the beginning, if not much explored, by Wimsatt and Beardsley. The entry in Shipley's *Dictionary* notes: ''Evidence that a work has a certain intentional meaning may be distinguished as 'internal' or 'external.' But this distinction is not one that can always be applied with certainty'' (230). Specifically it is noted that to know the meaning of individual words as they would have been understood by an author requires recourse to dictionaries of the time and perhaps to other texts, including those by the given author. As E. D. Hirsch and others have analyzed the processes necessary for determining what an author must have intended, the importance of certain kinds of external evidence has received much more attention. From this point of view, when Knapp and Michaels argue that "if meaning and intended meaning are already the same, it's hard to see how looking for one provides an objective method—or any sort of method—for looking for the other; looking for one just *is* looking for the other" (725); they fail to recognize that a process of translation is still required. The question remains, what does a reader who wishes to understand the author's intended meaning have to bring to the text in order to do so? Stated another way, the question becomes, "How much linguistic, cultural, and topical knowledge must a reader share with an author to interpret his or her operative intention?"

2d. The question of kinds of intent is best regarded from the point of view of SPEECH-ACT THEORY. In speech-act terms, the immediate intent of a sentence or passage is its *illocutionary* intent (the immediate understanding that the speaker or author intends), while the *perlocutionary* intent is the ultimate effect to which such an understanding may contribute. Michael Hancher defines the *final intention* (not to be confused with the author's final intention, as understood in editorial practice) as "an intention to *cause* an effect of one sort or another; it defines whatever the author wishes to accomplish *by means of* his completed work" (834). Final intention thus defined corresponds to perlocutionary intention. Alternative terminology can be drawn from Charles Altieri, who distinguishes three levels: *intention*, *plan*, and *project*. If, as speech-act theory assumes, the illocutionary act includes the intention that the illocutionary force of an utterance be grasped, the term intention may correspond to the interpretation of the illocutionary force of specific sentences, *plan* to the larger goal toward which the author aims, and *project* to the attitude toward life that the work as a whole appears to express (241–43).

3. The editor of a text is responsible for choosing between variant forms of the text and correcting inadvertent errors. In principle, the question confronted is not how the words on the page are to be interpreted, but what words the author intended to constitute the text. "All valid meaning is authorial meaning," writes Herschel Parker, "but in standard literary texts [published editions] authorial meaning may be mixed in with non-sense, skewed meanings, and wholly adventitious meanings which result from tampering with the text, by the author [in revision] or someone else" (ix). In practice, the choice between actual variants or between an existing form and possible corrections can hardly be made without reconstruction of authorial intention. G. Thomas Tanselle, considering the problem of deviations from externally determinable fact, writes, "In most instances, all there is to go on is the intention manifested in the work itself; the editor's decisions are based on an understanding of the internal workings of a particular act of expression" ("External Fact," 21). Questions that arise can involve deviations from externally determinable fact: "What should an editor do about internal inconsistencies?" "What errors of fact should be corrected?" "When should apparently inadvertently omitted words or punctuation be supplied?" More puzzling questions arise when an author has made revisions that introduce inconsistencies, create confusion for readers, or seem to affect the interpretation

of a passage. Such issues admit of no uniform solutions but must be resolved on a case-by-case basis. In general, contemporary editors endorse the same principles as set forth in "The Intentional Fallacy." In "The Editorial Problem of Final Authorial Intention" (1976), Tanselle insists that "The only direct evidence one has for what was in the author's mind is not what he says was there but what one finds in his work" (210), and in a later essay notes that "obviously a statement of intention does not necessarily match the actual realized intention, and editors are not concerned with statements of intention but authors' intentions as manifested in their works" ("External Fact," 32). Tanselle clarifies his use of author's intention in the 1976 essay by defining it in accordance with a formulation of Michael Hancher: "Active intentions characterize the actions that the author, at the time he finishes his text, understands himself to be performing in that text" (Hancher, 830; Tanselle, 175). Tanselle makes clear that each question of emendation or choice between variants is to be considered individually, but generally inclines toward the inclusion of the selection of the author's latest revision. This principle is modified by Steven Mailloux (whose work is cited without disapproval by Tanselle in his 1979 essay on "External Fact," 11n); Mailloux defines "active intentions" as characterizing "the actions that the author, *as he writes the text*, understands himself to be performing in that text" and goes on to argue that what an editor is actually pursuing are "inferred intentions" that "characterize the critic's description of the convention-based responses that the author, as he is writing, understands he will achieve as a result (at least in part) of his projected recognition of his intention" (99). Mailloux is thus arguing that the editor reconstructs what must have been the author's active intentions on the basis of the responses that could have been anticipated from the readers of the time. This allows an editor to decide between alternative versions on the basis of the work as an aesthetic whole, not simply the chronology of the differing versions.

4. Phenomenological *intentionality* is "the property or experience that consists in its being conscious 'of' or 'about' something" (Smith and McIntyre, xiii), or the "property of consciousness whereby it reflects or intends an object" (Runes, 164), or the "direction or application of the mind to an object; a conception formed by directing the mind to some object; a general concept" (*OED*, sense 11). This sense of intention, suggested by Franz Brentano and given currency by Edmund Husserl, lies at some distance from the question of authorial intention. Nevertheless, that which is set down in a text, literary or other, consists of objects of consciousness in the phenomenological sense, just as the readers' responses consist of a structure of intended objects. Intentionality in the phenomenological sense can thus be regarded as the process by which identifiable objects are constituted out of the chaos of sense impressions, memories, and so forth. Looked at in this way, it designates the process by which signifieds are marked off from the flow in the "floating realms of thought" (Saussure) or the objects to which signs correspond constituted from the succession of percepts (Peirce; see SEMIOTICS). Moreover, Hirsch, who has given particular attention

to the question of how intended meanings are construed from texts, looks to
Husserl for support for the proposition that ''Verbal meaning, being an intentional
object, is unchanging, that is, it may be reproduced by different intentional acts
and remains self-identical through all these reproductions'' (219). If this were
not the case, it would not be possible for a reader to reconstruct the author's
intended meaning. Looked at the other way round, ''the intentional object represented by a text is different from the intentional acts which realize it'' (241),
which is to say that the prospective intention is not the same thing as the realized
intention. More complex relationships between the phenomenological and more
traditional senses of intention in literary study are discussed by Georgia Warnke.

References

Altieri, Charles. *Act and Quality: A Theory of Literary Meaning and Humanistic Un-
    derstanding.* Amherst: University of Massachusetts Press, 1981.
Auerbach, Erich. *Literary Language and Its Public in Late Antiquity and in the Middle
    Ages.* New York: Pantheon Books, 1965.
Barthes, Roland. ''The Death of the Author.'' *Image-Music-Text.* Trans. S. Heath. New
    York: Hill and Wang, 1977.
Beardsley, Monroe. *Aesthetics: Problems in the Philosophy of Criticism.* New York:
    Harcourt, Brace and World, 1958.
Coomaraswamy, Ananda K. ''Intention.'' *American Bookman* 1 (1944): 41–48.
Davis, Walter A. *The Act of Interpretation: A Critique of Literary Reason.* Chicago:
    University of Chicago Press, 1978.
Derrida. ''Signature Event Context.'' *Glyph* 1 (1977): 172–97.
Dictionary of World Literature. Ed. Joseph T. Shipley. New York: Philosophical Library,
    1943.
Foerster, Norman. ''The Study of Letters.'' In *Literary Scholarship: Its Aims and Meth-
    ods.* Chapel Hill: University of North Carolina, 1941. Goethe's ''three questions''
    are found in Foerster's review of Manzoni's *Conti di Carmagnola*; the passage is
    translated in René Wellek's *History of Modern Criticism*, 1:223–24, and quoted
    in the original German in the notes (New Haven, Conn.: Yale University Press,
    1955).
Frye, Northrop. *Anatomy of Criticism.* Princeton, N.J.: Princeton University Press, 1957.
Grice, H. P. ''Meaning.'' *The Philosophical Review* 66 (1957): 377–88.
Hancher, Michael. ''Three Kinds of Intention.'' *Modern Language Notes* 87 (December
    1972): 829–35.
Hirsch, E. D. *Validity in Interpretation.* New Haven, Conn.: Yale University Press, 1967.
Juhl, P. D. *Interpretation.* Princeton, N.J.: Princeton University Press, 1980.
Knapp, Steven, and Walter Benn Michaels. ''Against Theory: Hermeneutics and De-
    construction.'' *Critical Inquiry* 8 (Autumn 1982): 723–42. Reprinted in *Against
    Theory*, ed. W. J. T. Mitchell. Chicago: University of Chicago Press, 1985.
Krieger, Murray. *The New Apologists for Poetry.* Minneapolis: University of Minnesota
    Press, 1965.
Mailloux, Steven. *Interpretive Conventions: The Reader in the Study of American Fiction.*
    Ithaca, N.Y.: Cornell University Press, 1982.
Parker, Herschel. *Flawed Texts and Verbal Icons.* Evanston, Ill.: Northwestern University
    Press, 1984.

Ransom, John Crowe. *The New Criticism*. Norfolk, Conn: New Directions, 1941.

Runes, Dagobert D. *Dictionary of Philosophy*. New York: Philosophical Library, 1983.

Smith, David Woodruff, and Ronald McIntyre. *Husserl and Intentionality*. Dordrecht, Holland: D. Reidel, 1982.

Spingarn, Joel. "The New Criticism." In *Criticism in America*. New York: Harcourt, Brace, 1924.

Tanselle, G. Thomas. "The Editorial Problem of Final Authorial Intention." *Studies in Bibliography* 29 (1976): 167–211.

———. "External Fact as an Editorial Problem." *Studies in Bibliography* 32 (1979): 1–47.

Warnke, Georgia. *Gadamer: Hermeneutics, Tradition, and Reason*. Stanford, Calif.: Stanford University Press, 1987.

Wimsatt, W. K. "Genesis: An Argument Resumed." In *Day of the Leopards*. New Haven, Conn.: Yale University Press, 1976.

———. "History and Criticism." In *The Verbal Icon*. Lexington: University of Kentucky Press, 1954. Reprinted from *PMLA* 66 (February 1951): 21–31.

Wimsatt, W. K., and Monroe C. Beardsley, "Intention." In *Dictionary of World Literature*, ed. J. T. Shipley. New York: Philosophical Library, 1943.

Wimsatt, W. K., and Monroe Beardsley. "The Intentional Fallacy." In *The Verbal Icon*. Lexington: University of Kentucky Press, 1954. Reprinted from *Sewanee Review* 54 (Summer 1946): 468–88.

Sources of Additional Information

There are plentiful discussions of authorial intention. David Newton–de Molina has collected fifteen essays or portions of books, beginning with W. K. Wimsatt and Monroe Beardsley's "The Intentional Fallacy" (see References above). T. M. Gang's "Intention" (*Essays in Criticism* 7, April 1957: 175–86) distinguishes intention from significance and practical from literary intentions, and defends seeking the author's intention so long as one is aware of what one is doing. Richard Kuhns's "Criticism and the Problem of Intention" (*Journal of Philosophy* 57, January 1960: 5–23) surveys various meanings and uses of "intention" and supports critical interest in intention as "what the work sustains as certain kind of experience, its focal effect" (22). W. V. Harris's *Interpretive Acts* (Oxford: Clarendon Press, 1988) seeks to define specifically what kinds of things readers assume that authors assume that readers will know or believe. Suresh Raval's "Intention and Contemporary Literary Theory" (*Journal of Aesthetics and Art Criticism* 38, Spring 1980: 261–77) presents the argument that neither the intentionalists nor the antiintentionalists can convert the other. One group conflates the intention of the speaker and the intentionality of the text while the other distinguishes between the two.

Exemplary of the issues raised in trying to relate events from an author's life to specific texts is the debate between Park Honan and Miriam Allott over the identity of Matthew Arnold's "Marguerite": see W. V. Harris's "The Lure of Biography: Who Was Marguerite and to Whom Does It Matter?" (*The Victorian Newsletter* 76, Fall 1989: 28–31).

A celebrated controversy over the status of the author vis-à-vis the text, and thus over intention, occurred in 1977 as a result of John Searle's reply to Derrida's "Signature Event Context" (see References above) eliciting a lengthy reply from Derrida. The first two essays appeared in *Glyph* 1 (1977: 172–208), and the third in *Glyph* 2 (1977: 162–251).

The canonic discussion of the choice of a copy-text and handling of the variations therefrom from which most later discussions start is W. W. Greg's "The Rationale of Copy-Text" (*Studies in Bibliography* 3, 1950–51:19–36).

Among the many interpretations of intentionality in the philosophic sense, John Searle's *Intentionality: An Essay in Philosophy of Mind* (Cambridge: Cambridge University Press, 1983) is of more than usual interest for literary studies. Volume 38 of *Dialecta* (1984) is made up of articles exploring a variety of aspects of intentionality.

INTERPRETATION   1. The understanding and/or explanation of words, allusions, sentences, portions of text, or texts as wholes. 2. The understanding and/or explanation of the meaning intended by an author through words, allusions, sentences, portions of texts or texts as wholes. 3. The understanding and/or explanation of implications of a word, allusion, sentence, portion of or entire text that were not necessarily or could not possibly have been intended by an author.

Consideration of the uses of the term "interpretation" leads quickly to the uses of the terms MEANING, HERMENEUTICS, *and* INTENTION. *The present entry seeks to distinguish the major senses of "interpretation" in literary criticism.*

1. The broadest sense of interpretation is simply "finding a meaning" (where "meaning" is also understood broadly). The appearance of the words "construction," explanation, "translation," "obtain information from," and "translate" in dictionary definitions of interpretation (see the OED) suggests a core sense of "translating in such a way as to increase understanding." Umberto Eco notes that "By interpretation (or criterion of interpretability) we mean the concept elaborated by Peirce, according to which every *interpretant* (either a sign, or an expression or a sequence of expressions that translate a previous expression), besides translating the Immediate Object or the content of the sign, also increases our understanding of it" (*Semiotics*, 43). Thus the simplest interpretation of single words occurs through the provision of better-known synonyms in the same language or translation of a word from a language a reader does not know into a familiar language.

However, the term is most often used in the twentieth century to refer to the pursuit of an understanding of, or the meaning of, a major portion or the whole of a text or discourse. Thus again Eco discriminates between "decoding" individual signs and "interpretation"; the latter "has rather been taken to mean understanding, on the basis of some previous decoding, the general sense of a vast portion of discourse. . . . Logically speaking this kind of interpretation is more akin to *inference*. Moreover, it is similar to that specific kind of inference that Peirce called *abduction*" (*Theory*, 131). Paul Ricoeur similarly uses "interpretation" to describe the "dialectic of explanation and understanding" in which two "moves" occur. "The first time, understanding will be a naive grasping of the meaning of the text as a whole. The second time, comprehension will be a sophisticated mode of understanding, supported by explanatory procedures" (74). Such formulations avoid restricting the term "interpretation" either to the author's consciously intended meaning or to meanings not so intended. Ricoeur, for instance, explicitly describes a dialectic between intended meaning and the *verbal meaning* of an autonomous text (29–30).

2. Although many an earlier writer related ''interpretation'' more or less to elucidation of an author's meaning, restriction of ''interpretation'' to the construction of the author's intended meaning is today especially associated with E. D. Hirsch. A formulation of the difference in *Validity in Interpretation* (1967) reads: ''*Meaning* is that which is represented by a text; it is what the author meant by his use of a particular sign sequence; it is what the signs represent. *Significance*, on the other hand, names a relationship between that meaning and a person, or a conception, or a situation, or indeed anything imaginable'' (8). P. D. Juhl's *Interpretation: An Essay in the Philosophy of Literary Criticism* goes beyond Hirsch in arguing that not only are there moral, practical, and psychological reasons for seeking to interpret the author's intended meaning, but ''there is a logical connection between statements about the meaning of a literary work and statements about the author's intention such that a statement about the meaning of a work *is* a statement about the author's intention'' (12).

George Dillon approaches the question from quite a different direction (see DISCOURSE ANALYSIS), but arrives at pretty much the same meaning of interpretation. For Dillon, reading occurs on three levels. The first, ''perception,'' is the identification of propositional structure. The second, ''comprehension,'' ''involves the integration of its propositional content into one's running tally of what is being described or argued in the passage'' (xvii). The third level is ''interpretation'' proper, ''where we relate the sense of what is going on to the author's constructive intention—why he is saying what he says, or what he is getting at in terms of the themes and meaning of the work'' (xx). Neither Hirsch nor Dillon believes that the attempt to reconstruct the author's meaning will always be successful or that the reconstruction of intended meaning constitutes the whole of the reader's activity, but for both it is the starting place.

3. The concept of interpretation as specifically *not* the author's intention derives from several theoretical programs. One is the principle that all interpretation, either of sense impressions or literature, is so closely tied to individual desires and perspectives that it can reflect only the observer's response. Friedrich Nietzsche is the foremost spokesmen for this position. ''To the extent to which knowledge has any sense at all, the world is knowable: but it may be interpreted *differently*, it has not one sense behind it, but hundreds of senses.—'Perspectivity.' '' For, ''[i]t is our needs that *interpret the world*; our instincts and their impulses for and against'' (15:12–13). Moreover, Ferdinand de Saussure's analysis of the value (roughly, meaning) of the signified as dependent on its place in the total system of signifieds within a language, that is, as defined by its relationship to all other signifieds, can be read as implying infinite regress. Jacques Derrida, arguing primarily from such an understanding of Saussure but also citing Nietzsche, contrasts interpretation as the pursuit of a single meaning or set of meanings (either sense 1 or sense 2) with delight in multiple meanings. ''There are thus two interpretations of interpretation, of structure, of sign, of

play. The one seeks to decipher, dreams of deciphering a truth or an origin which escapes play and the order of the sign, and which lives the necessity of interpretation as an exile. The other, which is no longer turned toward the origin, affirms play and tries to pass beyond man and humanism, the name of man being the name of that being who . . . has dreamed of full presence, the reassuring foundation, the origin and the end of play'' (292).

Wolfgang Iser's theory of READER RESPONSE regards the ''work itelf'' as existing between two poles: ''the artistic pole is the author's text and the aesthetic is the realization accomplished by the reader.'' For Iser, a text can be aesthetic in so far as it elicits a subjective, though guided, response. Therefore a text can never be said to have a single meaning: ''the interpreter's task should be to elucidate the potential meanings of a text, and not to restrict himself to just one'' (21–22). David Bleich, representing the variety of reader-response criticism that most strongly argues for the necessity of subjective interpretation, presents another form of the Nietzschean argument. ''Like the interpretation of dreams, the interpretation of an aesthetic object is motivated not by a wish to know the artist's intention—though this is an admissible enterprise in another context—but by the desire to create knowledge on one's own behalf and on behalf of one's community from the subjective experience of the work of art'' (93).

Quite different from any of these is the position of Susan Sontag in *Against Interpretation*; what she wishes to oppose is the identification of ''interpretation'' with the search for ''hidden meanings.'' ''The modern style of interpretation excavates, and as it excavates, destroys; it digs 'behind' the text, to find a sub-text which is the true one. The most celebrated and influential modern doctrines, those of Marx and Freud, actually amount to . . . aggressive and impious theories of interpretation'' (6–7).

References

Bleich, David. *Subjective Criticism*. Baltimore: Johns Hopkins University Press, 1978.
Derrida, Jacques. ''Structure, Sign, and Play in the Discourse of the Human Sciences.''
    In *Writing and Difference*. Trans. A. Bass. Chicago: University of Chicago Press,
    1978.
Dillon, George. *Language Processing and the Reading of Literature*. Bloomington: In-
    diana University Press, 1978.
Eco, Umberto. *Semiotics and the Philosophy of Language*. Bloomington: Indiana Uni-
    versity Press, 1984.
————. *A Theory of Semiotics*. Bloomington: Indiana University Press, 1976.
Hirsch, E. D. *Validity in Interpretation*. New Haven, Conn.: Yale University Press, 1967.
    In his 1960 piece, ''Objective Interpretation'' (*PMLA* 75, 463–79; reprinted in
    Validity in Interpretation) Hirsch distinguishes meaning and significance as fol-
    lows: ''The object of interpretation is textual meaning in and for itself and may
    be called the *meaning* of the text. The object of criticism, on the other hand, is
    that meaning in its bearing on something else (standards of value, present concerns,
    etc.) and this object may therefore be called the *relevance* of the text'' (464;
    ''relevance'' was changed to ''significance'' when Hirsch included the essay in
    the later volume [211]).

Iser, Wolfgang. *The Act of Reading*. Baltimore: Johns Hopkins University Press, 1978. Original German edition, 1976.

Juhl, P. D. *Interpretation: An Essay in the Philosophy of Literary Criticism*. Princeton, N.J.: Princeton University Press, 1980.

Nietzsche, Friedrich. *The Principles of a New Valuation*. Trans. Anthony M. Ludovici. In vol. 15 of *The Complete Works of Friedrich Nietzsche*. Ed. Oscar Levy. 1909–11; London: Russell and Russell, 1964.

Ricoeur, Paul. *Interpretation Theory*. Fort Worth: Texas Christian University Press, 1976.

Saussure, Ferdinand de. *Course in General Linguistics*. Ed. C. Bally and A. Sechehaye; trans. W. Baskin. New York: McGraw-Hill, 1966.

Sontag, Susan. *Against Interpretation*. New York: Farrar, Straus, and Giroux, 1964.

INTERTEXTUALITY   1. In its broadest usage, the mode of existence of all thought, language, and discourse. 2. More narrowly, the interaction of other utterances/texts (discourses) that produces a new utterance/text (discourse). 3. A synonym for allusion. 4. In one possible interpretation of Julia Kristeva, the process that produces the text from among the manifold possibilities of the mind's contents.

The word intertextuality enters, or at least assumes prominence in, literary theory and criticism through an essay by Julia Kristeva on Mikhail Bakhtin (1969), translated as "Word, Dialogue and Novel" in the 1980 Desire in Language. *There its sense is that "any text is constructed as a mosaic of quotations; any text is the absorption and transformation of another" so that "The notion of* intertextuality *replaces that of intersubjectivity" (66). It appears again in a somewhat more abstract formulation in her 1974* Revolution in Poetic Language *as the "transposition of one (or several) sign-system(s) into another" (59–60). The difficulty of Kristeva's writing in its personal blending of Freud, Lacan, Marxism, and* SEMIOTICS *appears to have precluded any general agreement about the inclusiveness of the term even in her own uses. Senses 1 through 3 are, therefore, like concentric circles delineating uses over which intertexuality ranges. It is to be noted that Bakhtin's* dialogism, *which lies behind Kristeva's* intertextuality, *also has a set of concentric senses.*

1. The global sense of intertextuality is possible because the meaning of a word prior to its use in a particular utterance/text depends on its previous uses, every actual utterance/text is dependent on (is a response to) other utterances/texts whether immediate or not, and every thought is defined against the social/cultural environment (which can itself be regarded as a system of texts), and because the individual mind can be regarded as a complex of assimilated concepts or texts. The generating metaphorical notion behind this usage is found in Emerson's "Every book is a quotation; and every house is a quotation out of all forests, and mines, and stone quarries; and every man is a quotation from all ancestors" (24).

2. Bakhtin's use of *dialogism*, which suggested *intertextuality* to Kristeva, is narrower in that it is restricted to language use, but within this area it is encom-

passing. His view, which has come to be influential, cannot be better represented than by a substantial quotation from Bakhtin:

> Indeed, any concrete discourse (utterance) finds the object at which it was directed already as it were overlain with qualifications, open to dispute, charged with value, already enveloped in an obscuring mist—or, on the contrary, by the ''light'' of alien words that have already been spoken about it. . . . The word, directed toward its object, enters a dialogically agitated and tension-filled environment of alien words, value judgments and accents, weaves in and out of complex relationships, merges with some, recoils from others, intersects with yet a third group. (276)

Tzvetan Todorov explicitly chooses *intertextuality* as his designation for the ''more inclusive'' meanings of Bakhtin's *dialogism*. However, in finding that ''Intertextuality belongs to discourse and not language'' (61), he stipulates a limitation that does not apply to the term in its most comprehensive linguistic use, since the lexical senses and connotations of an individual word can be regarded as intertextually produced—as Todorov himself seems to recognize elsewhere: ''words always already [have] been used and carry within themselves traces of preceding usage'' (63).

Given the primacy accorded language in the constitution of the human mind, it is possible, as noted by Walter B. Michaels, to regard the mind itself as an intertextual construct. ''The rhetoric of the community of interpretation emphasizes the role readers play in constituting texts, while the rhetoric of the self as sign in a system of signs emphasizes the role texts play in constituting consciousness—the strategy in each case is to collapse the distinction between the interpreter and what he interprets'' (401).

Literary historians have traditionally analyzed literary texts in terms of generic structures, literary conventions, character types, and traditional modes of conceptualizing reality. However, those critics and theorists who are currently emphasizing intertextuality are more radical in that they see texts as *primarily* transpositions of other texts. Thus Christopher Johnson writes: ''the theory of intertextuality states that no text is a harmonious, organic whole in itself, and is therefore not to be considered an autonomous isolated unit. It is rather the product of intersections of a whole corpus of texts which may be broadly defined as our 'culture.' . . . [A] given text is a function of its 'predecessors' '' (71). For Hillis Miller, ''A literary text is not a thing in itself, 'organically unified,' but a relation to other texts which are relations in their turn. The study of literature is therefore a study of intertextuality'' (334). Johnson's and Miller's dismissals of the concept of the organic unity of the text points to a corollary now frequently assumed to follow from the concept of intertextuality: a text is regarded not only as in dialogue with other texts, but also as in internal dialogue as aspects of the texts it has absorbed jostle and clash.

Strictly speaking, interest in intertextuality is not an interest in sources as these have traditionally been traced but rather in the presence of modes of thought and forms of expression that are carried along in the temporal flow of culture. Thus, Julia Kristeva comments in *Revolution in Poetic Language* that intertextuality "has often been understood in the banal sense of 'study of sources' " and therefore she finds it better to use the word *transposition* (60). "Intertextuality" is, nevertheless, occasionally to be encountered in the older sense of relations between earlier sources and texts they have influenced.

The notion behind *dialogism* and intertextuality is not a new one. E. E. Kellett wrote in 1933 that "In one sense *all*, or practically all, our writing is quotation. A thousand years of writing have given us a set of vocabularies, each appropriated to particular uses; and no man can write without employing multitudes of phrases the associations of which have been fixed long since and cannot be *deliberately* altered" (14).

3. What has traditionally been called ALLUSION can evidently be subsumed as a restricted form of intertextuality, a conscious and self-signaling form in which an author intends the reader to recognize a relationship between a portion or aspect of the immediate discourse and a portion or aspect of another discourse, recognition of which will enrich meaning.

4. A special sense which Christopher Johnson argues is the central one for Kristeva is psychoanalytic: intertextuality can be used to describe the way in which the mind produces utterances and texts. That is, it is a mode of exploring the relationship between what Kristeva calls the *phenotext* (the manifest discourse) and the *genotext* (the plurality of origins or forces in the individual mind that produce a phenotext that is both overdetermined and impoverished relative to the genotext). As Kristeva analyzes the *signifying process*, "one might see the relevance and subsequent articulation of the drives as constrained by the social code yet not reducible to the language system as a *genotext* and the signifying system as it presents itself to the phenomenological intuition as a *phenotext*" *Kristeva Reader*, (28).

References

Bakhtin, Mikhail. *The Dialogic Imagination*. Ed. M. Holquist: Trans. C. Emerson and M. Holquist. Austin: University of Texas Press, 1981.

Emerson, Ralph Waldo. "Plato, or the Philosopher." In vol. 4 of *Representative Men: The Collected Works of Ralph Waldo Emerson*. Ed. W. E. Williams and D. E. Wilson. Cambridge, Mass.: Belknap Press, Harvard University, 1987.

Johnson, Christopher M. "Intertextuality and the Psychic Model." *Paragraph* 2 (March 1988): 71–89.

Kellett, E. E. *Literary Quotation and Allusion*. 1933; Port Washington, N.Y.: Kennikat Press, 1969.

Kristeva, Julia. *The Kristeva Reader*. Ed. Toril Moi. New York: Columbia University Press, 1986.

———. *Revolution in Poetic Language*. Trans. M. Waller. New York: Columbia University Press, 1984. Portions appear in the *Kristeva Reader*.

———. "Word, Dialogue and Novel." in *Desire in Language*. Ed. Leon S. Roudiez; trans. T. Gora, A. Jardine, and L. Roudiez. New York: Columbia University Press, 1980.

Michaels, Walter Benn. "The Interpreter's Self: Peirce on the Cartesian 'Subject.' "

Georgia Review 31 (Summer 1977): 383–402. Reprinted in *Reader-Response Criticism*, ed. Jane Tompkins. Baltimore: Johns Hopkins University Press, 1980.

Miller, J. Hillis. "Stevens' Rock and Criticism as Cure, II." *Georgia Review* 30 (Summer 1976): 334.

Todorov, Tzvetan. *Mikhail Bahktin: The Dialogical Principle*. Trans. W. Godzich. Minneapolis: University of Minnesota Press, 1984.

IRONY   1. The assumption of a self-deprecating but inquiring manner in order to lead others into self-contradiction and logical error; this is generally distinguished as Socratic or behavioral irony. 2. Saying one thing in order to state the opposite; this is verbal irony. 3. A self-analytical recognition of the distance between aspiration and possibility, both as a human being and as an artist, usually leading to a paradoxical mixture of broad sympathy and detachment; this is Romantic irony. 4. The occurrence of an event the opposite of what would normally be expected or is desired; this is generally termed situational irony. 5. A balanced tension between concepts or emotions or responses; in a literary work, such tension is most often regarded as the result of the interaction between a word, image, or statement and the total context of the work. This sense of irony as an unresolvable but nevertheless stable tension found in literature and especially poetry, often known as contextual irony, arises in twentieth-century NEW CRITICISM. 6. The transformation of a belief in the ultimate absurdity or meaninglessness of existence into an attitude combining fatalism, a relish for absurdity, and dark humor; this is sometimes called existential or cosmic irony.

The order in which these senses are listed represents the order in which they entered the critical vocabulary, not necessarily that of their appearance in human discourse.

1. In Book 1 of Plato's *Republic*, Socrates, reporting a dialogic quest for the meaning of justice, pretends that he had been afraid of the angry questioning of Thrasymachus. "Thrasymachus, I said, with a quiver, have mercy on us. Our error, if we were guilty of any error, was certainly unintentional, and therefore you, in your wisdom, should have pity on us, and not be angry with us." Thrasymachus replies, "How characteristic of Socrates! . . . [T]hat's your ironical way! Did I not foresee—did I not tell you all that he would refuse to answer, and try irony or any other shift in order that he might avoid answering?" (2:158; 336–37).

Irony as yet had no other meaning than "the action of an *eiron*," that is, of the cunningly self-deprecating stage character who eventually triumphs over the strong and boastful but less intelligent individual. *Eiron* here is a disparaging term. In later classical literature, irony came to denote either the strategies of the weak but clever characters of drama or the Socratic mode of questioning; the latter, in turn, was understood either as mockery or witty urbanity (see Knox, Ch. 8).

Irony in the sense of the Socratic strategy of feigned ignorance appears not to have been recognized by medieval writers, although it was rediscovered in the Renaissance. Socrates again came to be regarded as the first ironist in the sense of one who pretends ignorance for serious purposes. Thus, Kierkegaard writes, "It is in Socrates that the concept of irony has its inception in the world" (47).

2. By the time of Quintilian, irony is understood very broadly as something which is the opposite of what is actually said, a meaning more or less parallel to the behavior of an *eiron* in pretending to be other than he is. Quintilian rather curiously distinguishes between irony as a trope, in which case the opposite meaning is immediately clear, and irony as a figure, in a more extended form resulting from "a sustained series of [ironic] tropes" (3:401). Irony as figure is explicitly linked to Socrates. However, as the Socratic disappeared as one of the senses of irony for medieval writers, the term came to mean simply the saying of the opposite of what one intended to be understood. This has remained the core sense through the Renaissance and the eighteenth century (when such irony was in particular vogue) to the present. In many instances, it is more accurate to say, as does Bishop Connop Thirwall in a central essay, "The Irony of Sophocles," that irony is achieved by a *contrast* rather than an *opposition* between what is said and what is meant. This sense is what Monroe Beardsley calls the "discursive use" of irony (256). Arthur Sidgwick's 1907 essay, "On Some Forms of Irony in Literature," qualifies Thirwall's view that irony is employed either in controversy or mock-controversy; it is also, finds Sidgwick, a mode of expressing especially powerful emotions through a contrast between what is said and the way it is said.

3. Romantic irony results from the recognition of the finiteness of the individual as against the multitude of contradictions encountered in an infinite world, and of the difference between art and life. D. C. Muecke sums up Romantic irony: "the irony of the fully-conscious artist whose art is the ironical presentation of the ironic position of the fully-conscious artist" (20). The notion of what is now called Romantic irony receives its first articulation in Friedrich Schlegel, writing in the last years of the eighteenth century and the early decades of the nineteenth. René Wellek weaves two quotations from Schlegel into a capsule statement: " 'Irony is a clear consciousness of the infinitely full chaos,' of the dark and inexplicable world, but it is also highly self-conscious, for irony is self parody, 'transcendental buffoonery' which 'rises above art, virtue, and genius' " (2:15). Romantic irony reconciles the finite and the infinite, the serious and the playful, through self-awareness of the paradoxes of the individual's relation to each pole. Schlegel's chief examples are Cervantes, Shakespeare, Sterne, and Goethe; the ultimate exemplar, however, is Socrates, as Ernst Behler's "The Theory of Irony in German Romanticism" illustrates. The Socratic model accounts for the Romantic ironist's self-control even when accepting human inability to penetrate to truths lying behind appearance. Irving Babbitt's strongly negative commentary on Romantic irony in *Rousseau and Romanticism* contrasts such irony with that of Socrates, but his charge that the Romantic ironist pleads the pursuit of the

infinite to avoid taking a stand suggests a parallel with the *eiron* of drama. (It is interesting to note that Babbitt's key objection to Romantic irony—that its irony is endless, 241–42—is restated using deconstructionist strategies by Paul de Man in "The Rhetoric of Temporality": "irony engenders a temporal sequence of acts of consciousness which is endless. . . . [I]rony is not temporary . . . but repetitive, the recurrence of a self-escalating act of consciousness," 202.)

Romantic irony receives a more comprehensive formulation in Karl Wilhelm Solger, for whom irony becomes the principle of all art, the source of its power of rising above and resolving contradictions.

4. Situational irony is the more comprehensive term for dramatic irony, which, in turn, subsumes Sophoclean or tragic irony. Though Romantic irony assumes a general irony in the structure of the world (the finite human desire to understand the intricacies of the infinite is a permanently ironic situation), Thirwall's essay of 1833, "On the Irony of Sophocles," is the first formally to explore what he called *practical irony*, which is now more often called *irony of events* or *situational irony*. Monroe Beardsley's designation is the *structure use* of irony (256). Its essence is a clash between intention and result, anticipation and fulfillment, expectation and event. Such irony is especially well suited to presentation in drama, where the spectator is able to observe the disjunction between intentions and hopes on the one hand and outcomes on the other. The standard paradigm is provided by Oedipus's search for the murderer of Laius, including, as it does, both direct irony of events and the kind of double-edged dialogue in which the audience is aware of meanings of which a speaker is unconscious.

Dramatic irony may be a matter of the audience seeing a meaning unintended by the speaker, of both the audience and one or more other characters recognizing the unintended meaning, or of a speaker intending a second meaning understood by the audience but not by the character being addressed (the latter case evidently involves verbal as well as situational irony). In addition, there exists the kind of narrative irony created by what Wayne Booth designates an "unreliable narrator" whom we judge by what we believe are the author's standards (Booth's section on this effect is titled "Secret Communion Between Author and Reader").

5. Whereas Socratic, verbal, and situational irony may rather easily be seen as specialized forms of the same basic contrast between appearance and reality, the New Critics, seeking a term which would embrace the tension between different intellectual or emotional forces existing within the same verbal structure, gave irony a much broader sense. The wellspring of this use of the term is I. A. Richards's *Principles of Literary Criticism*. Contrasting the "stable" poem which "is content with the full, ordered development of comparatively special and limited experience" (that is, development of a definite emotion, attitude, or mood, 249), with that which achieves a balance of heterogeneous impulses, Richards gives higher value to the second. The balance of opposing impulses satisfies his central criterion for evaluating actions, morality, and life in general: the satisfaction of as many impulses or "appetencies" as possible. Richards then

notes, as a means of more clearly differentiating the two kinds, that poems of the first, or stable, kind "will not bear an ironical interpretation" (250).

What is for Richards the test of superior poetry becomes for Cleanth Brooks a necessary condition of good poetry. The meaning of a poetic statement in poetry is "charged," "qualified," or "warped" by the context in which it appears, everything in the poem providing context for every other thing. This mutual qualification Brooks calls irony. In evaluating a poem, then, "we are forced to raise the question as to whether the statement grows properly out of a context; whether it acknowledges the pressures of the context; whether it is 'ironical'—or merely callow, glib, and sentimental" (732). (Richard's emphasis on the capacity of art to balance opposites and Brooks's assignment of the term irony to this capacity owe something to Solger.)

6. The rejection of belief in any stable point of reference that characterizes a large part of later-twentieth-century thought has been interpreted as the operation of a kind of desperate irony. If language cannot correspond to any nonlinguistic reality, if there is no center to the individual mind or personality, and if truth is wholly relative to human mental frameworks, the appropriate response, it is argued, can only be ironical. In *Ironic Vision in Modern Literature*, Charles Glicksberg regards human existence as plunged into what is best understood as a vast unpredictable and incomprehensible structure that demands an ironical response grimmer and less assured than Romantic irony.

> Irony in the modern age goes beyond the Sophoclean irony of fate, just as it goes beyond romantic irony. Grounded in a naturalistic outlook for the most part, it rejects the supernatural, the ideal of universal justice or moral laws, the concept of sin and atonement, the hope of redemption. . . . Men are blind to their true condition, but the ironic hero, in his quest for authenticity, at least refuses to be fooled. . . . He preserves his integrity by viewing all of existence through the perspective of irony. (10–11).

In *Horizons of Assent*, Alan Wilde similarly speaks of irony as "a mode of consciousness, a perceptual response to a world without unity or cohesion" (2). There are two components to ironical consciousness in this sixth sense. First, situational irony is raised to cosmic proportions; second, the assumption that existence is necessarily irrational is palliated by the cultivation of an ironic consciousness that finds pleasure, or at least relief, in seeking to reveal the omnipresence of irony. What Glicksberg calls cosmic irony, Wilde calls suspensive—the first term emphasizing the assumed absurdity of the world, the second, the response.

References

Babbitt, Irving. Chapter on Romantic Irony in *Rousseau and Romanticism*. Boston: Houghton Mifflin, 1919.
Beardsley, Monroe C. *Aesthetics: Problems in the Philosophy of Criticism*. New York: Harcourt, Brace and World, 1958.

Behler, Ernst. "The Theory of Irony in German Romanticism." in *Romantic Irony*, ed. Frederick Garber. Budapest: Akadémiai Kiadó, 1988.

Booth, Wayne. *The Rhetoric of Fiction*. 1961; 2d ed. Chicago: University of Chicago Press, 1983.

Brooks, Cleanth. "Irony as a Principle of Structure." In *Literary Opinion in America*, ed. Morton D. Zabel. New York: Harper, 1951. An earlier version appeared in *College English* 9 (1948): 231–37.

de Man, Paul. "The Rhetoric of Temporality," In *Interpretation: Theory and Practice*, ed. C. S. Singleton. Baltimore: Johns Hopkins University Press, 1969.

Glicksberg, Charles. *The Ironic Vision in Modern Literature*. The Hague: M. Nijhoff, 1969. Discusses the irony of writers such as Anatole France, Hardy, Dostoevsky, Mann, and Beckett. The ironist "may laugh at his predicament, which is that of all mankind, but his laughter is expressive of his despairing belief that there is nothing to be done. . . . The ironist is crucified on the cross of irony that he has built with his own hands" (16).

Kierkegaard, Søren. *The Concept of Irony* (1841). Trans. L. M. Capel. Bloomington: Indiana University Press, 1971. A difficult, somewhat indeterminately ironical, view of irony.

Knox, Dilwyn. *Ironia: Medieval and Renaissance Ideas on Irony*. Leiden, Netherlands: E. J. Brill, 1989. An important although awkwardly organized study.

Muecke, D. C. *Irony*. Critical Idiom Series. London: Methuen, 1970. A very useful and readable introduction.

Plato. *The Republic*. Vol. 2 of *The Dialogues of Plato*. Trans. B. Jowett. 4 vols. New York: Charles Scribner's Sons, 1907.

Quintilian. *The Instituto Oratoria*. Trans. H. E. Butler. 4 vols. Loeb Classical Library, London: Heinemann, 1922.

Richards, I. A. *Principles of Literary Criticism*. London: Routledge and Kegan Paul, 1948.

Sidgwick, Arthur. "On Some Forms of Irony in Literature." *Cornhill* 22 (1907): 497–508.

Solger, Karl Wilhelm. *Erwin* (1815). Berlin: Rudolf Kurtz, 1907.

Thirwall, Connop. "On the Irony of Sophocles." *The Philological Museum* 2 (1833): 483–536. Reprinted in vol. 3 of *Remains, Literary and Theological*, ed. J. S. Perowne. London: 1878.

Wellek, René. *The Romantic Age*. Vol. 2 of *A History of Modern Criticism, 1750–1950*. New Haven: Yale University Press, 1955. Important for an understanding of Friedrich Schlegel on irony.

Wilde, Alan. *Horizons of Assent*. Baltimore: Johns Hopkins University Press, 1981.

> Thus irony, as the typical form, at all levels, of this century's response to the problematics of an increasingly recessive and dissolving self and an increasingly randomized world, strives, by constantly reconstituting itself, to achieve the simultaneous acceptance and creation of a world that is both indeterminate and, at the same time, available to consciousness. (16)

Sources of Additional Information

For seven early definitions of irony translated from Spengel's *Rhetores Graeci*, see Appendix 2 (by Patricia Matsen) to Philip Rollinson's *Classical Theories of Allegory and Christian Culture* (Pittsburgh, Pa.: Duquesne University Press, 1981). Norman Knox's *The Word Irony and Its Context, 1560–1755* (Durham, N.C.: Duke University Press,

1961) sets out and exemplifies ten senses of the term; the most important of these for the neo-classical period, Knox finds, is "blame-by-praise."

The discussion of the several senses of irony does not address questions such as how irony is recognized or the problems of knowing the limits of a particular ironical construction. Wayne Booth's *A Rhetoric of Irony* (Chicago: University of Chicago Press, 1974) is the essential commentary on the interpretation of verbal irony. Booth explores the marks of irony, lays out the steps in reconstructing the intention of the ironist, considers the problem of how to know when to stop seeking further irony, and provides an extensive bibliography. He also strongly distinguishes between stable and unstable ironies; the most controversial aspect of the book is his preference for the first.

Other important essays on the recognition and interpretation of irony are Eleanor Hutchen's "The Identification of Irony" (*ELH* 27, 1960: 352–63) and Norman Knox's "On the Classification of Ironies" (*Modern Philology* 70, 1972: 53–62). Hutchen's overarching definition of irony is "the sport of bringing about a conclusion by indicating its opposite" (359), a definition that applies to situational and cosmic irony as well as Socratic and verbal so long as one imagines fate, the gods, or a similar force as the agent. Norman Knox's cogent essay, primarily a review of D. C. Muecke's *The Compass of Irony* (London: Methuen, 1969) and Glicksberg's *Ironic Vision* (see References above), identifies four variables that must be taken into consideration in classifying ironies: the "field of observation"; "the degree of conflict between appearance and reality"; the structure of relations between three roles, "victim, audience, author"; and "the philosophical-emotional" (comic, tragic, satiric, paradoxical; 53). One of the values of both essays is the recognition of the importance of comic as well as tragic irony.

An especially helpful study of irony is Muecke's *The Compass of Irony*. Muecke's approach is less historical than analytical: he distinguishes three grades of irony (overt, covert, and private) and four modes (the impersonal, the self-disparaging, the ingénu, and the dramatized); and distinguishes between the *irony of the impossible situation* and *corrective irony*. The chapter on Romantic irony is especially valuable. Somewhat more historical is the general discussion of irony in the first chapter of G. G. Sedgewick's *Of Irony, Especially in Drama* (Toronto: University of Toronto Press, 1935). Sedgewick argues that the entire situation of drama—the audience observing the action from outside—is essentially ironic.

For the development of the concept of Romantic irony, see the essays by Lowry Nelson, Jr.; Frederick Garber; Ernst Behler; and Raymond Immerwahr in *Romantic Irony*, ed. F. Garber (Budapest: Akadémiai Kiadó, 1988).

Morton Gurewitch's 1957 dissertation, *European Romantic Irony* (Ann Arbor: University Microfilms, 1986) is an interesting survey. "The identifying mark of the romantic ironist is his simultaneous commitment to exalted visions and to a renegade impulse which mockingly dissolves them" (73).

For anyone troubled by the irony of the seriousness with which critics seem to approach irony, D. J. Enright's *The Alluring Problem* is the proper tonic (New York: Oxford University Press, 1986).

L

LITERARY HISTORY   1. Any study of the language and historical contexts in which literary works were produced, and/or the lives of the authors. 2. The history of the succession of literary works, conventions, genres, or techniques, almost always including an explanation of temporal changes based on an implicit or explicit causal theory.

As a phrase rather than a single word, "literary history" has escaped the close attention of lexicographers. The OED, *treating the phrase under the word "literary," offers only "*literary history (e.g., of a legend, a historical personage or event, etc.): the history of the treatment of, and references to, the subject in literature." *Dictionaries of literary terms have generally passed over the phrase in silence. The first sense given above is not only the broader, but in fact the earlier and more common historically; however, only the second delineates a distinct scholarly activity.*

1. The whole of linguistic, historical, and biographical studies intended to provide the background for understanding a literary work is at times lumped together as literary history, a common use that is still less broad than Francis Bacon's usage: "History is Natural, Civil, Ecclesiastical, and Literary; whereof the three first I allow as extant, the fourth I note as deficient. For no man hath propounded to himself the general state of learning to be described and represented from age to age, as many have done the works of nature and the state civil and ecclesiastical" (183). An interesting twentieth-century example of the employment of the term as synonymous with all literary-historical research by a prestigious scholar will be found in Norman Foerster's "Literary Scholarship and Criticism" (1936). As René Wellek phrases it, this wide sense is equivalent to "study of literature in the past" ("Literary History," 115). This usage occurred especially in the 1930s and 1940s as spokesmen for the NEW CRITICS

were distinguishing CRITICISM, understood as the close reading of individual works of literature, from HISTORICAL SCHOLARSHIP or literary history in the broad sense, which they regarded as study *about* rather than *of* literature. When the author's biography and/or the cultural context is regarded as the source of causal explanation of a literary work, the process is often referred to as *genetic* literary history.

Though literary history generally declined in influence as a result of New Critical dominance, those who have continued to insist on its importance, including the journal *New Literary History*, founded in 1969, have tended to adopt a broad sense. New modes of relating texts to their cultural contexts associated with MARXIST LITERARY CRITICISM, FEMINIST LITERARY CRITICISM and New Historicism (see HISTORICISM) are frequently referred to as exercises in literary history; for example, the essays in *Toward a New American Literary History* (1980), edited by Louis Budd, Edwin Cady, and Carl Anderson, and *Reconstructing American Literary History* (1986), edited by Sacvan Bercovitch.

2. Generally, however, a distinction may be made between historical scholarship, research into specific questions of historical milieu or authorial biography, and the more restricted sense of literary history as a narrative of temporal succession, that is, as a chronological description and, usually, explanation of changes in structure, subject matter, and world view. Thus, René Wellek and Austin Warren's *Theory of Literature* regards literary history as "a view of literature which sees it primarily as a series of works arranged in chronological order and as integral parts of the historical process" (39).

However, this narrower use conceals a number of disparate interests and practices. Literary history has been used to describe endeavors as different as histories of national literature, histories of genre extending across national boundaries and/or historical epochs, histories of technical devices and characteristics, and histories of literary works between specific dates. Even in its narrower sense, therefore, the concept has been a fertile source of controversy. Conflicting answers are given to at least four different questions.

a. One issue is the relationship of literary history to literary criticism and literary theory. For example, while Matthew Arnold did not use the term literary history, his distinction between the historical interest of a work (for instance, as the earliest example of a new form or technique) and its proper evaluation, or *real estimate*, is still cogent. On the other hand, there is considerable debate in the latter twentieth century about whether there is such a thing as a proper evaluation, and a general agreement that the characteristics of texts regarded as worth tracing are functions of the time in which the literary history is written.

F. W. Bateson argues that literary history has to do with derivations, and criticism with evaluations ("Correspondence," 181). Less extreme is R. S. Crane's comment that "in a history propositions about minor and undistinguished works may be quite as relevant, narratively or causally, as anything that may be said about the major and distinguished works which alone, properly, interest the critical anthologist" (2:10). However, as René Wellek argued in Chapter 4 of Wellek and Warren's *Theory of Literature*, "Even the ascertaining of a date or title presupposes some kind of judgement, one which selects this particular book or event from the millions of other books and events" (40). The selection of authors and works considered in a given work of literary history is a function of evaluative judgments, interpretations of meaning, and of what relationships between authors, between works, between works and authors, or between works and the historical milieu in which they were written seem profitable for discussion. From the point of view of Ralph Cohen, the editor of *New Literary History*, looking back on that journal's first decade, even Wellek's warning against separation is insufficiently strong. From Cohen's point of view, literary criticism, theory, and history are themselves all literary genres, and all are historical. The differences between them have to do with "a particular combination of stresses these genres reveal (since they are obviously a family) rather than with the diachronic-synchronic distinction that is often insisted upon" (251). This question is evidently linked to debates over INTERPRETATION, historicism, and the relation of historical scholarship to criticism.

b. A second question is simply *what* is to be traced: a particular genre, a particular technique, choices of subject matter, or a concept or mode of thought. Each can claim to be a form of literary history, but major practical difficulties arise in attempts to combine these into a comprehensive study of literature even within such definite boundaries as "the lyric in the nineteenth century." One way of looking at this problem is R. S. Crane's suggestion that in the last analysis the subject matter of literary history is simply writers and/or readers. "A literary history, like any other history, is a narrative of the changing habits, beliefs, attitudes, tastes, and purposes of individual persons and groups or organizations of persons living in particular times and places; it is not a history of literature but of literary men" (7).

c. The question of what is to be traced through history can be asked in another way: What are the links being sought between the works considered? History is generally understood to be a narrative, not simply a chronological account. Hayden White states the usual view of history succinctly: "Difference implies change. Change implies cause" (100). If what historical narrative seeks are causal relationships, the problem of where to look for causes becomes central. Possible causes are as varied as (a) the influence of earlier authors and works, (b) readers' demands for novelty, and (c) the effects of socioeconomic or political contexts.

The first kind of cause produces source studies and histories of changes within generic types. The second tends to concentrate on changes wholly or largely separate from general cultural or socioeconomic influences, and thus to be characteristic of FORMALISM. The best-known such theory is that of the Russian Formalists: Boris Eichenbaum, summarizing the Formalist endeavor, writes, "We studied literary evolution insofar as it bore a distinctive character and only to the extent that it stood alone, quite independent of other aspects of culture" (*Russian Formalist Criticism*, 136). The result was a theory that regarded the function of literature as making the familiar strange and saw literary history as a record of the pursuit of new modes of defamiliarization as old ones became "automatized." Thus Shklovsky writes: "The purpose of the new form is not to express new content, but to change an old form which has lost its aesthetic quality" (*Russian Formalist Criticism*, 118). More recent versions of this sort of formalism tend to find an alternation between two forces—as foreseen, perhaps, by the dismissive comment in Medvedev/Bakhtin's *The Formal Method in Literary Scholarship* (1928): "All the formalist system needs is the existence of two mutually contrasting artistic terms" (166). David Lodge has described literary history as the alternate dominance of the metonymic and metaphoric principles, as does Hayden White in "The Problem of Change in Literary History" (108–9).

A reasonable, but nevertheless unexpected, development from the Russian Formalist's recognition of the importance of readers' responses emerges from Hans Robert Jauss's concept of an *aesthetic of reception*. "A literary work must be understood as creating a dialogue" (10), which dialogue changes over time. The original reception of a work for Jauss depends on its relation to what is expected, to the *horizon of expectation*; the different kinds of reception accorded the work throughout its history, equally worthy of study as the original reaction, will depend on an ever-changing horizon of expectation, part of which, as regards a given work, may be engendered by the history of previous responses. A somewhat similar position is set out by Robert Weimann in *Structuralism and Society in Literary History* (1976); Weimann argues for the dialectic relationship between the genesis and the later impact of a literary work, between *past significance* and *present meaning*.

Taking a different tack, F. W. Bateson, Josephine Miles, and William C. Spengemann, in somewhat different ways, have linked literary-historical changes to changes in the language itself. More recently, Alastair Fowler's *A History of English Literature* traces changes in literary kinds and forms: "Sometimes these have social or economic causes; but more often they are developments internal to literature—shifts in fashion, deeper movements, growth cycles, effects of compensation" (vii).

In a third category are the specifically external causes, whether broadly cultural or more specifically political or socioeconomic. Hippolyte Taine's *History of English Literature* (1873), written on the principle that race, surroundings, and epoch constitute the mainsprings of literary history, is perhaps the most famous example. An early-twentieth-century formulation of this understanding of literary history is that of Sir Sidney Lee in "The Place of English Literature in the Modern University" (1913): "In literary history we seek the external circumstance—political, social, economic, in which literature is produced" (8). Any such cause, it should be noted, can place emphasis either on explaining features of literary texts by an appeal to historical conditions or the illumination of historical conditions through literary texts. The first type can be said to be a history of the literature of X; the second, a literary history of X. Historicism, in one of its major senses, assumes that one can pursue both directions, since all aspects of the culture of a given period are mutually illuminating. Marxist criticism, on the other hand, tends to see literature as a reflection, or, more recently, a complex refraction, of the socioeconomic base or condition. Yuri B. Vipper thus describes the "philosophical base" of the Gorki Institute's *History of World Literature* as "historical monism, which takes its root in the works of Marx, Engels, and Lenin and presupposes a single process [in all national literatures] of social and cultural development" (546).

Certain "new historicist" writers seek to find the way in which literary texts reflect the relationships of power existing at the time of writing. Related but separable from this is recent concern for discovering in cultural, political, or socioeconomic terms why certain texts have achieved popularity, and thus power, as explored by Annette Kolodny and Jane Tompkins. Related to both is a new interest in the influence of literature on culture. The concept of literary history in terms of causal explanation of the temporal changes in literature is not necessarily central in certain of the above endeavors. The more interested the historian is in using literary texts to illuminate political, religious, or social conditions, the less focus there is likely to be on the sequential relationships between texts. Various balances between histories of aspects of literature and literary histories of aspects of culture are possible.

Moreover, chronological literary histories may be ordered so as to present very different visions of their subjects, as has become increasingly apparent as new literary histories of the United States have been prepared. The long-standard *Literary History of the United States*, edited by R. E. Spiller, W. Thorpe, T. H. Johnson, and H. S. Canby has, in recent years, been seriously challenged for its focus on a "mainstream" tradition of white, male authors, and a vision of American hope and expansion. Current histories, on the other hand, are emphasizing, and therefore making their selections, in such a way as to reflect tension, diversity, and conflict. Thus, the *Columbia Literary History of the United States* (ed. Emory Elliott) announces that it "does not . . . constitute a new consensus about the history of the literature of the United States. For many reasons . . . concurrence remains impossible at this time. There is today no unifying vision of a natural identity like that shared by many scholars at the closings of the two world wars. We have therefore sought to represent the variety of viewpoints that enliven current scholarship" (xii). Sacvan Bercovitch, the editor of the new Cambridge University Press history of American literature, speaks of the breakdown of both political and aesthetic consensus, and sees the only solution in making "a virtue of dissensus" (107). The influential essay by Annette Kolodny, "The Integrity of Memory: Creating a New Literary History of the United States" (1985), concludes with the invocation of an awareness "that if there was something uniquely 'American' about our nation and our literary inheritance, it was not a harmonious commonality or shared tradition, but diversity, division, discord" (307). The movement away from the seeking of a pattern or a set of causal relations explaining perceived directions of development in literary history parallels the reluctant conclusion of René Wellek (who has written repeatedly on the proper goals of literary history) in his 1973 "The Fall of Literary History":"Cause, in the sense as defined by Morris R. Cohen—'some reason or ground why, whenever the antecedent event occurs, the consequent must follow'—is, we must conclude, inapplicable to literary history" (72). "There is no progress, no development, no history of art except a history of writers, institutions, and techniques. This is, at least for me, the end of an illusion, the fall of literary history" (77). However, the causal relations obtaining in histories of literature and literary history can be less rigorously defined.

d. Whatever the chronological, national, or generic boundaries of a literary history; whatever the causal relations pursued; and whatever the proportional emphasis on understanding texts in terms of historical conditions and cultural history in terms of texts, some evaluative criteria must be chosen to limit the authors and texts included. If not one or more criteria of aesthetic success, then such criteria as typicality, ideological interest, popularity at the time of publication, significance in a cultural tradition, long-term canonical recognition, or relevance to a particular cultural phenomenon must necessarily lie behind the selection. Disagreements over which are the most significant criteria are part of the contemporary debate over what, if any specific, texts should constitute the literary CANON.

References

Arnold, Matthew. "The Study of Poetry" (1881). In vol. 9 of *The Complete Prose Works of Matthew Arnold*. Edited by R. H. Super. Ann Arbor: University of Michigan Press, 1960–77.
Bacon, Francis. *Advancement of Learning* (1605). Vol. 6 of *The Works of Francis Bacon*. Ed. J. Spedding, R. L. Ellis, and D. D. Heath. Boston: Taggard and Thompson, 1863.
Bateson, F. W. "Correspondence." *Scrutiny* 4 (1935): 181–85.
———. *English Poetry and the English Language: An Experiment in Literary History*. Oxford: Clarendon Press, 1934. "The real history of poetry is, I believe, the history of the changes in the kind of language in which successive poems have been written. *And it is these changes only that are due to the pressure of social and intellectual tendencies*" (vi–vii).
Bercovitch, Sacvan. "America as Canon and Context: Literary History in a Time of Dissensus." *American Literature* 58 (March 1986): 99–107.
Cohen, Ralph. "On a Decade of *New Literary History*." In *The Horizon of Literature*, ed. Paul Hernadi. Lincoln: University of Nebraska Press, 1982.
Columbia Literary History of the United States. General editor, Emory Elliott. New York: Columbia University Press, 1988.
Crane, R. S. "History versus Criticism in the Study of Literature." In vol. 2 of *The Idea of the Humanities* (Chicago: University of Chicago Press, 1967). Primarily an argument for greater attention to criticism, the essay seeks to define literary history as, like all history, "a discipline which has as its ultimate purpose the

discovery and verification of intelligible narrative propositions about the past''
(5).

Foerster, Norman. ''Literary Scholarship and Criticism.'' *English Journal* (College Edition) 25 (1936): 224–32.

Fowler, Alastair. *A History of English Literature*. Oxford: Basil Blackwell, 1987.

Jauss, Hans Robert. ''Literary History as a Challenge to Literary Theory.'' *New Literary History* 2 (Autumn 1970): 7–37. Essentially reprinted in *Toward an Aesthetic of Reception* (as first chapter). Trans. T. Bahti. Sussex: Harvester, 1982.

Kolodny, Annette. ''The Integrity of Memory: Creating a New Literary History of the United States.'' *American Literature* 57 (1985): 291–307.

Lee, Sir Sidney. ''The Place of English Literature in the Modern University'' (1913). Reprinted in *Elizabethan and Other Essays*. Oxford: Clarendon Press, 1929. ''Literary history ought to be no skeleton, no charnel house of dry bones. It should be a thing of flesh and blood, a living guide to the aspiration and practical endeavour of the author and a moving picture of his environment'' (8).

Literary History of the United States. Ed. R. E. Spiller, W. Thorp, T. H. Johnson, and H. S. Canby. New York: Macmillan, 1948. Later editions: 1953, 1963, 1974.

Lodge, David. ''Historicism and Literary History: Mapping the Modern Period.'' *New Literary History* 10 (Spring 1979): 547–55. Reprinted in *Working with Structuralism*. London: Routledge and Kegan Paul, 1981.

Medvedev, P. N./M. M. Bakhtin. *The Formal Method in Literary Scholarship* (1928). Trans. A. J. Wehrle. Baltimore: Johns Hopkins University Press, 1978. Originally published under Medvedev's name, the volume has also been attributed in whole or part to Bakhtin. Criticizes the Formalists for believing ''the series of literary history, the series of artistic works and their constructive elements, to be completely independent of other ideological series and of socioeconomic development'' (159).

Miles, Josephine. *The Continuity of Poetic Language*. Berkeley: University of California Press, 1951.

———. *The Vocabulary of English*. Berkeley: University of California Press, 1946.

Reconstructing American Literary History. Ed. Sacvan Bercovitch. Cambridge, Mass: Harvard University Press, 1986. In the introduction, Bercovitch describes the essays included as succeeding ''in using literary techniques to illuminate the dynamics of culture, and historical analysis to open up literary interpretation'' (ix).

Russian Formalist Criticism: Four Essays. Ed. Lee T. Lemon, and Marion J. Reis. Lincoln: University of Nebraska Press, 1965.

Spengemann, William C. ''American Things/Literary Things: The Problem of American Literary History.'' *American Literature* 57 (October 1985): 456–81. Spengemann questions the entire concept of a specifically ''American'' literature: ''We have American things, and we have literary things; but we have nothing typically American that can be called literary and nothing literary that can be called uniquely or specifically American'' (471). Spengemann argues that literary history can properly be a history of the literature written in one language and must include all literature written in that language.

Taine, Hippolyte. *History of English Literature*. Trans. H. Van Laun. 2 vols. Edinburgh: Edmonston and Hughes, 1873.

Toward a New American Literary History: Essays in Honor of Arlin Turner. Ed. Louis

J. Budd, Edwin H. Cady, and Carl L. Anderson. Durham, N.C.: Duke University Press, 1980.

Tompkins, Jane. *Sensational Designs: The Cultural Work of American Fiction, 1790–1860*. New York: Oxford University Press, 1985.

Vipper, Yuri B. "National Literary History in *History of World Literature*: Theoretical Principles of Treatment," *New Literary History* 16 (Spring 1985): 545–58.

Weimann, Robert. *Structure and Society in Literary History*. Charlottesville: University of Virginia, 1976.

Wellek, René. "The Fall of Literary History." In *The Attack on Literature*. Chapel Hill: University of North Carolina Press, 1982. Reprinted from *Geschichte: Ereignis und Erzählung*, ed. R. Kosseleck and W.-D. Stempel. Munich: Wilhelm Fink Verlag, 1973.

———. "Literary History." In *Literary Scholarship*, ed. N. Foerster. Chapel Hill: University of North Carolina Press, 1949. Wellek here offers a broad but bounded view of the activity of literary history: "[T]he process of interpretation, criticism, and appreciation has never been completely interrupted and is likely to continue indefinitely, or at least as long as there is no complete interruption of the cultural tradition. One of the tasks of the literary historian is the description of this process" (120).

Wellek, René, and Austin Warren. *Theory of Literature*. 1942; New York: Harcourt, Brace and World, 1956. The long-standing division of literature into literary theory, literary history, and literary criticism is set out straightforwardly in Chapter 4.

White, Hayden. "The Problem of Change in Literary History." *New Literary History* 7 (Autumn 1975): 97–111.

Sources of Additional Information

In "Six Kinds of Literary History," in *The Critical Significance of Biographical Evidence* (English Institute Essays for 1946, New York: Columbia University Press, 1947), René Wellek describes kinds of literary history, roughly in the order in which they arose: "as a (1) history of books; as (2) intellectual history; as the (3) history of national civilizations; as (4) sociological method; as (5) historical relativism; and, finally, as an (6) internal history of literary development" (113). Wellek here champions the last kind, but by 1973 he has abandoned the hope for its possibility. Beginning with the Renaissance, Wellek's *The Rise of English Literary History* (Chapel Hill: University of North Carolina Press, 1941) surveys the kinds of bibliographical and biographical compilations that, together with various essays on literature and criticism, lay behind the first true literary history in English, Thomas Warton's *History of English Poetry* (1774–81). R. S. Crane's "Critical and Historical Principles of Literary History" (in vol. 2 of *The Idea of the Humanities*, Chicago: University of Chicago Press, 1967) considers several of the major issues related to the writing of literary history and argues for a "history of forms" that focuses on the problems an author faced as an alternative to either *philological* or *dialectical* literary history.

For a brief summary of the effects of recent theoretical movements on the concept of literary history, see Alum Fakrul's "The Newer Criticism: New Directions in American Literary History" (*South Carolina Review* 21, Fall 1988: 65–68).

Emory Elliot's "New Literary History: Past and Present" (*American Literature* 57, December 1985: 611–21) explores the questions of theory, definition, and purpose confronting him as editor of the *Columbia Literary History of the United States* (See References above).

The pitfalls of conceptualizing literary history as a set of discrete periods are discussed by Claudio Guillén in "Second Thoughts on Currents and Periods" (in *The Disciplines of Criticism*, ed. P. Demetz, T. Greene, and L. Nelson, Jr., New Haven, Conn.: Yale University Press, 1968). "It is only a *certain* set of criteria" that makes possible a distinction between two periods—further, one can emphasize either continuity or difference. "Now, my main thesis is that a section of historical time should not be understood as a single entity, a bloc, a unity, but as a plural number of temporal currents, temporal levels, rhythms or sequences, running . . . simultaneously and side by side" (508).

Janusz Slawinski's "Reading and Reader in the Literary Historical Process" (*New Literary History* 19, Spring 1988: 521–39) develops the implications for literary history of the Jaussian program for an "aesthetics of reception" and the development of READER-RESPONSE theories generally. Texts may be considered not only in terms of the degree of their originality, but in terms of their *productivity*, defined as "the extent and variety of reactions [the text] has evoked in the course of the literary historical process" (535).

Among numerous discussions of the literary history as viewed from the point of view of feminist theory and criticism are Marilyn Williamson's "Towards a Feminist Literary History" (*Signs: Journal of Women in Culture and Society* 10, Autumn 1984: 136–47) and Lawrence Buell's "Literary History Without Sexism? Feminist Studies and Canonical Reception" (*American Literature* 59, March 1987: 102–14).

LITERATURE   1. Until late in the eighteenth century, polite learning, humanistic learning, belles lettres; that which was the source of wide and humane knowledge. 2. Imaginative, creative, artistic, or aesthetically oriented writing.

Definitions of "poetry" are often intended to apply as well to literature in sense 2.

Very much the same history of the term literature is to be found in Raymond Williams's Keywords, *René Wellek's "The Attack on Literature," and the first chapter of Terry Eagleton's* Literary Theory, *although with very different purposes and interpretive commentary (that is, neutral, conservative, and Marxist, respectively).*

1. René Wellek finds that "*litterae* in antiquity is simply the study of the arts and letters of the Greeks as far as they represent the Greek idea of man," and that in the Renaissance, "a clear consciousness of a new secular literature emerges and with it the terms *litterae humanae, lettres humains, bonnes lettres*, or as late as in Dryden, 'good letters' " (13). According to Raymond Williams, "literature" entered English in the fourteenth century "in the sense of polite learning through reading. . . . Thus a man of *literature*, or of *letters*, meant what we would now describe as a man of wide reading" (184).

2. In sense 1, "literature" carried a positive value. The identification of literature with texts of value continued as the meaning narrowed in the nineteenth century: thus the term is sometimes used descriptively, sometimes evaluatively. Literature in the narrower sense in which it embraces primarily poetry, prose fiction, drama, and the personal essay is sometimes distinguished as "imagi-

native," "creative," or "literature as art," but no single qualifying adjective seems adequate. A problem repeatedly noted is that certain sermons, philosophical essays, histories, and other prose works not intended or originally regarded as literature come to be considered literary.

There are at least nine bases on which literature in sense 2 has been defined. These are not necessarily incompatible, and some are overlapping: various of these criteria have been combined in a wide range of patterns by those who have attempted specific definitions.

a. An obvious criterion is value, for a wholehearted example of which one may take Sir Sidney Lee's 1913 statement: "It is needless to cite definitions of literature. We all know it to be the storehouse of the best thought and feeling, set forth in the most lucid, harmonious, and pleasure-giving forms, of which words are capable" (3). While for Lee such a characterization of literature is a happy one, Terry Eagleton's 1983 *Literary Theory: An Introduction* pursues the definition of literature as "a highly valued kind of writing" to the conclusion that what is called literature is that which supports an existing ideology and power structure (10, 14). Ultimately, for Eagleton, "Departments of literature in higher education . . . are part of the ideological apparatus of the modern capitalist state" (200).

b. Literature is generally associated with, and therefore not infrequently defined at least partially by, its ability to give pleasure. G. B. Harrison's definition is quite explicit: "Literature is a means of evoking pleasure in a reader by written words" (20).

c. Fictionality is a common criterion. While surveying a number of possible ways of defining literature in *Theory of Literature*, René Wellek and Austin Warren give particular emphasis to the fictional aspect of literature. "But the nature of literature emerges most clearly under the referential aspects. . . . The statements in a novel, in a poem, or in a drama are not literally true; they are not logical propositions" (25). David Lodge states in *The Modes of Modern Writing*, "I suggest that literary discourse is either self-evidently fictional or may be read as such, and that what compels or permits such reading is the structural organization of its component parts, its systematic foregrounding" (6–7).

J. M. Cameron has argued that the very purpose of literature is "the making of fictions"; Cameron goes on to develop a specific entailment of this fictionality.

> Fictitious descriptions are neither true nor false and this follows from their being fictions. . . . It follows from this that I could not give an *alternative* poetic description, for there could be no criterion (as there would be in the case of a real description) for deciding whether or not the alternative description had succeeded. The poetic description has the form of a description; but it exists only as *this* description, these words in this order. (136–37)

In *The Phenomenon of Literature*, Bennison Gray presents a similar argument and concludes that literature is not a particular use of language but rather a fictional statement, that is, an unverifiable one. "A work of literature is the

unverifiable moment-by-moment statement of an event'' (142). Under this definition as wielded by Gray, Eliot's *The Waste Land*, Blake's *The Marriage of
Heaven and Hell*, and Joyce's *Finnegans Wake* are excluded from literature
because they are not statements and cannot therefore be fictional. Though these
would be classed as literature under a definition based on the way they employ
language, Bennison remarks, ''it would be naive to claim that [such works] are
considered to be literature merely because they were composed by literary persons. The truth of the matter is that these works were intended to be literature
and have simply failed to be so by the criteria of the definition of literature as
fiction established here'' (144).

A variation on the criterion of fictionality as usually understood is that pursued
in an essay of Richard Ohmann's which, employing SPEECH-ACT analysis, defines
literature as discourse without illocutionary force. More fully: ''A literary work
is a discourse whose sentences lack the illocutionary forces that would normally
attach to them. . . . Specifically, a literary work *purportedly imitates* (or reports)
a series of speech acts, which in fact have no other existence'' (14).

Perhaps the most sophisticated approach to the fictionality of literature is that
derived from C. S. Peirce by John Sheriff, in which literature is understood as
what Peirce calls a *rhematic symbol*, a rheme being a sign of a possible but not
actual object.

> Peirce says, 'A rheme is any sign that is not true or false, like almost any single
> word except 'yes' and 'no'. . . . Since a poem (any work of literature) is experienced
> as a rhematic symbol, it is a distortion to equate it with a proposition or argument.
> . . . Anytime one says anything about the rheme produced by the sign, he is uncon-
> sciously allowing the interpretant (rheme) to become a new sign . . . which determines
> a new interpretant (an argument). In other words, he turns a sign of imaginative
> possibility into a proposition or argument. (68)

d. The power of literature to evoke emotions provides another possible criterion. The importance of emotion to the experience of poetry is assumed throughout Matthew Arnold's ''Study of Poetry.'' I. A. Richards, who admired Arnold,
made the stimulus of emotion rather than the communication of knowledge the
central differentiation between the emotive use of language in literature and the
referential use in science. ''Poetry affords the clearest examples of this subordination of reference to attitude. It is the supreme form of *emotive* language''
(273). Thomas C. Pollock's *The Nature of Literature* (1942) develops Richards's
distinction more elaborately.

> In *phatic communion*, one person uses words to come into relation with another. In
> *referential symbolism*, one person uses words to direct the attention of another to
> certain referents: if this is his controlling purpose, the use is *pure* referential: if his
> purpose is also to arouse attitudes or actions in connection with the referents, the
> use is *pragmatic*-referential. In *evocative symbolism*, one person uses words to evoke
> a controlled experience (E) in another: if he does this in order to express an experience
> of his own, the use is *literature (L)*: if his concern, however, is only to evoke an
> experience (E) in the other, the use is *pseudo-literature*. (195–96)

e. The Russian Formalists were much occupied with elucidating the defining characteristics of literature. Thus Roman Jakobson writes: "The subject of literary scholarship is not literature in its totality but literariness (*literaturnost*) i.e., that which makes of a given work a work of literature" (*Noveyshaya*, 11). This search for the basis of literariness led to Victor Shklovsky's concept of *defamiliarization*, of "making strange." "The purpose of art is to impart the sensation of things as they are perceived and not as they are known. The technique of art is to make objects 'unfamiliar,' to make forms difficult, to increase the difficulty and length of perception because the process of perception is an aesthetic end in itself and must be prolonged" (12).

f. The way in which language is employed can serve as a basis of definition. René Wellek and Austin Warren's chapter on "The Nature of Literature" gives almost as much importance to the language as to the fictionality of literature. "The resources of language are exploited much more deliberately and systematically. . . . Poetic language organizes, tightens, the resources of everyday language" (24). The classic statement of this way of defining literature is that of Roman Jakobson in "Linguistics and Poetics." After schematizing all verbal communication in terms of six aspects of language (addresser, context, message, contact, code, and addressee), Jakobson points out that different uses of language emphasize different factors. "The set (*Einstellung*) toward the MESSAGE as such, focus on the message for its own sake, is the POETIC function of language" (356).

g. The indirect, multiply suggestive quality of literature can define literature and or suggest how the literary is recognized. Thus Monroe Beardsley can say simply, "a literary work is a discourse in which an important part of the meaning is implicit" (126). Rather than defining literature, Umberto Eco seeks to explain the "aesthetic use of language." Essentially, Eco follows the lead given by Jakobson but with greater emphasis on ambiguity: the aesthetic text calls attention to itself by idiosyncratic uses of the standard codes of language that cause the text to be ambiguous and self-focusing. The literary text conveys the sense of a surplus of both expression and content, and thus of communicating too much. However, the aesthetic text is not simply ambiguous or chaotic; it is organized by a systematic rule so that "every deviation springs from a *general deviational matrix*" (271). Robert Scholes also builds on Jakobson's six factors: "Stated as simply as I can put it, we sense literariness in an utterance when any one of the six features of communication loses its simplicity and becomes multiple or duplicitous" (235).

h. For Paul de Man, employing a deconstructive extrapolation from Saussure (see SEMIOTICS, DECONSTRUCTION), the ambiguity of literature is understood as indeterminacy. "For the statement about language, that sign and meaning can never coincide, is what is precisely taken for granted in the kind of language we call literary" (*Blindness and Insight*, 17). In *Allegories of Reading*, he writes, "Literature as well as criticism—the difference between them being delusive—

is condemned (or privileged) to be forever the most rigorous and, consequently, the most unreliable language in terms of which man names and transforms himself'' (19).

i. The argument that literariness is not a property of texts but the name of a category that individual readers or society choose to apply to texts used in a certain way has been stated in a variety of forms in the twentieth century. For Louise Rosenblatt, ''The distinction between aesthetic and nonaesthetic reading . . . derives ultimately from what the reader does, the stance that he adopts and the activities he carries out in relation to the text'' (27). *Efferent* (information-seeking) reading concentrates on what can be used after the reading is finished. In contrast, ''At the aesthetic end of the spectrum . . . the reader's primary purpose is fulfilled *during* the reading event, as he fixes his attention on the actual experiences he is living through'' (27). For John Ellis, ''The category of literary texts is not distinguished by defining characteristics but by the characteristic use to which those texts are put by the community'' (50). For John Searle, '' 'literature' is the name of a set of attitudes we take toward a stretch of discourse, not a name of an internal property of the stretch of discourse, though why we take the attitudes we do will of course be at least in part a function of the properties of the discourse'' (59). For Stanley Fish, ''Literature is still a category, but it is an open category, not definable by fictionality, or by disregard of propositional truth, or by a statistical predominance of tropes or figures, but by what we decide to put in it'' (52).

As Searle suggests, the decision to regard a text as literature must be at least partially a function of its own characteristics, a matter that is left open by most of those who accept that what is literature is a result of an attitude toward, rather than a property of, texts. The question of what attributes cause readers to designate certain works as literary, and cause reasonably wide agreement about which texts are (descriptively as opposed to evaluatively) literature is, however, sometimes addressed by the suggestion that rather than one property shared by all texts regarded as literary, there are a number of characteristics, each of which may produce that judgment.

While Louise Rosenblatt insists that the reader can at least theoretically choose to read a text either aesthetically or efferently, she notes that reading certain texts aesthetically will be much more rewarding than reading others in that way. In any case, she specifically describes the use of what is read as literature in Coleridge's terms: ''The reader should be carried forward, not merely or chiefly by the mechanical impulse of curiosity, or by a restless desire to arrive at the final solution; but by the pleasurable activity of mind excited by the attractions of the journey itself'' (28). John Ellis somewhat similarly describes the difference in use: ''The use of texts in such a way that they are not regarded as limited to and functioning within the original circumstances of their origin is defining for literary texts'' (134). In both formulations, referential application interferes with the proper response to literature.

References

Arnold, Matthew. "The Study of Poetry" (1880). In vol. 9 of *The Complete Prose Works of Matthew Arnold*. Ed. R. H. Super. Ann Arbor: University of Michigan Press, 1960–77.

Beardsley, Monroe. *Aesthetics: Problems in the Philosophy of Criticism*. New York: Harcourt, Brace and World, 1958.

Cameron, J. M. "Poetry and Dialectic." In *The Night Battle*. London: Burns and Oates, 1962.

De Man, Paul. *Allegories of Reading*. New Haven: Yale University Press, 1979.

———. *Blindness and Insight*. New York: Oxford Univrsity Press, 1971.

Eagleton, Terry. *Literary Theory: An Introduction*. Minneapolis: University of Minnesota Press, 1983.

Eco, Umberto. *A Theory of Semiotics*. Bloomington: Indiana University Press, 1976. Pages 261–76 on the aesthetic text are of significant interest.

Ellis, John. *The Theory of Literary Criticism*. Berkeley: University of California Press, 1974.

Fish, Stanley. "How Ordinary is Ordinary Language?" *New Literary History* 5 (Autumn 1973): 41–54.

Gray, Bennison. *The Phenomenon of Literature*. The Hague: Mouton, 1975.

Harrison, G. B. *Profession of English*. 1962; New York: Doubleday/Anchor Books, 1967.

Jakobson, Roman. "Linguistics and Poetics." In *Style in Language*, ed. Thomas A. Sebeok. Cambridge, Mass.: MIT Press, 1960.

———. *Noveyshaya russkaya poeziya* (*Newest Russian Poetry*, 1921). The passage is quoted from p. 11 by Victor Erlich in *Russian Formalism: History—Doctrine*. The Hague: Mouton, 1955, p. 146.

Lee, Sir Sidney. "The Place of English Literature in the Modern University" (1913). In *Elizabethan and Other Essays*. Oxford: Clarendon Press, 1929.

Lodge, David. *The Modes of Modern Writing*. Ithaca, N.Y.: Cornell University Press, 1977.

Ohmann, Richard. "Speech Acts and the Definition of Literature." *Philosophy and Rhetoric* 4 (Winter 1971): 1–19.

Pollock, Thomas Clark. *The Nature of Literature*. Princeton, N.J.: Princeton University Press, 1942.

Richards, I. A. *Principles of Literary Criticism*. 1925; London: Routledge and Kegan Paul, 1948.

Rosenblatt, Louise. *The Reader, the Text, the Poem*. Carbondale: Southern Illinois University Press, 1978. Chapters 3 through 6 all bear on the question of what literature is.

Scholes, Robert. "Toward a Semiotics of Literature." In *What Is Literature?* ed. P. Hernadi. Bloomington: University of Indiana Press, 1978.

Searle, *Expression and Writing*. Cambridge: Cambridge University Press, 1979.

Sheriff, John. "Charles S. Peirce and the Semiotics of Literature." In *Semiotic Themes*, ed. Richard T. De George. Lawrence: University of Kansas Publications, 1981.

Shklovsky, Victor. "Art as Technique." In *Russian Formalist Criticism: Four Essays*. Ed. and trans. Lee T. Lemon and Marion J. Reis. Lincoln: University of Nebraska Press, 1965.

Wellek, René. "The Attack on Literature." In *The Attack on Literature and Other Essays*. Chapel Hill: University of North Carolina Press, 1982. Reprinted from *The American Scholar* 42 (December 1972): 27–42.

Wellek, René, and Austin Warren. *Theory of Literature*. 1949; New York: Harcourt, Brace and World, 1956.

Williams, Raymond. *Keywords: A Vocabulary of Culture and Society*. New York: Oxford University Press, 1985.

Sources of Additional Information

What Is Literature? ed. Paul Hernadi (Bloomington: Indiana University Press, 1978) brings together eighteen essays that explore the difficulties of defining literature. Of particular interest in this collection is Charles Altieri's "A Procedural Definition of Literature." Henryk Markiewicz's "The Limits of Literature" (*New Literary History* 4, Autumn 1972: 5–14) is an informed presentation of three properties of literariness: (a) fictionality, or the possible absence of an empirical referent, (b) figurality, or the presence of representational or nonrepresentational tropes, and (c) linguistic choices that are not purely referential.

The latter portion of John Guillory's "Canonical and Non-Canonical: A Critique of the Current Debate" (*English Literary History* 54, Fall 1987: 483–527) discusses literary language as a sociolect distinguishing classes.

LYRIC 1. In reference to classical Greek literature, poetry sung to the accompaniment of the lyre. 2. One of the three major kinds of poetry, the others being EPIC and dramatic. 3. As applied subsequent to the classical Greek period, and especially in reference to poetry of the Renaissance and after, a particular category of nondramatic poetry. The characteristics of this category most generally cited are first-person presentation, a sense of immediacy, expression of emotion, musicality, and brevity, though emphases differ among critics, and there remains considerable disagreement about the most essential nature of the lyric.

1. The name lyric originally designated that poetry written to be accompanied by the music of the lyre. Part of the confusion that has prevailed in the discussion of the lyric originates here, for, strictly speaking, such a definition excludes the elegy (meant to be accompanied by the flute), the ode sung by a chorus, and all nondramatic poetry not intended to be accompanied by music. Moreover, the term lyric is unknown in the classical period and appears to have originated among the scholars of Alexandria. The Alexandrians recognized nine *lyrikoi* or lyric poets, but have left little clarification of the term itself.

Aristotle, who distinguished the kinds of poetry by differences in their means (use of rhythm, harmony, and language), differences in their objects (that which was imitated), and differences in manner of imitation (narrative, dramatic, or mixed) had almost nothing to say about poetry that was neither narrative nor dramatic. In short, while the Greeks recognized a variety of kinds of non-epic, non-dramatic poetry as distinguished by meter, stanzaic form, and type of musical accompaniment, there appears to have been no term for some of these, while the term that was given general currency by the Alexandrian scholars suggests only one defining quality, one which is too narrow to apply to all even of the Greek poetry to which it has come to refer and which is irrelevant to poetry written since. Not even Roman poets wrote for lyre-ic accompaniment.

2. Though Aristotle did not explicitly divide poetry (which constituted by far the major part of what we would now call literature) into epic, dramatic, and lyric, his comments in the *Poetics* led to the Alexandrian categorization, and thence to the generally adopted triadic division. epic, dramatic, and lyric became fully established as the three universal forms, however, only in the eighteenth century (see GENRE). In England, "lyric" could serve especially well as the name of the third major form because its most important variety was understood to be the ode. In M. H. Abrams's words, "The soaring fortunes of the lyric may be dated from 1651, the year that Cowley's Pindaric 'imitations' burst over the literary horizon and inaugurated the immense vogue of the 'greater Ode' in England" (85). An important essay by Norman Maclean points out that while eighteenth-century poetry has seemed essentially nonlyrical to nineteenth- and twentieth-century readers, the age "regarded the highest form of the lyric—the Great Ode—as one of the supreme expressions of poetry and itself as a supreme epoch in the history of the lyric, with its first master, Cowley, at least rivaling Pindar, with Dryden secure among all competitors, and with Gray the last and the best" (408). Under the influence of the rediscovered Longinus, the Great or Pindaric Ode was identified with the sublime, while other forms of lyric poetry were grouped under the category of the Lesser Ode, which sought sweetness or beauty. However, by the end of the century, Lesser Odes that expressed passion were granted the possibility of a certain sublimity and, therefore, greater importance.

3. The twentieth century has seen numerous attempts to define the lyric more fully and to separate it from other forms of nondramatic poetry. The virtual disappearance of verse in drama and narrative accompanied by the recognition of the many varieties of poetry practiced in the nineteenth and twentieth centuries encouraged such differentiation. The role played by Francis Palgrave's *The Golden Treasury* (1861) in giving prominence to the lyric has been examined by Christopher Clausen. Just at the end of the last century, W. E. Henley's 1897 *English Lyric: Chaucer to Poe* insisted on the necessity of a "Lyrical Temperament" manifested in a poem with singleness of thought, feeling, and situation, and in which the " 'feeling' shall oblige us to forget the others, or at least to consider them chiefly essential to its triumphing expression" (vii–viii). Edward Reed constructed a working definition for his *English Lyrical Poetry* (1912): "all songs; all poems following classical lyrical forms; all short poems expressing the writer's moods and feelings in a rhythm that suggests music, are to be considered lyrics" (10). The most commonly cited characteristics are here set out: verse that either seems appropriate for a musical setting or is itself in some way "musical," is short, and expresses the writer's feelings (or at least feelings belonging to the voice or persona). Ernest Rhys's *Lyric Poetry* (1913) describes

the lyric as "a form of musical utterance in words governed by overmastering emotion and set free by a powerfully concordant rhythm" (vi). Rhys's emphasis is on emotional power above all else; thus he finds the lyrical in certain passages within long poems as well as in briefer ones.

M. R. Ridley's 1933 article "The Lyric" asks for agreement that "lyric is an expression, usually brief, of a personal feeling, whether that feeling is a transient emotional mood such as the excitement of a revel, or a long-continued emotional experience such as love of country" (112). What departs from the most common view here is the acceptance of emotion that does not represent an immediate mood as well as that which does. C. Day Lewis—who reflects Henley's criterion of singleness in the phrase "saying one thing at a time, without reservation" (5)—demands not so much emotion as verbal musicality, the "singing line." Emphasis on that criterion allows him to include the category of the "story lyric." Elder Olson's introduction to his *American Lyric Poems* (1964) gives special attention to brevity redefined not in terms of a poem's length but of "the brevity of the human behavior it depicts" (2) and insists that the core of lyric is personal response, not interpersonal action. Barbara Hardy's *The Advantage of Lyric* (1977) again looks primarily toward the expression of emotion through concentration: "Lyric poetry isolates feeling in small compass and so renders it at its most intense" (1).

Implicit in almost all such commentaries is the assumption that the lyric employs a first-person speaker; the distinction between drama, epic, and at least most other poetry has rested on this point since Aristotle. The first-person voice is not necessarily identified directly with that of the author. The New Critical principle of the autonomy of the poem explicitly excluded such identification, although the denial that one heard Whitman's, Wordsworth's, or Tennyson's voice speaking in their lyric poems has never been absolute (see AUTHOR). A different kind of distinction—one that does not deny that the first-person lyric voice is expressing a personally felt emotion while not insisting that the specific situation described or suggested by the poem has a direct biographical basis— is carefully traced by German writers as early as the middle of the nineteenth century. The concept of *Erlebnis*, as described by René Wellek, names "a quality of life" that "may come from the world of ideas or may be suggested by trivial circumstances, a chance meeting, the reading of a book, etc." In other words, it "means an experience, of whatever origin, intense enough to become the stimulus to creation" (250).

To a number of critics, the lyric voice has seemed oblivious of an audience. The most often-quoted formulation is that of John Stuart Mill. "Poetry and eloquence are both alike the expression or utterance of feeling. But if we may be excused the antithesis, eloquence is *heard*, poetry is *over*heard" (348). Mill was not in this remark trying to define the nature of the lyric but rather of poetry in general. He goes on to say, "All poetry is of the nature of soliloquy" (349). Nevertheless, he appears to have been thinking primarily of poetry of the lyric type, and T. S. Eliot and Northrop Frye, among others, have tied the distinction to the lyric. Eliot distinguishes three voices. "The first is the voice of the poet talking to himself—or to nobody. The second is the voice of the poet addressing an audience, whether large or small. The third is the voice of the poet when he attempts to create a dramatic character speaking in verse; when he is saying, not what he would say in his own person, but only what he can say within the limits of one imaginary character addressing another imaginary character" (6–7). The first voice represents for Eliot what is usually called lyric poetry, although he prefers the term *meditative verse*. Frye speaks of "the concealment of the poet's audience from the poet" (249). "The lyric poet normally pretends to be talking to himself or someone else: a spirit of nature, a Muse[,] . . . a personal friend, a lover, a god, a personified abstraction, or a natural object. . . . The poet, so to speak, turns his back on his listeners" (249). Opposing the Mill-Eliot-Frye notion that the lyric is a kind of soliloquy is W. R. Johnson's position in *The Idea of Lyric*. Johnson, a classicist, finds most Greek lyric partaking of what he calls the "I-You" form in which the first-person voice is evidently addressing an auditor or auditors, whether explicitly identified or not. Such address, he insists, is necessarily rhetorical. "What is essential, then, to lyric is rhetoric, and essential to this lyrical rhetoric . . . is the pronomial form and lyric identity, the dynamic configuration of lyrical pronouns that defines and vitalizes the situation of lyrical discourse" (23). For Johnson, the Greek lyric poet intended "lyrical discourse" (4), not the meditative soliloquy, the tendency to move toward which robbed much poetry of lyric power.

The immediacy of the emotions experienced is yet another characteristic generally ascribed to the lyric. The lyric has frequently been identified with a strong sense of the present (as the epic with the past, and the drama with the future). However, "lyric immediacy" can be felt less as the present than as timelessness. Wellek points out that in Emil Staiger's *Grundbegriffe der Poetik* (1946), the "time scheme is abolished for the lyrical mode" (237). Jonathan Culler's essay "Apostrophe" argues that the figure of apostrophe, frequently found in lyric poems and especially in the ode, establishes "what might be called a timeless present but is better seen as a temporality of writing. . . . Such considerations suggest that one distinguish two forces in poetry, the narrative and the apostrophic, and that the lyric is characteristically the triumph of the apostrophic" (149).

David Lindley's "Critical Idiom" volume on the lyric (1985) reviews all the above characteristics and finds that all require qualification. "We may then accept that many lyrics are short, many speak of heightened feeling in a poetic present and are uttered by a voice in the first person, and a significant number are written for music or out of a musical impulse. But many other poems we might wish to call 'lyrics' have few or none of these qualities" (4). In summary, by and large the current understanding of lyric is that poems that are not essentially narrative, that maintain a single tone, that reflect a moment in time and give a sense of immediacy, that express apparently personal emotion, that employ the first person, and in which the sound stratum pleasingly calls attention to itself, are certainly lyric, though deviations from the norm in one or more of these aspects do not necessarily disqualify a poem from membership in the category. What qualities among these a critic feels most important determine whether such marginal examples as *Lycidas*, the early version of *The Prelude*, or Browning's monologues are considered lyrics.

In addition to what might be called the majority opinion on the lyric, there are a number of stimulating positions that are eccentric (in the descriptive, not evaluative, sense). The first is explicit dissent from the Aristotelian doctrine that all poetry, including lyric, partakes of MIMESIS. Challenge came early in the history of English critical thought. Sir William Jones's essay "On the Arts called Imitative" (1771) disputes "the assertion of Aristotle that all poetry consists in imitation" (361); rather, "poetry was originally no more than a strong animated expression of the human passions" (364). Thomas Twining includes his disagreement with Aristotle (and Batteaux) in the notes to his translation of the *Poetics* (1789): "The Lyric Poet is not always, and essentially, an *imitator*, any more than the Epic. While he is merely expressing his own *sentiments*, in his own *person*, we consider him not as imitating;—we inquire not whether they are the assumed sentiments of the Poetic character, or even real sentiments of the writer himself; we do not even think of such distinction" (140).

The opposite position is taken by Gémino Abad, whose *Formal Approach to Lyrical Poetry* is an intriguing attempt to fill out the application to lyric of the Aristotelian Chicago School of critics with special attention to the work of Elder Olson. Interpreting the mimesis of the lyric as imitation of a mental activity or event, Abad begins by concentrating on the Aristotelian formal cause, that is, the object imitated. Of the four possible *magnitudes* of the represented object adopted from Olson, two yield classes of lyric: "the activity of a single character in a single closed situation" and "the activity of two or more characters in a single closed situation" (10). This system of classification allows for the inclusion of a great variety of poems, all of which, in effect, fall into the two magnitudes and are not didactic (the didactic is seen as rhetoric rather than imitation).

Other individual approaches are taken by Bennison Gray, Käte Hamburger, and Elder Olson in *The Phenomenon of Literature*, *The Logic of Literature*, and "Sailing to Byzantium: Prolegomena to a Poetics of the Lyric," respectively. Gray, who defines a work of literature as "the unverifiable moment-by-moment statement of an event" (142), is able to discard the term lyric by setting up for all of literature two genuses, the *unmediated* (to which belong the species monologue and dialogue) and the *mediated* (to which belong the species script, story, and serial). The lyric would fall within the unmediated genus, as do, for instance, fictional prose monologues. Käte Hamburger approaches the mimetic status of the lyric differently. Narrative and dramatic literature imitate reality and can be compared to it. However, statements by the "Lyric I" consist only of the statement-subject. "Something has taken place in the subject-object structure of these statements which never occurs in the informative statement. They have, so to speak, withdrawn from the object-pole and gone into a mutually interlocking order or contiguity, and have thereby taken on meaning-contents which in no way refer—at least not directly—to the object-pole" (248–49). Finally, Elder Olson finds that many lyrics can be analyzed as internal arguments (not necessarily about something external to the problems each explores). Thus they differ from mimetic forms of literature for all of which the constructive principle is the plot. In these lyric poems, "the principle is a tissue not of events but ideas, and the ordering of the poem will not be by necessity and probability, by the antecedents and consequents of action, but by dialectical priority and posteriority" (229).

References

Abad, Gémino H. *A Formal Approach to Lyrical Poetry*. Quezon City: University of Philippines Press, 1978. A rigorously pursued analysis.

Abrams, M. H. *The Mirror and the Lamp*. New York: Oxford University Press, 1953. The section, "The Lyric as Poetic Norm," pp. 84–88, is a standard brief source.

Clausen, Christopher. Chapter 4 in *The Place of Poetry*. Lexington: University Press of Kentucky, 1981.

Culler, Jonathan. "Apostrophe." In *The Pursuit of Signs*. Ithaca, N.Y.: Cornell University Press, 1981.

Eliot, T. S. *The Three Voices of Poetry*. New York: Cambridge University Press, 1954. For Eliot, *meditative verse* (his term for a portion of what is usually called lyric) is much less often found than poetry of the second voice (which addresses an audience). "The second voice is, in fact, the voice most often and most clearly heard in poetry that is not of the theatre: in all poetry, certainly, that has a conscious social purpose—poetry intended to amuse or to instruct, poetry that tells a story, poetry that preaches or points a moral, or satire which is a form of preaching" (24).

Frye, Northrop. *Anatomy of Criticism*. Princeton: Princeton University Press, 1971. Frye includes almost all but dramatic poetry under the heading of lyric since it is one of his four genres: epic, dramatic, lyric, and "fiction of the printed page."

Gray, Bennison. *The Phenomenon of Literature*. The Hague: Mouton, 1975. Many lyrics are literature in Gray's definition, but not all; what those that are literature have in common "is not reflected in their being lyrics but in their being fiction. The term 'lyric' is quite useless and ought to be discarded" (44).

Hamburger, Käte. *The Logic of Literature*. Trans. M. J. Rose. Bloomington: Indiana University Press, 1973.

Hardy, Barbara. *The Advantage of Lyric: Essays on Feeling in Poetry*. Bloomington: Indiana University Press, 1977. The volume contains chapters on Donne, Clough, Hopkins, Yeats, Auden, Dylan Thomas, and Plath.

Henley, William Ernest. *English Lyrics: Chaucer to Poe*. London: Methuen, 1897. An anthology of the English lyric.

Johnson, W. R. *The Idea of Lyric*. Berkeley: University of California Press, 1982. Emphasizes the fragmentary nature of what remains of Greek lyric. We try to ignore this; "*because* we know that Greek lyric is mere fragments, we act, speak, and write as if the unthinkable had not happened, as if pious bishops, careless monks, and hungry mice had not consigned Sappho and her lyrical colleagues to irremediable oblivion" (25).

Jones, Sir William. "On the Arts Called Imitative" (1771). In vol. 8 of *The Works of Sir William Jones*. 13 vols. London, 1807.

Lewis, Cecil Day. *The Lyric Impulse*. Cambridge: Harvard University Press, 1965.

Lindley, David. *Lyric*. Critical Idiom Series. London: Methuen, 1985. "The argument of the study has been, decidedly, that the only proper way to use the term 'lyric' is with precise historical awareness" (84).

Maclean, Norman. "From Action to Image: Theories of the Lyric in the Eighteenth Century." In *Critics and Criticism*, ed. R. S. Crane. Chicago: University of Chicago Press, 1952.

Mill, John Stuart. "Thoughts on Poetry and Its Varieties." In vol. 1 of *The Collected Works of John Stuart Mill*. Ed. J. M. Robson and J. Stillinger. Toronto: University of Toronto Press, 1981.

Older, Elder. Introduction to *American Lyric Poems*. New York: Appleton-Century-Crofts/ Goldentree Books, 1964.

————. "Sailing to Byzantium: Prolegomena to a Poetics of the Lyric." In *Five Approaches to Literary Criticism*, ed. W. S. Scott. New York: Macmillan, 1962. Reprinted from *University of Kansas City Review* 8 (1942): 209–19.

Palgrave, Francis Turner. *The Golden Treasury: Selected from the Best Songs and Lyric Poems in the English Language*. Cambridge: Macmillan, 1861.

Reed, Edward Bliss. *English Lyrical Poetry: From Its Origin to the Present Time* (1912). New York: Haskell House, 1967.

Rhys, Ernest. *Lyric Poetry*. London: J. M. Dent, 1913.

Ridley, M. R. "The Lyric." *Essays and Studies* 19 (1933): 112–36.

Smith, Barbara Herrnstein. *On the Margins of Discourse*. Chicago: University of Chicago Press, 1978.

Staiger, Emil. *Grundbegriffe der Poetik*. Zurich: Atlantis Verlag, 1946.

Twining, Thomas. *Aristotle's Treatise on Poetry. Translated with Notes*. London: Payne, 1789.

Wellek, René. "Genre Theory, the Lyric, and *Erlebnis*." In *Discriminations*. New Haven, Conn: Yale University Press, 1970.

Sources of Additional Information

F. B. Gummere's *The Beginnings of Poetry* (New York: Macmillan, 1908) seeks to reconstruct the origin of poetry from rhythmic communal chants and songs. In *Roots of Lyric: Primitive Poetry and Modern Poetics* (Princeton, N. J.: Princeton University Press, 1978), Andrew Welsh explores the structures of sound and image (Pound's *melopoeia* and *phanopoeia*; Frye's *Melos* and *Opsis*) on which poetry is built. "Our search is not for primal sources but for the basic structures of poetic language, whether they are found in a Bantu riddle or a poem by Donne, in a Cherokee charm or a song by Shakespeare" (23–24).

For a comprehensive discussion of Greek lyric, see C. M. Bowra's *Greek Lyric Poets* (London: Oxford University Press, 1961).

For an intriguing exploration of the lyric in English, see Yvor Winters's *Forms of Discovery: Critical and Historical Essays on the Form of the Short Poem in English* (Chicago: Alan Swallow, 1967). Jonathan Holden's *The Rhetoric of the Contemporary Lyric* (Bloomington: Indiana University Press, 1980) treats various questions of twentieth-century poetics and includes chapters on Stephen Dunn and John Ashbery. *Lyric Poetry: Beyond New Criticism*, ed. C. Hošek and P. Parker, is a miscellaneous collection of essays treating various theories, issues, and lyrics from certain twentieth-century points of view.

M

MARXIST LITERARY CRITICISM   Any criticism of literature based on the major principles of Karl Marx's analysis of history and social structure. Although an increasingly wide range of literary and cultural theories has been developed from Marx, the basic principles on which these rest are (1) that the whole history of humankind to the present moment is to be explained primarily on *materialist*, that is, economic, grounds, so that the *mode of production* (economic structure determining modes of producing and distributing goods) is the *base* on which the *superstructure* of institutions, ethics, aesthetics, and intellectual beliefs of a society is constructed; (2) that history primarily reflects a continuing struggle between socioeconomic classes; (3) that the interests of the classes, and especially the dominant class, are reflected in ideologies or modes and structures of thought so pervasive that most individuals are unconscious of their operation; (4) that capitalism (the dominant mode of production) must be destroyed (or else will destroy itself); (5) that recognizing and undermining the bourgeois ideology that justifies capitalism is an important contribution to that destruction; and (6) that Marxist theory should be accompanied and clarified by practical action against capitalism (*praxis* is a central Marxist term).

The most commonly cited summary quotation explaining the relation of base to superstructure and thus of literature to the economic ground is taken from Marx and Engel's The German Ideology:

> [W]e do not set out from what men say, imagine, conceive, nor from men as narrated, thought of, imagined, conceived, in order to arrive at men in the flesh. We set out from real, active men, and on the basis of their real life-process we demonstrate the development of the ideological reflexes and echoes of this life-process. The phantoms formed in the human brain are also, necessarily, sublimates of their

material life-process, which is empirically verifiable and bound to material premises. Morality, religion, metaphysics, all the rest of ideology and their corresponding forms of consciousness, thus no longer retain the semblance of independence. They have no history, no development; but men, developing their material production and their material intercourse, alter, along with this their real existence, their thinking and the products of their thinking. Life is not determined by consciousness, but consciousness by life. (47)

The result of this analysis is most commonly summarized as dialectical materialism. *That phrase is usually taken to refer to the relation between the material base and the cultural (ultimately ideological or* hegemonic*) superstructure; dialectic has also come to be understood as referring to the recognition of the multiplicity of relationships into which any phenomenon enters, between human activity and historical change, and between individual thinkers and their milieux.*

The translation of the Marxist view of history and society into literary-critical principles has been approached in a multitude of ways; these can, however, be very roughly grouped into four historical periods.

The first historical period is constituted by the somewhat fragmentary comments on literature by Marx and Engels, the treatments of literature by Lenin and Trotsky, and the early applications of Marxism to literature by other Russian writers. While Marx and Engels did not expect literature to offer open political advocacy, Lenin and Trotsky moved some way toward this, without, however, prescribing subject matter or strategies. The early attempts of Marxist linguists and critics to work out the literary ramifications of Marxism are characterized by considerable openness. Georgi Plekhanov's *Art and Social Life* (1913), for instance, rejected the subordination of aesthetics to propaganda. V. N. Voloshinov's 1929 *Marxism and the Philosophy of Language* used the base/superstructure model to argue against what Voloshinov calls the "abstract objectivism" of Saussure's emphasis on the closed, synchronic system of language. Voloshinov favors, rather, a focus on the concrete utterance within its total milieu, "the individual creative act of speech" (48). P. N. Medvedev's 1928 *Formal Method in Literary Scholarship* criticizes the formalist method for its failure to recognize the importance of ideologies, but does so in a way that indirectly defends aspects of Formalism. Moreover, while admitting the "correct and proper social demands" that Marxist criticism makes on literature, Medvedev states, "In order to carry out his social assignment, the poet must translate it into the language of poetry itself, formulate it as a purely poetic problem to be solved by the forces of poetry itself" (35). (Both the preceding works may have been written partly, largely, or wholly by M. M. Bakhtin—their authorship remains moot.)

During this phase, various American versions of Marxist thought appeared in the periodicals *The Masses* (1911–17) and *The Liberator* (1918–24). Max Eastman, Floyd Dell, Michael Gold, Upton Sinclair, and John Reed are names closely associated with these publications. V. F. Calverton, editor of *The Modern Quar-*

terly (1923–38) and author of *The Liberation of American Literature* (1932), was also an important Marxist writer in the 1920s.

The second major period begins in 1929, the year the great U.S. stock market crash initiated an economic depression that extended well beyond the United States, making Soviet communism seem an attractive alternative, and lasts a decade. Within the Soviet Union, Stalin's continuing moves toward a stronger state apparatus, collectivization, and personal power included the demand that literature and art directly reflect the doctrines of the Communist party. Specifically, what was expected was *socialist realism*, a blend of realism with the presentation of models of devotion to the cause and images of the perfected state toward which the Soviet Union was understood to be moving. The codification of this position by Andrei Zhdanov occurred at the first Soviet Writers' Conference (1934).

In the United States, *The New Masses*, founded in 1926, moved strongly toward endorsement of the principles enunciated by the Communist party under Stalin. Granville Hicks's "The Crisis in American Criticism," published in *The New Masses* in 1933, is an American translation of the principles of Soviet socialist realism. Worthy books "must deal with or be related to the central issues of life"; that is, "the novel must, directly or indirectly, show the effects of the class struggle." Moreover, "the author must be able to make the reader feel that he is participating in the lives described, whether they are the lives of bourgeois or of proletarian." Finally, the author should write from the viewpoint "of the vanguard of the proletariat," and therefore "should be, or try to make himself, a member of the proletariat" (11–12). *The Partisan Review*, established in 1934 and edited by Philip Rahv and William Phillips primarily to speak for a proletarian literature, initially supported official Communist party doctrine, but distanced itself over the next few years.

The formulations of the English Marxists Christopher Caudwell and Alick West are more sophisticated than those of the Soviet advocates of social realism, but they nevertheless reproduce a similar combination of desiderata: to inspire the proletariat and supply a vision of the world that the Communist revolution should ultimately produce. Writes Caudwell in *Illusion and Reality* (1937): "Today all bourgeois culture struggles in the throes of its final crisis. The contradictions whose tensions first drove on the development of society's productive forces are now wrecking them and a new system of social relations is already emerging from the womb of the old—that of communism" (306–7). Therefore, the choice is "between class art which is unconscious of its causality and is therefore to that extent false and unfree, and proletarian art which is becoming conscious of its causality and will therefore emerge as the truly free art of communism" (324–25).

However, by the end of 1939, the cumulative effect of the Spanish Civil War, the Stalinist purges, and finally the Soviet-Nazi nonaggression treaty of that year had driven many writers and critics outside Russia away from Stalinist communism if not theoretical Marxism; therefore, World War II and the years immediately following represent a kind of hiatus. The third phase of Marxist criticism came to prominence following the war, although most of those responsible had long been Marxist theorists. The rise of new, more sophisticated— but divergent—Marxist criticism was marked by the publication of Georg Lukács's championship of realism in the novel beginning with *Studies in European Realism* (1935–39), Lucien Goldmann's *The Hidden God* (1955), Theodor Adorno's *Noten zu Literatur* (1958–74), Walter Benjamin's posthumous *Illuminations* (1955) and *Understanding Brecht* (1968), and Pierre Macherey's *Theory of Literary Production* (1966). A highly influential figure, although one little concerned with literature per se, was Louis Althusser, whose *For Marx* (1965) and *Lenin and Philosophy* (1968) argue that the economic base is maintained by forces within the superstructure that he calls *ideological state apparatuses*: schools, the family, the media, the political system, and churches. The ideology that results thus becomes much more than a product of the base: It is seen as a force unconsciously operating for the maintenance of the status quo.

The significance of the interests, arguments, and developed positions of these writers is part of the continuing debate among Marxist critics. Here only certain major emphases of each can be indicated. Lukács represents a defense of the realistic novel as valuable for its honest presentation of the social structure (and therefore often unintentional illuminations of the capitalist ideology); while escaping the narrowness of socialist realism, however, his allegiance to realism makes it impossible for him to accept the modernism of writers like Proust, Joyce, and Kafka. Lukács writes in the 1970 Preface to a collection of his earlier essays: "My critical studies thus were directed against two fronts: against the schematic deadliness and impoverishment of socialist literature [as advocated by Zhdanov] and against those movements seeking salvation in following Western avant-garde schools. When I think back to this period now, more than thirty years later, I find this struggle on two fronts even more profoundly justified than I did then" (*Writer and Critic*, 8). Lucien Goldmann's *genetic structuralism* analyzes the thought structure or "vision" of texts as the product of the writer's social class or background. Adorno's sociologically oriented analysis of the text intends to find its objective (social) meaning rather than the intention of the author. Pierre Macherey seeks the conflicts among ideologies that produce gaps or silences in a text, pursuing what the text does *not* say. "Constrained by its essential diversity, the work, in order to say one thing, has at the same time to say another thing which is not necessarily of the same nature; it unites in a single text several different lines which cannot be apportioned. . . . What the work says is not one or other of these lines, but their difference, their contrast, the hollow which separates and unites them" (99–100). The goal of such analysis is not simply description but social intervention. Walter Benjamin is best known for his argument that the Marxist artist should challenge the forces affecting the production of art—a concept closely related to the *alienation effect* sought by his friend Bertolt Brecht.

Taken together, the major figures of this third phase decisively replaced the earlier naive or "vulgar" Marxist literary theory which had assumed a much more direct relation between base and superstructure. Benjamin, whose thought was partially a product of the Frankfurt School associated with the Institute for Social Research founded in 1923, died in 1940. Adorno died in 1969 and Lucien Goldmann, in some ways a discipline of Lukács, in 1970. Lukács, whose association with the Communist party dates from 1918, lived until 1971. The third phase which these men represent can be taken as continuing until the beginning of the 1970s.

The fourth phase, contemporary Marxist theory, is perhaps best represented by the strong continuing influence of Macherey and, in the Anglo-American context, the work of Fredric Jameson, Terry Eagleton, and Michael Ryan. Fredric Jameson is concerned to define more particularly the way in which Marxist, that is, dialectical, thinking will make possible the recognition of and opposition to the capitalist ideology even though, "particularly in the United States, the development of post industrial monopoly capitalism has brought with it an increasing occultation of the class structure through techniques of mystification practiced by the media and particularly by advertising in its enormous expansion since the onset of the Cold War." Dialectical thought for Jameson allows one to transcend the ideological by seeing interrelationships that raise thought to a more comprehensive level and by observing one's own thought process in such a way as "to reckon the [historical and immediate] position of the observer in the experiment itself" (*Marxism and Form*, xvii, 340). Both these activities are summed up in the opening sentences of the preface to *The Political Unconscious*. "Always historicize! This slogan [is] the one absolute and we may even say 'transhistorical' imperative of all dialectical thought" (9). Jameson never doubts that such dialectical thinking will support the essential Marxist analysis of the class struggle and historical materialism; indeed, "[t]he point is . . . that Marxism is not just one more theory of history, but on the contrary the 'end' or abolition of theories of history as such" (*Marxism and Form*, 321) Alternatively, as he states it in *The Political Unconscious*, "My position here is that only Marxism offers a philosophically coherent and ideologically compelling solution to the dilemma of historicism. . . . Only Marxism can give us an adequate account of the essential *mystery* of the cultural past" (19). Literary comprehension should, then, end in an understanding of the "*ideology of form*, that is, the symbolic messages transmitted to us by the existence of various sign systems which are themselves traces or anticipations of modes of production" (*Political Unconscious*, 76).

Eagleton's greatest emphasis, on the one hand, is on the continuing need for sophisticated analysis of the relationship between the economic base and the art that is part of the resulting superstructure, and, on the other hand, the need to understand the relations between the base and superstructure in art itself, that is, between "art as production and art as ideological" (*Marxism*, 74–75). Eagleton, following Macherey, explores these relations in literature by seeking the contradictions within the text. "It is important to recognize first of all that the necessity of the text is founded on the conflictual multiplicity of its meanings, and that to explain the work is therefore to distinguish the principle of its diversity" (*Against the Grain*, 14). Such criticism must be at the service of changing the socioeconomic structure: "Marxist criticism is not just an alternative technique for interpreting *Paradise Lost* or *Middlemarch*. It is part of our liberation from oppression" (*Marxism*, 76). The goal, then, is much more important than the method. "Any method or theory which will contribute to the strategic goal of human emancipation, the production of 'better people' through the socialist transformation of society is acceptable" (*Literary Theory*, 211).

Michael Ryan is best known for his attempt to bring Marxism and deconstruction together: "I will argue that deconstructive philosophy has positive implications for marxism and that these implications are not only philosophical, but political. One common conclusion promoted by both movements is that philosophy cannot be apolitical and that politics often rests upon philosophic or conceptual presuppositions" (1).

Ryan's argument speaks to the uneasy relationship between Marxist and poststructuralist theories generally (see STRUCTURALISM). On the one hand, the general tendency of Marxist critics to demote the author to the position of something like the vehicle through which ideologies express themselves and the Macherey-influenced denial of the unity of the text parallel much in poststructuralist thought. Jameson provides a typical statement of the former: "We are, I think, for the most part agreed to see the individual writer as the locus or working out of a certain set of techniques inherent in the available raw material itself" (*Marxism and Form*, 315). Terry Eagleton's formulation may be cited as typical of the second: "The postulate of the work's *unity*, which has always more or less haunted bourgeois criticism, must be unequivocally denounced" (*Against the Grain*, 14). Philip Goldstein has also argued for the compatibility of poststructuralist and Marxist criticism, suggesting that the combination incorporates valuable insights found separately in a variety of other modes of criticism.

On the other hand, poststructuralist criticism is frequently denounced by Marxists for being insufficiently political. That is, where poststructuralism questions many, if not all, assumptions of present culture very much as does Marxist criticism of bourgeois ideology, Marxist criticism assumes that at least its own basic analysis of the economic base and cultural superstructure is beyond question. The degree to which poststructuralism is political, or finally useful to Marxism, remains a matter of debate. In any case, the Marxist-oriented branch of NEW HISTORICISM that is identified with *cultural materialism* represents a particular application of Marxist criticism.

References

Adorno, Theodor. *Noten zu Literatur*. 4 vols. Berlin: Suhrkamp Verlag, 1958–74.
Althusser, Louis. *For Marx*. Trans. B. Brewster. London: New Left Books, 1969. Original French edition, 1965.
———. *Lenin and Philosophy and Other Essays*. Trans. B. Brewster. New York: Monthly Review Press, 1971. Original French edition, 1968.

Benjamin, Walter. *Illuminations*. Trans. H. Zohn. New York: Harcourt, Brace, World, 1968. Original German edition, 1955.

———. *Understanding Brecht*. London: NLB Press, 1973. Original German edition, 1968.

Caudwell, Christopher [Christopher St. John Sprigg]. *Illusion and Reality*. London: Macmillan, 1937.

Eagleton, Terry. *Against the Grain: Essays 1975–85*. London: Verso, 1986.

> The necessity of the text . . . is not the index of a cohering authorial will. . . . The necessity of the text—which is precisely what renders it *readable*, yields us a determinate object of analysis—inheres rather in the fact that the text *produces itself*—unfolds and activates its multiple lines of meaning without conformity to ''intention,'' pre-given normative model or external reality. The task of criticism is to discover in each text the laws of that self-production. (13)

———. *Literary Theory: An Introduction*. Minneapolis: University of Minnesota Press, 1983.

———. *Marxism and Literary Criticism*. Berkeley: University of California Press, 1976. ''Marxism is a scientific theory of human societies and of the practice of transforming them; and what that means, rather more concretely, is that the narrative Marxism has to deliver is the story of the struggles of men and women to free themselves from certain forms of exploitation and oppression'' (vii).

Goldmann, Lucien. *The Hidden God*. Trans. P. Thody. New York: Humanities Press, 1964. Original French edition, 1955.

Goldstein, Philip. *The Politics of Literary Theory: An Introduction to Marxist Criticism*. Tallahassee: Florida State University Press, 1990.

Hicks, Granville. ''The Crisis in American Criticism.'' (1933). In *Granville Hicks in The New Masses*, ed. J. A. Robbins. Port Washington, N.Y.: Kennimat Press, 1974.

Jameson, Fredric. *Marxism and Form*. Princeton, N.J.: Princeton University Press, 1971. Form is content. ''Thus it is a mistake to think, for instance, that the books of Hemingway deal essentially with such things as courage, love, and death; in reality, their deepest subject is simply the writing of a certain type of sentence, the practice of a determinate style'' (409).

———. *The Political Unconscious*. Ithaca, N.Y.: Cornell University Press, 1981. ''This book will argue the priority of the political interpretation of literary texts.'' The political perspective is seen as ''the absolute horizon of all reading and all interpretation'' (17).

Lukács, Georg. *Studies in European Realism*. Trans. E. Bone. London: Hillway, 1950. Original Hungarian and German essays, 1935–39.

———. *Writer and Critic and Other Essays*. New York: Grosset and Dunlap, 1971.

Macherey, Pierre. *A Theory of Literary Production*. Trans. G. Wall. London: Routledge and Kegan Paul, 1978. Original French edition, 1966.

Marx, Karl and Frederick Engels. *The German Ideology*. Ed. C. J. Arthur. New York: International Publishers, 1970.

Medvedev, P. N. [and/or Mikhail Bakhtin]. *The Formal Method in Literary Scholarship*. Trans. A. J. Wehrle. Baltimore: Johns Hopkins University Press, 1978. Original Russian edition, 1928.

Plekhanov, G. V. *Art and Social Life*. Trans. A. Rothstein. London: Lawrence and Wishart, 1953. Original Russian edition, 1913.

Ryan, Michael. *Marxism and Deconstruction: A Critical Articulation*. Baltimore: Johns
  Hopkins University Press, 1982.
Voloshinov, V. N. [and/or Mikhail Bakhtin]. *Marxism and the Philosophy of Language*.
  Trans. L. Matejka and I. R. Titunik. New York: Seminar Press, 1973. Original
  Russian edition, 1929. The basic argument anticipates much in speech-act theory.
  "The immediate social situation and the broader social milieu wholly determine—
  and determine from within, so to speak—the structure of an utterance" (3–4).
  "[W]hat is important for the speaker about a linguistic form is not that it is a
  stable and always self-equivalent signal, but that it is an always changeable and
  adaptable sign" (68).
West, Alick. *Crisis and Criticism*. London: Lawrence and Wishart, 1937.

Sources of Additional Information

Among the several dictionaries of Marxism, *A Dictionary of Marxist Thought*, ed. Tom
Bottomore (Cambridge, Mass.: Harvard University Press, 1983) provides especially good
essays on major terms.

A still useful though badly dated bibliography is Lee Baxandall's *Marxism and Aesthetics: A Selective Annotated Bibliography* (New York: Humanities Press, 1968), which
lists English-language books and articles treating the arts (including literature) from thirty-
six countries and authors from sixteen countries. Even more dated, but of interest for its
representation of the American view of Marxism in the early 1950s as well as for the
historical detail it makes available, is *Socialism and American Life*, vol. 1, ed. D. E.
Egbert and S. Persons (Princeton, N.J.: Princeton University Press, 1952). The second
volume, edited by T. D. S. Bassett, is a comprehensive bibliography to the date of
publication.

Marx and Engels on Literature and Art, ed. L. Baxandall and S. Morawski (St. Louis:
Telos Press, 1973), is made up of brief passages taken from the writings of Marx and
Engels together with a substantial introduction by Morawski that should be compared
with Peter Demetz's *Marx and Engels Among the Poets: Origins of Marxist Literary
Criticism*. Demetz traces the influences that shaped the literary/aesthetic views of Marx
and Engels and discusses Mehring, Plekhanov, and Lukács (trans. J. L. Sammons;
Chicago: University of Chicago Press, 1967; original German edition, 1959).

For the Frankfurt School, see Jay Martin's *The Dialectical Imagination*, chapter 6 of
which is titled "Aesthetic Theory and the Critique of Mass Culture" (Boston: Little,
Brown, 1973).

Marxism and Art: Essays Classic and Contemporary, ed. M. Solomon (New York:
Alfred Knopf, 1973), is a very helpful selection of major statements by Marxist thinkers
and writers accompanied by generous commentary. The collection of Marxist criticisms
of Kafka which makes up *Franz Kafka: An Anthology of Marxist Criticism*, ed. and trans.
Kenneth Hughes (Hanover, N.H.: University Press of New England, 1981), is fascinating
for the diversity of praise and blame it brings together. "Perhaps what unites all the
essays presented here, and what characterizes them as Marxist in their fundamental
concerns, is their commitment to . . . [Marx's] argument that 'it is not the consciousness
of men that determines their being, but, on the contrary, their social being that determines
their consciousness' " (p. viii). For a brief history of American Marxist literary criticism
in the first half of this century, see the chapter "Liberal and Marxist Criticism" in Walter
Sutton's *Modern American Criticism* (Englewood Cliffs, N.J.: Prentice-Hall, 1963).

Among the most interesting English Marxist critics (as opposed to theorists) is Arnold

Kettle, a number of whose essays have been gathered in *Literature into Liberation*, ed. G. Martin and W. R. Owens (Manchester, U.K.: Manchester University Press, 1988). Kettle's avoidance of technical and abstract, specifically Marxist, terminology makes him especially readable. A number of the points he makes anticipate more ponderously phrased views of later New Historicists. "The great artists of the bourgeois period are all highly critical, in some way or other, of bourgeois society and its values. This criticism is not always consciously formulated and seldom has an explicitly *political* slant. What the realist artists of the bourgeois period were doing was, above all, telling the truth" (27).

Raymond Williams's *Marxism and Literature* (Oxford: Oxford University Press, 1977) defines basic Marxist concepts in their relationship to literature, noting points at which Marxist commentators on literature have tended to oversimplify.

A strongly worded argument for carrying Marxist criticism into the classroom is Jim Merod's *The Political Responsibility of the Critic* (Ithaca, N.Y.: Cornell University Press, 1987): "The inability of professional textual study to address its own participation in the relentless commoditization of work and leisure . . . undermines the possibility that teachers and critics could make the imaginative and analytic work of reading an agent of social change" (7). An especially clear survey of the critical principles of Lukács, Macherey, Goldmann, and Adorno, and of the Marxist elements of Mikhail Bakhtin and Julia Kristeva, will be found in David Forgac's "Marxist Literary Theories," in *Modern Literary Theory*, ed. A. Jefferson and D. Robey (London: B. T. Batsford, 1982).

A salient and engaging critique of Marxist criticism's dismissal of the author (especially as exemplified in New Historicism) is Richard Levin's "The Poetics and Politics of Bardicide" (*PMLA* 105, May 1990: 491–502). "The Death of the Author enables these [Marxist] critics to wage—and to win—a kind of class war against the forces of evil, embodied in the text's hegemonic ideology, and therefore to achieve in this displaced and 'imaginary arena' their avowed political goals" (502).

MEANING   1. Any cognitive and/or emotional response to an external stimulus. 2. A response to a SIGN, that is, to a stimulus that causes its interpreter to take account of something other than, but related to, the stimulus. 3. That which a user of a sign system intends to convey. 4. The value or function of a discourse. 5. In the understanding of the Bible, and later of other works related to that tradition, edification and illumination as well as literal recording of events. 6. As applied specifically to language without regard to context of use: (a) the denotative and/or connotative senses in which a given word may be understood within a given language system; (b) the recognition of the results of the simultaneous amplification and limitation of the possible senses of the individual words when combined into a sentence; or (c) the recognition of one or more propositions and/or emotions or attitudes produced by the combination of sentences making up an individual discourse. 7. That which the utterance is understood as intended to convey within the full contextual situation of the utterance. 8. A relationship, often regarded as causal, between a context not taken into account by the author and the text produced. 9. A specifically defined intentional meaning or signification as opposed to significances that cannot be ascribed to intention.

One obvious difficulty in discussing meaning is the impossibility of avoiding the word itself in the explanation. One can, of course, construct a metalanguage in which meaning is given a specific meaning to be employed in discussing meaning in general, but adequate definition of the word meaning in the metalanguage requires a higher metalanguage. The meaning of meaning of meaning of meaning . . . is thus potentially an infinite series. In addition, meaning is employed in many different ways; Ogden and Richards distinguish sixteen uses.

1. The most basic sense of meaning would seem to be "to have in mind"; thus, meaning is most radically "that which is conveyed to a mind," where "that which" is understood to be a concept, attitude, or emotion. Though this extended sense of meaning does not appear even by implication in the *OED*, the multiplicity of the senses in which meaning has been used through the centuries evidently looks toward it.

2. The sense of meaning regarded not as response in general but as response to some sort of sign or series of signs (DISCOURSE) is ancient. This use includes responses to smoke as a sign of fire and high temperature as a sign of fever, as well as the utterance "yes" as a sign of assent. In the twentieth century, it underlies C. K. Ogden and I. A. Richards's influential *The Meaning of Meaning* (1923), which describes all perception, as opposed to mere awareness, as the result of sign situations (22). This sense of meaning is formulated most generally by Charles Morris (who prefers to avoid the term meaning itself) through his description of the processes of semiosis (1938). His semiotic description (see SEMIOTICS), very broadly stated, regards meaning as a *mediated-taking-account-of*, which is "mediated" because the taking account of is a response to a sign for something else (*Foundations*, 4).

3. Human employment of any sign system is generally assumed to be for the purpose of conveying a specific concept, attitude, or emotion to one or more other minds; the most common sense of meaning when applied to discourse has therefore been "that which the speaker or author intended to convey." Augustine explicitly distinguishes between natural signs (smoke as a sign of fire) and conventional signs (34; 2:1.2). H. P. Grice's twentieth-century differentiation of meanings into the *natural* sense where meaning is understood as a symptom or effect of a cause (cf. C. S. Peirce's *indices*) and the *nonnatural*, that is, meaning intended to be conveyed through a nonnatural sign system, speaks to the same distinction. Grice's formulation is " '*A* meant$_{nn}$ something by *x*' is (roughly) equivalent to '*A* intended by the utterance of *x* to produce some effect in an audience by means of the recognition of this intention' " where the subscript $_{nn}$ denotes nonnatural ("Meaning," 385).

4. Since at least the time of Plato, to ask the meaning has been to ask the significance or value of a discourse, or of certain kinds of discourse, or of discourse in general. Questioning of the value of discourse in general opens many issues. Does the use of language allow human beings to think about reality more accurately? Does it obscure how things "really" are, or does it create a reality (or realities) that is (are), in fact, the only reality (or realities) we can grasp? Do the specific kinds of discourse we call poetry or fiction imitate what is actual more or less fully and/or usefully than other discourse, or do they indeed

imitate a transcendent ideal instead? A very helpful survey of views of the value of poetry will be found in *The Princeton Encyclopedia of Poetry and Poetics*; aspects of the question of meaning posed in this way are considered under "Reference" and "Reality."

5. As applied primarily in the middle ages and Renaissance to the understanding of the Bible—and later works specifically constructed to follow a similar model of multileveled discourse—meaning was understood to exist on four levels: the literal, allegorical (practical illustration of principles of human life), tropological (moral), and anagogical (spiritual). The standard statement of the system is that by Dante in a letter to Can Grande, Della Scalla (see ALLEGORY).

6. In twentieth-century semantic analysis, the meaning of a word or utterance can be approached without regard to the external context of the utterance at three levels.

a. Lexical meaning: At the level of the word, meaning is the set of possible denotations and connotations as set out for instance in a dictionary. At this level exist major problems that have long vexed philosophers: if by denotations we mean primarily those ultimately nonlinguistic objects to which a word may refer, we immediately confront the question of the relationship between individual objects and the classes to which they belong (the cow to which a speaker is referring at a given moment and cows in general) and between objects that may be indicated ostensively ("the word 'pencil' means this object in my hand") and those concepts (honor, truth, procrastination) that cannot.

b. Propositional meaning: At the level of the sentence, knowledge of syntactic relations and the senses (designata or referents) of individual words are combined to produce the meaning of a sentence. However, to understand, for example, why a syntactically correct sentence may be judged meaningless, judge whether a paraphrase is accurate, or decide whether one proposition implies another requires the kind of compositional analysis now especially associated with the field of SEMANTICS.

c. Discourse meaning: Recognition of patterns of semantic coherence and conceptual juxtaposition are necessary but not sufficient conditions for the construction of the meaning of discourse beyond the sentence. Structures of coherence and conceptual patterns arise from the internal context (*co-text*) in any utterance or text of greater length than the single sentence. While semantics can be regarded as embracing the study of meaning generally, in practice, work in the field has been mostly confined to the study of meaning in individual words and single sentences. Therefore, concentration on the relations between sentences and between each sentence and the total text in which it appears is generally understood to be the province of DISCOURSE ANALYSIS, text linguistics, or, more rarely, text semantics.

7. The multiple senses of individual words, the dependence of much figurative language on context, and the manifold possibilities for indirectly expressing what one wishes to communicate require that any utterance be considered in its external (situational) context if the intended meaning of the author is to be grasped (see

CONTEXT). (For simplicity, as employed in the remainder of this entry, the term context designates external context.)

To use an example from Leech, "That boy is a girl" is nonsense when considered without context, but not if it is uttered as a way of pointing out that someone has mistaken the sex of a baby. Essentially the same distinction has been made using a variety of terminology. As indicated above, semantics is often regarded as the study of the meanings of utterances apart from context, but Paul Ricoeur distinguishes between language and discourse; and Ross Chambers between *meaning* and *meaningfulness*. French writers distinguish between *énoncé* and *énonciation*; H. P. Grice employs *timeless meaning* and *occasion meaning* in "Utterer's Meaning, Sentence-Meaning, and Word-Meaning." The difference is sometimes referred to as that between Saussure's *langue* and *parole*, though there is an ambiguity in this use since the same terms are sometimes used to distinguish the language regarded as comprehensive lexicon together with syntactical grammar from the syntactical arrangement of words into contextless sentences. In *The Meaning of Meaning*, Ogden and Richards recognize the importance of context in defining a sign as part of a context and of making the interpretation of a sign depend on the *sign situation*. The volume includes as an appendix an important essay by Bronislaw Malinowski that equates *context of situation* with the *sign-situation* (57, 308). Charles Morris's description of semiosis, which includes only four terms in his 1938 *Foundations of the Theory of Signs*, is elaborated to five terms in the 1964 *Signification and Significance*, the fifth being the conditions or context in which the sign operates.

The term pragmatics is sometimes applied to the study of meaning in context, as opposed to semantics as the study of meaning apart from context, though this usage can be confusing since pragmatics is also employed in other senses both broader and more restrictive.

8. In opposition to the identification of meaning with intention, it can be argued that since intended meanings cannot be directly known, the intended meaning of an utterance is irrelevant either in general or for certain purposes. A related form of the argument is that if it is necessary to know the context that the AUTHOR assumed the anticipated audience would share, to attempt to arrive at the author's meaning is futile. As Jonathan Culler makes the point that "total context is unmasterable, both in principle and in practice. Meaning is context bound, but context is boundless." Or again, "There is no limit in principle to what might be included in a given context, to what might be shown to be relevant to the performance of a particular speech act" (*Deconstruction*, 123–24).

It is equally possible to assert that what an author intended to convey is simply of lesser importance than what readers' present interests allow them to discover in a text. In this sense, meaning looks to the text less as a form of communication than as an object invested with meaning from outside. This sense of externally implied meaning was clearly stated by F. S. C. Schiller in a 1920 symposium on "The Meaning of 'Meaning' ": "What if Meaning be neither an inherent property of objects nor a static 'relation' between objects at all, not even between

the object and a subject, but essentially an *activity* or *attitude* taken up towards
objects by a subject and energetically projected into them?'' (389). The text,
then, is to be contextualized from the point of view of the reader's specific
interest; often, such interest is in tracing the ''causes'' of a text's structure or
apparent theme rather than in an author's presumably conscious intention, or in
using it as an illustration of a psychological, social, or political theory. Thus it
is possible, for instance, to speak of the meaning of a poem, play, or novel as
being a reflection of the power structure of the socioeconomic system of the time
it was written or of the psychological disposition (or difficulties or obsessions)
of the author.

9. In the light of the ramifications of the relation between intended meanings
and context, the third sense above can be stated more sharply. Though the degree
to which the understanding of an utterance can be, or ought to be, *re*constructions
of intended meanings varies widely between theoretical schools, it can plausibly
be argued that we always assume and attempt to construct the intended meaning
of any human utterance whatever other intellectual operations we subject it to.
Again, this is expressed through varying formulations, of which that quoted by
R. E. Innis from I. M. Schlesinger is perhaps the most succinct: ''Human nature
abhors a semantic vacuum'' (3). Hans Hörman's term for this demand of the
mind is *sense-constancy*.

Barbara Herrnstein Smith describes the understanding of the meaning of an
utterance in terms of inferring ''the motives and circumstances'' of the utterance
(*On the Margins*, 102) or finding ''the reasons for or *causes of*'' an utterance
(22), where such words as *motives* and *causes* are understood to bear on intention.
I. A. Richards comments in *The Philosophy of Rhetoric* that ''The mind will
always try to find connections and will be guided in its search by the rest of the
utterance and its occasion'' (126); Michael Stubbs points out in *Discourse Analysis* that ''however odd the utterance, hearers will do their utmost to make sense
of the language they hear, by bringing to bear on it all possible knowledge and
interpretations'' (5). The same force operates in interpreting literary texts; as
Peter Griffith writes, ''It seems as though people are constitutionally incapable
of treating anything in narrative as purely accidental or irrelevant'' (11).

The sense of meaning as that which an author intends to and succeeds in
conveying was clarified by E. D. Hirsch, who introduced an influential distinction
between *meaning* and *significance* in *Validity in Interpretation* (1967). Meaning
he defines as what the author intended to convey, or, more exactly, ''Verbal
meaning is whatever someone has willed to convey by a particular sequence of
linguistic signs and which can be conveyed (shared) by means of those linguistic
signs'' (31). Significance, on the other hand, is any cognitive or emotional
response, or any conceptual construction not intended by the author. Meaning
in this sense is a probabilistic reconstruction drawing on conventions and contexts
that the author either creates or can reasonably be assumed to have assumed;
significances are constructions produced when the text is placed in contexts other
than those that the author can assume or is likely to have assumed. For Hirsch,

understanding is the grasping of meaning, *interpretation* is the explanation of meaning, and *criticism* is the exploration of significance. For others, interpretation is the term for the pursuit of meaning itself. The goal of interpretation in either case is distinct not only from that of criticism in the Hirschean sense but from that of POETICS, the latter being the analysis not of the meaning of specific discourses but of the mechanisms that make meaning possible. Very much the same distinction between meaning and significance appears in the discrimination between *signification* and *significance* made by Charles Morris in 1964 in *Signification and Significance*.

Interpretation regarded as the understanding of words, sentences, and the discourse in terms of the author's intention is not, of course, a sequential but rather a recursive process constantly moving between various levels. Thus, George Dillon's model of reading includes *perception,* or the grasping of the propositional structure of a sentence, *comprehension,* or the "integration of its propositional content into one's running tally of what is being described or argued in the passage," and *interpretation,* or the relation of "the sense of what is going on to the author's constructive intention" (xvii–xx). Seymour Chatman's term *reading out,* which designates the mind's processing of that which one is reading, seems to parallel Hirsch's *understanding.*

Similarly, from a speech-act approach, J. L. Austin's word *uptake,* which describes an auditor's recognition of both the propositional content and the illocutionary force of an utterance, is close to Hirsch's interpretation, though full interpretation, especially as Dillon uses the term to describe the final step in processing discourse, would have to include a probabilistic construction of the utterer's perlocutionary intent (see SPEECH-ACT THEORY). A full understanding of the utterer's intention would thus include all five of the functions of language earlier catalogued by Ogden and Richards: In their terminology, "symbolization of reference" or *accuracy;* "expression of attitude to listener" or *suitability;* "expression of attitude to referent" or *appropriateness;* "promotion of effects intended" or *judiciousness;* and *support of reference,* that is, indication of the speaker's personal degree of certainty. The interpreter thus assumes that the author has attempted to make the utterance accurate, suitable, appropriate, judicious, and personal (234, 360ff.). In *Practical Criticism* (1929), Richards restates the first four functions as sense, tone, feeling, and intention, while dropping the fifth, the degree of certainty (181–82).

Roman Jakobson's well-known formulation of the six functions of language use, one of which dominates every utterance, derives from a different taxonomic principle but makes something of the same point: An utterance may be *emotive* (emphasizing the speaker's attitude), *conative* (intended primarily to affect the addressee), *referential* (emphasizing the contextual situation), *phatic* (establishing or keeping contact between speaker and addressee), *metalingual* (pursuing questions of meaning), or *poetic* (emphasizing the way in which the language is used). Recognition of which of the functions is dominant in a given use is a necessary part of recognizing the intended meaning.

References

Augustine. *On Christian Doctrine*. Trans. D. W. Robertson. Indianapolis: Bobbs-Merrill Library of the Liberal Arts, 1958.

Austin, J. L. *How To Do Things with Words*. Ed. J. O. Urmson and Marina Sbisà. 1962; Cambridge, Mass.:   ʼʻard University Press, 1975.

Chambers, Ross. *Meaning ι   Meaningfulness: Studies in the Analysis and Interpretation of Texts*. Lexington, Ky.: French Forum, 1979.

Chatman, Seymour. *Story and Discourse*. Ithaca, N.Y.: Cornell University Press, 1978.

Culler, Jonathan. *On Deconstruction*. Ithaca, N.Y.: Cornell University Press, 1982.

Dante Aligheri. "Epistle to Can Grande Della Scala." In *The Letters of Dante*. Ed. and trans. P. Toynbee. Oxford: Clarendon Press, 1920.

Dillon, George. *Language Processing and the Reading of Literature*. Bloomington: University of Indiana Press, 1978.

Grice, H. P. "Meaning." *The Philosophical Review* 66 (1957): 377–88. An essential essay.

———. "Utterer's Meaning, Sentence-Meaning, and Word-Meaning." *Foundations of Language* 4 (August 1968): 225–42.

Griffith, Peter. *Literary Theory and English Teaching*. Philadelphia: Open University Press, 1987.

Hirsch, E. D., Jr. *Validity in Interpretation*. New Haven, Conn.: Yale University Press, 1967.

Hörman, Hans. *Meaning and Context: An Introduction to the Psychology of Language*. New York: Plenum Press, 1968.

Innis, R. E. Introduction to Hörman's *Meaning and Context*.

Jakobson, Roman. "Linguistics and Poetics." In *Style in Language*, ed. Thomas A. Sebeok. Cambridge, Mass.: MIT Press, 1960.

Leech, Geoffrey. *Towards a Semantic Description of English*. Bloomington: University of Indiana Press, 1970.

Malinowski, Bronislaw. "The Problem of Meaning in Primitive Languages." Supplement 1 in Ogden and Richards, *The Meaning of Meaning*.

Morris, Charles W. *Foundations of the Theory of Signs*. Vol 1, no. 2 of the *International Encyclopedia of Unified Science*. Chicago: University of Chicago Press, 1938.

———. *Signification and Significance*. Cambridge, Mass.: MIT Press, 1964.

Ogden, C. K., and I. A. Richards. *The Meaning of Meaning*. 1923; 8th ed. New York: Harcourt, Brace, World, 1946. The starting point for a great part of twentieth-century discussion of the concept of meaning.

Princeton Encyclopedia of Poetry and Poetics. Ed. Alex Preminger, Rank J. Warnke and O.B. Hardison, Jr. Princeton, N.J.: Princeton University Press, 1974.

Ricoeur, Paul. *Interpretation Theory: Discourse and the Surplus of Meaning*. Fort Worth: Texas Christian University, 1976.

Richards, I. A. *The Philosophy of Rhetoric*. 1936; New York: Oxford University Press, 1965.

———. *Practical Criticism*. London: Kegan Paul, Trench, Trubner, 1929.

Schiller, F. C. S. "The Meaning of 'Meaning': A Symposium by F. C. S. Schiller, Bertram Russell, and H. H. Joachim." *Mind: A Quarterly Review of Psychology and Philosophy* n.s. 29 (October 1920): 385–414.

Smith, Barbara Herrnstein. *On the Margins of Discourse*. Chicago: University of Chicago Press, 1978.

Stubbs, Michael. *Discourse Analysis: The Sociolinguistic Analysis of Language*. Chicago: University of Chicago Press, 1983.

Sources of Additional Information

Further ramifications of H. P. Grice's influential description of meaning are developed in Grice's essay "Meaning" and P. Ziff's "On H. P. Grice's Account of Meaning," both in *Semantics*, ed. by D. Steinberg and L. Jakobits (Cambridge: Cambridge University Press, 1971); and also in Grice's "Utterer's Meaning and Intentions" in *Philosophical Review* 78 (April 1969): 147–77.

The complexities of formally describing the ways in which "meaning" is employed are examined in detail by Stephen R. Schiffer in *Meaning* (Oxford: Clarendon Press, 1972).

METAPHOR   1. The rhetorical device of giving something a name that belongs to another thing for the purposes of emphasis or ornament. 2. A trope in which one thing is referred to in terms of another in a way semantically inappropriate, and in which the inappropriateness triggers a meaning not derivable from semantics (that is, dictionary senses) alone.

"The 'most luminous and therefore the most necessary and frequent' (Vico) of all tropes, the metaphor, defies every encyclopedic entry. It has been the object of philosophical, linguistic, aesthetic, and psychological reflection since the beginning of time," writes Umberto Eco (Semiotics, 87). Although innumerable definitions of metaphor exist, essentially they are different formulations of the two historically distinct senses given above. The vast literature on metaphor (most of which has arisen in the last fifty years) reflects the difficulty of explaining the interrelated issues of how metaphors are recognized, how they are created and interpreted, and whether they make possible the communication of something that could not be expressed otherwise.

1. Aristotle's definition of metaphor in the *Poetics* laid the basis for the way in which metaphor was understood until well into the twentieth century. "Metaphor consists in giving the thing a name that belongs to something else; the transference being either from genus to species, or from species to genus, or from species to species, or on grounds of analogy." Aristotle clarifies the fourth kind: "That from analogy is possible whenever there are four terms so related that the second (B) is to the first (A), as the fourth (D) to the third (C); for one may then metaphorically put B in lieu of D, and D in lieu of B" (63; 1457b). In itself the definition would seem to make metaphor no more than a rhetorical ornament. On the other hand, Aristotle makes metaphor supreme among the "poetical forms." "[T]he greatest thing by far is to be a master of metaphor. It is the one thing that cannot be learnt from others; and it is also a sign of genius, since a good metaphor implies an intuitive perception of the similarity in dissimilars" (71; 1459a).

What seems to twentieth-century readers to be the same sort of ambiguity occurs in the discussion of metaphor in the *Rhetoric*. Aristotle writes that "it is from metaphor that we can best get hold of something fresh." "When the poet calls old age 'a withered stalk,' he conveys a new idea, a new fact, to us by means of the general notion of 'lost bloom,' which is common to both things." Immediately thereafter, however, he notes that "[t]he similes of the poets do the same," for the metaphor is just a shortened simile (186; 1410b).

Whether Aristotle saw the metaphor as more than a substitution based on resemblances that somehow produces the most effective of rhetorical flourishes, those who looked to him in framing their own definitions did not. For Trypho (first century B.C.), "Metaphor is expression transferred from the proper to the improper for the sake of emphasis or resemblance" (Matsen, 135). For Diomedes (A.D. fourth century), "Metaphor is the transferring of things and words from their proper signification to an improper similitude for the sake of beauty, necessity, polish, or emphasis." Such transfer occurs in four ways: "From animate being to animate being . . . [f]rom animate to inanimate[,] . . . from inanimate to animate, [and] from inanimate to inanimate" (Rollinson, 89–90). For Gregorius Corinthius (A.D. twelfth century), who adds a fifth species, "from action to action" to Diomedes's four, "Metaphor is a part of speech transferred for the sake of either emphasis or resemblance" (Matsen, 136). Six centuries later, Boswell reports Samuel Johnson's comment: "As to metaphorical expression, that is a great excellence in style, when it is used with propriety, for it gives you two ideas for one;—conveys the meaning more luminously and generally with a perception of delight" (855).

2. The twentieth-century reconsideration of the metaphor may be said to have begun, at least in the English-speaking world, with I. A. Richards's *Philosophy of Rhetoric* (1936), although the essence of Richards's view is derived from Coleridge's discussions of the imagination, which can be understood as largely a commentary on metaphor. (Richards's *Coleridge on Imagination* appeared two years before *The Philosophy of Rhetoric*.) Richards begins his chapter on metaphor by challenging the Aristotelian implication that "metaphor is something special and exceptional in the use of language, a deviation from its normal mode of working, instead of the omnipresent principle of all its free action" (90). Pointing to the growth of language through metaphorical coinages that eventually lose their metaphorical force, Richards notes that the "processes of metaphor in language, the exchanges between the meanings of words which we study in explicit verbal metaphors, are super-imposed upon a perceived world which is itself a product of earlier or unwitting metaphor" (108–9). Richards also provides what has become standard terminology: the *tenor* is the "underlying idea or principal subject which the *vehicle* or figure means" (emphasis added, 97). The tenor is that which is illuminated, and the vehicle that which illuminates it. In Dyer's line "My mind a kingdom is," mind is the tenor, kingdom the vehicle. The tenor need not be explicitly named: Emily Dickinson's "narrow Fellow in the Grass" is the vehicle, and snake the tenor.

Richards makes two more very significant contributions. First, he distinguishes "the tenor-vehicle antithesis" from the antithesis between "the metaphor (the double unit including tenor and vehicle) and its meaning'' (132). Second, grounding Richards's view is his understanding of the relation between word, concept, and thing, in which the concept or ''reference'' lying between and relating word and thing is a complex cluster of associations. Thus, a metaphor is not a matter of bringing two *words* into relation but rather involves two associated complexes or contexts. That is, metaphor is not simply a substitution of words or comparison of qualities, but ''a borrowing between and intercourse of *thoughts*, a transaction between contexts'' (94).

By general consent, the second major contribution to the study of metaphor was made by Max Black in his 1955 essay ''Metaphor.'' The *interaction* theory that Black here put foward in place of the traditional views of metaphor as substitution or comparison regards the vehicle or subsidiary subject as a filter through which to regard the tenor. In the metaphor ''man is a wolf,'' the characteristics commonly associated with wolves become the filter through which man is viewed. ''Any human traits that can without undue strain be talked about in 'wolf-language' will be rendered prominent, and any that cannot will be pushed into the background. The wolf-metaphor suppresses some details, emphasizes others—in short *organizes* our view of man'' (288). (Black notes that in the case of trivial metaphors, the substitution and comparison views of metaphor will in fact suffice.) Kenneth Burke is saying much the same thing in defining metaphor as ''a device for seeing something in terms of something else'' (''Four Major Tropes,'' 503), or, more cryptically, as giving ''perspective by incongruity'' (*Permanence*, 59ff.). Again, the definition given by George Lakoff and Mark Johnson is Blackian: ''The essence of metaphor is understanding and experiencing one thing in terms of another'' (5).

Nelson Goodman's 1976 discussion of metaphor in *Languages of Art* places emphasis on relations between schemas (systems of categorizing or sorting) rather than single objects or conceptions. ''What occurs is a transfer of a schema, a migration of concepts, an alienation of categories. Indeed, a metaphor might be regarded as a happy and revitalizing, even if bigamous, second marriage'' (73).

A fourth especially influential treatment of metaphor is that of John Searle (1979). Rejecting both substitution/comparison and interaction models, Searle draws on SPEECH-ACT THEORY in emphasizing that the difference created by a metaphor is not between the usual meaning of words and their meaning in the metaphorical utterance but between sentence meaning and utterer's meaning. He therefore concentrates on describing the process by which metaphors are recognized and interpreted as having a meaning other than sentence meaning. In answering how in a metaphorical utterance one understands that ''S is P'' conveys ''S is R,'' Searle gives the following rules. (a) ''Where the utterance is defective if taken literally [within a given context], look for an utterance meaning that differs from sentence meaning.'' (b) ''When you hear 'S is P' [and recognize the utterance as defective], to find possible values of R look for ways in which S might be like P, and to fill in the respect in which S might be like P, look for salient, well known, and distinctive features of *P* things.'' These features include what Black calls *associated commonplaces*—that is, qualities commonly associated with a thing whether or not necessary to its definition or true in fact (''Metaphor,'' 287). To restrict the resulting list, ''Go back to the *S* term and see which of the many candidates for the values of *R* are likely or even possible properties of *S*'' (105–6).

In *A Theory of Semiotics* (1976) Umberto Eco puts what seems essentially Searle's explanation in terms of semantic markers (see SEMANTICS). To say that ''Richard is a fox'' is to say that Richard and the fox share semantic markers. Such semantic markers are both connotative and denotative, the connotative ones representing culturally determined associations. Thus Eco writes in *Semiotics and the Philosophy of Language*, ''The success of a metaphor is a function of the sociocultural format of the interpreting subjects' encyclopedia [mental inventory of definitions and associated qualities]. In this perspective, metaphors are produced solely on the basis of a rich cultural framework'' (127).

The above sketches of major positions taken in certain seminal essays cannot begin to consider the many issues addressed in these and hundreds of other treatments of metaphor. A brief listing of the major such issues with an indication of what seems to be the majority position is all that can be attempted here.

a. As noted above, Aristotle made no strong distinction between metaphor and simile. For Joseph Priestley, ''A Metaphor hath already been defined, to be a simile contracted to its smallest dimensions'' (181). Middleton Murry states, ''it seems impossible to regard metaphors and similes as different in any essential property: metaphor is compressed simile'' (3). On the other hand, the less difference seen between metaphor and simile, the more emphasis will be placed on substitution rather than on comparison as the basis of a metaphor, and the less motivation there will be to explore interactions between the tenor and vehicle.

b. Another question is the degree to which metaphors announce themselves and achieve their effects through purely semantic anomalousness, and the degree to which they depend on the context of utterance. The question can be phrased as one of semantics versus pragmatics, competence versus performance, or sentence versus utterance. Although it is perhaps true that in the case of every metaphor it is possible to imagine a (perhaps far-fetched) situation in which it could be understood nonmetaphorically, many metaphorical sentences can immediately be understood as metaphors regardless of the immediate context of utterance (''Bill is a snake''). On the other hand, many sentences that operate metaphorically in context lose their metaphoricity if removed from it (Cleopatra's ''Dost thou not see my baby at my breast,/That sucks the nurse asleep?''). It can be argued that, in fact, metaphor operates only when a situation of utterance (even if this is simply the most common or likely situation) is explicitly opposed to the sentence when taken in isolation. Black speaks of the way in which ''recognition and interpretation of a metaphor may require attention to the *par-*

ticular circumstances of its utterance'' (277). Searle writes, ''It is essential to emphasize at the very beginning that the problem of metaphor concerns the relation between word and sentence meaning, on the one hand, and speaker's meaning or utterance meaning, on the other'' (77).

What seems generally agreed, in any case, is that if ''semantics'' is restricted to senses as found in a dictionary, most, if not all, metaphors depend on cultural if not immediate contexts. Thus Ina Loewenberg writes, ''Metaphorical utterances are identifiable only if some knowledge possessed by speakers which is decidedly not knowledge of relationships among linguistic symbols can be taken into account'' (331).

c. A question directly evoked by the vast number of ''dead'' metaphors in the language (as noted in Richards's essay) is whether there is any such thing as a literal meaning. On one view, all language is metaphorical; on the other, metaphor is anomalous. Those who wish to question the possibility of literal meanings often cite Nietzsche's famous equation of truths with a ''mobile army of metaphors, metonymies, anthropomorphisms . . . worn-out metaphors which have become powerless to affect the senses'' (2:180). However, just as Richards distinguishes what he calls *explicit* metaphor from metaphors no longer so recognized, and Black speaks of *extinct*, *dormant*, and *active* metaphors (''More about Metaphor,'' 26), Tzvetan Todorov comments, ''if everything is metaphor, then nothing is'' (14). (''Literal'' will be used in the remainder of this entry to designate language without active metaphors.)

d. A more complex question about the relationship between the metaphorical and literal is whether metaphors can be translated into other, literal language. Alternately formulated, the question is whether all, or most, nontrivial metaphors are instances of catachresis, filling in gaps in the language. Most current students of metaphor answer ''yes.'' In the words of Richards, ''The vehicle is not normally a mere embellishment of a tenor which is otherwise unchanged by it but . . . vehicle and tenor in cooperation give a meaning of more varied powers than can be ascribed to either'' (100). Such a concept of metaphor has a long history. Quintilian states that the metaphor ''adds to the copiousness of language . . . and finally succeeds in accomplishing the supremely difficult task of providing a name for everything. . . . A noun or a verb is transferred from the place to which it properly belongs to another where there is either no *literal* term or the *transferred* is better than the *literal*'' (303; VIII.vi.5.).

e. The previous question is related to another: is metaphor cognitively, and not simply rhetorically, creative? The positivist (now often referred to as the anticonstructivist) answer is that metaphors, like metaphysical conceptions, can only obscure the nature of reality. Rudolf Carnap's ''The Elimination of Metaphysics Through the Logical Analysis of Language'' is an especially thorough statement of positivist principles. The opposing constructivist position is that all human understanding of reality is interpretive: whatever may exist, and however it may exist separate from human consciousness, all human understanding of reality is constructed. Metaphors can be regarded as playing a major role in such construction. From this point of view, it is possible for Black to say of certain metaphors, "It would be more illuminating . . . to say that the metaphor *creates* the similarity than to say that it formulates some similarity antecedently existing" ("Metaphor," 284–85). Black comments in a later essay that such an assertion "is no longer surprising if one believes that the world is necessarily a world *under a certain description*—or a world seen from a certain perspective" ("More about Metaphor," 39–40). Paul Ricoeur writes that a metaphor "has more than an emotive value because it offers new information. A metaphor, in short, tells us something new about reality" (52–53). Ted Cohen writes: "I think of metaphor as the language's intrinsic capacity to surpass its own (putative) limits. It is the abiding device for saying something truly new—but something curiously new, for it is made out of already existent meanings" (671).

In *Metaphors We Live By* (1980) the argument is made by George Lakoff and Mark Johnson not simply that metaphors can help construct our understanding of reality but that thought itself is metaphorically structured in that there are certain large conceptual metaphors like "linguistic expressions are containers" ("Try to *pack* more meaning *into* fewer words") and "communication is sending" ("He didn't get the idea across") that structure not metaphorical language but thought itself. Abstract concepts especially are understood metaphorically (love is war). Mark Turner's *Death Is the Mother of Beauty* (1987) explores kinship metaphors as a way of exemplifying the principles that structure such metaphors: two examples are "causes are parents and effects are offspring" and "a prior related thing is an older sibling" (24). Turner further argues that, for instance, there are certain causal statements that cannot be accounted for other than by the underlying conceptual metaphor "causation is progeneration." Successful metaphors are not then just happy chances. Kinship metaphors "are motivated by our knowledge of kinship and our everyday experience with it. Not just any kinship metaphor is consistent with that knowledge and that experience" (16).

f. If metaphors help construct human understanding of reality, a corollary is that metaphors not only give insight but can equally be sources of confusion and conflict. If conceptual metaphors produce intellectual frames in which "facts" are understood, conflicts between frames cannot be resolved by appeal to facts. Recognition of the roles of large-scale conceptual metaphors and the frameworks they produce may be necessary to the resolution of social conflicts and the solving of certain kinds of social problems. Such issues move beyond the bounds of strictly literary theory, but it is obvious that literary metaphors may either reinforce conceptual frames or challenge them (although even successful counter-cultural metaphors cannot avoid appealing to some cultural basis or other). The relation of metaphor to society is cogently explored in the second of the groups of essays that make up the collection *Metaphor and Thought*, edited by Andrew Ortony.

Notes on Metaphor and Metonymy

A distinction between metaphor and METONYMY has long been recognized, even though the two fade into each other at the boundaries. (The first and second kinds of metaphor described by Aristotle are, in fact, both examples of metonymy if one takes synecdoche as a subtype of metonymy.) Roman Jakobson is responsible for a twentieth-century formulation of a strong difference between the two tropes. Noting that there appear to be two types of aphasia, one affecting the ability to recognize relations through similarity and the other the ability to recognize relations of contiguity, Jakobson identifies the first with the operation of metonymy and the second with the operation of metaphor. "In normal verbal behavior both processes are continually operative, but careful observation will reveal that under the influence of a cultural pattern, personality, and verbal style, preference is given to one of the two processes over the other" (76). The two processes are then further identified with literary, linguistic, and psychoanalytic distinctions. Metaphor is based on similarity, operates on the selection axis of utterance production, is the primary trope in Romanticism and symbolism, is central to poetry, and is to be associated with Freud's *identification* and *symbolism*; metonymy is based on contiguity, operates on the combination axis, is primary to realism, is of especial importance in prose, and is to be associated with Freud's *displacement* and *condensation*. David Lodge has developed Jakobson's argument into the assertion that the characteristic literature of each literary period will show a bias toward either metaphor or metonymy, while "at the highest level of generality at which we can apply the metaphor/metonymy distinction, literature itself is metaphoric and nonliterature metonymic" (109).

On the other hand, Gérard Genette, Paul de Man, and Jonathan Culler have all more recently argued that metaphors are dependent on metonymic processes; the argument is summed up in Culler's chapter "The Turns of Metaphor" in *Pursuit of Signs*. To some extent, the goal of these maneuvers is to undermine the traditional view of metaphor as the most important of tropes. Umberto Eco argues from more directly semiotic premises

that metaphors are produced by short-circuiting metonymic thought paths. "[E]ach metaphor can be traced back to a subjacent chain of metonymic connections which constitute the framework of the [linguistic] code" ("Semantics of Metaphor," 68).

References

Aristotle. *Poetics* (*Aristotle on the Art of Poetry*). Trans. I. Bywater. Oxford: Clarendon Press, 1909.

Black, Max. "Metaphor." *Proceedings of the Aristotelian Society* n.s. 55 (1954–55): 273–94. Reprinted in Black, *Models and Metaphors*. Ithaca, N.Y.: Cornell University Press, 1962. Also reprinted in *Philosophical Perspectives on Metaphor*.

———. "More about Metaphor." In *Metaphor and Thought*. Also published in *Dialectica* 3–4 (1977): 431–57.

Boswell, James. *The Life of Johnson*. London: Oxford University Press, 1953.

Burke, Kenneth. "Four Master Tropes." In *A Grammar of Motives*. Berkeley: University of California Press, 1969.

———. *Permanence and Change*. 1935; 3d ed. Berkeley: University of California Press, 1984.

Carnap, Rudolf. "The Elimination of Metaphysics Through Logical Analysis" (1932). Trans. Arthur Pap. In *Logical Positivism*, ed. A. J. Ayer. London: Allen and Unwin, 1959.

Cohen, Ted. "Figurative Speech and Figurative Acts." *The Journal of Philosophy* 72 (1975): 669–84. Reprinted in *Philosophical Perspectives on Metaphor*.

Culler, Jonathan. *The Pursuit of Signs*. Ithaca, N.Y.: Cornell University Press. 1981. Much of Culler's argument in the section cited turns on his designation of the similarity underlying metaphor as essential and the associations underlying metonymy as "accidental or contingent" (190).

De Man, Paul. Chapter 7 in *Allegories of Reading*. New Haven: Yale University Press, 1975.

Eco, Umberto. "The Semantics of Metaphor." In *The Role of the Reader: Explorations in the Semiotics of Texts*. Bloomington: Indiana University Press, 1979.

———. *Semiotics and the Philosophy of Language*. Bloomington: Indiana University Press, 1984.

———. *A Theory of Semiotics*. Bloomington: Indiana University Press, 1976.

Genette, Gérard. "Metonymie chez Proust." In *Figures III*. Paris: Seuil, 1972.

Goodman, Nelson. *Languages of Art*. Indianapolis: Bobbs-Merrill, 1968.

Jakobson, Roman. "Two Aspects of Language and Two Types of Aphasic Disturbances." In *Fundamentals of Language I*. The Hague: Mouton, 1956.

Lakoff, George, and Mark Johnson. *Metaphors We Live By*. Chicago: University of Chicago Press, 1980.

Lodge, David. *The Modes of Modern Writing: Metaphor, Metonymy, and the Typology of Modern Writing*. Ithaca, N.Y.: Cornell University Press, 1977.

Loewenberg, Ina. "Identifying Metaphors." *Foundations of Language* 12 (1975): 315–38. Reprinted in *Philosophical Perspectives on Metaphor*.

Matsen, Patricia. Appendix II (translations from Spengel's *Rhetores Graeci*) in Rollinson's *Classical Theories*.

Metaphor and Thought. Ed. Andrew Ortony. Cambridge: Cambridge University Press, 1979.

Murry, Middleton. "Metaphor." In *Countries of the Mind*. 2d series. London: Oxford University Press, 1931. "All metaphor and simile can be described as the analogy by which the human mind explores the universe of quality and charts the non-measurable world" (9).

Nietzsche, Friedrich. "On Truth and Falsity." In vol. 2 of *The Complete Works of Friedrich Nietzsche*. Ed. Oscar Levy. 15 vols. 1909–1913. Reprint. New York: Gordon Press, 1974.

Philosophical Perspectives on Metaphor. Minneapolis: University of Minnesota Press, 1981. An unusually valuable collection.

Priestley, Joseph. *Lectures on Oratory and Criticism*. Ed. V. M. Bevilacqua and R. Murphy. Carbondale: Southern Illinois University Press, 1965.

Quintilian. *The Instituto Oratoria*. Trans. H. E. Butler. 4 vols. Loeb Classical Library. London: Heinemann, 1922.

Richards, I. A. *Coleridge on Imagination*. New York: Harcourt, Brace, 1935.

———. *The Philosophy of Rhetoric*. New York: Oxford University Press, 1936.

Ricoeur, Paul. *Interpretation Theory*. Fort Worth: Texas Christian University Press, 1976.

Rollinson, Philip. *Classical Theories of Allegory and Christian Culture*. Pittsburgh: Duquesne University Press, 1981.

Searle, John. "Metaphor." In *Expression and Meaning*. Cambridge: Cambridge University Press, 1979. Reprinted in *Philosophical Perspectives on Metaphor*.

Todorov, Tzvetan. *Symbolism and Interpretation*. Trans. C. Porter. Ithaca, N.Y.: Cornell University Press, 1982. Original French edition, 1978.

Turner, Mark. *Death is the Mother of Beauty*. Chicago: University of Chicago Press, 1987.

Sources of Additional Information

There are two major bibliographies of metaphor. Warren Shibles's *Metaphor: An Annotated Bibliography and History* (Whitewater, Wis.: Language Press, 1971) lists more than 3,000 books and articles, annotating most. *Metaphor: A Bibliography of Post-1970 Publications*, ed. J. P. von Noppen. (Amsterdam: John Benjamins, 1985) contains 4,300 entries, some of which are annotated. In both bibliographies the annotations are in English regardless of the language of the original work. Terence Hawke's *Metaphor* (1972; London: Methuen, 1984) briefly surveys historical attitudes toward metaphor.

Ernst Robert Curtius's chapter "Metaphorics" in *European Literature and the Latin Middle Ages* gives examples of five families of metaphors with long ancestries: nautical, personal or kinship, alimentary, corporal, and theatrical (trans. W. Trask; London: Routledge and Kegan Paul, 1953).

Perhaps the best approach to the study of metaphor in the twentieth century is through the essays collected by Andrew Ortony in *Metaphor and Thought* and Mark Johnson in *Philosophical Perspectives on Metaphor* (for both see References above). The introductions by each editor are excellent; in addition, Johnson includes as a bibliography brief summaries of sixty important studies of metaphor.

The best-known twentieth-century argument for a semantic rather than pragmatic theory of metaphor is Robert J. Matthews's "Concerning a 'Linguistic Theory' of Metaphor" (*Foundations of Language* 7, 1971: 413–25). Matthews finds a model based on competency, that is, knowledge of the rules of semantic selection, to be adequate for an explanation of metaphor.

Two fully argued theories of metaphor that lie rather out of the mainstream are Liselotte Gumpel's *Metaphor Reexamined: A Non-Aristotelian Perspective* (Bloomington: Indiana University Press, 1984) and Michael C. Haley's *The Semeiosis of Metaphor* (Bloomington: Indiana University Press, 1988). Gumpel writes: "I begin with the startling assertion that the traditional metaphor does not exist in language, any more than does the solar movement across the sky. Like this movement, metaphor is based on sense impressions" (xii). Gumpel draws on Roman Ingarden and C. S. Peirce for basic concepts. Haley's analysis relies primarily on the work of Peirce, defining a metaphor as "an index pointing to an icon."

Gérard Genette's "Rhetoric Restrained" in *Figures of Literary Discourse* (trans. A. Sheridan; New York: Columbia University Press, 1951) traces the reduction of the concept of rhetoric to figures and tropes and then to metaphor: "at the beginning of the twentieth century, 'metaphor' was one of the rare terms to survive the great shipwreck of rhetoric" (114).

An interesting formulation of the effect of metaphor is William Empson's in *The Structure of Complex Words* (New York: New Directions, 1951):

> It seems to me that what we start from, in a metaphor as distinct from a transfer, is a recognition that "false identity" is being used, a feeling of "resistance" to it, rather like going into higher gear, because the machinery of interpretation must be brought into play, and then a feeling of richness about the possible interpretations of the word, which has now become a source of advice on how to think about the matter. (341)

Philip Wheelwright's *Metaphor and Reality* is a useful study of literary metaphor (Bloomington: Indiana University Press, 1962). For a monograph-length study of creativity through metaphor, see Carl Hausman's *Metaphor and Art: Interaction and Reference in the Verbal and Nonverbal Arts* (Cambridge: Cambridge University Press, 1989).

Colin Turbayne's *The Myth of Metaphor* goes beyond a demonstration of the way metaphors structure human concepts of reality to show the pernicious effects of taking literally the metaphor of the world as machine (2d ed.; Columbia, S.C.: University of South Carolina Press, 1970). Turbayne advocates rather the metaphor of the world as language. Defining the use of metaphor as intentional *sort-crossing*, he terms being used by metaphor, that is, taking a metaphor literally, *sort-trespassing*. In "Metaphor or Rhetoric: The Problem of Evaluation," Wayne Booth also comments on the cultural importance of metaphoric modes of thought (in *On Metaphor*, ed. Sheldon Sacks, Chicago: University of Chicago Press, 1979). Paul de Man's "The Epistemology of Metaphor," which appears in the same collection, employs poststructuralist strategies to argue that all attempts to banish tropes turn out to be tropes themselves.

Paul Ricoeur's *The Rule of Metaphor* (1975) is a carefully developed philosophical disquisition on metaphor in its relation to discourse in general, rhetoric, poetics, reference, and, ultimately, language as a whole (trans. R. Czerny; Toronto: University of Toronto Press, 1977). Much of the central argument of the book is summed up in "Metaphor and the Main Problem of Hermeneutics" (*New Literary History* 6, 1974–75: 95–110; reprinted in *The Philosophy of Paul Ricoeur*, ed. C. E. Reagan and D. Stewart (Boston: Beacon Press, 1978).

James Dickey's brief essay *Metaphor as Pure Adventure* is an unpretentious but stylish contemporary celebration of metaphor (Washington, D.C.: Library of Congress, 1968).

> [P]oets believe, with a high secret glee, that precisely because God made these things as they are (the star, the tree, the woman), because He made them so much themselves that they can be nothing *but* themselves, someone else—someone like a poet, say—can come along and compare a star to a woman, or to a tree, and accomplish something valuable by it. Poets believe that the things of this world are capable of making connections between each other that not God but men see, and they say so. (13).

METONYMY   The substitution of one term for another with which it is commonly associated: "the pen is mightier than the sword." Synecdoche, the naming of a part of a thing to signify the whole (or, occasionally, the substitution of whole for part), may be regarded as a special case of metonymy, though some critics and rhetoricians find the difference substantial enough to regard it as a separate trope.

For relationships between metonymy and METAPHOR, *see the note at the end of the entry on metaphor.*

In the Classical period, metonymy and synecdoche seem generally regarded as frequent and effective devices but not ones that stand out among others such as antiphrasis, hyperbaton, and metalepsis. Metonymy and synecdoche receive brief mention in Quintilian (A.D. first century). Metonymy may "indicate an invention by substituting the name of the inventor, or a possession by substituting the name of the possessor," that which is contained by that which contains, and cause by effect (313–17; VIII.vi.23–26). "Synecdoche has the power," he writes, "to give variety to our language by making us realise many things from one, the whole from a part, the *genus* from a *species*, things which follow from things which have preceded; or, on the other hand, the whole process may be reversed'' (311).

Diomedes (A.D. fourth century), defining metonymy simply as "a saying changed from one proper signification to another,'' gives six ways in which it can occur: "By means of that which is contained for that which contains"; "By means of the author or ruler for what is authored or the subject"; "By means of what does something for what it does"; and by the reverse of each of these (91). Synecdoche is understood in the usual way as the signifying of a part by the whole or the whole by a part.

As interest in figures as opposed to tropes declined, metonymy, like metaphor, received more attention. Joseph Priestley devoted a full lecture to it in his *Lectures on Oratory and Criticism* (1777). Priestley notes "the striking effect" of metonymy and synecdoche. "These terms are applied when, instead of the proper name of any thing or attribute, a name is borrowed from another object, which stands in any other relation to it than that of actual *resemblance*, which is referred to *metaphor*" (231). "It is almost endless to enumerate all the relations of things which afford a foundation for this figure of speech. Some of the principal of them are those of *cause and effect*, in all its varieties, *the subject and its attributes*, or circumstances; the *agent and the instrument; general and particular, abstract and concrete terms;* and *the whole and its part*, which alone is referred to *synecdoche*" (232). On the other hand, as Gérard Genette has pointed out, metonymy began to be thought of in the later eighteenth and the nineteenth centuries as primarily based on spatial contiguity rather than on the wide variety of relationships suggested by a Diomedes or a Priestley.

In the present century, metonymy and synecdoche have received increasing attention. Kenneth Burke thus includes them with metaphor and IRONY in his "four master tropes," tropes that represent for Burke central modes of human thought (metonymy thus represents a means of *reduction*, and synecdoche of *representation* in the particular senses in which Burke uses these words). Some writers have tended to assimilate metonymy to metaphor, not in order to diminish the importance of these tropes themselves but to identify them with what is frequently seen as the most significant trope. Terence Hawkes thus describes simile, synecdoche, and metonymy as "versions of metaphor's prototype" (2), and John Searle writes, "According to my account of metaphor, it becomes a matter of terminology whether we want to construe metonymy and synecdoche as special cases of metaphor or as independent tropes" (110). On the other hand, Roman Jakobson's concept of a linguistic opposition between metonymy and metaphor that reappears in a variety of human thought patterns has had significant influence (see METAPHOR).

References

Burke, Kenneth. "Four Master Tropes." In *A Grammar of Motives*. Berkeley: University of California Press, 1969.
Diomedes. [Concerning Tropes]. Translated as Appendix 1 in Philip Rollinson's *Classical*

Theories of Allegory and Christian Culture. Pittsburgh: Duquesne University Press, 1981.

Hawkes, Terence. *Metaphor*. Critical Idiom Series. London: Methuen, 1972.

Jakobson, Roman. "Two Aspects of Language and Two Types of Aphasic Disturbances." In *Fundamentals of Language 1*. The Hague: Mouton, 1956.

Priestley, Joseph. *Lectures on Oratory and Criticism* (1777). Ed. V. M. Bevilacqua and R. Murphy. Carbondale: Southern Illinois University Press, 1965.

Quintilian. *The Institutio Oratoria*. Trans. H. E. Butler. 4 vols. Loeb Classical Library. London: Heinemann, 1922.

Searle, John. "Metaphor." In *Expression and Meaning*. Cambridge: Cambridge University Press, 1979.

MIMESIS   1. Imitation. Mimesis carries the overriding sense of imitation or copying, the production of an iconic representation in which the similarity to the thing imitated is in itself the primary source of interest. 2. As employed in NARRATOLOGY, the use of dialogue (or the dramatic mode) in contrast to diegesis or pure narration without dialogue.

1. The controversies and attempted clarifications generated by the concept of mimesis in literary studies arise out of the question of what in fact is imitated in literature. Plato notoriously excludes poets from his ideal republic for imitating the objects of this world that are, in turn, simply imitations of ideal forms. Aristotle, on the other hand, accepts the imitation of human actions as a natural source of human pleasure and, perhaps, of knowledge. "Imitation is natural to man from childhood, one of his advantages over the lower animals being this, that he is the most imitative creature in the world, and learns at first by imitation. And it is also natural for all to delight in works of imitation" (9; 3.1448b). However, beyond contrasting Plato's concentration on the poet's representation of objects with Aristotle's on actions (a distinction rarely developed by later commentators), these generalizations do little to clarify the central question: What does literature imitate? Six answers are to be noted.

1a. The ideal forms, that is, Plato's ideas. While the traditional interpretation has been that Plato dismissed the poets from his ideal state, in 1928 J. Tate argued with some success that Plato in fact assumed the possibility of "good" imitation by those who had ascended to some grasp of the realm of ideas as well as "bad" imitation by those content with imitating existing objects as ordinarily perceived (that is, as imperfect copies of the ideal). "To sum up, there are two forms of imitation according to Plato. The first is the *merely* imitative, which imitates only the apparent nature of things which are apparent to the senses (*Rep*. 598b). . . . The second form of imitation is that which imitates the ideal world. This form can be achieved only by the man of understanding, who can recognize both the ideas in themselves and their images in the sensible world . . . (*Rep*. 402bc, 500 sqq.)" (23). On the other hand, D. A. Russell asserts in *Criticism in Antiquity* (1981), "We have no reason to think that [Plato] ever entertained the notion that poets and artists might aspire to copy directly the *ideai* of which objects in the visible world are themselves copies" (104).

1b. Generalized imitation. If, like Aristotle and most thinkers through the centuries, one rejects ideal forms as possible objects of imitation, a number of ways in which the literary work may imitate the world remain available. Four of these were outlined in 1789 in Thomas Twining's important essay "On Poetry Considered as an Imitative Art," only two of which Twining finds in Aristotle. The first is imitation of a generalized "reality" rather than of individual objects, persons, or actions. S. H. Butcher's well-known interpretation of the meaning of Aristotelian imitation is that art "eliminates what is transient and particular and reveals the permanent and essential features of the original" (150). "There is an ideal form which is present in each individual phenomenon but imperfectly manifested" (153). Thus, for Butcher the ideal pursued by art may be grasped by the artist through contemplation of the actual.

Butcher's concept of Aristotelian mimesis is very close to Twining's understanding of mimesis as *fiction*. Thus, fiction is the imitation "of nature, of real life, of truth in *general*, as opposed to that individual reality of things which is the province of the historian" (19).

1c. Direct imitation of another's speech. According to Twining, the other form of imitation recognized by Aristotle is that of *personation*, in which the author speaks as another person. That mimesis was understood by both Plato and Aristotle primarily as personation resulted from the dominant position of drama (and the importance of the rhapsode in orally presenting the epic) in Greek culture of the time. Evidently, personation in a somewhat different mode is central to the novel and the dramatic monologue. Since Plato appears to reserve the word mimesis for the presentation of direct speech as opposed to narrative, it is possible to see his condemnation of imitation as aimed at the impersonation of certain kinds of persons (see Russell, 102).

1d. Description. The third form of mimesis Twining distinguishes is *description*, as opposed to fictional narration. "In description, *imitation* is opposed to actual *impression*, external or internal: in fiction, it is opposed to *fact*" (119). Pointing out the very small amount of description, especially of nature, in Greek poetry, Twining notes that Aristotle did not concern himself with this form of mimesis.

1e. Sound. The fourth of Twining's forms of mimesis— also one not noted by Aristotle—is the imitation of sound in language. James Harris had previously commented on this aspect of imitation, which is made possible by differences between words in their "[a]ptness to be *rapidly* or *slowly* pronounced, and by the respective Prevalence of *Mutes*, *Liquids*, or *Vowels*" (70). The major portion of W. K. Wimsatt's "In Search of Verbal Meaning" is devoted to various ways in which the actual sound of language may be mimetic.

1f. Of perhaps minor interest are typographical arrangements such as the shaped poems of Herbert and Apollinaire. Wimsatt's essay cited previously briefly reviews other kinds of typographical mimesis.

1g. The imitation or evocation of other literary works. Mimesis is sometimes extended to include the partial imitation of other literary works (see ALLUSION).

1h. Imaginable individual phenomena. A modification of the notion of mimesis as the imitation of generalized experience sees literature as imitating not the general but the particular; the fictional instance is similar to the actual because it can be subsumed under categories of actual experience. This appears to have been the view of James Harris in "A Discourse on Music, Painting, and Poetry" (1744): "In entering upon this Inquiry, it is first to be observed, that the MIND is made conscious of the *natural world* and its Affections, and of other Minds and their affections, by the several *Organs of the Senses*. By the *same Organs*, these arts exhibit to the Mind *Imitations*, and imitate either Parts or Affections of the *natural World*, or else the Passions, Energies, and other Affections of *Minds*" (55–56).

John Crowe Ransom's "The Mimetic Principle" specifically disagrees with Butcher, denying that Aristotle "required the artistic imitation to emphasize the typical and eliminate the local and characteristic" (204). For Ransom, the value of literary mimesis, then, lies not in typicality but in the human love of imitation and the necessity enforced by art of contemplating rather than using the imitation. "An imitation is better than its original in one thing only: not being actual, it cannot be used, it can only be known" (197).

1i. Only language itself. It might be thought that the New Critics' concern for the work of literature as an autonomous structure would have excluded the idea of mimesis. However, as the citation from Ransom under (g) above suggests, that the literary work imitates nonliterary and nonlinguistic experience seems rarely to have been challenged. (One pungently phrased nineteenth-century dissent is that of E. S. Dallas in his *Poetics* of 1852: "Greatly in vogue at one time, the commonplace of criticism, always at hand, and if not always of service, at least always officious, the definition [of literature as imitation] seems now, like a physician in good old age, to have retired from practice. It is no longer in request," 121.) In recent decades, those who extrapolate Ferdinand Saussure's principle of the arbitrariness of the relation between signifier and signified into the doctrine that the signified itself is an arbitrary construction, or extend the belief that ultimate reality is unknowable into the doctrine that mimesis is impossible because there is nothing outside language for it to imitate, have generally taken language, or at least literary language, as either mimetic only of itself or as play. One such response is represented by Gérard Genette: "Now then, for reasons that have been set forth a thousand times (and not only by me), I believe there is no imitation in narrative because narrative, like everything (or almost everything) in literature, is an act of language. And, therefore, there can be no more imitation in narrative in particular than there is in language in general" (42).

Another kind of response is represented in Mihai Spariosu's belief that "the original [pre-Platonic] meaning of mimesis reflects what Heidegger and [Eugen] Fink call the 'ecstatic play of the world,' which is the opposite of imitation" (iii). An especially interesting reinterpretation is that of James S. Hans in *Imitation and the Image of Man*, which argues for a "non-linear kind of imitation that is articulated through the play between differences, that is dialectical and recursive rather than objective and linear'' (xvii). In a way different from Tate's reinterpretation of Plato sixty years earlier, Hans sees Plato's theory of imitation as referring ''to an active process rather than a set of objects or states of mind. Instead of focusing on the representation of objects in the external world— something Plato was right to be concerned about—the older mimetic theory [that which Plato would approve] is based on imitating the dialectical process we see embodied in the Socratic dialogue'' (14).

2. Gérard Genette's contrasting of mimesis with diegesis goes back to Plato's distinction between story-telling by simple narrative and by mimesis or the representation of direct speech (*The Republic*, sections 392c–395; and see also *Sophist*, section 267). Mimesis used in this restricted sense refers to the same object of imitation as (1c) above—Twining's *personation*—but the force of its use as one of a pair of contrasting terms perhaps justifies considering this use as a separate sense (see Genette's *Narrative Discourse*, 162ff., and *Narrative Discourse Revisited*, 18, 43, 45).

References

Aristotle. *On the Art of Poetry*. Trans. I. Bywater. Oxford: Clarendon Press, 1909.

Butcher, S. H. *Aristotle's Theory of Poetry*. 2d ed. London: Macmillan, 1898. An influential study, although it has frequently been challenged.

Dallas, Eneas Sweetland. *Poetics*. London: Smith, Elder, 1852.

Genette, Gérard. *Narrative Discourse*. Trans. J. E. Lewin. Ithaca, N.Y.: Cornell University Press, 1980. Originally published as *Discours du récit* in 1972.

———. *Narrative Discourse Revisited*. 1983; Ithaca, N.Y.: Cornell University Press, 1988.

Hans, James S. *Imitation and the Image of Man*. Philadelphia: J. Benjamins, 1987.

Harris, James. ''A Discourse on Music, Painting, and Poetry.'' In *Three Discourses*. 1744; 2d ed. London: John Nourse, 1765.

The Republic and *Sophist*. In vols. 2 and 3 of *The Dialogues of Plato*. Trans. B. Jowett. New York: Scribner, 1911.

Ransom, John Crowe. ''The Mimetic Principle.'' In *The World's Body*. New York: Charles Scribner's Sons, 1938.

Russell, D. A. *Criticism in Antiquity*. London: Duckworth, 1981.

Spariosu, Mihia, ed. *Mimesis in Contemporary Theory*, vol. 1. Amsterdam: John Benjamins, 1984.

Tate, J. '' 'Imitation' in Plato's Republic.'' *Classical Quarterly* 22 (January 1928): 16–23. An important essay.

Twining, Thomas. ''On Poetry Considered as an Imitative Art.'' In *Aristotle's Treatise on Poetry*. Trans. T. Twining. London: 1789. Essential.

Wimsatt, W. K. ''In Search of Verbal Meaning.'' In *Day of the Leopards*. New Haven, Conn.: Yale University Press, 1976.

Sources of Additional Information

Richard McKeon's ''Literary Criticism and the Concept of Imitation in Antiquity'' (*Modern Philology* 34, August 1936: 1–35, reprinted in *Critics and Criticism*, ed. R. S. Crane, Chicago: University of Chicago Press, 1952), is a standard treatment of the meanings of mimesis for Plato and Aristotle. "Whereas for Plato the term 'imitation' may undergo an infinite series of gradations of meaning, developed in a series of analogies, for Aristotle the term is restricted definitely to a single literal meaning" (16). For further development of J. Tate's interpretation of Plato's view of mimesis, see his "Plato and 'Imitation' " (*Classical Quarterly*, 26, July-October 1932; 161–69). In *Mimesis: Plato's Doctrine of Artistic Imitation and Its Meaning to Us* (*Philosophia Antiqua*, vol. 3; Leiden: E. J. Brill, 1949), W. J. Verdenius discusses the implications of Plato's view of the "weakness of art" and the "poorness of its images," concluding that the artist's realization of these characteristics of art nevertheless "seems to enable him to reveal something of what is behind appearances" (37).

For an extensive study of mimesis in the eighteenth century, see John D. Boyd's *The Function of Mimesis and Its Decline* (Cambridge, Mass.: Harvard University Press, 1988): "This book attempts to study the critical concept of the function of mimesis within its tradition, its characteristics and minimal demands, and their implications in context, especially as conceived by Aristotle and as they appeared during the decline of this concept in eighteenth-century England" (2). Herbert Lindenberger's "The Mimetic Bias in Modern Anglo-American Criticism" in *Mimesis in Contemporary Theory*, vol. 1, ed. Mihai Spariosu (Amsterdam: John Benjamins, 1984), examines the often concealed reliance on mimesis in C. S. Lewis, T. S. Eliot, F. R. Leavis, R. S. Crane, and others.

The Chicago School of criticism argues that allegory is not a form of mimesis; thus Elder Olsen writes, "The construction of such mimetic poetry as epic, tragedy, and comedy is very different [from didactic allegory]; these are ordered, not to a doctrine, but to a plot" ("William Empson, Contemporary Criticism, and Poetic Diction," in *Critics and Criticism*, ed. R. S. Crane, Chicago: University of Chicago Press, 1952, 67).

Erich Auerbach's celebrated *Mimesis* (1946; trans. W. Trask, Princeton, N.J.: Princeton University Press, 1953) traces changes in the representation of reality from Homer forward; the volume does not, however, offer a theory of mimesis, but rather implies Auerbach's own preference for a mixture of styles and a concern for everyday life, both of which were foreign to Classical practice.

MODERN   1. Literature contemporary with the period in which the word is employed. 2. Literature and art from the Renaissance to the present.

1. "Modern" comes into currency with the meaning "just now," or "originating in the current age" in the sixteenth century; it has been possible to use the word and its derivatives to refer to literature contemporary with oneself at any time since. It was thus employed in the quarrel between advocates of the superiority of contemporary over ancient literature in the seventeenth and eighteenth centuries—a type of the recurrent opposition that Ernst Curtius reminds us "is a constant phenomenon of literary history and literary sociology." Thus, he points out, Aristarchus (c. 250–150 B.C.) contrasted the "moderns," the *neoteroi*, with Homer, and among the Romans the difference between ancients and moderns is the subject of comment, for example, by Terence and Cicero (Curtius, 251).

2. Recorded history of the Western world has frequently been divided into three great eras, ancient, medieval, and modern, with the modern period beginning with the Renaissance. The overarching worldview is seen as undergoing a

critical change in the Renaissance as human nature and achievement become the focus of thought, initiating a new humanism and new reliance on rationality. The full significance of the Renaissance appears not to have been fully recognized until late in the nineteenth century: Jacob Burckhardt and J. A. Symonds provided the canonical explorations.

References

Burckhardt, Jakob. *The Civilization of the Renaissance in Italy*. Trans. S. G. C. Middlemore. Oxford: Phaidon Press, 1944.
Curtius, Ernst Robert. *European Literature and the Latin Middle Ages*. London: Routledge and Kegan Paul, 1953.
Symonds, John Addington. *The Renaissance in Italy*. 7 vols. London: Smith, Elder, 1875–86.

MODERNISM   1. An Anglo-American literary movement, the major period of which extended from roughly 1912 to 1930. 2. A reaction against nineteenth-century cultural and aesthetic values extending across Europe and including the United States. 3. A reaction to Renaissance humanism that began at least as early as the latter third of the nineteenth century and extends to the present.

1. Modernism is the name that came to be given to the literature and art that seemed to critical observers in the early years of the twentieth century to differ significantly from nineteenth-century norms. Delineation of a modernist movement has been especially important in English and American literary criticism. From the English point of view, it was perhaps especially easy to begin to contrast the modern with Romantic and high Victorian thought, art, and literature. However, because what had been described as modern in, for instance, the 1920s began to seem dated, the anomaly of designating a fixed period by a term that had hitherto referred to that which was characteristic of the present became evident.

There are two very distinguishable strands in late-nineteenth- and early-twentieth-century literature, as evidenced in the correspondence between Henry James and H. G. Wells, Virginia Woolf's essay on Arnold Bennett, and D. H. Lawrence's essay on Galsworthy. Stephen Spender's 1963 *Struggle of the Modern* sets out the influential distinction between *moderns* and *contemporaries*. James, Joyce, Eliot, Pound, Lewis, Lawrence, Woolf, and Beckett ("that heroic survivor") figure as the central moderns, and Shaw, Wells, Galsworthy and Bennett as major representatives of the contemporaries. The "moderns," writes Spender, were "deliberately setting out to invent a new literature as the result of their feeling that our age is in many respects unprecedented, and outside all the conventions of past literature and art" (x). Eliot's *Waste Land*, Pound's *Cantos*, Joyce's *Ulysses*, and the later Yeats of *The Tower* are central literary exemplars. More specifically, the moderns (later termed modernists) reacted with dislike to the effects of technology and the apparent direction of cultural development, while the contemporaries, although they could also revolt against the aspects of society they did not like, were likely to think "that, on the whole, the duty of writers is to enlist their art in the cause of progress" (x). Paul Fussell, writing many years later, constructs a very similar distinction:

> A *Modernist* is a late-nineteenth- or twentieth-century artist or artistic theorist who has decided to declare war on the received, the philistine, the bourgeois, the sentimental, and the democratic. . . . A Modern . . . is capable of incorporating into his work contemporary currents of thought and emotion without any irritable need to quarrel with the past—intellectually, psychologically, or technically. A Modern can embrace the past and not just feel but enjoy its continuity with the present. (584)

It is possible to distinguish a tradition embraced by antimodernist writers; for instance Geoffrey Harvey's *The Romantic Tradition in English Poetry* traces a line from Wordsworth through Tennyson, Hardy, Kipling, and Housman to Auden, Betjeman, and Larkin.

The modernists' consciousness of being modern is central to their work: Graham Hough writes, "This consciousness of modernity is a distinctly modern thing; it is largely the work of the revolutionary generation itself" (5). Donald Davie speaks of modern poetry as "something different, in important ways, from the poetry of the past" (147).

The general characteristics of modernist writing have been variously formulated, but for most critics they include the dismissal of earlier notions of decorum in both diction and subject matter, depreciation of the meaning of history, the creation of discontinuity, and complex allusiveness. Lawrence Gamache has given a useful summation of characteristics of modernism as they have been developed by commentators since Spender:

> (1) a preoccupation with the present, usually urban and technical rather than rural and agricultural in its sense of place and time, is related to the loss of a meaningful context derived from the past, from its forms, styles, and traditions; (2) this sense of loss gives rise to a search for a new context—cosmopolitan, not provincial, in scope—and for new techniques to evolve an acceptable perception of reality, often, paradoxically, in the form of an attempt to rediscover roots in the depths of the past; (3) but this search tends to an increasingly relativistic, inward, often disillusioned vision and a compulsive need to develop techniques to embody it. (33)

Irving Howe wrote in 1978 that "modernism despairs of human history, abandons the idea of a linear historical development, falls back upon the notion of a universal *condition humaine* or a rhythm of eternal occurrence, yet within its own realm is committed to ceaseless change, turmoil, and re-creation" (8). Ihab Hassan cites seven characteristics: urbanism, technologism, dehumanization, primitivism, eroticism, antinomianism, and experimentalism (35–37).

In contrast to these attempts to characterize modernism by its relation to the surrounding culture, certain critics have concentrated on formal or technical qualities. A tendency to view human experience spatially rather than temporally has come to seem a further important characteristic. Joseph Frank's "Spatial Form in Modern Literature" (1945) influentially argued that modern literature "is moving in the direction of spatial form"; writers like Eliot, Pound, Proust, and Joyce "ideally intend their readers to apprehend their work spatially, in a moment of time, rather than as a sequence" (8–9). Frank linked this characterization to Worringer's distinction between the *naturalistic* and the *linear-geometric* styles—the canceling or weakening of the distinction between past and present represents the latter. The same contrast had much earlier been employed by T. E. Hulme, who foresaw, and encouraged, a "re-emergence of geometrical art" as humans recognized their lack of harmony with nature (78).

For Donald Davie, "What is common to all modern [modernist] poetry is the assertion or the assumption (most often the latter) that syntax in poetry is wholly different from syntax as understood by logicians and grammarians" (148). "Syntax" here refers to the movement of thought rather than grammatical syntax only. David Lodge, drawing on Jakobson's characterization of the difference between metaphoric and metonymic thought, has argued that the most basic characteristic of modernist literature as a whole is "a metaphoric (symbolist or mythopoeic) representation of experience" (177). Sanford Schwartz links the modernist preoccupation with spatiality to the opposition between conscious surface and unconscious depth as the *before-and-after* paradigm of the nineteenth century gave way to the *surface-and-depth* paradigm (5).

The relationships of the Anglo-American modernists to earlier English literature have been much and variously explored. The European symbolist movement is generally regarded as having had a strong influence on modernism, although Imagism was the proximate begetter. The importance of Imagism has been especially developed by Stephen Spender and Graham Hough. Carol Christ has emphasized the continuities in intention between the modernist and Victorian poets which existed despite the modernists' sense of their opposition. In *Axel's Castle*, Edmund Wilson describes European modernism generally as a "second flood" of romanticism (1–2), and Robert Langbaum has more recently traced the influence of ROMANTICISM. David Lodge sees modernism largely as a reaction to nineteenth-century REALISM (125), while Michael Bell presents it as a combination of naturalism (social and biological determinism) and symbolism (18).

If the proper beginning date of literary modernism is moot—Malcolm Bradbury and James McFarlane choose the 1890s; Peter Faulkner, 1910; Graham Hough, 1914—how late it continues is even more debatable. There is disagreement about whether Yeats and Wallace Stevens ought to be included. Faulkner, Hemingway, and dos Passos are sometimes included (as, for instance, by Julian Symons), as are John Crowe Ransom, Allen Tate, and Robert Penn Warren (for instance, by Monroe Spears). There is more unanimity that, as Bernard Bergonzi writes, "By 1930 . . . the seminal texts had been written, though major canonical texts continued to appear in the 1930s and 40s" (xvi).

There is a close relationship between Anglo-American modernism and what came to be known as the NEW CRITICISM, although this was not fully recognized in the early years of their mutual reinforcement. T. S. Eliot's early critical writing—so influential with the New Critics—cleared the way for his own and other modernists' poetic practice, as, to a lesser extent, did that of Ezra Pound. The New Critical emphasis on the autonomy of the individual work, the necessity of close reading, the value of tension and irony, and the distinction between the poet's subjective consciousness and the work itself was largely congruent with the modernists' own high valuation of complexity, ironic challenging of social norms, and preference for distancing the author from direct statement. The previously remarked interest in spatial form is an index of the compatibility of the literature and criticism of a given period: the New Critical emphasis on elucidating the overall pattern of a text was eminently suitable for the analysis of works meant to interest less through anticipation of the temporal, cause-and-effect succession than through tension and correspondences within the structure of the work as a whole.

The political tendencies of Anglo-American modernism began to receive particular attention with the advent of World War II. The political conservatism (for example, in Yeats and Eliot), if not fascism (for example, in Pound and Lewis) of modernist writers made the elitism associated with modernism seem considerably more sinister. Those who strongly distinguish a postmodernist movement from modernism proper frequently see POSTMODERNISM as having become populist and antifascist. More recently, critics of Marxist orientation have insisted on the connection between the "social technological modernization" they deplore and literary modernism (Huyssen, 4).

2. When one steps outside the group of Anglo-American authors primarily identified with modernism and seeks either the roots of modernism or the outlines of the larger, multinational tendencies in literature and art to which the Anglo-American modernists seem allied, the dates of the precursors, if not the center, of modernism are pushed back earlier, and the complexities of definition increase. Richard Ellmann and Charles Feidelson's anthology of criticism and theory, *The Modern Tradition: Backgrounds of Modern Literature*, finds seminal influences as early as the mid-eighteenth century. The Introduction to *Modernism*, edited by Malcolm Bradbury and James McFarlane, sees the whole of the phenomena of modernism—one of the "cataclysmic upheavals of culture" (19–20)—as beginning to gather force from the 1850s. Janko Lavrin, writing in 1935 and finding the terms "modern" and "modernism" already hackneyed, included Anatole France, born in 1844, in his *Aspects of Modernism: From Wilde to Pirandello*. There is little question that Proust, Valéry, Gide, Mann, Rilke, and Kafka belong to the larger modernist movement, as do Picasso, Matisse, Braque, Stravinsky, Schoenberg, and Diaghilev; cubism, futurism, dadaism, surrealism, and vorticism represent associated aspects of the revolt against early-twentieth-century social and aesthetic norms.

3. In its widest sense, modernism extends to the present. Once modernism is seen as a large-scale change in Western thought and the arts generally, it is possible to regard it not as the latest development of the era that opened with the Renaissance but as initiating a fourth era that collides directly with the general cultural values existing roughly from the sixteenth through the nineteenth century.

As early as 1924, T. E. Hulme was predicting the "break up of the Renaissance humanistic attitude" (78). An influential 1925 essay by José Ortega y Gassett, "The Dehumanization of Art," found that the arts were moving away from the usual human interests and responses: "preoccupation with the human content of the work is in principle incompatible with aesthetic enjoyment proper" (9). Irving Howe wrote in 1963, "in much modern literature one finds a bitter impatience with the whole apparatus of cognition and the limiting assumptions of rationality"; moreover, "modernism despairs of human history" and "abandons the idea of a linear historical development" (7–8). Georg Lukács, writing from a Marxist perspective in the late 1950s, found international modernism as exemplified by writers like Kafka, Robert Musil, Joyce, and Beckett to be not only a denial of the social nature of humanity but also an "attenuation of reality and dissolution of personality" in which "[m]an is reduced to a sequence of unrelated experiential fragments" (26). In 1961, Lionel Trilling cited "the disenchantment of our culture with culture itself" so that the "characteristic element of modern literature . . . is the bitter line of hostility to civilization that runs through it." (3). Frank Kermode's *The Sense of an Ending* (1967) insists on the modernist assumption of an apocalyptic ending. Monroe K. Spears suggests 1870 as the beginning of modernism as a mode of conceiving the world, linking it to the thought of Nietzsche, Freud, Frazer, and Marx, whose "Dionysian" views of the world undercut the liberal humanism and rationality of the era that began in the Renaissance. Ricardo Quinones gives greater psychological and philosophical significance to the modernists' desire to spatialize, locating it as a decisive break with the Renaissance. "If a key conquest of the Renaissance was the modern notion of time, one so crucial to the mentality of our industrialized societies, then it is not surprising that in a time of disenchantment with that industrial base, the formative concept of time should itself undergo revision" (25).

References

Bell, Michael. *1900–1930*. London: Methuen, 1980.

Bergonzi, Bernard. *The Myth of Modernism*. Brighton, U.K.: Harvester Press, 1986.

Bradbury, Malcolm, and James McFarlane, "The Name and Nature of Modernism." In *Modernism*, ed. M. Bradbury and J. McFarlane. Harmondsworth, U.K.: Penguin, 1976.

Christ, Carol T. *Victorian and Modern Poetics*. Chicago: University of Chicago Press, 1984.

Davie, Donald. *Articulate Energy: An Inquiry into the Syntax of English Poetry*. London: Routledge and Kegan Paul, 1955.

Faulkner, Peter. Introduction to *A Modernist Reader*. London: Batsford, 1986.

Frank, Joseph. "Spatial Form in Modern Literature" (1945). In *The Widening Gyre: Crisis and Mastery in Modern Literature*. New Brunswick, N.J.: Rutgers University Press, 1963.

Fussell, Paul. "Modernism, Adversary Culture, and Edmund Blunden." *Sewanee Review* 94 (October-December 1986): 583–601.

Gamache, Lawrence B. "Toward a Definition of 'Modernism.' " In *The Modernists: Studies in a Literary Phenomenon, Essays in Honor of Harry T. Moore*, ed. Ian MacNiven and Lawrence B. Gamache. Rutherford, N.J.: Fairleigh Dickinson University Press, 1987.

Harvey, Geoffrey. *The Romantic Tradition in English Poetry*. London: Macmillan, 1986.

Hassan, Ihab. *The Postmodern Turn*. Columbus: Ohio State University Press, 1987.

Hough, Graham. *Reflections on a Literary Revolution*. Washington, D.C.: Catholic University of America Press, 1960. Important study of Imagism and its influence.

Howe, Irving. *The Decline of the New* (1963). New York: Harcourt, Brace and World, 1978.

Hulme, T. E. *Speculations*. New York: Harcourt, Brace, 1924.

Huyssen, Andreas. "Critical Theory and Modernity." *New German Critique* 26 (Spring/Summer 1982): 3–11.

James, Henry. *Henry James and H. G. Wells: A Record of their Friendship* . . . Ed. L. Edel and G. N. Ray. Urbana: University of Illinois Press, 1958.

Kermode, Frank. *The Sense of an Ending*. London: Oxford University Press, 1967.

Langbaum, Robert. *The Poetry of Experience*. New York: Random House, 1957.

Lavrin, Janko. *Aspects of Modernism: From Wilde to Pirandello*. London: Stanley Nott, 1935.

Lawrence, David Herbert. "John Galsworthy" (1928). In *Selected Essays*. Ed. A. Beal. London: Heinemann, 1955.

Lodge, David. *The Modes of Modern Writing: Metaphor, Metonymy, and the Typology of Modern Literature*. Ithaca, N.Y.: Cornell University Press, 1977.

Lukács, Georg. "The Ideology of Modernism." In *Realism in Our Time*. 1958; Trans. J. Mander and N. Mander. New York: Harper and Row, 1962.

The Modern Tradition: Backgrounds of Modern Literature. Ed. Richard Ellmann, and Charles Feidelson, Jr. New York: Oxford University Press, 1965. An excellent resource for tracing the roots of modernism.

Ortega y Gasset, José: *The Dehumanization of Art*. 1925: Trans. W. A. Trask, Garden City, N.Y.: Doubleday Anchor, 1956.

Quinones, Ricardo J. *Mapping Literary Modernism: Time and Development*. Princeton, N.J.: Princeton University Press, 1985.

Schwartz, Sanford. *The Matrix of Modernism*. Princeton, N.J.: Princeton Unversity Press, 1985.

Spears, Monroe K. *Dionysus and the City: Modernism in Twentieth-Century Poetry*. New York: Oxford University Press, 1970.

Spender, Stephen. *The Struggle of the Modern*. London: Hamish Hamilton, 1963. Central for its early delineation of the specific modernist characteristics.

Symons, Julian. *Makers of the New: The Revolution in Literature, 1912–1939*. New York: Random House, 1987.

Trilling, Lionel. "On the Teaching of Modern Literature" (1961). In *Beyond Culture*. New York: Viking Press, 1965.

Wells, H. G. See James, Henry.

Wilson, Edmund. *Axel's Castle*. 1931; New York: Scribner's, 1959. A classic study of Symbolism.

Woolf, Virginia. "Mr. Bennett and Mrs. Brown" (1924). In *Collected Essays*. Ed. Leonard Woolf. 4 vols. New York: Harcourt, Brace and World, 1967.

Sources of Additional Information

Alastair Davies's *Annotated Critical Bibliography of Modernism* (Brighton, U.K.: Harvester Press, 1982) includes separate annotated bibliographies of Yeats, Lewis, Lawrence, and Eliot. *A Modernist Reader: Modernism in England, 1910–1930*, ed. Peter Faulkner (London: Batsford, 1986) is a convenient collection of contemporary statements associated with the rise of modernism. Robert M. Adams's "What Was Modernism?" (*Hudson Review* 31, Spring 1978: 1933) is an especially readable rapid survey which places modernism as "a cultural trend most clearly discernible between 1905 and 1925" (33). *Literary Modernism*, ed. Irving Howe (New York: Fawcett, 1967) is an equally helpful collection of major critical essays on modernism. *Modernism*, ed. Malcolm Bradbury and James McFarlane (Harmondsworth, U.K.: Penguin, 1976), contains thirty-four widely ranging essays. Harry Levin's "What Was Modernism" (in *Massachusetts Review* 1, 1960: 609–30, and reprinted in *Refractions*, New York: Oxford University Press, 1966) is an important reassessment which opened reconsideration of the modernists. C. K. Stead's *Pound, Yeats, Eliot and the Modernist Movement* (London: Macmillan, 1986) provides a valuable discussion of the relation of the modernists to Symbolism and Imagism. Among useful treatments of specialized aspects is Jacob Korg's *Language in Modern Literature: Innovation and Experiment* (New York: Barnes and Noble, 1979), which emphasizes the delight in new forms of order in literature that was felt by Stein, Hulme, Eliot, Lewis, Pound, Joyce, Williams, and Cummings.

MYTH CRITICISM 1. Assessment of the role of classical mythology in literary texts. 2. The identification of literature, and especially poetry, as mythic in itself. 3. The analysis of authors' total worldviews as represented in their works and as they function as enabling structures. 4. The elucidation of mythic patterns as underlying the various kinds or genres of literature. 5. The recognition of mythic patterns in a specific literary work, whether or not explicitly alluded to. Many myth critics insist that such recognition must be followed by an analysis of the function of the mythic pattern or elements identified. 6. Criticism of attitudes and beliefs that heavily influence or control society; the exploration of ideologies.

Myth criticism is a somewhat awkward term that has come to designate the consideration of the role of myth in literature. It is not to be confused with philosophical, anthropological, or psychological criticism of myth as a phenomenon of human culture or the study of specific myths by means of one of these disciplines. Criticism of myth, to give such endeavors a name, leads into a vast field of theory and countertheory about such issues as whether myths embody truth, or are intended to do so; whether the most essential thing about a myth is that it is believed (or not believed); and whether myths arise out of rituals, from stories of actual lives (euhemerism), or from primitive attempts to explain central aspects of experience. Such issues are not the provenance of myth criticism proper, although certain approaches to the relations between myth and literature are linked to specific positions on these issues.

It should also be understood that what is under discussion here are meanings now associated with the word myth. The Greek term mythos *was broader, designating narrative generally; Aristotle uses it to refer to plot. The word does not appear to enter English as a designation for stories of gods and heroes until early in the nineteenth century.*

Finally, it should be noted that in most contemporary uses, myth criticism includes only senses 4 and 5.

1. By the time of Plato, debate over the truth and seemliness of the stories of the Greek Olympians was already in progress; in *The Republic*, Plato specifically rejects allegorical interpretations intended to uncover indirectly expressed truths in myths (2:201; 378d). The controversy had to do with the ''truth'' or value of mythological events, especially as incorporated in Homer's narratives, and not directly with the relation of myth to literature; but obviously the position taken on the issue affects judgments about works in which myth appears. The debate continued into the Christian era, the early church believing it necessary to deny truth or value to classical mythology. In general, the allegorical understanding of myth returns only with the Renaissance, where it exists alongside what might best be called a culturally evocative function. As Douglas Bush notes in the introduction to the standard study of Renaissance uses of classical mythology, ''the myths have constituted for modern poets a kind of poetic shorthand of infinite imaginative and emotional value'' (x).

The pendulum swings again in the eighteenth century as Voltaire and others dismiss mythical ''superstition,'' although the then little known Giambattista Vico was arguing by the middle of the century that myths represent a ''poetic metaphysic,'' an early stage through which every ''nation'' must pass. James Engell makes the interesting argument that it was precisely the eighteenth-century writers' revolt against conventional and decorative allusion to classical myth that led to the transformation of the idea of myth into a source of imaginative power.

In the nineteenth century, the Romantic concept of myth as the foundation for literature produced a new perspective on the relation between myth and literature (see sense 2), although the uses of classical mythology and, therefore, the central attitude toward it continued alongside the elevation of myth as a way of grasping experience that could be more important than reason or logic.

2. Friedrich Schlegel and Friedrich Schelling are the major figures in the development of the view that all poetry is mythic and that great poetry requires a vision of the absolute possible only through the imaginative cohesion of a mythology. Obviously, in this sense myth designates something more than Greek and Roman mythology; it designates a comprehensive vision (as opposed to metaphysical explanation) of the world clothed in narrative. Unfortunately, Schlegel believes, modern poets have no operative myths on which to draw. Coleridge expresses a version of the same view of the role of myth in the earliest poetry in a lecture of 1825:

> Long before the entire separation of metaphysics from poetry, that is, while yet poesy, in all its several species of verse, music, statuary, &c. continued mythic;— while yet poetry remained the union of the sensuous and the philosophic mind;—

the efficient presence of the latter in the *synthesis* of the two, had manifested itself
in the sublime *mythus* . . . concerning the *genesis*, or birth of . . . reason in man.
(2:334–35)

Better known are the opening paragraphs of Shelley's 1821 *Defense of Poetry*,
which describe poets' insights in terms that echo the German Romantics' concept
without using the term myth (a term that would be introduced into the vocabulary
within the decade). Philip Wheelwright is a twentieth-century representative of
the same tradition: "Myth . . . is not in the first instance a fiction imposed on
one's already given world, but is a way of apprehending that world" and "myth
is more than simple envisionment; it is a way of envisionment that *tends toward
story form*" (166). Literature, at least the greatest literature, is mythic in that it
participates in the same kind of imaginative response to the world that created
classical mythology.

The identity of myth and literature has been argued in a reverse way by Richard
Chase. In an essay of 1946, Chase argues against the idea that myth is a substructure in the nature of a philosophy, theology, or worldview. Rather, "*a myth
is a story, myth is narrative or poetic literature.* . . . Myth is a mode of cognition,
a system of thought, a way of life, only as art is" ("Notes," 339). Thus, "Myth
is not the 'indispensable substructure' of poetry. Poetry is the indispensable
substructure of myth. Myth is a less inclusive category than poetry" (340).
Chase's *Quest for Myth* (1949) surveys the history of approaches to the understanding of myth against the background of his belief that "myth is literature
and therefore a matter of aesthetic experience and the imagination" (vi).

3. If great literature demands an undergirding mythology and no such mythology is available, the only hope for the writer is to create one. This is the
position Schelling comes to in his *Philosophy of Mythology*, the background of
which Haskell Block traces to Herder. Among English Romantics, Blake and
Shelley are the primary examplars of the creation of personal myth; Yeats is the
third great example. The renewed feeling of a need for a grounding mythology
among twentieth-century poets is associated with an expansion of the meaning
of myth well beyond the sense in which it designates narratives describing the
deeds of gods and men; it has acquired a sense something like "vision of the
world or of the possibilities of human experience." Thus commentators refer to
the myths of poets like T. S. Eliot, Hart Crane, and Dylan Thomas. Such personal
myths may incorporate elements from classical or anthropological myths while
remaining essentially individual constructions. In *Ancient Myth in Modern Poetry*, Lillian Feder has examined the influence of various approaches to the
meaning and function of myth on four twentieth-century poets who adapt (primarily classical) myth to their own uses: Yeats, Pound, Eliot, and Auden.

4. Myth criticism in its two most central contemporary senses (4 and 5) dates
from the interest in myth that began to develop in the second half of the nineteenth
century, fostered in part by the debate between Max Müller and Andrew Lang.
Müller, applying a strictly philological approach, argued that in the early history
of the language, myths developed through confusions engendered by metaphoric,

homonymic, and polynomic uses of the names of the gods found in the Veda. The supreme Vedic deity, Dyaus, is a sun god; all myths are thus ultimately solar myths. Müller's great challenger, Andrew Lang, argued that myths are simply residues of primitive belief and custom.

A major new impetus was generated by Sir James Frazer's *The Golden Bough* (initial version, 1890) and the subsequent work of the Cambridge anthropologists, Gilbert Murray (actually at Oxford), F. M. Cornford, and Jane Harrison. Though the major interest of the Cambridge anthropologists was the origin of myths, their investigation of myths in primitive cultures led to the increasing recognition of the widespread dispersion of similar myths. If these commonalities cannot be explained by transmission from one culture to another, the alternative appears to be that the human mind (or human experience as processed by the mind) is so constructed that certain modes of thought and correlative narratives are produced by all peoples. (An early version of this view appears in Vico's belief that all cultures go through the same sequence of intellectual stages.) Maude Bodkin's *Archetypal Patterns in Poetry* (1934) draws on the psychological theories of Carl Jung rather than the researches of the anthropologists to make much the same argument. Moreover, if there are certain common themes, motifs, or modes of thought, it can be argued that there is, in fact, a basic narrative of which all others are modifications. The famous development of this latter view is that of Joseph Campbell in *The Hero with a Thousand Faces*, which sets out the theory of the *monomyth*: "A hero ventures forth from the world of common day into a region of supernatural wonder: fabulous forces are there encountered and a decisive victory is won: the hero comes back from this mysterious adventure with the power to bestow boons on his fellow man" (30). A succinct statement of Campbell's conception of myth is his essay "Bios and Mythos: Prolegomena to a Science of Mythology," in which he develops Adolf Bastian's argument for universal Elementary Ideas modified by geography and history.

Building on the belief that narratives of myth are thus somehow essentially related to the structure of the human mind, Northrop Frye's *Anatomy of Criticism* produces a set of taxonomies of literary kinds on the basis of an ordered set of archetypes. All genres of literature, he suggests, are derived from the quest myth. This argument for basing a set of classifications on foundational archetypes of human experience is given its most direct statement in Frye's "Archetypes of Literature," published six years before the *Anatomy*, in which the basic myths themselves are seen as resulting from the four-phase solar, seasonal, and life cycles. The "dawn, spring and birth phase" of these cycles, for example, lies behind myths "of the hero, of revival and resurrection, of creation and . . . of the defeat of the powers of darkness, winter and death." The corresponding genres are romance and dithyrambic and rhapsodic poetry ("Archetypes of Literature," 104). This portion of Frye's total system is further developed in the third essay of *Anatomy of Criticism* (1957), where COMEDY has now become the genre associated with spring while ROMANCE is associated with summer. While

Frye's is an immense, and to some extent arbitrary, structure, Harold Watts's "Myth and Drama" uses the structures of myth to illuminate just the two major dramatic genres, comedy and TRAGEDY.

5. The pursuit of mythic patterns in individual texts (whether intentional or unintentional, overt or implied) also develops more or less directly from the work of Frazer and the Cambridge anthropologists; their conclusions are regarded by many myth critics as having been validated by Freud's theories of the unconscious. The analysis of such patterns has most often assumed that myths express fundamental human responses to life which are finally inexpressible in any other way. Stanley E. Hyman cites Gilbert Murray's 1914 "Hamlet and Orestes" as perhaps the earliest cogent examination of the myths and ritual underlying literary tragedy (87). Northrop Frye's term for the presence of myth in literary texts is *displacement*. He sees a continuum of myth, romance (in a broader sense than that which he identifies with spring or summer), and REALISM. Romance reveals displaced myth: "The central principle of displacement is that what can be metaphorically identified [with an archetype] in a myth can only be linked in romance by some form of simile: analogy, significant association, incidental accompanying images, and the like" (*Anatomy*, 137). John Vickery unequivocally states the importance of myth criticism. "First, the creating of myths, the mythopoeic faculty, is inherent in the thinking process and answers a basic human need. Second, myth forms the matrix out of which literature emerges both historically and psychologically. As a result, literary plots, characters, themes, and images are basically complications and displacements of similar elements in myths and folktales" (ix).

For evident reasons, myth criticism has focused particularly on tragedy. One especially interesting example is Richmond Hathorn's *Tragedy, Myth and Mystery*, which sees myth as "a tissue of symbolism clothing a mystery" (25). Reason deals with problems, myths with mysteries arising from the foundational situation. That "a human being stands as a finitude in the midst of an infinite cosmos" (29) informs the genre of tragedy. Herbert Weisinger's approach to tragedy explicitly takes the anthropological reconstruction of the basic myth and ritual model as the "seedbed of tragedy." "The myth and ritual pattern of the ancient Near East, which is at least six thousand years old, centers in a divine king who was killed annually and who was reborn in the person of his successor" (31). "The paradox of the fortunate fall . . . is the shorthand symbol for the meaning of the myth and ritual pattern as a whole; compressed into it is the entire range of significance of a complex of belief and action which for many centuries in many forms has been able to provide a satisfactory answer to a deeply rooted need of man, his longing for order, for rationality, and, above all, for life" (269).

A set of assumptions about the intellectual and spiritual forces acting on late-nineteenth- and early-twentieth-century poets widely held by the middle of this century is set forth concisely in Kimon Friar and Malcolm Brinnin's essay "Myth and Metaphysics: An Introduction to Modern Poetry." Amalgams of allusion to myth, creation of personal myths, and use of Symbolist devices are seen as resulting from "the modern poet's search for a mythology that might replace that of the disintegrating Christian culture" (421). For Friar and Brinnin, "Faust was perhaps the last great epic in which the mythology of Christianity could be used with structural validity" (424). This sense of myth is obviously close to sense 2, especially in the principles cited from Vickery above, but in rather seeking to identify myth and literature, it stresses the need for culturally validated myths on which a writer can draw.

R. S. Crane summarizes with irony at least the less cautious examples of myth criticism in this fifth sense.

> Our end is accomplished . . . when we have established the presence in poems of patterns of action, character, and imagery concerning which we can say that they are patterns originating not in the artistic purposes and inventions of the poets but in antecedent history or prehistory or in human nature itself, our assumption being that the profounder meanings of poems are a function always of the original meanings of the archetypes they embody. (135)

Perhaps the best-known attack on myth criticism is Philip Rahv's "The Myth and the Powerhouse." "The cultism of myth is patently a revival of romantic longings and attitudes" (637), and "the craze for myth is the fear of history" (642). Further, "[t]o take the fact that myth is the common matrix of many literary forms as an indication that myth is literature or that literature is myth is a simple instance of the genetic fallacy" (639).

Recent writers on myth and literature have tended to be at least as much interested in what the text that alludes to or incorporates myth is suggesting about that myth as in what the myth contributes to the interpretation of the text. John Vickery comments that in modern writers, literature becomes "the interpreter of myth insofar as it, explicitly or implicitly, establishes an attitude, a point of view toward specific myths" (*Myths and Texts*, 186).

6. Although sense 6 has not in the past been strictly a part of literary criticism, the contemporary trend toward linking literary and cultural criticism has brought the old popular sense of myth as a false belief into literary-critical currency. Such myths are sometimes regarded as consciously constructed, sometimes as simply having crept into a culture; they are also usually seen as destructive or at least absurd, but they can be regarded as agents of progress. The latter is the case in Georges Sorel's influential *Reflections on Violence*: "Experience shows that the *framing of a future, in some indeterminate time*, may, when it is done in a certain way, be very effective, and have very few inconveniences; this happens when the anticipations of the future take the form of those myths, which enclose with them all the strongest inclinations of a people, of a party or of a class" (124–25).

On the other hand, Frank Kermode distinguishes between *fictions*, including fictions that are necessary ways of making sense of the world, and *myths*, which are fictions accepted as fact. "Fictions can degenerate into myths whenever they are not consciously held to be fictive. In this sense anti-Semitism is a degenerate fiction, a myth" (39). Roland Barthes's analysis of petit-bourgeois cultural attitudes linked to twenty-eight "mythologies"—ranging from professional wrestling and the advertising of detergents to Einstein's mind—is one of the best-known examples. "I resented seeing Nature and History confused at every turn, and I wanted to track down, in the decorative display of *what-goes-without-saying*, the ideological abuse which, in my view, is hidden there" (11). Robert Clark's *History, Ideology and Myth in American Fiction, 1823–52* examines the American "myth of the innocent in the garden," which "presents us with an inversion of real conditions and a wish-fulfilment of the values contained in Democratic ideology" (12–13).

Note on Terminology

There is considerable inconsistency in the use of terms in this area, but it may be helpful to note the most frequent usages. Mythic is usually an honorific term implying the tapping of universal resonances; mythical most often carries the sense of illusory or untrue. To some degree, mythology, which has almost lost its sense as "the study of myths" while acquiring that of "a body of myths," is most frequently employed to designate primarily Greek, Roman, and Northern European stories of gods and heroes. Narratives of gods and humans (including accounts of the creation of the world or the appearance of the first people) collected by anthropologists tend to be referred to simply as myths. A typical definition is that of *The Princeton Encyclopedia of Poetry and Poetics*: "Myth may be defined as a story or a complex of story elements taken as expressing, and therefore as implicitly symbolizing, certain deep-lying aspects of human and trans-human existence" (538).

References

Barthes, Roland. *Mythologies*. Trans. A. Lavers. New York: Hill and Wang, 1975. Original French edition, 1957.

Block, Haskell M. "The Myth of the Artist." In *Literary Criticism and Myth*, ed. Joseph Strelka. University Park: Pennsylvania State University Press, 1980.

Bodkin, Maude. *Archetypal Patterns in Poetry*. London: Oxford University Press, 1934.

Bush, Douglas. *Mythology and the Renaissance Tradition in English Poetry*. 1932; New York: W. W. Norton, 1963.

Campbell, Joseph. "Bios and Mythos: Prolegomena to a Science of Mythology." In *Myth and Literature*, ed. J. B. Vickery. Reprinted from *Psychoanalysis and Culture*, ed. G. B. Wilbur and W. Muensterberger. New York: International Universities Press, 1951.

———. *The Hero with a Thousand Faces*. Princeton, N.J. Princeton University Press, 1949. The volume opens as follows:

> Whether we listen with aloof amusement to the dreamlike mumbo jumbo of some red-eyed witch doctor of the Congo, or read with cultivated rapture thin translations from the sonnets of the mystic Lao-tse; now and again crack the hard nutshell of an argument of Aquinas, or catch suddenly the shining meaning of a bizarre Eskimo fairy tale: it will be always the one, shape-shifting yet marvelously constant story that we find, together with a challengingly persistent suggestion of more remaining to be experienced than will ever be known or told. (3)

Chase, Richard. "Notes on the Study of Myth." *Partisan Review* 13 (Summer 1946): 338–46. Reprinted in *Myth and Literature*.

————. *Quest for Myth*. Baton Rouge: Louisiana State University Press, 1949.

Clark, Robert. *History, Ideology and Myth in American Fiction, 1823–52*. London: Macmillan, 1984.

Coleridge, Samuel Taylor. "On the Prometheus of Aeschylus." In *The Literary Remains of Samuel Taylor Coleridge*. Ed. H. N. Coleridge. 2 vols. London: William Pickering, 1836.

Crane, R. S. *The Languages of Criticism and the Structure of Poetry*. Toronto: University of Toronto Press, 1953.

Engell, James. "The Modern Revival of Myth: Its Eighteenth-Century Origins." In *Allegory, Myth, and Symbol*, ed. Morton Bloomfield. Cambridge, Mass.: Harvard University Press, 1981.

Feder, Lillian. *Ancient Myth in Modern Poetry*. Princeton, N.J.: Princeton University Press, 1971.

Frazer, James. *The Golden Bough*. London: Macmillan, 1890 (the first, one-volume edition). The completed 12-volume edition was published by Macmillan, 1911–1915.

Friar, Kimon, and Malcolm Brinnin. "Myth and Metaphysics: An Introduction to Modern Poetry." In *Modern Poetry: American and British*. New York: Appleton-Century-Crofts, 1951. The essay comments briefly on the use of myth in Eliot, Hart Crane, Joyce, Yeats, and Pound.

Frye, Northrop. *Anatomy of Criticism*. Princeton, N.J.: Princeton University Press, 1957.
————. "The Archetypes of Literature." *Kenyon Review* 13 (Winter 1951): 92–110. Reprinted in *Myth and Literature*.

Hathorn, Richmond Y. *Tragedy, Myth and Mystery*. Bloomington: Indiana University Press, 1966.

Hyman, Stanley Edgar. "The Ritual View of Myth and the Mythic." In *Myth: A Symposium*, ed. Thomas A. Sebeok. Philadelphia: American Folklore Society, 1955. Reprinted in *Myth and Literature*. Hyman's essay opens with a helpful brief summary of the development of the Cambridge School of anthropology.

Kermode, Frank. *The Sense of an Ending*. London: Oxford University Press, 1967.

Lang, Andrew. "Mythology and Fairy Tales." *Fortnightly Review* 19 (May 1873): 618–31. This article was the first of Lang's attacks on Müller. His major work on the subject is *Myth, Ritual, and Religion*. 2 vols. London: Longmans, Green, 1887.

Müller, Friedrich Max. "Comparative Mythology." In *Oxford Essays*. 4 vols. Oxford: J. W. Parker, 1855–58. This is Müller's first essay on mythology. His major work on the subject is *Contributions to the Science of Mythology*. 2 vols. London: Longmans, Green, 1897.

Murray, Gilbert. "Hamlet and Orestes" (1914). In *The Classical Tradition in Poetry*. Oxford: Oxford University Press, 1927.

Myth and Literature: Contemporary Theory and Practice. Ed. J. B. Vickery. Lincoln: University of Nebraska Press, 1966. This extensive collection serves as an excellent introduction to the issues of most importance in understanding the relationships between myth and literature. Vickery notes that myth criticism "affords a unifying point of view which more nearly than any other derives from literature itself" (x).

Plato. *The Republic*. In vol. 2 of *The Dialogues of Plato*. Trans. B. Jowett. New York: Charles Scribner's Sons, 1907.

Princeton Encyclopedia of Poetry and Poetics. Ed. A. Preminger, F. J. Warnke, and O. B. Hardison. Princeton, N.J.: Princeton University Press, 1974.

Rahv, Philip. "The Myth and the Powerhouse." *Partisan Review* 20 (November-
    December 1953): 635–48. Reprinted in *Myth and Literature*.
Sorel, Georges. *Reflections on Violence* (1906). Trans. T. E. Hulme and J. Roth. New
    York: Collier Books, 1961.
Vickery, John B. *Myths and Texts: Strategies of Incorporation and Displacement*. Baton
    Rouge: Louisiana State University Press, 1983. Vickery's emphasis is on the
    functions of mythical allusion and structuring in literature.
Vico, Giambattista. *The New Science* (1725, 1744). Trans. T. G. Bergin and M. H.
    Fisch. Ithaca, N.Y.: Cornell University Press, 1948.
Watts, Harold. "Myth and Drama." In *Myth and Literature*. Reprinted from *Cross
    Currents* 5 (Spring 1955): 154–70.
Weisinger, Herbert. *Tragedy and the Paradox of the Fortunate Fall*. East Lansing:
    Michigan State College Press, 1953.
Wheelwright, Philip. *The Burning Fountain*. Bloomington: Indiana University Press,
    1954.

Sources of Additional Information

Standard treatments of classical mythology in English poetry are Douglas Bush's
Mythology and the Renaissance Tradition in English Poetry (1932; New York: Norton,
1963) and *Mythology and the Romantic Tradition in English Poetry* (1937; New York:
Norton, 1963). The latter actually treats the period from 1680 to 1935; both include
appendices listing poetry based on mythology. G. S. Kirk's *Myth: Its Meaning and
Functions in Ancient and Other Cultures* represents much contemporary thinking on both
classical mythology and myths of many other cultures (Cambridge: Cambridge University
Press, 1970).

For the relationships of the Romantic view of myth developed by the Schlegels and
Schelling to their general literary and philosophical concerns, see the second volume of
René Wellek's *A History of Modern Criticism, 1750–1950* (5 vols.; New Haven, Conn.:
Yale University Press, 1955).

Jung discusses the relationship between literature and the archetypes belonging to the
collective unconscious in "On the Relation of Analytical Psychology to Poetry" (1922)
and "Psychology and Literature" (1930) in *The Spirit in Man, Art, and Literature* (trans.
R. F. C. Hull; vol. 15 of *The Collected Works of C. G. Jung*. Ed. H. Read, M. Fordham,
and G. Adler, New York: Pantheon, 1953–).

Ernst Cassirer's work is constantly cited in discussions of literature and myth, although
the relevance of his work to the question is indirect. His most frequently cited volumes
are *An Essay on Man* (New Haven, Conn.: Yale University Press, 1944) and *The Philosophy of Symbolic Forms* (3 vols; trans. R. Manheim; New Haven, Conn.: Yale University Press, 1953–57).

Paul A. Cantor's *Creature and Creator: Myth-Making and English Romanticism* (Cambridge: Cambridge University Press, 1984) intriguingly argues that Romantic writers
"follow the gnostic pattern of pushing their narratives further and further back in time,
in a quest for the absolute origin which would make all other creation accounts seem
displaced and derivative" (xii).

Richard M. Dorson's "The Eclipse of Solar Mythology," in *Myth: A Symposium*, ed.
Thomas A. Sebeok (Philadelphia: American Folklore Society, 1955) is a fascinating
discussion of the debate over Max Müller's theory of solar mythology in the latter half
of the nineteenth century.

The effect on the reader of the incorporation of myth into literature (displacement), not often dir ctly discussed, is examined by John J. White in "Mythological Fiction and the Reading Process" in *Literary Criticism and Myth*, ed. Joseph Strelka (University Park: Pennsylvania State University Press, 1980). "A work of fiction prefigured by a myth is read in such a way that our reactions to character and plot are transformed by an awareness of the mythological precedent. . . . Prefigurations arouse expectations in the reader which may or may not be fulfilled, and in any case will probably be satisfied in unexpected ways" (77). William Righter's *Myth and Literature* (London: Routledge and Kegan Paul, 1975) succinctly sums up the shifts in questions asked of myth in the ancient world ("Is it literally true?"), in the Renaissance ("What kind of hidden truth might it contain?"), and in the twentieth century ("What place does the phenomenon of myth occupy among the languages of mankind?") (8). He also sums up four theories of myth: the functional, the psychological, the religious, and that of symbolic form (15–23).

For a carefully developed position that is skeptical of the value of myth except as a guide to the ways in which the mind works, see David Bidney's "Myth, Symbolism, and Truth" in *Myth: A Symposium*, ed. Thomas A. Sebeok (see above).

> To my mind, contemporary philosophers and theologians, as well as students of literature in general, who speak of the 'indispensable myth' in the name of philosophy and religion, and anthropologists and sociologists who cynically approve of myth because of its pragmatic social function, are undermining faith in their own disciplines and are contributing unwittingly to the very degradation of man and his culture which they otherwise seriously deplore. (14)

More directly polemic is Wallace W. Douglas's "The Meanings of 'Myth' in Modern Criticism" (*Modern Philology* 50, February 1953, 232–42).

> [W]ith the problem formulated as it is and with the discussion carried on as it is, the result has been to turn attention away from literature as literature and to import into criticism confusing terms and concepts drawn from a social science that is itself so insight-ridden as to be peculiarly agreeable to critics who in other contexts seem to feel that the sin without name is that of committing a social science. (242)

N

NARRATIVE   1. The process of telling or recounting, in any medium, one or more actual or fictional events. 2. The "content" of the narration, the story told. 3. The plot, that is, the story regarded under the aspect of cause. 4. The total form in which the story is told. 5. An explanation of a state of affairs by means of a story.

For critical approaches to specific aspects of narrative structure, see NARRA-TOLOGY. *A difficulty in the use of the term narrative is its tendency to shift between the first four of the above meanings, a tendency all the more confusing in that a number of the synonyms for narrative in one sense or another tend to shift as well.*

1. The sense of narrative as an account, recounting, or telling is evident in its use in E. M. Forster's frequently quoted definition of a story: "We have defined a story as a narrative of events arranged in their time-sequence" (130), in which the narrative is evidently not the same thing as story or the event-content but rather the process of presenting the story. The importance of the act of recounting is evidently what Robert Scholes and Robert Kellog have in mind in saying, "By narrative we mean all those literary works which are distinguished by two characteristics: the presence of a story and a story-teller" (4). It is this sense of narrative that Genette calls *narration*, usually translated as *narrating* (*Narrative Discourse*, 27).

2. In common use, however, narrative easily replaces the term story as used by Forster above: "he launched into a complicated narrative." The essential constituent of a narrative as a story is an event or sequence of events. Thus, descriptions of scenes or statements of information do not qualify as narratives (stories) unless they imply events. Forster's oft-quoted example of a story is "The king died and then the queen died" (130). Gerald Prince's *Narratology*

(1982) defines a narrative as "the representation of *at least two* real or fictive events or situations in a time sequence, neither of which presupposes or entails the other" (4), thus importing Forster's definition into contemporary critical discourse (for Prince's earlier, more complex definition, see sense 3 below). For Genette in 1988, a "minimal narrative" is clearly defined in terms of events alone: "Nothing more than 'The king died' is necessary" (*Narrative Discourse Revisited*, 20). Whether, however, Genette's term *histoire* applies to this or the next sense of narrative is not clear.

3. Narrative can also refer to plot; again, as defined by Forster, plot is "a narrative of events, the emphasis falling on causality" so that " 'The king died, and then the queen died of grief' is a plot (103)." What Gerald Prince calls a "minimal story" in his much more detailed description is evidently the same thing as Forster's *plot*. "A minimal story consists of three conjoined events. The first and third events are stative, the second is active. Furthermore, the third event is the inverse of the first. Finally the three events are conjoined by three conjunctive features in such a way that (a) the first event precedes the second in time and the second precedes the third, and (b) the second event causes the third" (*Grammar of Stories*, 31). Thus, Forster's example fits nicely enough if restated as "The king died, then the queen was grief-stricken, then the queen died."

A historian's recounting of events that suggests or states causal relationships but avoids devices for appealing to the reader's interest is presumably still plotted.

4. Narrative is also employed, as for instance by Genette, as a synonym for the tale as told rather than the bare story content, that is, in the sense of *récit* or *discourse* as opposed to *histoire* or *fable*. It is not always clear whether narrative in this sense of discourse is being opposed to story (as in narrative sense 2) or plot (as in narrative sense 3). "The queen died and then it was found that her death was caused by grief over the death of the king" is a minimal narrative as contrasted with Forster's story, "The king died and then the queen died," as well as with Forster's plot, "The king died and then the queen died of grief."

On the other hand, plot is, at times, given a meaning something like "the story as given interest by the order in which the events are related, the choice of point of view, and the choice of narrator"; so defined, plot and narrative in this fourth sense have largely the same meaning. The same distinction between the story and the constructed narrative (in the sense of discourse or recit) is evidently what H. W. Leggett had in mind in his comment in *The Idea in Fiction* (1934), "To a great extent what is commonly called construction in fiction simply means folding a story so that, in the telling, it shall more effectively unfold itself to the reader" (26). The term plot as opposed to story in the standard translations of the Russian Formalists designates the whole of the manner in which the story is told, not a plot as defined by Forster; it is the term translated as story that corresponds to Forster's notion of the plot as the combination of the temporal and causal. Thus, Boris Tomashevsky wrote, "We must emphasize that a story requires not only indications of time, but also indications of cause" (*Russian Formalist Criticism*, 66) and Victor Shklovsky: "The plot of *Eugene Onegin* is, therefore, not the romance of the hero with Tatyana, but the fashioning of the subject of this story as produced by the introduction of interrupting digressions" (Lemon and Reis, 57).

William Labov's work with oral narratives suggests that even the most apparently unsophisticated accounts of events tend to be structured so as to capture and hold the hearer or reader's interest; that is, the basic story is made "tellable." What he calls the "natural narrative," the form in which a spontaneous oral account is given, is likely to include (1) an "abstract," a kind of introductory summary or reflection; (2) an "orientation" that places the story in time and/or place and/or situation; (3) the "complicating action"; (4) "evaluation," that is, some means of indicating the importance or point of the account; (5) the resolution; and (6) a coda that gives the story a definite close (363–70). It is evident that literary texts generally modify and complicate this scheme to a greater or lesser extent, but the need to give form to the story content seems almost universal. The bare, unaccommodated story or *histoire* almost never occurs; even collections of plot summaries suggest causal structures; and whenever the recounting of events—whether actual or fictional, whether presented orally or in written form—is intended to be of interest in itself (to be something more than the giving of information, as in a witness's testimony in a courtroom), narrative in this fourth sense as *récit* or discourse is the result.

Evidently, historians' attempts to recount actual events (irrespective of the degree to which accuracy is actually achieved) are given at least minimal structuring devices and are thus narratives in this fuller sense.

5. Narrative is at times used to designate an account of reality accepted in order to legitimate cultural or scientific "truth," that is, as a rationale. Thus, François Lyotard writes of *metanarratives* and *grand narratives* that have given social legitimation to certain forms of knowledge and purposes in the modern period (and are questioned by POSTMODERNISM).

References

Forster, E. M. *Aspects of the Novel*. New York: Harcourt, Brace, 1927.

Genette, Gérard. *Narrative Discourse: An Essay in Method*. Trans. J. E. Lewin. Ithaca, N.Y.: Cornell University Press, 1980. Original French edition, 1972, in a volume entitled *Figures III*.

———. *Narrative Discourse Revisited*. Trans. J. E. Lewin. Ithaca, N.Y.: Cornell University Press, 1988. Original French edition, 1983.

Labov, William. "The Transformation of Experience in Narrative Syntax." In *Language in the Inner City*. Philadelphia: University of Pennsylvania Press, 1972.

Leggett, H. W. *The Idea in Fiction*. London: George Allen and Unwin, 1934.

Lyotard, François. *The Postmodern Condition: A Report on Knowledge*. Trans. G. Bennington and B. Massumi. Minneapolis: University of Minnesota Press, 1984.

Prince, Gerald. *A Grammar of Stories*. New York: Mouton, 1973.

————. *Narratology: The Form and Functioning of Narrative.* New York: Mouton, 1982.

Russian Formalist Criticism. Ed. Lee T. Lemon and Marion J. Reis. Lincoln: University of Nebraska Press, 1965.

Scholes, Robert, and Robert Kellog. *The Nature of Narrative.* New York: Oxford University Press, 1966.

Sources of Additional Information

Drawing on the work of Labov, Mary Louise Pratt's *Toward a Speech Act Theory of Literary Discourse* (Bloomington: University of Indiana Press, 1977) argues for major parallels between literary and everyday narrative structures. Jacques Lacan's psychoanalytical view of narrative is the subject of ten essays published as *Lacan and Narration* under the editorship of Robert Con Davis (Baltimore: Johns Hopkins University Press, 1985; these originally appeared in the December 1983 issue of *Modern Language Notes*, 98). Ann Banfield's "Narrative Style and the Grammar of Direct and Indirect Speech" (*Foundations of Language* 10, 1973:1–39) argues that the use of free indirect speech can result in narrative without a true narrator. J. Hillis Miller's essay "Narrative" in *Critical Terms for Literary Study*, ed. Frank Lentricchia and Thomas McLaughlin (Chicago: University of Chicago Press, 1990) explores the reasons human beings desire narratives.

NARRATOLOGY   1. The study or science of narrative structure, inclusive of all narratives, not only those regarded as "literary." 2. The body of theory and terminology describing the possible formal structures of literary narrative. Narratology in both the first and second senses derived its primary impulse from STRUCTURALISM. 3. Broadly, commentary on the story content and thematic strategies as well as the structure of fictional narrative.

1. The specific term narratology (*narratologie*) was introduced by Tzvetan Todorov in 1969 in *Grammaire du Décaméron*, where it is described as a new science applicable to popular stories, myths, film, dreams, and all other discourses with narrative structure (10). However, though Todorov is inclusive as to genre and narrative structure generally, the intent of his analysis of the stories of the *Décaméron* is to describe them in terms of a structure analogous to language and presumed to be universal. Characters are thus regarded as nouns, actions as verbs, and attributes (states, qualities, and conditions) as adjectives. Since 1969, rather different approaches to the analysis of narrative, some considerably antedating the introduction of the term, have been placed under this rubric. Vladimir Propp's *Morphology of the Folktale* (1958), which sets out thirty-one functions that may be filled (in invariant order) by the dramatis personae of the tale, is frequently taken as the earliest example of true narratological analysis. Other central examples are Lévi-Strauss's analysis of myth in *Structural Anthropology* (1958), the narrative theories of A. J. Greimas, which began to appear in 1966, and Roland Barthes's "Introduction to the Structural Analysis of Narratives" (1966), which describes narrative structure at the levels of function, action, and narration. Gerald Prince's *A Grammar of Stories* (1973) seeks to represent dia-

grammatically the way in which "a finite number of explicit rules could account for the structure of all the sets and only the sets [of elements making up narrative] which are generally and intuitively recognized as stories" (5).

2. In a more specific sense, narratology designates the investigation of the range of formally describable devices employed in presenting narrative sequences. The most influential of these has been Gérard Genette's *Narrative Discourse* (1972). Here, using Proust for illustrative texts, Genette distinguishes between (1) the "story" (*histoire*) or "the signified or narrative content"; (2) the narrative (*récit*) or "the signifier, statement, discourse or narrative text itself"; and (3) narrating (*narration*) or the "act of the narrating taken in itself" (26–27). He then pursues the relation between the time of the story and the time of the narrative under the terms *order, duration,* and *frequency*; the relation between the story and the narrator under the term *voice*; and the relationship between the narrative and the narrator under *mood*. So influential has been Genette's analysis that a brief summary of his major terminological distinctions may be useful. *Anachronies* are dislocations between the temporal orders of story and narrative, that is, any portion of the narrative that jumps ahead or behind the point in the story at which the narrative has arrived. Forward anachronies are *prolepses*, and backward ones are *analepses*. The temporal distance leaped over in an anachrony constitutes its *reach* (*portée*), and the length of the anachronic narrative is its *extent* (*amplitude*). The *duration* of a narrative or portion thereof is defined as the relation between the physical (page) length of the text and the story time presented.

Basic narrative movements governing duration are (in ascending order of speed) *ellipsis, summary, scene,* and *descriptive pause*. Frequency comprises four possibilities: "narrating once what happened once," "narrating n times what happened n times" (both examples of singulative narrative), "narrating n times what happened once" (repeating narrative), and "narrating one time what happened n times" (iterative narrative). The most important concept discussed under the heading mood is focalization, where *zero focalization* is roughly omniscient narrative, *internal focalization* is narration from the point of view of one or more characters, and *external focalization* refers to narration in which the narrator never goes behind the words and actions of characters to enter their minds. Three forms of characters' speech are also considered under mood: *narrated, transposed* (indirect), and *reported* (direct).

Under the umbrella term voice Genette includes the temporal relation of the narrator to the story as *subsequent* (past tense), *prior* (future tense), *simultaneous* (present contemporaneous), and *interpolated* ("between the moments of action" as in the epistolary novel). Narrative levels define the relations between narrators and that narrated (narrators may stand outside the narratives they present, be included in their own narratives, or be included in those of other narrators, yielding the *extradiagetic, intradiagetic,* and *metadiagetic* levels). As Genette insists in *Narrative Discourse Revisited* (1983), his analysis "bears on the narrative and the narrating, not on the story," that is, content (154).

The single device that has been most discussed within the field of narratology is free indirect discourse (*le style indirect libre*, or *erlebte Rede*). It is to be distinguished from direct discourse ("He said, 'I will go.' "), and tagged indirect discourse ("He said that he would go."); in free indirect discourse (FID), the corresponding form would be "He would go." In his useful discussion and illustration of the free indirect style, *The Dual Voice* (1977), Roy Pascal cites a 1912 article by Charles Bally as the first analysis of the form, while pointing to even earlier recognitions of it. Dorrit Cohn, who refers to this form of narration as *narrated monologue*, produced a cogent essay on the technique in 1966. Brian McHale's "Free Indirect Discourse: A Survey of Recent Accounts" (1978) summarizes much previous discussion and argues that the usual attempt to describe FID in purely grammatical terms, or as "derived" from indirect discourse, is inadequate. McHale suggests that categorization of narrative discourse should proceed from an analysis of kinds of literary representation, and distinguishes seven degrees of mimesis, of which FID is one. FID can thus be recognized by contextual features, idiom and register, and content, as well as by grammatical features. Characteristic of FID is possible ambiguity as to whether the reader is being presented with speech or thought, as to the amount of the utterance to be attributed to the narrator and that to be attributed to a character (frequent), and as to whether the passage is to be read as empathetic or ironic.

Seymour Chatman's *Story and Discourse* (1978) sums up much narratological theory to the date of publication, while demonstrating its applicability to the cinema as well as written narrative, and adding supplementary observations.

3. Until the 1960s, methods for analyzing poetry were much in advance of those for narrative. The chapter on narrative fiction in the fifth edition of René Wellek and Austin Warren's *Theory of Literature* (1956) begins, "Literary theory and criticism concerned with the novel are much inferior in both quantity and quality to theory and criticism of poetry" (212). Nevertheless, analysis of the structure of fiction of course has a long history prior to the advent of the structuralism that begot narratology in its restricted contemporary senses. Sustained discussion in England and the United States can be said to begin with Henry James's prefaces and essays on fictional techniques (James E. Miller has grouped his comments by topics and provided a useful index in *Theory of Fiction: Henry James*). James himself noted in *The Art of Fiction* (1884) that "only a short time ago it might have been supposed that the English novel was not what the French call *discutable*. It had no air of having a theory, a conviction, a consciousness of itself behind it" (375–76). Percy Lubbock's influential *Craft of Fiction* (1921) codified a Jamesian approach to point of view contrasting scenic and panoramic (dramatic versus pictorial) presentation. In *Technique of the Novel* (1928), Carl Grabo, like Lubbock, discusses strategies in narrative rather than presenting a system of formal techniques; thus his discussion of the tempo of narration (to be compared with that of Genette) notes that psychological time is speeded up by close causal sequencing or focusing on a single center of interest, and slowed by cutting back and forth between groups of characters and putting

emphasis on the incoherence of experience as well as by the addition of detail and narrator's commentary. E. M. Forster's *Aspects of the Novel* (1927) offers a leisurely account of such matters as the differences between story and plot and between flat and round characters. Cleanth Brooks and Robert Penn Warren's influential textbook *Understanding Fiction* (1943) encouraged close reading of fiction, with particular attention to the internal structure of metaphor and symbol. Joseph Frank's "Spatial Form in Modern Literature" (1945) analyzes ways in which modern fiction substitutes a spatial, or at least nontemporal, pattern for chronological structure. Erich Auerbach's *Mimesis: The Representation of Reality in Western Literature* (1946) acutely analyzes modes by which narrative reflects historically determined concepts of reality. Such studies go well beyond the techniques of narration that are now the specific topics of narratology, reaching to such matters as the overall worldview of an author. Exemplary of one kind of general approach to the novel at the middle of the twentieth century is Douglas Grant's essay of 1951, "The Novel and Its Critical Terms," which defines character as "a symbolic representation of the attitudes of man as they are generally but imprecisely realized in the novelist's society" (426) and structure as "the moral and aesthetic order of a novel" (429).

Closer analysis of formal techniques resulted from interest in stream-of-consciousness narrative as exemplified by Lawrence Bowling's *PMLA* article of 1950 and book-length studies by Robert Humphrey (1954) and Melvin Friedman (1955), behind all of which stands Edouard Dujardin's *Le Monologue interieur* (1931). Wayne Booth's *The Rhetoric of Fiction* (1961), best known for its arguments undercutting twentieth-century slogans about the superiority of showing to telling, of realism of treatment, and of the objectivity and invisibility of the author, brought new attention to the question of types of narration. The concepts of the *reliable* versus *unreliable* narrators and of the *implied author* enter critical discourse in Booth's book. Wolfgang Iser, whose *Implied Reader* appeared in Germany in 1972, has been influential in the investigation of a different aspect of fiction, the way in which the reader interacts with the text in the process of reading, anticipating, filling in gaps, and correcting his or her own assumptions and expectations as these prove erroneous (see READER-RESPONSE). Mikhail Bakhtin's *Problems of Dostoevsky's Poetics* (published 1929, but given recognition outside of Slavic studies only in the 1970s) and his essays on the novel first published in 1975 as *The Dialogic Imagination* introduced the concepts of dialogism, double voicing, hybridization, heteroglossia, and polyphony in narrative fiction (see Note 2).

As is evident from the above highly selective list, very central questions were being explored by the 1960s: the importance of dimensions of structure other than the chronological; the relationship between fictional narrative and reality; the subtly differentiated range of techniques and resulting effects possible; the necessary activity of the reader and the role of the reader's knowledge, beliefs, and expectations; and, finally, the possible distances between the author as an individual existing prior to and outside the text, the authorial personality and values implied by the text itself, and the narrator. Though too diffuse or too much concerned with the content of narratives to fit fully under the stricter definition of narratology, these earlier-twentieth-century studies provide necessary supplements to its designedly restricted approach. As Gerald Prince has phrased it, narratology in its usual narrower definition (sense 1) "asks some important questions that pertain to all narratives—including nonverbal and nonextant ones—and only to narratives," while "it cannot (and does not attempt to) account for or provide all the possible interpretations of a given set of narratives"; nor does it enter the realm of evaluation at all ("Narrative Analysis," 182, 185).

Notes

1. Narratological theorists are not in full agreement in their terminology. In the following list, what seems the most common term is given followed either by the most generally agreed definition or a list of more or less alternative terms without entering into subtle discriminations between the various systems of categorization.

> Story (Forster, Todorov, Genette, Chatman, Rimmon-Kenan) = fabula (Russian Formalists), histoire, narration (Barthes), diégèse (Genette);
>
> Discourse, as opposed to story (Todorov, Chatman) = récit, narrative (Genette), text (Rimmon-Kenan), sjužet (Russian Formalists);
>
> Indirect discourse (McHale, Chatman) = narrated monologue (Cohn), transposed speech (Genette);
>
> Free indirect style (Pascal) = le style indirect libre (Bally), erlebte Rede (Lerch), free indirect discourse (Genette), represented speech and thought (Banfield);
>
> Direct discourse of thought or speech (Chatman, McHale) = reported speech (Genette); of thought = quoted monologue (Cohn);
>
> Narrative summary of character's words (Chatman) = narrated or narratized speech (Genette);
>
> Internal analysis (Bowling) = psycho-narration (Cohn);
>
> Interior monologue (Dujardin, Bowling, Humphreys) = immediate speech (Genette), quoted monologue (Cohn).

2. Bakhtin's terminology has entered critical commentary so widely and is employed in so many extended senses that a summary of the meanings he gave his terms may be helpful.

> Dialogism: The principle that the meaning of all words is shaped by their previous uses in the ongoing human dialogue, and that all discourse is a response to, and to be understood only in relation to, other discourse. Though all discourse is unavoidably dialogic, some discourse suppresses awareness of the dialogic background and thus appears monologic.
>
> Double-voicing: The effect of one or more additional voices within speech that is formally attributed to a single speaker.
>
> Heteroglossia: The simultaneous existence of multiple dialects, professional argots, social registers, and ideological orientations within a national language. Bakhtin is primarily interested in the clash of ideologies, where ideology means essentially an individual's dominant value system.

Hybridization: Double-voicing occurring within a single syntactical structure without markers such as quotation marks to differentiate it.

Polyphony: The representation in fiction of the ultimate dialogism of the world in which neither the author's voice nor that of any character is so privileged as to have the final word about any character; alternatively, literature in which the ideological conflict is never resolved, and thus in which neither the author nor any character becomes the standard of judgment.

References

Auerbach, Erich. *Mimesis: The Representation of Reality in Western Literature*. Trans. W. R. Trask. 1953; Princeton, N. J.: Princeton University Press, 1968. Original German edition, 1946. Classic examination of modes of realistic narrative.

Bakhtin, Mikhail, M. *The Dialogic Imagination: Four Essays*. Ed. Michael Holquist, trans. C. Emerson and M. Holquist. Austin: University of Texas Press, 1981. Original Russian Publication, 1975. Includes the lengthy essays "Epic and Novel," "From the Prehistory of Novelistic Discourse," "Forms of Time and the Chronotope in the Novel," and "Discourse in the Novel," the last of which is of special importance to narratology.

————. *Problems of Dostoevsky's Poetics*. Ed. and trans. Caryl Emerson. Minneapolis: University of Minnesota Press, 1984. Original Russian edition, 1929. Important for an understanding of Bakhtin's concepts of *polyphony*, *carnivalization*, and *microdialogue*.

Bally, Charles. "Le Style indirect libre en français modern." *Germanisch-Romanische Monatsschrift* 4 (1912): 549–56, 597–606. Earliest treatment of free indirect discourse.

Banfield, Ann. *Unspeakable Sentences: Narration and Representation in the Language of Fiction*. Boston: Routledge and Kegan Paul, 1982. An approach to the representation of characters' discourse from assumptions of Chomskian generative grammar.

Barthes, Roland. "Introduction to the Structural Analysis of Narratives." In *Image-Music-Text*. Trans. S. Heath. New York: Hill and Wang, 1977. Original French essay, 1966. This essay appears in Barthes's *The Semiotic Challenge*. Trans. R. Howard. New York: Hill and Wang, 1988.

Booth, Wayne. *The Rhetoric of Fiction*. 1961; Chicago: University of Chicago Press, 1983. Classic analysis of the relations of author and narrator to narrative.

Bowling, Lawrence E. "What Is the Stream of Consciousness Technique?" *PMLA* 65 (June 1950): 333–45. Important early formulation of the distinctions within stream-of-consciousness narration.

Brooks, Cleanth, and Robert Penn Warren. *Understanding Fiction*. New York: F. S. Crofts, 1943. Standard textbook applying New Critical methods to the analysis of narrative fiction.

Chatman, Seymour. *Story and Discourse*. Ithaca, N.Y.: Cornell University Press, 1978. Very useful presentation of various narratological concepts in both textual and cinematic narrative.

Cohn, Dorrit. "Narrated Monologue: Definition of a Fictional Style." *Comparative Literature* 18 (Spring 1966): 97–112. Clearly presented analysis of free indirect discourse.

Dujardin, Edouard. *Le Monologue interieur*. Paris: Albert Messein, 1931.

Forster, E. M. *Aspects of the Novel*. New York: Harcourt, Brace, 1927. Thoughtful commentary on the novel by an author who loves literature rather than theory.

Frank, Joseph. "Spatial Form in Modern Literature." *Sewanee Review* 53 (1945): 221–40, 453–56, 643–53. An expanded version appears in Frank's *The Widening Gyre* (New Brunswick, N.J.: Rutgers University Press, 1963).

Friedman, Melvin. *Stream of Consciousness: A Study in Literary Method.* New Haven, Conn.: Yale University Press, 1955. A standard study.

Genette, Gérard. *Narrative Discourse: An Essay in Method.* Trans. J. E. Lewin. Ithaca, N.Y.: Cornell University Press, 1980. Original French edition, 1972, in *Figures III.* Essential; initiates a new mode of discussing the handling of temporal order, perspective, narrative focus, and voice in narrative.

———. *Narrative Discourse Revisited.* Trans. J. E. Lewin. Ithaca, N.Y.: Cornell University Press, 1988. Original French edition, 1983. Genette's clarifications, restatements, and defenses of his treatment of narrative structures in *Narrative Discourse* with comments on the systems of certain of his critics and other narratologists.

Grabo, Carl H. *Technique of the Novel.* New York: Charles Scribner's Sons, 1928.

Grant, Douglas, "The Novel and Its Critical Terms." *Essays in Criticism* 1 (October 1951): 421–29.

Greimas, Algirdas Julien. *On Meaning: Selected Writings in Semiotic Theory.* Trans. P. J. Perron and F. H. Collins. Minneapolis: University of Minnesota Press, 1987. The essays "The Elements of Narrative Grammar," "A Problem of Narrative Semiotics: Objects of Value," "Actants, Actors, and Figures," and "Toward a Theory of Modalities" included here offer a good introduction to various aspects of Greimas's theory of narrative.

Humphrey, Robert. *Stream of Consciousness in the Modern Novel.* Berkeley: University of California Press, 1954.

Iser, Wolfgang. *The Act of Reading: A Theory of Aesthetic Response.* Baltimore: Johns Hopkins University Press, 1978. Original German edition, 1976. Important study of the way in which the reader responds to narrative in the process of reading, and the way in which such responses alter the reader's perceptions of the world.

———. *The Implied Reader.* Baltimore: Johns Hopkins University Press, 1974. Original German edition, 1972.

James, Henry. "The Art of Fiction." In *Partial Portraits.* London: Macmillan, 1888. Reprinted from *Longman's Magazine* 4 (September 1884): 502–21.

———. *Theory of Fiction: Henry James.* Ed. James E. Miller. Lincoln, University of Nebraska Press, 1972.

Lévi-Strauss, Claude. *Structural Anthropology.* Trans. C. Jacobson and B. Schoepf. New York: Basic Books, 1963. Original French edition, 1958.

Lubbock, Percy. *The Craft of Fiction.* London: Jonathan Cape, 1921. Important discussion of narrative fiction strongly influenced by the theory and practice of Henry James. Lubbock's commentary is broader and more cogent than most contemporary references to it suggest.

McHale, Brian. "Free Indirect Discourse: A Survey of Recent Accounts." *PTL* 3, no. 2 (April 1978): 249–87. Excellent survey that goes on to argue for a seven-level categorization of modes of presentation of characters' words and thoughts rather than the usual three types.

Pascal, Roy. *The Dual Voice: Free Indirect Speech and Its Functioning in the Nineteenth-Century European Novel.* Manchester, U.K.: Manchester University Press, 1977. Helpful presentation of free indirect discourse with consideration of its use in

Goethe, Austen, Büchner, Dickens, Eliot, Trollope, Flaubert, Zola, and Dostoevsky. Very useful history of the early discussion of the style.

Prince, Gerald. *A Grammar of Stories*. New York: Mouton, 1973.

————. "Narrative Analysis and Narratology." *New Literary History* 13 (Winter 1982): 179–88. The goal is the description of a narrative by diagrams or symbols; thus, "S stat + CT$_t$ + S act + CT$_t$ + CT$_e$ + S stat^{-1}" symbolizes "John was happy, then John met a woman, then, as a result, John was unhappy" (35).

Propp, Vladimir. *Morphology of the Folktale*. Trans. L. Scott, revised by L. A. Wagner. 1958; Austin: University of Texas Press, 1968. Origin of an approach to literature of major importance for structuralism and having a strong influence on some forms of narratology.

Todorov, Tzvetan. *Grammaire du Décaméron*. The Hague: Mouton, 1969.

Wellek, René, and Austin Warren. *Theory of Literature*. 1949; 3rd ed. New York: Harcourt, Brace, 1956.

Sources of Additional Information

Several good general introductions to narratology exist, each of which suggests particular additions or modifications to the generally received formulations. Mieke Bal offers a highly systematic approach in *Narratology: Introduction to the Theory of Narrative* (trans. C. van Boheemen; Toronto: University of Toronto Press, 1985). Gerald Prince's *Narratology: The Form and Functioning of Narrative* (New York: Mouton, 1982) and Shlomith Rimmon-Kenan's *Narrative Fiction: Contemporary Poetics* (London: Methuen, 1983) are equally useful; the latter includes a strong bibliography. Tzvetan Todorov's *Introduction to Poetics* summarizes a considerable amount of narratological theory on pages 27–46 (trans. R. Howard; Minneapolis: University of Minnesota Press, 1981). Prince's *A Dictionary of Narratology* (Lincoln: University of Nebraska Press, 1987) is a valuable reference.

The chapter entitled "Reported Speech and Internal Monologue in Flaubert" in Stephen Ullmann's *Style in the French Novel* (Oxford: Basil Blackwell, 1964) is a frequently cited treatment of free indirect discourse. Claude Bremond's *Logique de Récit* modifies Propp's morphological approach to present a grammar of fictional roles (Paris: Editions du Seuil, 1973).

Roland Barthes's notorious *S/Z* (trans. R. Miller; New York: Hill and Wang, 1974) analyzes Balzac's "Sarrasine" through the application of five codes presumed applicable to all narrative. Franz Stanzel's *A Theory of Narrative* presents an idiosyncratic but interesting examination of person, mode, and voice (trans. C. Goedsche; Cambridge: Cambridge University Press, 1984; original German edition, 1979). Dorrit Cohn's review of Stanzel ("The Encirclement of Narrative," *Poetics Today*, 2, no. 2, 1981:157–81) provides a useful comparison with Genette's system. Käte Hamburger presents a cogent argument for the atemporality of third-person narrative (events described in the past tense are neither past nor present) and the transformation of deictic into symbolic terms in fictional narrative in *The Logic of Literature* (trans. Marilynn Rose; Bloomington: Indiana University Press, 1973, pp. 59–134).

Dorrit Cohn's *Transparent Minds: Modes for Presenting Consciousness* (Princeton, N.J.: Princeton University Press, 1978) is an important study of the various ways in which consciousness is narrated; Brian McHale's review, "Islands in the Stream of Consciousness" (*Poetics Today*, 2, no. 2, 1981: 183–91) is especially cogent.

For a modern study of a narrational technique that breaks free of the all-too-common patterns of narratological commentary, see Mark Lambert's *Dickens and the Suspended Quotation* (New Haven, Conn.: Yale University Press, 1981), which arrives at conclusions about the use of tags and the relationship between Dickens and his readers more comprehensive than the title suggests.

The Nature of Narrative by Robert Scholes and Robert Kellog is an excellent historical and theoretical study of narrative that considers aspects of narrative well beyond the interests of contemporary narratological analysis; its bibliographical appendix is important in itself. Richard Stang's *The Theory of the Novel in England, 1850–1870* reaches beyond the twenty years of its title to survey a great deal of the significant nineteenth-century commentary on the art of the novel (New York: Columbia University Press, 1959).

NEW CRITICISM   1. A particular approach to criticism: the general concept of the critic's task is regarded as the understanding and evaluation of the individual work through close, careful reading with as little reference to the author's biography, literary history, or the characteristics of the culture at the period of composition as possible. From the beginning, poetry has been the primary interest of critics associated with the New Criticism, although in theory the approach can be applied to all literature. Inasmuch as New Critical principles are now rarely directly promulgated, it might seem that they should be referred to in the past tense, but in terms of actual practice, they have retained much of their influence. 2. Evidently, whatever is the reigning critical method or theory in any culture at any time can be referred to as "the new criticism."

1. The name New Criticism derives from the title of John Crowe Ransom's volume of 1941 treating the poetic criticism of I. A. Richards, William Empson, T. S. Eliot, and Yvor Winters, together with commentary on Charles Morris's theory of signs. Ransom used the term broadly; thus, after citing a passage from Empson, he commented, "Writings as acute and at the same time as patient and consecutive as this have not existed in English criticism, I think, before Richards and Empson. They become frequent now; Richards and Empson have spread quickly. That is a principal reason why I think it is time to identify a powerful intellectual movement that deserves to be called a new criticism" (111). Despite such praise, Ransom disagreed with the views of all four men at least as often as he endorsed them. Moreover, as Cleanth Brooks commented in "In Search of the New Criticism" (1983–84), "[Lewis] Carroll never told us what either a snark or a boojum was; no more circumstantial was the man who, more or less by accident, gave the New Criticism its name" (41).

Ransom's evaluations of the critical principles of Richards and Eliot are somewhat idiosyncratic, but there is general agreement that the two men were responsible for much of the intellectual atmosphere in which the New Criticism blossomed. Neither saw poetry as primarily an expression of thought, although where Richards regarded concepts as simply the necessary source of the emotions in which he was interested, Eliot sought the integration of thought and feeling. Richards advocated close reading, especially in *Practical Criticism* (1929); even though Eliot was often most concerned with comparing works, he also looked to the qualities of the works themselves (Eliot's sense of "tradition" had more to do with comparative evaluation than literary history). Richards sharply divided the values of poetry from those of science, while Eliot, drawing on T. E. Hulme, opposed the confusion of the moral and intellectual.

To the extent that Ransom's book urges a specific view, it is his belief that poetry consists of a logical structure supporting a texture of detail that fills out what would otherwise be abstract. "The texture of a poem is the heterogeneous character of its detail, which either fills in the logical outline very densely or else overflows it a little" (163). This texture, which distinguishes poetry from scientific discourse, is all-important. "I suggest," wrote Ransom, "that the differentia of poetry as discourse is an ontological one. It treats an order of existence, a grade of objectivity, which cannot be treated in scientific discourse" (281). As a result, "[t]he world of art is the actual world which does not bear restriction; or at least is sufficiently defiant of the restrictiveness of science, and offers enough fullness of content to give us the sense of actual objects" (293).

New Criticism quickly came to have a more diffuse meaning as it was associated not only with the already diverse critical practices of Richards, Empson, Eliot, and Winters, but also with those of Cleanth Brooks, Robert Penn Warren, Allen Tate, and R. P. Blackmur. It came, indeed, to be regarded as an especially American movement, although certain of F. R. Leavis's principles put the *Scrutiny* group in loose alliance. What is essential in the study of English literature, wrote Leavis, is "that appreciative habituation to the subtleties of language in its most charged and complex uses which the literary critical discipline is" (38).

A group so diversely situated in time, place, and interests can hardly be regarded as a school; what was shared was a reaction against either impressionistic commentary or the reduction of the study of literature to biography, philology, or historical facts. Thus, Cleanth Brooks wrote in 1983: "The name was ill-chosen—and was not, by the way, chosen by the so-called 'New Critics' themselves. In any case, they were not a cohesive group marching under one banner. Probably their only common trait was their reaction against the reigning historicism and their renewed respect for the structure and inner workings of the poem or novel or drama in question" (*Rich Manifold*, 39). To the extent that New Critical principles became codified, this occurred primarily through Cleanth Brooks and Robert Penn Warren's *Understanding Poetry* (1938) and René Wellek and Austin Warren's *Theory of Literature* (1949), both highly influential textbooks. These were welcomed as pointing the way to what might be done in the classroom beyond the transmission of information about author and milieu; the value of New Criticism as a pedagogic method was largely responsible for its success.

The central emphases of New Criticism regarded as a whole are (a) the autonomy of the work; (b) the total experience of the work; (c) the organic, internally unified nature of the individual work; (d) the importance of complexity, and especially irony and paradox, which are harmonized in the work but not necessarily resolved; (e) the need for close scrutiny of diction, syntax, metaphor, and imagery; and (f) the responsibility of the critic to make critical judgments.

Each of these emphases or principles—which will be considered separately—has been the subject of controversy.

a. By the autonomy of the work is meant that the goal of the critic is to understand and evaluate the literary text in itself, not to seek to illuminate the text by, nor use the text to, illuminate the author's biography, the peculiar character of the age, or literary history. For the New Critics generally, these latter endeavors are not in themselves illegitimate, but they are not literary criticism. (See INTENTION, HISTORICAL SCHOLARSHIP, and LITERARY HISTORY).

The irrelevance of an author's statement of his or her intention was especially insisted upon by W. K. Wimsatt and Monroe Beardsley's "The Intentional Fallacy" (1946), an essay that came to be regarded as a central statement of New Critical doctrine. Frequently misread as denying the validity of any consideration of the author's intention, the essay, as Wimsatt explained in "Genesis: A Fallacy Revisited" (1968), was directed against any attempt to derive an author's intention from authorial statements external to the text. The point is not that the reader may not infer authors' intentions from the text in question, but that the meaning or intentionality actually expressed by that text cannot be established by any prior or subsequent statement of its author. This point of view is supported by Ransom's description of the alteration and enriching of the poet's originally conceived propositional meaning by the exigencies of form (including rhyme and meter).

Obviously, problems arise as soon as one asks if the recognition of contemporary allusions, the knowledge of the contemporary senses of words, or the unusual or unique senses that authors at times assign to words are not relevant. Moreover, critics with political preoccupations have chastised the New Critics for divorcing literature from the necessarily ideological conflicts of actual experience. Criticizing the concept of autonomy from another direction, contemporary Marxist critics (see MARXIST LITERARY CRITICISM) attack New Criticism for failing to recognize that its interpretations assume what they see as a shared, if unrecognized, elitist, capitalist, humanist ideology (see HUMANISM). Thus, Terence Hawkes: "New Criticism's high regard for ''ambiguity,'' its admiration of polysemous structures, represent no real leaning towards ''total'' criticism so much as a bourgeois commitment: the stances it prizes most—sophistication, wit, poise—are those of a decaying aristocracy revered by a sycophantic middle-class" (155).

b. The insistence on regarding the poem as an experience rather than a communication, with particular concern for the emotional rather than cognitive properties of the poem, derives primarily from I. A. Richards, who, with C. K. Ogden in *The Meaning of Meaning* (1923) and then in his *Principles of Literary Criticism* (1924) and *Science and Poetry* (1926) sought to distinguish literature, and especially poetry, from scientific discourse, and thus assert the importance of its role in an increasingly scientific age. "A statement may be used for the sake of the *reference*, true or false, which it causes. This is the *scientific* use of language. But it may also be used for the sake of the effects in emotion and attitude produced by the reference it occasions. This is the *emotive* use of language" (*Principles*, 267). Ransom's critical summation of Richards on this point is succinct: "In other words, poetry is a very good thing, but it has no rating as a way of knowing the world. Its service is not cognitive but psychological" (8). One way of viewing what Richards was attempting to do is to see him in the tradition of Kant's distinction between the aesthetic, moral, and philosophical/ scientific.

Both the principles that poetry is essentially experiential, not cognitive, and that it is autonomous (as defined above) raise the question of the grounds of the meaning of the words within a poem if they are without reference. Murray Krieger's *The New Apologists for Poetry* (1956) explores the problem of how a poem can be autonomous if its very words must take their meaning from outside the poem. The argument that poetry is necessarily also referential and propositional, that "the fact of the *coerciveness* of reality, that power possessed by objects outside of ourselves to compel human interpretations and judgments to move in one direction rather than another" (10) cannot be ignored by poet or reader has been made in detail by Gerald Graff in *Poetic Statement and Critical Dogma* (1970). However, it should be noted that a distinction can be made between the words in a poem that are readily understood to have sense without reference to specific existence (Keats's Grecian urn) and abstract statements of presumably universal propositions ("truth is beauty").

Related to the problem of referentiality is that of belief. In *Principles of Literary Criticism*, Richards specifically differentiates between scientific beliefs based on knowledge and emotive beliefs (including religious beliefs) that are, in fact, "objectless." "To excite a serious and reverent attitude is one thing. To set forth an explanation is another" (286). In the chapter "Doctrine in Poetry" in *Practical Criticism*, Richards distinguishes more fully between emotional and intellectual beliefs to argue that one does not have to accept the author's beliefs (or, presumably, the general cultural beliefs of a time) to respond appropriately to a work. However, the role of belief in determining the reader's response has been an important point of debate. John Crowe Ransom commented in *The New Criticism*, "I would question decidedly whether there can be any important effects in emotion and attitude flowing from what the subject knows to be nonsense or falsehood" (39–40). Gerald Graff's *Poetic Statement and Critical Dogma* explores the problem of belief from several directions.

The distinction between the emotional and the cognitive has not been regarded as necessarily absolute. Most of the New Critics found the great value of poetry in its power of presenting both at once. Ransom sought an "ontological" critic who could respond to the fullness of being that is captured by poetry. Allen Tate frequently describes literature in terms like "knowledge of a whole object" and the "complete knowledge, the full body of experience that [the poem] offers us" (105). In R. P. Blackmur's words, "Poetry is the game we play with reality; and it is the game and the play—the game by history and training, the play by instinct and need—which make it possible to catch hold of reality at all" (422).

c. The concept of the poem as an organic, unified structure descends from Coleridge through I. A. Richards. The term actually encompasses a number of different concepts. It implies the achievement of a kind of harmony out of apparently discordant impulses. Thus Richards writes, "The equilibrium of opposed impulses, which we suspect to be the ground-plan of the most valuable aesthetic responses, brings into play far more of our personality than is possible in experience of a more defined emotion" (*Principles*, 251). It may also refer to a union of form and content. As William Van O'Connor wrote in 1949, "[T]he new criticism objects to the old dichotomy of content and form. The principle, simply enough, is that we know in part what a writer says by the way he says it" (66). Equally important is the concept of the organic growth of the work through the agency of the imagination as opposed to a mere mechanical structuring. The notion of organic growth is perhaps also reflected in Ransom's notion of the way in which the exigencies of rhyme and meter add texture to both the meaning and the sound (a view echoed later by Murray Krieger). A more specific sense of organic form is reflected in Joseph Frank's description of *spatial form*, the retrospective perception of the whole of a structure that has been temporally and sequentially unfolded in the process of reading. (See ORGANIC UNITY.)

The critical assumption of organic unity or harmony governed the interpretation of literature, especially LYRIC poetry, until quite recently. Though some works were found to be ambiguous in meaning, the more consistent and determinate the interpretation and the more it accounted for in the work, the better it was judged to be. With the arrival of poststructuralism (see STRUCTURALISM), especially DECONSTRUCTION, the argument that all texts, or at least all interesting texts, are self-subverting, self-contradictory, or indeterminate has gained adherence among a substantial number of critics.

d. Richards's insistence on the poise or balance of oppositions reappears in Cleanth Brooks's analyses of the paradox and irony that generate the complexity necessary for better poetry. An especially interesting statement of this position is R. P. Warren's "Pure and Impure Poetry" (1943). From early on, however, New Criticism has been faced with the charge that it is unable to account for the value and pleasure of works lacking in irony and paradox: for example, the simple evocative lyric or eighteenth-century poetry with its carefully crafted diction.

e. Close reading or careful explication of the text, with attention to multiple meanings, functional ambiguities, structures of symbols, and evocative patterns of imagery naturally resulted from concentration on the work as an autonomous organic structure. As far as possible, each significant word and each image are to be regarded as simultaneously contributing to and illuminated by a context internal to the work. I. A. Richards's *Practical Criticism*, while insisting that "many, if not most, of the statements in poetry are there *as a means* to the manifestation and expression of feelings and attitudes" (180), equally insists that the poet's "control of our thoughts is ordinarily his chief means to the control of our feelings, and in the immense majority of instances we miss nearly everything of value if we misread his sense'' (184). William Empson's *Seven Types of Ambiguity* (1930), cited with approval by Ransom in *The New Criticism*, contributed strongly to both theory and practice. Further support was derived from Cleanth Brooks and R. P. Warren's *Understanding Poetry* and later *Understanding Fiction*. The founding of *The Explicator* in 1942 reflected the new interest. Though at times criticized both for over-privileging the complex and for a tendency to produce the over-ingenious, the techniques of close reading or explication have become indispensable tools even in the hands of poststructuralist critics who repudiate New Critical thought as whole.

All the principles so far stated in one way or another support the New Critical denial of the possibility of paraphrase (the motto, ''the heresy of paraphrase'' first appears as a chapter title in Brooks's *The Well Wrought Urn*).

f. Finally, evaluative judgments, though perhaps not strictly required by other New Critical tenets, are a natural concomitant. If organic unity or an equilibrium among opposed modes of thought and a complex harmony of emotions constitute the essence of poetry, the absence of either complexity or unity, however these are defined, becomes a substantive fault. The very process of explication or elucidation then naturally implies a judgment of worth; it was easy enough for the New Criticism to associate itself with the traditional sense of the critic as one who separates the chaff from the grain for the benefit of the ordinary reader. Thus, William Van O'Connor writes in ''A Short View of the New Criticism'': ''The job of the critic is to help us perceive the nature and worth of the literary work'' (70).

2. Examples of the use of ''new criticism'' as the contemporary criticism of a given time and country are Joel Spingarn's chapter titled ''The New Criticism'' in his *Creative Criticism* of 1925, Edwin B. Burgum's 1930 anthology *The New Criticism* (which includes selections from Richards and Eliot but also from Spengler, Croce, Santayana, Bosanquet, and Haldane among the sixteen critics represented), and Laurent LeSage's *The French New Criticism* (1967), which treats the French movement in criticism arising out of Sartre and Heidegger, and including Bachelard, Barthes, Blanchot, Richards, Starobinski, and Goldmann.

References

Blackmur, R. P. *The Lion and the Honeycomb*. New York: Harcourt, Brace, 1955.
Brooks, Cleanth. ''In Search of the New Criticism.'' *The American Scholar* 53 (Winter 1983–84): 41–53.
————. *The Rich Manifold*, ed. J. M. Ditta. Columbia, Mo. *Missouri Review*, 1983. A retrospective view of the New Criticism by one of its leading figures.
————. *The Well Wrought Urn*. New York: Harcourt, Brace, 1947.
Brooks, Cleanth, and R. P. Warren. *Understanding Fiction*. New York: F. S. Crofts, 1943.
————. *Understanding Poetry*. New York: Henry Holt, 1938.
Burgum, Edwin Berry. *The New Criticism: An Anthology of Modern Aesthetics and Criticism*. New York: Prentice-Hall, 1930.

Coleridge, Samuel Taylor. The standard edition is now *The Collected Works of Samuel Taylor Coleridge* under the general editorship of Kathleen Coburn. London: Routldge and Kegan Paul; Princeton, N.J.: Princeton University Press, 1969–. For the core of Coleridge's organicism, see Chapter 13 of the *Biographia Literaria*, in vol. 7, pt. 1 of the *Collected Works*, and Lecture 8 of the 1812–13 Lectures on Belles Lettres, in vol. 5, pt. 1, pp. 493–95.

Empson, William. *Seven Types of Ambiguity*. London: Chatto and Windus, 1930.

Frank, Joseph. "Spatial Form in Modern Literature." *Sewanee Review* 53 (1945): 221–40, 453–56, 643–53. An expanded version appears in Frank's *The Widening Gyre* (New Brunswick, N.J.: Rutgers University Press, 1963).

Graff, Gerald. *Poetic Statement and Critical Dogma*. Evanston; Ill.: Northwestern University Press, 1970.

———. "What Was New Criticism." In *Literature Against Itself*. Chicago: University of Chicago Press, 1979. Graff writes: "If the New Critics were formalists, they were extremely reluctant ones, driven to formalism against the grain of their own temperaments by their reaction against the mechanical 'mimetic' rationality of industrialism and positivistic science" (146).

Hawkes, Terence. *Structuralism and Semiotics*. Berkeley: University of California Press, 1977.

Krieger, Murray. *The New Apologists for Poetry*. Minneapolis: University of Minnesota Press, 1956. One of Krieger's major points, taken from Hulme, is that the freshness of poetry results from the transformation of the original thought as it seeks expression in poetic form. "Thus for Hulme there can be no pre-existing fresh idea for which the poet seeks fresh embodiment. The idea becomes fresh as it is worked by him across the grain of language habits" (67).

Leavis, F. R. *Education and the University*. London: Chatto and Windus, 1943.

LeSage, Laurent. *The French New Criticism*. University Park: Pennsylvania State University Press, 1967.

O'Connor, William Van. "A Short View of the New Criticism." *College English* 11 (November 1949): 63–71.

Ogden, C. K., and I. A. Richards. *The Meaning of Meaning*. London: Kegan Paul, 1923.

Ong, Walter J. "The Meaning of the New Criticism." In *Twentieth-Century English*, ed. W. S. Knickerbocker. New York: Philosophical Library, 1946.

Ransom, John Crowe. *The New Criticism*. Norfolk, Conn.: New Directions, 1941.

Richards, I. A. *Practical Criticism*. London: Kegan Paul, 1929. Richards's experiment with students' readings of unidentified poems and his theoretically oriented commentary on the results.

———. *Principles of Literary Criticism*. London: Kegan Paul, 1924.

———. *Science and Poetry*. London: Kegan Paul, 1926. A succinct statement of Richards's point of view in the 1920s.

Spingarn, J. E. *Creative Criticism*. New York: Harcourt, Brace, 1925.

Tate, Allen. "Literature as Knowledge" (1941). In *Essays of Four Decades*. New York: Swallow, 1968.

Warren, R. P. "Pure and Impure Poetry." *Kenyon Review* 5 (Spring 1943): 228–54. An often-cited example of the New Critics' general antipathy to the English Romantic poets, and especially Shelley.

Watson, George. *The Discipine of English*. London: Macmillan, 1978.

Wellek, René, and Austin Warren. *Theory of Literature*. New York: Harcourt, Brace, 1949.

Wimsatt, W. K. "Genesis: A Fallacy Revisited." In *The Disciplines of Criticism*, ed. P. Demetz, T. Greene, and L. Nelson. New Haven, Conn.: Yale University Press, 1968. Reprinted in *The Day of the Leopards* (New Haven, Conn.: Yale University Press, 1976) as "Genesis: An Argument Resumed."

Wimsatt, W. K., and Monroe Beardsley. "The Intentional Fallacy." *Sewanee Review* 54 (Summer 1946), 468–87.

Sources of Additional Information

Ewa M. Thompson's *Russian Formalism and Anglo-American New Criticism* (The Hague: Mouton, 1971) usefully compares the two kinds of formalist criticism.

William Elton's *A Glossary of the New Criticism* (Chicago: Modern Poetry Association, 1949) is a helpful guide to the meanings attached to New Critical terminology at the time it was displacing other modes of critical discussion, though by 1956 David Daiches describes the *Glossary* as "comical."

There are a number of thoughtful analyses of New Criticism formulated during the years of its greatest influence. Father Walter Ong's "The Meaning of the New Criticism" in *Twentieth-Century English*, ed. W. S. Knickerbocker (New York: Philosophical Library, 1946) examines the ways in which the New Critic escapes the Cartesian dichotomy between mind and matter. Robert W. Stallman's "The New Critics," in *Critiques and Essays in Criticism*, ed. Stallman (New York: Ronald Press, 1949), comments, "The structure of critical ideas and the practical criticism that British critics—Leavis, Turnell, Empson, Read—and American critics—Ransom, Tate, Brooks, Warren, Blackmur, Winters—have contrived upon the foundations of Eliot and Richards constitute an achievement in criticism the like of which has not been equalled in any previous period in our literary history" (506). Cleanth Brooks's "My Credo: The Formalist Critics" (*Kenyon Review* 13, Winter 1951:72–81) announces and briefly comments on ten "articles of faith." Also useful is Walter Sutton's chapter in *Modern American Criticism* (Englewood Cliffs, N.J.: Prentice-Hall, 1963). More questioning are the comments of David Daiches's "The 'New Criticism': Some Qualifications" in *Literary Essays* (Edinburgh: Oliver and Boyd, 1956).

David Robey's "Anglo-American New Criticism" in *Modern Literary Theory*, ed. Ann Jefferson and David Robey (London: Batsford, 1982) is an excellent brief study of New Critical thought. For an entertainingly Marxist assessment of the New Criticism, and especially the Cambridge movement led by F. R. Leavis, see pages 30–53 of Terry Eagleton's *Literary Theory: An Introduction* (Minneapolis: University of Minnesota Press, 1983). John Fekete, who is more doctrinaire in attacking the New Criticism and other influential approaches to literature of the 1970s, writes in *The Critical Twilight* (London: Routledge and Kegan Paul, 1977) that his study "must oppose modern critical theory for being the theoretical face of capitalist transformation, identify it as a neocapitalist practice, and affirm itself as a moment of revolutionary praxis, thus providing the social ontological ground for its methodological attitude in the struggle for the historical validation of its truth" (xvi).

A latter-day defender of at least a portion of New Critical thought and practice is Gerald Graff; Chapters 9–12 of Graff's *Professing Literature: An Institutional History* (Chicago: University of Chicago Press, 1987) consider New Criticism in the total context of the development of the study of vernacular literature in the United States. René Wellek's "The New Criticism" in vol. 6 of *A History of Modern Criticism, 1750–1950* (New Haven, Conn.: Yale University Press, 1986; originally published in *Critical Inquiry* 4, 1978, 611–624) constitutes a vigorous defense of the New Critics; the chapter precedes essays on Ransom, Brooks, Warren, Blackmur, Burke, Winters, and Wimsatt. George Watson's brief discussion of the New Critics in *The Discipine of English* (London: Macmillan, 1978) is an interesting summary from the point of view of an English critic.

On specific debated issues: J. Timothy Bagwell's *American Formalism and the Problem of Interpretation* (Houston, Tex.: Rice University Press, 1986) argues that an author's intention as he or she may formulate it outside the work itself must fail to be adequate to the work in the same way as are all paraphrases. "My arguments suggest that literature (in the sense of a function of language that transcends not only canons but possibly even texts) is something which is to be understood rather than explicated" (102). Monroe Beardsley develops the difference between intentions internal and external to the text (in a less polemic manner than the earlier "The Intentional Fallacy," see References above) in *Aesthetics: Problems in the Philosophy of Criticism* (New York: Harcourt, Brace, 1958, 17–29). William Empson's *The Structure of Complex Words* (New York: New Directions, 1951) is a detailed examination of the interrelation of the cognitive and emotive meanings of words; the two functions of words cannot be separated. R. S. Crane's "Cleanth Brooks; or, the Bankruptcy of Critical Monism" is a critique both of Brook's concept of irony and the grounds of his distinction between poetry and science (*Modern Philology*, 45, May 1948:226–45; reprinted in *Critics and Criticism*, Chicago: University of Chicago Press, 1952).

O

ORGANIC UNITY   1. The result of a process of growth in the author's mind similar to the growth of plants or animals so that the resulting work has been internally shaped. 2. Perfect adjustment of parts to the whole so that nothing is lacking and nothing superfluous. 3. Complete interdependence of all parts or aspects of a work, so that the alteration of one would alter the others. 4. Identity of form and content. 5. A high degree of unity.

Uses of "organic unity" frequently include more than one of the above senses; nevertheless, almost always one of these is primary. "Organic unity" is to be distinguished from the concept of UNITY *or harmony understood as order, completeness, or the absence of contradiction.*

1. The comparison of the work of art to a living thing goes back at least to Socrates's conclusion in *Phaedrus*: that "every discourse ought to be a living creature, having its own body and head and feet; there ought to be a middle, beginning, and end, which are in a manner agreeable to one another and to the whole" (1:568; 264c). The importance of the concept in the nineteenth and twentieth centuries, however, derives from a combination of the Kantian idea of purposiveness without purpose as developed in *The Critique of Judgment* with ideas that appear to have been generally in the air, perhaps from Leibnitz through Karl Philip Moritz (see Benziger) that received influential statement in Schlegel. The concept makes its definitive entrance into English literary theory through Coleridge, whose best-known statement is an almost exact translation of a passage in Schlegel. Coleridge's words, which appear among the extant fragments of his lectures on Shakespeare, are as follows:

> The form is mechanic when on any given material we impress a predetermined form, not necessarily arising out of the properties of the material, as when to a mass of clay we give whatever shape we wish it to retain when hardened. The organic form,

> on the other hand, is innate; it shapes as it develops itself from within, and the
> fullness of its development is one and the same with the perfection of its outward
> form. Such is the life, such the form. Nature, the prime genial artist, inexhaustible
> in diverse powers, is equally inexhaustible in form. (1:224)

The botanical metaphor is of major importance in Coleridge's concept of the
poet or of the mind of genius. M. H. Abrams comments in *The Mirror and the
Lamp*, ''Indeed, it is astonishing how much of Coleridge's critical writing is
couched in terms that are metaphorical for art and literal for a plant; if Plato's
dialectic is a wilderness of mirrors, Coleridge's is a very jungle of vegetation''
(169). Coleridge's contrast between the mechanical and the organic is closely
related to that between the fancy and the IMAGINATION, and that between the
externally shaped copy and the unique product of an internal principle interacting
with external circumstance. ''Before I go further, I may take the opportunity of
explaining what is meant by mechanic and organic regularity. In the former the
copy must appear as if it had come out of the same mould with the original; in
the latter there is a law which all the parts obey, conforming themselves to the
outward symbols and manifestations of the essential principle'' (2:170). Largely
under the influence of I. A. Richards, the analogy between the lyric poem and
the growth of a plant or embryo became central to the New Critics (see NEW
CRITICISM). The introductory essay of Cleanth Brooks and Robert Penn Warren's
influential *Understanding Poetry* is explicit: ''The relationship among the elements in a poem is . . . all important, and it is not a mechanical relationship but
one which is far more intimate and fundamental. If we should compare a poem
to the make-up of some physical object it ought not to be a wall but to something
organic like a plant'' (19). Norman Holland's ''Why Organic Unity?'' develops
a strictly psychological explanation for the unity of the literary work in which
that unity is not wholly dependent on conscious planning. Literary unity is organic
in that it is created through the same processes Freud attributes to the making
of dreams and serves a psychological function ''as a synthesis and compromise
of conflicting demands'' (29). Therefore, ''a text is literary to the extent a search
for unity in it is rewarded'' (30).

However, the concept of organic form thus stated is the source of significant
problems. A major one, as Abrams and Benziger, among others, have pointed
out is the difficulty of reconciling the idea of a self-evolving poem with any
degree of freedom or choice in the poet. R. Jack Smith has explored the possible
substitution of the notion of ''general intention'' or ''organic center'' for that
of a specific authorial intention as a way of avoiding this difficulty. G. N. G.
Orsini suggests that ''To render less paradoxical this determination of the parts
by the whole in the aesthetic process, let us put it this way: the unity is antecedent,
not prior, only logically or ideally, not chronologically'' (17).

The power of the concept of organicism as an explanation for scientific and
philosophic thought as well as aesthetic creation is suggested in two collections
of essays. *Organic Form: The Life of an Idea*, edited by George Rousseau (1972),
draws together essays treating biological, aesthetic, and specifically literary or-

ganicism. *Approaches to Organic Form*, edited by Frederick Burwick (1987), which builds on Rousseau's volume, includes essays on Anglican natural theology, utopian literature, Goethe's aesthetics, the relation of the concept of organicism to that of energy, language theory, and the influence of the concept of organicism on Victorian and modernist thought. Philip C. Ritter's "Organic Form: Aesthetics and Objectivity in the Study of Form in the Life Sciences" in the Rousseau volume is especially interesting. However, Burwick's introduction warns against confusing true and metaphorical organicism. "As long as the reciprocity can be convincingly determined between the organism and the patterns or products of its activity, the argument of 'organic form' is capable of rigorous analogy. It should be recognized, however, that many critics wield the term 'organic form' purely as metaphor and avoid all claims of genetic or physiological priority" (x). René Wellek similarly warns against the degree to which Günther Müller and Horst Oppel have employed the concept: "The analogy between the work of art and a living being is so strongly exploited by these two authors that they are in constant danger of obliterating the distinction between art and life, between a work of art made by man and an animal or tree" (64).

2. The organic metaphor easily, though not necessarily, leads to the position that in the organic work nothing is either superfluous or lacking. The article "Aesthetics, Problems of" in the *Encyclopedia of Philosophy* of 1967 tells us that "the central criterion" for the judgment of art, "the one most universally recognized, is unity (sometimes called organic unity)." Further, "In the unified object, everything that is necessary is there, and nothing that is not necessary is there" (1:43). In *The Analysis of Art* (1926), before stating that "[t]he ancient law of organic unity is the master principle of aesthetic form; all other principles serve it," De Witt Parker defines organic unity as meaning that "each element in a work of art is necessary to its value, that it contains no elements that are not thus necessary, and that all that are needful are there" (36, 34).

In "Organic Unity Reconsidered," Catherine Lord explicitly challenges so absolute an interpretation: "Every part of the work of art is not equally important when importance means prominence or impact" (263), and "[t]he concept of grades of relevance leads, almost logically, to the conclusion that subtraction and addition do not necessarily diminish the value of the work of art as whole" (264). Her argument is not that the metaphor exaggerates the organicity of the work of art, but rather that true organisms are constituted partly by features that are not essential. Looking to Aristotle, she writes, "Not all attributes of an organism are a part of its essence, but it is a part of the essence of an organism to have accidents, non-essential features. If, then, we liken a work of art to a living creature, we should expect it to exhibit accidents" (264). W. K. Wimsatt also argues that the organic metaphor is frequently carried too far when it is asserted that everything in a poem is an organic part. "A 'loose' conception of poetic organicism is, in short, what I am arguing for" (76).

The organistic notion that a successful poem lacks nothing essential can be taken as an argument for literature's self-sufficiency or autonomy. Thus in "The

Poem as Organism'' (1940), Cleanth Brooks uses organistic principles to restrict interpretation to what is provided by the total context within the poem itself, as opposed, for instance, to knowledge of the author's life. In *The New Apologists for Poetry* (1956) Murray Krieger explores the practical difficulties of trying to remain totally within the world of the poem in this way. ''On the one hand there is the need to maintain the context as self-contained; that is, the need to keep out any meaning not necessitated by the organic and closed system of mutual interrelations among the terms which make up the context. . . . On the other hand, however, there is the difficulty—indeed, if language is considered primarily as referential, the impossibility—of consistently maintaining an unqualified organicism'' (135).

3. Organicism can also be interpreted as implying such a degree of interdependence between all the parts of a work of art that the modification of any one aspect necessarily modifies all the others. For example, Morris Weitz's *Philosophy of the Arts* (1950) states that in the organic ''internally constituted'' work, ''[e]very element, every characteristic, every relation, even that of mere serial order, makes a difference to every other'' (52). In *The Basis of Criticism in the Arts* (1946), Stephen Pepper writes of the organistic criteria of beauty as being ''the degree of integration and the amount of material integrated. . . . The maximum of integration is a condition where every detail of the object calls for every other and no feeling demands are unfulfilled. Or negatively, it is a condition where no detail can be removed or altered without marring or even destroying the value of the whole'' (79). Catherine Lord denies this conclusion as well as that of the impossibility of adding to or subtracting from the organic work. G. N. G. Orsini also questions so absolute an interpretation of organicism and suggests that it is possible to avoid being misled by the organic metaphor through substitution of such terms as ''intrinsic unity'' or T. E. Hulme's ''intensive manifold'' (27).

4. Organicism is sometimes understood to mean the identity or inseparability of form and content in the literary text or aesthetic object. Herbert Read's definitions of organic (romantic) and abstract (classical) form provide a well-known example.

> *Organic form*: When a work of art has its own inherent laws, originating with its very invention and fusing in one vital unity both structure and content, then the resulting form may be described as *organic*.
> *Abstract Form*: When an organic form is stabilised and repeated as a pattern, and the intention of the artist is no longer related to the inherent dynamism of an inventive act, but seeks to adapt content to predetermined structure, then the resulting form may be described as *abstract*. (3–4)

In ''Concepts of Form and Structure in Twentieth-Century Criticism,'' René Wellek at one point refers to the ''insight of organicism'' as ''the unity of content and form'' (65), and in the essay ''The Revolt Against Positivism in Recent European Literary Scholarship,'' he refers to the Russian Formalists' conception of the literary work as the "sum of all the devices employed in it" as an essentially organic notion.

5. Organic at times is meant simply as a quantitative term of praise. As James Benziger comments, "At times the word organic seems to be no more than a mere intensive: to say that a painting has *organic form* is to say that it has "lots of form"; a poem with *organic unity* is a poem with "lots of unity" (24).

References

Abrams, M. H. *The Mirror and the Lamp.* New York: Oxford University Press, 1953. Pages 167–77 constitute a most helpful discussion of "Coleridge's Mechanical Fancy and Organic Imagination."

Approaches to Organic Form. Ed. Frederick Burwick. Dordrecht, the Netherlands: D. Reidel, 1987.

Benziger, James. "Organic Unity: Leibnitz to Coleridge." *PMLA* 66 (March 1951): 24–48. Explores the relationship between organicism and pantheism; argues that Schlegel and Coleridge wished to turn a distinction in degree into a distinction in kind.

Brooks, Cleanth. "The Poem as Organism." In the *English Institute Annual for 1940.* New York: Columbia University Press, 1941. Opposes the logical as well as the mechanical to the organic; specifically argues for the importance of the internal context of the poem over biographical interpretation.

Brooks, Cleanth, and Robert Penn Warren. *Understanding Poetry.* New York: Henry Holt, 1938.

Coleridge, Samuel Taylor. *Coleridge's Shakespearean Criticism.* Ed. Thomas M. Raysor. 2 vols. London: Constable, 1930.

The Encyclopedia of Philosophy. Ed. Paul Edwards. 8 vols. New York: Macmillan, 1967.

Holland, Norman. "Why Organic Unity?" *College English* 30 (October 1968): 19–30.

Krieger, Murray. *The New Apologists for Poetry.* Minneapolis: University of Minnesota Press, 1956. Examines certain of the problems raised by the New Critics' reliance on a theory of organicism; in particular: "The poem must in one sense, as a special form of discourse, be nonreferential, even as it must be referential to be any form of discourse at all" (22).

Lord, Catherine. "Organic Unity Reconsidered." *Journal of Aesthetics and Art Criticism* 22 (Spring 1964): 263–68.

Organic Form: The Life of an Idea. Ed. George Rousseau. London: Routledge and Kegan Paul, 1972. Includes a bibliography of books and essays treating biological, aesthetic, and literary organicism from 1823 to 1970.

Orsini, G. N. G. "The Organic Concept in Aesthetics." *Comparative Literature* 21 (Winter 1969): 1–30.

Parker, De Witt. *The Analysis of Art.* New Haven, Conn.: Yale University Press, 1926.

Pepper, Stephen C. *The Basis of Criticism in the Arts.* Cambridge, Mass.: Harvard University Press, 1946.

Plato. *Phaedrus.* In vol. 1 of *The Dialogues of Plato.* Trans. B. Jowett. New York: Charles Scribner's Sons, 1911.

Read, Herbert. *Form in Modern Poetry.* London: Sheed and Ward, 1932.

Ritter, Philip C. "Organic Form: Aesthetics and Objectivity in the Study of Form in the Life Sciences." In *Organic Form: The Life of an Idea.*

Smith, R. Jack. "Intention in an Organic Theory of Poetry." *Sewanee Review* 56 (Autumn 1948): 625–33.

Weitz, Morris. *Philosophy of the Arts*. Cambridge, Mass.: Harvard University Press, 1950.

Wellek, René. "Concepts of Form and Structure in Twentieth-Century Criticism" and "The Revolt Against Positivism in Recent European Literary Scholarship." In *Concepts of Criticism*. New Haven, Conn.: Yale University Press, 1963. A general survey of various approaches to the identification of form and content.

Wimsatt, William K. "Organic Form: Some Questions about a Metaphor." In *Organic Form: The Life of an Idea*. Argues that the organic metaphor has been carried too far, denying that "the poem itself, the hypostasized verbal and mental act, looks in any way like an animal or a vegetable" (69).

Sources of Additional Information

A history of the concept of organicism from Plato's *Phaedrus* foreword is outlined in G. N. G. Orsini's "The Ancient Roots of a Modern Idea" in *Organic Form: The Life of an Idea* (see References above). Orsini finds that the terms "organic" and mechanical mean pretty much the same thing until the eighteenth century.

For a detailed exploration of Coleridge's concept of organicism, see Gordon McKenzie's *Organic Unity in Coleridge* (*University of California Publications in English*, Berkeley 7, no. 1, 1939: 1–108). "The entire range of Coleridge's thought presents a mind which is trying to find a rational philosophic justification for an intuitive emotional belief" (5). G. N. G. Orsini sums up the scholarship concerning Coleridge's adaptation of A. W. Schlegel's distinction between organic and mechanical form in "Coleridge and Schlegel Reconsidered" (*Classical Literature* 16, Spring 1964: 97–118). David Stempel argues in "Coleridge and Organic Form" for the influence of David Hume as well as Kant on Coleridge's idea of organicism (*Studies in Romanticism* 6, Winter 1967: 89–97).

Prior to tracing the resulting opposition in Shelley's *Defense of Poetry*, J. D. Bone explores the opposed notions of being and becoming, both implicit in the general Romantic notion of organicism ("Organicism and Shelley's *A Defense of Poetry*" in *Approaches to Organic Form* [see References above]). "The idea of the 'organic' contained for the Romantic period in Britain notions of both completeness and the impossibility of completedness, of a state of true being (the 'organic whole') and a state of truth which was eternal becoming (the 'infinity' of the organic)" (195).

Richard Harter Fogle's "Organic Form in American Criticism: 1840–1870" examines the form and adequacy of the organicism of American writers between 1840 and 1870 (in *The Development of American Literary Criticism*, ed. Floyd Stovall. 1955; New Haven, Conn.: College and University Press, 1964). "In the 1840's the idea of organicism could be inhaled from the atmosphere; as a method for literary criticism it derives from the general change in man's vision of reality. The world was no longer a mechanism, but a living organism; no longer a smoothly running watch, but now a growing tree" (83).

Two approaches to an organic unity that are careful to point to the analogy between the aesthetic work and biological growth are Harold Osborne's chapter in *Aesthetics and Criticism* (London: Routledge and Kegan Paul, 1955) and I. A. Richards's "How Does a Poem Know When It Is Finished?" (in *Parts and Wholes*, ed. D. Lerner; Cambridge, Mass.: MIT Press, 1963; reprinted in I. A. Richards, *Sciences and Poetries*, New York: Norton, 1970). Osborne argues that the parts of a whole exist as parts only in relation to the whole, but that it is not true that any completed work could not have been changed for the better by the artist. Richards emphasizes "the dependence of what any word or phrase can do in the poem upon what its other words and phrases can do there" (117).

For a reply to the view of Marxist critics like Terry Eagleton that the principle of organicism is to be equated with a conservative ideology (*Literary Theory: An Introduction*, Minneapolis: University of Minnesota Press, 1983, 47ff.), see James McGeachie's "Organicism, Culture, and Ideology in Late Victorian Britain: The Uses of Complexity" in *Approaches to Organic Form* (see References above).

P

PLURALISM (literary critical) 1. The principle that readers' interpretations and responses will necessarily vary within certain limits. 2. The principle that no one set of theoretical assumptions or methodological approaches and no one critical vocabulary can adequately describe a text or exhaust its possible meanings or significances.

Critical pluralism is to be distinguished from both theories of the fundamental indeterminacy of all discourse and most of the varieties of READER-RESPONSE *criticism. The argument for radical indeterminacy is grounded finally in the lack of any necessary correspondence between word and thing, or, more technically, between signifier and signified, so that any attempt to fix meaning leads simply from* SIGN *to sign (each word or sign deriving its value from its place in the total system—the language), and thus to an infinite regress. On these grounds, the meaning of any critical statement about a* TEXT *is as indeterminate as the text itself. In particular, deconstructionists (see* DECONSTRUCTION*) see themselves as operating at a level that transcends (while undercutting) the literary-critical endeavor. As Christopher Fynsk writes, "To represent deconstruction as one method among many others that may be set forth within an either/or choice is to suspend its claims or presuppositions and to operate in terms that are radically foreign to it" (7).*

For the most part, reader-response theories—whether based on the necessity of literary and/or cultural conventions, or on individual differences in experience and/or psychological makeup—are theories about how readers necessarily respond emotionally or intellectually (interpretively), not about possible modes of critical analysis. By and large, most reader-response theories validate only one approach (through the study of the conventions of discourse communities or of psychological structures, and so forth), although the selected approach itself recognizes a range of responses, as in definition 1.

Critical pluralism is also to be distinguished from cultural pluralism, which has to do with the question of the literary CANON.

1. What may be called the weak sense of pluralism derives from the insistence on the variation, from reader to reader, of interpretation of, experience of, or response to a particular text. René Wellek and Austin Warren's formulation in *Theory of Literature* (1948) is well known: "[T]he real poem must be conceived as a structure of norms, realized only partially in the actual experience of its many readers. Every single experience . . . is only an attempt—more or less successful and complete—to grasp this set of norms or standards" (150). For I. A. Richards (*Principles of Literary Criticism*, 1948), a poem is "a class of experiences which do not differ in any character more than a certain amount, varying for each character, from a standard experience" (226–27). Theodore Redpath, pointing out that Richards is speaking of the poem rather than its meaning (as are Wellek and Warren) and that Richards goes on to identify the "standard experience" as the author's own contemplation of the poem (see AUTHOR), states the principle somewhat differently: "Perhaps the meaning of a poem is a class of similar experiences, one or other of which those words in that order and arranged in that form, *ought* to evoke in a reader familiar with the language (or languages) in which the poem is written" (21).

It may be noted that in all three of these statements there is at least an implication of an ideal experience or interpretation from which readers necessarily deviate on the basis of individual differences, and that there is a limit to the permissible degree of deviation even though this cannot be explicitly formulated (since it is impossible to achieve, or to know if one has achieved, the ideal). A more general formulation that omits any reference to standard experiences or norms, or to limits or boundaries, is that of Tzvetan Todorov in *Introduction to Poetics* (1981): "Every work is rewritten by its reader, who imposes upon it a new grid of interpretation for which he is not generally responsible but which comes to him from his culture, from his time, in short from another discourse; all comprehension is the encounter of two discourses: a dialogue" (xxx). Behind all those who recognize inevitable differences between the experiences of readers of the same text is the distinction made by Suzanne Langer between concepts and conceptions. What is necessary to communication is only a shared concept rather like a dictionary definition. "But just as quickly as the concept is symbolized to us, our own imagination dresses it up in a private, personal *conception*" (58).

2. The second, strong sense of pluralism concerns itself more with the many different aspects of a text that may be of interest and/or the underlying assumptions that generate both the kinds of questions asked and the kinds of answers that will be regarded as adequate. Within this general sense, however, there are varying emphases. Stanley Edgar Hyman's *The Armed Vision* (1948) empirically explores the strengths and weaknesses of a number of different critical approaches. While imagining the ideal critic who would synthesize "every practical technique or procedure," retaining the strengths and avoiding the weaknesses of each, he

sees such a program as impossible, primarily because knowledge and skill would be demanded from too many disciplines. "In the future we can expect that the burden of having a working command of every field of man's knowledge applicable to literary criticism will grow increasingly difficult to bear, and eventually simply become impossible" (394–95). R. P. Blackmur argues from the impossibility of adequately describing a text: "[T]here is no vicar for poetry on earth. Poetry is idiom, a special and fresh way of saying, and cannot for its life be said otherwise; and there is, finally, as much difference between words used about a poem and the poem as there is between words used about a painting and the painting" (381). In this situation, "Any rational approach is valid to literature and may be properly called critical which fastens at any point upon the work itself" (379). It is also necessary, then, to see the limits within which each critic works. "Once we reduce, in a man like Irving Babbitt, the magnitude of application of such notions as the inner check and the higher will, which were for Babbitt paramount—that is, when we determine the limits within which he really worked—then the massive erudition and acute observation with which his work is packed become permanently available" (380). In *The Literary Critics* (1962), George Watson links the need for different forms of criticism to the wide range of works that have been regarded as literary: "Anyone, indeed, who supposes that there is one method apt to every critical adventure must be vastly underestimating the immense variety of the thousands of documents called English literature" (219).

The best-known, most insistently presented, and most closely argued statements of critical pluralism are to be found in the Chicago School of critics, especially in Elder Olson and R. S. Crane, and in Wayne Booth's attempt to go beyond not only the explicitly argued pluralism of the Chicago school represented by Crane, but also the implicit pluralisms of Kenneth Burke and M. H. Abrams. Crane's version of pluralism is at the center of *The Languages of Criticism and the Structure of Poetry* (1953).

> What I would propose . . . is that criticism is not, and never has been, a single discipline, to which successive writers have made partial and never wholly satisfactory conclusions, but rather a collection of distinct and more or less incommensurable "frameworks" or "languages," within any one of which a question like that of poetic structure necessarily takes on a different meaning and receives a different kind of answer from the meaning it has and the kind of answer it is properly given in any of the rival critical languages in which it is discussed. (13)

Therefore, the pluralistic critic "would take the view that the basic principles and methods of any distinguishable mode of criticism are tools of inquiry and interpretation rather than formulations of the 'real' nature of things and that the choice of any special 'language,' among the many possible for the study of poetry, is a practical decision to be justified solely in terms of the kind of knowledge the critic wants to attain" (31). Variations on this position can be found in Crane's "The Critical Monism of Cleanth Brooks," "Questions and Answers in the Teaching of Literary Texts," and "Criticism as Inquiry." The ease with which a critic falls into the belief that his or her own method is the most appropriate talisman is explained by Crane through the principle of the *dialectical fallacy*: "the tacit assumption that what is true in your theory as a dialectical consequence must also be, or tend to be, true in actuality—that if you can so read a literary work as to reveal in it the particular kind of meaning or structure that is entailed by your definition . . . or by your formula for the author or his age, you have sufficiently demonstrated that it has that kind of meaning or structure" ("Criticism," 40).

Elder Olson pursues the same argument in more detail and with more rigor. In "An Outline of Poetic Theory," he writes, "I propose that the number of possible critical positions is relative to the number of possible philosophical positions and that the latter is determined by two principal considerations: (1) the number of aspects of a subject which can be brought into discussion, as constituting its *subject matter*; (2) the kinds of basic dialectic which may be exerted upon that subject matter" (547). Listing five major aspects of the text (essentially reflecting focus on the text, the author, the audience, the use of the text, and what the text may be taken as a sign of), Olson discusses two major philosophical orientations or dialectics, the integral and the differential. Each of the ten resulting possible combinations is subject to further focalizations. Olson's "The Dialectical Foundations of Critical Pluralism" is a yet more detailed analysis of possible philosophical bases that result in different critical practices. Dialectics (philosophical systems) may be oriented in six basic ways depending on the relation adopted between things, thoughts, and words, and reliance on the principles of either likeness or difference (integration and differentiation). These six dialectics may be applied to the text regarded as product, activity, passivity, instrument, faculty, or sign; further, each aspect may be discussed in terms of any one of the four Aristotelian causes (formal, material, efficient, and final).

Wayne Booth's *Critical Understanding: The Powers and Limits of Pluralism* (1979) seeks to justify both a variety of modes of understanding "intentions as inferable from the text" (265) and a variety of modes of *overstanding*, that is, of going beyond the boundaries of a text, asking of it "improper" questions that violate its intentions. For Booth the goal is to "treat critical modes not as positions to be defended but as locations or openings to be explored." A critical mode or topic "is not a position on which one stands, not a pedestal from which one looks out upon a world of error. Rather, it is an inhabited place in which a valued activity can occur among all those who know how to find their way in" (339). Booth gives special emphasis to the difficulty (but critical responsibility) of being fair to other critical modes.

References

Blackmur, R. P. "A Critic's Job of Work" (1935). In *Language as Gesture*. New York: Harcourt, Brace, 1952.
Booth, Wayne. *Critical Understanding: The Powers and Limits of Pluralism*. Chicago: University of Chicago Press, 1979. The most extensive treatment of the question of pluralism.
Crane, R. S. "The Critical Monism of Cleanth Brooks." In *Critics and Criticism*, ed.

R. S. Crane. Chicago: University of Chicago Press, 1952. Reprinted from *Modern Philology* 45 (May 1948): 226–45.

———. "Criticism as Inquiry; or, The Perils of the 'High Priori Road' " (1957). In vol. 2 of *The Idea of the Humanities*. 2 vols. Chicago: University of Chicago Press, 1967.

———. *The Languages of Criticism and the Structure of Poetry*. Toronto: University of Toronto Press, 1953. Crane's most developed statement of pluralism. "The moral is surely that we ought to have at our command, collectively at least, as many different critical methods as there are distinguishable major aspects in the construction, appreciation, and use of literary works" (192).

———. "Questions and Answers in the Teaching of Literary Texts" (1953). In vol. 2 of *The Idea of the Humanities*. 2 vols. Chicago: University of Chicago Press, 1967.

Fynsk, Christopher. "The Choice of Deconstruction." In *The Textual Sublime*, ed. H. J. Silverman and G. E. Aylesworth. Albany: State University of New York Press, 1990.

Hyman, Stanley. *The Armed Vision*. 1948; New York: Vintage Books, 1955.

Langer, Suzanne K. *Philosophy in a New Key*. 1942; New York: New American Library, Mentor Books, 1948.

Olson, Elder. "The Dialectical Foundations of Critical Pluralism." In *On Value Judgments in the Arts*. Chicago: University of Chicago Press, 1976. Reprinted from *Texas Quarterly* 9 (Spring 1966): 202–30. Seeks to prove that pluralism is demanded by the properties of language and necessary modes of thought. "In the first place, language is necessarily abstractive or selective. That is, it is impossible for language to signify the totality of existence; if it did, it would be nonsignificant" (334).

———. "An Outline of Poetic Theory." In *Critics and Criticism*, ed. R. S. Crane. Chicago: University of Chicago Press, 1952. Reprinted in *On Value Judgments in the Arts*. "[P]luralism is possible both in philosophy and in criticism because criticism is a department of philosophy" (547).

Redpath, Theodore. "The Meaning of a Poem." In *On Literary Intention*, ed. D. Newton–de Molina. Edinburgh: University of Edinburgh Press, 1974.

Richards, I. A. *Principles of Literary Criticism*. London: Routledge and Kegan Paul, 1948.

Todorov, Tzvetan. *Introduction to Poetics*. Trans. R. Howard. Minneapolis: University of Minnesota Press, 1981.

Watson, George. *The Literary Critics*. 1962; London: Hogarth Press, 1986.

Wellek, René, and Austin Warren. *Theory of Literature*. 1948; New York: Harcourt, Brace and World, 1956.

Sources of Additional Information

A set of interestingly linked essays extending from 1972 to 1977 demonstrates the degree to which the question of critical pluralism is related to other central issues of contemporary criticism. In a review of M. H. Abrams's *Natural Supernaturalism* published in *Diacritics* (2, Winter 1972: 6–13), J. Hillis Miller questions the entire methodology of the book for assuming the possibility of interpreting texts and discovering UNITY—both denied by Derridean DECONSTRUCTION. In the same year, Abrams's "What's the Use of Theorizing about the Arts?" appeared in the collection *In Search of Literary*

Theory, ed. by Morton W. Bloomfield (Ithaca, N.Y.: Cornell University Press, 1972). Here Abrams's argument that all criticism presupposes theory leads him to espouse a pluralistic view of criticism.

> [C]ritical definitions and theories may be discrepant without conflict, and mutually supplementary instead of mutually exclusive, since each delimits and structures its field in its own way. . . . No theory is adequate to tell the whole story, for each one has limits correlative with its powers. As a speculative instrument, it has its particular angle and focus of vision, and what for one speculative instrument is an indistinct or blank area requires an alternative speculative instrument if it is to be brought into sharp focus for inspection. (25)

Abrams defends the importance of theory and the necessity of pluralism in "A Note on Wittgenstein and Literary Criticism" (*ELH* 41, Winter 1974: 541–54). In a very different way, Wayne Booth questions in "M. H. Abrams: Historian as Critic, Critic as Pluralist" how Abrams reconciles his theoretical pluralism with his magisterially presented interpretation of romanticism in *Natural Supernaturalism*; Abrams replies in the same issue of *Critical Inquiry* (2, Spring 1976: 411–45 and 447–64, respectively). This exchange led to essays by Booth, Abrams, and Miller published under the general title "The Limits of Pluralism" in *Critical Inquiry* 3 (Spring 1977: 407–47). Although none of these essays is directly focused on the grounds or practice of pluralism, the whole set moves between defenses of pluralism, questions of its limits, and the question of whether deconstruction is actually a denial of pluralism.

Although not usually thought of as pluralist, E. D. Hirsch's principles as argued in *Validity in Interpretation* (New Haven, Conn.: Yale University Press, 1967) and *The Aims of Interpretation* (Chicago: University of Chicago Press, 1976) can be understood as a form of pluralism in their presentation of both *meaning* and *significance* (cf. Wayne Booth's *understanding* and *overstanding*). What Hirsch calls meaning—the author's intended meaning as realized in the text—is the goal of interpretation. A plurality of procedures must be employed to narrow the class into which the text falls in order to arrive at an interpretation. Further, there is no necessary limit to the number of significances that may be explored (that is, there is a plurality of purposes for which a critic may elect to use a text).

In the context of a poststructuralist FEMINIST LITERARY CRITICISM, Elizabeth Meese argues against a prescriptive criticism in the final chapter of *Crossing the Double-Cross* (Chapel Hill: University of North Carolina Press, 1986). "In response to the complexity resulting from multicentering moves, we need to conceive of feminist criticism, indeed as Culler suggests, all criticism, as an infinite progression that refuses to identify a center because it is always decentered, self-displacing and self-contradictory" (150).

Paul B. Armstrong's "The Conflict of Interpretations and the Limits of Pluralism" (*PMLA* 98, May 1983: 341–52) defends pluralism while attempting to suggest that there are criteria of validity. "Literary criticism is a pluralistic universe, but there are limits to its pluralism" (349).

POETICS 1. As employed by Aristotle in the *Poetics*, exploration of the structures, requirements, capabilities, and purposes of the various types or species of poetry. 2. Any treatment of poetry in general. Librarians thus tend to classify books on prosody, on how to write poetry, and on how to read poetry together under the rubric poetics. 3. The exploration of the characteristics that distinguish literature from other uses of language. 4. The techniques, practices, and devices of specific authors. 5. The elucidation of the systems that make MEANING in literature (and, by extension, in all DISCOURSE) possible. 6. Overarching theories explaining the nature of LITERATURE.

All the above senses with the exception of the second (the loosest and broadest) agree in excluding interpretation (explication) of the meaning of individual texts and at least the greater part of HISTORICAL SCHOLARSHIP *and* LITERARY HISTORY.

1. Aristotle's *Poetics* opens, "Our subject being Poetry, I propose to speak not only of the art in general but also of its species and their respective capacities; of the structure of plot required for a good poem; of the number and nature of the constituent parts of a poem; and likewise of any other matters in the same line of inquiry" (3; 1447a). Aristotle's concern thus centers on how poems are made, the Greek *poiem* from which *poetikos* is derived having the meaning "to make" or "to create." Since the *Poetics* that has come down to us remains focused on tragedy, the range of what Aristotle might have regarded as necessary to a comprehensive discussion is not wholly clear. Nevertheless, Aristotle's discussion of the six elements—plot or fable, characters, diction, thought, spectacle, and melody—places action, character depiction (including form of narration), diction, spectacle (presumably including in nondramatic works the use of imagery), melody (including prosody), and thought (which for Aristotle is the "[t]hought of the personages [characters]," 55; 1456a) within the subject matter of poetics. Since the *Poetics* seeks to explain the principles of success in tragedy, it can be taken as a manual for the writing and judging of tragedy (and, to some extent, of poetry in general). In R. S. Crane's words, "The primary aim of poetics, for Aristotle, is the discovery and statement of the principles which govern poets when they make good poems; these, it is assumed, will also be the principles by which the specifically *poetic* qualities of existing poems are to be judged" (43). Generous interpretation of this first sense allows the inclusion of such works as Horace's *Ars Poetica* (c. 15 B.C.), Puttenham's *The Arte of English Poesie* (1589), Pope's *Essay on Criticism* (1711), and E. S. Dallas's *Poetics* (1852).

2. Any discussion of poetry in general, as opposed to interpretation of an individual work, has been loosely regarded as belonging to poetics, especially in library classification systems. This has allowed textbooks on how to understand (interpret) poetry to fall under the same class as those studies that are today most often specifically differentiated from them: studies of the nature of poetry and the principles that make poetic meaning possible (see senses 5 and 6). The Library of Congress cataloging system dating from 1915 groups studies of prosody, methods of poetic composition, and the interpretation of poetry under the PN1039 to PN1049 range; divisions within the range are by language, not topic.

3. The application of the word poetics to literature as a whole is essentially a twentieth-century shift. Initiated primarily by the Russian Formalists' pursuit of the principle(s) differentiating literature from other discourse, of the specific

quality that produces literariness, it migrated into the structuralist vocabulary. Criticism was too broad a term to designate the investigation of the structures of literature in general as opposed to the meanings of individual texts; poetics, now applied to prose as well as verse, became the preferred term. Roman Jakobson, a major link between Russian Formalism and literary theory in Western Europe, England, and the United States, thus defined the term in 1958: "Poetics deals summarily with the question, *What makes a verbal message a work of art?* Because the main subject of poetics is the *differentia specifica* of verbal art in relation to other arts and in relation to other kinds of verbal behavior, poetics is entitled to the leading place in literary studies" (350). Tzvetan Todorov, another of the major conduits bringing Russian Formalist and French structuralist thought to Anglo-American criticism, described poetics in 1966: "what it studies is not poetry or literature but 'poeticity' or literariness" (*Poetics*, 33). (On literariness, see LITERATURE and FORMALISM.)

4. The Russian Formalists' focus on the *devices* employed by individual authors as well as in literary texts generally has led to the designation of the styles, techniques, and dominant characteristics of specific authors, genres, and schools as their "poetics." The practice has become common in English only recently, as in, for example, Jean Hytier's *The Poetics of Paul Valéry* (1966), Coburn Freer's *The Poetics of Jacobean Drama* (1981), Marianne Shapiro's *The Poetics of Ariosto* (1988), and Robert Dale's *The Poetics of Prosper Mérimeé* (1966).

5. The incorporation of much Russian Formalist thought into the early structuralist movement led to the structuralists' use of "poetics" to describe their major interest, the structures that make possible the interpretation of literary works (as opposed to the production of interpretations of specific works). The basic structures that make meaning possible can be regarded as either innate or as adopted conventions. Structuralists like Roland Barthes (in his early work) raise the possibility that "Corresponding to the *language faculty* postulated by Chomsky, there is perhaps in people a *literature faculty*, an energy of discourse" (75). On the other hand, Jonathan Culler argues in *Structuralist Poetics* that the goal of such a poetics is the description of a culturally derived *literary competence*. In either case, poetics, which Barthes calls "the science of language," is to be "a science of the *conditions* of content, that is to say of forms: it will concern itelf with the variations of meaning engendered, and, so to speak, *engenderable* by works" (73–74).

6. The amalgamation of Russian Formalist and structuralist thought, together with the ever-growing interest in theory—as opposed to CRITICISM or INTERPRETATION—has led to the extension of "poetics" to include all investigation into the nature and function of literature as well as into that which makes possible its interpretation. In his 1981 *Introduction to Poetics*, Todorov contrasts poetics with *interpretation* on the one hand and with what he calls *science* (the application of external systems of analysis, or what E. D. Hirsch calls *criticism*), on the other. "In contradistinction to the interpretation of particular works, [poetics]

does not seek to name meaning, but aims at a knowledge of the general laws that preside over the birth of each work. But in contradistinction to such sciences as psychology, sociology, etc., it seeks these laws within literature itself. Poetics is therefore an approach that is at once "abstract" and "internal" (6–7).

Thus, the first issue of the journal entitled *Poetics: International Review for the Theory of Literature* (1971) announced that it would be "interested exclusively in theoretical and methodological work" (5). The first issue of *PTL: A Journal of Descriptive Poetics and Theory of Literature* (January 1976) states, "PTL is a journal devoted to the development of poetics, the systematic study of literature" (1).

References

Aristotle. *On the Art of Poetry*. Trans. I. Bywater. Oxford: Clarendon Press, 1909.
Barthes, Roland. *Criticism and Truth*. Trans. K. P. Keuneman. Minneapolis: University of Minnesota Press, 1987. Original French edition, 1966.
Crane, R. S. *The Languages of Criticism and the Structure of Poetry*. Toronto: University of Toronto Press, 1953.
Culler, Jonathan. *Structuralist Poetics*. Ithaca, N.Y.: Cornell University Press, 1975.
Jakobson, Roman. "Linguistics and Poetics." In *Style in Language*, ed. Thomas A. Sebeok. Cambridge: MIT Press, 1960.
Todorov, Tzvetan. *Introduction to Poetics*. Trans. R. Howard. Minneapolis: University of Minnesota Press, 1981. Original French edition, 1968.
————. *The Poetics of Prose*. Trans. R. Howard. Ithaca, N.Y.: Cornell University Press, 1977. Original French edition, 1971.

Sources of Additional Information

Wilbur Samuell Howell's *Poetics, Rhetoric, and Logic* (Ithaca, N.Y.: Cornell University Press, 1975), and especially the first essay, "Aristotle and Horace on Rhetoric and Poetics" argues that despite attempts to confound the two, Aristotle and Horace both kept poetics, as the principles of poetry (necessarily mimetic), distinct from those of rhetoric (which is nonmimetic).

Chapter 9 of Roger Fowler's *Literature as Social Discourse*, "Linguistics and, and Versus, Poetics" (Bloomington: Indiana University Press, 1981) argues the value of keeping poetics and linguistics separate, but complementary, disciplines.

POSTMODERNISM   The complex of dominant cultural characteristics of the period from World War II to the present. There are, however, varying and sometimes contradictory emphases within this broad definition: (a) literature, and art generally, since World War II; (b) the major direction of social, political, and economic development since World War II and the accommodation of art and literature within this development; (c) the resistance to the dominant forces of society by art and literature, and especially politically oriented critical theorizing, since World War II; and (d) a tendency recurring throughout history to oppose and parody the reigning social norms and the dominant forces in a culture.

Certain writers tend either to use postmodernism as a synonym for poststructuralism or to take the latter as the theory underlying the former. However,

although poststructuralism has evidently had its effect both on many recent
literary works and on contemporary intellectual currents, the motivations behind
neither postmodern literature nor postmodern thought can be adequately sub-
sumed under poststructuralist arguments. It is preferable to keep the two terms
separate. (See STRUCTURALISM.*)*

Critics' positions on the questions of whether there is such a thing as postmodernism (or anti- or neo-modernism), and, if so, how it is defined, depend
largely on their understanding of MODERNISM, their political beliefs, and whether
their primary focus is on the literature or the critical theorizing of the postmodern
decades. Thus a critic like Monroe Spears, who regards modernism as ending
the era of liberal HUMANISM, sees modernism and postmodernism as phases of
a new era extending indefinitely into the future. It is possible to argue that the
very awkwardness of a term that designates both "the present time" and a
historical phenomenon inevitably generated the necessity of declaring at least a
new phase with a new name: a literary movement could not continue over many
decades under a label meaning "just now." Frank Kermode finds the characteristics of the two eras sufficiently similar to speak of *palaeo-modernism* and
neo-modernism. On the other hand, William Spanos, who regards modernism
as the end of traditions originating in the Renaissance, hails postmodernism as
necessarily being directly opposed to modernism in that it inaugurates a new
historical era.

a. Irving Howe and Harry Levin were perhaps the first to adopt the term
postmodern, applying it generally to literature written after World War II. Ihab
Hassan was influential in focusing attention on what was new in this literature;
typical in its use of postmodernist literary techniques of discontinuity to write
about postmodernist literature is his "POSTmodernISM," first published in
1971. In this essay, postmodernism appears to carry further the seven characteristics Hassan had used to define modernism. Hassan's 1982 essay "Toward
a Concept of Postmodernism," which cites himself and Leslie Fiedler as the
first to employ the term with approbation, condenses many of the characteristics
he had found in modernism into a single term. His *indeterminance* combines
indeterminacy ("ambiguity, discontinuity, heterodoxy, pluralism, randomness,
revolt, perversion, deformation," 92) and immanence ("the capacity of mind
to generalize itself in symbols, intervene more and more into its own nature, act
upon itself through its own abstractions and so become, increasingly, immediately, its own environment," 270). In Hassan, as frequently elsewhere in discussions of postmodernism, the theoretical assumptions of postmodernist critics
and the characteristics of postmodernist art and literature are explicitly seen as
parallel. Douwe Fokkema offers a somewhat parallel list of postmodern characteristics: a preference for fragments over coherence, the avoidance of explanation or selection of what is described, the cultivation of contradiction and
verbosity, and a tendency to discuss the process of writing what is being written.

Other critics have discussed postmodernism in terms primarily of its formal
characteristics rather than social or political relevance. David Lodge, building

on Roman Jakobson's theory that discourse is primarily metaphorical and me-
tonymical, sees what Stephen Spender called the "contemporary" writers of the
first half of the century as representing experience through metonomy, the "modernists" as representing it metaphorically, and postmodernism as the attempt to
create a new form of discourse (see METONYMY and METAPHOR).

> Stated most baldly, Jakobson's theory asserts that any discourse must connect its
> topics according to either similarity or contiguity, and will usually prefer one type
> of connection to the other. Postmodernist writing tries to defy this law by seeking
> some alternative principle of composition. To these alternatives I give the names:
> Contradiction, Permutation, Discontinuity, Randomness, Excess, and The Short
> Circuit. (13)

The intent is to deny meaningful patterns in the text, or at least ensure that any
found are understood to be illusory impositions of the reader. Gerald Graff writes,
"In its literary sense, postmodernism may be defined as the movement within
contemporary literature and criticism that calls into question the traditional claims
of literature and art to truth and human value" (32). Graff further distinguishes
two forms of postmodern literature, one that portrays an all-embracing relativism
as a deprivation, and one that celebrates that relativism (55ff.).

Brian McHale finds that postmodernist fiction is dominated by ontological
rather than epistemological issues (xii). Postmodernist fiction thus asks ontological questions such as, "Which world is this?" "What is to be done with it?"
and "Which of my selves is to do it?" (10). Jerome Klinkowitz believes that
postmodernist literature and art shifts the center of interest from the result to the
creative act, "from product to maker and from artwork to performer" (6). Thus,
"what is confronted in a novel or painting is not a form to be admired but rather
the problematic action of an individual at work with his or her materials" (4);
moreover, now, "instead of the totalitarian ideology of the referent we can glory
in the act of production" (9). The political resonance of such a statement suggests
the strong political current running through much postmodernist writing. Linda
Hutcheon, joining with those who see postmodernism as an assault on "liberal
humanism," argues that "Postmodernism teaches that all cultural practices have
an ideological subtext which determines the conditions of their production of
meaning" (xii–xiii) and is therefore "fundamentally contradictory, resolutely
historical, and inescapably political" (4). Postmodernist texts relate parodically
to traditions, conventions, and genres—as does postmodern art and architecture,
analysis of the latter being especially favored among postmodernist critics.

b. Polemical, politically oriented criticism, influenced heavily by one or more
varieties of neo-Marxism, explicitly links postmodern literature and art to the
present state of society. Discussion of literature becomes inseparable from an
analysis of the existing socioeconomic, specifically capitalist, cultural system.
Paul Bové finds that postmodern critics "all conceive the postmodern and their
own critical practices as alternatives both to the established values and beliefs
of our mass culture and to the habitual linguistic forms of critical practice which
legitimate those values" (4). Fredric Jameson's "Postmodernism and the Con-

sumer Society'' notes that the formerly subversive styles of modernism have now been accommodated by society; a countercultural postmodernism must therefore react against these. This is possible, however, only through pastiche; parody is no longer possible because the norms against which parody is judged no longer exist. Nor in these days of corporate capitalism and population explosion is there any longer a ''bourgeois individual subject'' against which to react. For critics like Jameson, postmodernist literature and art is less a challenge to ''late capitalism'' than a capitulation. As he writes in ''Postmodernism, or the Cultural Logic of Late Capitalism,'' having recognized the ability of the capitalist system to turn art into a commodity, postmodernist writers and artists accept their role as the production of commodities; thus, postmodernist architecture, which is seen as a reaction against the ''elitist'' and ''authoritarian'' architecture of modernism (54) is under the ''patronage of multinational business'' (57). For postmodernists like Jameson, ''the whole global, yet American, postmodern culture is the internal and superstructural expression of a whole new wave of American military and economic domination throughout the world: in this sense, as throughout class history, the underside of culture is blood, torture, death and horror'' (57). Terry Eagleton's ''Capitalism, Modernism, and Postmodernism'' reinforces Jameson's analysis: late capitalism ''proclaims that if the artefact is a commodity, the commodity can always be an artefact'' (62). Admitting that the work of art is simply a commodity (68), for Eagleton postmodernism is postmetaphysical: the world is what it is.

c. Hal Foster points out in the introduction to *The Anti-Aesthetic: Essays on Postmodern Culture* (xii) that there are two postmodernisms; though both oppose themselves to modernism, one celebrates the status quo while the other resists it. This is evident in the Marxist postmodernists' antagonism to the social accommodation of much postmodernist literature and art. The distinction can also be seen in the fact that while to some critics postmodernist and poststructuralist are terms that can equally be applied to most contemporary literary theory, Andreas Huyssen charges the poststructuralists (as opposed to the postmodernists) with evading questions of politics and their arguments against referentiality with strengthening conservative positions. From Huyssen's point of view, Paul de Man's work ''drives the literary modernism debate back into the academic ghetto from which critics like Benjamin and Adorno have tried to free it'' (11).

d. On the other hand, William Spanos is able both to identify present postmodernism with an inherent mode of human thought found in marginalized, carnivalized, and parodic literature of the past and to combine elements of the deconstructive approach of Jacques Derrida, the analysis of the *archival* or *epistemic* initiated by Michel Foucault, and Marxists' challenge to the social order (see DECONSTRUCTION and MARXIST LITERARY CRITICISM). For Spanos, the modernist spatialization was the last phase of the Western humanistic tradition; postmodernism recognizes the importance of the temporal dimension, especially the inescapable influence of culture at every historical moment. Thus, ''*post-*

modern describes a literature that radically interrogates the authorizing logocentric forms and rhetorics of the entire literary tradition culminating in modernism in order to retrieve and explore the temporality—and the differences that temporality disseminates—that these 'spatial forms' have repressed by exclusion or assimilation and forgotten'' (195).

References

The Anti-Aesthetic: Essays on Postmodern Culture. Ed. Hal Foster, Port Townsend, Wash.: Bay Press, 1983.

Bové, Paul A. "The Ineluctability of Difference." In *Postmodernism and Politics*, ed. Jonathan Arac. Minneapolis: University of Minnesota Press, 1986.

Eagleton, Terry. "Capitalism, Modernism and Postmodernism." *New Left Review* 152 (1983): 60–73.

Fokkema, Douwe. *Literary History, Modernism, and Postmodernism*. Amsterdam: J. Benjamins, 1984. A fertile discussion in a brief compass.

Graff, Gerald. "The Myth of the Postmodern Breakthrough." In *Literature Against Itself*. Chicago: University of Chicago Press, 1979.

Hassan, Ihab. "POSTmodernISM." *New Literary History* 3 (Fall 1971): 5–30. Reprinted in *Paracriticisms: Seven Speculations of the Times*. Urbana: University of Illinois Press, reprinted in 1975. Also *The Postmodern Turn*. Columbus: Ohio State University Press, 1987.

———. "Toward a Concept of Postmodernism." In *The Dismemberment of Orpheus: Toward a Postmodern Literature*, 2d. rev. ed. Madison: University of Wisconsin Press, 1982. Reprinted in *The Postmodern Turn*. Columbus: Ohio State University Press, 1987. A standard formulation.

Howe, Irving. "Mass Society and Postmodern Fiction." *Partisan Review* 26 (1959): 420–36.

Hutcheon, Linda. *A Poetics of Postmodernism*. New York: Routledge, 1988. An exceptionally substantial and well-informed study.

Huyssen, Andreas. "Critical Theory and Modernity: Introduction." *New German Critique*, no. 26 (Spring-Summer 1982): 3–11.

Jameson, Fredric. "Postmodernism and the Consumer Society." In *The Anti-Aesthetic*.

———. "Postmodernism, or the Cultural Logic of Late Capitalism." *New Left Review*, no. 146 (1984): 53–59.

Kermode, Frank. "Modernisms." In *Innovations*, ed. Bernard Bergonizi. London: Macmillan, 1968.

Klinkowitz, Jerome. *Rosenberg/Barthes/Hassan: The Postmodern Habit of Thought*. Athens: University of Georgia Press, 1988.

Levin, Harry. "What was Modernism?" *Massachusetts Review* 1 (1960): 604–30. Reprinted in *Refractions*. New York: Oxford University Press, 1966.

Lodge, David. *Working with Structuralism*. London: Routledge and Kegan Paul, 1981.

McHale, Brian. *Postmodernist Fiction*. London: Methuen, 1987.

Spanos, William V. "Postmodern Literature and Its Occasion." In *Repetitions: The Postmodern Occasion in Literature and Culture*. Baton Rouge: Louisiana State University Press, 1987. Reprinted from *Krisis* 3/4 (1985).

Spears, Monroe. *Dionysus and the City: Modernism in Twentieth-Century Poetry*. New York: Oxford University Press, 1970.

Sources of Additional Information

Ihab Hassan's *The Dismemberment of Orpheus* (Madison: University of Wisconsin Press, 1982) and *Paracriticisms: Seven Speculations of the Times* (Urbana: University of Illinois Press, 1975) convey the experimentalism and fragmentariness that is in part characteristic of postmodernist critical writing.

Much of the discussion of postmodernism continues to occur in a political rather than an essentially literary context. Jürgen Habermas's "Modernity versus Postmodernity" in *New German Critique* (no. 22, Winter 1981, 3–14 and reprinted in *The Anti-Aesthetic* [see References above] as "Modernity—An Incomplete Project") has been the object of attacks by critics of the Marxist orthodoxy for failing to trace postmodernist phenomena to a crisis engendered by "late capitalism." François Lyotard's arguments in *The Postmodern Condition: A Report on Knowledge* (Minneapolis: University of Minnesota Press, 1984) that the basis of postmodernism is doubt of *metanarratives* (narratives that legitimate forms of knowledge) and that society has now adopted efficiency and *performativity* as its central (nonhumanistic) values have been incorporated in one way or another in much of the politically oriented writing on postmodernism. Peter Burger's *Theory of the Avant-Garde* (trans. Michael Shaw; Minneapolis: University of Minnesota Press, 1984) prefers the term *avant-garde* to postmodernism. "Modernism may be understandable as an attack of traditional writing techniques, but the avant-garde can only be understood as an attack meant to alter the institutionalized commerce with art" (xv); the target is "mass culture" and the "culture industry" (xviii). In *The Politics of Postmodernism* (London: Routledge, 1989), Linda Hutcheon considers the political challenge of postmodernism defined as "self-conscious, self-contradictory, self-undermining statement" (1). David Harvey's *The Condition of Postmodernity* (Oxford: Basil Blackwell, 1989) is a survey of postmodernism as a general cultural phenomenon, with particular attention to its reflection of the compression of space and time in the contemporary technological culture. Charles Newman's *The Postmodern Aura: The Act of Fiction in an Age of Inflation* (Evanston, Ill.: Northwestern University Press, 1985) describes postmodernism as the "inflation of discourse."

On the other hand, for an appreciative commentary on early postmodernist writing which emphasizes its refreshing qualities, its "delight in design" with "the highest premium on art and joy," and its quality of "ethically controlled fantasy," see Robert Scholes's *The Fabulators* (New York: Oxford University Press, 1967) and his later version, *Fabulation and Metafiction* (Urbana: University of Illinois Press, 1979).

PRAGMATICS   1. The third "dimension" of SEMIOTICS as formulated by Charles Morris, "the science of the relation of signs to interpreters," or, somewhat more narrowly, of language to its users. 2. Less broadly, as generally employed in Anglo-American linguistics and philosophy, the study of MEANING in CONTEXT as opposed to SEMANTICS, the study of lexical meaning. 3. Most narrowly, the investigation of indexicality or deixis, that is, the terms that link discourse to a specific speaker, audience, or moment.

PRAGMATICS *and* PRAGMATISM: *It might seem that the relationship between pragmatics as a division of semiotics and pragmatism as a philosophical principle have little more in common than the fact that Peirce and Morris both looked to the same Greek root for a word that would convey the idea of use or practice. However, Morris specifically stated that pragmatics was "coined with reference* *to the term 'pragmatism.' " Pragmatism "has directed attention more closely to the relation of signs to their users than had previously been done and has assessed more profoundly than ever before the relevance of this relation in understanding intellectual activities. The term 'pragmatics' helps to signalize the achievements of Peirce, James, Dewey, and Mead within the field of se-miotic" (*Foundations, *29–30; see also* Pragmatic Movement, *23–24*). Peirce linked the interpretant (roughly, concept) to habits of response, and Morris's own thought went further in this direction. "The semantical rule has as its correlate in the pragmatical dimension the habit of the interpreter to use the sign vehicle under certain circumstances and, conversely, to expect such and such to be the case when the sign is used" (*Foundations, *32*). If, then inter-pretants are habits of action in the presence of a given sign, signs are interpreted in a way analogous to the pragmatist's rule for interpreting concepts by their effects. Moreover, in either case the interpretation of the effects is contextual. That is why the historical web of thought that circles pragmatics and pragmatism is of importance for literary theory.*

1. In developing the concern for semiotics as the relation of signs to their interpreters, Morris gave the field very broad scope, as evidenced by two separate definitions: "Since most, if not all, signs have as their interpreters living or-ganisms, it is a sufficiently accurate characterization of pragmatics to say that it deals with the biotic aspects of semiosis, that is, with all the psychological, biological, and sociological phenomena which occur in the functioning of signs" (*Foundations*, 30). "Pragmatics is the aspect of semantics concerned with the origin, uses, and effects of signs" (*Signification*, 44). Any psychological or social response to a sign would fall under pragmatics taken in this sense.

2. Pragmatics in its most usual Anglo-American use designates the study of how specific intentional meaning is conveyed and interpreted in a specific con-textual situation. That is, it is concerned especially with the ways in which choices are made by users within a given context either to limit possible inter-pretations or to express something indirectly, and how their addressees respond to the interaction of context and form of expression. An early use of pragmatism as an emphasis on interpretation through context occurs in Bronislaw Mali-nowski's "The Problem of Meaning in Primitive Language" which appeared as a supplement in C. K. Ogden and I. A. Richards's *The Meaning of Meaning* of 1923. "We can say that language in its primitive function and original form has an essentially pragmatic character; that it is a mode of behaviour, an indispensable element of concerted human action. And negatively: that to regard it as a means for the embodiment or expression of thought is to take a one-sided view of one of its most derivative and specialized functions" (316). It is interesting to note that this was written before Peirce's doctrine of signs was generally known (perhaps the first careful summary of which appeared as part of Appendix D to *The Meaning of Meaning*) and fifteen years before Morris's *Foundations of the Theory of Signs*.

The contextual emphasis can be seen in Teun van Dijk: "Linguistic pragmatics is a formal reconstruction of an assumed system of rules enabling a native speaker to relate one or more discourses of a natural language with one or more appropriate contexts, and conversely'' (26). Elizabeth Bates is more succinct: ''Pragmatics is perhaps best defined as rules governing the use of language in context'' (420). Jerrold Katz puts greater emphasis on indirection: ''A pragmatic theory deals with the various mechanisms real speakers use in order to exploit the richness of the context in order to produce utterances whose meaning in the context diverges predictably from the meaning of the sentences of which they are tokens'' (15).

Pragmatics in this sense draws on theories of the speech act, of presupposition and inference, and on Grice's Cooperative Principle (see SPEECH-ACT THEORY). All these areas address users' (both authors' and audiences') expectations about language use that make possible conversational implicature (the recognition of intentionally indirect communication).

Study of the development of language skills in young children is heavily concerned with pragmatics, the use of language under particular contextual conditions. Children must acquire not only a vocabulary and a competence in syntax, but such skills as ''the ability to repair conversational errors'' and ''the ability to use inference in interpreting meaning in stories'' (Rees, 7).

3. The restriction of pragmatics to the domain of indexicals or ''shifters'' as it is by Richard Montague is not uncommon among linguists. The operation of indexicals is more complex than it might seem and is clearly a central link to context, although one perhaps more important in speech than writing. For examples of investigations into the role of indexicals, see Susan Bean's *Symbolic and Pragmatic Semantics: A Kannada System of Address*, and Michael Silverstein's ''Shifters, Linguistic Categories, and Cultural Description.''

Note

The importance of pragmatics (especially in the second sense) for literary studies lies not only in the fact that all interpretation draws upon context, but that indirection (through IRONY, METAPHOR, METONYMY, litotes, and so forth) is especially common in those texts that have traditionally been regarded as literary. For example, a dialogue in a novel occurs in a local context and the context of the novel as a whole (both of these are sometimes referred to as *co-text*), and the external contexts of the knowledge of genre, character traits, and everyday experience that readers bring to the text.

References

Bates, Elizabeth. ''Pragmatism and Sociolinguistics in Child Language.'' In *Normal and Deficient Child Language*, ed. D. Morehead and A. Morehead. Baltimore: University Park Press, 1976.

Bean, Susan S. *Symbolic and Pragmatic Semantics: A Kannada System of Address*. Chicago: University of Chicago Press, 1978.

Dijk, Teun A. van. ''Pragmatics and Poetics.'' In *Pragmatics of Language and Literature*.

Katz, Jerrold. *Propositional Structure and Illocutionary Force*. New York: Crowell, 1977.

Malinowski, Bronislaw. ''The Problem of Meaning in Primitive Languages.'' Supplement

1 of *The Meaning of Meaning*, ed. C. K Ogden and I. A. Richards. 1923; New York: Harcourt Brace, 1946.

Montague, Richard. "Pragmatics." In *Formal Philosophy: Selected Papers*, ed. R. H. Thomason. New Haven, Conn.: Yale University Press, 1974.

Morris, Charles. *Foundations of the Theory of Signs*. Chicago: University of Chicago Press, 1938. The history of pragmatics as a philosophical and linguistic term begins here.

————. *The Pragmatic Movement in American Philosophy*. New York: George Braziller, 1970.

————. *Signification and Significance*. Cambridge, Mass.: MIT Press, 1964.

Pragmatics of Language and Literature. Ed. Teun A. van Dijk. New York: American Elsevier, 1976.

Rees, N. "An Overview of Pragmatics, or What Is in the Box?" In *Pragmatics: The Role in Language Development*, ed. John V. Irwin. La Verne, Calif.: Fox Point Publishing, 1982.

Silverstein, Michael. "Shifters, Linguistic Categories, and Cultural Description." In *Meaning in Anthropology*, ed. Keith H. Basso and Henry A. Selby. Albuquerque: University of New Mexico Press, 1976.

Sources of Additional Information

An especially useful introduction to the central questions of pragmatics (including presupposition, conversational implicature, and speech acts) and to the range of definitions that have been given to the term in S. C. Levinson's *Pragmatics* (Cambridge: Cambridge University Press, 1983).

Radical Pragmatics, ed. Peter Coles (New York: Academic Press, 1981), is a collection of essays attempting to show "that aspects of meaning previously taken as integral to the literal meaning of a construction are in fact due to the application of conversational implicature to a more restricted literal meaning" (xii). Gerald Gazdar's *Implicature, Presupposition, and Logical Form* (New York: Academic Press, 1979), which defines pragmatics as meaning less truth conditions, is a technical argument for the place of contextual conditions in the determination of meaning, resulting in the principle that the important relationships of implicature and presupposition are those of consistency, not entailment. Richard Montague's essays "Pragmatics" and "Pragmatics and Intensional Logic" are logical formulations of the concept of pragmatics in relation to truth and context (see References above).

PRAGMATISM   1. The doctrine developed by Charles Sanders Peirce that the meaning of a concept is the sum of its conceivable effects. 2. Various amplifications and modifications of Peirce's doctrine, the best known of which perhaps is that of William James. 3. Recently, the new pragmatism or neo-pragmatism, primarily associated with Richard Rorty, which denies the possibility of grounding any proposition in reality or an absolute principle of value. Also known as *anti-essentialism* and *anti-foundationalism*.

On the relationship of pragmatism to PRAGMATICS, *see that entry.*

1. Peirce's definition of the principle of pragmatism appeared as a maxim in an essay entitled "How to Make Our Ideas Clear" in the *Popular Science Monthly*

for January 1878, although without the direct use of the term: "Consider what effects, that might conceivably have practical bearings, we conceive the object of our conception to have. Then, our conception of these effects is the whole of our conception of the object" (5.401). The maxim was specifically attached to the term in Peirce's definition of "Pragmatic and Pragmatism" which was contributed to Baldwin's *Dictionary of Philosophy and Psychology* (1902). It is to be noted that Peirce introduces his maxim as a means by which metaphysics may be "largely cleared up" (5.2); it is intended to lead toward (though not necessarily to attain) true opinion and thus a knowledge of reality. "The opinion which is fated to be ultimately agreed to by all who investigate, is what we mean by truth, and the object represented in the opinion is the real" (5.407).

2. William James is credited with calling attention to the term pragmatism and the maxim that defines it in a lecture of 1898. Though James cited Peirce's maxim, his own use diverged toward a principle for validating belief in addition to addressing metaphysical disputes. The position that he endorses (and which is generally shared by John Dewey and F. S. C. Schiller) is "that ideas (which themselves are but part of our experience) become true just in so far as they help us to get into satisfactory relation with other parts of our experience" (58). Peirce's maxim proved to be a fertile engenderer of doctrines that at least sounded similar and claimed the name pragmatism. A. O. Lovejoy, writing in 1908, just ten years after William James had revived the term and started it on its way to popularity, distinguished thirteen senses of pragmatism. Peirce's well-known reaction to the shifts in the meaning of his term was to abandon it, with Peircean irony, in an article in the 1905 *Monist*. "So then, the writer, finding his bantling 'pragmatism' so promoted, feels that it is time to kiss his child good-by and relinquish it to its higher destiny; while to serve the precise purpose of expressing the original definition, he begs to announce the birth of the word 'pragmaticism,' which is ugly enough to be safe from kidnappers" (5.414).

3. Richard Rorty's influential arguments against the possibility of meta-physics, of knowledge as an accurate representation of reality, or of any foundational theory of knowledge, as presented in *Philosophy and the Mirror of Nature* (1979), has subsequently come to be assimilated by Rorty to the tradition of pragmatism as understood by William James and John Dewey. Rorty's philosophical heroes in the 1979 volume are Wittgenstein, Heidegger, and Dewey, who "are in agreement that the notion of knowledge as accurate representation, made possible by special mental processes, and intelligible through a general theory of representation, needs to be abandoned" (6). Though Rorty there parallels his own view of philosophy with that of earlier pragmatists, it is only in slightly later essays like "Nineteenth-Century Idealism and Twentieth-Century Textualism" (see *Consequences of Pragmatism*) that he espouses the pragmatism of Dewey and especially William James. Rorty's position as pragmatist is best stated in the introduction to *Consequences of Pragmatism* (1982) in which he accepts William James's formulation: The true is "the name of whatever proves itself to be good in the way of belief, and good,

too, for definite, assignable reasons'' (xxv). Therefore, for Rortian pragmatism, ''true sentences are not true because they correspond to reality, and so there is no need to worry what sort of reality, if any, a given sentence corresponds to—no need to worry about what 'makes' it true'' (*Consequences*, xvi). This is explicitly a return to Jamesian, not Peircean, pragmatism. Where Peirce's pragmatism was a means of getting a clear conception of things—of understanding the meaning of a concept—Jamesian pragmatism is a means of defining what is true without regard to any notion of correspondence with reality. Though Rorty would presumably agree with Peirce's insistence that pragmatism ''will serve to show that almost every proposition of ontological metaphysics is either meaningless gibberish—one word being defined by other words, and they by still others, without any real conception ever being reached—or else is downright absurd'' (5.423), Rorty explicitly discounts Peirce's importance. Peirce's ''contribution to pragmatism was merely to have given it a name, and to have stimulated James'' (*Consequences*, 161). Hardly compatible with James's definition of truth is Peirce's: ''The opinion which is fated to be ultimately agreed to by all who investigate, is what we mean by truth, and the object represented in this opinion is the real'' (5.407). All forms of commentary on literature would for Rorty become part of an ongoing ''conversation'' of which the goal is edification rather than truth. ''I shall use 'edification' to stand for this project of finding new, better, more interesting, more fruitful ways of speaking'' (*Philosophy and the Mirror*, 360).

The new pragmatists' final position is similar to utilitarianism without the explicit principle of the greatest happiness of the greatest number as the criterion on which to make choices between alternatives. The central problem that has been pointed out in the Rortian/Jamesian or ''new'' pragmatism is the evident one: By what criteria can one judge what is ''good in the way of belief,'' or know whether the culture toward which pragmatism looks is better than the tradition of Platonic, Cartesian, or Kantian philosophy, or whether new ways of speaking are an improvement? In the words of Carl Rapp, ''the obstinate questioner who keeps asking what 'better' means is advised to change the subject. You will know it when you see it, he is told . . . you will just know it, it will feel better'' (130). The criticism that the new pragmatism envisions an essentially aimless conversation will be found in Anthony J. Cascardi's ''Geneaology of Pragmatism'': ''For Rorty . . . 'edification' is a rough synonym for 'abnormal discourse' (his term) and comes to mean something close to 'unbuilding.' As such, it provides no further or more detailed information about the nature of the ''conversation of mankind'' as he would envision it and works at cross purposes to the larger aims of pragmatism as Dewey imagined them to be'' (303). Charles Reeves writes, ''Rorty has yet to make his seem a road worth taking. There are in the new terrain of 'pragmatism' too few signposts, too few indications of the goals to be pursued or the motives which might prompt our pursuit'' (355).

The foremost literary critic claiming the title of pragmatist, Stanley Fish, expanded the argument that the interpretation of literature always depends on the conventions of an *interpretive community* in the final essays collected in *Is There a Text in This Class?* (1980) to broader claims against the possibility of theory having consequences. "Foundationalist theory has no consequences because its project cannot succeed, and antifoundationalist theory has no consequences because, as a belief about how we got our beliefs, it leaves untouched (at least in principle) the beliefs of whose history it is an explanation" ("Consequences," 115). Rorty emphasizes the impossibility of stepping outside language; Fish emphasizes the impossibility of getting outside one's beliefs and communally determined modes of thought and action.

One of the major criticisms of the Fishean view is obviously, again, that there are no criteria against which to judge arguments. Thus, Carl Rapp writes: "[N]o argument can succeed because of its cogency. If it wins, it just wins, and that is that" (134). As Rapp goes on to point out, such an attitude supports the view that all human endeavor is simply a struggle for power, while suggesting that the intellectual who understands that everything is just a game should simply look on to see which idealogy wins.

References

Cascardi, Anthony. "The Genealogy of Pragmatism." *Philosophy and Literature* 10 (October 1986): 295–302.
Fish, Stanley. "Consequences." *Critical Inquiry* 11 (March 1985): 433–58. Reprinted in *Against Theory: Literary Studies and the New Pragmatism*, ed. W. J. T. Mitchell. Chicago: University of Chicago Press, 1985.
———. *Is There a Text in This Class?* Cambridge, Mass.: Harvard University Press, 1980.
James, William. *Pragmatism: A New Name for Some Old Ways of Thinking.* 1907; London: Longmans, Green, 1940.
Lovejoy, Arthur O. *The Thirteen Pragmatisms and Other Essays.* Baltimore: Johns Hopkins University Press, 1963. All these essays are related to pragmatism in some way.
Peirce, Charles Sanders. *Collected Papers.* Ed. Charles Hartshorne and Paul Weiss (vols. 1–6) and A. W. Burks (vols. 7–8). Cambridge, Mass.: Harvard University Press, 1931–35, 1958. Volume 5 is primarily dedicated to pragmatism and pragmaticism. The collected papers are conventionally cited by volume and paragraph numbers. A new edition of Peirce is appearing; see Sources of Additional Information below.
Rapp, Carl. "Ideology and the New Pragmatism." *Modern Age: A Quarterly Review* 31 (Spring 1987): 125–37.
Reeves, Charles Eric. "Deconstruction, Language, Motive, Rortian Pragmatism and the Uses of 'Literature.' " *Journal of Aesthetics and Art Criticism* 44 (Summer 1986): 351–56.
Rorty, Richard. *Consequences of Pragmatism (Essays 1972–1980).* Minneapolis: University of Minnesota Press, 1982.
———. *Philosophy and the Mirror of Nature.* Princeton, N.J.: Princeton University Press, 1979.

Sources of Additional Information

A useful survey of the development of philosophical pragmatism is H. S. Thayer's *Meaning and Action: A Critical History of Pragmatism* (1968; Indianapolis: Hackett, 1981).

A new edition of Peirce's writings arranged in chronological order is in process of publication through the Indiana University Press under the general editorship of Max H. Fisch; volume 1 appeared in 1982; twenty volumes are projected. For a survey of Peirce's thought in all the areas he considered, see Thomas A. Goudge's *The Thought of C. S. Peirce* (Toronto: University of Toronto Press, 1950).

For consideration of the relationship between Peirce's doctrine of signs and pragmatism, see John J. Fitzgerald's *Peirce's Theory of Signs as Foundation for Pragmatism* (The Hague: Mouton, 1966); Max H. Fisch's "Peirce's General Theory of Signs," in *Sight, Sound, and Sense*, ed. T. A. Sebeok (Bloomington: University of Indiana Press, 1978); and Arthur Skidmore's "Peirce and Semiotics: An Introduction to Peirce's Theory of Signs" in *Semiotic Themes*, ed. Richard T. De George (Lawrence: University of Kansas Press, 1981).

The new pragmatism has been much influenced by Thomas Kuhn's *The Structure of Scientific Revolutions* (1962; Chicago: University of Chicago Press, 1970). Kuhn conceives of science as a succession of explanatory paradigms rather than the progressive discovery of the nature of reality, each paradigm ushered in by a burst of *abnormal science* followed by the tidying up of the paradigm in *normal science*. An influential argument against the importance of literary theory from a new pragmatist position is that of Walter Benn Michaels and Steven Knapp in "Against Theory" (*Critical Inquiry* 8, Summer 1982: 723–42). This essay was reprinted together with a number of responses as *Against Theory*, ed. W. J. T. Mitchell (Chicago: University of Chicago Press, 1985). For the effect of the revived and revised pragmatism on editing practices, see Leonard N. Neufeldt, "Neopragmatism and Convention in Textual Editing: With Examples from the Editing of Thoreau's Autograph Journal" (*Analytical and Enumerative Bibliography* n.s. 1, 1987: 227–36). Frank Lentricchia's "The Return of William James" (*Cultural Critique* 4, Fall 1986: 5–31) presents a "new historical" (anticapitalist) case for the importance of the renewed interest in William James while disagreeing with the conservative ramifications of the new pragmatism generally. Cornel West's *The American Evasion of Philosophy: A Genealogy of Pragmatism* (Madison: University of Wisconsin Press, 1989) combines a historically oriented defense of American pragmatism with a vision of that pragmatism as a weapon against destructive forces in American culture. "The fundamental argument of this book is that the evasion of epistemology-centered philosophy—from Emerson to Rorty—results in a conception of philosophy as a form of cultural criticism in which the meaning of America is put forward by intellectuals in response to distinct social and cultural crises" (5).

Pragmatism and its adjectival form lends itself to individual uses in or related to literary discourse: for an example of pragmatism in its least specialized sense (with the meaning "practical"), see Terry Eagleton's "Two Approaches in the Sociology of Literature" (*Critical Inquiry* 14, Spring 1988: 469–76) in which the political use is regarded as the pragmatic one. Jürgen Habermas's "universal pragmatics" is the principle that "anyone acting communicatively" raises universal validity claims (see "What Is Universal Pragmatics?" in *Communication and the Evolution of Society*, trans. Thomas McCarthy, 1976; Boston, 1979).

PSYCHOLOGICAL/PSYCHOANALYTIC CRITICISM   The use of a psychological or psychoanalytic theory to explain one or more of the following:
the general processes of literary creativity; the origin of the literary work in
the individual author's mind; the thoughts and actions of a character in a
literary work; the structure of a literary work; or readers' responses.

Psychoanalytical criticism only becomes possible with Sigmund Freud's publication of *The Interpretation of Dreams* in 1900; psychological criticism as a
name for a specific approach to literature is hardly known before that. However,
assumptions about psychological phenomena have always had a substantial place
in commentary on literature. The mental activities underlying literary creativity,
the sources of readers' interest in the characters and events comprising literary
works, the appeal of certain generic forms, and the degree of both the agreement
and disagreement among readers of the same text naturally engender speculation.
Moreover, both the literary critic and the psychoanalyst are connoisseurs of the
symbolic. What Peter Brooks has written about the reason for literary interest
in psychoanalysis applies, in fact, to all theories of mental activity: ''We continue
to dream of a convergence of psychoanalysis and literary criticism because we
sense that there ought to be, that there must be, some correspondence between
literature and psychic process, that aesthetic structure and form, including literary
tropes, must somehow coincide with the psychic structures and operations they
both evoke and appeal to'' (4).

Socrates considers the source of creative activity in Plato's *Ion*: ''For all good
poets, epic as well as lyric, compose their beautiful poems not as works of art,
but because they are inspired and possessed. And as the Corybantian revelers
when they dance are not in their right mind, so the lyric poets are not in their
right mind when they are composing their beautiful strains (1:223; 533d–534a).
Coleridge's explorations of the processes of the poet's imagination belong to the
same line of inquiry. Although in *The Lives of the Poets* Samuel Johnson consciously keeps lives and works separate, there is evidently some assumption of
a relationship behind the very idea of such a conjunction. The most influential
French critic of the nineteenth century, Charles Augustine Sainte-Beuve, was
committed to the assimilation of biography and literary creation. A different sort
of non-Freudian literary-critical exploration is John Livingston Lowes's pursuit
of the sources of Coleridge's ''Rime of the Ancient Mariner'' and ''Kubla Khan''
in *The Road to Xanadu*. The ''humours'' psychology of the Renaissance is the
best-known example of a pre-Freudian mode of exploring the springs of *characters'* personalities and actions. I. A. Richards's theory of art as the harmonizing
of as many apparently conflicting impulses as possible is an early-twentieth-
century, but not directly Freudian, approach to the value *readers* find in literature.

Brief accounts of Freudian theory easily fall into distorting oversimplification.
However, Freud's own single-sentence summary of 1923 reads: ''The assumption
that there are unconscious mental processes, the recognition of the theory of
resistance and repression, the appreciation of the importance of sexuality and of
the Oedipus complex—these constitute the principal subject-matter of psycho-

analysis and the foundations of its theory'' (18:247). To this must be added Freud's belief that the unconscious is like a reservoir, storing experiences, especially rationally inadmissable fears and socially unacceptable (largely sexual) desires, from at least the moment of birth; and that recognition by the conscious ego of the unacceptable contents of the unconscious is blocked by the socially created censor, the superego; however; these contents gain expression in disguised forms through compulsive actions and, what is of greatest importance for their interpretation, in dreams. The central psychical strategies for slipping past the superego are *substitution*, in which a similar but acceptable object is substituted for the repressed one, and *condensation*, which is a fusion of several meanings into a single image or word. The relationship to literature that immediately leaps from this Freudian theorizing is the parallel between unconscious fantasies and their manifestation in the actual dream, on the one hand, and, on the other, the repressed fantasies of the writer and their transmogrified manifestation in the texts produced by the writer. This line of thought can suggest that the writer is especially poorly adapted to reality, a victim of fantasies that can only be controlled by fashioning them into poems, plays, or novels. Freud at times seems to incline to this view, but at other times he regards artists and creative writers as differing from other humans primarily through the possession of a capacity for giving interest to the form in which their fantasies are presented. Louis Fraiberg summarizes this view: "The writer is, naturally, subject to the same motivating forces as everyone else; he differs in his as yet unexplained ability to embody his fantasies in forms which are attractive to others" (31).

Freud himself applied his theory to, and found confirmation in, literature. In addition to *Oedipus Rex*, he considers the motivation of characters in *Hamlet*, *Macbeth*, *The Merchant of Venice*, *The Brothers Karamazov*, *Rosmersholm*, and C. F. Myers's *Die Richterin*. *Delusion and Dreams in Jensen's Gradiva* (1907) analyzes the dreams of the character Norbert Hanold. In this latter study, Freud writes that "creative writers are valuable allies and their evidence is to be prized highly, for they are apt to know a whole host of things between heaven and earth of which our philosophy has not yet let us dream" (9:8). Freud's most generalized commentary on the sources of literary creativity is the essay "Creative Writers and Day-Dreaming." "The creative writer does the same as the child at play. He creates a world of phantasy which he takes very seriously— that is, which he invests with large amounts of emotion—separating it sharply from reality" (9:144). Moreover, "[a] strong experience in the present awakens in the creative writer a memory of an earlier experience (usually belonging to his childhood) from which there now proceeds a wish which finds its fulfillment in the creative work" (9:151).

Two persons close to Freud have produced the most often cited early applications of his theories. Ernest Jones's "The Oedipus Complex as an Explanation of Hamlet's Mystery" (1910) begins by explaining Hamlet's actions but moves to the attribution of similar mental conflicts to Shakespeare himself; Marie Bonaparte's *Life and Works of Edgar Allen Poe: A Psycho-Analytic Interpretation*

(1933) traces practically everything in Poe's works to an unconscious necrophilia resulting from a fixation on his mother, who died before he was three.

The literary-critical uses of, partial borrowings from, and modifications to Freud's thought have been expectedly various (American critics have been particularly responsive to Freudian theory). Van Wyck Brooks's *The Ordeal of Mark Twain* (1920) is not wholly psychoanalytical in its method, but it calls on Freud to help explain the frustrations and bitterness Brooks finds in Twain. Ludwig Lewisohn's *Expression in America* (1932) seeks psychoanalytical support in condemning American Puritanism and its effect on American literature. Lionel Trilling's "Freud and Literature" (1940) is an influential essay that attempts a balanced account of Freud's contribution. Edmund Wilson's *The Wound and the Bow* (1941) draws on certain portions of Freud's work to argue for the connection between neurosis and artistic power—the essays on Dickens, Kipling, and Hemingway have had considerable influence. Hanns Sachs's *The Creative Unconscious* (1942) gives particular attention to the importance of suitable form (in prosody, narrative progression, diction, and so forth) in the expression of the transformed unconscious fantasy.

Charles Mauron inaugurated a long series of studies of the *personal myths*—the particular contributions of a writer's unconscious—with *Mallarmé l'Obscur* (1941). Frederick Hoffman's *Freudianism and the Literary Mind* (1945) pursues the differential influence of Freudianism on James Joyce, D. H. Lawrence, Sherwood Anderson, Waldo Frank, Franz Kafka, and Thomas Mann. Ernst Kris's *Psychoanalytic Exploration in Art* (1952) gives much more emphasis to the role of the conscious mind (or ego) than Freud. In *Fiction and the Unconscious* (1957), Simon Lesser goes yet further in tracing the interplay of the instincts with the ego and superego; his particular contribution, however, is in shifting the focus from the creative process to the role that the topography of the psyche plays in the response of the reader. Leslie Fiedler's *Love and Death in the American Novel* (1960) draws heavily but quite indirectly on Freud and Jung (their names scarcely appear). For Fiedler, like Van Wyck Brooks, the major traits of American literature emerge from the absence of any "real sexuality" in American life: the result is a largely concealed gothicism. Norman Holland's *The Dynamics of Literary Response* (1968) is like Lesser's study in seeking to understand the reader's response rather than the creative process or the characteristics of the resulting text, but it gives much more emphasis to the gratification of fantasy. "In effect, the literary work dreams a dream for us. It embodies and evokes in us a central fantasy; then it manages and controls that fantasy by devices that, were they in a mind, we would call defenses, but, being on the page, we call 'form' " (75). Holland's 1975 book, *5 Readers Reading*, moves from the general effect of literature to an argument that each reader responds in terms of a personal *identity theme* which represents his or her characteristic way of coping with experience. Harold Bloom's *The Anxiety of Influence* (1973) transforms the individual's rivalry with the father into a complex six-stage response to some earlier writer who is both model and competitor to be transcended.

Until the 1970s, the primary rival to an essentially Freudian psychoanalytical approach to literature was that of Carl Jung. Rather than concentrating on the lasting effects of infantile sexuality in the unconscious, Jung finds a universal mental structure of responses, the *collective unconscious*. Jung's appeal has been twofold. First, what is universal is not a set of reactions to the fact of sexual differentiation but a set of tendencies to respond in similar ways to certain archetypal situations. The basis for symbolic relationships within the psyche, and therefore symbolic structures in literature, becomes much broader. It is important here to note that the inherited archetypes are not themselves images— rather, each may be represented by a variety of symbolic images. Second, even though the Oedipal conflict and its expression is for Freud unavoidable, and therefore not in itself pathological, these experiences do constitute the source of pathological disturbances; to find this conflict at the center of a literary work suggests an uncomfortably close relationship between mental disturbances and literature. Jung thus writes of the analysis of literature: "The psychologist who follows Freud will of course be inclined to take the writings in question as a problem in pathology. . . . [H]e will try to account for the curious images of the vision by calling them cover-figures and by supposing that they represent an attempted concealment of the basic experience" (183). The word vision here is important: the true artist, for Jung, is not alleviating psychic discomfort but rather pursuing a vision.

The very conception of archetypes leads the critic to search for mythical patterns rather than repressed desires underlying literary works. The best known adaptation of Jung—and it is an adaptation that departs in certain ways from Jungian theory—is Maud Bodkin's *Archetypal Patterns in Poetry* (1934). (For an appreciative evaluation of Bodkin and the degree to which she avoids a facile reduction of literary construction to Jungian patterns, see Walter Sutton's chapter, "Psychological and Myth Criticism," in *Modern American Criticism.*) More recent is Bettina Knapp's *A Jungian Approach to Literature* (1984), which analyzes ten texts drawn from different periods and cultures. In proper Jungian fashion, Knapp carefully distinguishes the general background (the *ectype*) for each text from the archetypes operative in it.

Although specifically Freudian and Jungian criticism have continued to appear, both are generally on the defensive by the 1970s. Frederick Crews's account of Freudian literary criticism, "Reductionism and Its Discontents" (1975), which distinguishes between the necessarily reductive nature of any critical analysis and the reductionism that fails to admit the fact of reductiveness, states a position that might have been endorsed by the majority of those making use of the psychoanalytical approaches at the time. However, the 1970s saw the beginning of a wide dissemination of the thought of the French psychoanalyst Jacques Lacan, who devoted himself to rethinking Freud in a way that is both a return to the essence of Freud's insights and a significant revision of them.

In a 1976 essay, Morse Peckham called for a rapproachement between psychology and language. Psychology "must begin with higher cognitive activity, including its own. And that means it must begin with language, which is not the instrument of higher cognitive activity but is higher cognitive activity itself'' (64). Lacan's development of psychoanalysis in this direction, long in the making, was then just beginning to achieve significant recognition outside France: the English translation of a selection from Lacan's *Ecrits* appeared in 1977, five years after a volume of *Yale French Studies* (48) was devoted to Lacan. Associated with the structuralist movement through his concentration on the role of language in mental processes, Lacan finds that Freud's understanding of the function of language, both as the medium through which psychoanalysis occurs and as a structuring mechanism within the mind, has been largely underestimated. Lacan's writing is unusually difficult—so much so that his commentators, balked in translating his arguments into other terms, tend to repeat variations of his formulations. In essence, however, Lacan regards language as that which allows humans to think about, and not simply speak about, a reality (*the Real*) that is distanced from them by the very process that produces language. (Cf. Saussure's statement on language's power to give form to what would otherwise be a chaos of responses to sense reports: "Without language, thought is a vague, uncharted nebula. There are no pre-existing ideas, and nothing is distinct before the appearance of language," 112.) The unconscious is formed through the structuring of human desire by means of language. Further, the acquisition of language by the individual divides the *Imaginary* state, in which the child is aware of an (illusory) self, from the *Symbolic* state that makes possible participation in the social structure.

Lacan's emphasis on the role of language is a significant reorientation that fits his psychoanalytical thought comfortably into the intense contemporary focus on the powers of language—in theories of literature and human activity generally—and allows a relatively easy melding with deconstructive thought. At the same time, whereas older psychoanalytic studies were challenged for not taking the aesthetic qualities of a text sufficiently into account, there is skepticism among many critics today about the existence of specifically aesthetic qualities.

Since a common deconstructive and poststructuralist move is the application of a theory or strategy to itself, it is not surprising to encounter essays like Jacques Derrida's "Coming into One's Own," which reads Freud in Freudian terms or his "The Purveyor of Truth," which treats Lacan in a somewhat Lacanian manner, as well as Barbara Johnson's "The Frame of Reference: Poe, Lacan, Derrida," which provides a deconstructive reading of Derrida's deconstructive reading of Lacan's psychoanalytical reading of Poe. Careful readers without Lacan's investment in psychoanalysis or Derrida or Johnson's investment in deconstruction have also been reading Freud simply as a textual construction. Stanley Fish's "Withholding the Missing Portion: Power, Meaning, and Persuasion in Freud's 'The Wolf-Man,' " discusses Freud's famous analysis of the primal scene lying behind the wolf-man's neuroses as, finally, a triumph of rhetorical persuasion:

> One might say then that at the conclusion of the case history the primal scene emerges triumphant as both the end of the story and its self-authenticating origin; but what

is really triumphant is not this particular scene, which after all might well have assumed a quite different shape if the analysis had taken the slightest of turns, but the discursive power of which and by which it has been constructed. (938)

Christine Brooke-Rose, who is skeptical of the value of psychoanalytical theory in casting light on literature, also encourages reading such theory as literature. "Thus it seems to me more dangerous . . . to 'use' psychoanalysis in literary criticism, but fascinating and enriching to consider it, at its best, as a literary text, as Nietzsche's texts are literary texts" (35). There is also an increasing tendency to read in both directions. Shoshanna Felman, a strongly psychoanalytically oriented critic, has become well known not only as an advocate of bringing French and American psychoanalytic theory into dialogue but of making the relation between psychoanalysis and literature truly mutual in ways that allow each to illuminate the other. "We would like to suggest that, in the same way that psychoanalysis points to the unconsciousness of literature, *literature, in its turn, is the unconscious of psychoanalysis*" (10).

References

Bloom, Harold. *The Anxiety of Influence*. London: Oxford University Press, 1973.

Bodkin, Maud. *Archetypal Patterns in Poetry: Psychological Studies of Imagination*. London: Oxford, 1934. Essential for the psychoanalytic approach to myth.

Bonaparte, Marie. *The Life and Works of Edgar Allen Poe: A Psycho-Analytic Interpretation*. Trans. J. Rodker. London: Imago, 1949. Original French edition, 1933.

Brooke-Rose, Christine. "Id is, is Id?" In *Discourse in Psychoanalysis and Literature*.

Brooks, Peter. "The Idea of Psychoanalytic Literary Criticism." In *Discourse in Psychoanalysis and Literature*. "The detour through psychoanalysis forces the critic to respond to the erotics of form, that is to an engagement with the psychic investments of rhetoric, the dramas of desire played out in tropes" (17).

Brooks, Van Wyck. *The Ordeal of Mark Twain*. New York: E. P. Dutton, 1920.

Crews, Frederick. "Reductionism and Its Discontents." In *Out of My System: Psychoanalysis, Ideology, and Critical Method*. New York: Oxford University Press, 1975. Reprinted from *Critical Inquiry* 1 (May 1975): 547–58. All the essays making up the volume are of interest both in themselves and as a record of changes in Crews's understanding of psychoanalytical criticism over a period of years.

Derrida, Jacques. "Coming into One's Own." In *Psychoanalysis and the Question of the Text*.

————. "The Purveyor of Truth." In *The Post Card: From Socrates to Freud and Beyond*. Trans. A. Bass. Chicago: University of Chicago Press, 1987. Partially reprinted in *The Purloined Poe: Lacan, Derrida & Psychoanalytic Reading*. Original essay published in French in 1975.

Discourse in Psychoanalysis and Literature. Ed. S. Rimmon-Kenan. London: Methuen, 1987.

Felman, Shoshanna. "To Open the Question." In *Literature and Psychoanalysis; The Question of Reading: Otherwise*, ed. Shoshanna Felman. Baltimore: Johns Hopkins University Press, 1982.

Fiedler, Leslie. *Love and Death in the American Novel*. New York: Stein and Day, 1960, 1966.

Fish, Stanley. "Withholding the Missing Portion: Power, Meaning and Persuasion in Freud's 'The Wolf-Man.' " *Times Literary Supplement*, 29 August 1986, 935–38. An expanded version appears in Fish's *Doing What Comes Naturally*. Durham, N.C.: Duke University Press, 1989.

Fraiberg, Louis. *Psychoanalysis and American Literary Criticism*. Detroit, Mich.: Wayne State University Press, 1960. Fraiberg summarizes Freud's views in the opening chapter and gives a chapter each to nine American critics who made use of Freudian insights.

Freud, Sigmund. *The Complete Psychological Works*. Ed. J. Strachey. 24 vols. London: Hogarth Press, 1959.

Hoffman, Frederick J. *Freudianism and the Literary Mind*. Baton Rouge: Louisiana State University Press, 1945.

Holland, Norman. *The Dynamics of Literary Response*. New York: Oxford University Press, 1968.

————. *5 Readers Reading*. New Haven, Conn.: Yale University Press, 1975.

Johnson, Barbara. "The Frame of Reference: Poe, Lacan, Derrida." In *Psychoanalysis and the Question of the Text*. Reprinted in *Untying the Text*, ed. R. Young. London: Routledge and Kegan Paul, 1981; also reprinted in *The Purloined Poe*.

Jones, Ernest. "The Oedipus Complex as an Explanation of Hamlet's Mystery." *The American Journal of Psychology* 21 (January 1910): 2–113. Expanded in *Hamlet and Oedipus*. New York: W. W. Norton, 1949.

Jung, Carl. *Modern Man in Search of a Soul*. Trans. W. S. Dell and C. F. Baynes. New York: Harcourt, Brace, 1933. See especially Chapter 8, "Psychology and Literature." "The secret of artistic creation and of the effectiveness of art is to be found in a return to the state of *participation mystique*—to that level of experience at which it is man who lives, not the individual, and at which the weal or woe of the single human being does not count, but only human existence" (198–99).

Knapp, Bettina. *A Jungian Approach to Literature*. Carbondale: Southern Illinois University Press, 1984.

Kris, Ernst. *Psychoanalytic Explorations in Art*. New York: International Universities Press, 1952.

Lacan, Jacques. *Ecrits: A Selection*. Trans. A. Sheridan. New York: Norton: 1977. Original French edition, 1966.

Lesser, Simon O. *Fiction and the Unconscious*. Boston: Beacon Press, 1957.

> It is my assumption that as we read we unconsciously *understand* at least some of a story's secret significance; to some extent our enjoyment is a product of this understanding. But some readers go on to try to account for the effect a story has had upon them. . . . It is in connection with these later critical activities . . . that psychoanalytical concepts are likely to prove invaluable. (15)

Lewisohn, Ludwig. *Expression in America*. New York: Harper, 1932. Later titled *The Story of American Literature*.

Lowes, John Livingstone. *The Road to Xanadu*. Boston: Houghton Mifflin, 1927.

Mauron, Charles. *Mallarmé l'Obscur*. Paris: Denöel, 1941.

Peckham, Morse. "Psychology and Literature." In *Literary Criticism and Psychology*, ed. Joseph Strelka. University Park: Pennsylvania State University Press, 1976.

Plato. *Ion*. In vol. 1 of *The Dialogues of Plato*. Trans. B. Jowett. 4 vols. New York: Scribner, 1911.

Psychoanalysis and the Question of the Text. Ed. Geoffrey Hartman. Baltimore: Johns Hopkins University Press, English Institute Papers, 1976–77, 1978.

The Purloined Poe: Lacan, Derrida & Psychoanalytic Reading. Ed. J. P. Miller and W. J. Richardson. Baltimore: Johns Hopkins University Press, 1988. Brings together Poe's "The Purloined Letter," Lacan's seminar on the story, analyses of the seminar, Derrida on Lacan, and other essays on either Poe's story or the readings of it, including portions of Marie Bonaparte's psychoanalytic study of Poe.

Sachs, Hanns. *The Creative Unconscious*. Boston: Sci-Art Publishers, 1942.

Saussure, Ferdinand. *Course in General Linguistics*. Ed. Charles Bally and Albert Sechehaye; trans. W. Baskin. New York: McGraw-Hill, 1966. Original French edition, 1915.

Sutton, Walter. *Modern American Criticism*. Englewood Cliffs, N.J.: Prentice-Hall, 1963.

Trilling, Lionel. "Freud and Literature." *The Kenyon Review* 2 (Spring 1940): 152–73; revised version printed in *The Liberal Imagination*. New York: Viking Press, 1950.

Wilson, Edmund. *The Wound and the Bow*. New York: Oxford University Press, 1941. The central assumption of the volume is fully evident in the final essay: "one feels in the *Philoctetes* a more general and fundamental idea: the conception of superior strength as inseparable from disability" (235).

Sources of Additional Information

Peter Gay's *Freud: A Life for Our Time* includes a fine bibliographical essay (New York: Norton, 1988). Elizabeth Wright's "Modern Psychological Criticism" in *Modern Literary Theory*, ed. Ann Jefferson and David Robey (London: Batsford, 1986), gives an excellent overview of the relation of literature criticism to psychoanalysis. The first fifty pages of Norman Holland's *Psychoanalysis and Shakespeare* (New York: McGraw-Hill, 1966) comprise a useful, if highly optimistic, summary of the application of Freud to literature. "Quite simply, it has become possible in this century to answer with some certainty the traditional puzzles about literature: What is the nature of inspiration? The creative process? How do we respond to literature? . . . How does literature have a moral effect? (3). *Holland's Guide to Psychoanalytic Psychology and Literature-and-Psychology* (New York: Oxford University Press, 1990) is, as its title suggests, a quite personal guide to material treating the application of psychoanalytic theory to literature.

For a thoughtful, balanced examination of the values and limits of the application of psychoanalytic methods to literature, see Meredith Anne Skura's *The Literary Use of the Psychoanalytic Process* (New Haven, Conn.: Yale University Press, 1981).

A collection of historically important essays on Freud from a literary point of view stretching from Leonard Woolf in 1914 to Harold Bloom in 1978 has been gathered by Perry Meisel in *Freud: A Collection of Critical Essays* (Englewood Cliffs, N.J.: Prentice-Hall, 1981). Claudia C. Morrison's *Freud and the Critic* (Chapel Hill: University of North Carolina Press, 1968) is an interesting history of reaction to Freud, primarily in the United States and of early attempts at critical application. Appendix A, "A Chronology of Events Relevant to the Acceptance of Freud's Ideas in the United States," is useful.

Two rich essays by Jung explicitly distinguish his mode of approaching literature from that of Freud, elucidate the difference between *introverted* or *psychological* and *extraverted* or *visionary* literature, and describe the appeal of the archetype: "On the Relation of Analytical Psychology to Poetry" (1922) and "Psychology and Literature" (1930).

PSYCHOLOGICAL/PSYCHOANALYTIC CRITICISM

Both are found in *The Spirit in Man, Art, and Literature* (trans. R. F. C. Hull), in vol. 15 of *The Collected Works* (New York: Pantheon, 1953–). For a helpful essay on the use of Jung in literary criticism, see James Baird's "Jungian Psychology in Criticism" in *Literary Criticism and Psychology*, ed. Joseph Strelka (University Park: Pennsylvania State University Press, 1976). *Psychological Perspectives on Literature: Freudian Dissidents and Non-Freudians*, ed. Joseph Natoli (Hamden, Conn.: Archon, 1984) collects essays applying the thought of Adler, Jung, Reich, and Fromm to literature.

For a condensed criticism of Norman Holland's theory of identity themes in readers, see Jonathan Culler's "Prolegomena to a Theory of Reading" in *The Reader in the Text*, ed. Susan R. Suleiman and Inge Crosman (Princeton, N.J.: Princeton University Press, 1980).

The essays primarily by and about Lacan in *Yale French Studies* 48 (1972) have remained seminal. Malcolm Bowie's "Jacques Lacan" in *Structuralism and Since*, ed. J. Sturrock (Oxford: Oxford University Press, 1979), is a clearly written introduction to Lacan. *Lacan and Narration: The Psychoanalytic Difference in Narrative Theory*, ed. Robert Con Davis (Baltimore: Johns Hopkins University Press, 1983), is a useful collection of essays by various hands (originally published in *Modern Language Notes* 98, December 1983: 843–1036). Davis's introductory essay gives the flavor of the whole.

> Narration—irremediably diachronic *and* synchronic—repeats and represents unconscious desires in the only way the unconscious can be known: as a sequence of opportunities for linguistic substitution and (re)combination. The potential for continuity and unity in such sequences makes possible the "gaps" or "lapses" that indicate the "Other" scene of signification, the repressed scene of writing not a part of manifest narration but which (like a buoy, or series of buoys) holds it up and enables it to exist at all. (853)

Also useful for an understanding of Lacan are Shoshanna Felman's *Jacques Lacan and the Adventure of Insight* (Cambridge, Mass.: Harvard University Press, 1987) and *The Works of Jacques Lacan: An Introduction*, by Bice Benvenuto and Roger Kennedy (London: Free Association Books, 1986).

Peter Brooks's *Reading for the Plot* (New York: Knopf, 1984) is an influential application of psychoanalytical theory to the structure of narrative.

For approaches to myth that acknowledge the work of Freud and Jung and yet seek to go beyond it, see Richard Chase's *Quest for Myth* (Baton Rouge: Louisiana State University Press, 1949) and Erich Fromm's *The Forgotten Language* (New York: Holt, Rinehart and Winston, 1951). Fromm writes: "The myths of the Babylonians, Indians, Egyptians, Hebrews, Greeks are written in the same language as those of the Ashantis or the Trukese. The dreams of someone living today in New York or Paris are the same as the dreams reported from people living some thousand years ago in Athens or in Jerusalem" (7).

Françoise Meltzer's essay on the term "Unconscious" in *Critical Terms for Literary Study*, ed. Frank Lentricchia and Thomas McLaughlin (Chicago: University of Chicago Press, 1900) is an excellent summary of its use in Freud and Lacan.

R

READER   1. The actual, "real" reader; the person who is reading or has read a text. 2. The potential reader as assumed or imagined by the author, often designated as "the intended reader." 3. The reader—or, more properly, the reader's responses—as guided or implied by the text, most often designated "the implied reader."

For theories of the ways in which actual readers interpret and react to what they read, see READER-RESPONSE; *for further consideration of what readers must know to understand what they read, see* CONTEXT.

1. The reader considered in general may be regarded as simply an abstract function, as in Roman Jakobson's famous six-factor schema for any use of language (spoken or written) in which an *addresser* sends a *message*, by means of a *contact*, to an *addressee* within a *context* using an at least partially common CODE that is a communicative channel, such as a text. Any actual use of language brings all six factors into play.

Less abstractly, to think of a reader as a function is quite different from thinking of the reader as a receptacle for receiving messages. That the reader is not simply a passive recipient, taking in a text as an object, but an active contributor to the process of reading is implied in both the long history of HERMENEUTICS and the nineteenth-century discussions of HISTORICISM. As Wolfgang Iser states in *The Act of Reading*, "If interpretation has set itself the task of conveying the meaning of a literary text, obviously the text itself cannot have already formulated that meaning" (18). Understanding is possible only if readers bring the knowledge and experience to the text that will allow them to recognize implied links and fill in omitted information on the basis of what they know to be usual.

But the concept of a reader's mind as not simply reconstructing an encoded meaning but shaping the outcome of the encounter with the text, which leads to the present variety of reader-response theories, is more radical. It is not, however, an uncommon position in the first half of this century. Though the reader's contribution did not begin to be formally explored until the 1960s, its importance seems to have been on its way to general recognition until the New Critical focus on the autonomy of the text pushed the reader as well as the author into the background (see NEW CRITICISM). This has so frequently been forgotten that it is worthwhile to cite instances. One may begin with George Edward Woodberry in 1913: "The fact is that a work of art, being once created and expressed, externalized, is gone from the artist's mind and returns to the world of nature; it becomes a part of our external world, and we treat it precisely as we treat the rest of that world, as mere material for our own artist-life which goes on in our own minds and souls in the exercise of our own powers in their limitations"(66). Woodberry further speaks of the "paradox which I often maintain, that it is not the poet, but the reader, who writes the poem" (71). Ernest Kellett writes in 1933: "It is a truth often forgotten, and yet obvious on the least consideration, that every book has many authors. There is the so-called writer, and there are the readers, every one of whom contributes his share: it is the combination of these that makes the alloy we call 'book' " (65). T. S. Eliot succinctly states in *The Use of Poetry and the Use of Criticism* (1933), "The poem's existence is somewhere between the writer and the reader; it has a reality which is not simply the reality of what the writer is trying to 'express,' or of his experience of writing it, or of the experience of the reader or of the writer as reader" (30). Louise Rosenblatt's *Literature as Exploration* (1938) is based on the principle that all literary experience is an "*interaction* between the reader and the work" (42); the necessity of the interaction is underlined by Rosenblatt's distinction in her later *The Reader, the Text, the Poem* (1978) between the text as a set of signs and the poem as the result of the reader's interaction with the text (12). From H. W. Leggett's *The Idea in Fiction* of 1934: "In truth, the Idea of a story only takes final shape when the story is written and it is only completely communicated when the reader shares, collaborates, in the work of creation" (153). Finally, F. W. Bateson wrote in 1950, "Criticism has not paid sufficient attention to this problem of the poets' audiences. . . . The first point, then, that must be made is that a poem only becomes a poem, in the ordinary sense of the word, when it is read. Up to that stage it is only so many black marks on a piece of white paper" (69).

That readers necessarily must draw on their own experience in the interaction suggests that there is, in fact, no generic reader, only readers of various abilities, interests, and backgrounds at various temporal and cultural distances from the context in which the text they may read was produced. Walter Slatoff develops this point strongly in *With Respect to Readers* (1970). "When we begin to contemplate the extent to which individual differences shape literary experiences it becomes understandable why we have clutched so desperately at theories and ways of talking which permit us to ignore those differences and have tried to relegate them to provinces labeled 'psychology' or 'taste' '' (31–32). Since reading is an act, readers' experiences of the text will necessarily be active, not passive; Slatoff therefore explores the variety of reasons for which readers may differ in finding certain aspects of a text irritating, pleasurable, questionable, intellectually stimulating, or offensive. (Though Slatoff is among those emphasizing the active role of the reader, he does not offer a reader-response theory or privilege the values of a certain kind of reading, and is therefore not usually noticed as a reader-response critic.)

2. If most communication, especially that through written texts, requires not only a sharing of the language (lexical items and syntactical rules) but the sharing of certain conventions, a certain amount of knowledge, and at least some attitudes, the author evidently must proceed on the basis of assumptions about the readers that he or she anticipates. Peter Rabinowitz designates these anticipated readers as the *authorial audience*; authors ''design their books rhetorically for some more or less specific *hypothetical* audience, which I call the *authorial audience*. Artistic choices are based upon these assumptions—conscious or unconscious—about readers, and to a certain extent, artistic success depends on their shrewdness, on the degree to which actual and authorial audience overlap'' (21). M. M. Bakhtin in particular has insisted on the author's sense of readers' likely responses:

> The listener and his response are regularly taken into account when it comes to everyday dialogue and rhetoric, but every other sort of discourse as well is oriented toward an understanding that is ''responsive.'' . . . Responsive understanding is a fundamental force, one that participates in the formulation of discourse, and it is moreover an *active* understanding, one that discourse senses as resistance or support enriching the discourse. (280)

3. Wolfgang Iser is responsible for the currency of the term *implied reader*: ''This term incorporates both the prestructuring of the potential meaning by the text, and the reader's actualization of this potential through the reading process. It refers to the active nature of this process—which will vary historically from one age to another—and not to a typology of possible authors'' (*Implied Reader*, xii). As a number of critics have pointed out (see especially Samuel Weber's ''Caught in the Act of Reading''), there are difficulties in this formulation. First, since Iser endows texts with a degree of indeterminacy that allows a range of possible interpretations, the structure of the text (which is determinate) would seem to have to be differentiated from the responses (*realizations, actualizations,* or *concretizations,* in variations of the terminology that Iser has adopted from Roman Ingarden) that are to some degree indeterminate. Moreover, Iser at times writes of the ''prestructuring of the potential meaning'' as a quality of the text without reference to the author while at other times he writes as though accepting the intentionalist view that the structure of a text reflects, though it may not fully or effectively incorporate, an author's active intentions (see INTENTION).

Jon-K. Adams has pointed out another kind of confusion, exemplified by W. Daniel Wilson, who has himself identified the ambiguities in Iser's discussion of the implied reader. Wilson comments at one point that the implied reader "can be defined as the attitudes and judgments demanded of the real reader by the text" (856), but earlier he defines the implied reader as "the behavior, attitudes, and background—presupposed or defined, usually indirectly, in the text itself—necessary for a proper understanding of the text" (848). In the latter formulation, the implied reader is identified with Rabinowitz's authorial audience rather than the textual structure that guides the reader's response. Walter Ong's engaging and frequently cited "The Writer's Audience Is Always a Fiction" participates in the same confusion, at times referring to the author's need to imagine an audience while at other times referring to the reader as being cast in a role by the author. Hypothesizing the audience almost certainly helps an author in the strategic construction of a text that will in turn imply the reader's possible responses, but the authorial audience and the implied reader are not the same.

Thus, there are three possible ambiguities. First, the "implied reader" may refer to a structure producing a range of implied realizations as opposed to the range of realizations itself. Second, it may refer either to the actual (realized) intentions of the author *or* to the implications of the text regarded wholly without reference to authorial intention. Third, the phrase may refer either to the response-producing structure of the text in one of the above forms or to the kind of reader the author assumed necessary to understand the structure he or she creates. However one resolves the three questions, one can accept Wilson's formulation that "the implied reader is a function of no more and no less than the overall meaning (that is, the overall interpretation) of the text" (858), the implications of the formulation will vary according to one's choices among these alternatives.

Though the critical community is far from agreement, in its most common acceptation, implied reader seems to designate the range of responses created by a text that reflects (though not necessarily perfectly) the author's active intention as mediated by that author's assumptions about the anticipated audience.

There is a further distinction within the overall notion of the implied reader that was little considered prior to Peter Rabinowitz's *Before Reading* (1987). The reader responding to the structure of the work, and understanding it in a way presumably within the range of possibilities authorized by the structure, must also in some sense accept the incidents of the narrative, whether, as Rabinowitz notes, these include fairy godmothers, young men turning overnight into giant insects, or young girls joining March Hares for underground tea parties. Rabinowitz thus points out that there is what he calls a *narrative audience* that accepts, but does not necessarily believe, the possibility of the events portrayed. As members of the narrative audience, readers must accept for the nonce not only what they know to be fictional events that did not actually occur but also fictional events that they believe could not possibly occur.

The implied reader and the *narratee* (the person the narrator of the story appears to be addressing, to the extent that there is such a person) are not infrequently confused, and in cases where there is no hint of a narratee within the text, nothing in fact is to be gained by trying to separate them. Nevertheless, the two are, in principle, and often in fact, different. When, for instance, one says that a narrator is to be regarded ironically, the narrator is being judged against standards suggested by the implied author to the implied reader, while a narratee would not necessarily exhibit recognition of the irony. Wilson, who prefers the term *characterized reader* to narratee, comments that "the characterization may be achieved directly, when the narrator addresses or refers to this [characterized] reader or when the reader is heard to speak. But the characterized reader can also be determined indirectly, by uncovering implicit assumptions about a reader in the text. Most often, the indirectly portrayed characterized reader will correspond to the implied reader" (855–56).

In Seymour Chatman's well-known diagram of the "narrative-communication situation," the implied author and implied reader are said to be *immanent"* to the situation, while the narrator and narratee are regarded as optional (151). However, it seems more accurate to say that there is always a narrator speaking at least to an assumed narratee, just as there is always an implied author and an implied reader. In some cases, the narrator and implied author and/or the implied reader and narratee are indistinguishable while in other cases—most obviously when there is an internal (*intradiegetic* or *characterized*) narrator and a directly characterized narratee—the members of each pair are clearly quite separate. In these latter cases, the implied author seems almost to be speaking to the implied reader over the heads of the narrator and narratee.

References

Adams, Jon-K. *Pragmatics and Fiction*. Amsterdam: John Benjamins, 1985.
Bakhtin, M. M. *The Dialogic Imagination*. Trans. C. Emerson and M. Holquist. Austin: University of Texas Press, 1981.
Bateson, F. W. *English Poetry: A Critical Introduction*. London: Longmans, 1950.
Chatman, Seymour. *Story and Discourse*. Ithaca, N.Y.: Cornell University Press, 1978.
Eliot, T. S. *The Use of Poetry and the Use of Criticism*. 1933; London: Faber and Faber, 1964.
Iser, Wolfgang. *The Act of Reading*. 1976; Baltimore: Johns Hopkins University Press, 1978.
———. *The Implied Reader: Patterns of Communication in Prose Fiction from Bunyan to Beckett*. Baltimore: Johns Hopkins University Press, 1974.
Jakobson, Roman. "Closing Statement: Linguistics and Poetics." In *Style and Language*, ed. Thomas A. Sebeok. Cambridge, Mass.: MIT Press, 1960.
Kellett, Ernest E. *Literary Quotation and Allusion*. 1933; Port Washington, N. Y. Kennikat Press, 1969.
Leggett, H. W. *The Idea in Fiction*. London: George Allen and Unwin, 1934.
Ong, Walter J., S.J. "The Writer's Audience is Always a Fiction," *PMLA* 90 (January 1975): 9–21.
Rabinowitz, Peter J. *Before Reading: Narrative Conventions and the Politics of Interpretation*. Ithaca, N.Y.: Cornell University Press, 1987. Suggests new insights into what might have seemed an exhausted topic.

Rosenblatt, Louise. *Literature as Exploration*. New York: Appleton-Century-Crofts, 1938; Rev. ed., 1968.

————. *The Reader, the Text, the Poem*. Carbondale: Southern Illinois University Press, 1978. A wide-ranging defense of the reader's role.

Slatoff, Walter J. *With Respect to Readers*. Ithaca, N.Y.: Cornell University Press, 1970. An important book not yet outdated in that it approaches readers' responses from a variety of perspectives and avoids pretentious critical argots.

Weber, Samuel. "Caught in the Act of Reading." In *Demarcating the Disciplines: Philosophy, Literature, Art*. Minneapolis: University of Minnesota Press, 1986.

Wilson, W. Daniel. "Readers in Texts." *PMLA* 96 (October 1981): 848–63. An important essay for sorting out the considerable number of terms that have been employed for similar but not always identical purposes.

Woodberry, George Edward. "Two Phases of Criticism: Historical and Aesthetic" (1913). In *Criticism in America*. New York: Harcourt, Brace, 1924.

Sources of Additional Information

Oscar Wilde's "The Critic as Artist" (*Intentions*. London: Osgood, McIvaine, 1891) is a paradoxically structured foreshadowing of the recognition of the creativity of the reader, although Wilde was more interested in the consciously willed creation of the critic than the necessary participation of the reader.

Walker Gibson's "Authors, Speakers, Readers, and Mock Readers" (*College English* 11, February 1950: 265–69) and Gerald Prince's "Introduction to the Study of the Narratee" (*Poetique*, no. 14, 1973: 177–96) are frequently cited essays on the roles created for readers and the variety of kinds of narratee respectively. Both have been reprinted in *Reader-Response Criticism*, ed. Jane P. Tompkins (Baltimore: Johns Hopkins University Press, 1980).

Full understanding of Wolfgang Iser's conception of the reader's relationship to the structure of a text requires acquaintance with Roman Ingarden's *The Literary Work of Art*, ed. G. G. Grabowicz (Evanston, Ill.: Northwestern University Press, 1973).

READER-RESPONSE THEORY   An umbrella term embracing various theories that share an emphasis on the reader's construction of the meanings he or she finds in a text but differing in their explanations of the ways in which such construction necessarily does, or in some cases should, take place. All are explanations of what readers actually do; they are thus theories of INTERPRETATION and therefore have a place in HERMENEUTICS.

The major varieties of reader-response theory follow, most of which are discussed from different perspectives under other entries.

It is useful to regard the various reader-response theories as ranged along a continuum from an objective pole, at which reconstruction of meaning intentionally embodied in a text is the primary goal, to a subjective pole, at which each reader is understood to construct a meaning linked to his or her individuality.

a. Toward the objective end is the approach of DISCOURSE ANALYSIS, as represented, for instance, by George Dillon. Dillon pursues the ways in which readers *perceive* the propositional structure of a sentence, *comprehend* it by integrating it into the structure of "what is being described or argued," and *interpret* the author's "constructive intention"; that is, "why he is saying what he says" (*Language Processing*, xx). Such processing of what is read is seen to depend heavily on grammatical rules and general interpretive conventions, although, as Dillon points out elsewhere, "no stretch of writing absolutely determines what is constructed from it; it only shapes or guides the reader's construction of a meaning. Readers always go beyond what is explicitly stated, drawing inferences, enriching the text with pieces of personal knowledge, evaluating and interpreting it in terms of personal beliefs and values, interests and purposes" (*Constructing Texts*, xi).

b. Since the process of reading requires continuous perception, comprehension, and interpretation (to use Dillon's terms), the order in which propositions and implications are encountered (that is, constructed) is of major importance. The *affective stylistics* in the early work of Stanley Fish finds that the very process of adjusting and correcting perceptions of the propositional meaning of a sentence as it is read continues to influence our response. Fish's argument here exemplifies what may be called *temporally oriented* reader-response theories, as does Wolfgang Iser's idea of the *wandering viewpoint* of the reader. Expectations are constantly aroused and then fulfilled, modified, or disappointed. Whichever resolution actually occurs becomes part of the background out of which new expectations arise. Until the end of the text is reached, writes Iser, the confirmation or contradiction of each expectation becomes a part of the remembered background at the place in the text at which the reader has arrived. "It is clear, then, that throughout the reading process there is a continual interplay between modified expectations and transformed memories" (*Act of Reading*, 111). Menakhem Perry's "Literary Dynamics: How the Order of the Text Creates Its Meanings" explores in detail the importance of narrative order.

c. What can be thought of as "low" STRUCTURALISM that locates in shared conventions the structures making interpretation of language possible is well represented by the earlier work of Jonathan Culler. The chapter "Literary Competence" from his *Structuralist Poetics* is perhaps the best-known statement of the operation of shared literary conventions. *Literary competence* becomes the name for awareness of the conventions that govern the interpretation of literature, a class of conventions within the totality of those that Dillon explores.

d. A special case that in one sense does and another sense does not belong toward the objective end of the range is the new pragmatism (see PRAGMATISM) espoused in the later work of Stanley Fish. In explaining interpretation in terms of interpretive communities sharing interpretive conventions, Fish emphasizes the role of convention in producing interpretive agreement. However, in seeing interpretive communities as unstable and their conventions as without ultimate grounding, and moreover in finding no imperative for the interpreter to try to read as though a member of the interpretive community to which the author belongs or belonged, Fish gives no privilege to reconstruction of the author's intended meaning.

e. Paradigms of interpretation are frequently in competition. The interpretive conventions of a given paradigm may be criticized from outside, though never from a position that is not within some other paradigm. New normative principles of interpretation may be opposed to existing conventions. (By principles here are simply meant assumptions that are consciously recommended; conventions are assumptions employed so automatically that they are not necessarily brought to awareness.) Contemporary examples of *normative* reader-response criticism that seeks to undermine certain conventions while championing others are FEMINIST CRITICISM and MARXIST LITERARY CRITICISM.

f. Further from the objective pole than those systems focusing on interpretive conventions are a range of critics and theorists interested primarily in the *affective* response of readers. They are less interested in the conventions through which interpretation occurs than in the reader's feelings of pleasure, identification, discomfort, or distaste as he or she relates what is being read to personal experiences and values and to a personal orientation to the world. This strong concern for the affective side of reading has led critics like Walter Slatoff and Louise Rosenblatt to explore the complex interaction or transaction between reader and text (see READER). The act of reading literature is seen both as an experience pursued for its own sake and as deriving meaning from its relationship to other experiences. Thus Rosenblatt writes:

> The transaction is basically between the reader and what he senses the words as pointing to. The paradox is that he must call forth from memory of his world what the visual and auditory stimuli symbolize for him, yet he feels the ensuing work as part of the world outside himself. The physical signs of the text enable him to reach through himself and the verbal symbols to something sensed as outside and beyond his own personal world. (21)

g. The emphasis on the sense of interacting with something beyond oneself, on the response to otherness and difference more than to shared conventions produced by interaction with the text, is equally characteristic of the approach associated with phenomenology. Influenced by Husserl's analysis of the way in which the mind constitutes the objectives of its consciousness, Roman Ingarden developed an influential model that sees the reader as actualizing or concretizing, in fleshing out and filling in details around, a situation that is only *schematized*, that is necessarily less than fully determined or definitively outlined in the text. "If, e.g., a story begins with the sentence: 'An old man was sitting at a table,' etc., it is clear that the represented 'table' is indeed a 'table' and not, for example, a 'chair'; but whether it is made of wood or iron, is four-legged or three-legged, etc., is left quite unsaid and therefore—this being a purely intentional object—*not determined*" (249). As developed by Wolfgang Iser in *The Implied Reader* and *The Act of Reading*, Ingarden's process of actualization leads to the idea of a productive tension in which the reader is pulled toward a view of the world implicit in the text (see the discussion of the implied reader under READER), even while actualizing the text in a manner contingent on his or her individuality. In the process, the world as it ought to be becomes evident although it is not directly portrayed; it is the unformulated negative of values represented in both the text and in the reader's experience.

h. Iser does not really address the question of the degree to which the different values, social contexts, and interpretive conventions of different historical periods produce different actualizations and, indeed, different *negativities*. Hans Robert Jauss has done so, however, by recommending shifting analysis from the response of the individual hypothetical readers to those of actual readers of the text since it first appeared. Looking back to the phenomenological current flowing from Ingarden, Jauss is looking also to the philosophical hermeneutics of Gadamer and addressing the central problem of HISTORICISM. For Jauss, the impossibility of sufficiently re-entering the thought and attitudes of an earlier period is offset by the Gadamerian celebration of the fusion of the historical horizon of the reader with the horizon in which the text was produced and with all succeeding horizons. The response of readers in each succeeding period is sought; the important work will be the one already distanced from the assumptions of its own time even when it appears and thus capable of inducing new negativities from period to period.

i. If one thinks of Rosenblatt, Slatoff, Ingarden, Iser, and Jauss (different though their central preoccupations are) as somewhere near the center of the objective/subjective range, balancing the uniqueness of the individual reader and context of reading against the unchangingness of the textual structure, psychological commentary marks an evident step toward greater subjectivity. Norman Holland's *5 Readers Reading* argues that each reader's response is a function of that reader's personal psychological identity, of his or her habitual way of strategically interpreting and coping with experience. For Holland, more of what the reader responds to is the result of what the reader brings to the text, less is the function of the propositional and formal structures within the text.

j. Well to the subjective end of the spectrum is David Bleich's application of the *subjective paradigm* to the reading of literature. Bleich goes beyond the positions of Slatoff and Rosenblatt, who point to the importance of the associations and experiences that each reader brings to the text, although in fact his view is an extrapolation from it. At the end of her chapter on "Evoking the Poem," Rosenblatt writes, "Interpretation involves primarily an effort to describe in some way the nature of the lived-through evocation of the work" (70). For Bleich, the explanation of the reader's response to the process of reading the text moves away from an interest in the construction of the text to concentrate on the psychological explanation of the individual reader's responses. Where Ingarden speaks of actualizing the work, or Rosenblatt of evoking the poem, Bleich speaks of the reader's response as a symbolization of the work; interpretation then is a *resymbolization* in which one interprets not the work but only one's response. Using the analogy of responding to a mountain perceived as "magnificent," Bleich writes, "In this instance, the response is an act of symbolization; if I then conceptualize the symbolization, I will have interpreted my perceptual experience of the mountain. I will not, however, have interpreted the mountain, whose status as a real object is no longer relevant to me'' (98). Much of Bleich's approach is compatible with the new pragmatism of Richard Rorty and Stanley Fish, although in making the purpose of the resymbolization self-understanding, Bleich turns from Rorty's "edification," in which an understanding of that which is experienced is presumably as important as self-understanding, as therapeutic use. His term *subjective criticism* is an accurate rubric for the endeavor.

One can, then, roughly describe one end of the reader-response spectrum as "conventionalist," the center as "transactionalist," and the other end as "subjectivist." Steven Mailloux's chart of reader-response theories is similar: on one side is subjectivism, which produces a psychological model of reading; in the middle is phenomenology, which produces an intersubjective model; on the other side is structuralism, which produces a social model of reading.

References

Bleich, David. *Subjective Criticism*. Baltimore: Johns Hopkins University Press, 1978.
Culler, Jonathan. *Structuralist Poetics*. Ithaca, N.Y.: Cornell University Press, 1975.
Dillon, George. *Constructing Texts*. Bloomington: Indiana University Press, 1981. Though primarily concerned with a theory of composition, the volume looks to both the author and the reader: "The title of this work . . . is calculatedly ambiguous, embracing the activities of reader and writer, comprehension and composition" (xi).
————. *Language Processing and the Reading of Literature*. Bloomington: University of Indiana Press, 1978.
Fish, Stanley. *Is There a Text in This Class?* Cambridge, Mass.: Harvard University Press, 1980. This volume reprints essays reflecting major positions Fish has taken over the years. The investigation of the effects of the order of reading sentences will be found in "Literature in the Reader"; "Interpreting the *Variorum*" announces Fish's turn toward regarding interpretation as solely a function of the conventions of interpretive communities.
Holland, Norman. *5 Readers Reading*. New Haven, Conn.: Yale University Press, 1975.
Ingarden, Roman. *The Literary Work of Art*. Trans. George G. Grabowicz. 1960; Evanston, Ill.: Northwestern University Press, 1973.
Iser, Wolfgang. *The Act of Reading*. Baltimore: Johns Hopkins University Press, 1978. Clarifies and develops the theoretical argument exemplified by Iser's exploration of a series of English novels in the *Implied Reader*. Original German edition, 1976.
————. *The Implied Reader*. Baltimore: Johns Hopkins University Press, 1974. Original German edition, 1972.
Jauss, Hans Robert. *Aesthetic Experience and Literary Hermeneutics*. Trans. M. Shaw. Minneapolis: University of Minnesota Press, 1982.
————. *Toward an Aesthetic of Reception*. Trans. T. Bahti. University of Minnesota Press, 1982.
Mailloux, Steven. *Interpretive Conventions: The Reader in the Study of American Fiction*. Ithaca, N.Y.: Cornell University Press, 1982. The first two chapters offer detailed analyses and comparisons of major forms of reader-response criticism.

Perry, Menakhem. "Literary Dynamics: How the Order of a Text Creates Its Meanings."
      Poetics Today 1 (Autumn 1979): 35–64, 311–61.
Rosenblatt, Louise. *The Reader, the Text, the Poem.* Carbondale: Southern Illinois University Press, 1978.
Slatoff, Walter. *With Respect to Readers.* Ithaca, N.Y.: Cornell University Press, 1970.

Sources of Additional Information

The introduction to *Reader-Response Criticism*, ed. Jane P. Tompkins (Baltimore: Johns Hopkins University Press, 1980) gives a helpful charting of various theories and concepts associated with reader-response criticism. The volume itself is an extremely useful collection of essays illustrating varieties of reader-response criticism under Tompkins's broad definition (a portion of the issues and concepts she includes are discussed under the present READER entry). *The Reader in the Text: Essays on Audience and Interpretation* (Princeton, N.J.: Princeton University Press, 1980), ed. Susan R. Suleiman and Inge Crosman, is less useful as an introduction, but helpfully illustrates applications of a variety of reader-response approaches. Both the volume edited by Tompkins and that by Suleiman and Crosman include substantial bibliographies.

Though SPEECH-ACT THEORY is not generally thought of as a type of reader-response theory, in its assumption that the recognition of illocutionary force, especially indirectly expressed illocutionary force, is dependent on the appropriate response to certain conventions (as formulated most influentially by H. P. Grice), it has an evident degree of congruence with the reader-response movement.

REALISM   1. The European and American movement, particularly in prose fiction and drama, dating roughly from 1850 to the early decades of the twentieth century, that opposed itself to what were regarded as the sentimental, idealized, or romantic in literature, and especially the novel. 2. Specific techniques, scenes, or local effects in a literary work that produce verisimilitude. 3. As socialist realism, the depiction of the underlying economic and social forces as these were understood by Karl Marx together with suggestions of the ideal socialist world toward which Marx saw history inexorably moving.

This entry is devoted to realism as a literary term only; the philosophical uses are much more complex. For the contrast between realism and romance, see ROMANCE.

1. The realism that arises in the middle of the nineteenth century was an international movement in the sense that it occurred in many countries; however, in the first decades its development in each national literature was largely independent, and there are marked differences from country to country (and indeed among the realists of each country). Differences are manifest between the works of the Goncourts, Flaubert, and Zola in France; Eliot, Trollope, and Gissing in England; Howells, James, Dreiser, and Norris in the United States; Tolstoy, Dostoevsky, Chekov, and Turgenev in Russia; Brandes, Bjørnson, and Ibsen in Scandinavia; and Galdós in Spain. All these writers display certain important characteristics of realism, but the anomalies of such a grouping suggest the difficulties of arriving at a single definition.

Although the purpose of literary realism is evidently to reflect reality more accurately, "reality" is so variously understood—both philosophically and in terms of what one's own experience suggests is true to life—that defining realism in terms of its relation to reality is not a useful exercise. George Becker notes that many statements about realism "address themselves to three ideas simultaneously, the appeal to the average reader, the use of average characters, and the use of ordinary events" (*Realism*, 68). These principles rule out styles and techniques of writing intended to appeal primarily to the sophisticated reader and characters and events that are rare, special, or improbable. Such an approach is a version of the common strategy of defining realism in terms of the assumptions and attitudes of the readers for whom it was written. Edwin Cady speaks of realism as the "common vision" achieved when the novelist induces "imaginative experience within his reader consonant with the reader's communal experience" (20). After surveying several approaches to describing realism, René Wellek settles for "the objective representation of contemporary social reality" (253). For David Lodge, realism is "the representation of experience in a manner which approximates closely to descriptions of similar experience in nonliterary texts of the same culture" (25).

Agreement on what constitutes an objective representation, social reality, or communal experience—or how the illusion of these is produced—is complicated by the necessity of distinguishing at least four characteristics of realism which are combined in various proportions in various national literatures and in specific literary works within those literatures.

a. Realism of subject matter. The goal of realism is to treat the whole of life (though not, of course, in a single work). This means including all social classes as opposed to concentration on the upper and middle classes, including the humdrum details of life as well as the crises, and including the unpleasant and previously unmentionable aspects of human existence. Moreover, nothing in human life is to be idealized, romanticized, or sentimentalized.

It hardly need be said that any description of human experience is necessarily selective. There is wide room for debate over the point at which the portrayal of the grimmer and more unpalatable facts of existence becomes unrealistic through overemphasis. Whether a depiction of sexual love romanticizes or a portrayal of an apparently unselfish action idealizes remains a judgment of the individual reader. Nevertheless, there is little disagreement that realism as a movement has emphasized large new areas of deserving subject matter, foremost among which is the life of the poor. Thus the Goncourt brothers write in 1865:

> Living in the nineteenth century, at a time of universal suffrage, and democracy, and liberalism, we asked ourselves whether what are called "the lower orders" had no claim upon the Novel; whether the people—this world beneath a world—were to remain under the literary ban and disdain of authors who have hitherto maintained silence regarding whatever soul and heart they might possess. (iii)

b. Realism of language. While totally accurate reproduction of the individual variations in speech is not possible in a text, it is easier to judge whether the language used by characters seems to violate their social class, education, and experience than to agree on whether the plot, details, action, and emphasis are realistic.

The narrator's voice is a major problem to the extent that realism requires that that voice not call attention to itself. Fully realistic principles seem to dictate that figurative, witty, poetic, and abstract language must be avoided in external (third-person) narration, as is anything that may be construed as authorial commentary. The goal for many realists becomes the disappearance of the author—which in practice means avoiding anything that bestows on the implied author a personality or point of view.

c. Realism of structure. Thinking almost certainly of choices both in the language and in structure, R. L. Stevenson remarks in "A Note on Realism" (1883), "This question of realism, let it then be clearly understood, regards not in the least degree the fundamental truth, but only the technical method, of a work of art" (71). Structure, however, is a complex matter.

First, realism tends to banish not only fantasy but the improbable. Though unlikely things do occur in human experience, realists were reacting, and have continued to react, against the degree to which the romantic and idealist writers trafficked in the improbable. William Dean Howells, the foremost nineteenth-century American advocate of realism, employs the comparison between a natural grasshopper and an artificial one "made up of wire and card-board, very prettily painted in a conventional tint and . . . perfectly indestructible." The realist must reject the ideal grasshopper, though "I will own that I think . . . that the people who have been brought up on the ideal grasshopper, the heroic grasshopper, the impassioned grasshopper, the self-devoted, adventureful, good old romantic card-board grasshopper, must die out before the simple, honest, and natural grasshopper can have a fair field" (11–12). The improbable is further ruled out by a writer like Zola, who regards his novels as scientific experiments, the novelist being both observer and experimentalist. "The observer [in the novelist] gives the facts as he has observed them, suggests the point of departure. . . . Then the experimentalist appears and introduces an experiment, that is to say, sets his characters going in a certain story so as to show that the succession of facts will be such as the requirements of the determinism of the phenomena under examination call for" (8).

Realism also tends to eschew the imposition of a pattern of significance through the use of orienting METAPHOR or symbolism, the continual IRONY of events, coincidence, or the fortuitous rounding-off of a sequence of events. The relation to the SYMBOL and large-scale metaphor is particularly interesting. While insisting that "[i]t is impossible for any work of art not to be both realistic and symbolical," Albert Guérard noted in 1940 that the "symbolical" (in which he includes the metaphorical) is the literary mode that most contrasts with realism. Roman Jakobson's 1956 contrast between organization by METONYMY and organization by metaphor, particularly as developed by David Lodge, identifies realism (and prose) with metonymy and romanticism and symbolism (and poetry) with metaphor.

d. Realism of total vision or orientation. References are frequently made to the philosophical dimension of literary realism, and there is a rough relation between the direction of realism in literature and one of the later meanings of realism in philosophy: in the words of sense 1.b.(a) of the *OED*, "Belief in the real existence of matter as the object of perception." That is, literary realism rejects the idealism that seeks a realm of forms or essences beyond sense perception. In fact, while literary realists of the nineteenth century and early decades of the twentieth appealed to what they understood as empiricism, positivism, or the methods of science, they did not rely on a developed philosophical underpinning. On the other hand, what writers or critics select as the essentials of human experience (and regard as a realistic proportioning of emphases among these), and what they believe to be the most effective narrative language and structuring will evidently depend on their visions of human life. It will also depend on whether the writer's goal is to give the greatest possible illusion of life within a particular environment or to criticize the social structure that produces that environment. The form and degree of each of the first three characteristics is thus governed by the writer's total orientation.

Naturalism, which is more or less a synonym for realism through the nineteenth century, is generally employed in the twentieth to designate a variety of realism that both regards humans as without the free will they necessarily believe they have—as beings determined by heredity and environment—and emphasizes all that is unpleasant and uninspiring. Naturalism is associated more with French literature, especially with Zola, than with English, Russian, or American literature, though it can be found to some extent in all. Hippolyte Taine's well-known formula for explaining literary history—race, moment, and milieu— becomes a naturalist mode of regarding the individual if race is taken to mean primarily heredity, and milieu, the total environment. "In the eyes of the naturalist man is not a reasoning creature who is independent, superior, healthy in himself, capable of achieving truth and virtue by his own efforts, but a simple force, of the same order as other creatures, receiving from circumstance his degree and his direction" ("Balzac," 106).

Each of the above characteristics evidently creates difficulties for the realist. (a) Though one can argue that happiness is as real and frequent as its opposite, literature that is optimistic and that celebrates the joys of life rather than depicting its monotony, pain, or injustice is unlikely to be claimed for realism. Essentially defined as it is by opposition to romanticism and idealism, what is understood as literary realism depicts life as a whole as gray, if not grim. (b) The language of a dispassionate and wholly objective external narrator is likely to seem flat and uninteresting, if not actually cumbersome. (c) The more the realist writer obeys the injunction to avoid neat patterning, the more shapeless and inartistic the resulting work is likely to seem. Moreover, as Albert Guérard points out, the most successful realistic works are likely to be metaphorical or symbolic as a whole even if they seem to avoid metaphor and symbol. "The melancholy end of a certain Emma Bovary is fit for a brief coroner's report; but thanks to

Flaubert, we realize that we all have 'Bovaryism' in our hearts, and we see ourselves dissected under the symbol of the village doctor's wife'' (169). (d) In terms of total vision, the realist who sees human experience as largely joyless is indeed faced with a dilemma: writers who see a preponderance of disappointment, unhappiness, and pain as the result of the social structure can hardly help making at least an indirect plea for reform; writers who see these as unavoidably engendered by the human condition can hardly help conveying an irremediable despair.

The fact is that the most successful writers have not strongly exhibited all four characteristics. The narrative language of Flaubert and the Goncourts, while hardly sparkling, is carefully chosen; the realism of George Eliot does not deny her narrators choice phrasing; and Tolstoy is openly, at times flagrantly, the philosophic commentator. Critics find symbolic patterns in Flaubert and Dostoevsky, and even more obviously in Zola; contrived ironies in Maupassant; and careful structuring in the English realists. The English realists remained reticent in their treatment of sex and the less salubrious aspects of human life, as did the early-twentieth-century American realists.

2. Realism as local verisimilitude or a portrayal of life that will be accepted as plausible and in some sense typical of course greatly antedates realism as a literary movement: Erich Auerbach's celebrated *Mimesis* surveys examples of ''the interpretation of reality through literary representation or 'mimesis' '' (554) from Homer to Virginia Woolf. Indeed, even the wildest fantasy includes realistic details. Part of the effect of fantasy lies in the contrast between realistic detail and improbable event. However, in general, neither local effects produced by description, characters' modes of speaking, nor the avoidance of the coincidental and improbable were specifically described as realism until literary realism as a mode of writing was recognized in the latter part of the nineteenth century. As is frequently the case, the phenomenon preceded the name. J. P. Stern's *On Realism* is a stimulating study of the term in its more historically comprehensive sense. Stern interestingly discriminates the several meanings of realism ''in life'' from the meanings intended in the application of the term to literature (40).

3. Socialist realism as enunciated by A. A. Zhdanov at the First All-Soviet Writers' Congress (1934) defines literary realism in terms of the Marxist conception of reality. ''[T]he truthfulness and historical concreteness of artistic portrayal should be combined with the ideological remoulding and education of the toiling people in the spirit of socialism. This method in *belles lettres* and literary criticism is what we call the method of socialist realism'' (21). Its best-known spokesman is Georg Lukács, for whom realism requires a penetration of the surface of experience to the historical process that has led to capitalism and is to lead to the socialist state envisioned by Marx. Of socialist realism, Lukács writes, ''Portrayal of the overall process is the precondition for a correct construction. Why is this? Because only portrayal of the overall process can dissolve the fetishism of the economic and social forms of capitalist society, so that these appear as what they actually are, i.e. (class) relations between people'' (*Essays*,

53). "Since [socialist realism's] ideological basis is an understanding of the future, individuals working for that future will necessarily be portrayed from the inside. . . . Socialist realism is able to portray from the inside human beings whose energies are devoted to the building of a different future" (*Contemporary Realism*, 95–96).

References

Auerbach, Erich. *Mimesis: The Representation of Reality in Western Literature*. Trans. W. R. Trask. Princeton, N.J.: Princeton University Press, 1953. Original German edition, 1946.

Becker, George J. *Realism in Modern Literature*. New York: Frederick Ungar, 1980. An essential study of European, English, and American realism from 1850 to the mid-twentieth century. Good bibliography.

Cady, Edwin H. *The Light of Common Day*. Bloomington: Indiana University Press, 1971.

Documents of Modern Literary Realism. Ed. George J. Becker. Princeton, N.J.: Princeton University Press, 1963. A very helpful collection of essays on realism, including statements both for and against. The introductory essay is unusually comprehensive.

Goncourt, Edmond, and Jules de Goncourt. "Preface" to *Germinie Lacerteux*. 1865; Paris: Société des Beaux-arts, n.d. Also translated by G. J. Becker in *Documents of Modern Literary Realism*.

Guérard, Albert. *Preface to World Literature*. New York: Henry Holt, 1940.

Howells, William D. *Criticism and Fiction*. New York: Harper, 1891. See pp. 1–17.

Jakobson, Roman. "Two Aspects of Language and Two Types of Aphasic Disturbances." *Fundamentals of Language I* (The Hague: Mouton, 1956).

Lodge, David. *The Modes of Modern Writing*. Ithaca, N.Y.: Cornell University Press, 1977.

Lukács, Georg. *Essays on Realism*. Trans. D. Fernbach. Cambridge, Mass.: MIT Press, 1980. Original German edition, 1971.

———. *The Meaning of Contemporary Realism*. Trans. J. Mander and N. Mander. London: Merlin Press, 1963. Original German edition, 1957. The volume opposes critical realism to modernism and then opposes socialist realism to critical realism. Kafka is taken as an example of modernism, and Mann as an example of critical realism. "This then is the crucial distinction. Socialist realism differs from critical realism, not only in being based on a concrete socialist perspective, but also in using this perspective to describe the forces working towards socialism *from the inside*" (93).

Stern, J. P. *On Realism*. London: Routledge and Kegan Paul, 1973.

Stevenson, R. L. "A Note on Realism" (1883). In *Essays Literary and Critical*. London: Heinemann, 1932 [Tusitala edition of the *Works*].

Taine, Hippolyte. "Balzac" (1880). Portions translated by G. J. Becker in *Documents of Modern Literary Realism*.

Wellek, René. "The Concept of Realism in Literary Scholarship." In *Concepts of Criticism*. New Haven, Conn.: Yale University Press, 1963. Traces the use of the term from the beginning of the nineteenth century and surveys a variety of discussions of realism in different national literatures.

Zhdanov, A. A. "Soviet Literature—The Richest in Ideas, The Most Advanced Literature.'' In *Problems of Soviet Literature: Reports and Speeches at the First Soviet Writers' Congress*, ed. H. G. Scott. New York: International Publishers, n.d. A brief portion is translated in *Documents of Modern Literary Realism*.

Zola, Emile. "The Experimental Novel.'' In *The Experimental Novel*. 1880; New York: Cassell, 1893. Also translated in *Documents of Modern Literary Realism*.

Sources of Additional Information

For nineteenth-century French realism, see Harry Levin's *The Gates of Horn* (New York: Oxford University Press, 1963), which treats Stendhal, Balzac, Flaubert, Zola, and Proust. Levin closely links realism to the bourgeois consciousness: "This period of bourgeois capitalism, roughly from 1789 to 1939, happens by no accident to be the heyday of the realistic novel'' (81). In *French Realism: The Critical Reaction, 1830– 1870*, Bernard Weinberg examines French critical comment on nine French novelists (New York: Modern Language Association, 1937).

Everett Carter's *Howells and the Age of Realism* (Philadelphia: Lippincott, 1954) focuses on the preeminent nineteenth-century American spokesman for realism in fiction. William W. Demastes's *Beyond Naturalism: A New Realism in American Theatre* (New York: Greenwood Press, 1988) treats the realism of recent American playwrights including David Mamet, Sam Shephard, and David Rabe. *Realism and Naturalism in Nineteenth-Century American Literature* (Carbondale: Southern Illinois University Press, 1984) is a collection of Donald Pizer's essays. Pizer finds specifically American characteristics: American realism is "ethically idealistic'' (2) in a way that French realism is not; and American naturalists were not trying "to demonstrate the overwhelming and oppressive reality of the material forces present in our lives'' but "to represent the intermingling in life of controlling force and individual worth'' (28).

Ione Williams's *The Realist Novel in England* (Pittsburgh: University of Pittsburgh Press, 1974) treats English novelists during the whole of the nineteenth century. Elizabeth Ermarth's *Realism and Consensus in the English Novel* (Princeton, N.J.: Princeton University Press, 1983) examines the conventions of realism, especially in regard to the treatment of time, from Defoe to James. "I argue that fictional realism is an aesthetic form of consensus, its touchstone being the agreement between the various viewpoints made available by a text'' (ix–x). Marshall Brown's "The Logic of Realism: A Hegelian Approach'' (*PMLA* 96, March 1981: 224–38) is a searching examination of the manifold characteristics of realism as it developed from early-nineteenth-century Romanticism. Common to much realism, he finds, is "the silhouetting of animated coup de theatre against static tableaux'' (231), a structural characteristic that parallels Hegel's *dialectic of reality* in the *Science of Logic*. In *The Realistic Imagination: English Fiction from Frankenstein to Lady Chatterly* (Chicago: University of Chicago Press, 1981), George Levine strongly defends the achievement of the English realistic novel. English realism "defines itself against the excesses, both stylistic and narrative, of various kinds of romantic, exotic, or sensational literature'' (5). However, "No major Victorian novelists were deluded into believing that they were in fact offering an unmediated reality; but all of them struggled to make contact with the world out there, and, even with their knowledge of their own subjectivity, to break from the threatening limits of solipsism, of convention, and of language'' (8).

In *Introduction to Russian Realism*, Ernest Simmons examines "the inception and development of certain aspects of realism in significant works of six major Russian authors'' (3): Pushkin, Gogol, Dostoevsky, Tolstoy, Chekhov, and Sholokhov. George

Bisztray's *Marxist Models of Literary Realism* (New York: Columbia University Press, 1978) focuses on Marxist theorists: Lukács, Gorky, Mehring, Plekhanov, Garaundy, and Fischer.

REFERENCE 1. In a loose sense, the representation of a world close to the world of human experience; MIMESIS. 2. The concept or thought represented by a word or expression. 3. The relation between the objects named in utterances (specifically, in sentence utterances) and the objects themselves. 4. In grammar and DISCOURSE ANALYSIS, the processes by which a word or expression acquires its semantic interpretation through its relation to another word or expression, as in the functioning of pronouns. 5. The relation between a TEXT and the "world" it creates.

For senses 2 and 3, see also FICTION.

1. While the mimetic basis of literature has been explicitly recognized since classic Greek thought, the question of what precisely is imitated by a text admits of disparate answers. However, in the broadest sense, reference (or mimesis) may be regarded as the necessarily imperfect resemblance of events, characters, and objects presented through the language of the text to the world as commonly understood by those to whom it is addressed. This is not as trivial an observation as it may seem. The world as experienced (where experience is defined as the joint product of sense-data, the concepts made available through language, and beliefs and attitudes acquired from the culture to which the individual is exposed) enables that individual as reader: (a) to understand the statements made by and events narrated in a text (the simplest, most sentimental love story and *Romeo and Juliet* both depend on the conventions of romantic love and knowledge of sexual drives); (b) to fill in the gaps in the narrative (a scene in a novel set in a restaurant need not include all the details of entering, ordering, paying, and so forth); (c) to translate external characteristics of a character into probable personal traits (Uriah Heep's writhing); (d) to recognize departures from "reality" (the adventures of Wells's time traveler), and thus differentiate, at the extremes, fantasy from REALISM; and (e) to recognize relations with and allusions to other texts. (Functions [a] through [d] seem to be what Linda Hutcheon calls *extratextual reference*; function [e] seems to be what she calls *intertextual reference*, 9.)

2. The most familiar use of reference to designate the concept or thought which in some way stands between an extra-linguistic object or state of affairs, on the one hand, and a word or expression, on the other, is that of C. K. Ogden and I. A. Richards in *The Meaning of Meaning*. However, there have been a number of other influential formulations of the relationships between word, concept, and object; the diverse terminology employed has made generalized discussion of these relationships unusually difficult. The basic relationship is often diagrammed as a triangle with the linguistic representation or sign-vehicle situated at the left-hand base angle, the concept at the apex, and the nonlinguistic

object at the right-hand base angle. Ogden and Richards's terms for the three are *symbol*, *reference*, and *referent*, respectively; Ferdinand de Saussure's terms are *signifier* and *signified* for the first two (he has no standard designation for the third); Charles S. Peirce's most usual terms are *sign* or *representamen*, *interpretant*, and *object*; Charles Morris employs *sign-vehicle, interpretants*, and *designata*; Gottlob Frege's terms are *Zeichen, Sinn*, and *Bedeutung*, which are translated variously as sign, sense, and referent; or sign, reference, and referent; or sign, sense, and nominatum. P. F. Strawson uses *expression* and *meaning* for the first two, and generally a circumlocution for the third. (A convenient set of comparative diagrams appears on pages 184–85 of Anna Whiteside's essay "Theories of Reference" in *On Referring in Literature*.)

Although the terms used to designate the three points on the diagrammatic triangle (that is, the three components of the relationship) correspond very roughly, they cannot be regarded as synonyms: each formulation carries with it special presuppositions and emphases. Each, however, clearly separates the concept (reference, interpretant, sense) from both the word/expression (symbol, sign, representamen) and the object or state of affairs (referent, nominatum). Within this entry, expression, reference, and referent will be employed where necessary as standardizing terms.

Of the questions that arise in connection with the expression-reference-referent relationship, the one most directly relevant to literary study is the status of expressions that appear to refer to something that does not exist, such as "the prime minister of the United States," "Iago," or "Heathcliff." A related question (of less direct importance in literary study) is whether two expressions can have the same referent ("the inventor of the telephone" and "Alexander Graham Bell"). Charles Morris, a follower of Peirce and one of the pioneers of SEMIOTICS, had no difficulty with the question of reference to the nonexistent:

> A sign must have a designatum; yet obviously every sign does not, in fact, refer to an actual existent object. . . . The designatum of a sign is the kind of object which the sign applies to, i.e., the objects with the properties which the interpreter takes account of through the presence of the sign vehicle. And the taking-account-of may occur without there actually being objects or situations with the characteristics taken account of. . . . No contradiction arises in saying that every sign has a designatum but not every sign refers to an actual existent. Where what is referred to actually exists as referred to the object of reference is a *denotatum*. (5)

(Morris is here stipulating specific meanings for designatum and denotatum; both are employed in other ways by other writers.)

Morris's explanation of the possibility of reference to objects that do not in fact have extralinguistic existence is basically the same as that suggested by Gottlob Frege and developed by P. F. Strawson, whose approaches to the problem are the ones now generally accepted, although nuances and possible modifications are still debated. By defining the term sense (roughly, dictionary meaning) as a general description, and the referent as that object or state that fits that description, Frege is able to explain both how several expressions, each having its own sense, can have the same referent and how a word or expression can have sense without a referent (as do unicorn, manticore, troll, Polonius, Stephen Daedalus, Erewhon, and Casterbridge). "In hearing an epic poem," writes Frege, "apart from the euphony of the language we are interested only in the sense of the sentences and the images and feelings thereby aroused. . . . Hence it is a matter of no concern to us whether the name 'Odysseus,' for instance, has reference, so long as we accept the poem as a work of art" (63). Strawson takes a further step in arguing that the reference of a word or expression is a function of the context in which it is used. He formulates the point as follows:

> The actual unique reference made, if any, is a matter of the particular use in the particular context; the significance of the expression used is the set of rules or conventions which permit such references to be made. Hence we can, using significant expressions [expressions with Fregean senses], refer in secondary ways, as in make-believe or in fiction, or mistakenly think we are referring to something in the primary way when we are not, in that way, referring to anything. (181)

Thus "the King of France" always has significant sense, but only in the context of certain historical periods does it have a referent.

Strawson thus regards reference as a matter of PRAGMATICS, not SEMANTICS, of use or utterance, not dictionary meaning, of *parole*, not *langue*. Similarly, John Lyons writes, "it is the speaker who refers (by using some appropriate expression): he invests the expression with reference by the act of referring" (1:177). John Searle summarily comments, "In the sense in which speakers refer, expressions do not refer any more than they make promises or give orders" (155). For Gilbert Ryle, "The use of an expression, or the concept it expresses, is the rôle it is employed to perform, not any thing or person or event for which it might be supposed to stand" (144). This pragmatic viewpoint parallels the basis of Morris's distinction between words with designata only and those with denotata, for the semiotic relationship between sign vehicles, interpretants, and designata always takes into account "the agents of the process," or the interpreters (4). Morris also explains the relationship in another way: "A designatum is not a thing, but a kind of object or class of objects—and a class may have many members, or one member, or no members" (5). Morris's designatum, then, is essentially the description associated with what Strawson calls the meaning (reference), and not, as a hasty attempt to bring the explanations into correspondence might suggest, a form of the referent. To sum up, bringing together terms that are roughly synonymous as far as they relate to the issue at hand, what Ogden and Richards called the reference is a sense, description, class, or type, which may or may not have a referent, denotatum, or existent token.

3. The question of the actual existence of an object or state arises most often not in regard to a single word or expression but in the form of sentences (actually statements or propositions). "The prime minister of the United States is a Republican." "There's a unicorn in the garden." "In the late summer of that year we lived in a house in a village that looked across the river and the plain to the mountains." "Morley was dead, to begin with." Bertrand Russell's Theory of

Descriptions was formulated to address the problems caused by Russell's belief that such sentences assert the existence of the subjects about which they make statements. Russell's view, a form of what Umberto Eco calls the *referential fallacy* (58), has been attacked from a number of directions. The central objection is that Russell evidently regards reference as semantic, while in recent years the same major shift toward pragmatic rather than semantic determination of meaning has occurred in the intrepretation of sentences as well as of individual words and expressions. Strawson states what is the most common contemporary point of view:

> To give the meaning of an expression (in the sense in which I am using the word) is to give *general directions* for its use to refer to or mention particular objects or persons; to give the meaning of a sentence is to give *general directions* for its use in making true or false assertions. . . . So the question of whether a sentence or expression *is significant or not* has nothing to do with the question of whether the sentence, *uttered on a particular occasion*, is, on that occasion, being used to make a true-or-false assertion or not, or of whether the expression is, on that occasion, being used to refer to, or mention, anything at all. (171,172)

As compared to Russell, Strawson's argument is that no *assertion* of existence is made in such statements as "Morley was dead"; there is merely an *implication* of existence. The context of the utterance may cancel the implication, as it does in literary fictions. A. P. Martinich, approaching the question from the point of view of SPEECH-ACT THEORY, suggests that what is specifically involved is the conversational implicature—that is, in evidently nonfictional uses, the hearer/reader assumes H. P. Grice's Cooperative Principle is in force and therefore further assumes that whatever is referred to exists. (Speech-act theory in fact suggests that nonfictional utterances that the hearer/reader recognizes as implying the existence of something the utterer knows that the hearer/reader knows to be nonexistent will be taken as violations of the Cooperative Principle intended to produce indirect illocutionary force.)

However, in recognizably fictional discourse, the maxims of the Cooperative Principle do not apply to the narrative voice as they do in conversational or nonfiction modes of discourse. The statement in nonfiction prose that Gladstone resided for a time at Number 10 Downing Street implies Gladstone's existence, while Dickens's narrator's statement that Nicholas Nickleby resided for a time at Dotheboys Hall results not from semantic differences but simply from different contexts of utterance. While a word or expression may be said to presuppose the existence of a referent, presuppositions are a function of the expectations associated with mode of discourse. Gillian Brown and George Yule, citing Talmy Givón, write, "We shall take the view that the notion of presupposition required in discourse analysis is pragmatic presupposition, that is, 'defined in terms of assumptions the speaker makes about what the hearer is likely to accept without challenge' '' (29).

That actual persons, places, and events appear in fiction is sometimes regarded as a major complication. However, since the description associated with the sense of a word or expression remains in force, all uncontradicted descriptive characteristics remain available. In the case of Gladstone appearing in a novel, the reader imports all the attributes that he/or she happens to associate with the name Gladstone (if any) unless the narrative explicitly denies them, just as a reader assumes unless told otherwise that houses that appear in fiction have doors and windows, that dogs appearing in fiction have four legs, and that characters in fiction are pursuing the normal biological course from birth to death.

There is evidently a distinction between the discourse of the narrator of a novel and that of a character within it. While the events narrated (whether presented by an overt narrator or through a covert narrator who merely sets down dialogue) are understood not to imply existence, the actual dialogues of the characters are understood to have their usual implications for the characters participating in them (in other words, Grice's Cooperative Principle is in force between characters). Further, there is of course a distinction between the discourse of the narrator of a work of fiction and discourse about the work by a reader or a critic, but again, the difference is in the situation of utterance, not the semantic qualities of the words that make up the utterance. Cocktail party conversation about Hercule Poirot is understood to have reference to a character who exists in a fictional world (if reference to that world were impossible, one could not make true or false statements about it). That a person who is ignorant of Agatha Christie's detective might assume that the mention of Hercule Poirot implied existence outside the novel illustrates the function of total context in determining reference.

4. In grammar and discourse analysis, reference (sometimes termed *co-reference*) designates one kind of cohesion within a text. Personal and demonstrative pronouns provide the obvious example of reference, but in the standard treatment, *Cohesion in English*, M. A. K. Halliday and Ruqaiya Hasan explore what they call comparative reference. Two of their examples follow. "The other squirrels hunted up and down the nut bushes; but Nutkin gathered robin's pin-cushions off a briar bush." "The blow would have knocked anyone else cold. The champ just leaned to one side, then straightened again" (78–79). Occasionally, reference is used as an overall term for all five of the relationships producing cohesion as explored by Halliday and Hasan; these are, in addition to reference or co-reference, substitution, ellipsis, conjunction, and lexical cohesion.

Anphoric references are to the preceding text: "The dog slipped out of its collar" is a single-sentence example. *Cataphoric* references are to subsequent text: "It's the same dog we saw the last time we were here." References that require their meanings to be found in the situation of utterance rather than the utterance itself are *exophoric*; those whose meaning is found within the text are *endophoric*. "Well, that's life!" spoken by one person to another when they have just experienced a disappointment is exophoric; the same statement made by a narrator who has just described a situation of disappointment is endophoric.

5. It is commonly said that literature, especially drama and fiction, creates a

world. That is, the concatenation of statements making up the text creates or projects an intelligible extended set of relations about which it is possible to make true and false statements. "After a series of misunderstandings and misadventures Tom Jones is united with Sophia" and "Hamlet kills Polonius" are true within that set of relations; "Elizabeth Bennet tries desperately to get Mr. Collins to propose to her" and "Iago proves a true friend to Othello" are not. The relations between the propositions making up the text are presumably what Linda Hutcheon calls *intratextual reference* which creates a coherent *heterocosm*.

The relation of such created worlds to the reader's understanding of reality is seen by Paul Ricoeur as a special kind of reference.

> Writing such as fiction rejoins reality, however, at another, more fundamental level than the one on which [the] descriptive, confirmative, didactic form of discourse we call ordinary language functions. My thesis is that the suspension of a first-order reference, such as is achieved by fiction and poetry, is the condition of the possibility for yielding a second-order reference. This second-order reference no longer touches the world at the level of manipulable objects, but at the deeper level which Husserl designated by the term "life-world" (*Lebenswelt*) and Heidegger by that of being-in-the-world (*in der Welt-sein*). (25)

Note on Reference and Reality

To avoid possible confusion, it may be useful to state explicitly that the "reality" to which words have reference, and to which the question of existence is relevant, is that shared by a particular culture. Cultures share both common beliefs and awareness of contesting beliefs. That is, individuals are aware of the existence and distribution within the culture of beliefs and attitudes that they do not themselves accept. Human conceptions of reality reflect the culturally created systems of knowledge, beliefs, attitudes, and practices described in Peter Berger and Thomas Luckman's *The Social Construction of Reality*, not an ultimate reality independent of human perceptions and conceptions and only to be known, in Peirce's words, as "brute, irrational insistency" (6, 340). Language may, of course, be employed in attempts to explore or describe ultimate reality—literary texts frequently do so employ it—but the reference or sense of words that determines their possible referents, even in tropes, is necessarily derived from cultural reality.

References

Berger, Peter L., and Thomas Luckman. *The Social Construction of Reality*. Garden City, N.Y.: Doubleday, 1966.

Brown, Gillian, and George Yule. *Discourse Analysis*. Cambridge: Cambridge University Press, 1983. Includes a cogent discussion of grammatical/discourse reference (co-reference) in the context of discourse analysis as a whole.

Eco, Umberto. *A Theory of Semiotics*. Bloomington: Indiana University Press, 1976. Eco discusses reference in terms of semiotic codes, pointing out that "[s]emiotics is mainly concerned with signs as social forces" (65).

Frege, Gottlob. "On Sense and Reference" (1892). Trans. M. Black. In *Translations from the Philosophical Writings of Gottlob Frege*. Ed. P. Geach and M. Black. Oxford: Basil Blackwell, 1952. Although this essay glances only tangentially at literature, it has been as influential in the discussion of reference in literary fictions as in the scientific uses of language, in which Frege was primarily interested.

Grice, H. P. "Logic and Conversation." In *Syntax and Semantics III*. New York: Academic Press, 1975. While this essay is not directly concerned with speech-act theory, it has become central to that field.

Halliday, M. A. K., and Ruqaiya Hasan. *Cohesion in English*. London: Longman, 1976. Includes an extensive discussion of grammatical/discourse reference and the ways in which it produces cohesiveness.

Hutcheon, Linda. "Metafictional Implications for Novelistic Reference." In *On Referring in Literature*.

Lyons, John. *Semantics*. 2 vols. Cambridge: Cambridge University Press, 1977. The whole of Chapter 7 is valuable not only in distinguishing reference, sense, and denotation, but also in clarifying the various systems of terminology that have been used to mark these distinctions.

Martinich, A. P. *Communication and Reference*. Berlin: de Gruyter, 1984.

Morris, Charles W. *Foundations of the Theory of Signs*. Vol. 1, no. 2 in *Foundations of the Unity of Science*. Chicago: University of Chicago Press, 1938. An essential discussion from the point of view of Peircean semiotics.

Ogden, C. K., and I. A. Richards, *The Meaning of Meaning*. 1923; New York: Harcourt, Brace, 1946.

On Referring in Literature. Ed. Anna Whiteside and Michael Issacharoff. Bloomington: Indiana University Press, 1987.

Peirce, Charles Sanders. *Collected Papers*. 8 vols. Ed. C. Hartshorne and P. Weiss (vols. 1–6) and A. W. Burks (vols. 7–8). Cambridge, Mass.: Harvard University Press, 1931–58. See especially vol. 2.

Philosophy and Ordinary Language. Ed. C. E. Caton. Urbana: University of Illinois Press, 1963. An important collection of essays by philosophers associated with "ordinary-language" philosophy; many of these essays are relevant to the problems of reference.

Ricoeur, Paul. "Philosophical and Theological Hermeneutics." *Studies in Religion* 5 (1975–76): 14–43.

Russell, Bertrand. "On Denoting." *Mind* 14 (1905): 479–93. Reprinted in *Logic and Knowing*, ed. R. C. Marsh. London: Allen and Unwin, 1956.

Ryle, Gilbert. "The Theory of Meaning." In *Philosophy and Ordinary Language*. Reprinted from *The Philosophical Review* 62 (1953): 167–86.

Saussure, Ferdinand de. *Course in General Linguistics*. Ed. Charles Bally and Albert Sechehaye; trans. W. Baskin. New York: McGraw-Hill, 1966.

Searle, John R. *Expression and Meaning: Studies in the Theory of Speech Acts*. Cambridge: Cambridge University Press, 1979.

Strawson, P. F. "On Referring." In *Philosophy and Ordinary Language*. Originally published in *Mind* 59 (1950): 320–344. An essential essay.

Whiteside, Anna. "Theories of Reference." In *On Referring in Literature*.

Sources of Additional Information

As noted in the commentary above, in reading discussions of reference, especially in senses 2 and 3, one must be aware both that there is no fully accepted standard terminology and that terms used by different writers that seem synonymous may not be fully so.

The clearest introduction to the issue of reference in senses 2 and 3 is perhaps Leonard Linsky's article on "Referring" in *The Encyclopedia of Philosophy*, ed. Paul Edwards (8 vols. New York: Macmillan, 1967). Kent Bach's *Thought and Reference* (Oxford:

Clarendon Press, 1987) is an extended treatment; Leonard Linsky's "Reference and Referents" in *Philosophy and Ordinary Language* (see References above) is useful in clearing certain confusions. Linsky notes, for example, "These famous philosophical examples, the round square, the golden mountain, are just the things we do *not* talk about (except in telling a story or a fairy tale or something of the kind)." Such an expression "does not occur in isolation from some larger context" (85). Chapter 4 of John R. Searle's *Speech Acts: An Essay in the Philosophy of Language* (Cambridge: Cambridge University Press, 1969) addresses problems of reference.

Three different approaches to the meaning of reference in literary fictions will be found in Charles Morris's "Esthetics and the Theory of Signs" (*The Journal of Unified Science* [*Erkenntnis*] 8, 1938–40, 131–50), Jon-K. Adams's *Pragmatics and Fiction* (Amsterdam: John Benjamins, 1985), and Françoise Meltzer's "Renaming in Literature: Faces of the Moon" in *On Referring in Literature* (see References above).

RHETORIC 1. Language chosen and arranged for the purpose of persuasion, together with the study of persuasive discourse. 2. The use of figures and tropes. 3. The effective use of language.

It is not appropriate in a dictionary of literary concepts to review the developments in rhetorical theory, or the differences in emphases in treatments of rhetoric over time. Although the history of rhetoric as a concept from the contest between Socrates and the Sophists in the fifth century B.C., *through Aristotle, Cicero, Quintilian, and Ramus, to Whateley, Campbell, and Blair, and then to Burke, Richards, and Perelman, bears on literature at many points, only a broad outline of the relations between thought about rhetoric and thought about literature can be sketched here.*

1. The central classical definition of rhetoric is that of Aristotle: "the faculty of observing in any given case the available means of persuasion" (24; I.2.26–27). That Aristotle spoke of finding the *means* of persuasion rather than simply skill in persuasion has been regarded as evidencing Aristotle's sensitivity to the charge that the purpose of rhetoric was to make the worse seem the better. While the authority of Aristotle has preserved his formal definition, rhetoric in this first sense is much more commonly understood as, in the straight-forward phrasing of sense 1.a in the *OED*, "The art of using language so as to persuade or influence others." In any case, Aristotle's distinction between poetry as the art of imitation and rhetoric as the art of persuasion established definite but nevertheless debatable boundaries. The classical analyses of rhetoric were all developed with almost exclusive reference to the function of persuasion. Rhetoric was thus divided into three major types according to purpose: deliberative (to persuade an audience such as a legislative assembly to adopt a policy), forensic (to persuade judges of guilt or innocence), and epideictic (to praise or blame persuasively on ceremonial occasions, or, more generally, to display one's command of the rhetorical art). The sources of persuasion were divided into ethos (that which contributes to the speaker's credibility and appearance of trustworthiness), logos (that which gives rational support to the argument), and pathos (that which gives

emotional support). The necessary components of a persuasive speech were categorized as invention, disposition (arrangement), style, memory, and oral delivery. The MIMESIS or imitation that Aristotle believed was essential to poetry finds no real place among these categories; presumably, Aristotle would not have written separate treatises on rhetoric and poetics if he had not thought that the two kinds of discourse were essentially different. (The argument that the Aristotelian distinction between rhetorical and poetic discourse ought to be preserved has been forcefully made in the twentieth century by Wilbur Samuel Howell, though how sharp the division between the two in Aristotle's mind remains a moot issue.

2. Over the centuries, the importance of memory and oral delivery declined as written forms of argument increased; while invention and disposition remained important, the analysis of style gained in importance, especially where the sixteenth-century Petrus Ramus's reassignment of both invention and disposition to the realm of logic rather than that of rhetoric had influence. Style, especially its analysis through the classification of figures (word and sound patterns like alliteration and chiasmus [see FIGURE]) and tropes (thought patterns such as METAPHOR and METONYMY) came to seem more and more the essential constituent of rhetoric. This sense remains strong. For instance, in Jonathan Culler's comments on the role of rhetoric in the interpretation of literature, it is the response to figures and tropes that he primarily has in mind. "Rhetorical theory," writes Culler in *Structuralist Poetics* (1975), "thought to justify various features of literary works by naming them and specifying which figures were appropriate to particular genres" (179). The continuing value of training in rhetoric can be seen if it is recognized that "[t]he repertoire of rhetorical figures serves as a set of instructions which readers can apply when they encounter a problem in the text" (181). A similar argument is found in Culler's *Pursuit of Signs* (1981). "A second topic that could serve as the basis for course work at the graduate level is the revival of rhetoric and rhetorical categories to describe the production of meaning in discourse. Literature has often been thought of as the prime example of figurative language and therefore as the privileged object for rhetorical analysis (215–16). Brian Vickers's *Classical Rhetoric in English Poetry* gives a brief history of rhetoric, but in analyzing specific poems, his focus is on the figures they employ. Gérard Genette traces and protests the historical reduction of rhetoric first to a preoccupation with figures, then to an interest primarily in metaphor and metonymy, and finally to metaphor defined so as to include tropes generally.

3. As Edward Corbett points out, despite the influence of Aristotle's distinction between rhetorical and poetic discourses, when Horace adds the improving or useful (that is, didactic) function to poetry, persuasion enters poetic theory and the distinction begins to fade (*Rhetorical Analyses*, xiv–xv). At about the same time, Ovid was bridging the difference through the large-scale importation of rhetorical figures into poetry. Not long afterward, Quintilian makes literature the subject of Book 10 of his *Institutio Oratoria*. Curtius writes, "Here and

there in Quintilian's treatise the subject of rhetoric is transformed into something wholly different—into the humanistic recognition of literary studies as the highest good in life'' (67).

As rhetorical study became more closely associated with written texts, and especially from the early Renaissance on, it became less distinct from a study of belles lettres while its application to forms of spoken discourse broadened. After all, mimesis may be employed in the service of persuasion, while epideictic rhetoric appears to give much the same pleasure as mimetic discourse. Moreover, the characters who speak *within* mimetic discourse, whether prose fiction, drama, or poetry, are constantly employing rhetoric. The shift is fully evident by the eighteenth century. George Campbell's well-known definition in *The Philosophy of Rhetoric* (1776) makes ''eloquence'' or rhetoric the ''art or talent by which discourse is adapted to its end,'' where four ends are considered: ''to enlighten the understanding, to please the imagination, to move the passions, or to influence the will'' (1). By the time Hugh Blair focuses the opening chapters of his *Lectures on Rhetoric and Belles Lettres* (1783) on taste defined as ''[t]he power of receiving pleasure from the beauties of nature and of art'' and, like Quintilian, devotes the final ten of his forty-seven chapters to literature, the old distinction had lost most of its power.

The twentieth century has seen a continued broadening of the concept of rhetoric. On the one hand, in consonance with the identification of rhetoric with the study of prose composition generally that goes back at least to Blair (5), rhetoric has increasingly become the preferred term for the principles of good writing. The opening sentence of Edward Corbett's *Classical Rhetoric for the Modern Student* thus reads: ''This book endeavors to present a coherent, realistic art of composition—an adaptation of classical rhetoric'' (xi).

At the same time, Kenneth Burke's redefinition of rhetoric as ''identification,'' or, less cryptically, as ''the use of language as a symbolic means of inducing cooperation in beings that by nature respond to symbols,'' gives a much less narrow meaning to rhetoric even in the sense of persuasion (*Rhetoric of Motives*, 567). Burke employs an even broader definition: ''the use of language in such a way as to produce a desired impression upon the hearer or reader. . . . In accordance with the definition we have cited, effective literature could be nothing else but rhetoric'' (*Counter-Statement*, 210). I. A. Richards's view of rhetoric as the ''study of verbal understanding and misunderstanding'' (23) in the 1936 *Philosophy of Rhetoric* is at least as comprehensive as Burke's; only a little less broad is Wayne Booth's concept in *The Rhetoric of Fiction*, where rhetoric refers to the whole of the techniques for transmitting a fictional world to the reader. Thus, alongside its more limited sense, rhetoric is today frequently given a meaning something like Edward Corbett's ''strategies of discourse directed to a definite audience for a definite purpose'' (*Classical Rhetoric*, 31).

An influential argument against breaking down the distinction between rhetoric and poetics has been mounted by Wilbur Samuel Howell, a number of whose essays on the issue are gathered in *Poetics, Rhetoric, and Logic*. Howell insists on an Aristotelian distinction: "poetry accomplishes its purposes by means of the poetic mimesis or fiction, whereas oratory proceeds to its goal by using statements and proof" (22). Nevertheless, for Howell, literature embraces both: rhetoric produces "literature of statement" while poetics is responsible for "literature of symbol" (32). "[T]he poetical utterance differs from the rhetorical utterance by virtue of the fact that the words used in the latter refer directly to states of reality, and that the words used in the former refer directly to things that stand by deputy for states of reality. These things that stand by deputy for other things I shall call symbols" (217–18).

The ramifications of the largely expanded sense of rhetoric are of considerable importance. "Rhetorical analysis," that is, the analysis of the totality of strategies found in persuasive discourse (practiced primarily in university speech departments after the early part of the twentieth century), seeks to elicit from the text as full an understanding as possible of the author's purposes and the intended effects on a given audience. In Corbett's words, "Rhetorical criticism seeks simply to ascertain the particular posture or image that the author is establishing in this particular work in order to produce a particular effect on a particular audience" (*Rhetorical Analyses*, xix). It thus opposes the formalisms of NEW CRITICISM and STRUCTURALISM which attempt to ignore or bracket authorial intention, the specific situation, and the probable effects on a specific audience. It equally opposes the poststructuralist dismissal of the author, adoption of the entire system of language (rather than the situation of utterance) as the boundary of its commentary, and the consequent insistence on indeterminacy. Unlike such approaches, rhetorical analysis gives prominence to the *effect* of the given discourse in a *particular situation*. Further, it reduces or cancels the distinction between literature and all other forms of discourse. It thus parallels some of the concerns of READER-RESPONSE THEORY, SPEECH-ACT THEORY, DISCOURSE ANALYSIS, MARXIST LITERARY CRITICISM, New Historicism, and reception aesthetics. Terry Eagleton's Marxist-oriented *Literary Theory* recommends a shift from literary theory to rhetoric because rhetoric "saw speaking and writing not merely as textual objects, to be aesthetically contemplated or endlessly deconstructed, but as forms of *activity* inseparable from the wider social relations between writers and readers, orators and audiences, and as largely unintelligible outside the social purposes and conditions in which they were embedded" (206). Where Marxists are interested in rhetoric as a tool for analyzing how ideologies they oppose are maintained and for effecting particular kinds of social change, the model of rhetoric as persuasion in the most comprehensive sense makes it a means of effecting change across human thought and institutions. One central statement of this position is Lloyd Bitzer's influential essay, "The Rhetorical Situation." "In short, rhetoric is a mode of altering reality, not by the direct application of energy to objects, but by the creation of discourse which changes reality through the mediation of thought and action. The rhetor alters reality by bringing into existence a discourse of such a character that the audience, in thought and action, is so engaged that it becomes mediator of change" (4). It is a single step from this position to the argument that rhetoric creates the way in which the human mind understands reality; and one more step to the position that different understandings produce different insights.

References

Aristotle. *Rhetoric*. Trans. W. R. Roberts. With the *Poetics*. New York: Random House, Modern Library, 1954.

Bitzer, Lloyd. "The Rhetorical Situation." *Philosophy and Literature* 1 (Winter 1968): 1–14.

Blair, Hugh. *Lectures on Rhetoric and Belles Lettres* (1783). Halifax, U.K.: Wm. Milner, 1847.

Booth, Wayne. *The Rhetoric of Fiction*. Chicago: University of Chicago Press, 1961; 1983.

Burke, Kenneth. *Counter-Statement*. 1931; Chicago: University of Chicago Press, 1957.

———. *A Rhetoric of Motives* (1950). With *A Grammar of Motives*. New York: World, 1962.

Campbell, George. *The Philosophy of Rhetoric* (1776). Ed. Lloyd Bitzer. Carbondale: Southern Illinois University Press, 1963.

Corbett, Edward P. J. *Classical Rhetoric for the Modern Student*. 1965; New York: Oxford University Press, 1971.

———. *Rhetorical Analyses of Literary Works*. New York: Oxford University Press, 1969. Includes fourteen examples of rhetorical analysis of literary works. The discussion of the relationship between literature and rhetoric in the introduction is of first importance. "When rhetorical criticism is applied to imaginative literature, it regards the work not so much as an object of aesthetic contemplation but as an artistically structured instrument of communication" (xxii). "A critic becomes 'rhetorical' when he tries to show that the choices from among the available options were made in reference to subject-matter or genre or occasion or purpose or author or audience—or some combination of these" (xxiv).

Culler, Jonathan. *The Pursuit of Signs*. Ithaca, N.Y.: Cornell University Press, 1981.

———. *Structuralist Poetics*. Ithaca, N.Y.: Cornell University Press, 1975.

Curtius, Ernst Robert. *European Literature and the Latin Middle Ages*. New York: Pantheon, 1953.

Eagleton, Terry. *Literary Theory: An Introduction*. Minneapolis: University of Minnesota Press, 1983.

Genette, Gérard. "Rhetoric Restrained." In *Figures of Literary Discourse*. Trans. A. Sheridan. New York: Columbia University Press, 1982.

Howell, Wilbur Samuel. *Poetics, Rhetoric, and Logic: Studies in the Basic Disciplines of Criticism*. Ithaca, N.Y.: Cornell University Press, 1975.

Richards, I. A. *The Philosophy of Rhetoric*. 1936; Oxford: Oxford University Press, 1965.

Vickers, Brian. *Classical Rhetoric in English Poetry*. London: Macmillan, 1970. The volume includes "A Concise History of Rhetoric" and gives useful examples of figures in classical literature, the Bible, and English literature.

Sources of Additional Information

The above entry has not considered the long history of dyslogistic uses of the term rhetoric as dishonest, pretentious, gaudy, or empty. Wayne Booth cogently protests the continuing use of rhetoric with the pejorative meaning of "men try[ing] to change each other's minds without giving good reasons for change" (6) in "The Revival of Rhetoric" (included in *New Rhetorics*, ed. Martin Steinmann, Jr. New York: Charles Scribner's Sons, 1967). Roland Barthes's "The Old Rhetoric and the New" (1970), which appears in a translation by R. Howard in *The Semiotic Challenge* (New York: Hill and Wang, 1988) employs rhetoric as a name for all those uses of language that Barthes rejects. "[A]ll our literature, formed by Rhetoric and sublimated by humanism, has emerged from a politico-judicial practice . . . in those areas where the most brutal conflicts—of money, of property, of class, are taken over, contained, domesticated, and sustained by state power, where state institutions regulate feigned speech and codifies [sic] all recourse to the signifier; this is where our literature is born" (93).

Not only has the relationship between rhetoric and poetics long been a matter of debate, but the rhetorical or oratorical tradition has been opposed to the philosophical since Plato opposed the Sophists. For a survey of the two traditions, see Bruce Kimball's *Orators and Philosophers* (New York: Teachers College Press, Columbia University, 1986) and chapters 2 and 3 of Brian Vickers's *In Defence of Rhetoric* (Oxford: Clarendon Press, 1988).

Kenneth Burke's comments on rhetoric are spread fairly well across the body of his work; the relationship between rhetoric as language intended "to induce corresponding acts" is opposed to poetics, which "could still be concerned with symbolic action for its own sake" (see pp. 296–97, 302 of *Language as Symbolic Action*, Berkeley: University of California Press, 1966). See also his "Rhetoric Old and New" (*Journal of General Education* 5, April 1951: 203–9; reprinted in *New Rhetorics*, ed. Martin Steinmann, Jr.; New York: Charles Scribner's Sons, 1967). "The key term for the old rhetoric was 'persuasion' and its stress was upon deliberate design. The key term for the 'new' rhetoric would be 'identification,' which can include a partially 'unconscious' factor in appeal" (*New Rhetorics*, 63).

Daniel Fogarty's *Roots for a New Rhetoric* (1959; New York: Russell and Russell, 1968) usefully surveys the contributions to rhetorical theory of Burke, I. A. Richards, and General Semantics theory, emphasizing the movement toward regarding rhetoric as an instrument for achieving cooperation.

A further step beyond the view that different rhetorics produce different understandings of reality is Paul de Man's argument in *Blindness and Insight* (New York: Oxford University Press, 1971) that insights are correlatives of the blindnesses in one's own understanding. "Critics' moments of greatest blindness with regard to their own critical assumptions are also the moments at which they achieve their greatest insight" (109).

ROMANCE   1. Originally a French designation for literature written in the vernacular rather than Latin, and, by transference, the most common type of such literature as it emerged in the twelfth century: fictional accounts of martial adventures or courtly love written in verse, and, somewhat later, in prose. 2. Since the eighteenth century, any narrative of supernatural, incredible, or highly improbable incidents, or of high adventure, or of events and characters that seem more symbolic than realistic.

Though exceptions can be adduced, romance, whether medieval or modern, is frequently associated closely with wish fulfilment. Gillian Beer writes, "Romance is always concerned with the fulfilment of desires" (12); Northrop Frye's influ-

ential section "The Mythos of Summer: Romance" in Anatomy of Criticism *opens, "The romance is nearest of all literary forms to the wish-fulfilment dream" (186).*

1. "Romance as we know it begins with the knight in a land of faerie, alone and pale, on a mysterious quest, facing exotic and completely improbable trials that have, nevertheless, ritual implications" (4), writes Eleanor T. Lincoln. What Gillian Beer calls "a peculiar vagrancy of the imagination" (4) is the characteristic mark of the treatment of the knightly warfare and courtly amours that are the subjects of the medieval romance. That the medieval romance is to be distinguished from EPIC is generally agreed; the bases of the distinction are less settled. For example, the *chanson de geste* is regarded as closer to epic than romance when romance is regarded as primarily treating affairs of love, but the *chanson de geste* can also be regarded as a type of romance. Nathaniel Griffin argues in an essay of 1923 that the romance always succeeds the epic because it is a modification of the epic for a later time. "By a romance we commonly mean a tale of an improbable or, better, of an incredible character. In this respect the romance differs from the epic, which was once, though now, of course, to the modern reader no longer, a credible tale" (56). W. P. Ker sees romance succeeding epic as the heroic age gives way to the age of chivalry. "Whatever Epic may mean, it implies some weight and solidity; Romance means nothing if it does not convey some notion of mystery and fantasy" (4). On the whole, the romance also has less structure: the events it portrays tend to follow each other without much concern for causal explanation, subordination of the less to the more important, or establishment of an authorial perspective. However, for an exploration of the "interlaced" structure of narration in the romance, see Chapter 5 of Eugène Vinaver's *The Rise of Romance*.

The subject matter of the medieval romance has four major sources: Matter of France (centered on Charlemagne), Matter of Britain (centered on King Arthur), Matter of Rome (including tales of Alexander and from the Orient as well as tales from the Trojan War), and Matter of England (which includes various English tales such as *Guy of Warwick*). Standard examples of the medieval romance are the Arthur legends of Chrétien de Troyes, Benoit de Sainte Maure's *Roman de Troie*, Gottfried von Strassburg's *Tristan and Isolt*, *Havelock the Dane*, *Sir Gawain and the Green Knight*, and, if the *chanson de geste* is to be included, *The Song of Roland*, the earliest of example of the Matter of France. The form continues, with modifications, into the Renaissance: Boiardo's *Orlando innamorato*, Ariosto's *Orlando furioso*, Tasso's *Gerusalemme liberata*, and Spenser's *Faerie Queene* are examples. *The Faerie Queene* is more allegorical than is normally true of the romance form, but the discussion of the medieval romance by scholars and critics writing in English centers around the romance traditions found in that poem. Patricia Parker's essay "Romance," in *The Spenser Encyclopedia*, is a comprehensive summary of the traditions and motifs incorporated by Spenser.

"The romance," writes John Stevens, "stands to medieval literature as the novel stands to the literature of the nineteenth and twentieth centuries. It is the major secular genre from the time of Chrétien de Troyes (*c.* 1180) to Chaucer (d. 1400)'' (15). Indeed, the rejection of the traditional romance form is apparent only in the seventeenth century; a decisive turn is represented by Cervantes's *Don Quixote* (1605, 1615), a work that stands by itself in point of time and mode as a romance that satirizes the conventions of the romance.

2. The term romance gradually acquired its present extended applications from the eighteenth century on, coming to be retrospectively applied to Greek and Roman fiction outside the older epic genre (e.g., the Greek *Argonautica*, Longus's *Daphnis and Chloe*, Heliodorus's *Ethiopia*, and Apuleius's *The Golden Ass*), later eighteenth- and early nineteenth-century tales of horror, and nineteenth- and twentieth-century narrative fiction that deviates from REALISM in some way.

As Arthur Johnson's *Enchanted Ground* demonstrates, interest in the earlier romances remained strong in the eighteenth century even though the dismissive attitude of Samuel Johnson was also common: ''almost all the fictions of the last age will vanish, if you deprive them of a hermit and a wood, a battle and a shipwreck'' (3:20). The more appreciative attitude toward medieval romance essentially begins with Bishop Richard Hurd's *Letters on Chivalry and Romance* of 1762. Hurd's comparison of the ''enchanted ground'' of the romance with eighteenth-century norms of literary taste is often quoted: ''What we have gotten by this revolution . . . is a great deal of good sense. What we have lost, is a world of fine fabling'' (120).

In 1750 Johnson described the contemporary ''comedy of romance'' as ''precluded from the machines and expedients of the heroic romance,'' so that it can ''neither employ giants to snatch a lady away from the nuptial rites, nor knights to bring her back from captivity'' (3:19); nevertheless, before the end of the century, the supernatural horrors of the Gothic romances were claiming an enormous readership. Walpole's *The Castle of Otranto* (1765) is the major English precursor; Mrs. Radcliffe's *A Sicilian Romance* (1790) and *The Mysteries of Udolpho* (1794), Matthew Gregory Lewis's *The Monk* (1797), Mary Shelley's *Frankenstein* (1817), and Charles Maturin's *Melmoth the Wanderer* (1820) are central examples. (The term Gothic as originally applied to earlier romances meant medieval with a pejorative connotation, as in *OED* sense 3a; the term then became transferred to fictions trading in supernatural horror, as romance became the standard term for the kind of medieval works now designated by that term.)

Whereas the medieval romance is defined partly by contrast to the epic, the later romance has been defined chiefly by contrast with the realistic novel. Clara Reeve's *The Progress of Romance Through Times, Countries, and Manners* (1785) is the early significant statement of the distinction. ''The Romance is an heroic fable, which treats of fabulous persons and things.—The Novel is a picture of real life and manners, and of the times in which it is written. The Romance in lofty and elevated language, describes what never happened nor is likely to happen.—The Novel gives a familiar relation of such things, as pass every day before our eyes, such as may happen to our friend, or to ourselves" (1:111). Other famous definitional statements are those of Nathaniel Hawthorne, Henry James, and Robert Louis Stevenson. In the Preface to *The House of Seven Gables*, Hawthorne comments that the novel "is presumed to aim at a very minute fidelity, not merely to the possible, but to the probable and ordinary course of man's experience." However, although the romance "sins unpardonably, so far as it may swerve aside from the truth of the human heart," it "has fairly a right to present that truth under circumstances, to a great extent, of the writer's own choosing or creation" (1). James, on the whole no friend of the romance, writes, "The only *general* attribute of projected [that is, literary] romance that I can see . . . is the fact of the kind of experience with which it deals—experience liberated, so to speak; experience disengaged, disembroiled, disencumbered, exempt from the conditions that we usually know to attach to it" (xvii). As the three definitions suggest, the modern romance is not to be defined either in terms of subject matter or GENRE, but of manner of treatment; it is a mode, not a genre.

The list of works reasonably described as romances in terms of the definitions of Reeve, Hawthorne, and James is extensive, and not confined to prose fiction. In addition to the Gothic romances of the end of the eighteenth and beginning of the nineteenth centuries, the following are among the most frequently cited examples: Keats's "Eve of St. Agnes"; Disraeli's *Lothair*; Tennyson's *Idylls of the King*; most of Hawthorne and much of Melville; Morris's prose and verse tales; Meredith's *Harry Richmond*; Conrad's *Shadow Line*; Tolkien's *The Lord of the Rings*; the "Southern Gothic" narratives of Faulkner, Welty, McCullers, and Oates; and, arguably, science fiction.

References

Beer, Gillian. *The Romance*. London: Methuen, Critical Idiom Series, 1970.

Frye, Northrop. *Anatomy of Criticism*. Princeton, N.J.: Princeton University Press, 1957.

Griffin, Nathaniel E. "The Definition of Romance." *PMLA* 38 (March 1923): 50–70.

Hawthone, Nathaniel. *The House of Seven Gables*. Centenary Edition. Columbus: Ohio State University Press, 1965.

Hurd, Richard. *Letters on Chivalry and Romance*. London, 1762. Reprint. New York: Garland, 1971. Essential. "The spirit of Chivalry, was a fire which soon spent itself: But that of *Romance*, which was kindled at it, burnt long, and continued its light and heat even to the politer ages" (3–4).

James, Henry. *The American*. New York Edition. New York: Charles Scribner's Sons, 1907.

Johnson, Arthur. *Enchanted Ground: The Study of Medieval Romance in the Eighteenth Century*. London: Athlone Press, 1964.

Johnson, Samuel. *The Rambler*, no. 4 (31 March 1750). In vol. 3 of *The Yale Edition of the Works of Samuel Johnson*. New Haven, Conn.: Yale University Press, 1969.

Ker, W. P. *Epic and Romance: Essays on Medieval Literature*. London: Macmillan, 1922.

Lincoln, Eleanor Terry. Introduction to *Pastoral and Romance: Modern Essays in Criticism*, ed. Lincoln. Englewood Cliffs, N.J.: Prentice-Hall, 1969. The volume collects an interesting variety of essays on both the medieval and the modern romance.

Parker, Patricia. "Romance." In *The Spenser Encyclopedia*, ed. A. C. Hamilton. Toronto: Toronto University Press, 1990. The essay very usefully summarizes both the types of romance and various elements of romance found in works of other kinds to the time of Spenser.

Reeve, Clara. *The Progress of Romance Through Times, Countries, and Manners.* Colchester, U.K.: Keymer, 1785. Reprinted New York: Garland, 1970.

Stevens, John. *Medieval Romance: Themes and Approaches.* New York: Norton, 1974. Steven's focus is on medieval romance but he examines it as a permanent kind of idealistic experience. In the Middle Ages the major experiences treated in the romance are "idealized love, idealized social living, idealized valour or integrity, idealized religious aspiration" (227).

Vinaver, Eugène. *The Rise of Romance.* Oxford: Oxford University Press, 1970.

Sources of Additional Information

George Saintsbury's *The Flourishing of Romance and the Rise of Allegory* (New York: Charles Scribner's Sons, 1897) offers a readable, if old-fashioned, survey of the medieval romance. The most helpful brief account of the medieval romance is that in the *Princeton Encyclopedia of Poetry and Poetics*, ed. Alex Preminger (Princeton, N.J.: Princeton University Press, 1974). An especially influential study of a twelfth-century romance is Erich Auerbach's "The Knight Sets Forth," in *Mimesis* (Princeton, N.J.: Princeton University Press, 1953; original German edition, 1946). A standard reference is *Le Roman*, fascicule 12 of the *Typologie des sources du moyen âge occidental*, ed. J. C. Payen and F. N. M. Diekstra et al. (Turnhout, Belgium: Brepols, 1975).

Robert Louis Stevenson delightfully defends the romance in two well-known essays first published in *Longman's Magazine*: "A Gossip on Romance" (1882) and "A Humble Remonstrance" (1884; both reprinted in volume 29 of the Tusitala Edition of Stevenson's works, London: Heinemann, 1924). From the former: "The desire for knowledge, I had almost added the desire for meat, is not more deeply seated than this demand for fit and striking incident" (122); "English people of the present day are apt, I know not why, to look somewhat down on incident, and reserve their admiration for the clink of teaspoons and the accents of the curate" (124).

Richard Chase provides a twentieth-century statement of the distinction between romance and novel ("Novel vs. Romance," in *Pastoral and Romance*, ed. E. T. Lincoln [see References above]).

> The novel renders reality closely and in comprehensive detail. It takes a group of people and sets them going about the business of life. . . . By contrast the romance, following distantly the medieval example, feels freer to render reality in less volume and detail. It tends to prefer action to character, and action will be freer in romance than in a novel, encountering, as it were, less resistance from reality. (282–83)

Kenneth Graham's *English Criticism of the Novel, 1865–1900* (Oxford: Clarendon Press, 1965) notes various discussions of the role of the Romance during the period treated. Jay MacPherson's "Romance Since Spenser (English)," in *The Spenser Encyclopedia*, ed. A. C. Hamilton (Toronto: Toronto University Press, 1990) ranges widely in bringing a variety of examples of literature in English since Spenser under the umbrella of romance. "Most Gothic novels are in some sense about the grip of the past on the present: the young hero (or heroine) from whom its secrets are hidden is tyrranized by them, and their revelation sets him free" (620).

ROMANTICISM   1. As first applied to literature in the seventeenth century, a way of designating the form and content of works differing from Greek and Roman models. 2. A general European reaction against, or movement away from, neo-classicism in the latter half of the eighteenth century and extending through the greater part, if not the whole, of the nineteenth century. 3. In England, the period from 1789 (the date of publication of Blake's *Songs of Innocence*) or at latest 1798 (the date of Wordsworth and Coleridge's *Lyrical Ballads*) to at least 1822 (the year of Shelley's death), and perhaps encompassing the first third or even half of the nineteenth century as well. 4. An orientation dominant in certain historical periods and always present in humanity which is variously characterized as giving preference to the IMAGINATION over the reason, to the transcendental over the empirical, to the contemplation of the infinite rather than the finite, and/or to the belief that human beings are basically good rather than evil.

The aspects of Romanticism receiving major emphasis vary not only among the four senses listed above but also according to whether primary focus is on literature or culture in general, and even within these categories, it varies from scholar to scholar. In an influential essay of 1924, "On the Discrimination of Romanticisms," A. O. Lovejoy argues that there are so many, and often conflicting, ways in which the term Romanticism is used that no common denominator can be found. "The word 'romantic' has come to mean so many things that, by itself, it means nothing. It has ceased to perform the function of a verbal sign" (232). However, a considerable number of the essays on Romanticism since have argued that there is, in fact, a common core of meaning.

1. The original use of the term Romanticism as far as literary history is concerned appears to have been in the seventeenth century in reference to works that were outside the traditions of Greek and Roman literature. René Wellek writes: "The term 'romantic poetry' was used first of Ariosto and Tasso and the medieval romances from which their themes and 'machinery' were derived. It occurs in this sense in France in 1669, in England in 1674, and certainly Thomas Warton understood it to mean this when he wrote his introductory dissertation to his *History of English Poetry* (1774)" (131).

2. A movement opposing various characteristics of neo-classicism that can broadly be termed romantic (although the term itself was applied retrospectively) arose in various European countries in the eighteenth century. Jacques Barzun writes in *Classic, Romantic and Modern*, "For our present purpose, historic romanticism can be defined as comprising those Europeans whose birth falls between 1770 and 1815, and who achieved distinction in philosophy, statecraft,

and the arts during the first half of the nineteenth century'' (8). In the last years of the eighteenth century and in the early 1800s a considerable discussion of the differences between ancient and modern or classical and romantic developed; Wellek cites A. W. Schlegel's pronouncements as the most influential of these. ''Schlegel formulated the contrast, classical and romantic, as that between the poetry of antiquity and modern poetry, associating romantic with progressive and Christian. He sketched a history of romantic literature which starts with a discussion of the mythology of the Middle Ages and closes with a review of the Italian poetry of what we would today call the Renaissance'' (135).

Definitions of and emphases on the characteristics of the movement as a whole vary among its historians. Referring to nineteenth-century writers on literature and aesthetics, Wellek states, ''[O]n the whole there was really no misunderstanding about the meaning of 'romanticism' as a new designation for poetry, opposed to the poetry of neoclassicism, and drawing its inspiration and models from the Middle Ages and the Renaissance'' (151–52). The characteristics of this poetry he defines succinctly: ''imagination for the view of poetry, nature for the view of the world, and symbol and myth for poetic style'' (161). Morse Peckham, who devotes a number of essays to the question of the meaning of romanticism, argues in ''Toward a Theory of Romanticism'' (1951) that despite Lovejoy's earlier essay denying a central meaning to Romanticism, Lovejoy actually did define its major characteristic in the final chapters of *The Great Chain of Being* as a mode of thought that developed in the late eighteenth and early nineteenth centuries and which was wholly different from the tradition of human thought since Plato. The movement was from ''static dynamism,'' the concept of the world as machine-like, to ''dynamic organism,'' the idea of the world as organized like a living thing. ''Hence the new thought is organicism. Now the first quality of an organism is that it is not something made, it is something *being* made or growing.'' For this reason, ''change becomes a positive value, not a negative value'' (10). The degree to which Peckham's and Wellek's well-known summations of European romanticism are compatible has been a matter of debate between them; most scholars find belief in the power of imagination and the principle of organicism central to the European Romantic movement. A later formulation by Peckham aligns Romanticism more strongly with contemporary poststructuralist views: ''What the first couple of generations [of Romantic writers] had in common was the realization that the thing to be explained was not the nature of the world but rather that the most important thing men do is to create explanations of the world'' (''Romanticism,'' 78).

Among those who have found in Romanticism an essentially unhealthy orientation, the New Humanists Irving Babbitt and Paul Elmer More are perhaps best known; both find it a form of egoism seeking an impossible vision of the infinite, and wish to combat it, particularly as it manifests itself in the thought of Rousseau. ''Now, the romantic movement, beneath all its show of expansion and vitality, seems to me at its heart to be . . . a drift towards distintegration and disease,'' writes More (viii). And, ''[i]f I had to designate very briefly this underlying principle which gives to historic romance a character radically different from the mystery and wonder of classic art, I should define it as that expansive conceit of the emotions which goes with the illusion of beholding the infinite within the stream of nature itself instead of apart from the stream'' (xiii). F. L. Lucas, finding more value in Romanticism, nevertheless regards it primarily as an escape: ''Romantic literature is a dream-picture of life; providing sustenance and fulfillment for impulses cramped by society or reality'' (35–36). In *The Romantic Agony*, Mario Praz concentrates on a current of masochism and sadism running through Romanticism and comments, ''In no other literary period, I think, has sex been so obviously the mainspring of works of imagination'' (vii).

3. It is much easier to delineate English Romantic poetry than the European Romantic movement, although disagreement about various aspects of the English Romantic movement is not uncommon. The fullest consensus is found in naming Wordsworth, Coleridge, Shelley, and Keats as the four major English Romantic poets. Byron is most frequently made the fifth, but the increasing attention given to Blake in recent decades has tended to displace Byron. Burns is at times proposed as the sixth or seventh important Romantic poet. The English movement, of course, extends well beyond the half-dozen poets with whom it is chiefly identified. Ernest Bernbaum's *Guide Through the Romantic Movement* treats Hazlitt, Scott, Southey, Campbell, Landor, Moore, Hunt, De Quincey, and Carlyle as well as the major poets.

C. M. Bowra places the close of the Romantic phase of English poetry at the death of Shelley in 1822; however, if the Romantic impulse is associated primarily with a turn away from neo-classicism and a high valuation of the imagination (however defined), then the whole of the nineteenth century, both in poetry and in prose, can be argued to be essentially romantic. Yeats's claim, ''We are the last romantics'' (''Coole Park and Ballylee, 1931'') is invoked in Graham Hough's *The Last Romantics*, which traces currents from Ruskin to Yeats. In addition, many an author of the eighteenth century can be regarded as pre-Romantic: Bernbaum's *Guide* lists some forty figures from Shaftesbury to Cowper. The Romanticism that More questions is rather surprisingly represented in *The Drift of Romanticism* by Beckford, Newman, Pater, Fiona Macleod, Nietzsche, and Huxley.

While differing in their emphases, scholars and critics looking primarily to the Romantic poets assign a reasonably consistent constellation of characteristics. A well-known early-twentieth-century formulation is by Theodore Watts-Dunton: Romantic poetry represents the ''Renasence of Wonder,'' the earlier period of wonder having ended with Milton. ''The phrase, the Renasence of Wonder, merely indicates that there are two great impulses governing man, and probably not man only, but the entire world of conscious life: the impulse of acceptance— the impulse to take unchallenged and for granted all the phenomena of the outer world as they are—and the impulse to confront these phenomena with eyes of inquiry and wonder'' (237–38). Walter Jackson Bate traces the way English empiricism led to individualism and the preference for the particular over the general. "Empiricism, having disposed of the mind as a strictly rational instrument, was increasingly forced to fall back on the immediate feeling of the individual" (129). For C. M. Bowra, the "single characteristic which differentiates the English Romantics from the poets of the eighteenth century is to be found in the importance which they attached to the imagination and in the special view they held of it" (1). In other words, Blake, Coleridge, Wordsworth, Shelley, and Keats all believed "that the creative imagination is closely connected with a peculiar insight into an unseen order behind visible things" (271). Richard Harter Fogle finds the principle of Romanticism in "the principle of vital growth, manifested in poetry by organic unity, or a oneness of form and content not superimposed from the outside by mechanical rules but organically proceeding from the interaction of the poet's mind with his materials" ("Romantic Movement," 113).

In *The Mirror and the Lamp*, M. H. Abrams stresses the shift to the expressive function of poetry. "Repeatedly romantic predications about poetry, or about art in general, turn on a metaphor which, like 'overflow,' signifies the internal made external. The most frequent of these terms was 'expression' " (48). Thus, "[i]n the main . . . romantic critics substituted the presentation of a world that is instinct with the poet's feelings for the depiction of the universal and typical as the property which distinguishes poetry from descriptive discourse" (56).

Whatever the order of precedence, the primacy of the individual imagination, which yields insights beyond what can be granted by the senses; belief in the principle that human creations should develop organically; pursuit of the particular rather than the general; and a sense of wonder or awe before the natural world and before intimations of a transcendent power are the characteristics most generally associated with English Romantic poetry.

In American literature, writers such as Bryant, Brockden Brown, Poe, Hawthorne, Longfellow, Emerson, Thoreau, Melville, and Whitman all evidence important qualities associated with the Romantic movement, but the term is much less helpful as a description of nineteenth-century literary and intellectual currents in the United States than in England or on the Continent. The influence of English Romantic poetry, especially of Coleridge, and the principle of organic form (see ORGANIC UNITY) on American critical thought is explored in R. H. Fogle's "Organic Form in American Criticism, 1840–1870."

4. Romanticism, as opposed to Greek and Roman classicism and eighteenth-century neo-classicism, can also be taken as an attitude toward life that becomes dominant at certain times but is always present in a culture as, in Morse Peckham's words, "a general and permanent characteristic of mind, art, and personality, found in all periods and in all cultures" ("Toward a Theory," 3).

Note

The following is a selection of statements contrasting classicism and Romanticism, some focused primarily on literature and some on basic philosophical principles. (Bernbaum's *Guide* lists twenty-eight definitions of "Romantic," some contrasting it with classicism.)

August Wilhelm Schlegel.

> Ancient poetry and art is a rhythmical *nomos*, a harmonious promulgation of the eternal leg-
> islation of a beautifully ordered world mirroring the eternal Ideas of things. Romantic poetry,
> on the other hand, is the expression of a secret longing for the chaos which is perpetually
> striving for new and marvelous births, which lies hidden in the very womb of orderly creation.
> . . . [Greek art] is simpler, clearer, more like nature in the independent perfection of its separate
> works; [Romantic art], in spite of its fragmentary appearance, is nearer to the mystery of the
> universe. (Quoted from Schlegel's *Lectures on Dramatic Art and Poetry* in Wellek's *A History
> of Modern Criticism*, 2:59)

Samuel Taylor Coleridge. (Though Coleridge does not here use the terms classic and
romantic, he is closely following A. W. Schlegel's distinction, including the identification
of the Romantic with the Christian.)

> The Greeks changed the ideas into finites, and these finites into *anthropomorphi*, or forms of
> men. Hence their religion, their poetry, nay, their very pictures become statuesque. With them
> the form was the end. The reverse of this was the natural effect of Christianity; in which finites,
> even the human form, must, in order to satisfy the mind, be brought into connexion with, and
> be in fact symbolical of, the infinite; and must be considered in some enduring, however
> shadowy and indistinct, point of view, as the vehicle or representative of moral truth. (From
> Lecture 10 of the 1818 series in Raysor's *Coleridge's Miscellaneous Criticism*, 148)

Johann Wolfgang von Goethe. "The classical is the healthy; the romantic is the dis-
eased" (*Werke*, 38:283).
Walter Pater.

> The "classic" comes to us out of the cool and quiet of other times, as the measure of what a
> long experience has shown will at least never displease us. And in the classical literature of
> Greece and Rome, as in the classics of the last century, the essentialy classical element is that
> quality of order in beauty, which they possess, indeed, in a pre-eminent degree, and which
> impresses some minds to the exclusion of everything else in them.
>   It is the addition of strangeness to beauty, that constitutes the romantic character in art; and
> the desire of beauty being a fixed element in every artistic organisation, it is the addition of
> curiosity to this desire of beauty, that constitutes the romantic temper. (*Appreciations*, 245–
> 46)

Irving Babbitt. "A thing is romantic when it is strange, unexpected, intense, superlative,
extreme, unique, etc. A thing is classical, on the other hand, when it is not unique, but
representative of a class" (4). There are two main paths for man: "he may develop his
ethical self—the self that lays hold of unity—or he may put his main emphasis on the
element within him and without him that is associated with novelty and change" (*Rousseau
and Romanticism*, 49).
T. E. Hulme.

> Here is the root of all romanticism: that man, the individual, is an infinite reservoir of possi-
> bilities; and if you can so rearrange society by the destruction of oppressive order then these
> possibilities will have a chance and you will get Progress. . . . One can define the classical quite
> clearly as the exact opposite of this. Man is an extraordinarily fixed and limited animal whose
> nature is absolutely constant. It is only by tradition and organization that anything decent can
> be got out of him. (116)

Moreover,

> [t]he romantic, because he thinks man infinite, must always be talking about the infinite. . . .
> What I mean by the classical in verse, then, is this. That even in the most imaginative flights

there is always a holding back, a reservation. The classical poet never forgets this finiteness, this limit of man. (*Speculations*, 119–20)

F. L. Lucas. The recurring qualities of Romanticism are:

Remoteness, the sad delight of desolation, silence and the supernatural, winter and dreariness; vampirine love and stolen trysts, the flowering of passion and the death of beauty; Radcliffe horrors and sadistic cruelty, disillusion, death, and madness; the Holy Grail and battles on the Border; the love of the impossible. (24–25)

The qualities of the classic are:

Grace, self-knowledge, self-control; the sense of form, the easy wearing of the chains of art hidden under flowers, as with some sculptured group that fills with life and litheness its straitened prison in the triangle of a pediment; idealism steadied by an unfaltering sense of reality; lamp and midnight-oil, rather than the wine-cup. (*The Decline and Fall of the Romantic Ideal*, 28)

Albert Guérard. "Classicism is restraint, Romanticism is urge; if these plain terms be accepted, it will be evident that the two tendencies are not parallel, independent, mutually exclusive; they are part of a single whole, they *must* co-exist in every work of art" (*Preface to World Literature*, 164).

Jacques Barzun. "Classicism is . . . stability within known limits; romanticism is expansion within limits known and unknown" (58). "To suppose that one can have classicism without authoritarianism is like supposing that one can have braking power without friction. Conversely, romanticism is not simply love of ease or impatient rebellion. It is a different way of fulfilling human wants after the breakdown of an attempt at eternal order" (*Romanticism and the Modern Ego*, 58, 69–70).

References

Abrams, M. H. *The Mirror and the Lamp*. 1953; New York: Norton, 1958. An important exploration of Romantic thought.

Babbitt, Irving. *Rousseau and Romanticism*. 1919; Boston: Houghton Mifflin, 1965.

Barzun, Jacques. *Classic, Romantic and Modern*. 1943; 2d ed. Boston: Little, Brown and Company, 1961. Considers the total European culture including all the arts. "Romanticism as a European phenomenon . . . comes of age between 1780 and 1830, and remains undisputed master of the field until about 1850" (98).

———. *Romanticism and the Modern Ego*. Boston: Little, Brown, 1947.

Bate, Walter Jackson. *From Classic to Romantic*. 1946; New York: Harper and Row, 1961. Analyzes the general philosophical currents; the role of associationist theory is given particular attention.

Bernbaum, Ernest. *Guide Through the Romantic Movement*. 1930; 2d ed. New York: Ronald Press, 1949. A standard guide to the English Romantic poets which includes a dated, though still useful, bibliography.

Bowra, C. M. *The Romantic Imagination*. Cambridge, Mass.: Harvard University Press, 1957. "So far from thinking that the imagination deals with the non-existent, they [the English Romantic poets] insist that it reveals an important kind of truth. They believe that when it is at work it sees things to which ordinary intelligence is blind and that it is intimately connected with a special insight or perception or intuition" (7).

Coleridge, Samuel Taylor. *Coleridge's Miscellaneous Criticism*. Ed. Thomas M. Raysor. Cambridge: Harvard University Press, 1936.

Fogle, Richard Harter. "Organic Form in American Criticism, 1840–1870." In *The Development of American Literary Criticism*, ed. Floyd Stovall. Chapel Hill: University of North Carolina Press, 1955.

———. "The Romantic Movement." In *Contemporary Literary Scholarship*, ed. L. Leary. New York: Appleton-Century-Crofts, 1958.

Goethe, Johann Wolfgang von. "Maximen und Reflexionen." In vol. 38 of *Sämtliche Werke*. Jubiläums-ausgabe. Stuttgart: J. S. Cotta, 1902–7.

Guérard, Albert. *Preface to World Literature*. New York: Henry Holt, 1940. Chapter 9 on Classicism and Romanticism is a brief, highly readable interpretation of classicism as discipline and Romanticism as rebellion.

Hough, Graham. *The Last Romantics*. 1947; London: Methuen, 1961.

Hulme, T. E. "Romanticism and Classicism." In *Speculations*. London: Kegan Paul, Trench, Trubner, 1924. A constantly cited essay.

Lovejoy, A. O. "On the Discrimination of Romanticisms." *PMLA* 39 (June 1924): 229–53.

Lucas, F. L. *The Decline and Fall of the Romantic Ideal*. Cambridge: Cambridge University Press, 1936. " 'Romance' means first a certain language; then a certain type of literature composed in that language; then the epithet 'romantic' is applied to the unreality associated with that type of literature; or to the temperament associated with that type of unreality; or to the literary forms associated with that type of temperament" (18–19).

More, Paul Elmer. Preface. In *The Drift of Romanticism*. Shelburne Essays, 8th Series. Boston: Houghton Mifflin, 1913.

Pater, Walter. *Appreciations*. 1889; London: Macmillan, 1911.

Peckham, Morse. "Romanticism: The Present State of Theory." In *The Triumph of Romanticism*. Columbia, S.C: University of South Carolina Press, 1970.

———. "Toward a Theory of Romanticism." In *The Triumph of Romanticism*. Columbia, S.C.: University of South Carolina Press, 1970. Reprinted from *PMLA* 66 (March 1951): 5–23.

Praz, Mario. *The Romantic Agony*. Trans. A. Davidson. 1933; London: Oxford University Press, 1951.

Schlegel, August Wilhelm. *Lectures on Dramatic Art and Poetry* (1809–1811). Quoted from vol. 2, p. 59 of René Wellek's *A History of Modern Criticism, 1750–1950*, New Haven, Conn.: Yale University Press, 1955.

Watts-Dunton, Theodore. *Poetry and the Renasence of Wonder*. London: Herbert Jenkins, 1916.

Wellek, René. "The Concept of Romanticism in Literary History" (1949). In *Concepts of Criticism*. New Haven, Conn.: Yale University Press, 1963. A major survey.

Sources of Additional Information

Ernest Bernbaum's "The Romantic Movement" in *The English Romantic Poets: A Review of Research* (New York: Modern Language Association, 1956) is a valuable bibliographical essay despite its datedness. For an examination of the specific character of the imagery of the English Romantic poets, see W. K. Wimsatt's "The Structure of Romantic Nature Imagery" in *The Verbal Icon* (Lexington: University Press of Kentucky, 1954).

If we think of a scale of structures having at one end logic, the completely reasoned and abstracted, and at the other some form of madness or surrealism, matter or impression unformed and undisciplined (the imitation of disorder by the idiom of disorder), we may see metaphysical and neoclassical poetry as near the extreme of logic (though by no means reduced to that status) and romantic poetry as a step toward the directness of sensory presentation (though by no means sunk into subrationality). (116)

M. H. Abrams's *Natural Supernaturalism* (New York: Norton, 1971), a major study, stresses the "secularization of inherited theological ideas and ways of thinking" in the Romantic movement; it seeks to show that "Romantic thought and literature represented a decisive turn in Western culture" (12, 14).

For a Marxist revisionist approach, see Jerome J. McGann's *The Romantic Ideology* (Chicago: University of Chicago Press, 1983).

For a comprehensive overview of the Continental Romanticism as well as the English, see Volume 2 of René Wellek's *History of Modern Criticism: 1750–1950*. New Haven, Conn.: Yale University Press, 1955.

S

SATIRE   1. As the designation of a specific genre, formal verse satire, a poem in which the satirist, usually speaking in the first person, attacks one or more individuals, an institution, or some form of general human viciousness or folly. 2. As what is frequently called either Menippean or Varronian satire, an attack as above, but carried out in the form of a loosely constructed narrative or an ironic essay, usually in the third person. 3. As the designation of a tone, or attitude, or style of writing, any use of comedy, IRONY, or ridicule to reveal vice or folly.

All three senses of satire are believed to have been derived from the Latin lanx satura, *"full or mixed dish" (see Highet, 231–33), first used literarily to describe works treating a variety of subjects or written in a variety of styles. During the greater part of the Renaissance, the term was thought to derive from the Greek satyr plays as set out in the fourth-century preface to the plays of Terence by Aelius Donatus. This assumed etymology was attacked but not immediately destroyed by Isaac Causabon's* De Satyrica Graecorum Poesi et Romanorum Satira *(1605).*

In considering satire in senses 1 and 2 especially, the importance of not confusing the speaker—whether the apparent speaker in a formal satire, the narrator of a satiric story, or a character in a play—with the AUTHOR *has increasingly been recognized. Maynard Mack's "The Muse of Satire" (1951) argues that "The contours of a formal verse satire . . . are not established entirely or even primarily by a poet's rancorous sensibility; they are part of a fiction" (194). Alvin Kernan similarly protests that the actual author must be distinguished from what he calls the satirist, a persona that is partly the result of convention. "Now it would be nonsense to argue, as the biographical critic does, that all authors of satire are straightforward, honest, pessimistic, indignant men who dislike ostentatious rhetoric, come from the country, and have simple moral codes" (22). "Satirist" as used below refers to the persona, not the flesh-and-blood author*.

1. As a specific genre, the formal verse satire is found primarily in Roman literature of the first century B.C. and first century A.D., with Arisosto in Italy, Mathurin Régnier and Nicolas Boileau in France, and in English literature from the end of the sixteenth century to the early nineteenth. It is regarded as having originated with Lucilius (180–102 B.C.), and reached its height in Roman Literature in Horace, Persius, and Juvenal. The well-known statement of Quintilian, *"satira quidem tota nostra est"* (satire belongs to us [Romans] alone, 4:53; X.1.93) is best understood as referring to such verse satire, written in hexameters, as practiced after Lucilius, most eminently by the three great Roman satirists.

The Roman models were decisive in establishing the central tradition of English verse satire in which the satirist delivers his thrusts directly (Gilbert Highet thus calls this form of satire the *monologue*). The greatest influence was that of Juvenalian style, which is harsher, less compromising, and more in pursuit of the knave than the fool. Mary Claire Randolph writes, "From observation and study of the classical satires, then, the English Renaissance satirist learned these elementary things about form: that satires were usually written in clusters of indeterminate number, sometimes introduced by separate prologue or preface; that their lengths were extremely variable; and that they were semidramatic and monometric" (180). The satires of Ariosto (in terza rima) and Régnier were also influential in establishing the conventions of verse satire. From at least the time of the *Virgidemiarum* (1598) of Joseph Hall, the conventions coalesced into a definite English genre. Hall, who thought of himself as the first English satirist, had the Roman tradition directly in view. As David Worcester points out, Hall "felt himself bound to verse, to the decasyllabic couplet, to roughness of versification and rudeness of manner. He must closely imitate Horace, Persius, and Juvenal[,] . . . indulge in darksome innuendo, feel a divine mission, and burn with wrath as he wields the flail" (4). The license in versification, diction, and violation of taste found in these models seemed further authorized by the Renaissance etymology of the word satire from the satyr plays. O. J. Campbell thus explains "Satire, [critics of the Renaissance] thought, was in origin a rude form of ridicule designed to purge simple men of their faults and was composed to serve as the characteristic utterance of crude sylvan gods—hence its harshness and license" ("The Elizabethan Satyr-Satirist," 84).

Dryden's *A Discourse Concerning the Original and Progress of Satire* (1693) pointed toward further regularization: the verse satire should be unified by focus on a single target and should use the pentameter couplet. Beyond this, Dryden quotes a definition of satire from Daniel Heinsius:

> Satire is a kind of poetry, without a series of action, invented for the purging of our minds; in which human vices, ignorance, and errors, and all things besides, which are produced from them in every man, are severely reprehended; partly dramatically, partly simply, and sometimes in both kinds of speaking; but, for the most part, figuratively, and occultly; consisting in a low familiar way, chiefly in a sharp and

pungent manner of speech; but partly, also, in a facetious and civil way of jesting; by which either hatred, or laughter, or indignation, is moved. (2:100)

Dryden generally approves this description, except for the phrase "consisting in a low and familiar way of speech," which, he comments, is true of Horace but not of all satire.

The central English tradition—in which the poem is in heroic couplets and the satirist directly mounts his attack—is exemplified by Hall, Butler (*The Elephant in the Moon*), Dryden (*The Medall*), Pope (*Imitations of Horace*), Johnson (*The Vanity of Human Wishes*), and Byron (*English Bards and Scotch Reviewers*). It is obvious that some of the best-known satires of the writers just mentioned depart in at least some way from the norm: Butler's *Hudibras* employs the octosyllabic couplet, and Byron's *Don Juan* uses ottava rima; *Hudibras*, Dryden's *Absalom and Achitophel*, Pope's *Dunciad*, and (more or less) Byron's *Don Juan* are satiric narratives rather than monologues. However, all lie on the boundary, if not actually within the genre, of the formal verse satire.

The unity of even these formal verse satires lies in the attitude they reflect: indignation toward vice and folly expressed through the more or less humorous depiction of their grotesqueness and absurdity.

Of particular interest is the relationship between formal verse satire, with its first-person commentator, and Renaissance drama. O. J. Campbell points out that some of Shakespeare's most problematic plays are dominated by the satiric spirit. "During the first decade of the seventeenth century Shakespeare began to give freer rein to his satiric spirit and to grind it to a sharper edge. Indeed some of the dramas that he wrote during these years, notably *Troilus and Cressida*, *Measure for Measure*, *Coriolanus*, and *Timon of Athens*, are not only filled with the harsh spirit of formal satire, but in construction they also display distinguishing characteristics of the genre" (*Shakespeare's Satire*, viii). What in essence happens is that the satirist is made a character who is himself satirized. Alvin Kernan, examining the satire in the comedies of Jonson and Marston as well as the tragedies of Shakespeare, Tourneur, Webster, and Marston, argues that the impulse to put satire in the mouth of a character gives way to the construction of dramas in which character and event are self-satirizing. "Satire appears to have had too narrow a range for the more gifted [Renaissance] dramatists, and they turned their 'satiric' plays into examinations of the credentials of satire itself and explorations of the validity of the satiric sense of life. In doing so they inevitably subordinated satire to tragedy or comedy, and left it to the next age to become the great period of English satire" (246).

2. Where the satiric attack announces itself through the absurdity of the events narrated or enacted on the stage rather than through direct commentary, the work is generally regarded as Menippean or Varronian satire. (Menippus was a third-century Greek who wrote burlesque narratives mixing prose and verse; Varro wrote such works in Latin in the first century B.C.) Though this term was originally applicable only to satire mixing poetry and prose, any extended satire that resists classification as formal verse satire—including farce, burlesque, and

parody—is likely to be regarded as Menippean. It thus has a much wider range, both chronologically and generically, than formal verse satire. Langland's *Piers Plowman*, Petronius's *Satyricon*, Erasmus's *Praise of Folly*, Shakespeare's *Timon*, Jonson's *Volpone*, Swift's *A Tale of a Tub* and *Gulliver's Travels*, Peacock's short novels, and Twain's *A Connecticut Yankee in King Arthur's Court* fall in this category.

If the eighteenth-century is the golden age both of English verse satire, as represented by Pope and Johnson, and of the non-novelistic narrative, mock essay, and general farrago represented respectively by Swift's *Gulliver's Travels*, *A Modest Proposal*, and *A Tale of a Tub*, the latter part of the eighteenth century sees the richest satire shifting to the novel in Fielding, Smollett, and Sterne, where it has largely remained.

3. Certainly the satiric attitude antedates specific literary uses. Robert Elliott traces the satiric impulse back to legends of Greek, Arab, and Irish "satirists" who had the magical power to kill or injure merely through their words. Matthew Hodgart quotes the anthropologist Paul Radin: "I know of no tribes where satires and formal narratives avowedly humorous have not attained a rich development. Examples of every conceivable form are found, from broad lampoon and crude invective to subtle innuendo and satire based on man's stupidity, his gluttony, and his lack of a sense of proportion" (34–35). G. L. Hendrickson has explored the various forms of satire inherent in Greek thought and writing long before the Roman verse satire. Incidental satire does not adhere to any set form; it seems to be able to make use of, and thus at least partially transform, any genre. Drama and the novel are, however, the forms in which works are most likely to be spiced with satire without becoming wholly satirical. COMEDY is likely to include patches of satire; O. J. Campbell, for instance, points to the elements of satire in Shakespeare's comedies where the fool is a source of laughter (e.g., Launce in *Two Gentlemen of Verona*); he finds satire as evident in the tragedies (e.g., the figure of Osric in *Hamlet*).

It is as hard to draw the line between a satire (a work satirical in essence) and a work containing satire as it is to draw the line between formal satire and Menippean. *Candide* seems a satire; *Rasselas* seems an apologue with satirical portions. Which Restoration comedies fall primarily within comedy and which within satire is a matter of debate. Fielding's *Shamela*, *Joseph Andrews*, and *Tom Jones* form a graded series. Dickens's *Bleak House* can be described as "a satire on the legal system" but would not generally be described simply as "a satire." *Huckleberry Finn* is filled with satire, but to call it "a satire" will seem to most readers reductive. From one point of view, exact categorization is neither necessary nor possible. On the other hand, the problems that arise from attempting to read a work not essentially a satire as if it were, or a work containing incidental satire as if it were wholly a satire, have been insightfully considered by Sheldon Sacks in the first chapter of *Fiction and the Shape of Belief*.

In summary the essential ingredients of satire are humor, a target against which the humor is directed, and, at least until this century, an at least implicit

ideal against which the target of the satire may be compared. Further characteristics frequently cited are vividness in describing folly or vice, which generally
leads to the depiction of the unpleasant, obscene, or nasty; an apparent intention
either to punish or cure; the evocation of a mixture of amusement and contempt;
and the projection of a personal inability to abide wickeness or folly. Patricia
Spacks adds the production of a sense of uneasiness. Given the variety of kinds
of writing generally regarded as satirical, it is not surprising that while most
critics would agree that all or most of these characteristics are relevant, there
are important differences of emphasis. It should also be noted that with the
exception of the first (vividness), all these characteristics derive from subjective
responses that the author is presumed to have intended to produce.

Various modes of categorization reflect the differing interests of critics. Thus,
the scaffolding of Northrop Frye's *Anatomy of Criticism* leads him to discriminate
between satire that employs convention as its norm, that which questions conventions, and that which is radical in its questioning, doubting even common
sense. Edward Rosenheim differentiates persuasive from punitive satire. David
Worcester emphasizes the importance of irony in all satire, while Frye is interested in the differences within satire. Louis Bredvold points out that satire is
frequently seen as a contamination of the comic, but Ronald Knox finds humor
without satire to be "a perversion, the misuse of a sense." The critics who give
primary attention to its humor think of satire somewhat differently than the ones
who concentrate on the bite of its criticism; critics who emphasize the satirist's
underlying idealism or desire to reform society respond somewhat differently
from those who emphasize the satirist's hatred for evil and the evil-doer.

References

Bredvold, Louis I. "A Note in Defense of Satire." *ELH* 7 (December 1940): 253–64.
Campbell, O. J. "The Elizabethan Satyr-Satirist and His Satire." In *Satire: Modern
      Essays in Criticism*, ed. Ronald Paulson. Englewood Cliffs, N.J.: Prentice-Hall,
      1971.
————. *Shakespeare's Satire*. London: Oxford University Press, 1943.
Dryden, John. "A Discourse Concerning the Original and Progress of Satire" (1693).
      In Vol. 2 of *Essays of John Dryden*. Ed. W. P. Ker. 2 vols. Oxford: Clarendon
      Press, 1900.
Elliott, Robert C. *The Power of Satire: Magic, Ritual, Art*. Princeton, N.J.: Princeton
      University Press, 1960.
Frye, Northrop. *The Anatomy of Criticism*. Princeton, N.J.: Princeton University Press,
      1957. See the section titled "The Mythos of Winter."
Hendrickson, G. L. "Satura Tota Nostra Est." In *Satire: Modern Essays in Criticism*.
      Reprinted from *Classical Philology* 22 (January 1927): 46–60.
Highet, Gilbert. *The Anatomy of Satire*. Princeton, N.J.: Princeton University Press,
      1962. An important study; the contents pages give an excellent summary of the
      points discussed, making the volume especially convenient for reference.
Hodgart, Matthew. *Satire*. London: Weidenfeld and Nicolson, 1969.
Kernan, Alvin P. *The Cankered Muse: Satire of the English Renaissance*. New Haven,

Conn.: Yale University Press, 1959. The introductory chapter, which is reprinted
in *Satire: Modern Essays in Criticism*, is a cogent commentary on satire generally.

Knox, Ronald A. "On Humour and Satire." In *Satire: Modern Essays in Criticism*.
Reprinted from *Essays in Satire*. London: Sheed and Ward, 1928. An essay
attempting to distinguish humor from satire: "The humourist runs with the hare;
the satirist hunts with the hounds" (59).

Mack, Maynard. "The Muse of Satire." In *Satire: Modern Essays in Criticism*. Reprinted
from *The Yale Review* 41 (1951): 80–92. Important essay emphasizing the structure
that the author gives to the satire.

Quintilian. *Institutio Oratoria*. Trans. H. E. Butler. 4 vols. Loeb Classical Library.
Cambridge: Harvard University Press, 1936.

Radin, Paul. "Primitive Literature: Nature and Evolution." In *The World Through Literature*, ed. Charlton Laird. London: Peter Owen, 1959.

Randolph, Mary Claire. "The Structural Design of Formal Verse Satire." In *Satire:
Modern Essays in Criticism*. Reprinted from *Philological Quarterly* 21 (1942):
368–84.

Rosenheim, Edward, Jr. *Swift and the Satirist's Art*. Chicago: University of Chicago
Press, 1963.

Sacks, Sheldon. *Fiction and the Shape of Belief: A Study of Fielding*. Berkeley: University
of California Press, 1964.

Satire: Modern Essays in Criticism. Ed. Ronald Paulson. Englewood Cliffs, N.J.: Prentice-Hall, 1971. An excellent collection of essays on satire.

Spacks, Patricia Meyer. "Some Reflections on Satire." In *Satire: Modern Essays in
Criticism*.

Worcester, David. *The Art of Satire*. Cambridge, Mass.: Harvard University Press, 1940.

Sources of Additional Information

Good general surveys of English satire from its earliest appearances will be found in
Hugh Walker's *English Satire and Satirists* (London: J. M. Dent, 1925) and James
Sutherland's *English Satire* (Cambridge: Cambridge University Press, 1958).

John Heath-Stubbs's *The Verse Satire* is an unusually valuable little volume; its focus
is on English verse satire though it begins with the Romans (London: Oxford University
Press, 1969). The exemplary passages provided by Heath-Stubbs are convenient references. For a survey of earlier English formal verse satire from Wyatt to Richard Braithwaite, see Raymond MacDonald Alden's *The Rise of Formal Satire in England Under
Classical Influence* (Philadelphia: Publications of the University of Pennsylvania, vol. 7,
no. 2, 1899).

Ronald Paulson's *Satire and the Novel in Eighteenth-Century England* (New Haven,
Conn.: Yale University Press, 1967) and *The Fictions of Satire* (Baltimore: Johns Hopkins
University Press, 1967) are standard critical studies. The latter examines the kinds of
fictions created to support various satires.

"The Medical Concept in English Renaissance Satiric Theory" by Mary Claire Randolph (*Philological Quarterly* 21, 1942: 368–84, and reprinted in *Satire: Modern Essays
in Criticism* [See References above]) explores the large amount of medical imagery
employed in and used to describe Renaissance satire. She finds such imagery pointing
back to the primitive idea of the actual destructive power of satire among the Celts as
well as to its assumed curative function. Fred Norris Robinson surveys the magical (and
presumably lethal) powers ascribed to what were called satirists in early Irish legends

("Satirists and Enchanters in Early Irish Literature" in *Satire: Modern Essays in Criticism*, ed. Ronald Paulson [see References above]).

For a pleasant survey of types of satire supported by exemplary passages, see Arthur Pollard's *Satire* (London: Methuen, 1970).

Somewhat curiously, satire in American literature (other than in specific works and writers) has received almost no attention. Lewis P. Simpson's "The Satiric Mode: The Early National Wits" points out the lack of humor in the satires written in the early Republic (in *The Comic Imagination in American Literature*, ed. Louis D. Rubin, New Brunswick, N.J.: Rutgers University Press, 1973).

SEMANTICS 1. Having to do with meaning, especially that of human language. 2. In an early and brief narrowing of the meaning by Michel Bréal, the study of the laws through which other than phonetic changes occur in the language. 3. The study of the relation between signs and what they signify. 4. The study of the meanings of words as defined by their "sense," that is, by their relation to other words (lexical items). 5. The attempt to account for the non-grammatical knowledge necessary to explain an individual's linguistic competence through componential analysis.

This entry seeks to discriminate the various senses of semantics; for the definition and problems associated with MEANING, *see that entry.*

1. In its earliest and broadest sense, semantic, for which the *Oxford English Dictionary* (*OED*) reports no use earlier than 1894, meant "relating to signification or meaning"; its plural, semantics, appears in the *OED* as equivalent to semasiology, "which deals with the meaning of words, sense-development and the like"—semasiology having appeared in English only in 1857—and in competition with sematology, which dates from 1831. John Lyons retains this broad meaning in his 1968 *Introduction to Theoretical Linguistics*: "Semantics may be defined, initially and provisionally, as 'the study of meaning' " (400).

2. In his still-cited *Semantics: Studies in the Science of Meaning* of 1897, Michel Bréal announced, "Leaving aside the phonetic changes which belong to physiological grammar, I propose to study the intellectual causes which have influenced the transformation of our languages" (5). An example of such a cause is "The Law of Specialisation," that is, "the substitution of invariable independent exponents for exponents that are variable and dependent" (13). This is the "science of Semantics" that C. K. Ogden and I. A. Richards reject as disappointing because its metaphorical locutions "conceal the very facts which the science of language is concerned to elucidate" (3–4). A note in Saussure's *Course in General Linguistics* (26n) indicates that in 1915, Bally and Sechahaye, Saussure's editors, regarded semantics as the study of "changes in meaning."

3. Charles Morris's *Foundations of the Theory of Signs* (1938) defined the *semantical dimension* of semiosis (see SEMIOTICS) as the "relations of signs to the objects to which the signs are applicable" (6) or, in another formulation, "Semantics deals with the relation of signs to their designata and so to the objects

which they may or do denote'' (21). It is to be noted that by describing semantics as the study of the relation of the SIGN to designata or denotata, and not to the *interpretant* (to use his term), Morris was focusing on the relation to the ''objects'' designated while at the same time recognizing that the object need not necessarily exist. He was further concerned to deny the belief that ''languages mirror (correspond with, reflect, are isomorphic with) the realm of nonlinguistic objects'' (26).

4. In asking how it is that utterances can be said to have meaning, semantics has increasingly focused on explaining and defining more exactly such phenomena as synonymy, homonymy, polysemia, and antonymy, as those can be explained as the result of lexical systems, that is, the relations between words (signs, lexical items), not between words and nonlinguistic objects. ''As far as the empirical investigation of the structure of language is concerned, the sense of a lexical item may be defined to be, not only dependent upon, but identical with, the set of relations which hold between the item in question and other items in the same lexical system'' (Lyons, 443). In Geoffrey Leech's words: ''A criterion of 'meaningfulness,' for a philosopher, will tend to revolve around the evaluation of sentences for truth and falsehood. For a linguist, on the other hand, 'meaningfulness' must be dealt with by reference to what utterances make good sense, or fail to make good sense, to the people whose linguistic knowledge and behavior he is studying'' (4). As Leech points out, semantics is not concerned with context. Thus, ''That girl is a boy'' is semantically unacceptable, though it could meaningfully be said ''in reply to a person who had mistaken the sex of a baby'' (11).

5. Componential analysis was introduced by J. J. Katz, J. A. Fodor, and P. M. Postal in the early 1960s. The definition of semantics remains quite general: ''Semantics is the study of linguistic meaning. It is concerned with what sentences and other linguistic objects express, not with the arrangement of their syntactic parts or with their pronunciation'' (Katz, 1). The compositional approach is, however, focused on finding the answer to the standard questions of semantics: ''What are synonymy and paraphrase?'' ''What is semantic ambiguity?'' ''What is entailment?'' through analysis of the semantic (and syntactic) markers of a word. Thus, the word ''chair'' has as semantic markers ''(Object), (Physical), (Non-living), (Artifact), (Furniture),'' and so on (Katz, 40). These make the statements, ''The chair was growing right outside'' or ''He falsified the chair'' meaningless in themselves. The difference between syntactic and semantic markers is exemplified in noting that the celebratedly anomalous sentence ''Colorless green ideas sleep furiously'' is syntactically but not semantically acceptable.

Whether pursuing compositional or more traditional analyses, semanticists continue to be concerned with the ways in which words can be used without anomaly (''The stick chased the dog,'' ''Uncles are female,'' ''a naked nude'' are examples of anomaly), and with the information that is given by a sentence without respect to context of use (''The car was red'' presupposes the existence of the car and entails that the car was colored).

References

Bréal, Michel. *Semantics: Studies in the Science of Meaning* (1897). Trans. Mrs. Henry
    Crust. New York: Dover, 1964.
Katz, Jerrold J. *Semantic Theory*. New York: Harper and Row, 1972.
Leech, Geoffrey N. *Towards a Semantic Description of English*. Bloomington: University
    of Indiana Press, 1970.
Lyons, John. *Introduction to Theoretical Linguistics*. Cambridge: Cambridge University
    Press, 1968.
Morris, Charles W. *Foundation of the Theory of Signs*. Vol 1, no. 2 of the *International
    Encyclopedia of Unified Science*. Chicago: University of Chicago Press, 1938.
Ogden, C. K., and I. A. Richards. *The Meaning of Meaning*. 1923; Harcourt, Brace and
    World, 1946.

Sources of Additional Information

Allan Keith's *Linguistic Meaning* (2 vols; London: Routledge and Kegan Paul, 1986)
is an excellent source for the meaning and use of specific semantic terms.

Stephen Ullmann's *Semantics: An Introduction to the Science of Meaning* (New York:
Barnes and Noble, 1962) is an eminently readable account of the state of semantic theory
just prior to the publication by Jerrold Katz and Jerry Fodor of "The Structure of a
Semantic Theory" (*Language* 39, 1963, 170–210). The introductory chapter briefly traces
kinds of interest in the meaning of words from Thucydides and Plato to the twentieth
century.

An Integrated Theory of Linguistic Descriptions, by Jerrold J. Katz and Paul M. Postal
(Cambridge, Mass.: MIT Press, 1964) combines the semantics of Fodor and Katz with
Chomsky's concept of generative grammar.

SEMIOTICS   1. The study of signs and signification as founded by Charles
Sanders Peirce. 2. The science of signs as founded by Ferdinand de Saussure,
his term for which was *semiology* (*sémiologie*). 3. More broadly, the study
of signs conceived as encompassing, if not reconciling, the contributions of
both Peirce and Saussure and developments therefrom to include the study of
communication as well as signification. "Semiology" is sometimes used in
this same inclusive sense. 4. More broadly, the pursuit of a general science
that might serve as the ground of all others. 5. An approach to the unification
of the sciences and/or a new understanding of human existence. 6. In a use
of semiotic peculiar to Julia Kristeva and her followers, pertaining to the
preoedipal psychic forces, and thus opposed to the *Symbolic Order* as defined
by Jacques Lacan.

*Though they had no influence on each other, Charles Sanders Peirce (1839–
1914) and Ferdinand de Saussure (1857–1913) share in the founding of the field
of semiotics as broadly defined. Interest in the nature of language, the relation
of words to things, and the concept of the* SIGN *generally have, of course, a
history extending back at least to Classical Greece; the term semiotic is sometimes
retrospectively applied to earlier such investigations. However, Peirce and Saus-*

*sure essentially initiated fresh approaches to the question of what signs are and
how they function.*

1. Peirce took the term semiotic from Locke's use of it at the the the close of *An
Essay Concerning Human Understanding* (in the form *semeiotiká*, 1690), in
which Locke classed all human understanding as being of "the nature of things
as they are in themselves," "that which man himself ought to do . . . for the
attainment of any end, especially happiness," or "the ways and means whereby
the knowledge of both the one and the other of these is attained and communicated." The third branch might be called a "doctrine of signs," the role of
which would be "to consider the nature of signs, the mind makes use of for the
understanding of things, or conveying its knowledge to others" (2:460–61).

Peirce's definition of what he saw as a new science is well known: "I am,
as far as I know, a pioneer, or rather a backwoodsman, in the work of clearing
and opening up what I call *semiotic*, that is the doctrine of the essential nature
and fundamental varieties of possible semiosis" (5.488). *Semiosis* Peirce defined
as "an action, an influence, which is, or involves, a cooperation of *three* subjects,
such as a sign, its object, and its interpretant, this tri-relative influence not being
in anyway resolvable into actions between pairs" (5.484). Peirce thought logic
in its largest sense to be the same thing as semiotic, and thus as constituted by
a grammar, a logic in the narrower sense, and a rhetoric. The grammar largely
consists of a complex classification of signs, and the logic explores questions
of the nature of deduction and induction, while the rhetoric remained inchoate
(see Zeman). Consequently, a discussion of Peirce's semiotics generally revolves
itself into an examination of his categorization of signs.

For Peirce, the sign only existed in relation to an object and an interpretant.
One of his formulations, then, is "[t]he Sign creates something in the Mind of
the Interpreter, which something, in that it has been so created by the sign, has
been, in a mediate and *relative* way, also created by the Object of the Sign,
although the Object is essentially other than the Sign. And this creature of the
sign is called the Interpretant" (8.179). In the influential monograph *Foundations
of the Theory of Signs*, Peirce's most direct disciple, Charles W. Morris, elaborated the factors constituting semiosis as follows: "that which acts as a sign
[the *sign vehicle*], that which the sign refers to [the *designatum*], and that effect
on some interpreter in virtue of which the thing in question is a sign to that
interpreter [the *interpretant*]" (*Foundations*, 3). Following Peirce, he insists that
"[t]he properties of being a sign, a designatum, an interpreter, or an interpretant
are relational properties which are taken on by participating in the functional
process of semiosis. Semiotic, then, is not concerned with the study of a particular
kind of object, but with ordinary objects in so far (and only so far) as they
participate in semiosis (4). The study of semiotics Morris divided into three
dimensions: the semantical ("the relations of signs to the objects to which the
signs are applicable"); the pragmatical ("the relation of signs to interpreters");
and the syntactical ("the formal relation of signs to one another") (6). The object
is to determine rules governing each dimension: "Syntactical rules determine

the sign relations between sign vehicles; semantical rules correlate sign vehicles with other objects; pragmatical rules state the conditions in the interpreters under which the sign vehicle is a sign'' (35). Each of the three dimensions was later subdivided into pure, descriptive, and applied (*Signs*, 219–20).

Of Peirce's three trichotomies of signs, only that which describes the relationship of the sign to the object has been generally adopted. To simplify, the *icon* is related by resemblance (a portrait, onomatopoetic language); the index by a concomitance (smoke is an index of fire); and the symbol by conventional, that is arbitrary, association. (To avoid a possible confusion, it should be noted that what Peirce calls an index, Aristotle, in describing the materials of an enthymeme, called a sign; see Corbett, p. 76.) The terms used in the other two trichotomies are *qualisign, sinsign, legisign,* and *rheme, dicent,* and *argument.*

An example of the terminological disagreements that have figured prominently in the history of the field is the quarrel over semiotic versus semiotics. Although semiotic is the term used by Peirce and Morris, semiotics has now become standard. (The final "s" of semiotics is not a sign of plurality but of the Greek origin of the word.)

2. Saussure's famous founding statement is: "A science that studies the life of signs within society is conceivable; it would be a part of social psychology and consequently of general psychology; I shall call it *semiology.* . . . Semiology would show what constitutes signs, what laws govern them" (16). Saussure defined a sign as the combination of a concept (the signified) and a sound-image or its tangible written form (the signifier) (66). Approaching the sign as a linguist, Saussure is concerned most fully with the relation between the sounds employed in language and the concepts they convey. A "slice" of sound is arbitrarily associated with a slice of what would otherwise be "a vague, uncharted nebula" or "an indefinite plane of jumbled ideas" (112). Saussure is not interested in tracing the source of the "shapeless and indistinct mass" (111) that is thought; in other words, he is not interested in the status of the object (referent). His concern, rather, is with (a) the arbitrariness of the signifier/signified link (where the association is not arbitrary, Saussure would speak of a *symbol*; thus, his use of symbol would encompass Peirce's *icon* and *index*), (b) the interdependence of both components of the sign for their existence as signifier or signified (nothing is a signifier without a signified, and vice versa), and (c) the mutually defining nature of signs, both signifiers and signified gaining their values only through their differences. The value (or, to simplify, the meaning) of a signified is the result of the place it occupies in the total system of language. Thus the argument— which Saussure himself did not make—that any attempt to understand a sign in itself leads to an infinite regress.

The work of Roland Barthes, whose *Elements of Semiology* builds primarily on Saussure, shows special interest in systems of signs other than those in language, and analyzes food, clothing, and furniture as systems of signification. His well-known assertion that semiology as the study of all signs should be seen as part of linguistics, rather than the reverse, is essentially a way of saying that linguistics is the model for understanding all "collections of objects" that function as sign systems, for "they enjoy the status of system only insofar as they pass through the relay of language" (10).

3. The importance of the investigations of the nature of the sign carried out by Peirce and Saussure was given substantial recognition during neither of their lives, and the gradual assimilation of Peirce's thought by philosophers and of Saussure's by linguists resulted in two distinct schools. Saussure's emphasis on language as a system in which each sign is defined by other signs rather than by correspondence with the "real" object to which it refers could be taken as underpinning for the argument of Edward Sapir and Benjamin Whorf for the interrelationship of culture and language, for the Russian Formalists' doctrine of the autonomous, self-referential nature of the literary text, and for Claude Lévi-Strauss's analysis of myth and cultural systems as ordered analogously to language. It thus came to be seen as a foundation for all structuralist thought (see STRUCTURALISM). Peirce's concern for the relationship of the sign to both its object and its interpreter, which links his doctrine of signs to his pragmatic theory, has led literary theorists to an interest in that theory, while the increasing interest in the role of language in thought has led to a revived interest in pragmatism among philosophers.

The relationship between semiotics and semiology has been the subject of much discussion. The two terms are at times employed as though interchangeable or a matter of linguistic preference (sémiology was earlier the preferred term in France, although it now appears to have been overtaken by sémiotique; semiotics is the most usual term in the United States, while semiology appears to remain the British preference).

However, separating the terms can continue to signal a useful distinction. Since Peirce included the object in his definition of sign, while Saussure concerned himself almost wholly with the sound (or written) image and the concept to which it was united, semiology can be regarded as emphasizing that language is a closed system of mutually defining signs, while semiotics takes account of extra-linguistic objects (though not conceived through a naive realism), and has tended to give greater attention to signs' contexts of use.

4. By including what he called indices among the forms of signs, Peirce was evidently pursuing natural as well as intentional signs. Morris makes the breadth of semiotic subject matter explicit: "Semiotic has for its goal a general theory of signs in all their forms and manifestations, whether in animals or men, whether normal or pathological, whether linguistic or nonlinguistic, whether personal or social" (Signification, 1). However, a fuller investigation of nonlinguistic and non-human uses of signs awaited later writers. Margaret Mead early recognized the potential breadth of semiotics by defining it as "patterned communication in all modalities" (quoted by Sebeok, Contributions, 22). Thomas Sebeok, one of the major inheritors of Peircean semiotic thought, writes, "The subject matter of semiotics—ultimately a mode of extending our perception of the world—is the exchange of any messages whatever and of the systems of signs which

underlie them" (*Contributions*, 1). He thus subdivides the field into *anthropo-semiotics* ("man's species-specific signaling systems"), *zoosemiotics* (the "study of animal communication in the broadest sense"), and *endosemiotics* (the study of "cybernetic systems within the body") (3).

The wide range of phenomena that can be regarded as amenable to semiotic analysis has caused most of its commentators to regard it not as a specific science or discipline but rather as an interdisciplinary field. Sebeok specifically chooses to describe semiotics as a "doctrine of signs" rather than a theory or a science (ix). Umberto Eco's "Semiotics: A Discipline or an Interdisciplinary Method?" lists almost two dozen areas of semiotic activity (for instance, meteorology, medicine, art, music, and the study of tactile communication) in arguing that the core of semiotics is the study of "referring back," an activity too omnipresent to belong to a single discipline. Moreover, Eco's *A Theory of Semiotics* makes explicit that there are two semiotic endeavors: a theory of codes (a semiotics of signification) and a theory of sign production (a semiotics of communication) (3–4). "Every act of communication to or between human beings . . . presupposes a signifying system as its necessary condition" (9), but actual production of a message "requires that the sender should foresee, and the addressee isolate, a complex network of *presuppositions* and of possible inferential *consequences*" (152). Knowledge of such presuppositions and consequences is presumably what Peirce meant by *collateral observation* (8.179).

On the other hand, it has been argued that semiotics is most profitably understood in relation to one or another specific discipline. Max H. Fisch has emphasized that Peirce's investigation of signs developed out of his preoccupation with logic, and suggests that Peirce's reference to interpreters' minds was a reluctant concession for the sake of clarity (see especially pp. 55–56). In this connection, one may note that in the passage from which Peirce took the term semiotic, Locke commented that the doctrine of sign is "aptly enough" called "logic" (461). In contrast, Charles Morris came increasingly to move toward a biological explanation: "The present study is based on the conviction that a science of signs can be most profitably developed on a biological basis and specifically within the framework of the science of behavior" (*Signs*, 2). As a recent example, Kaja Silverman asserts "the centrality of psychoanalysis to semiotics" and emphasizes sexual difference "as an organizing principle not only of the symbolic order" but of semiotics (vii–viii).

There are warnings against too imperialistic a conception of semiotics, as in Rulon Wells's "Criteria for Semiotics" and Arthur Skidmore's essay arguing against the possibility of a general theory of signs.

> If the concept of the sign relation is to be rich and complex enough to cover human language, it is going to leave out, or be inapplicable to, non-linguistic signs such as bee dances or wax impressions. On the other hand, if one's concept of sign is to be broad enough to extend to anything that might be called significant or a sign, it will lack the subtlety and complexity required to explain anything about human language. (Skidmore, 48–49)

5. Even greater claims than wide interdisciplinary utility have been and are made for semiotics—claims at least partially supported by the current preoccupation with language in discipline after discipline. Charles Morris announced in 1938 that "[t]he concept of the sign may prove to be of importance in the unification of the social, psychological, and humanistic sciences" (2) and that "it does not seem fantastic to believe that the concept of the sign may prove as fundamental to the sciences of man as the concept of the atom has been for the physical sciences or the concept of the cell for the biological sciences" (*Foundations*, 42). David Sless is explicit that "[t]he central argument which this book will develop is that the semiotic point of view can reach into every aspect of the world, providing a set of unifying ideas from which we can see the world afresh" (2). In contrast to structuralist emphases on language as a prison, Sless celebrates what he calls the *letness*, or creativity, of language (159). Thomas Sebeok's "Ecumenicalism in Semiotics" announces that "the scope of semiotics encompasses the whole of oikoumenē, the entirety of our planetary biosphere" (181–82). Behind such imperialism lies one version at least of Peirce's own vision:

> It seems a strange thing, when one comes to ponder over it, that a sign should leave its interpreter to supply a part of its meaning; but the explanation of the phenomenon lies in the fact that the entire universe–not merely the universe of existents, but all that wider universe, embracing the universe of existents as a part, the universe which we are all accustomed to refer to as "the truth"—that all this universe is perfused with signs, if it is not composed exclusively of signs. (5.448n)

Given the ease with which any text can be talked about as a system of signs and the prestige of the term, it is not surprising that a good many rather traditional terms and approaches have been rechristened. When Jonathan Culler speaks of a "semiotics of literature which would attempt to describe in a systematic fashion the modes of signification of literary discourse and the interpretive operations embodied in the institution of literature" (*Pursuit*, 12), he appears to be describing what has usually been called poetics. In reviewing Michael Riffaterre's *Semiotics of Poetry*, Culler in fact speaks of one of the two activities between which Riffaterre wavers as "descriptive semiotics or poetics." The other activity Culler finds in the book, a genetically based mode of interpretation, seems even less specifically "semiotic." The *semiotic square* around which A. J. Greimas builds a structuralist mode of analyzing narrative is the traditional logical square. Susan Tiefenbrun's "The State of Literary Semiotics: 1983" is largely a review of a variety of approaches to linguistics, structuralism, and literature from Saussure through the Russian Formalists and the Prague school, to the New Criticism, Jakobson, structuralists such as Todorov, Barthes, and Greimas, and then to Derrida, Lacan, and Foucault.

There are a variety of books and articles that have, in fact, drawn on the main currents of semiotics for their foundations. John K. Sheriff returns to Peirce's classification of signs to argue that a literary work falls into the category of *rhematic symbols*, a rheme being, according to Peirce, "a sign . . . of qualitative

possibility, that is as representing such and such a kind of possible Object''
(Peirce, 2.250; Sheriff, 65). Maria Corti's *Introduction to Literary Semiotics*
considers literature as an ''information and communication system'' structured
on ''various planes and levels'' (7), and, returning to a central insight of Saussure's while drawing on the work of Mukařovsky, Corti recognizes that ''a
semiological conception of literature has the advantage of creating a network of
relations between the signs of the literary series and those of other series, thus
avoiding a unilateral approach to texts as pure literary objects or as direct wit-
nesses of a reality which is external to them'' (16).

6. In *Revolution in Poetic Language* and later, Julia Kristeva adapts Jacques
Lacan's psychoanalytic distinction between the Imaginary and Symbolic orders
into an opposition between the pre-Oedipal drives (semiotics) and their expression
as modified by language and the social constraints it embodies (symbolism).
While basic psychic drives ''involve pre-Oedipal semiotic functions and energy
discharges that connect and orient the body to the mother'' (27), ''the *symbolic*—
and therefore syntax and all linguistic categories—is a social effect of the relation
to the other, established through the objective constraints of biological (including
sexual) differences and concrete, historical family structures'' (29).

References

Barthes, Roland. *Elements of Semiology* (1964). Trans. A. Lavers. London: Jonathan
    Cape, 1967. Barthes pursues an essentially Sausurrian view.
Corti, Maria. *An Introduction to Literary Semiotics*. Trans. M. Bogat and A. Mandelbaum.
    Bloomington: Indiana University Press, 1978.
Corbett, Edward P. J. *Classical Rhetoric for the Modern Student*. 2d ed. New York:
    Oxford University Press, 1971.
Culler, Jonathan. *The Pursuit of Signs: Semiotics, Literature, Deconstruction*. Ithaca,
    N.Y.: Cornell University Press, 1981.
———. ''The Semiotics of Poetry: Two Approaches.'' In *Semiotic Themes*.
Eco, Umberto. ''Semiotics: A Discipline or an Interdisciplinary Method.'' In *Sight,
    Sound, and Sense*, ed. Thomas A. Sebeok.
———. *A Theory of Semiotics*. Bloomington: Indiana University Press, 1976. An essential
    book.
Fisch, Max H. ''Peirce's General Theory of Signs.'' In *Sight, Sound and Sense*. An
    especially valuable study; discriminates the stages of Peirce's development of his
    theory of signs and enumerates major unanswered questions.
Greimas, A. J. *On Meaning: Selected Writings in Semiotic Theory*. Minneapolis: Uni-
    versity of Minnesota Press, 1987.
Kristeva, Julia. *Revolution in Poetic Language*. Trans. M. Walker. New York: Columbia
    University Press, 1984. Original French edition, 1974.
Locke, John. *An Essay Concerning Human Understanding*. Ed. Alexander Campbell
    Fraser. 2 vols. Oxford: Clarendon Press, 1894.
Morris, Charles W. *Foundations of the Theory of Signs*. Vol. 1, no. 2 of the *International
    Encyclopedia of Unified Sciences*. 1938; University of Chicago Press, 1960.
———. *Signification and Significance*. Cambridge, Mass.: MIT Press, 1964.
———. *Signs, Language and Behavior*. New York: Prentice-Hall, 1946. Contains a
    useful glossary of terms as used by Morris.

Peirce, Charles Sanders. *Collected Papers of Charles Sanders Peirce*. Ed. Charles Hart-shorne and Paul Weiss (vols. 1–6) and A. W. Burks (vols. 7–8). 8 vols. Cambridge, Mass.: Harvard University Press, 1931–35, 1958. Peirce's best-known statements of his theory of signs occur in the letters to Lady Welby printed in Volume 8; the more detailed discussion appears, however, in Book 2 of Volume 2. So interrelated are Peirce's investigations into logic, signs, and pragmatism that the attempt fully to understand Peirce's thought on any one of these subjects inevitably leads to the others. The *Collected Papers* are traditionally cited by volume and paragraph number.

A Perfusion of Signs. Ed. Thomas A. Sebeok. Bloomington: Indiana University Press, 1977.

Sapir, Edward. *Selected Writings in Language, Culture, and Personality*. New York: Harcourt, Brace, 1921.

Saussure, Ferdinand de. *Course in General Linguistics*. Ed. Charles Bally and Albert Sechehaye; trans. W. Baskin. 1959; New York: McGraw-Hill, 1966. The *Cours de linguistique général* was first published in French, 1915.

Sebeok, Thomas. *Contributions to the Doctrine of Signs*. Bloomington: University of Indiana, 1976. Sebeok is a major force in the development of Peircean semiotics.

———. "Ecumenicalism in Semiotics." In *A Perfusion of Signs*.

Semiotic Themes. Ed. Richard T. De George. Lawrence: University of Kansas Press, 1981.

Sheriff, John K. "Charles S. Peirce and the Semiotics of Literature." In *Semiotic Themes*. An important, well-informed study.

Sight, Sound and Sense. Ed. Thomas A. Sebeok. Indiana University Press, 1978.

Silverman, Kaja. *The Subject of Semiotics*. New York: Oxford University Press, 1983.

Skidmore, Arthur. "Peirce and Semiotics: An Introduction to Peirce's Theory of Signs." In *Semiotic Themes*.

Sless, David. *In Search of Semiotics*. Totawa, N. J.: Barnes and Noble, 1986.

Tiefenbrun, Susan W. "The State of Literary Semiotics." *Semiotica* 51, nos. 1/3 (1984): 7–44. Excellent bibliography.

Wells, Rulon S. "Criteria for Semiosis." In *A Perfusion of Signs*.

Whorf, Benjamin Lee. *Language, Thought, and Reality*. Ed. John B. Carroll. Cambridge, Mass.: MIT Press, 1956.

Zeman, J. Jay. "Peirce's Theory of Signs." In *A Perfusion of Signs*.

Sources of Additional Information

The *Encyclopedic Dictionary of Semiotics*, ed. Thomas Sebeok (3 vols.; Berlin: Mouton de Gruyter, 1986), is an exceptionally helpful and authoritative guide to a broad and confusing field. The generously detailed entries treat three types of subjects: "Entries tracing the historical background and range of present usage of terms"; "Evaluative biographical sketches"; and "Expositions of the impact of semiotics on various traditional arts and sciences" (vi). Sebeok's "Semiotics: A Survey of the State of the Art" (*Current Trends in Linguistics* 12, 1974: 211–64) provides a very helpful introduction to the general field and includes a substantial bibliography.

The relations between the terms semiotics and semiology are discussed by Umberto Eco in *A Theory of Semiotics* (p. 30; see References above) and at greater length by Thomas Sebeok in "Semiotics and Its Congeners" in his *Contributions to the Doctrine of Signs* (pp. 47–58; see References above). Brief sketches of precursors to the semiotics/

semiology developed by Peirce and Saussure will be found in Keith Percival's "Ferdinand de Saussure and the History of Semiotics" (*Semiotic Themes*, see References above), Susan Tiefenbrun's "The State of Literary Semiotics: 1983" (*Semiotica* 51, 1984: 7–44), and in the Appendix to Charles Morris's *Signs, Language and Behavior* (see References above).

For commentary on Saussure, Jonathan Culler's *Ferdinand de Saussure* (Ithaca, N.Y.: Cornell University Press, 1986) is very helpful; for briefer summaries, see Fredric Jameson's Marxist commentary in *The Prison-House of Language* (Princeton, N.J.: Princeton University Press, 1972, 6–22) or Robert Scholes's *Structuralism in Literature* (New Haven, Conn.: Yale University Press, 1974, 13–22). George Watson's "The Stacked Deck of Language" (*The Sewanee Review* 93, Summer, 1985: 412–27) gives a lively argument against the novelty of many of the formulations for which Saussure is generally given credit; that the structuralist "discovery" that human beings are to be regarded as at the mercy of language was a commonplace at the turn of the century is made evident by Lady Welby's satire on that position in "A Royal Slave" (*The Fortnightly Review* 62, 1 September 1897: 432–34). One may also consult Jeremy Bentham's *Essay on Logic* (in vol. 8 of *The Works of Jeremy Bentham*, ed. John Bowring (Edinburgh: William Tait, 1843). "What is now pretty generally, and the same time, pretty clearly understood is, that the connexion between a word and its import is altogether arbitrary, the result of tacit convention and long-continued usage; . . . the short proof is the infinite diversity of languages,—the infinite multitude of signs by which, in the different languages, the same object has been found presented" (238).

For commentary on Peirce see Douglas Greenlee's *Peirce's Concept of the Sign* (The Hague: Mouton, 1973). A standard general study is Thomas Goudge's *The Thought of C. S. Peirce* (Toronto: University of Toronto Press, 1950). *Writings of Charles Peirce: A Chronological Edition* is in progress from the University of Indiana Press under the general editorship of Max H. Fisch. The correspondence between Peirce and Lady Victoria Welby, in which much of Peirce's theory of signs was set forth, has been printed in *Semiotics and Significs*, ed. Charles S. Hardwick (Bloomington: Indiana University Press, 1977). Lady Welby's own contributions to the field have not received the attention they deserve: see Susan Petrilli's "Victorian Lady Welby and Significs: An Interview with H. J. Schmitz" (in *The Semiotic Web: 1987*, ed. Thomas Sebeok; Berlin: Mouton de Gruyter, 1987).

Charles Morris's "Esthetics and the Theory of Signs" (*The Journal of Unified Science* 8, 1939–40: 131–50) specifically addresses the functioning of signs in art, including literature.

An interesting example of the many extensions of the term in individual instances is Michael Riffaterre's *Semiotics of Poetry* (Bloomington: Indiana University Press, 1978), where semiosis is the term used to describe the discovery of the key word or proposition that gives a poem its unity.

SIGN 1. Anything that represents, that is, that calls up the thought of something else. 2. In the Peircean tradition, that which mediates between the interpretant (concept) and its object. 3. In the Saussurian scheme, that which results from the arbitrary union of a signified (concept) and a signifier (sound image or graphic representation) within a collectivity (group sharing a language).

Any consideration of signs leads naturally into the history of theories of the origin of language and language's relation to non-linguistic reality, beginning with Plato's Cratylus. *Adequate consideration of the subject would require a volume in itself. The present entry is intended only to provide a quick reference to theories of the sign that are of special interest in the twentieth century. For summaries of the systems into which the definitions of Saussure and Peirce fit, see* SEMIOTICS.

1. Probably the most influential comprehensive definition of the sign is that of Augustine: "A sign is a thing which causes us to think of something beyond the impression the thing itself makes upon the senses" (34; II.1.1). The breadth of this definition is evident from the opening of the treatise. "All doctrine concerns either things or signs, but things are learned by signs. Strictly speaking, I have here called a 'thing' that which is not used to signify something else, like wood, stone, cattle, and so on; but not that wood concerning which Moses cast it into bitter waters that their bitterness might be dispelled, nor that stone which Jacob placed at his head (8; I.2.2). In the seventeenth century, John Poinsot, following but also seeking to correct Augustine, defines the sign as "[t]hat which represents something other than itself to a cognitive power" (25). For Augustine and his followers, the approach to an understanding of the word was through an understanding of the signs of which words are the most important subclass. However, general usage tended to make a distinction between words and signs, signs being anything except words that stand for, represent, or indicate something else. The importance of remembering that words are, after all, signs became evident in the rigorous analyses of the place and function of the sign in thought and communication in the work of Charles Sanders Peirce in the United States and Ferdinand de Saussure in Switzerland. Thus, according to Peirce's broad definition: "A sign . . . is something which stands for something in some respect or capacity" (2.228).

2. Peirce, approaching the sign from the point of view of the logician, sought from the beginning to incorporate the sign's relationship to reality into his definition. Thus he wrote, "I define a *Sign* as anything which on the one hand is so determined by an Object and on the other so determines an idea in a person's mind, that this latter determination, which I term the *Interpretant* of the sign, is thereby mediately determined by that Object" (8.343). By object, Peirce refers in the basic instance to a sense perception; by interpretant (not to be confused with interpreter) he refers to a mental concept of the object. Objects need not be sense perceptions; they may be purely conceptual. Indeed, any attempt to analyze the interpretant in itself leads to an infinite regress since an interpretant thus becomes a sign (object).

3. Saussure defined a sign as a combination of a concept (the signified) and a sound image or its tangible written form (the signifier) (66). The sign is the result of the arbitrary association of certain sounds with a certain idea or concept. "Language can . . . be compared with a sheet of paper: thought is the front and the sound the back; one cannot cut the front without cutting the back at the same time; likewise in language, one can neither divide sound from thought nor thought from sound" (113). For Saussure, then, the sign exists only as a combination

of sound or its representation (the *signifier*) and thought (the *signified*), the latter being roughly equivalent to Peirce's interpretant.

Note

Ducrot and Todorov have noted that studies of signs tend to move from the study of the relations within the sign, or even between signs as they exist in the system of *langue* (language as a total system at a synchronic moment), to their motivated use within society (92).

References

Augustine. *On Christian Doctrine*. Trans. D. W. Robertson. Indianapolis: Bobbs-Merrill, Library of Liberal Arts, 1958.

Ducrot, Oswald, and Tzvetan Todorov. *Encyclopedic Dictionary of the Sciences of Language* (1972). Trans. C. Porter. Baltimore: Johns Hopkins University Press, 1979.

Peirce, Charles Sanders. *Collected Papers of Charles Sanders Peirce*. Ed. C. Hartshorne and P. Weiss (vols. 1–6) and A. W. Burks (vols. 7–8). 8 vols. Cambridge, Mass.: Harvard University Press, 1931–35, 1958.

Poinsot, John. *Tractatus de Signis: The Semiotic of John Poinsot* (1632). Trans. J. Deely. Berkeley: University of California Press, 1985.

Saussure, Ferdinand de. *Course in General Linguistics*. Ed. Charles Bally and Albert Sechehaye; trans. W. Baskin. 1959; New York: McGraw-Hill, 1966.

SPEECH-ACT THEORY   A perspective on language use (*parole*) that regards utterances as both presenting propositions and causing effects, that is, as both constative and performative. The major relevance of speech-act theory for literary study has been through its explanation of how language can imply meanings not present in the dictionary senses of the words used nor in the literal meanings of the sentence(s) they constitute. It has thus led to the study of the principles of context-generated expectations that make possible the indirect expression of attitudes and propositions.

Much of what has been written in the field of speech-act theory treats technical, linguistic, logical, or philosophic matters about which there is continuing disagreement. The following commentary seeks to outline the aspects of the total field about which there is a fair share of (although not necessarily total) agreement and that appear to have the greatest relevance for the understanding of literature.

The origin of speech-act theory can be given with precision: it arose out of the William James Lectures delivered at Harvard University in 1955 by J. L. Austin and subsequently published as *How to Do Things with Words*. Austin begins by making and exploring a distinction between constatives (utterances that are true or false) and performatives (utterances that perform an action). Examples of performatives are: "I'll bet you ten dollars Seabiscuit wins the Derby," "I pronounce you man and wife," and "I bequeath half my estate to Greenpeace." In the course of analyzing both kinds of utterances, Austin discriminates a locutionary act (the uttering of a set of words), an illocutionary act (the creation of a certain force; for instance, that of a promise, threat, or suggestion), and a perlocutionary act (an effect that results from the communication of both the locution and the illocution). ("I'll be there tonight" is a locution that could have the illocutionary force of, among other possibilities, a simple statement, a promise, or a threat, depending on the circumstances in which it is spoken, and that could bring about the perlocutionary effects of, among other possibilities, reassurance, happiness, fear, or anger.)

In the course of the lectures, his exploration of the operation of locutionary meaning and illocutionary force leads Austin to question the original distinction between constatives and performatives. It turns out that constatives can have a performative aspect and performatives a constative aspect; the important distinction proves to be that between the locution and its illocutionary force. "The doctrine of the performative/constative distinction stands to the doctrine of locutionary and illocutionary acts in the total speech act as the *special* theory to the *general* theory" (148).

From the point of view of literary study, the distinction between locution, illocution, and perlocution has proved useful, but the major contribution has developed from Austin's explicit recognition that illocutionary force is often communicated by indirection or insinuation. On the simplest level, one does not have to use the words bet or promise (or their synonyms) to convey the appropriate intention: "Ten dollars on the bay" or "I'll be sure to be here by five" adequately perform the actions of betting and promising. Further, Austin's linking of illocutionary force to the context ("I'll bet ten dollars on Penn State" cannot be understood as a bet if the speaker and addressee already know the outcome of the game) suggests an importance to the role of CONTEXT that has proved central for speech-act theory.

John Searle's *Speech Acts* (1969) clarifies the results at which Austin's lectures arrived and develops a number of ramifications and corollaries. Searle distinguishes the simple utterance of words, the utterance act, and the propositional acts of referring and predicating from the illocutionary acts of "stating, questioning, commanding, promising, etc." "Utterance acts consist simply in uttering strings of words. Illocutionary and propositional acts consist characteristically in uttering words in sentences in certain contexts, under certain conditions and with certain intentions" (24–25). He thus gives additional emphasis to the function of contexts outside the utterance in producing illocutionary force.

Although the view of language use that Searle develops in *Speech Acts* bears on literary study at a number of points, the aspect of speech-act theory that has so far proved most relevant has arisen from the work of H. P. Grice, most specifically from his 1975 essay "Logic and Conversation." Grice's major interest has not been speech-act theory but questions of what is meant by MEANING, the difference between the meaning of a sentence and the meaning of the utterer, and the way in which the latter is determined. "Logic and Conversation" does not, in fact, mention Austin, Searle, or speech-act theory, but the concept of *implicature* there developed explains the way in which the expectations of the hearer, which are functions of context, produce interpretations of the speaker's intention that could not be gathered from the speech act taken out of the context of its utterance. The general principle governing conversation Grice calls the *Cooperative Principle* (CP): "Make your conversational contribution such as is required, at the stage at which it occurs, by the accepted purpose or direction of the talk exchange in which you are engaged" (45). Four maxims of the CP are the expectation that an utterance will be relevant to the situation and that its quality (truth), quantity, and manner will be appropriate. When a speaker appears to openly flout or violate the Cooperative Principle by saying something irrelevant or obviously untrue, or by saying too much or too little, the hearer assumes the presence of implicature. Grice offers a "general pattern" for interpreting implicature.

> He has said that *p*; there is no reason to suppose that he is not observing the maxims, or at least the CP; he could not be doing this unless he thought that *q*; he knows (and knows that I know that he knows) that I can see the supposition that he thinks that *q* IS required; he has done nothing to stop me thinking that *q*; he intends me to think, or is at least willing to allow me to think, that *q*; and so he has implicated that *q*. (50)

The importance of context (which is to be understood to include shared conventions) has already been mentioned. The illocutionary force of "It's hot in here" depends on such extralinguistic matters as whether the room in which the locution is uttered is hot, comfortable in temperature, or cold; whether strong emotions are being expressed at the time; whether something might be explained by the room's temperature; and whether something might be done about an uncomfortable temperature. Relevant contexts must, of course, be shared: Kent Bach and Robert Harnish speak of *mutual contextual beliefs*. Alternatively, the total context surrounding an utterance is sometimes called the *situation*, as by Claude Germain, who restricts context to the linguistic context. In *The Concept of Situation in Linguistics*, Germain writes, "In this work, the term *situation* will indicate *the set of facts known by the speaker and the listener at the moment the speech act occurs*" (15). (The speech within a specific situation is also sometimes referred to as *enunciation* as opposed to *utterance*, that is, speech regarded in abstraction from its nonlinguistic context.)

Equally important is the assumption that the speaker intends the hearer to correctly understand the proposition conveyed by, and the illocutionary force of, the utterance. Austin's term is *uptake*: the illocutionary act is not successful unless uptake is achieved, that is, unless it is understood as the kind of illocutionary act intended. Moreover, the addressee must know that the illocutionary force *was* intended. Bach and Harnish phrase this principle in general terms as the *communicative presumption* or "the mutual belief prevailing in a linguistic community to the effect that whenever someone says something to somebody, he or she intends to be performing some identifiable illocutionary act" (12).

Though Austin, Searle, Grice, and indeed most speech-act theorists, have chosen their examples and focused their investigations on oral conversation, the relevance of the distinction between propositional content and illocutionary force, the workings of implicature that make indirect expression of meaning possible, and the assumption of a mutual understanding of context and intention are evidently applicable to written texts and literature generally. As Mary Louise Pratt was one of the first to argue, speech-act theory helps break down qualitative boundaries between ordinary speech, texts in general, and texts regarded as literary. She writes, "Grice's account of rule-breaking in conversation clearly shows that intentional deviance does occur routinely outside literature. And the fact that Grice's account seems perfectly able to handle deviance within literature as well shows that there are no clear grounds for distinguishing the way deviance occurs in the two supposedly opposed realms of discourse" (200). Pratt notes particularly implicatures created by the violation of genre (Tristram Shandy's flouting of the conventions of the autobiography and Sterne's simultaneous flouting of those of the novel), by the violation of narrative conventions (Benjy's narrative in *The Sound and the Fury*), and by the violation of what readers know and expect the author to know they know (the opening sentence of *Pride and Prejudice*).

For speech-act theory, implicature is also the principle underlying the understanding of tropes, the first step in the interpretation of which, in speech-act terms, is the recognition of a violation of the Cooperative Principle. Either the dictionary meanings of the words used violate expected usage, or the proposition violates expectations appropriate to the context. The second step is the recognition that the violation results from the presence of METAPHOR, METONYMY, synecdoche, or IRONY. John Searle's chapter on metaphor in *Expression and Meaning* and Ted Cohen's essay "Figurative Speech and Figurative Acts" exemplify the application of speech-act theory to figurative (that is, tropic) usage.

An increasing interest in speech-act verbs (that is, verbs that name illocutionary forces—command, promise, and plead, for example) suggests a somewhat different kind of relevance for the understanding of literature. Searle has pointed out that "there is no one-to-one correspondence between illocutionary verbs and illocutionary forces. . . . Many possible illocutionary forces do not have a corresponding verb in English nor even a corresponding illocutionary force indicating device, and frequently one and the same illocutionary force is named by several non-synonymous verbs" (Searle and Vanderveken, 179). Nevertheless, Thomas Ballmer and Waltraud Brennenstuhl suggest that "the verbs denoting speech acts, speech activities, or various aspects of linguistic behavior can be taken as an indication of what the speakers of a language regard as relevant in their linguistic behavior" (3); in Anna Wierzbicka's words, "The set of English speech act verbs reflects a certain interpretation of the world of human actions and interactions" (10). Various approaches have been taken to the analysis of these verbs. Following Austin's division of "the *illocutionary forces* of an utterance" (he estimates that there are between 1,000 and 10,000 such forces) into five classes (150–51), a number of other classifications have been developed.

However, analytical inventories and dictionaries appear to be more useful than taxonomies that fit the speech-act verbs into a dozen or fewer classes. In *Foundations of Illocutionary Logic*, Searle and Vanderveken have worked out logical statements of the illocutionary senses of over a hundred verbs. Ballmer and Brennenstuhl's *Speech Act Classification* offers a taxonomic structure of "8 model groups, 24 models and typifications, 600 categories, and 4800 speech act verbs" (5). For example "implore" belongs to the Emotion Model, and to the category "Appeal to a Higher Authority." Wierzbicka's *English Speech Act Verbs: A Semantic Dictionary* treats 37 groups averaging a half-dozen verbs each. Explications of each verb are given by using the simplest words to sketch the total situation in which the illocutionary force of the verb is appropriate. The explication of "implore" is as follows:

> I say: I want you to do X. I want you to understand that it will be more than bad for me if you don't do it. I know that you don't have to do what I say I want you to do. I assume that you don't want to do it. I feel something bad because of that. I want you to imagine how I feel. I think if you imagine how I feel you will feel something because of that and will do what I say I want you to do. I say this because I want to cause you to do it. (55)

Since much of a reader's understanding of a literary text is dependent on assigning an appropriate illocutionary force to the locutions presented in a lyric poem or essay, or made by a narrator in a novel or by the characters of a novel or a play, such inventories suggest the number of fine distinctions in illocutionary force possible in our culture. They further remind us that the imputing of illocutionary force by readers (not necessarily consciously) is basic to the understanding of the voice of a persona or narrator and of the personalities, motives, and interactions of characters. Moreover, Wierzbicka's scheme is especially useful in illuminating the relationship between the contextual situation surrounding an utterance and its illocutionary force.

References

Austin, J. L. *How to Do Things with Words*. Ed. J. O. Urmson and M. Sbisá. Cambridge, Mass.: Harvard University Press, 1975.

Bach, Kent, and Robert M. Harnish. *Linguistic Communication and Speech Acts*. Cambridge, Mass.: MIT Press, 1979. A broad-ranging theory of the relationships between speech acts and communication generally.

Ballmer, Thomas, and Waltraud Brennenstuhl. *Speech Act Classification: A Study in the Lexical Analysis of English Speech-Activity Verbs*. Berlin: Springer-Verlag, 1981.

Cohen, Ted. "Figurative Speech and Figurative Acts." *Journal of Philosophy* 7 (November 1975): 669–84.

Germain, Claude. *The Concept of Situation in Linguistics*. Trans. B. J. Wallace. Ottawa: University of Ottawa Press, 1979. Original French edition, 1973.

Grice, H. P. "Logic and Conversation." In *Syntax and Semantics 3*. New York: Academic Press, 1975. An immensely influential essay.

Pratt, Mary Louise. *Toward a Speech Act Theory of Discourse*. Bloomington: Indiana

University Press, 1977. Pioneering endeavor in the application of speech act theory to literature.

Searle, John. *Expression and Meaning*. Cambridge: Cambridge University Press, 1979. Chapters on a number of topics of interest for the understanding of literature: Indirect Speech Acts, The Logical Status of Fictional Discourse, Metaphor, Literal Meaning, and the question of reference.

————. *Speech Acts*. Cambridge: Cambridge University Press, 1969.

Searle, John R., and Daniel Vanderveken. *Foundations of Illocutionary Logic*. Cambridge: Cambridge University Press, 1985.

Wierzbicka, Anna. *English Speech Act Verbs: A Semantic Dictionary*. Sydney: Academic Press, 1987.

Sources of Additional Information

Chapter 8 of Keith Allan's *Linguistic Meaning* (2 vols., London: Routledge and Kegan Paul, 1986) is a very helpful survey of the principles of speech act theory and certain of the debated issues. Chapter 2 of *Interpretive Acts* by Wendell Harris (Oxford: Clarendon Press, 1988) summarizes speech-act theory; the following three chapters treat the kinds of context relevant to the interpretation of literary texts.

For Grice's exploration of questions related to the interpretation of meaning as these are related to speech act theory, see "Meaning" in *The Philosophical Review* (66, 1957), "Utterer's Meaning, Sentence-Meaning, and Word-Meaning" in *Foundations of Language* (4, August 1968:225–42), "Utterer's Meaning and Intentions" in *The Philosophical Review* (78, April 1969:147–77), and "Further Notes on Logic and Conversation" in *Syntax and Semantics* (9, 1978:41–58). Chapter 2 of Charles Altieri's *Act and Quality* (Amherst: University of Massachusetts Press, 1981) links Wittgenstein, Austin, and Grice.

David Holdcroft's *Words and Deeds: Problems in the Theory of Speech Acts* (Oxford: Clarendon Press, 1978) relates speech-act theory to questions of truth conditions. "[W]e can say that someone understands S's locution if, given that S has uttered a sentence x, he knows what possible state of affairs has to obtain for x to express a truth" (167). Jerrold J. Katz's *Propositional Structure and Illocutionary Force* (New York: Thomas Y. Crowell, 1977) finds a greater role for syntactic and semantic competence in the interpretation of illocutionary force than Searle.

Recognition of the importance of implication in literature of course long predates speech-act theory. Two interesting twentieth-century examples are I. A. Richards's discussion of four kinds of meaning in *Practical Criticism* (London: Kegan Paul, Trench, Trubner, 1929) and Irvin Ehrenpreis's *Acts of Implication: Suggestion and Covert Meaning in the Works of Dryden, Swift, Pope, and Austen* (Berkeley: University of California Press, 1978). Richards adds to the Sense of what is said, Feeling, Tone, and Attitude, the latter three being sensitive to context. Ehrenpreis writes of the notion of implication: "I suggest that in most speech we do not consciously or deliberately either speak out or veil our meaning. We merely say what we have to say in a context that supports, directs, and limits meaning" (4).

STRUCTURALISM   1. The methodological principle that human culture is made up of systems in which a change in any element produces changes in the others; in general, cultural systems are regarded as structured on the model of language. 2. Specifically, literary structuralism seeks to explain the structures underlying literary texts either in terms of a grammar modeled on that of language or in terms of Saussure's principle that the meaning of each word depends on its place in the total system of language. Four basic types of theoretical or critical activities have been regarded as structuralist: the use of language as a structural model, the search for universal *functions* or actions in literature, the explanation of how meaning is possible, and the poststructuralist denial of objective meaning. 3. Increasingly, from the beginning of the 1980s, structuralism as a term has been restricted to designation of the first of the four activities included under sense 2, the direct or metaphorical application of linguistic categories to literary work.

1. Structuralism is founded primarily on the work of Ferdinand de Saussure and has been regarded by at least some structuralists as constituting the science of signs for which Saussure saw his work as the ground. Commentators who have focused on the earlier phases of structuralism have tended to identify structuralism with the semiology that Saussure desiderated. Thus, Jonathan Culler comments, "It would not be wrong to suggest that structuralism and semiology are identical" (6). (However, see SEMIOTICS.) Structuralism, having arisen out of linguistic theory, has always retained a basic preoccupation with language. The element of Saussure that was initially most influential was his emphasis on language as a system of interrelated and mutually defining signs that were not in any necessary correspondence with non-linguistic reality. For Saussure, the signifieds to which signifiers relate are marked off by language itself. Although the Russian Formalists and the Prague Linguistic Circle applied these insights directly to literature, and their work later influenced the direction of literary structuralism (primarily through Roman Jakobson), structuralism as a term for a method of investigation in various fields, and subsequently as a general movement, originated with the anthropologist Claude Lévi-Strauss; seminal early works are the essay "L'Analyse structurale en linguistic et en anthropologie" (1945) and *Triste Tropiques* (1955). By regarding cultural phenomena as organized like a language, that is, as systems of signs whose meanings derive from their differential relationship, Lévi-Strauss found a way to approach both myths and such systems within society as the division of tribes into clans and rules governing kinship relationships. The most influential aspects of Lévi-Strauss's work have been the Saussurean emphases on synchronic systems, in which elements operate in the same way as signs in general and words in particular, on the correlative notion that the elements of a system are to be understood in terms of their functions within it, and on the retrieval of hidden formal relationships as opposed to surface content.

Subsequent commentators emphasize different aspects of both Saussure's theory and Lévi-Strauss's use of it. David Robey writes:

> Inspired by a famous passage in Saussure's *Cours de linguistique général*, and founded in the anthropology of Lévi-Strauss, this new science (as it claims to be) has grown out of the supposition that the theories and methods of structural linguistics

are directly or indirectly applicable to the analysis of all aspects of human culture, in so far as all of these, like language, may be interpreted as systems of signs. (2)

Roland Barthes defines structuralism in terms of its reconstitutive activity.

> The goal of all structuralist activity, whether reflexive or poetic, is to reconstruct an "object," in such a way as to manifest thereby the rules of functioning (the "functions") of this object. The structure is therefore actually a *simulacrum* of the object, but it is a directed, *interested* simulacrum, since the imitated object makes something appear which remained invisible or, if one prefers, unintelligible in the natural object. ("Structuralist Activity," 214–15)

Barthes regards the phenomena in which he is interested (which may be menu items or fashions as well as texts in the usual sense) as systems of signs; the mode of analyzing these systems is set forth in his *Elements of Semiology* (1964). For Jean-Marie Benoist, "An analysis is structural if, and only if, it displays the content as a model, i.e., if it can isolate a formal set of elements and relations in terms of which it is possible to argue without entering upon the significance of the given content (8). The shift from content to form is here especially evident.

Less explicit and more controversial is the principle apparently assumed by Lévi-Strauss and certain other structuralists that the human mind is structured to operate in certain ways. Such a view can of course be found among other investigators of linguistic phenomena. Central to Benjamin Whorf's 1941 "Language, Mind, and Reality" is the argument that

> in linguistic and mental phenomena, significant behavior . . . [is] ruled by a specific system or organization, a "geometry" of form principles characteristic of each language. This organization is imposed from outside the narrow circle of the personal consciousness, making of that consciousness a mere puppet whose linguistic maneuverings are held in unsensed and unbreakable bonds of pattern. . . . And now appears a great fact of human brotherhood—that human beings are all alike in this respect. (257)

Michael Lane, one of the earlier commentators on structuralism, notes, "there seems to be general, if implicit agreement among certain structuralists, notably Lévi-Strauss in anthropology, Roman Jakobson in linguistics, Jean Piaget in psychology, and François Jacob in biology, that there is in man an innate, genetically transmitted and determined mechanism that acts as a structuring force" (15). Terence Hawkes writes in 1976, "the ultimate quarry of structuralist thinking will be the permanent structures into which individual human acts, perceptions, stances fit, and from which they derive their final nature" (18). However, later structuralist thinking moves away from the presumption of universal structuring.

Two of Lévi-Strauss's modes of analysis that had an immediate vogue but have become somewhat less common are the reliance on resolving phenomena into binary oppositions (for example, the raw and the cooked) and his use of such binary contrasts in *homologies* (*a* is to *b* as *c* is to *d*). Employed especially in comparing variant versions of myths, homology in Lévi-Strauss retains part of the heritage from its original biological use while losing a portion of its rigor. (Biological homologies are fundamental similarities due to commonality of descent; a definition that can apply to cultural homologies as well. However, where biology seeks to demonstrate the commonality of descent, this is generally either assumed or overlooked in cultural analysis.)

2. By regarding literature as a subsystem defined by its difference from the system of all other uses of language, and regarding the text as a system in which the content is a function of the form, Russian FORMALISM moved toward the divorce of the text from the process of its creation, the history of the elements that make it up, and its place in cultural history. Russian Formalism sought the source of the literariness of literature; this emphasis on literature's difference from other discourse is embodied in Roman Jakobson's well-known description of literature as having its primary orientation toward the message (rather than the other five factors of verbal communication: addresser, context, contact, code, and addressee), which led toward a heavily linguistic analysis of the message (see "Closing Statement").

Literary structuralism per se, which originated as, and to a considerable extent has remained, a French movement, shares with Russian Formalism the common background in Saussure; indeed, Jakobson, a leading member of both the Russian Formalists and the Prague Linguistic Circle, introduced Lévi-Strauss to the work of Saussure in 1944.

Four major types of application of structuralism to texts are to be distinguished. Strictly speaking, the purpose of none of these is the interpretation of an individual text; rather, each attempts to demonstrate principles of structuration in literature or discourse generally. One—which has largely fallen from favor—is the application, direct or metaphorical, of linguistic categories to literary works. The most basic assumption here is put simply by Roland Barthes: "If a working hypothesis is needed for an analysis whose task is immense and whose materials infinite, then the most reasonable thing is to posit a homological relation between sentence and discourse insofar as it is likely that a similar formal organization orders all semiotic systems" ("Introduction to Structural Analysis," 83). Though all structuralism derives from theories of language, this type is here designated *linguistic structuralism*. Examples are Tzvetan Todorov's suggestion in a 1966 paper that means for structuring literary works may be "projections of rhetorical devices" ("Language and Literature," 127–29) and his 1969 *Grammaire du Décaméron*, which treats characters as nouns, actions as verbs, and so forth. Such applications are perhaps more metaphorical than direct. The most famous example of direct application is the 1962 linguistic analysis of Baudelaire's "Les Chats" by Roman Jakobson and Lévi-Strauss (to which Michael Riffaterre gave an equally well-known reply, pointing out that many of the grammatical and linguistic structures cited by Jakobson and Lévi-Strauss have no effect on a reader).

A second mode of concentrating on structure, practiced first by the Russian

Formalist Vladimir Propp, is to be found in a variety of attempts to discover a set of functions (necessary relations, roles, or types of actions) that are basic to narrative. (Structuralist critics and theorists have concentrated primarily on fictional narrative.) Where Propp discovers thirty-one *functions* in the Russian folktale, Claude Bremond seeks to resolve the action of narratives into triadic sequences, in each of which a possibility is either developed or not, and A. J. Greimas analyzes narratives into six essential *actants* or roles. Roland Barthes combines several modes of analysis in "Introduction to the Structural Analysis of Narratives." "It is proposed to distinguish three levels of description in the narrative work: the level of '*functions*' (in the sense this word has in Propp and Bremond), the level of '*actions*' (in the sense this word has in Greimas when he talks of characters as actants) and the level of '*narration*' (which is roughly the level of 'discourse' in Todorov)" (88). Anglo-American interest in structuralism was, for a considerable time, strongly focused on this second type, as is apparent from Robert Scholes's *Structuralism in Literature* (1974) and Jonathan Culler's *Structuralist Poetics* (1975). The general type of structuralist analysis is now most often referred to as NARRATOLOGY; for convenience, the older practice can be designated *narratological structuralism*. The most influential narratologist is Gérard Genette.

The third direction of structuralism is toward the development of systems of POETICS that will explain how MEANING is possible; it can be thought of as *poetics-seeking structuralism*. From the beginning, literary structuralism has been seen primarily as an explanation of the ways in which structures create meaning, and not as a mode of explicating the meanings of specific texts (although a number of explications based on structuralist premises have been carried out). The essay originally contributed by Todorov to the 1968 collection *What Is Structuralism?* under the title "Poétique" led to his brief volume *Introduction to Poetics* (1973). Poetics is defined by Todorov as distinct from interpretation: it "aims at a knowledge of the general laws that preside over the birth of each work" (*Introduction*, 6). Jonathan Culler's *Structuralist Poetics* similarly argues that structuralism "helps one to envisage . . . a poetics which strives to define the conditions of meaning" (viii). However, Culler here shifts the structuralist emphasis from analysis of the structure within a text to the structure of the interpretive conventions that the reader brings to the text in order to produce meaning; that is, to interpret it.

The fourth form of literary structuralism focuses on the consequences of regarding language as constituting human understanding of reality rather than merely providing the means of communicating that understanding. To view language thus is to undermine the possibility of using it to refer to a reality beyond that which it creates; paradoxically, language controls what can be communicated while denying the possibility of communicating a univocal meaning (since there is no extralinguistic reality against which language can be compared). The resulting stance has sometimes been called *high* structuralism to distinguish it from the *low* structuralism associated with senses 2 and 3, but *ideological* is an equally appropriate designation (the current designation is *poststructuralism*—see the discusion of this term under sense 3 below). This type of structuralism, which has exerted a major influence on literary theory even though it is not primarily concerned with literary criticism, is, to a greater or lesser extent, polemical, antimetaphysical, and ideological.

Arguments for the ideological type of structuralism are authorized by a reading of Saussure that extrapolates the principle that the value of a word depends on its place in the total language (the synchronically viewed system of relationships between words) into the principle that meaning is constantly deferred from word to word within the language. At the same time, emphasis on the existence of language as a prerequisite for individual utterances (*parole*) and as an inherited set of structural (and semantic) possibilities suggests that the individual mind, the subject, is no more than a product of language. This demotion of the subject is an inherent tendency in all structuralism, as is the subordination of content to form. Jean-Marie Benoist writes in 1975, "instead of referring the works under consideration to the probable or problematic intentions of the author, the critic develops his analysis of the text in its various levels of meaning." Therefore "the possibilities of interpretation remain open, and the end of critical activity is a network of *relational invariants* proceeding from the system of relationships that can be deciphered in the text or work of art" (10). Thus,

> [i]f the freedom of the text is asserted against the almighty rule of the "author-generator," and the meaning is accepted as being simply relational, the inevitable result is a challenge to the very notion of the *subject*. The subjectivity of the author becomes of minor importance in the elucidation of the text, and the supposed subject of the work—"what it is about"—disappears when the signifying plane is brought into the foreground. (13)

It should further be noted that just as Saussure's theorizing applied to all uses of language, ideological structuralists generally do not differentiate qualitatively between the operation of language in literature and its operation in other discourse.

Primarily associated with the fourth form of structuralism are Roland Barthes (in his later work), Jacques Lacan, Michel Foucault, Jacques Derrida, and, less frequently, Louis Althusser. (Both Althusser and Lacan have denied the label.) Of these, only Barthes is primarily a literary critic, but the theorizing of all has been appropriated for use by literary criticism. The direction in which Barthes moves after *Elements of Semiology* (1964) emerges fully in *S/Z* (1970). There, explicitly rejecting the attempt of "the first analysts of narrative . . . to see all the world's stories (and there have been ever so many) within a single structure," Barthes celebrates the "difference" of the individual text and goes on to announce that "the goal of literary work (of literature as work) is to make the reader no longer a consumer, but a producer of the text," which in turn requires that the text be writerly (*scriptible*) rather than readerly (*lisible*) (3–4). "To interpret a text is not to give it a (more or less justified, more or less free) meaning, but on the contrary to appreciate what *plural* constitutes it" (5).

The psychoanalyst Lacan's reading of Freud insists on the unalterably linguistic realm in which psychoanalysis works and proceeds to find the basis of the psychoanalytic undertaking in the nature of language rather than in what a patient's language can report. The unconscious for Lacan is structured like a language—indeed, to have structure is for Lacan to be like a language. Derrida's DECONSTRUCTION of texts finds that discourse is necessarily self-contradictory because it is denied grounding in a nonlinguistic reality or *presence*, and thus is necessarily indeterminate in meaning. Derrida celebrates that sort of interpretation "which is no longer turned toward the origin [and which] affirms play and tries to pass beyond man and humanism" (292).

The cultural historian Foucault analyzes the beliefs and practices of historical periods as functions of the structure of thought that the prevailing discourse governs. In each period the conflict between power and desire produces a specific world or *episteme*. Foucault's comment in a 1966 interview sums up much of ideological structuralist thought.

> The breach [with the previous generation of thinkers, in particular the existentialists] became complete when Lévi-Strauss demonstrated for societies and Lacan demonstrated for the unconscious that their "sense" presumably is nothing but a kind of surface effect, a foam. On the other hand, that which penetrates most deeply into us, that which was there before we were, that which holds us together in time and space—that is indeed the *system*. The "I" is destroyed (think of modern literature). We now speak of "one." (Quoted in Broekman, 2)

The Marxist Louis Althusser recognizes the power of the cultural superstructure to create unconscious ideologies that not only arise from the economic base but also affect it. For each of these forms of poststructuralism, all meaning is relative to specific frames of reference, that is, to humanly constructed systems.

3. The term structuralism is now applied most frequently to the first of the four types (the linguistic) only. The second type having been subsumed under narratology, the third (poetics-seeking) has shifted from a concern for conventions to an insistence on the artificiality and pluralicity of reading conventions, in which form it is allied with "the new pragmatism" [see PRAGMATISM, sense 3], and the fourth type (ideological) is now most frequently referred to as poststructuralism.

Poststructuralism is a curious term inasmuch as the four writers most frequently cited as poststructuralists—Barthes, Lacan, Derrida, and Foucault—figured in the 1970s simply as leading French structuralists. For instance, the 1972 collection, *The Structuralists from Marx to Lévi-Strauss*, includes Barthes, Foucault, and Lacan; Jan Broekman's 1971 *Structuralism*, Fredric Jameson's 1972 *The Prison-House of Language*, and Jean-Marie Benoist's 1975 *The Structural Revolution* all unhesitatingly include Barthes, Derrida, Foucault, and Lacan simply as structuralists. By the 1980s, however, a clear distinction is being made: thus Peter Griffith's 1987 *Literary Theory and English Teaching* includes a chapter on "Structuralism and the Science of Narrative," which features Propp, Barthes, and Genette, and another titled "Post-Structuralism and the Escape of Signification." Ann Jefferson's 1986 essay on "Structuralism and Post-Structuralism" in *Modern Literary Theory* similarly divides structuralism and poststructuralism.

References

Althusser, Louis. *Lenin and Philosophy*. Trans. B. Brewster. New York: Monthly Review Press, 1968.
———. *Reading Capital*. Trans. B. Brewster. New York: Pantheon, 1970. Original French edition, 1965.
Barthes, Roland. *Elements of Semiology*. London: Cape, 1967. Original French edition, 1964.
———. "Introduction to the Structural Analysis of Narratives." In *Image—Music—Text*. Trans. S. Heath. New York: Hill and Wang, 1977. This essay also appears in *The Semiotic Challenge*. Trans. R. Howard. New York: Hill and Wang, 1988. Original French edition, 1985.
———. "The Structuralist Activity" (1963). In *Critical Essays*. Trans. R. Howard. Evanston, Ill.: Northwestern University Press, 1972.
———. *S/Z*. Trans. R. Miller. New York: Hill and Wang, 1974. Original French edition, 1970.
Benoist, Jean-Marie. *The Structural Revolution*. Trans. A. Pomerans. London: Widenfeld and Nicolson, 1978. Original French edition, 1975. Essays in the volume relate structuralism to a number of philosophical and literary traditions.
Bremond, Claude. *Logique du récit*. Paris: Seuil, 1973.
Broekman, Jan M. *Structuralism: Moscow—Prague—Paris*. Trans. J. F. Beekman and B. Helm. Dordrecht: D. Reidel, 1974. Original German edition, 1971. Traces structuralism from the Russian Formalists to the several directions of development in France.
Culler, Jonathan. *Structuralist Poetics: Structuralism, Linguistics, and the Study of Literature*. Ithaca, N.Y.: Cornell University Press, 1975. The first portion explores and critiques major applications of structuralist principles to literature, especially to narrative; the second half sketches a poetics based on readers' literary competence, that is, familiarity with literary conventions.
Derrida, Jacques. "Structure, Sign, and Play in the Discourse of the Human Sciences." In *Writing and Difference*. Trans. A. Bass. Chicago: University of Chicago Press, 1978. Lecture originally delivered in 1966.
Foucault, Michel. *The Archaeology of Knowledge*. Trans. A. Sheridan-Smith. New York: Pantheon, 1972. Original French edition, 1969.
———. *The Order of Things*. New York: Pantheon, 1970. Original French edition, 1966.
Genette, Gérard. *Narrative Discourse: An Essay in Method*. Trans. J. E. Lewin. Ithaca, N.Y.: Cornell University Press, 1980.
Greimas, A. J. *Semantique Structurale*. Paris: Larousse, 1966.
Griffith, Peter. *Literary Theory and English Teaching*. Milton Keynes, U.K.: Open University Press, 1987.
Hawkes, Terence. *Structuralism and Semiotics*. Berkeley: University of California Press, 1976. A useful survey including various contributions to and formulations of structuralist insights, beginning with Vico.
Jakobson, Roman. "Closing Statement: Linguistics and Poetics." In *Style and Language*, ed. Thomas A. Sebeok. Cambridge, Mass.: MIT Press, 1960. Reprinted in *The Structuralists from Marx to Lévi-Strauss*.

Jakobson, Roman, and Claude Lévi-Strauss. "Charles Baudelaire's 'Les Chats.' " In *The Structuralists from Marx to Lévi-Strauss*.

Jameson, Fredric. *The Prison-House of Language: A Critical Account of Structuralism and Russian Formalism*. Princeton, N.J.: Princeton University Press, 1972. Sees the privileged object of structuralism as "the unconscious value system or system of representations which orders social life at any of its levels, and against which the individual, conscious social acts and events take place and become comprehensible" (101). Criticizes structuralists for focusing on the synchronic without sufficient attention to diachronic change.

Jefferson, Ann. "Structuralism and Post-Structuralism." In *Modern Literary Theory: A Comparative Introduction*, ed. Ann Jefferson and David Robey. London: B. T. Batsford, 1986.

Lacan, Jacques. *Ecrits: A Selection*. Trans. A. Sheridan. New York: Norton, 1977.

Lane, Michael, ed. *Structuralism: A Reader*. London: Jonathan Cape, 1970.

Lévi-Strauss, Claude. "L'Analyse structurale en linguistique et en anthropologie." *Word* 1 (April 1945): 33–53.

———. *Triste Tropiques*. Trans. J. Weightman and D. Weightman. New York: Atheneum, 1974. Original French edition, 1955.

Propp, Vladimir. *Morphology of the Folktale* (1928). Trans. Laurence Scott. 1958; Austin: University of Texas Press, 1968.

Qu'est-ce que le Structuralism? Ed. François Wahl. Paris: Editions du Seuil, 1968.

Riffaterre, Michael. "Describing Poetic Structures: Two Approaches to Baudelaire's *Les Chats*." In *Structuralism*, ed. J. Ehrmann. Garden City, N.Y.: Doubleday Anchor, 1970. Reprinted from *Yale French Studies* 36/37 (1966): 200–242.

Robey, David, ed. *Structuralism: An Introduction*. Oxford: Clarendon Press, 1973. A useful commentary. "Structuralism in literary theory . . . is not concerned with the interpretation of individual works. It is a general science, the object of which is the system or series of systems of conventions and procedures (in the last analysis signs) which constitute the distinctive features of literature as a whole" (3).

Saussure, Ferdinand de. *Course in General Linguistics*. Ed. Charles Bally and Albert Sechehaye; trans. W. Baskin. New York: McGraw-Hill, 1966. Original French edition, 1915.

Scholes, Robert. *Structuralism in Literature*. New Haven, Conn.: Yale University Press, 1974. A helpful treatment of structuralist approaches to narrative.

The Structuralists from Marx to Lévi-Strauss. Edited by Richard and Fernande De George. Garden City, N.Y.: Doubleday Anchor, 1972.

Todorov, Tzvetan. *Grammaire du Décaméron*. The Hague: Mouton, 1969.

———. *Introduction to Poetics*. Trans. Richard Howard. Minneapolis: University of Minnesota Press, 1981. Original French edition, 1973.

———. "Language and Literature." In *The Languages of Criticism and the Sciences of Man*, ed. Richard Macksey and Eugene Donato. Baltimore: Johns Hopkins University Press, 1970. Originally delivered as a lecture in 1966.

Whorf, Benjamin. "Language, Mind, and Reality." (1941). In *Language, Thought, and Reality: Selected Writings of Benjamin Lee Whorf*. Ed. J. B. Carroll. Cambridge, Mass.: MIT Press, 1956.

Sources of Additional Information

Jurij Striedter's *Literary Structure, Evolution, and Value: Russian Formalism and Czech Structuralism Reconsidered* (Cambridge, Mass.: Harvard University Press, 1989) gives special attention to the Prague structuralists Mukařovsky and Felix Vodička; a major section considers the relation of the Prague structuralists to literary questions currently under debate.

Although he was not operating from structuralist principles, Northrop Frye's *Anatomy of Criticism* (Princeton, N.J.: Princeton University Press, 1957) is often regarded as structuralist in its view of the whole of literature as a structure classifiable into universal categories and in what seems an implicit appeal to an innate structure of the human mind.

Structuralism, especially of the ideological sort, gained new prominence in the United States as a result of the 1966 Johns Hopkins symposium "The Languages of Criticism and the Sciences of Man." Papers there presented appear in the volume of that title edited by Richard Macksey and Eugene Donato (Baltimore: Johns Hopkins University Press, 1970).

Structuralism and Since: From Lévi-Strauss to Derrida, ed. J. Sturrock (Oxford: Oxford University Press, 1979) contains an excellent series of essays on major structuralists (Dan Sperber on Lévi-Strauss; John Sturrock on Roland Barthes; Hayden White on Michel Foucault; Malcolm Bowie on Jacques Lacan; and Jonathan Culler on Jacques Derrida).

For some of the best examples of the application of structuralist thought to individual texts (a procedure questioned by certain structuralists), see the collection of Tzvetan Todorov's essays titled *The Poetics of Prose* (trans. R. Howard; Ithaca, N.Y.: Cornell University Press, 1977).

In *Figures of Literary Discourse* (trans. A. Sheridan; Oxford: Blackwell, 1982) Gérard Genette moves from the argument that structuralist analysis is most valuably applied to literature that is distant temporally and/or culturally from the reader to a call for equal recognition of the contributions of hermeneutics and structuralism. The two should be regarded as complementary: "on the subject of the same work, hermeneutic criticism might speak the language of the resumption of meaning and of internal recreation, and structural criticism that of distant speech and intelligible reconstruction" (15). Art Berman's *From the New Criticism to Deconstruction* (Urbana: University of Illinois Press, 1988) "examines the various attempts to absorb, transform, and integrate structuralism and post-structuralism, to make them applicable as critical methods within the Anglo-American [empiricist] critical environment" (6).

For a critique of the *antirationality* of the ideological structuralism of Derrida, Lacan, and Foucault from the point of view of the German hermeneutic tradition, see Manfred Frank's *What Is Neo-Structuralism?* (trans. S. Wilke and R. Gray; Minneapolis: University of Minnesota Press, 1989).

STYLE   1. An evaluative term referring to correctness and clarity in writing and speaking. 2. One of several kinds or modes of writing or speaking. The primary ancient divisions were between the ornate, middle, and plain, or between the Attic and Asiatic. 3. The differentiating qualities in the writing of an individual author, or of a particular group of writers or period. 4. A term of praise for qualities in addition to clear exposition; applied most often specifically to literature. 5. The expressive or affective qualities of discourse as opposed to the strictly semantic and syntactic sense (propositional substance). 6. The manner of speaking or writing characteristic of DISCOURSE in a particular situation. In one kind of situation a formal style is expected, in another a casual style.

All senses of style assume the possibility of choices in the use of language, although some emphasize it more than others. In Stephen Ullmann's words, "There can be no question of style unless the speaker or writer has the possibility of choosing between alternate forms of expression" (Style; 6).

1. Style is derived from the Latin *stilus*, the pointed instrument for writing on wax or other suitable surfaces; by analogy with the correct (legible) use of the stylus, the term came to signify the clear and correct use of language. Aristotle states in the *Rhetoric*, "Style to be good must be clear, as is proved by the fact that speech which fails to convey a plain meaning will fail to do just what speech has to do" (167; 1404b). He goes on to say that positive adornment is useful, but his emphasis is on appropriateness and naturalness. The discussion of diction in the *Poetics* is quite similar.

This sense of the term lies behind the second of the three meanings distinguished by Middleton Murry, style as "technique of exposition" (8). It also lies behind those works that give general advice on good writing or style. Well-known examples are Herbert Spencer's *The Philosophy of Style* (1852), G. H. Lewes's *Principles of Success in Literature* (1865), and Walter Pater's "Style" (1889). The several principles elucidated in contemporary composition textbooks that are designed primarily to produce clear, serviceable prose descend from the same conception of style.

2. Classical rhetoric at least from Cicero on developed Aristotle's concept of appropriateness into the recognition of at least three styles, the ornate (later, the grand), the middle, and the plain, a distinction maintained by Puttenham in the sixteenth century. A somewhat differently oriented set of distinctions is that between the Attic and the Asiatic. The former, associated with Greece at the height of its power, is restrained and always tempered by the subject and situation; the latter, associated with the later Greek culture of Asia Minor, is luxuriant or grandiloquent. Concern for the separation of styles according to subject matter largely disappeared by the middle of the nineteenth century.

3. The existence of individual styles was, of course, recognized in antiquity and well understood in the Renaissance. Puttenham writes in 1589 that style is "a certain contrived form and quality, many times natural to the writer, many times his peculiar by election and art, and such as either he keepeth by skill, or holdeth on by ignorance, and will not or peradventure cannot easily alter into any other. . . . So we say that Cicero's style, and Salust's were not one, nor Caesar's and Livy's, nor Homer's and Hesiod's, nor Erasmus' and Budaeus' stiles" (148). In the nineteenth century, however, renewed emphasis begins to be placed on the elements making up individual styles as methods are developed for more accurately describing these (see STYLISTICS). Helmut Hatzfeld's *Don Quixote als Wortkunstwerk* (1927) and Franz Dornseiff's *Pindars Stil* (1921) are early-twentieth-century examples. At the same time, the characteristic styles of particular literary groups and periods received additional attention, partly in connection with the study of the stylistic characteristics of individual languages initiated by Charles Bally. F. W. Bateson's *English Poetry and the English*

Language (1934) and Stephen Ullmann's *Style in the French Novel* (1964) represent varieties of this interest.

In twentieth-century analyses, the style of the individual author is almost always regarded as an index of the qualities of his or her mind and concomitant aesthetic strategies. Thus, Donald Freeman writes, "a poet's deployment of his language's transformational apparatus, its syntactic patterns, not only reflects cognitive preferences, a way of seeing the world; perhaps more importantly, it reflects the fundamental principles of artistic design by which the poet orders the world that is the poem" (20).

Linguists tend to use the term *idiolect* for the characteristics of an individual's speaking and writing that are produced by a combination of the linguistic resources (lexical and syntactic) available to him or her and habitual choices within those resources. The term is less often applied to literary texts than to discourse as a whole; however; given the range of meanings of style, it is a useful designation.

4. The *Oxford English Dictionary* (*OED*) entry on style gives as sense 13b, "A good, choice or fine style," and cites from 1589, "All this is but bad English, when wilt thou come to a stile?" This evaluative sense is common: to say a writer "has style" is to give praise. By identifying style as "[a]n informing spirit running through a composition" and "that factor of a work of art which preserves in every part some sense of the form of the whole" (10), W. C. Brownell both stipulates the sense he assigns to the word style and makes it a term of commendation. A yet stronger honorific force is at times given to the word: René Wellek cites Goethe's use to designate the highest reaches of art (74). Such a sense is one of the three distinguished by Middleton Murry's influential study: "Style, as the highest achievement of literature" (8).

5. Sense 14, in the *OED* reads, "Those features of literary composition which belong to form and expression rather than to the substance of the thought or matter expressed." The first date associated with this sense in English is 1577, but it evidently is related to the rhetorical tradition that understands figures and tropes as ornament. Although neither Cicero nor Quintilian explicitly separates substance and style, such references as Cicero's to the "flowers of language and gems of thought" and Quintilian's to adornment "with suitable figures" could suggest that style is an external wrapping. Thus, the third book of Puttenham's *The Arte of English Poetry* is titled "Of Ornament"; in the opening sentence, the reader is told, "so is there yet requisite to the perfection of this art, another manner of exornation, which resteth in the fashioning of our maker's language and style, to such purpose as it may delight and allure as well the mind as the ear of the hearers with a certain novelty and strange manner of conveyance, disguising it no little from the ordinary and accustomed" (137).

Whatever the case in the older tradition, contemporary discussions of style insist that it is not a synonym for ornament. There are, however, two perspectives on the issue. The view that every alternate phrasing—every phonological, lexical, or syntactic choice—produces a different MEANING is usually called stylistic monism. The strongest way of stating this is that the same thing cannot be said in two different ways; all choices between ways of saying things are, thus, choices of what is said. The opposing view, stylistic dualism, holds that the same content or sense can be conveyed in more than one way, and that paraphrase is possible. Actually, the difference between the two is not as great as it seems: by meaning, monists generally intend to designate everything that is conveyed, and thus include the emotional and attitudinal, while dualists explicitly distinguish content, sense, or reference from emotional or attitudinal accompaniments. The dualists' distinction parallels that of I. A. Richards in *Practical Criticism*, where meaning is divided into four aspects: sense, feeling, tone, and intention (181–82). W. K. Wimsatt uses an intriguing simile: "A study of verbal style, though it ought to deal only with meaning, ought to distinguish at least two interrelated levels of meaning, a substantial level and another more like a shadow or gesture" (202). Louis Milic speaks simply of two kinds of meaning, "*represented* or *cognitive* meaning" and "*affective* or *expressive* meaning" (2). Stephen Ullmann's differentiation appears to separate the two in a way that makes it more difficult to subsume them both under the umbrella meaning. "Everything that transcends the purely referential and communicative side of language belongs to the province of expressiveness; emotive overtones, emphasis, rhythm, symmetry, euphony, and also the so-called '*evocative*' elements which place our style in a particular register (literary, colloquial, slangy, etc.) or associate it with a particular milieu (historical, foreign, provincial, professional, etc.)" (*Language and Style*, 10). Nevertheless, the term expressiveness, which Ullmann adopts from Charles Bally, remains much closer to sense or content (to use the older term) than to ornament.

In fact it proves difficult to adhere fully to monism or dualism. When, in the essay "Style," Pater writes of the transcribing of the writer's "sense of fact" (9—10) or of the search for the "unique word, phrase, sentence, paragraph, essay, or song, absolutely proper to the single mental presentation or vision within" (29), he seems to be a monist. When he writes of soul as "a quality of style" distinct from mind (25), he is on the edge of dualism. One may debate whether Middleton Murry was speaking from a monist or dualist position when he says, "Style is a quality of language which communicates precisely emotions or thoughts, or a system of emotions or thoughts peculiar to an author" (71). He seems closer to the dualist position when he drops the word thought in formulating what he calls "the central problem of style," that is, how the writer is to "compel others to feel the particularity of his emotion" (75). Wimsatt in effect meets the problem head on: "The term *verbal style*, if it is to have any clear use, must be supposed to refer to some verbal quality which is somehow structurally united to or fused with *what* is being said by the words, but is also somehow to be distinguished from *what* is being said" (202). E. L. Epstein's epigrammatic "Style is the regard that *what* pays to *how*" opens a survey that keeps the two separate, although he concludes, "In the long run, the *what* is created by the *how*" (80). The fact seems to be that critics tend to monism when they wish to deny that style is detachable and to dualism when they wish to discuss how literary effects are achieved or explain features that call attention to themselves.

6. Sometime in the sixteenth century, style came to have a sense something like "manner as governed by the occasion." This sense is evidently related to the distinction between levels that belongs to sense 2, although here the occasion or situation rather than the subject is controlling. Thus, the *usage-scale* by which Martin Joos designates style in *The Five Clocks* (frozen, formal, consultative, casual, intimate) is related to situations of use. The linguist's usual term for the styles or types of discourse distinguished by the situations in which they are used is *register*. It is important to recognize that what is called the style of a specific discourse is a product of style both in sense 3 (idiolect) and sense 6 (register).

References

Aristotle. *Rhetoric*. Trans. W. R. Roberts. New York: Random House, Modern Library Edition, 1954.

Bally, Charles. *Traité de stylistique française*. Heidelberg: C. Winter, 1919–21.

Bateson, Frederick W. *English Poetry and the English Language*. Oxford: Clarendon Press, 1934.

Brownell, W. C. *The Genius of Style*. New York: Charles Scribner's Sons, 1924.

Epstein, E. L. *Language and Style*. London: Methuen, New Accents Series, 1978. Epstein divides style into public and private games played by the poet and the reader. The first consists of sound patterns, intonation (modes of conveying tone), and syntax; the second consists primarily of word choice.

Freeman, Donald C. "The Strategy of Fusion: Dylan Thomas's Syntax." In *Style and Structure in Literature*, ed. Roger Fowler. Ithaca, N. Y.: Cornell University Press, 1975.

Joos, Martin. *The Five Clocks*. New York: Harcourt, Brace, Jovanovich, 1967. An engaging examination of the functions of five styles in sense 6 (manner in relation to situation).

Lewes, George Henry. *Principles of Success in Literature*. Boston: Allyn and Bacon, 1891. Lewes lists five laws of style: Economy, Simplicity, Sequence, Climax, and Variety (127), all of which ultimately flow from the master principle of sincerity. First published in *The Fortnightly Review* in 1865.

Milic, Louis T. "Introductory Essay." In *Stylists on Style: A Handbook with Selections for Analysis*, ed. Louis T. Milic. New York: Charles Scribner's Sons, 1969. "Style might be described as that aspect of a piece of writing that we *perceive* but do not *observe*, what we respond to in writing without being aware of it" (1). Milic sketches various ways of analyzing style: quantitatively, by propositional reduction, and by logical diagram.

Murry, J. Middleton. *The Problem of Style*. London: Oxford University Press, 1922. An influential early-twentieth-century investigation of the meaning of style.

Pater, Walter. "Style" (1888). In *Appreciations*. London: Macmillan, 1911.

Puttenham, George. *The Arte of English Poesie*. Ed. G. D. Willcock and A. Walker. Cambridge: Cambridge University Press, 1936. (The spelling of the passages quoted from Puttenham have been modernized here.)

Richards, I. A. *Practical Criticism*. London: Kegan Paul, Trench, Trubner, 1929.

Spencer, Herbert. *The Philosophy of Style*. Boston: Allyn and Bacon (1892). For Spencer, style is grounded in the principle of economy, that is, "of economizing the reader's or hearer's attention" (3). Originally published in *The Westminster Review* in 1852.

Ullmann, Stephen. *Language and Style*. New York: Barnes and Noble, 1964. Includes four essays treating stylistics which contain useful observations on the general subject of style.

————. *Style in the French Novel*. Oxford: Basil Blackwell, 1964.

Wellek, René. "Stylistics, Poetics, and Criticism." In *Literary Style: A Symposium*, ed. Seymour Chatman. London: Oxford University Press, 1971.

Wimsatt, W. K. "Verbal Style: Logical and Counterlogical." In *The Verbal Icon*. Lexington: University Press of Kentucky, 1954.

Sources of Additional Information

An interesting collection of statements on style, mostly from the nineteenth and early twentieth centuries, is assembled in Paul M. Fulcher's *Foundations of English Style* (New York: F. S. Crofts, 1927).

For a clear, concise presentation of the relationship between dialects, registers, idiolects, and individual styles, see Chapter 4 of *The Linguistic Sciences and Language Teaching* by M. A. K. Halliday, Angus McIntosh, and Peter Strevens (Bloomington: Indiana University Press, 1964).

The introduction to Geoffrey Leech's *Style in Fiction: A Linguistic Introduction to English Fictional Prose* (London: Longman, 1981) offers an incisive summary of the strengths and weaknesses of the arguments of both the monist and dualist positions on the relation of style to sense (form to content). The later chapters treat style in relation to lexical choices, grammatical choices, figures of speech, cohesion, and coherence.

Examples of the wide range of questions that fall under the general topics of style and stylistics will be found in *Style in Language*, ed. Thomas A. Sebeok (Cambridge, Mass.: M.I.T. Press, 1960); *Literary Style: A Symposium*, ed. S. Chatman (London: Oxford University Press, 1971); and the introduction and first three chapters in *Style and Structure in Literature*, ed. Roger Fowler (Ithaca, N. Y.: Cornell University Press, 1975). Fowler's introduction to the latter volume is particularly recommended for its summary of the "new stylistics."

STYLISTICS   1. The analysis of texts to discover characteristic features that may help in the identification of the author or the date of composition. 2. The study of the totality of the choices available for expressive effect in a given language. 3. The analysis of the phonological, semantic, and syntactic characteristics of a text or set of texts. Such analysis may be undertaken either on the assumption that these characteristics reflect the mind of the author or in order to understand the functions served or effects produced.

The above division of stylistics on the basis of type of application is useful in avoiding certain confusions; however, the term is sometimes used comprehensively to include all three.

Although any comment on the STYLE *of a* DISCOURSE *presupposes attention to the constituents of that style, prior to the middle of the nineteenth century such comments were largely impressionistic. The word stylistics itself is found in German in the first half of the nineteenth century; the* OED *gives the date 1846 for the appearance of the English term stylistic in reference to the science or study of style. As the term is now almost always used, stylistics is closely associated with linguistics, although the exact relationship remains debatable, as is the degree to which linguistics may be more scientific than literary criticism in general.*

1. The earliest attempts at more objective or scientific analysis appear to have been statistical studies undertaken to address questions of attribution and dating. Anthony Kenny cites T. C. Mendenhall's studies of average word length and the frequency of words of various lengths (two-letter, three-letter, and so forth) as the first attempt at a statistical analysis of an element of style. More complex sets of characteristics were being investigated by the end of the century, such as word order, rhythm, vocabulary, collocations of certain words, and the use of superlatives. Statistical analyses of the kinds described by Kenny in *The Computation of Style* are essential for attribution and dating studies, since these depend on the comparison of specific texts. The significant differences between texts often can be found only by trial and error (the differences may prove to be as unremarkable as between choices of prepositions or preference for one of two nearly synonymous words).

2. The burgeoning of stylistics as a distinct field occurs in the early twentieth century as the linguistic theories of Ferdinand de Saussure suggested a range of new approaches. The most direct development from Saussure is represented by the work of Charles Bally, who sought to form an inventory of resources for expressiveness in French. As René Wellek notes (65), such a study in one way parallels the cataloguing of stylistic devices by rhetoricians from Greek antiquity on. However, the twentieth-century approach, a part of the "new stylistics," differs in seeking to describe rather than recommend, and in making use of linguistics for techniques of analysis and description. David Crystal and Derek Davy's *Investigating English Style* (1969) exemplifies such a stylistic approach to the English language.

3. In the analysis of individual texts and the works of individual authors, stylistics, or the "new stylistics," also draws heavily on linguistics. However, although the importance of linguistics for stylistic studies is widely agreed, the relationship is conceived in a number of different ways. Crystal and Davy state: "Linguistics is the academic discipline which studies language scientifically. Stylistics, studying certain aspects of language variation, is therefore essentially a part of this discipline" (9). Geoffrey Leech and Michael Short subordinate stylistics to linguistics a little less positively, regarding stylistics as "the (linguistic) study of style" (13). However, Stephen Ullmann writes, "Stylistics is not a branch of linguistics; it is a parallel science which examines the same problems from a different point of view" (10). For G. W. Turner, "*Stylistics* means the study of style, with a suggestion, from the form of the word, of a

scientific or at least a methodical study'' (8). René Wellek suggests that however the relation of stylistics to linguistics is understood, when the stylistician turns to literary texts, ''the study of style then has to come to grips with poetics and the theory of style'' (67).

The issue is not merely terminological; it is intertwined with the question of how one identifies the stylistically significant features of a text. For Leo Spitzer, who is regarded as the most important figure of the new stylistics, the first step is necessarily intuitive, or at least unmethodical: the text is read and reread until some feature calls attention to itself. ''And suddenly, one word, one line stands out, and we realize that, now, a relationship has been established between the poem and us'' (27). An analysis of the significance or function of that feature then begins. For some analysts, stylistic features are recognized at least in part by their deviation from a norm. Ullmann writes, ''The expressive force of a device depends in no small measure on whether it deviates from ordinary usage''; this ''principle of deviation from the norm'' (9) also seems essential to Spitzer's technique. However, although certain kinds of deviation from everyday use stand out, it is difficult to define ''normal'' language with much specificity, especially when differences induced by history, dialect, GENRE, and register are taken into account.

Much more methodical are analyses that examine every area of text construction in which choices can be made—in sound, vocabulary, and grammar. The classic example is the exhaustive examination of Baudelaire's ''Les Chats'' by Roman Jakobson and Claude Lévi-Strauss, who analyze the poem as a structure of linguistic structures. René Wellek's comment is representative: ''They have demonstrated the parallelism, correspondences, reiterations, and contrasts convincingly, but I fail to see that they have or could have established anything about the aesthetic value of the poem'' (73). While stylisticians would answer that stylistics is not intended to illuminate aesthetic values, Michael Riffaterre raises incisive questions: Are all the strictures that linguistic analysis may discover relevant to the effect of the poem, and are all the significant structures such as to be captured by linguistic analysis? For Riffaterre, what are to be noted by the stylistician are those elements or structures to which readers actually respond. By tabulating what readers comment on, one can discover the stylistic devices that are truly germane.

Without necessarily accepting Riffaterre's method, most stylisticians now accept that not all phenomena that can be linguistically described are relevant to stylistic effect and that not all effects can be linguistically described. Anne Cluysenaar commented in 1975: ''[T]he problem of selection has been the (not always recognized) bone of contention in recent controversies over the relevance of linguistics to literary criticism. I take the view that, if we want to pick out from amongst the mass of linguistic features in any text those that are of *special* importance to the reader[,] . . . our criteria of selection cannot remain wholly linguistic'' (16). Cluysenaar goes on to point out that the same linguistic feature will have different effects in different contexts. For Stephen Ullmann, this is the *principle of polyvalency*: "The same device of style may give me a variety of effects" and "the same effect may be obtained from a number of different devices" (9).

As a generalization, one may note that it is evidently necessary to have some reason to believe that a feature is stylistically significant, whether because it is a deviation from some normative expectation, or it seems to constitute an internal pattern, or experience with other texts suggests that it might be worth exploring. An alternative is simply to approach each text with a checklist of questions that will elicit possibly significant features; Leech and Short suggest nineteen such questions (75–80). The number of characteristics analyzed in a given text will depend on how many recommend themselves for one of the above reasons.

There are two other obvious variants among stylistic analyses of individual texts: the methodologies employed and the goals envisioned. Methodology is largely a function of the features considered. Examination of syntactical structures, sentence or word length, or type of vocabulary in a lengthy work requires statistical analysis. Louis Milic's *Quantitative Approach to the Style of Jonathan Swift* is a representative example. At the other end of the spectrum, a critic interested in style may simply note what seem to be especially effective passages and try to discover the means by which the effectiveness has been achieved. Methods here may be no more complex than a close examination of one's own process of response (as in Stanley Fish's *affective stylistics*); trying out different syntactical structures, substituting what seem to be synonymous words, or looking for patterns, as Anne Cluysenaar's *Aspects of Literary Stylistics* demonstrates. Between Milic and Fish in point of technicality falls a method like that described by Richard Ohmann in "Generative Grammars and the Concept of Literary Style." Here Ohmann applies rule-governed transformations to sentences from several authors to determine which transformations affect the style and the kind of transformations favored by the author.

The final variant is the goal sought by the stylistic analyses. One frequent goal is insight into the working of the author's mind. A statement by Richard Ohmann is often quoted: "stylistic preferences reflect cognitive preferences" (*Shaw*, 22). In his earlier work, Leo Spitzer seeks to link whatever stylistic feature interests him to the psychology of the author, although in his later studies he links it to the total organization of the text. An elaborate attack on attempts to move from a description of stylistic features to an understanding of the habitual form of an author's thought is developed by Stanley Fish in "What Is Stylistics and Why Are They Saying Such Terrible Things About It?" and in a sequel published a few years later. In Fish's own summary, the focus in the first essay is "on the arbitrary relationship between the specification of formal patterns and their subsequent interpretation"; the second essay argues that "formal patterns are themselves the product of interpretation and that therefore there is no such thing as a formal pattern, at least in the sense necessary for the practice of stylistics" ("What Is Stylistics? II," 144).

The debate continues, but there seem to be some general agreements among the majority of current writers on stylistics. First, as noted above, no feature or device has an invariable significance—whatever significance there is depends on the CONTEXT. Second, although the examination of a single passage in a novel or long poem is perhaps less a matter of examining style than of analyzing technique, the explanation of felt differences in the total manner of writing (between Swift and Mill, Pope and Hopkins, or Fielding and Faulkner, to take extremes) is a legitimate aim of stylistics whether or not the results bear on interpretation of either the author's mind or the intended meaning. Third, the aim of stylistic analysis of a text is not necessarily to demonstrate that the form mimes the content (or more accurately, that certain stylistic features in some way imitate what is taken to be the propositional meaning). Style, the dimension of expressiveness, may function primarily to qualify or otherwise comment on what would seem to be an accurate paraphrase of a text's propositional content.

While most of the work in stylistics in this third sense has focused on individual texts or authors, a series of studies in the 1950s and 1960s by Josephine Miles examines the characteristics of poetry in English from the seventeenth to the twentieth centuries. Miles concentrates on the proportion of adjectives, nouns, and verbs in a generous selection of poets in each period (this yields information about syntactic preferences), and the words most frequently used by each poet and in particular decades (this yields information about the sounds of poetry as well as vocabularies). While the information Miles gathers is presented in tabular form, her commentary on the stylistic qualities of individual poets and representative poems is illuminating.

References

Cluysenaar, Anne. *Aspects of Literary Stylistics*. New York: St. Martin's Press, 1975.
Crystal, David, and Derek Davy. *Investigating English Style*. Bloomington: Indiana University Press, 1969.
Fish, Stanley. "Literature in the Reader: Affective Stylistics." *New Literary History* 2 (Autumn 1970): 123–62. Reprinted in *Is There a Text in This Class?* Cambridge, Mass.: Harvard University Press, 1980.
———. "What Is Stylistics and Why Are They Saying Such Terrible Things About It?" In *Approaches to Poetics*, ed. Seymour Chatman. New York, Columbia University Press, 1973. Reprinted in Stanley Fish, *Is There a Text in This Class?* Cambridge: Mass.: Harvard University Press, 1980.
———. "What Is Stylistics and Why Are They Saying Such Terrible Things About It?— Part II." In *The Question of Textuality*, ed. W. V. Spanos, P. A. Bové, and D. O'Hara. Bloomington: Indiana University Press, 1982. Reprinted in Stanley Fish, *Is There a Text In This Class?* Cambridge, Mass.: Harvard University Press, 1980.
Jakobson, Roman, and Claude Lévi-Strauss. " 'Les Chats' de Charles Baudelaire." *L'Homme* 2 (1962): 5–21.
Kenny, Anthony. *The Computation of Style*. Oxford: Pergamon Press, 1982. Although the book is devoted primarily to the explanation of statistical methods, the first chapter cites a number of interesting examples of the application of statistical analysis to questions of attribution and dating.
Leech, Geoffrey N., and Michael H. Short. *Style in Fiction: A Linguistic Introduction*

to *English Fictional Prose*. London: Longman, 1981. An important presentation of the significant elements of style in fiction and their effects.

Mendenhall, T. C. "The Characteristic Curves of Composition." *Science* 9 (11 March 1887): 237–46.

Miles, Josephine. *The Continuity of Poetic Language: Studies in English Poetry from the 1540's to the 1940's*. Berkeley: University of California Press, 1951.

—— —. *Eras and Modes in English Poetry*. Berkeley: University of California Press, 1964. These two are perhaps the most central of Miles's many studies.

Milic, Louis T. *A Quantitative Approach to the Style of Jonathan Swift*. The Hague: Mouton, 1967.

Ohmann, Richard. "Generative Grammars and the Concept of Literary Style." *Word* 20 (December 1964): 423–39. The brief comments on twelve approaches to stylistics made at the beginning of this essay are insightful.

———. *Shaw: The Style and The Man*. Middletown, Conn.: Wesleyan University Press, 1962.

Riffaterre, Michael. "Describing Poetic Structures: Two Approaches to Baudelaire's 'Les Chats.' " In *Structuralism*, ed. Jacques Ehrmann. Garden City, N.Y.: Doubleday Anchor, 1970. Reprinted from *Yale French Studies* 36/37 (1966): 200–242.

Spitzer, Leo. "Linguistics and Literary History." In *Linguistics and Literary History*. Princeton, N.J.: Princeton University Press, 1948. An important essay by a major figure in the history of stylistics that clearly sets forth Spitzer's method and the assumptions behind it. "Whoever has thought strongly and felt strongly has innovated in his language; mental creativity immediately inscribes itself into language, where it becomes linguistic creativity" (15).

Turner, G. W. *Stylistics*. Harmondsworth, U.K.: Penguin, 1973.

Ullmann, Stephen. *Style in the French Novel*. Oxford: Basil Blackwell, 1964. The Introduction gives a helpful overview of portions of the history and methodology of stylistics.

Wellek, René. "Stylistics, Poetics, and Criticism." In *Literary Style: A Symposium*, ed. Seymour Chatman. Oxford: Oxford University Press, 1971. A brief but important commentary on stylistics.

Sources of Additional Information

The bibliography of stylistics is vast, partly because the boundaries are not at all well defined; rhetorical, speech-act, and narratological approaches can often be regarded as studies in stylistics. The basic bibliography is Helmut Hatzfeld's *Critical Bibliography of the New Stylistics Applied to the Romance Languages, 1900–1952* (Chapel Hill: University of North Carolina Press, 1953), which was extended to 1960 in a revised 1966 edition. Three standard bibliographies are *Style and Stylistics: An Analytical Bibliography*, ed. Louis Milic (New York: Free Press, 1967); *English Stylistics: A Bibliography*, ed. R. W. Bailey and D. Burton (Cambridge, Mass.: MIT Press, 1968); and *Bibliography of Stylistics and Related Criticism, 1967–83*, ed. James R. Bennett (New York: MLA, 1986).

Roger Fowler's brief introductory essay in *Style and Structure in Literature* (Ithaca, N.Y.: Cornell University Press, 1975) is helpful, not least in its summaries of the arguments of the three essays on stylistics that follow. Fowler's comment that stylisticians analyze surface structures while structuralists analyze "deeper, more abstract patterns" (11) cuts through a certain amount of confusion. Louis Milic's introductory essay in

Stylists on Style (New York: Scribner's, 1969) reviews several approaches to stylistic analysis, including the methods of Propositional Reduction and the Logical Diagram. The brief sections on "Concepts of Style" and "Stylistics" in David Lodge's *Language of Fiction* (London: Routledge and Kegan Paul, 1966) consider a number of the important issues. More comprehensive are the four essays on stylistics in Stephen Ullmann's *Language and Style* (New York: Barnes and Noble, 1964) and G. W. Turner's highly readable *Stylistics* (Harmondsworth, U.K.: Penguin, 1973).

The range of stylistic studies can be gathered from major anthologies that include *Style in Language*, ed. Thomas A. Sebeok (Cambridge, Mass.: MIT Press, 1960); *Essays on the Language of Literature*, ed. S. Chatman and S. R. Levin (Boston: Houghton Mifflin, 1967); and *Literary Style: A Symposium*, ed. S. Chatman (London: Oxford University Press, 1971).

An important essay on the question of synonymity (another way of formulating the debate between stylistic monism and dualism) is E. D. Hirsch's "Stylistics and Synonymity" (*Critical Inquiry* 1, March 1975: 559–79), which argues that synonymity is in fact possible. A significant corollary of the argument is the position at which Hirsch arrives concerning the relationship between stylistics and interpretation: "Stylistics cannot be a reliable method of determining meaning, or a reliable method of confirming an interpretation, but neither can any other method perform those feats . . . [however] stylistics may indeed provide clues that help induce interpretive guesses, and may indeed provide evidence that helps shift the weight of probability from one interpretation to another" (577).

An excellent survey of the stylistic features that are characteristic of poetry, in which poetry is approached in terms of deviations from everyday discourse, is Geoffrey Leech's *A Linguistic Guide to English Poetry* (London: Longman, 1969). Patterns of sound, metre, lexical and semantic deviation, and figurative language are among the characteristics examined.

SYMBOL 1. Broadly, anything that, through convention, resemblance, or association, is recognized as representing or standing for a second thing. 2. Language presenting images that evoke, and perhaps help give insight into, that which cannot be directly perceived, such as spiritual truths, transcendent patterns, or things-in-themselves. 3. In relation to French *Symboliste* poetry and thought, an image with the effective but unexplainable power of evoking particular emotions, moods, or synaesthetic relations. 4. Most commonly in the twentieth century, an image that, by calling attention to itself, also suggests an (often indefinite or ambiguous) idea or thing. A presentation that is understood as a representation as well. 5. A SIGN having a meaning beyond its immediate meaning. Tzvetan Todorov places all indirect discursive meaning under the term verbal symbolism. Thus, all forms of indirection—symbols in sense 4, allegory, tropes, and the forms of indirection that H. P. Grice calls implicature, which are the major focus of study in SPEECH-ACT THEORY—are instances of symbolism in this sense.

For the psychoanalytical perspective on symbols, see also PSYCHOLOGICAL/ PSYCHOANALYTICAL CRITICISM.

1. The comprehensive English sense of symbol is also the oldest. Described in twentieth-century terms, it includes both what Ferdinand de Saussure called a sign and C. S. Peirce called a symbol (in which the relationship between signified and signifier is arbitrary) and what Saussure called a symbol and Peirce called on index or icon (in which there is some association or resemblance between signifier and signified). (See SEMIOTICS.) Thus, all natural language C. K. Ogden and I. A. Richards characterize words as symbols in their influential 1923 *Meaning of Meaning*), all signification assigned within a particular system (such as the notations used in symbolic logic), all culturally conventional sig-nifications like those of the flag, all "natural" symbols resulting from common associations (water with life), and all nonce symbols created by and operative only within a given text or situation (Melville's white whale) fall within this meaning. Kenneth Burke generally uses symbol in this overarching sense, as when he speaks of the human being as "the symbol-using animal" (*Language*, 3) or the symbolic as "representative" (*Philosophy*, 22). Poetry for Burke is a *symbolic act* because he sees poetry as act and all acts as symbolic. In this sense, symbol includes both ALLEGORY and METAPHOR (thus, Guérard speaks of met-aphor as the *first degree* of the symbol). Conventional symbols, schematized symbols (those assigned a fixed meaning in fields outside literature, such as psychoanalysis), and contextual symbols (those given symbolic weight by the text itself) may all be significant for the interpretation of a text.

2. In a much more restricted sense, symbolism in language, and especially literature, is understood to be a use of signs that points beyond routine or literal senses or meanings. Philip Wheelwright sums up the use of symbol in this sense in *The Burning Fountain*. "It is enough for our purposes that we understand a symbol as that which means or stands for something more than (not necessarily separate from) itself, which invites consideration rather than overt action, and which characteristically (although not perhaps universally) involves an intention to communicate" (24). An alternative formulation is that of Paul Ricoeur: "I define 'symbol' as any structure of signification in which a direct, primary, literal meaning designates, in addition, another meaning which is indirect, secondary, and figurative and which can be apprehended only through the first" (*Conflict*, 12–13).

The symbol in this sense is usually distinguished from both metaphor and allegory. The distinction between symbolism in this more specific sense and allegory appears to date no further back than the very end of the eighteenth century. An 1824 maxim of Goethe's (No. 279) in which the distinction is directly judgmental is a standard reference. "There is a great difference whether the poet seeks the particular for the universal or sees the universal in the particular. Out of the first method arises allegory, where the particular serves only as an example of the universal; the latter procedure, however, is really the nature of poetry; it speaks forth a particular, without thinking of the universal or pointing to it" (quoted in Adams, 52–53). Coleridge's famous separation of symbolism from allegory in *The Statesman's Manual* (1816) is equally invidious.

> Now an Allegory is but a translation of abstract notions into a picture-language which is itself nothing but an abstraction from the objects of the senses. . . . On the other hand a Symbol . . . is characterized by a translucence of the Special in the Individual or of the General in the Especial or of the Universal in the General; above all by the translucence of the Eternal through the Temporal. It always partakes of the Reality which it renders intelligible; and while it enunciates the whole, abides itself as a living part in that Unity, of which it is the representative. (30)

The symbol as described by Goethe and Coleridge is often designated the "Romantic symbol." There are three important points to be made about such symbols.

a. In saying that the symbol partakes of that which it represents, Coleridge makes the relationship between the symbol and that which is symbolized essential (at least synecdochic or metonymic), rather than arbitrary, a point that has been variously repeated. For instance, Albert Guérard notes that in the symbol there is "actual correspondence between the sign and the thing signified" (171), and Elder Olson comments that the "materials of the concept of the symbol . . . must be drawn from some part of the concept of the symbolized, without which the latter could not be" (583).

b. Goethe and Coleridge both see the symbol as representing something that conceptual language cannot express. Goethe is especially explicit on this point. "The symbolic changes the phenomenon into the idea, the idea into the image, in such a way that the idea remains always infinitely active and unapproachable in the image, and will remain inexhaustible even though expressed in all languages" (quoted in Adams, 57). Yeats, commenting on lines from Burns, is equally explicit on this point. "But, when all are together, moon and wave and whiteness and setting Time and the last melancholy cry, they evoke an emotion which cannot be evoked by any other arrangement of colours and sounds and forms" (155–56). Albert Guérard compresses this view of the symbol as the "attempt to express (or adumbrate) the inexpressible" (497).

c. From regarding the symbol as a means of evoking that which is otherwise incommunicable to regarding it as a revelation of God's purposes, or an ideal realm, is a short step. Coleridge's reference to the "translucence of the Eternal through and in the Temporal" suggests such correspondence. Carlyle's language is similar. "In the Symbol proper . . . there is ever, more or less distinctly and directly, some embodiment and revelation of the Infinite; the Infinite is made to blend itself with the Finite, to stand visible, and as it were, attainable there" (166). Even though the view of symbolism as communicating what is otherwise incommunicable leads toward the view of it as a revelation of the transcendental, there is a distinction between the two: one who accepts the first does not have to accept the second. Charles Chadwick's definition of symbolism captures the two possibilities. "Symbolism can, then, be finally said to be an attempt to penetrate beyond reality to a world of ideas, either the ideas within the poet, including his emotions, or the Ideas in the Platonic sense that constitute a perfect supernatural world towards which man aspires" (6).

3. The Romantic experience of moments of communion with the Holy Spirit, or of seeing through Nature into the heart of things (see ROMANTICISM), faded as the century went on, to be replaced by a curious mingling of egotism and despair in the French Symbolist movement. Symbol, as understood by the French Symbolist poets writing in the second half of the nineteenth century and by those whom they influenced, is allied to the third mode of regarding the symbol in sense 2. The main current of such symbolism is represented by Charles Baudelaire, Paul Verlaine, Arthur Rimbaud, and Stéphane Mallarmé; its influence is found in such writers as Rainer Maria Rilke, Stefan George, Alexander Blok, and W. B. Yeats. The semiorthodox system which lies behind Coleridge's belief in the transcendental power of the symbol or Carlyle's less orthodox religious sense takes on a coloring more mystical than religious. Critical commentaries on these Symbolists reflect different emphases. C. M. Bowra summarizes French Symbolism as "a mystical form of aestheticism" (3); for him, "The essence of Symbolism is its insistence on a world of ideal beauty, and its conviction that this is realised through art" (6). Anna Balakian finds three constants: "ambiguity of indirect communication; affiliation with music; and the 'decadent' spirit" (101), where decadence is defined as "the haunting awareness of man's mortality" (116). Charles Chadwick writes, "Symbolism can therefore be defined as the art of expressing ideas and emotions not by describing them directly, nor by defining them through overt comparisons with concrete images, but by suggesting what these ideas and emotions are, by re-creating them in the mind of the reader through the use of unexplained symbols" (2–3). The mystical or magical attitude characteristic of French Symbolism tends to include a belief in correspondences between certain objects or images and certain emotions or ideas, and/or correspondences between objects of the different senses (synaesthesia). Baudelaire's poem "Correspondences" is the most famous statement of the synaesthetic doctrine: "perfumes, sounds, and colors correspond." Yeats's comment on Burns's lines, cited above, imply an interaction between sounds and colors. Almost immediately after this passage, we find a sweeping explanation of such effects. "All sounds, all colours, all forms, either because of their preordained energies or because of long association, evoke indefinable and yet precise emotions, or, as I prefer to think, call down among us certain disembodied powers, whose footsteps over our hearts we call emotions" (156–57). However the "preordained energies" and "disembodied powers" are interpreted, Yeats evidently wishes to invoke more than "association" resulting from experience.

4. The New Critics assigned major importance to the symbol while partially redefining it (see NEW CRITICISM). In opposing the growing prestige of science, the New Critics contrasted the suggestively indefinite symbol with the sterility of the definite sign, and the expression of human emotion through linguistic symbols with the analysis of formal reasoning through logical symbols. The successful work of literature is regarded as representing the complexity of reality through its inner tensions while bringing a sense of unity and harmony to those tensions, often through a structure of symbols. The high value given the symbol

as opposed to the allegorical abstraction defined by the Romantic view is maintained, though the underlying patterns made visible by the symbolic structure become expressions of human wisdom rather than transcendent insight. Some New Critics tended to regard the symbol as a strong form of metaphor, one likely to be more central to the meaning of a work but also likely to be more ambiguous. "The symbol may be regarded . . . as a metaphor from which the first term has been omitted" (634) wrote Cleanth Brooks and Robert Penn Warren in *Understanding Poetry* (1938). Indeed, the similarities between symbol and metaphor have led critics to specify where the difference lies. Roland Bartel, summing up a distinction frequently met with over the last fifty years, writes, "A symbol expands language by substitution, a metaphor by comparison and interaction. A symbol does not ask a reader to merge two concepts but rather to let one thing suggest another" (61).

The absence of a definite, even if unstated, second term tends to produce an element of ambiguity in the symbol which the New Critics have cited as a source of additional richness (much the same notion is expressed in the "surplus of signification" that Paul Ricoeur attributes to the symbol (*Interpretation Theory*, 55). At the same time, New Critical commentary once again broadens the concept of the literary symbol by singling out conventional, archetypal, and Freudian symbols as well as contextual symbols (those images to which the structure of the work itself gives symbolic status).

The tendency to give substantial attention to while broadening the meaning of literary symbolism has not been confined to the New Critics. Whatever the presuppositions of critics writing on the symbol in literature from the 1930s to the present, the direction has been away from the transcendental or mystical and toward a concern for images that call strong attention to themselves. Thus Northrop Frye writes in *Anatomy of Criticism* (1957) that symbol "in this essay means any unit of any literary structure that can be isolated for critical attention" (71). Paul Ricoeur's formulation is similar if more detailed. "Poetics . . . if we understand this term in its broad sense, understands symbols to be the privileged images of a poem, or those images that dominate an author's works, or a school of literature, or the persistent figures within which a whole culture recognizes itself, or even the great archetypal images which humanity as a whole—ignoring cultural differences—celebrates" (*Interpretation Theory*, 53). Wilbur Samuel Howell employs symbol as a synonym for Aristotle's MIMESIS (31).

5. Paul Ricoeur employs symbol to designate signs "whose intentional texture calls for a reading of another meaning in the first, literal, and immediate meaning" (11–12). Tzvetan Todorov's similar scheme, as set forth in *Symbolism and Interpretation*, cuts across a number of common categorizations: symbols in sense 1 are divided into *signs* and *symbols* (not on the basis by which these are distinguished by Saussure), and E. D. Hirsch's *meaning* is divided into *direct* and *indirect*. On the other hand, by grouping under the umbrella term symbol any expression in which a knowledge of the meaning of the signs is not sufficient for an understanding of the meaning expressed, Todorov extends the term to

include all tropes and discursive expressions that the hearer knows to be indirect because they violate what H. P. Grice calls the *Communicative Presumption* (and Todorov calls *pertinence*). For Todorov, symbols are recognized through certain indices: contradiction, discontinuity, and cultural implausibility. "We might divide these indices . . . into two large groups: they derive from the establishment of a relation between the given segment and either other utterances belonging to the same *context* (syntagmatic indices) or else the shared knowledge of a community, with its *collective memory* (paradigmatic indices)" (30).

At the same time, Todorov brings together the fields of RHETORIC and HERMENEUTICS through the implicit assumption that the first is concerned with ways of communicating an intended meaning and the second with ways of determining intended meaning.

References

Adams, Hazard. *Philosophy of the Literary Symbolic*. Tallahassee: Florida State University Press, 1983.

Balakian, Anna E. *The Symbolist Movement: A Critical Appraisal*. New York: Random House, 1967. An important study of French symbolists and writers they influenced.

Bartel, Roland. *Metaphors and Symbols: Forays into Language*. Urbana, Ill.: National Council of Teachers of English, 1983.

Bowra, C. M. *The Heritage of Symbolism*. London: Macmillan, 1943. An influential study focusing on Valéry, Rilke, Stefan George, Blok, and Yeats.

Brooks, Cleanth, and Robert Penn Warren. *Understanding Poetry*. New York: Henry Holt, 1938.

Burke, Kenneth. *Language as Symbolic Action*. Berkeley: University of California Press, 1966.

———. *The Philosophy of Literary Form: Studies in Symbolic Action*. Baton Rouge: Louisiana State University Press, 1941.

Carlyle, Thomas. "Symbols." Book 3, Chapter 3 of *Sartor Resartus*. Boston: Estes and Lauriat, Centennial Edition, 1885. Original serial publication, 1833–34.

Chadwick, Charles. *Symbolism*. London: Methuen, 1971. A study of the French symbolists.

Coleridge, Samuel Taylor. *The Statesman's Manual* (1816). In *Lay Sermons*. Ed. R. J. White, vol. 6 in *The Collected Works*, ed. K. Coburn. 16 vols. London: Routledge and Kegan Paul, 1969–84.

Frye, Northrop. *Anatomy of Criticism*. Princeton, N.J.: Princeton University Press, 1957.

Grice, H. P. "Logic and Conversation." In *Syntax and Semantics, III*. New York: Academic Press, 1975.

Guérard, Albert. *Preface to World Literature*. New York: Henry Holt, 1940. Though often regarded as outdated, Guérard's discussions of particular literary categorizations are frequently still cogent.

Howell, Wilbur Samuel. *Poetics, Rhetoric, and Logic*. Ithaca, N.Y.: Cornell University Press, 1975.

Ogden, C. K., and I. A. Richards. *The Meaning of Meaning*. London: Kegan Paul, Trench, Trubner, 1923.

Olson, Elder. "A Dialogue on Symbolism." In *Critics and Criticism*, ed. R. S. Crane. Chicago: University of Chicago Press, 1952. Raises a number of important issues.

Ricoeur, Paul. *The Conflict of Interpretations*. Ed. D. Ihde. Evanston, Ill.: Northwestern
    University Press, 1974.
———. *Freud and Philosophy*. Trans. D. Savage. New Haven, Conn.: Yale University
    Press, 1970.
———. *Interpretation Theory*. Forth Worth: Texas Christian University Press, 1976.
Todorov, Tzvetan. *Symbolism and Interpretation*. Trans. C. Porter. Ithaca, N.Y.: Cornell
    University Press, 1982. Original French edition, 1978.
Wheelwright, Philip. *The Burning Fountain*. Bloomington: Indiana University Press,
    1954. A stimulating study of literary symbolism.
Yeats, William Butler. "The Symbolism of Poetry" (1900). In *Essays and Introductions*.
    New York: Macmillan, 1961.

Sources of Additional Information

Ernst Cassirer's philosophical arguments pursuing the ways in which human beings
seize reality symbolically and thus divide and classify it according to their needs had
considerable impact on literary critics in the middle decades of this century. See *The
Philosophy of Symbolic Forms* (trans. R. Manheim; 3 vols.; New Haven: Yale University
Press, 1953–55) and *An Essay on Man: An Introduction to a Philosophy of Human
Culture* (New Haven, Conn.: Yale University Press, 1944). See also Suzanne Langer's
Cassirer-influenced *Philosophy in a New Key* (Cambridge, Mass.: Harvard University
Press, 1942). William York Tindall's *The Literary Symbol* (Bloomington: Indiana Uni-
versity Press, 1955) considers the symbol in the context of general literary theory.

Arthur Symons's *The Symbolist Movement in Literature* (London: Heinemann, 1899)
is a near contemporary account of *Symbolisme*; C. M. Bowra's *The Heritage of Symbolism*
and Anna E. Balakian's *The Symbolist Movement: A Critical Appraisal* (both cited in
References above) are broader historical accounts. *Symbolism: A Bibliography of Symbolism as an International and Multi-Disciplinary Movement*, comp. David L. Anderson
(New York: New York University Press, 1975), is usefully organized. *The Symbolist
Movement in the Literature of the European Languages* (Budapest: Akadémiai Kiadó,
1982) is an extensive collection of essays on Symbolism as an international movement.

There is no comprehensive discussion of the symbol from the strictly New Critical
point of view; the best starting points are, perhaps, portions of Cleanth Brooks and Robert
Penn Warren's *Understanding Poetry* (New York: Henry Holt, 1938) and Brooks's *The
Well Wrought Urn* (New York: Harcourt, Brace, 1947).

Correctives to the overly zealous pursuit of symbols are Harry Levin's "Symbolism
and Fiction" in *Contexts of Criticism* (New York: Athenaeum, 1963); Mary McCarthy's
"Settling the Colonel's Hash" (*Harper's Magazine* 208, February 1954:68–75); and Saul
Bellow's "Deep Readers of the World, Beware!" (*New York Times Book Review* 64, 15
February 1959:1,34). *Literary Symbolism*, ed. Maurice Beebe (San Francisco; Calif.:
Wadsworth, 1960), is a useful collection of essays and excerpts including the McCarthy
and Bellow essays.

Sigmund Freud's psychoanalytical theories (1900) brought a restricted but widely
known and very influential meaning to the word symbol: the disguises under which
repressed, rationally inadmissable desires (usually sexual) appear in dreams and myths.
While denying that a dictionary of fixed symbolic meanings was possible, Freud accepted
as a general principle that "All elongated objects . . . represent the male member," while
"Small boxes, chests, cupboards, and ovens correspond to female organs." Moreover,
"[s]teep inclines, ladders, and stairs . . . are symbolic representations of the sexual act"

(*The Interpretation of Dreams* in *The Basic Writings of Sigmund Freud*, ed. A. A. Brill, New York: Modern Library, 1938, 371–72). Although a number of critics were quick to search the canon for such symbols, as Harry Levin has commented, "Nature abounds in protuberances and apertures. Convexities and concavities, like Sir Thomas Browne's quincunxes, are everywhere. The forms they compose are not always enhanced or illuminated by reading our sexual obsessions into them" (194). Demurring from Freudian orthodoxy, Erich Fromm (*The Forgotten Language*, New York: Holt, Rinehart and Winston, 1951) interprets dream and myth symbols as transformations of human feelings and knowledge generally, while Carl Jung, from 1912 on, increasingly finds in the symbolism of dreams and myths the embodiment of a *collective unconscious* (see *The Basic Writings of C. G. Jung*, ed. Violet Staub de Laszlo, New York: Modern Library, 1959).

T

TEXT   1. Any written or printed DISCOURSE. 2. An authoritative or primary discourse. 3. The literary object (poem, novel, or essay) in itself. 4. The material representation (words as printed on a page or spoken aloud) as opposed to the work experienced as literature. 5. Any collocation of phenomena that may be interpreted as a system of signs. 6. As enunciated by Roland Barthes, the *text* is opposed to the *work*; where the work signifies a specific set of determinable meanings that are "consumed" by the reader, the text is irreducibly plural in meaning and produces activity in the reader. It may indeed be regarded as "productivity" rather than as a means of communication. 7. For certain poststructuralists, all texts are interweavings of previous texts.

1. Traditionally, text signified a written or printed version of any use of language—novel, play, poem, philosophical disquisition, law, letter, or recipe—although it was most often used for documents of continuing importance and interest. As suggested by its derivation from *texere*, "to weave," text implied an entity in which the parts (from the words of a single sentence to a succession of arguments in a treatise or incidents in a narrative) were intended to exist as a coherent whole. One way of describing such coherence is as *texture* that is dependent on cohesion and coherence. "A text has texture, and this is what distinguishes it from something that is not a text. It derives this texture from the fact that it functions as a unity with respect to its environment" (Halliday and Hasan, 2). (Texture in this sense is not to be confused with its use to designate the concrete details that appear in or the phonetic qualities of a discourse, especially a poetic one, or the somewhat more specialized use of this term by John Crowe Ransom.)

2. As is evident from senses 1d and 2 of the *OED*, the term text has often been employed in ways that suggest authority or authenticity: the original wording

as opposed to translations, corrupt or condensed versions, commentaries, or critical apparatus. Something of this sense is associated with the term textbook.

3. Literary critics associated with New Critical principles stressed that the literary object they sought to understand was the structure of thought and language found in the text itself, without regard for announced or assumed authorial intentions, readers' personal responses, presumed literary influences, or specific historical circumstances. While the New Critics continued to speak indifferently of works and texts, the French structuralist critics' use of the term has led to a common choice of text over work as a way of emphasizing a disassociation between the author and what is written.

4. Louise Rosenblatt has used text and work to describe another distinction, that between the text as a structure of potential meanings and the "literary work," which exists only as the result of a transaction between the text and a reader. "Instead of functioning as a rigid mould, the text is seen to serve as a pattern which the reader must to some extent create even as he is guided by it. The text presents limits or controls; the personality and culture brought by the reader constitute another type of limitation on the resultant synthesis, the lived-through work of art" (129). Both Louise Rosenblatt (13–14) and Barbara Herrnstein Smith (46) compare texts to scores and readings to performances.

5. The science of semiology projected by Saussure was to include all human sign systems; that of SEMIOTICS projected by C. S. Peirce took all signs as its province. Any phenomenon that can be regarded as a system of interpretable signs (for example, clothes, photography, or toys) is therefore described by certain investigators as a text. Interpretations of texts can also be regarded as texts. Thus, Robert Scholes writes in *Textual Power* (1985): "The response to a text is itself always a text. Our knowledge is itself only a dim text that brightens as we express it" (20). For a critic like Walter Benn Michaels, "The self, like the world, is a text" (401). It should be noted, however, that many critics continue to make the (at least implied) assumption that a defining characteristic of a text is that it is an intentionally constructed expression of a meaning consciously intended by a particular person or group.

6. In "From Work to Text," Roland Barthes valorizes the text as essentially a structure of language that is unclassifiable by traditional taxonomies and that defers interpretive closure, disseminates many meanings, exists without a relationship to the author, is produced by the reader, and is the source of joy. On the other hand, the work for Barthes is a material artifact that fills a recognizable role and presents interpretable meanings, speaks univocally, is tied to its author, is consumed by the reader, and at the most gives mere pleasure. The distinction between text and work in this 1971 essay largely parallels those that Barthes sets out in different ways in other essays. In the terminology of the 1960 essay "Authors and Writers," the author (*écrivain*) is engaged in an activity, produces writing that is *intransitive*, and serves as a "priest," while the writer (*écrivant*) performs a function, produces writing that is transitive in that it is intended as "an instrument of communication" (147) and has the role of a clerk. Essentially

the same distinction appears in the opposition that Barthes sets up in *S/Z* between the writerly (*scriptible*) and the readerly (*lisible*) text, and in the opposition in the 1973 *The Pleasure of the Text*, between texts that produce joy or bliss (*jouissance*, which includes a sexual connotation) and those that produce simple pleasure.

Not only for Barthes but also for a number of French critics writing after the late 1960s, text is the preferred word to designate a discourse which, rather than expressing a meaning ultimately existing beyond the text, produces "meaning effects" through opening up an infinite play of signs. For Julia Kristeva, the *productive* text is seen to open a gap between everyday uses of language and a "working" of language that communicates nothing: "Any 'literary' text may be envisioned as productivity. Literary history since the end of the 19th century has given us modern texts which, even structurally, perceive themselves as a production that cannot be reduced to representation" (*Kristeva Reader*, 86). (To avoid confusion, it should be noted that Kristeva's distinction between the geno-text and the pheno-text is not between two types of text but between the prelinguistic impulses that seek to find expression in language and the resulting text; see *Kristeva Reader*, 120–23.)

7. For Kristeva and others, any text is an assemblage of materials from other texts (see INTERTEXTUALITY). Thus, Kristeva defines a text as "a translinguistic apparatus that redistributes the order of language by relating communicative speech, which aims to inform directly, to different kinds of anterior or synchronic utterance. . . . [I]t is a permutation of texts; an intertextuality: in the space of a given text, several utterances, taken from other texts, intersect and neutralize each other" ("Bounded Text," 36).

References

Barthes, Roland. "Authors and Writers" (1960). In *Critical Essays*. Trans. R. Howard. Evanston; Ill.: Northwestern University Press, 1972.

———. "From Work to Text." (1971). In *Image—Music—Text*. Trans. S. Heath. New York: Hill and Wang, 1977.

———. *The Pleasure of the Text*. Trans. R. Miller. New York: Hill and Wang, 1975. Original French edition, 1973.

———. *S/Z*. Trans. R. Miller. New York: Hill and Wang, 1974. Original French edition, 1970.

Halliday, M. A. K., and Ruqaiya Hasan. *Cohesion in English*. London: Longmans, 1976.

Kristeva, Julia. "The Bounded Text" (1969). In *Desire in Language*. Trans. T. Gora, A. Jardine, and L. S. Roudiez. New York: Columbia University Press, 1980.

———. *The Kristeva Reader*, ed. Toril Moi. New York: Columbia University Press, 1986.

Michaels, Walter Benn. "The Interpreter's Self: Peirce on the Cartesian 'Subject.' " *Georgia Review* 31 (Summer 1977): 383–402.

Ransom, John Crowe. *The New Criticism*. Norfolk, Conn.: New Directions, 1941. See especially the final chapter, "Wanted: An Ontological Critic," with its definition of the poem as "a loose logical structure with an irrelevant texture" (280).

Rosenblatt, Louise. *The Reader, the Text, the Poem*. Carbondale: Southern Illinois University, 1978

Scholes, Robert. *Textual Power: Literary Theory and the Teaching of English*. New Haven, Conn.: Yale University Press, 1985.

Smith, Barbara Herrnstein. *On the Margins of Discourse*. Chicago: University of Chicago Press, 1978.

Sources of Additional Information

In "The Representation of Text-Types" (*Textual Pratice* 2, Spring 1988:22–29), Seymour Chatman gives the clearest statement of the consequences of the linearity of both written and printed texts. "What distinguishes a text from other communicative structures is its capacity to order the timing of its consumption by the audience. Not only does its discourse work in time, but it regulates the audience's temporal access to the information it generates" (22).

Writing of texts in general, Dominick LaCapra interestingly defines the text as "a situated use of language marked by a tense interaction between mutually implicated yet at the same time contestatory tendencies" ("Rethinking Intellectual History and Reading Texts," in *Modern European Intellectual History*, ed. D. LaCapra and S. L. Kaplan; Ithaca, N.Y.: Cornell University Press, 1982: 49). The essay surveys the issues associated with the relations between the text and the author's intention, the author's life, society, culture, the author's corpus, and modes of discourse.

THEORY   1. The attempt to state the principles of literature. 2. More frequently, the attempt to state the principles by which CRITICISM and/or INTERPRETATION of literary works should proceed. 3. The attempt to ground the interpretation and/or criticism of literature in a more "basic" discipline such as philosophy, psychology, or linguistics. 4. Theoretical arguments that theories of literature are self-invalidating. 5. In a special sense that is associated with the Frankfurt School's use of the terminology, "critical theory" may refer to analyses of literature or other aspects of culture from the point of view of social/political theories that oppose the existing culture as the product of monopoly capitalism.

There are special difficulties in defining theory in literary studies: if theory is thought of as an explanatory generalization inductively arrived at, few theoretical discussions of literature can be accommodated. Those that have been—Aristotle's account of tragedy is an example—are as much descriptive as explanatory and are generally subject to the limitations of genre, culture, and historical period. A theory, according to Coleridge, "supposes the general idea of cause and effect" (1:464); literary theories whose explanatory structures are based squarely on cause-and-effect relationships are rare. If theory is distinguished from hypothesis on the traditional basis that a hypothesis can be confirmed as theory if it successfully predicts as-yet-unexamined phenomena, few readers expect any predictive power from literary theories.

1. Theories of literature per se have generally attempted (a) to define what literature is, (b) to explain what value it has, or (c) to explore the ways in which

psychological, aesthetic, or literary effects are achieved in literature. The third endeavor, most often pursued in relation to a single genre, is often distinguished as POETICS. Aristotle's *Poetics* addresses all three issues in varying degrees, defining poetry (effectively, literature) as the art of imitation, finding the value of poetry in its mimetic power—"Man is differentiated from other animals because he is the most imitative of them, and he learns his first lessons through imitation, and we observe that all men find pleasure in imitations" (110)—and specifically analyzing the characteristic effects of tragedy and their production by means of the six components of the tragic work. Horace's *Ars Poetica* again sets out the principles to be observed by the successful poet, although in passing he makes the famous suggestion that the aim of poetry is the combination of the pleasant and the useful. Proclus's essay "The Nature of Poetic Art," an answer to the treatment of the poets in Plato's *Republic*, defines and evaluates three kinds of poetry in relation to the three "lives" (or faculties) of the soul.

Exemplary of the recurrent return over the centuries to the evidently closely related questions of the nature and the value of literature are Sidney's "Apologie for Poetrie" (1598), Shelley's "Defense of Poetry" (1821), and I. A. Richards's *Principles of Literary Criticism* (1925), which, despite its title, is much more concerned with the nature of literature than the procedures of criticism. Claims for both the distinctiveness and value of a class of specifically literary texts has progressively decreased in the twentieth century (see LITERATURE).

Theories of the essential characteristics of literary texts that produce the effects on readers essential to, expected of, and necessary for the success of the literary text evidently depend on at least implicit assumptions about the nature and value of literature, but nevertheless are reasonably distinct. Twentieth-century examples derive especially from structuralist investigations like that of Vladimir Propp into the essential components of the folktale.

2. The principles of criticism have as often been the subject of literary theory as the principles of literature, though their extended discussion appears later in history. Pope's *Essay on Criticism* (1711) is a standard example of the mixture, and it is to be noted that, in fact, the *Essay* constitutes advice to authors at least as much as to critics. Matthew Arnold's "Function of Criticism at the Present Time" essentially opens the question (at least in the Anglo-American context) of what the critic should be about, though its primary focus is on what criticism should accomplish. Certainly New Critics such as John Crowe Ransom, Allen Tate, and R. P. Blackmur were very much concerned to define the role of the critic, but their essays on the topic did not generally appeal to any theoretical framework (see NEW CRITICISM). Fuller discussion of the meanings of CRITICISM will be found under that entry, but it is significant that René Wellek and Austin Warren's *Theory of Literature*, which was first published in 1942 and is a standard reference for almost a generation of graduate students, first aligns literary theory with poetics (7), then speaks of the theory of literature as actually a "theory of literary criticism" and a "theory of literary history" (39). The bulk of the volume is then devoted to elucidating "The Extrinsic Approach to the Study of Liter-

ature'' (through biography, psychology, history of ideas, and so forth) and ''The Intrinsic Study of Literature'' (consisting of attention to such aspects as euphony, style, image, myth, and genre). In other words, Wellek and Warren provide less a theory than a description of some of the things that critics do.

Nevertheless, the movement from HISTORICAL SCHOLARSHIP to theory-based criticism was significant enough by 1967 for R. S. Crane to warn against the increasing application of a priori systems and the *dialectical fallacy*, that is, ''the tacit assumption that what is true in your theory as a dialectical consequence must also be, or tend to be, true in actuality'' (40).

3. Aristotle's *Poetics* was presumably intended to be read as part of a total philosophy, but for centuries most theoretical discussion of literature was developed wholly within the context of literature and its study. (Certainly from at least the time of Baumgarten and Kant, theories of general aesthetics blossomed, but aesthetics as a philosophical study of judgments about beauty and as a specifically literary theory are quite different things.) Efforts to anchor the practice of criticism at a ''higher'' level of conceptualization (philosophy), on a more ''scientific'' foundation (psychology, anthropology, or linguistics), or on a more ''socially relevant'' system of thought (Marxism) become important in the twentieth century. Thus, Freud, Jung, Marx, Saussure, G. E. Moore, F. H. Bradley, Nietzsche, Wittgenstein, Peirce, Husserl, Heidegger, and, most recently, Derrida and Foucault have been laid under contribution, the results varying among the adherents of each of these figures almost as much as among those who build on different prophets. The development of complex and sophisticated theories of what literature is, what it does, and how it is understood is a phenomenon of the second half of the twentieth century; the emergence of theory in the present sense is indeed usually dated around 1960 (see Griffith, 1–2, and de Man, 5–6). The decades since have seen an increasing preoccupation with theory and a belief in the autonomous value of theory elaborated for its own sake rather than for the aid it can give in understanding literature.

Theories of language, whether drawn from linguistics, philosophy, or psychology, have been the major source of this change. Paul de Man writes, ''The advent of theory, the break that is now so often being deplored and that sets it aside from literary history and from literary criticism, occurs with the introduction of linguistic terminology in the metalanguage about literature. By linguistic terminology is meant a terminology . . . that considers reference as a function of language and not necessarily as an intuition'' (8).

4. The perhaps surprising result by the 1980s has been a partial convergence as philosophy, linguistics, and the social sciences have all moved (though hardly monolithically) toward a high degree of relativism, much of it based on the belief that language cannot engage reality and, indeed, that the language of one text can hardly say anything useful or meaningful about another text. Theorists thus come to deny the possibility of theory; there is an evident irony (in which some find as much delight as others despair) in the long desired interdisciplinary confluence of theory and the strong desire for more rigorous theorizing in lit-

erature having resulted in a denial of the possibility of theory. Murray Krieger describes what has happened: where once there were "words about words about words: theoretical statements about critical statements about the verbal sequences we call literary works" (*Words*, 6), theory now questions the possibility of theory. Similarly, theorists question "the capacity of words . . . to reach outside themselves to refer to the world when that world has already been prearranged for them" (14). In Paul de Man's words, "It is . . . not *a priori* certain that literature is a reliable source of information about anything but its own language" (11). As Gregory Jay and David Miller argue in the introduction to *After Strange Texts*, theory that frames the activity of literature cannot at the same time frame or ground itself: the search for an ultimate frame or ground can lead only to infinite regression (6).

Stanley Fish defines theory as a model intended to govern practice (110) and goes on to deny such a possibility not only to literary theory but to theory in general. The first wave of dedicated theorists demonstrated that the apparent argument or theme of a literary text is undermined by dependence on an illegitimate hierarchy or essential contradiction (DECONSTRUCTION), or its use of a necessarily self-reflexive structure of language that can engage nothing beyond itself (various poststructuralist schools; see STRUCTURALISM), or because it assumes a coherent ego rather than recognizing that the human being is the intersection of linguistic codes (as in much poststructuralism), or because it fails to recognize that it simply assumed or endorsed a socioeconomic political power structure (see MARXIST LITERARY CRITICISM).

Moreover, if literature is suspect, why should it be privileged over criticism, and why indeed should either be privileged over theory? Such a question can lead to an absolute leveling of all discourse, but it equally as often has led to the insistence that theory is literature. The second wave of theorists, which overlaps rather than replaces the first, transfers skeptical analyses to the same theories that earlier found the literary texts hollow.

The form of vocabulary, diction, and structure of argument has shifted as much as the issues and targets. By 1977, Mary Louise Pratt was noting that "[t]he overriding tendency to disguise all notions of intention, perception, and value by converting them into textual attributes has a conspicuous stylistic effect on almost all [Russian] formalist and structuralist writings. They are a grammarian's goldmine of agentless passives, statives, reflexives, and attributives, all with conspicuously nonhuman subjects" (74). Describing the style of an adherent of the newer theorizing, Elizabeth Bruss comments, "The proof is meandering, elements circulate and overlap. . . . There is little or no attribution machinery. . . . Glancing blows and playful allusions replace official footnotes, making . . . [the] text seem more porous . . . full of minute fissures through which concepts seep in and leak out, impossible either to claim or entirely disclaim" (7).

As early as 1978, George Watson was sounding a warning against the skepticism of criticism: "Much of the most fashionable criticism in the Western

World since 1968 has based itself on an extreme insistence that poems, plays and novels have no independent reality in themselves, that they do not and cannot describe any reality outside themselves, and that the critic in his turn cannot seriously hope to describe them. . . . If that is what criticism does, then what criticism does is not worth doing'' (34).

The responses to the efflorescence of theory, especially theory that sees literature as political and ideological because, paradoxically, language does not connect it to a grounding reality, are predictably various. Paul de Man, remarking that "resistance to theory is a resistance to the use of language about language" (12), regarded the new theorizing as necessary and inevitable. A critic like Murray Krieger is both exhilarated by the omnipresence of theoretical debate and made uneasy by the concomitant depreciation of the role of literature (see "Literary Invention"); Marxists of various schools are happy to see what they regard as late capitalist ideologies being undercut while uneasy at the implication that their own system of thought is equally vulnerable. One Marxist approach is simply to deny that literature constitutes a class of texts that is in any way definable, to proclaim that university departments of literature have existed only to maintain bourgeois discourse, and to assert that literary theory is, in fact, a chimera, or at least is pursuing a self-negating process. Thus, Terry Eagleton writes, "If literary theory presses its own implications too far, then it has argued itself out of existence. . . . This, I would suggest, is the best possible thing for it to do" (204). Feminist critics may be pleased with the help that the newest theories give in overthrowing patriarchal and male-chauvinist modes of thought while also wary that these weapons may be turned against them (see Spivak, 184–86).

On the other hand, the position of those many theorists who argue that language can only refer to itself appears simple absurdity to theorists like the historian Hayden White. Full understanding occurs only when the mind imposes its own patterns. White sides with what he calls *normal criticism*, which believes that criticism

> not only *has* sense but *makes* sense of experience. . . . [However,] we witness the rise of a movement in literary criticism which raises the critical question only to take a grim satisfaction in the impossibility of ever resolving it or, at the extreme limit of thought, even of asking it. Literature is reduced to writing, writing to language, and language, in a final paroxysm of frustration, to chatter about silence. (262)

At the same time, White finds much of the impulse for the kind of theorizing he calls "absurdist" to arise from the repression of "the dark side of civilized existence" (269).

There is yet a third stance. Critics like Stanley Fish appear content with the position that human beings will always believe in some sort of norm, theoretical position, or ideology in order to have grounds for their decisions. A variation of this position is that adopted by Steven Knapp and Walter Benn Michaels in a controversial 1982 essay titled "Against Theory," which argues that no theory is necessary to explain how meaning is grounded in authorial intention since the two are identical. Curiously enough, neither that essay nor the majority of responses to it as gathered in the volume *Against Theory* (edited by W. J. T. Mitchell) consider that a theory may be required to explain how the author's intention is expressed in and to be recovered from the text—a point noted by Stanley Cavell in "The Division of Talent" (especially page 524)—or whether there is not a place for theories about the legitimacy of doing other things after the author's intention has been recognized.

5. The "Critical Theory" that grew out of what has come to be known as the Frankfurt School (founded in 1923 as the Institute of Social Research in affiliation with the University of Frankfurt) came to be strongly interested in the cultural ramifications of the capitalist system from which its leading thinkers (including Max Horkheimer, Herbert Marcuse, Theodor Adorno, and, in the second generation, Jürgen Habermas) wished to emancipate the Western World. According to Horkheimer, Critical Theory "says that the basic form of the historically given commodity economy on which modern history rests contains in itself the internal and external tensions of the modern era: it generates these tensions over and over again in an increasingly heightened form . . . it finally hinders further development and drives humanity into a new barbarism" (227). Although Critical Theory meant somewhat different things to different members of the group, and although present neo-Marxist movements largely separate themselves from the program of the Frankfurt School, the association between contemporary Marxist literary criticism, theory regarded as general cultural critique, and the antipositivist, anticapitalist Critical Theory has led to the use of the term Critical Theory to designate neo-Marxist analyses of culture, including literature.

References

Against Theory. Ed. W. J. T. Mitchell. Chicago: University of Chicago Press, 1985.

Arnold, Matthew. "The Function of Criticism at the Present Time" (1864). In vol. 3 of *The Complete Prose Works of Matthew Arnold*. Ed. R. H. Super. Ann Arbor: University of Michigan Press, 1960–77.

Aristotle. *Poetics*. Trans. O. B. Hardison. In *Classical and Medieval Literary Criticism*, ed. A. Preminger, O. B. Hardison, and Kevin Kerrane. New York: Frederick Ungar, 1974. The sentence quoted is from Section 4.

Bruss, Elizabeth. *Beautiful Theories*. Baltimore: Johns Hopkins University Press, 1982.

Cavell, Stanley. "The Division of Talent." *Critical Inquiry* 11 (June 1985): 519–38.

Coleridge, Samuel Taylor. *The Friend*. Ed. Barbara E. Rooke. In *The Collected Works*. Ed. K. Coburn. 16 vols. Princeton, N.J.: Princeton University Press, 1969–84.

Crane, R. S. "Criticism as Inquiry; or, The Perils of the 'High Priori Road.' " In *The Idea of the Humanities*. 2 vols. Chicago: University of Chicago Press, 1967.

De Man, Paul. "The Resistance to Theory." In *The Resistance to Theory*. Minneapolis: University of Minnesota Press, 1986. Originally published in *Yale French Studies* 63 (1982): 3–20.

Eagleton, Terry. *Literary Theory*. Minneapolis: University of Minnesota Press, 1983.

Fish, Stanley. "Consequences." *Critical Inquiry* 11 (March 1985): 433–58. Reprinted in *Against Theory*.

Griffith, Peter. *Literary Theory and English Teaching*. Philadelphia: Milton Keynes, 1987.

Horkheimer, Max. "Traditional and Critical Theory." Trans. W. J. Greenstreet. In *Critical Theory: Selected Essays*. New York: Herder and Herder, 1972.

Jay, Gregory, and David Miller, eds. *After Strange Texts: The Role of Theory in the Study of Literature*. University: University of Alabama Press, 1985.

Knapp, Steven, and Walter Benn Michaels. "Against Theory." *Critical Inquiry* 8 (Summer 1982): 723–42. Reprinted in *Against Theory*.

Krieger, Murray. "Literary Invention and the Impulse to Theoretical Change." *New Literary History* 18 (Autumn 1986): 191–208.

———. *Words about Words about Words*. Baltimore: Johns Hopkins University Press, 1988.

Pratt, Mary Louise. *Toward a Speech Act Theory of Literary Discourse*. Bloomington: University of Indiana Press, 1977.

Proclus. "The Nature of Poetic Art." Trans. Thomas Taylor; rev. Kevin Kerrane. In *Classical and Medieval Literary Criticism*, ed. A. Preminger, O. B. Hardison, and Kevin Kerrane. New York: Frederick Ungar, 1974.

Propp, Vladimir. *The Morphology of the Folktale*. Trans. Laurence Scott. Austin: University of Texas University Press, 1968.

Richards, I. A. *Principles of Literary Criticism*. 1924; London: Routledge and Kegan Paul, 1948.

Spivak, Gayatri Chakravorty. "Displacement and the Discourse of Woman." In *Displacement: Derrida and After*, ed. Mark Krupnick. Bloomington: Indiana University Press, 1983.

Watson, George. *The Discipline of English*. London: Macmillan, 1978.

Wellek, René, and Austin Warren. *Theory of Literature*. 1942; New York: Harcourt, Brace, World, 1956.

White, Hayden. "The Absurdist Moment in Contemporary Literary History" (1976). In *Tropics of Discourse*. Baltimore: Johns Hopkins University Press, 1978.

Sources of Additional Information

Murray Kreiger's "Literary Invention and the Impulse to Theoretical Change" (*New Literary History* 18, 1986: 191–208) is a genial commentary on the inevitable succession of literary theories, each of which attempts to universalize itself before losing prominence to the next fashionable theory.

A cogent set of essays that approach black literature employing various aspects of contemporary literary theory will be found in *Black Literature and Literary Theory*, ed. Henry Louis Gates, Jr. (London: Methuen, 1984).

Convenient accounts of the Frankfurt School are Richard A. Brosio's *The Frankfurt School: An Analysis of the Contradictions and Crises of Liberal Capitalist Society* (Muncie; Ind.: Ball State University, 1980) and Tom Bottomore's *The Frankfurt School* (London: Tavistock, 1984).

Nine essays responding to Steven Knapp and Walter Benn Michaels's *Critical Inquiry* article "Against Theory" as well as two replies from the original authors are collected in *Against Theory: Literary Studies and the New Pragmatism*, ed. W. J. T. Mitchell (Chicago: University of Chicago Press, 1985).

TRAGEDY   1. Drama of that kind exemplified by the extant plays of Aeschylus, Sophocles, and Euripides and described by Aristotle in the *Poetics*.
2. In the medieval period, the fall of the mighty conceived under the image
of the wheel of fortune. 3. Since the Renaissance, a conception of a class of
literary works that includes not only the Greek tragedies but also a number
of Renaissance, neo-classical, and nineteenth- and twentieth-century plays and
novels. In this sense, tragedy is defined primarily in terms of a vision of human
life rather than in terms of specific formal elements.

*All three of the above senses are to be distinguished from the looser common
use in which serious accidents, misfortunes, and disasters in general are regarded as tragic. R. B. Heilman has commented with special incisiveness on
the confusions incident to this popular use.*

1. As traced with special clarity in A. E. Haigh's standard *The Tragic Drama
of the Greeks* (1896), Greek tragedy arose out of the choral dances at the spring
festivals honoring Dionysus. The source of the name *tragodia*, "goat-song,"
remains moot. Thespis introduced an actor (answerer) into the choral dithyramb
in the sixth century; Aeschylus, whose first play appeared in 499 B.C., introduced
a second actor and what were to become the traditional padded costumes and
thick-soled shoes; Sophocles introduced the third actor. The first definition of
Greek tragedy is necessarily taken from Aristotle:

> A tragedy, then, is the imitation of an action that is serious and also, as having
> magnitude, complete in itself; in language with pleasurable accessories ["rhythm
> and harmony or song"], each kind brought in separately in the parts of the work
> [some portions in verse only, some in song]; in a dramatic, not in a narrative form;
> with incidents arousing pity and fear, wherewith to accomplish its catharsis of
> emotions. (17; 5.1449b)

To this summary description must be added two other Aristotelian formulations. The first is the necessity of unity of plot: a single action is to be represented
"with its several incidents so closely connected that the transposal or withdrawal
of any one of them will disjoin and dislocate the whole" (27; 8.1451a). In
addition, the protagonist should be "a man not pre-eminently virtuous and just,
whose misfortune, however, is brought upon him not by vice and depravity but
by some error of judgment [*hamartia*], of the number of those in the enjoyment
of great reputation and prosperity" (35; 13.1453a). Ingram Bywater's notes to
his translation of the *Poetics* and the commentaries of F. L. Lucas and S. H.
Butcher are standard references for twentieth-century discussions of the *Poetics*.

2. Roman tragedy, modeled on that of the Greeks, is represented centrally by
Seneca (A.D. first century), while, according to Haigh, performances of Greek
tragedy continued until the fourth century. Tragic drama then disappears almost
completely until the Renaissance. The medieval conception of tragedy looked
to a NARRATIVE, not dramatic, form, and to a combination of Christian morality
and Fortune regarded partly as aleatory and partly as a wheel that, having carried
a person of note to the highest possible point, inevitably carries that person down

to sorrow and destruction. The best known statement of the medieval view of tragedy is that of Chaucer in the "Prologue to the Monk's Tale":

> Tragedie is to seyn a certeyn storie,
> As olde bookes maken us memorie,
> Of hym that stood in greet prosperitee,
> And is yfallen out of heigh degree,
> Into myserie, and endeth wrecchedly.

Fortune is regarded, in words from the thirteenth-century *Carmina Burana*:

> O Fortune, you are like the moon,
> ever changing
> ever waxing and waning.
> This hateful life first savages us,
> and then, at a whim, solaces,
> like a gambler in a senseless game.
> It causes power and poverty alike
> to dissolve like the melting of ice.

Raymond Williams comments: "There might be particular sins which led to the falls, and at times these would be examined, in the light of the doctrine of Fortune as the ministering agent of Providence. But behind the particular sins was a more general sin: that of trusting to Fortune in the sense of seeming worldly success at all. The pride of the world involved all other vices, and the remedy was to put no trust in the world but to seek God" (22–23). Such an effect was, of course, reinforced by the principle that one's experience in this world was of little importance as long as one was rewarded with bliss in the next.

3. Enormously influential, Aristotle's description of tragedy is open to interpretation at a number of points. What constitutes a single action? Does the principle of unity deny subplots? What is meant by catharsis? Is the great error or tragic flaw to be understood as a moral lapse? Intertwined with such questions is the most important one: assuming the authoritativeness of Aristotle's analysis of Greek tragedy (and accurate interpretation thereof), how relevant is it to works of later centuries that have been regarded as tragedies? To put the question another way, to what degree can a text diverge from the Aristotelian description and still usefully be described as a tragedy?

Generally, critics and commentators have attempted to answer these questions in terms that will allow the inclusion of both Greek tragedy and many at least of what the Renaissance considered tragedies, including, of course, the great Shakespearean tragedies; the number of works accepted as tragedies in succeeding centuries varies greatly. The ways in which the Aristotelian analysis is interpreted, modified, or challenged depends largely on the particular writer's philosophy, beliefs, and personal responses to literary texts. Hegel's concept of tragedy grows directly out of his logic of synthesis: tragedy for him results from the clash of two human values, both of which are positive in themselves. Though the persons who have made these values their own are destroyed, the conflict itself is resolved in such a way as to produce a new stability. "Over and above mere fear and tragic sympathy we have therefore the feeling of *reconciliation*, which tragedy reaches for in virtue of its vision of eternal justice, a justice which exercises a paramount force of absolute constringency on account of the relative claim of all merely contracted aims and passions" (4:300). Equally based in a total personal vision of existence is Nietzsche's *The Birth of Tragedy*. For Nietzsche, the combination of suffering and ecstasy represented by the Dionysian myth represents the truth of human existence, while the calmness of the Apollonian vision of the world is a necessary illusion. "The Greek knew and felt the terrors and horrors of existence: to be able to live at all, he had to interpose the shining dream-birth of the Olympian world between himself and them" (1:34–35). Dionysus represents the ultimate unity of the world, a sense of which can be conveyed only by music; Apollo presides over the individuating illusion (the world forces ultimately care nothing for the individual). The reconciliation of the two occurs in tragedy. "The one truly real Dionysus appears in a multiplicity of forms, in the mask of a fighting hero and entangled, as it were, in the net of an individual will. As the visibly appearing god now talks and acts, he resembles an erring, striving, suffering individual: and that, in general, he *appears* with such epic precision and clearness, is due to the dream-reading Apollo" (1:81–82). The audience of the tragedy become spectators of existence as a whole, finding a justification impossible in individual experience. Nietzsche's primary interest is in the great epoch of Greek tragedy, which he sees beginning to fail as early as Euripides and his Socratic, theoretical rather than mythical, mode of thought. "Greek tragedy had a fate different from that of all her older sister arts: she died by suicide, in consequence of an irreconcilable conflict; accordingly she died tragically, while they all passed away very calmly and beautifully in ripe old age" (1:86).

The influence of Hegel visible in Nietzsche is found in another way in A. C. Bradley, who frames a definition intended to embrace both Greek and Shakespearean tragedy. "So that, by way of summary, we may now alter our first statement, 'A tragedy is a story of exceptional calamity leading to the death of a man in high estate,' and we may say instead (what in its turn is one-sided, though less so), that the story is one of human actions producing exceptional calamity and ending in the death of such a man" (16). Herbert Weisinger's *Tragedy and the Paradox of the Fortunate Fall* is a central example of theorizing built on anthropological investigations (specifically, on those of the group known as the Cambridge School). The audience's response to tragedy arises from the deep archetype of rebirth, which is metamorphosed under the Christian mode of thought to the paradox of the fortunate fall. The resulting definition: "Tragedy occurs when the accepted order of things is fundamentally questioned only to be the more triumphantly affirmed" (266). Northrop Frye, whose discussion of tragedy as "The Mythos of Autumn" requires a definition that will stretch from the origins of tragedy to the present, finds that "[w]hether the context is Greek, Christian, or undefined, tragedy must lead up to an epiphany of law, of that which is and must be'' (208). Further, tragedy seems to Frye to include strong elements of both fate and violation of the moral law—neither exploration sufficing by itself.

In T. R. Henn's view, "It is beyond all question that the values stated or questioned in the tragic experience are of the utmost moral importance, both individually and collectively'' (286). Tragedies set forth certain values; Henn's list begins with Courage, Temperance, Liberality, Magnificence, and Magnanimity. All tragedy from ancient Greek times to the present is to be judged in terms of its "enrichment of the human spirit,'' of which Henn finds less in tragedy after Shakespeare. His final, explicitly Christian, point of view: "Tragic evil becomes recognizable as the assertion of the will beyond the limits proper to the individual's relationship to his fellows and his God'' (289–90).

George Steiner, for whom " 'tragedy' encloses . . . in a single span both the Greek and the Elizabethan example'' (192) emphasizes that "[t]he tragic personage is broken by forces which can neither be fully understood nor overcome by rational prudence'' (10). The forces that act are capricious and unjust. Modern serious plays fail to achieve the tragic because they deny full human responsibility and assume that all problems can be addressed by social action. But, "The destiny of Lear cannot be resolved by the establishment of adequate homes for the aged'' (128). Raymond Williams, writing from an essentially Marxist point of view, argues that to attempt to define the sense of the tragic too rigidly is an error: "the varieties of tragic experience are to be interpreted by reference to the changing conventions and institutions'' (46). His real interest is in demonstrating that although immediate results of revolutions driving toward full human liberation, toward "absolute humanity,'' will necessarily include tragedy, such revolutions are essential.

R. B. Heilman's approach to an understanding of the nature of tragedy is uniquely focused on an analysis of the two major classes of literature he distinguishes. The central characteristic of tragedy for Heilman is division within the protagonist; the individual is torn between two moral imperatives, between an imperative and an impulse (strong desire), or between two impulses. On the other hand, where the conflict is not within the character but between the character and outside forces, the result is melodrama. Significant reclassification occurs as a result of the distinction: *Oedipus the King* remains a tragedy, but *Oedipus at Colonus* moves toward melodrama; *King Lear* remains tragic, but *Richard III* is to be understood as melodrama; Ibsen's *John Gabriel Borkman* is a tragedy, but *An Enemy of the People* is melodrama.

Richard Sewall understands the tragic sense of life as "this sense of ancient evil, of 'the blight man was born for,' of the permanence and mystery of human suffering, that is basic to the tragic sense of life'' (6). Concentrating on this tragic vision rather than on structure and form, Sewall's discussion of tragedy ranges not only through the centuries but across genres into the realm of the novel, treating *Job, Oedipus, Doctor Faustus, King Lear, The Scarlet Letter, Moby-Dick, The Brothers Karamazov,* and *Absalom, Absalom*. Dorothea Krook's careful formulation of what she believes are in practice recognized as universal elements of tragedy also leads her to say that the finest examples of tragedy in the modern era are novels: she cites *Moby-Dick*, *The Brothers Karamazov*, *Middlemarch*, and *The Secret Agent*. The universal elements she finds are an act (or condition) of shame or horror, resultant suffering, resultant knowledge (but not necessarily self-knowledge), and an affirmation of "an order of values transcending the values of the human order" (15).

References

Aristotle. *On the Art of Poetry*. Trans. I. Bywater. Oxford: Clarendon Press, 1909.

Bradley, A. C. *Shakespearean Tragedy: Lectures on Hamlet, Othello, King Lear, and Macbeth*. London: Macmillan, 1904. A study that cannot be ignored, although it is constantly criticized.

Carmina Burana. Trans. Norma Condee. Unpublished.

Chaucer, Geoffrey. "The Prologue to the Monk's Tale." *The Poetical Works of Chaucer*. Ed. F. N. Robinson. Boston: Houghton Mifflin, 1933.

Frye, Northrop. "The Mythos of Autumn." In *Anatomy of Criticism*. Princeton, N.J.: Princeton University Press, 1957.

Haigh, A. E. *The Tragic Drama of the Greeks*. Oxford: Clarendon Press, 1896. An essential reference.

Hegel, Georg Wilhelm Friedrich. *The Philosophy of Fine Art*. Trans. F. P. B. Osmaston. 4 vols. London: G. Bell and Sons, 1920.

Heilman, R. B. *Tragedy and Melodrama: Versions of Experience*. Seattle: University of Washington Press, 1968. An important study.

Henn, T. R. *The Harvest of Tragedy*. London: Methuen, 1956. "Alone of all artistic forms tragedy offers no apology for its incidental didacticism" (286).

Krook, Dorothea. *Elements of Tragedy*. New Haven, Conn.: Yale University Press, 1969.

Lucas, F. L. *Tragedy: Serious Drama in Relation to Aristotle's Poetics*. 1927; London: Hogarth Press, 1957.

Nietzsche, Friedrich. *The Birth of Tragedy*. In vol. 1 of *The Complete Works of Friedrich Nietzsche*. Ed. Oscar Levy. 18 vols. New York: Gordon Press, 1974. Highly influential, partially through its stylistic qualities: "Platonic dialogue was as it were the boat in which the shipwrecked ancient poetry saved herself together with all her children: crowded into a narrow space and timidly obsequious to the one steersman, Socrates, they now launched into a new world, which never tired of looking at the fantastic spectacle of this procession" (109). Through the combination of myth with the music of tragedy, "the tragic spectator in particular experiences . . . the sure presentiment of supreme joy to which the path through destruction and negation leads; so that he thinks he hears, as it were, the innermost abyss of things speaking audibly to him" (160).

Sewall, Richard B. *The Vision of Tragedy*. New Haven, Conn.: Yale University Press, 1959. An emphasis on the inevitable tragedy of existence. "More than Prometheus or Oedipus, Job is the universal symbol for the western imagination of the mystery of undeserved suffering" (9).

Steiner, George. *The Death of Tragedy*. New York: Hill and Wang, 1963. An unusually stimulating book in which Steiner reminds the reader that tragedy is not a universal genre—it is particularly Western—and attempts to assess the reasons for the decline in modern literary tragedy that he finds. *Job* is not tragic because Jehovah is finally just. Rather, "the *Iliad* is the primer of tragic art. In it are set forth the motifs and images around which the sense of the tragic has crystallized during nearly three thousand years of western poetry: the shortness of heroic life, the exposure of man to the murderousness and caprice of the inhuman, the fall of the City" (5).

Weisinger, Herbert. *Tragedy and the Paradox of the Fortunate Fall.* East Lansing: Michigan State College Press, 1953.

Williams, Raymond. *Modern Tragedy.* London: Chatto and Windus, 1966.

Sources of Additional Information

The anthropological explanation of the origin of Greek tragedy is stated in its essential form in the "Excursus on the Ritual Forms Preserved in Greek Tragedy" contributed by Gilbert Murray to Jane Harrison's *Themis: A Study of the Social Origins of Greek Religion* (2d. ed., Cambridge: Cambridge University Press, 1927). Murray finds five elements— the *Agon* (contest), *Pathos* (ritual death), Messenger bringing news of the death, *Threnos* (lamentation), and *Anagnorisis* (recognition)—which, belonging to the myth of Dionysus, were carried over into Greek tragedy, most clearly in the plays of Euripides. H. D. F. Kitto's *Greek Tragedy* (London: Methuen, 1939) devotes extensive examination to the art of twenty-nine Greek plays.

Hegel's various writings on tragedy are usefully brought together in *Hegel on Tragedy*, edited by A. Paolucci and H. Paolucci (Garden City, N.Y.: Doubleday Anchor, 1962).

A stimulating study of the use of verse in English tragedy is to be found in Moody E. Prior's *The Language of Tragedy* (Gloucester, Mass.: Peter Smith, 1964). "The use of verse may be regarded as a sign that the criterion of appropriateness in diction is not reportorial exactness, or even a freely interpreted concern with faithfulness to the actual circumstances governing dialogue in life, but the needs of art; it represents an intention of using all possible means to gain appropriate artistic ends without being hampered by the demands of verisimilitude (6). Thus, "[t]he language of poetry is generally directed away from the literal and toward the symbolic, and it functions so as to increase the relevant implications and suggestions at any given point and to establish associations and correspondences between analogous or unlike things" (12).

The volume *Tragedy* written by Clifford Leech for the Critical Idiom series (London: Methuen, 1969) gives a common-sense summary of major issues in the understanding of tragedy, especially those arising out of Aristotle's *Poetics*. Oscar Mandel's *A Definition of Tragedy* (New York: New York University Press, 1961) builds the following definition which is especially intended to exclude all that is not essential to tragedy (neither an "ethical direction" nor emotional effect are necessary for Mandel): "A protagonist who commands our earnest good will is impelled in a given world by a purpose, or undertakes an action, of a certain seriousness and magnitude, and by that very purpose or action, subject to that same given world, necessarily and inevitably meets with grave spiritual or physical suffering" (20). The volume is devoted to considering the usual problems raised in the discussion of tragedy in the light of this definition.

A standard survey of English tragedy from the beginnings to the Romantic movement is Ashley Thorndike's *Tragedy* (1908; New York: Cooper Square Publishers, 1965).

U

UNITY 1. In older uses, the result of obedience to the unities of place, time, and action in drama, especially TRAGEDY, as incorrectly derived from Aristotle. 2. Harmony, coherence, and/or interrelatedness of all aspects of a work.

For a discussion of the assumptions that the successful work exhibits the functional relevance of everything included in the TEXT, *or evidence of an internal development like that of a seed growing into a plant, see* ORGANIC UNITY.

1. As is generally well known, the one form of unity prescribed by Aristotle in the *Poetics* is that of action: "just as in the other imitative arts one imitation is always of one thing, so in poetry the story, as an imitation of action, must represent one action, a complete whole, with its several incidents so closely connected that the transposal or withdrawal of any one of them will disjoin and dislocate the whole" (27; 9.1451a). He mentions that tragedies are generally confined to a single revolution of the sun but does not set this forth as necessarily a virtue. Nevertheless, that the action of a drama should not only be unified but should also be confined to one place and be limited to the occurrences of a single day came to be regarded as Aristotelian "rules"—primarily as the result of Lodovico Castelvetro's 1570 commentary accompanying his translation of the *Poetics*.

The value of unity of action has been generally accepted (although whether the principle proscribes subplots has been a matter of debate), while the other two unities have a considerable history of controversy. That Greek tragedy generally did observe the unities of place and time was very likely largely due to the role of the chorus. As F. L. Lucas points out, "it was unlikely that the same dozen old men should reappear, all together now at Athens, now at Sparta, now at Thebes; still more, that they should punctually reassemble at intervals of years" (170).

Along with other English writers of the time, Sir Philip Sidney assumed the propriety of adherence to the dramatic unities. *Gorboduc* he found "faultie both in place and time, the two necessary Companions of all corporall actions. . . . [T]he *Stage* should always represent but one place, and the uttermoste time presupposed in it, should bee both by Aristotelian precept, and common reason, but one day" (72). However, Shakespeare and Renaissance drama in general moved the action across miles and, at times, years, and English drama has never felt tightly bound by the unities of place and time. In the seventeenth-century French theater, on the other hand, Corneille and Racine regarded the unities as prescriptive rules.

Samuel Johnson's dismissal of the unities of time and place is well known:

> The objection arising from the impossibility of passing the first hour at Alexandria, and the next at Rome, supposes, that when the play opens the spectator really imagines himself at Alexandria, and believes that his walk to the theatre has been a voyage to Egypt, and that he lives in the days of Antony and Cleopatra. Surely he that imagines this may imagine more. He that can take the stage at one time for the palace of the Ptolemies, may take it in half an hour for the promontory of Actium. (7:76–77)

2. The principle that a work should be unified in the sense of being complete, harmonious, and without evident excrescences can be regarded as a criterion of either interpretation or evaluation; in practice, it is frequently employed in both ways. In interpretation, unity has, until recent decades, been almost universally invoked as the criterion for interpretive adequacy. The more aspects of a work that are explained, related, or shown to cast light on each other, the more successful the interpretation. To show that some portion of the narration, plot, dialogue, or apparent symbolism seems anomalous from the perspective of a given interpretive commentary has been generally regarded as demonstrating incompleteness, if not error. Where a work does not appear to admit of any comprehensive interpretation, it has been regarded as an at least partial failure. It is worth noting that works that seem so simple and unproblematic that no apparent intellectual activity is required to discover their unity are generally dismissed as trifling. Unity, in other words, is taken to mean "unity in diversity," the harmony of disparate parts or the resolution of oppositions and differences, and not simple consistency or agreement. Thus the work that either fails to demand interpretive explanation or fails to yield sufficiently to it is adversely evaluated. Jonathan Culler, who does not accept the proposition that successful works are necessarily unified, has pointed out that at least the convention of unity powerfully affects critical practice. This he illustrates by a survey of various critical analyses of Blake's "London" (58).

A common, but not always explicit, assumption behind the use of unity or harmony as either an interpretive or evaluative criterion is that the author either consciously intends or unconsciously strives for a work in which all the major parts are meaningfully related, in which nothing is finally anomalous, and in which apparent contradictions are introduced only to be resolved (see AUTHOR and INTENTION). R. S. Crane has commented in regard to any kind of practical criticism:

> We shall have to assume that any poetic work, like any other production of human art, has, or rather is, a definite structure of some kind which is determined imme- diately by its writer's intuition of a form to be achieved in its materials by the right use of his medium, and, furthermore, that we can arrive at some understanding of what this form actually is and use our understanding as a principle in the analysis and criticism of the work. (165)

Walter Davis's formulation in *The Act of Interpretation* (1978) is that "[p]urpose coincides with structure because it gives birth to it" (3).

The general principle of unity can be formulated in other terms. In *The Foundation of Aesthetics*, C. K. Ogden, I. A. Richards, and James Wood employ the term *equilibrium* to express a richness and complexity that are nevertheless balanced in a work of art (75, 91). Eugene Paul Nassar prefers the term *continuity*: "Sensitivity to the true tone and continuity of a piece, and the ability to articulate with accuracy and precision his sensitivity—this is the first and most important job of a critic" (13).

Note

That the expectation of unity is more a cultural convention or psychological demand than a recognition of the actual nature of literary works is an argument that has been made from several theoretical bases. Walter Slatoff, for instance, wrote in 1970: "[A] great many works, especially those which interest us most, are less closed and unified than much of our criticism indicates. . . . The strength of our desire to see closures is indicated by the fact that every time a critic discovers a countercurrent he tries to insist that it is the main stream" (158–59). Recent movements in critical theory, those associated with poststructuralism (see STRUCTURALISM), revisionism, or, most specifically, DECON- STRUCTION, have more strongly denied that a work ever achieves substantial unity or that the goal of the critic should be to seek and elucidate an essential unity.

References

Aristotle. *On the Art of Poetry*. Trans. I. Bywater. Oxford: Clarendon Press, 1909.
Crane, R. S. *The Languages of Criticism and the Structure of Poetry*. Toronto: Toronto University Press, 1953.
Culler, Jonathan. "Prolegomena to a Theory of Reading." In *The Reader in the Text*. Princeton, N. J.: Princeton University Press, 1980.
Davis, Walter. *The Act of Interpretation*. Chicago: University of Chicago Press, 1978.
Johnson, Samuel. "Preface to Shakespeare" (1765). In vol. 7 of the *Yale Edition of the Works of Samuel Johnson*. New Haven, Conn.: Yale University Press, 1968.
Lucas, F. L. *Tragedy: Serious Drama in Relation to Aristotle's Poetics*. 1927; London: Hogarth Press, 1957.
Nassar, Eugene Paul. *The Rape of Cinderella*. Bloomington: Indiana University Press, 1970.
Ogden, C. K., I. A. Richards, and James Wood. *The Foundations of Aesthetics*. London: George Allen and Unwin, 1922.

Sidney, Sir Philip. *The Defense of Poesie* (1595). Cambridge: Cambridge University
     Press, 1904.
Slatoff, Walter J. *With Respect to Readers*. Ithaca, N. Y.: Cornell University Press,
     1970.

Sources of Additional Information

Joel Spingarn's *Literary Criticism in the Renaissance* (New York: Columbia University
Press, 1908) traces the entry and early history of the principle of the unities in Italy,
France, and England (89–106, 206–13, and 290–92, respectively). The section on the
Italian critics (the source for the view of the unities held in the other two countries) is
particularly informative, tracing the comments on the unity of time from Cinto prior to
Castelvetro's addition of the unity of place.

The propriety of the unities is one of the subjects of debate in the first third of Dryden's
"An Essay on Dramatic Poesy" (the standard edition is that of W. P. Ker in *Essays of
John Dryden*, 2 vols.; New York: Russell and Russell, 1961).

The seventeenth- and eighteenth-century controversy over the necessity and interpretation of the unities may be traced in J. W. H. Atkins's *English Literary Criticism: 17th
and 18th Centuries* (London: Methuen, 1951).

Coleridge also rejected the unities of time and place; his various comments are most
easily traced in *Coleridge's Criticism of Shakespeare*, ed. R. A. Foakes (London: Athlone
Press, 1989).

Barbara Herrnstein Smith's study of how poems end (*Poetic Closure*, Chicago: University of Chicago Press, 1968) argues that the reader must be aware of the unity of the
total poem.

> Closure occurs when the concluding portion of a poem creates in the reader a sense
> of appropriate cessation. It announces and justifies the absence of further develop-
> ment; it reinforces the feeling of finality, completion, and composure which we
> value in all works of art; and it gives ultimate unity and coherence to the reader's
> experience of the poem by providing a point from which all the preceding elements
> may be viewed comprehensively and their relations grasped as part of a significant
> design. (36)

Index of Concepts and Terms

This index of concepts and terms includes the major entry of each concept (these pages numbers are given in *italics*) together with those references to a term or concept that substantially contribute to its understanding. It does not list the various senses of the 70 concepts for which there are separate entries—such a listing opens each entry. Because so many literary terms have senses specific to particular scholars or critics, where appropriate the name of the writer (or one of the writers) associated with that particular use is given in parentheses.

Index of Names

This index includes critics, theorists, and editors of collections of essays cited in the text for each entry. Citations in the References and Sources of Additional Information sections are not included.

About the Author

WENDELL V. HARRIS is Professor of English at Pennsylvania State University. His academic specialities in literary theory and Victorian literature are reflected in his previous books including *British Short Fiction of the Nineteenth Century*, *The Omnipresent Debate*, and *Interpretive Acts*.